新东方
NEW ORIENTAL

D1430336

浓缩雅思词汇精华，把握雅思考试规律

IELTS Vocabulary

孙涛 梅晗·编著

雅思词汇胜经

群言出版社
Qunyan Press

图书在版编目（CIP）数据

雅思词汇胜经 / 孙涛，梅晗编著. —北京：群言出版社，
2009（2012.9 重印）

ISBN 978-7-80256-009-3

Ⅰ．雅… Ⅱ．①孙…②梅… Ⅲ．英语—词汇—高等教育—
自学参考资料 Ⅳ．H313

中国版本图书馆 CIP 数据核字（2009）第 080483 号

雅思词汇胜经

出 版 人	范 芳
责任编辑	孙春红
封面设计	贾臻臻
出版发行	群言出版社（Qunyan Press）
地 址	北京东城区东厂胡同北巷 1 号
邮政编码	100006
网 站	www.qypublish.com
读者信箱	bj62605588@163.com
总 编 办	010—65265404 65138815
编 辑 部	010—65276609 65262436
发 行 部	010—62605588 62605019
经 销	新华书店
读者服务	010—65220236 65265404 65263345
法律顾问	中济律师事务所
印 刷	北京四季青印刷厂
版 次	2012 年 9 月第 1 版第 6 次印刷
开 本	787mm×1092mm 1/16
印 张	25.75
字 数	530 千
书 号	ISBN 978-7-80256-009-3
定 价	49.00 元

新东方图书策划委员会

主任　俞敏洪

委员　（按姓氏笔画为序）

王　强　　包凡一

仲晓红　　沙云龙

陈向东　　张洪伟

邱政政　　汪海涛

周成刚　　徐小平

谢　琴　　窦中川

前　言

　　整整一年的时间，经过无数次的讨论、否定、修改与校验，这 7838 个雅思词汇终于结集出版了。迄今距离我编写的第一本雅思词汇书《雅思词汇精选》出版已经快六年时间了，记得当时自己还是个青涩的雅思教师，转眼间已步入而立之年。随着一堂堂课、一场场讲座的累积，感觉雅思之于自己越来越像花朵之于园丁，草药之于中医，太熟悉了，以至于可以不断地悟出一些东西。

　　词汇对于任何一个"烤鸭"来讲，都是一个很大的挑战，但现在很多正在起步的"烤鸭"可能还在用对付四六级、托福甚至是 GRE 的办法来对付雅思考试。如果参加大学英语四六级考试，我们可以按照《大学英语教学大纲通用词汇表》进行准备，干净利索；如果参加 GRE 考试，我们也可以抱着俞敏洪老师的 GRE 词汇红宝书反复背诵，因为 GRE 考查的是认知、逻辑能力，考生要面对用英语写成的专业文章，因此对词汇识记的广度和深度要求较高，这样我们只能死记硬背，倒也痛快。就算是跟雅思最接近的托福考试，也可以通过反复记忆单词来取得比较好的分数，因为词汇量大对于阅读来讲无疑有很大的帮助，而且托福考试的口语和写作评分标准（Speaking / Writing Rubrics）中，没有对词汇提出明确的专项要求，而是更重视宏观任务的完成和话题的延展。可面对雅思考试的时候，很多考生突然感觉仅有背单词的执着和热情好像还是不太够用，有很多词汇量很大、听力和阅读考了满分的考生，在写作或口语上却总迈不过 6 分这个坎儿。当然，造成写作、口语分数不高的原因有很多——因为语法、发音、词汇等都是雅思考试中写作或口语部分的评分标准，我们在其中任何一项上出现问题都会导致分数不理想。但不可否认，对词汇的掌握不符合雅思考试的要求是其中一个重要的原因，雅思写作和口语的评分标准（Band Descriptors）对词汇提出了专门的要求，而且明确界定出各个分数级别间的差异，这一点决定了雅思词汇的准备是有别于其他的英语测试的，雅思词汇的识记应该更"雅思"一些。

　　可能是因为英语专业出身的缘故吧，我在济南外国语学校读中学、在北外读英国社会研究、在英国读教育学的时候反而没怎么在意过单词。一直以来对单词的态度就是"死磕"，遇到不认识的就背，到后来发现不认识的单词越来越少，做功课、写论文轻松了很多。可这种"持久战"式的背单词法并不适合所有的英语学习者，不是每个人都可以把语言当专业去学，也不是每个人都有 12 年的英语学习经历。对于大部分读者来讲，他们需要在有限的时间内去突破词汇的限制，并实现语言能力的提升。

　　在雅思词汇的学习上更是如此，我们的目标应该是从雅思考试的特点和标准出发，按照符合雅思考试规律的方法来积累词汇，并争取在较短的时间内实现 test-taking performance 的提升。那应该怎样准备雅思词汇才能更有效地提高成绩呢？

1. 要准备真正"雅思"的词汇。

　　所谓真正"雅思"的词汇，就是真正在雅思考试中出现过或者多次出现过的词汇，就像本书中的词汇，都取自于雅思考试语料库（其中收录了 Cambridge IELTS 1-7、雅思机经以及权威雅思出版物中的所有文字材料）。

2. 针对雅思听、说、读、写采取不同的词汇学习方法。

　　听力和阅读词汇以识记为主，认识即可；本书中收录了剑桥真题系列中所有的听力词汇，并单独附列在书后，以听录音、练拼写为主；阅读除了要准备 6 分核心、7 分高分词汇外，本书还提供了阅读真题认知词汇，以认识、读懂例句为目标。就口语、写作而言，以熟记 6 分核心、7 分高分词汇的发音和背诵例句为主。本书提供了词汇学习的四个步骤(参见"如何使用本书")来帮助考生真正有针对性地准备雅思词汇。

3. 针对 6 分核心、7 分高分词汇，要融背诵、朗读、记忆例句和练习为一体，做到真正会使用这些词汇。

　　在雅思词汇学习过程中，我们往往背得多，练得少；学得多，用得少。在本书中，希望通过"如何使用本书"和练习题部分来帮助考生把重心放在单词的"使用"而不是"识记"上。

　　与以前编写《雅思词汇精选》不同的是，这次我不是一个人在战斗。我邀请到了我的同事——北京新东方学校的梅晗老师加入到编写过程中，他在多年的雅思词汇和雅思阅读的教学中积累了丰富的素材，并对雅思词汇有精深的理解。本文开头时提到的整整一年的讨论、修改，大都是和他一起进行的。这次是与梅晗老师第一次合作，他的敬业和才华让人敬佩，他的贡献也让本书多了更多时尚的元素。此外，不得不提的还有我现在的直接领导——新东方教育科技集团常务副总裁、新东方雅思研究院院长周成刚老师和把我领入新东方的北京新东方学校国外部英联邦项目主任何钢老师，自我编写第一本雅思书籍开始，他们就一直给予我专业的指导和无私的支持。

　　不知道几年之后我会不会再出版一本雅思词汇书，雅思总是那么熟悉可有时候又会不时给我新的灵感。不管怎样，希望与各位正在奋斗着的"烤鸭"一同进步。

编者

如何使用本书

Step 1

附录 1：2000 个最常用词汇	
先进行单词测试，如果下列 10 个单词都认识，则可跳过 Step 1，直接开始 Step 2： advice　　　　bottom　　　　condition　　　　detail　　　　encourage freedom　　　　guide　　　　length　　　　mention　　　　quality 如果有单词不认识，则需要先熟悉"2000 个最常用词汇"。	
单词数量	2000
建议学习时间	1 周（每天 1-1.5 小时）
学习方法	突击式，每天 400 个单词，最后两天集中复习，复习时可以将英文单词盖住，根据右栏的中文解释迅速说出对应单词及其拼写。
学习目标	识记即可。

Step 2

6 分词汇	
6 分词汇为雅思核心级词汇，必须熟练掌握，对阅读、写作、口语用处极大。	
单词数量	共 42 个单元，1764 个单词。
建议学习时间	7 周（每天 1.5-2 小时）
学习方法	通过例句记住单词，反复熟悉单词英文解释和例句，最后通过练习题加以巩固。
学习目标	音、义、用皆通。

注：建议在进行 Step 2 的同时开始学习"附录 2：听力真题场景词汇"。

附录 2：听力真题场景词汇	
该部分收录了 Cambridge IELTS 2-7 中的听力词汇，基本上涵盖了雅思听力中所有的场景和常见词汇。由于该部分有很多词汇、词组与"6 分词汇"部分重合，因此记忆负担不大。	
单词数量	2000
建议学习时间	与"6 分词汇"同步
学习方法	通过听力真题学习单词，然后练习拼写。
学习目标	能听懂，会拼写。

Step 3

7分词汇	
7分词汇为雅思高分词汇，如果识记得当，可以帮助考生在写作、口语中创造词汇亮点。7分要求使用得当，因此在识记7分单词时重心不在量，而在正确使用。	
单词数量	共28个单元，1064个单词。
建议学习时间	如果目标为保5争6，建议4周时间(每天1.5-2小时)突击学习；如果目标为保6争7，建议6周时间(每天1.5-2小时)细致学习。
学习方法	尽量通过记忆例句来记住单词，最后通过练习题加以巩固。
学习目标	音、义、用准确。

Step 4(Optional)

附录3：阅读真题认知词汇	
该部分收录了雅思阅读真题中的纯认知词汇，如 beiji(白鳍豚)、counting house(老式的账房)等，在阅读过程中即使不了解他们的意思也不妨碍考生做对题目，但这些词的存在会对考生阅读的流畅感和自信心产生很大影响，所以如果复习时间还够的话，可以突击浏览一下这些词汇。	
单词数量	1010
建议学习时间	2周
学习方法	纯粹混个眼熟。
学习目标	对中文意思有印象即可。

单词释义中所用符号说明

adj.	= adjective 形容词	AmE	= 美国英语
adv.	= adverb 副词	fig.	= figurative 比喻的
conj.	= conjunction 连词	derog.	= derogative 贬义的
prep.	= preposition 介词	[同]	= 同义词
pron.	= pronoun 代词	[反]	= 反义词
n.	= noun 名词	[近]	= 近义词
v.	= verb 动词		
fml.	= formal 用于正式文体		
infml.	= informal 用于非正式文体		
BrE	= 英国英语		

目 录

6 分词汇

✓ **abstract** [ˈæbstrækt]   [同] theoretical [反] concrete

adj. based on general ideas or principles rather than specific examples or real events 抽象的

The research shows that pre-school children are capable of thinking in *abstract* terms. 研究表明学龄前儿童有抽象思维能力。

n. a short written statement containing only the most important ideas in a speech, article, etc. 摘要；概要

✓ **abundance** [əˈbʌndəns]   [同] sufficiency [反] lack

n. a large quantity of something 大量，充足

There is an *abundance* of evidence to support the research findings. 有大量的证据来支持研究结果。

✓ **abuse**   [同] ①misapply, make ill use of ②ill-treat

① *v.* [əˈbjuːz] to deliberately use something for the wrong purpose or for your own advantage 滥用

Biometrics raises thorny questions about privacy and the potential for *abuse*. 生物测定学引发了关于隐私以及该学科有可能被滥用等棘手问题。

② *n.* [əˈbjuːs] cruel or violent treatment of someone 虐待

Child *abuse* is a worldwide problem affecting children from birth to 18 years of age. 儿童虐待是个影响从刚出生到 18 岁之间儿童的全球性问题。

✓ **baggage** [ˈbægɪdʒ] Package

n. (esp. AmE) the cases, bags, boxes, etc. carried by sb. who is traveling (=luggage) 行李

When you arrive at an airport in Australia, you may be greeted in the *baggage* hall by a detector dog, wearing a little red coat bearing the words 'Quarantine'. 当你到达澳大利亚的机场时，你会在行李大厅遇到穿着印有"检疫"字样红外套的稽查犬。

✓ **candidate** [ˈkændɪdeɪt]   [同] applicant, seeker

n. a person who is trying to be elected or is applying for a job (竞选或求职的)候选人，申请人

If a woman *candidate* manages to get on a shortlist, then she has probably already proved herself to be an exceptional *candidate*. 如果一位女候选人能进入最后的角逐，就已经证明她是个很出色的候选人了。

✓ **canteen** [kænˈtiːn]

n. a place where food and drink are served in a factory, a school, etc. 食堂，餐厅

The *canteen* was absolutely packed and I had to wait for ages. 食堂里人满为患，我得等上好长时间。

capable [ˈkeɪpəbl] be ~ of doing   [同] able, competent [反] incapable

adj. having the ability or qualities necessary for doing sth. 有能力的，有才能的

Even very tiny babies are *capable* of grasping and remembering a concept. 即使是很小的孩子

也能领会和记住一个概念。

✓ capacity [kə'pæsəti] [同] ability

n. ①the amount of space a container, room, etc. has to hold things or people 容量 ②the ability to do sth. 能力

The *capacity* of the environment to sustain economic development and population is finite. 环境承受经济的发展和人口的能力是有限的。

✓ capital ['kæpɪtl]

n. a large amount of money that is invested or is used to start a business 资本；资金

Cheap labour may make Chinese clothing competitive in America, but if delays in shipment tie up working *capital* and cause winter coats to arrive in spring, trade may lose its advantages. 廉价劳动力可能会让中国的服装产品在美国富有竞争力，但如果运货过程中的耽搁套牢了营运资金并导致冬装在春天才运送到，那服装贸易就没什么优势可言了。

✓ data ['deɪtə]

n. facts or information used in deciding or discussing sth. 资料，数据

Very little *data* is available. 现有的资料十分不足。

✓ date ['deɪt]

① *n.* specific numbered day of the month, or specific year, usu. given to show when sth. happened or is to happen 日期；日子；年份

Times change, and one of the most significant changes to *date* is the rise of globalization. 时代在变，全球化的兴起成为迄今为止最为显著的变化之一。

② *v.* to have existed since a particular time in the past 存在，追溯

The first weather stations in the far north *date* back just 50 years. 在（地球）最北边的最早的气象站也不过存在了 50 年之久。

✓ economy [ɪ'kɒnəmi]

n. the system by which a country's money and goods are produced and used, or a country considered in this way 经济

Low interest rates will help the *economy*. 低利率有助于经济。

✓ edition [ɪ'dɪʃn] [同] version

n. the form in which a book is published 版本（出版形式）

She collects first *editions* of Victorian novels. 她收集维多利亚时代的初版小说。

✓ facilitate [fə'sɪlɪteɪt] [同] ease

v. (fml.) to make an action or a process possible or easier 促进；促使；使便利

Standard teaching *facilitates* learning. 标准化教学有利于学习。

✓ facilities [fə'sɪlətɪz]

n. buildings, services, equipment, etc. that are provided for a particular purpose 设施；设备

The school has excellent sporting *facilities*. 这个学校有良好的运动设施。

✓ gamble ['gæmbl] [同] bet, try one's luck

v. to spend (money) by playing games of chance, etc. for money 用（钱）赌博

He *gambled* all his winnings on the last race. 他把赢得的钱全压在最后一场赛马上了。

✓ gang [gæŋ]

n. group of young people, usu. males in their teens and early twenties, who are typically troublesome（闹事的青少年，通常指男性）一群，一伙

Gangs of New York 纽约黑帮（著名电影）

✓ hairdresser ['heədresə(r)]

n. a person who cuts, washes, and arranges people's hair in particular styles 理发师

I'm going to the *hairdresser* after work. 下班后我去做头发。

identification [aɪˌdentɪfɪˈkeɪʃn] [同] recognition

n. official papers or cards, such as your passport, that prove who you are 身份证明

Do you have any *identification*? 有没有可以证明你身份的证件？

identify [aɪˈdentɪfaɪ] [同] determinate

v. to show, prove, etc. who or what sb./sth. is; recognize sb./sth. (as being the specified person or thing) 确认、证明某人或某事物；鉴别出（系某人或某物）

Identifying genetically talented individuals is only the first step. 鉴别出天生有才能的个体仅仅是第一步。

idiom [ˈɪdiəm]

n. a group of words that has a special meaning that is different from the ordinary meaning of each separate word 习语；成语；惯用语

The English language has many *idioms*. 英语有很多惯用语。

（have two left feet 意思是"极笨拙"）

idle [ˈaɪdl] [近] ①inactive [同] ①②busy

①*adj.* not working or producing anything 闲散的；不工作的或没有工作的

Many people were *idle* during the depression. 在萧条时期，很多人都无事可做。

②*v.* to do nothing; waste time 无所事事；浪费时光；闲荡

Stop *idling* and help me clean up. 别游手好闲的，来帮我打扫打扫吧。

jar [dʒɑː(r)]

n. cylindrical container, usu. made of glass 广口瓶

I keep my paint-brushes in old jam *jars*. 我把画笔存放在旧果酱瓶里。

jealous [ˈdʒeləs] [近] envious

adj. feeling or showing resentment of sb.'s advantages, achievements, etc.; envious 嫉妒的；羡慕的

This can sometimes cause problems with other siblings who may feel *jealous* even though they themselves may be bright. 这样做有时会使兄弟姐妹感到嫉妒，尽管他们本身可能很聪明。

labour [ˈleɪbə(r)] [近] work

n. work, especially physical work; all the people who work for a company or in a country 劳动；劳力

Cheap *labour* may make Chinese clothing competitive in America. 廉价劳动力可能使中国的服装在美国富有竞争力。

lack [læk] [近] need

v. to be without (sth.); have less than enough of 没有（某事物）；缺乏；缺少；不足

Some houses still lack basic amentities such as bathrooms. 有些住宅仍没有像卫生间这样的基本设施。

magnify [ˈmæɡnɪfaɪ] [同] enlarge [反] minify

v. ①to make sth. look bigger than it really is, for example by using a lens or microscope 放大

②to make something seem more important than it really is 夸大，夸张

The image is *magnified* by a series of lenses within the telescope. 图像由望远镜里的若干镜头加以放大。

naive [naɪˈiːv] [同] innocent, simple

adj. lacking experience of life, knowledge or good judgement and willing to believe that people always tell you the truth 缺乏经验的；幼稚无知的；轻信的

to be politically *naive* 对政治一无所知

overview [ˈəʊvəvjuː]

n. (fml.) short general description(without unnecessary details); survey 综览；概观；概述

Can you give us a quick *overview* of the history of the bear family? 你能给我们简要地介绍一下熊类家族的历史吗?

pension [ˈpenʃn]

n. sum of money paid regularly by the State to people above a certain age and to widowed or disabled people, or by an employer to a retired employee 养老金；抚恤金；退休金

Even hourly employees receive benefits such as *pension* contributions and medical insurance. 甚至小时工也能领取养老金和医疗保险等福利。

perceive [pəˈsiːv]　　　　　　　　　　　　　　　　[同] detect

v. ①to understand or think of something or someone in a particular way 理解；认为 ②(fml.) to become aware of (sb./sth.); notice; observe 意识到；注意到

Many students *perceive* that on-the-job training is more important than college. 很多学生认为在职培训比大学的学习重要。

percent [pəˈsent]

n./adj. an amount out of a total of 100 parts 百分比

a 10 *percent* increase in house prices 房价涨幅 10%

percentage [pəˈsentɪdʒ]

n. an amount expressed as if it is part of a total which is 100 百分数；比例

The *percentage* of women students at the university has increased steadily. 大学里的女生比例有了稳定的增长。

responsible [rɪˈspɒnsəbl]　　　　　　　　　　　　　[同] accountable

adj. having the job or duty of doing sth. or taking care of sb./sth., so that you may be blamed if sth. goes wrong 有责任的；承担义务的

Even if parents no longer live together, they each should continue to be *responsible* for their children. 即使父母不再共同生活，他们也要分别对子女负责。

restore [rɪˈstɔː(r)]　　　　　　　　　　　　　　　[同] recover

v. to bring back a situation or feeling that existed before 恢复(某种情况或感受)

The most recent operation *restored* his sight. 最近的一次手术使他恢复了视力。

restrain [rɪˈstreɪn]　　　　　　　　　　　　　　　[同] inhibit

v. to stop sb./sth. from doing sth., esp. by using physical force (尤指用武力)制止；管制

The disease can be *restrained* long enough for scientists to discover an antidote. 这种病可以被控制足够长的时间来让科学家们寻找一种治疗方法。

setback [ˈsetbæk]

n. a difficulty or problem that delays or prevents sth., or makes a situation worse 挫折；阻碍

The team suffered a major *setback* when their best player was injured. 最优秀的队员受了伤，使得这支队伍的实力大打折扣。

severe [sɪˈvɪə(r)]

adj. strict or harsh in attitude or treatment; imposing stern discipline 严格的；严厉的；苛刻的；纪律严明的

be *severe* with one's children 对子女很严

✓ **shabby** ['ʃæbi]

adj. in poor condition through much use or being badly cared for (指东西) 因为使用过久或照管不善而破旧的

a *shabby* dress 破旧的连衣裙

✓ **shallow** ['ʃæləʊ] [同] superficial [反] deep

adj. not deep 浅的

The beach itself is very clean and the water is *shallow* and safe. 海滩本身很干净，水很浅也很安全。

yield [jiːld]

① *v.* to produce or provide sth., for example a profit, result or crop 出产 (作物) ; 产生 (收益、效益)

The research has *yielded* useful information. 这项研究提供了有用的资料。

② *n.* the total amount of crops, profits, etc. that are produced 产量 ; 产出 ; 利润

Subsidies for pesticides and artificial fertilizers encourage farmers to use greater quantities than are needed to get the highest economic crop *yield*. 政府在杀虫剂和人造化肥上的补贴鼓励了农民对其过量使用以达到最高的经济作物产出量。

✓ **youngster** ['jʌŋstə(r)] [同] juvenile

n. (infml.) a young person or a child 年轻人 ; 少年 ; 儿童

The camp is for *youngsters* aged 8 to 14. 这次夏令营是为 8 至 14 岁的少年儿童安排的。

Take the Test ➤➤

一、英汉互译

抽象的	obstrack	abundance	大量
设施	facilities	canteen	食堂
身份证明	identification	restrain	抑制
概述	overview	setback	挫折
退休金	pension	youngster	年青人

二、翻译句子

1) 有大量的证据来支持研究结果。(abundance)

There is an abundance of evidence to support the research findings

2) 环境承受经济的发展和人口的能力是有限的。(capacity)

3) 很多学生认为在职培训比大学的学习重要。(perceive)

Many students perceive the on-the-job training is

4) 大学里的女生比例有了稳定的增长。(percentage)

✓ **abandon** [əˈbændən]　　　　　　　　　　　　　　　[同] desert, forsake [反] reclaim

v. to leave a thing or place, esp. because it is impossible or dangerous to stay 离弃；舍弃

Over the past 40 years, most people have ***abandoned*** their nomadic ways, but they still rely heavily on nature to provide food and clothing. 在过去的 40 年里，大部分人放弃了游牧生活，但他们仍然在很大程度上依赖大自然提供衣食来源。

✓ **abnormal** [æbˈnɔːml]　　　　　　　　　　　　　　　　　　　　　　[反] normal

adj. very different from usual in a way that seems strange, worrying, wrong, or dangerous 反常的，变态的

an ***abnormal*** level of cholesterol 胆固醇值不正常

absorb [əbˈsɔːb]　　　　　　　　　　　　　　　　　　　　　　　　[反] give out

v. to take in liquid, gas, or another substance from the surface or space around 吸收

The moisture is ***absorbed*** by thirsty plants. 湿气被干渴的植物所吸收。

✓ **bacteria** [bækˈtɪərɪə]

n. (plural of bacterium) a type of very small organism that lives in air, earth, water, plants and animals, often one which causes a disease 细菌

Bacteria grow best in hot, damp conditions, and are often to be found in most domestic bathrooms and kitchens. 细菌适宜在湿热的条件下生长，在大多数的家庭厨房和浴室里都能发现它们。

✓ **badminton** [ˈbædmɪntən]

n. game for two or four people played with rackets and shuttlecocks on a court with a high net 羽毛球运动

badminton tournament 羽毛球巡回赛

✓ **cafeteria** [ˌkæfəˈtɪərɪə]　　　　　　　[同] coffee shop, lunchroom

n. a restaurant where you choose and pay for your meal at a counter and carry it to a table 自助餐厅；自助食堂

In addition to a small ***cafeteria*** at the new center, the main Visitors' Center has many meal choices. 除了新中心的小餐厅外，主游客接待中心还有很多吃饭的地方。

✓ **calculate** [ˈkælkjuleɪt]　　　　　　[同] compute, estimate

v. to work (sth.) out by using numbers or one's judgment; estimate 计算；推算

It has been ***calculated*** that the world's population will double by 2050. 据推算，世界人口在 2050 年将要增加一倍。

✓ **calendar** [ˈkælɪndə(r)]　　　　　　　　　　　　　　[同] programme

n. a page or a series of pages showing the days, weeks and months of a particular year, esp. one that you hang on a wall 日历；挂历

a ***calendar*** for 2010 2010 年日历

✓ **campus** [ˈkæmpəs]

n. the buildings of a university or college and the land around them（大学、学院的）校园，校区
Students are allowed to park their cars on the *campus*. 校园里允许学生停车。

✓ **cancel** [ˈkænsl] [同] drop, call off
v. to decide that sth. that has been arranged will not now take place 取消；撤销
All flights have been *cancelled* because of bad weather. 因天气恶劣，所有航班均被取消了。

✓ **damage** [ˈdæmɪdʒ] [同] injury/injure
n./v. loss of value, attractiveness or usefulness caused by an event, accident, etc. 损失；损害；损毁
Government policies have frequently compounded the environmental *damage* that farming can cause. 政府的政策往往加重了种植业引发的环境破坏。

✓ **damp** [dæmp] [反] dry
adj. not completely dry; slightly wet 不完全干燥的；潮湿的
Don't sleep between *damp* sheets. 睡觉时不要用潮湿的被褥。

✓ **dash** [dæʃ] [同] rush
v. move suddenly and quickly; rush 猛冲；突进
I spent three weeks reading and doing general research and then I *dashed* the writing off very quickly. 我花了三周的时间阅读并做了广泛的研究，之后很快就把文章写完了。

✓ **ease** [iːz] [反] burden
n. lack of difficulty 容易；不费劲
He passed the exam with *ease*. 他轻而易举地通过了考试。

✓ **ecology** [iˈkɒlədʒi]
n. the way in which plants, animals, and people are related to each other and to their environment, or the scientific study of this 生态关系；生态学
Maria set out to catalog species according to their *ecology* and their sexuality. 玛莉亚开始根据生态关系和性特征对物种进行分类。

✓ **fabric** [ˈfæbrɪk] [同] material
n. cloth used for making clothes, curtains, etc. 织物；布料
She bought some *fabric* to make shirts from. 她买了些做衬衫的布料。

✓ **fabulous** [ˈfæbjələs] [同] wonderful
adj. (infml.) extremely good or impressive 极好的；绝妙的
The room has *fabulous* views across the lake. 这间房有着极佳的湖景。

✓ **gallery** [ˈgæləri]
n. covered walk or corridor partly open at one side; colonnade 走廊；柱廊
Its oak wall consists of a grassy mound and the front is a long glass *gallery*. 成排的橡树立于覆盖着青草的土堆之上，而它的正面是一条长长的玻璃走廊。

✓ **habitat** [ˈhæbɪtæt]
n. natural environment of an animal or a plant; home（动物或植物的）自然环境；栖息地
This creature's (natural) *habitat* is the jungle. 这种动物的（天然）栖息地是丛林。

✓ **ideal** [aɪˈdiːəl] [同] ①flawless, perfect
①*adj.* satisfying one's idea of what is perfect; most suitable 理想的；完美的；最合适的
ideal weather for a holiday 度假的理想天气
②*n.* person or thing regarded as perfect 完美的人或事物
She's looking for a job, but hasn't found her *ideal* yet. 她在找工作，但还未找到最理想的。

idealism [aɪˈdɪəlɪzɪəm]

n. the belief that you should live your life according to high standards and principles, even when they are very difficult to achieve 理想主义；唯心论

the ***idealism*** of the younger generation 年轻一代的理想主义

√ **identical** [aɪˈdentɪkl]　　　　　　　　　　　　　　　　　　　　　　[同] same

adj. the same 同一的

Just ahead of me are two buildings that look like ***identical*** twins. 在我正前方是两栋如同双胞胎般一模一样的建筑。

√ **jail** [dʒeɪl] = gaol

n. (=gaol) prison 监狱

The castle had been used as a ***jail***. 那城堡曾用作监狱。

√ **jam** [dʒæm]

traffic jam 交通堵塞 = congestion of traffic.

n. sweet substance made by boiling fruit with sugar until it is thick, usu. preserved in jars, etc. 果酱

He spread some strawberry ***jam*** on his toast. 他把草莓酱涂在了烤面包片上。

v. to squeeze sb./sth. (into a space) so that he/it cannot move out 将某人 / 某物塞（进某空间）不能出来

The ship was ***jammed*** in the ice. 轮船卡在冰中间无法驶出。

keen [kiːn]　　　　　　　　　　　　　　　　　　　　　　　　　[同] enthusiastic

adj. eager; enthusiastic 热切的；热情的；热心的

Scientists are increasingly ***keen*** to find out what's going on. 科学家们越来越热切地想探明究竟。

√ **lab** [læb]

n. (infml.) laboratory 实验室

I'll meet you outside the science ***lab***. 我将在科学实验室外面见你。

√ **label** [ˈleɪbl]　　　　　　　　　　　　　　　　　　　　　　　　[同] ①②tag

①*n.* piece of paper, cloth, metal, etc. on or beside an object and describing its nature, name, owner, destination, etc. 标签；标记

I read the information on the ***label*** before deciding which jam to buy. 我先看看果酱标签上的说明再决定买哪种。

② *v.* to attach a label onto sth. or write information on sth. 做标记，贴标签

Label the diagram clearly. 清晰地标注图表。

√ **magnet** [ˈmæɡnət]

n. ①a piece of iron or steel that can stick to metal or make other metal objects move towards itself 磁铁 ② person or thing that has a powerful attraction 有强大吸引力的人或物

The region has become a ***magnet*** for small businesses. 这个地区很吸引小企业。

√ **magnificent** [mæɡˈnɪfɪsnt]　　　　　　　　　　　　　　　[同] grand, gorgeous

adj. extremely attractive and impressive; deserving praise 壮丽的；宏伟的

The seven-day holiday includes a ***magnificent*** book giving the local history. 七天的假期计划包含一本精美的介绍当地历史的书。

√ **naked** [ˈneɪkɪd] *the naked eye 肉眼*　　　　　　　　　　　　[同] nude

adj. not wearing any clothes 裸体的；裸露的

The planet should be visible to the ***naked*** eye. 这颗行星肉眼就能看得见。

√ **overseas** [ˌəʊvəˈsiːz]　　　　　　　　　　　　　　　　　　　[同] ①②abroad

① *adv.* to or in a foreign country that is across the sea 在海外，在国外

He plans to study *overseas*. 他打算去国外读书。

② *adj.* [ˈəʊvəsiːz] coming from, existing in, or happening in a foreign country that is across the sea 海外的，国外的

overseas students 海外留学生

✓ **oversee** [ˌəʊvəˈsiː]   [同] monitor

v. to watch over and control (sb./sth.); supervise 监督，监视(某人/某物)

You must employ someone to *oversee* the project. 你得雇个人监督这一工程。

✓ **peer** [pɪə(r)]

n. person who is equal to another in rank, status or age (官阶、等级、年龄)同等的人 ；凝视

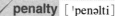

Teenagers often start smoking because of *peer* pressure. 青少年开始吸烟通常是由于同龄人间的相互影响。

✓ **penalty** [ˈpenəlti]   [同] fine

n. thing imposed as a punishment(e.g. imprisonment or a fine) 施加的惩罚(如监禁、罚款)

People who work reduced hours pay a huge *penalty* in career terms. 那些工作减少工时的人在职业中会受到很重的惩罚。

✓ **resort** [rɪˈzɔːt]

n. a place where a lot of people go on holiday vacation 旅游胜地；度假胜地

There are beach *resorts* all along the coast on this part of the island. 在岛的这一边，沿岸有许多海滨胜地。

✗ **resource** [rɪˈsɔːs]

n. a supply of sth. that a country, an organization or a person has and can use, esp. to increase their wealth 资源；财力

The fundamental conditions and *resources* for health are peace, shelter, education, food and so on. 健康的基本条件和来源是要有和平的环境，有避身之处，能接受教育，有食物等等。

✓ **response** [rɪˈspɒns]   [同] answer

n. a spoken or written answer (口头的或书面的)回答；答复

I received an encouraging *response* to my advertisement. 我的广告宣传有了令人鼓舞的回应。

✓ **sequence** [ˈsiːkwəns]   [同] order

n. the order that something happens or exists in 前后顺序

The system follows a logical *sequence*. 该系统遵循逻辑顺序。

✓ **series** [ˈsɪəriːz]   [同] succession

n. number of things, events, etc. of a similar kind, esp. placed or occurring one after another 一系列的事物

There will be a *series* of demonstrations. 将会有一系列的证实。

✓ **session** [ˈseʃn]   [同] ②conference

n. ①single continuous period spent in one activity (进行某活动连续的)一段时间 ②a formal meeting or group of meetings, especially of a law court or parliament 会议

After several *sessions* at the gym, I feel a lot fitter. 我在健身房锻炼了几次，觉得身体好多了。

worship [ˈwɜːʃɪp]   [同] ①adore ②adoration

①*v.* to love and admire sb. very much, esp. so much that you cannot see their faults 爱慕；崇拜(尤指达到看不到缺点的地步)

Christians *worship* God. 基督教徒信仰上帝。

②*n.* a strong feeling of love and respect for sb./sth. 崇拜；爱慕

What she feels for him is akin to **worship**. 她对他的感情近乎崇拜。

wrap [ræp]　　　　　　　　　　　　　　　　　　　　　　　[同] enfold　[反] unwrap

v. to cover sth. completely in paper or other material, for example when you are giving it as a present 包，裹（礼物等）

He spent the evening **wrapping** up the Christmas presents. 他花了一个晚上的时间包圣诞礼物。

wrap up

Take the Test ≫

一、英汉互译

羽毛球	badminton	bacteria	细菌
自助餐厅	Cafeteria	ecology	生物学
标记	Label	habitat	栖息地
同龄人	peer	identical	相同的
前后顺序	sequence	penalty	

二、翻译句子

1）据推算，世界人口在 2050 年将要增加一倍。（calculate）
_____

2）我花了三周的时间阅读并做了广泛的研究，之后很快就把文章写完了。（dash off）
_____

3）在我正前方是两栋如同双胞胎般一模一样的建筑。（identical）
_____

4）青少年开始吸烟通常是由于同龄人间的相互影响。（peer）
_____

Few things are impossible in themselves; and it is often for want of will, rather than of means, that man fails to succeed.

事情很少有根本做不成的；其所以做不成，与其说是条件不够，不如说是由于决心不够。

——法国作家 罗切福考尔德（La Rocheforcauld, French writer）

Word List 3

✓ academic [ˌækəˈdemɪk]　　　　　　　　　　　　　　　　[同] scholastic

adj. relating to education, esp. at college or university level 学业的，学术的

This new welfare service is open to all students at London's *academic* institutions. 这项新的福利措施适用于伦敦学术机构的所有学生。

✓ academy [əˈkædəmi]

n. an official organization which encourages the development of literature, art, science, etc. 学院，学会

Having won 6 *Academy* Awards, *The Godfater* is the greatest mafia film of all time. 获得 6 项奥斯卡大奖的《教父》是迄今为止最棒的意大利黑帮电影。

✓ access [ˈækses]

① *n.* the opportunity or right to use something or to see sb./sth. （使用或见到某人／某物的）机会，权利

Our teachers have *access* to an extensive range of materials, including the very latest in language teaching technology. 我们的老师可以使用大量的材料，包括最先进的语言教学技术方面的。

② *v.* (fml.) to reach, enter or use something 到达；使用

Listening to lectures in many ways is just giving you information that you could *access* for yourself in the library. 从很多方面而言，听讲座只不过是让你得到了你本来可以自己在图书馆获得的信息。

✓ balance [ˈbæləns]

n./v. condition that exists when two opposites are equal or in correct proportions 均衡状态；均势

Most insects are quite harmless and play an essential role in maintaining the *balance* of nature.

多数的昆虫不仅无害还在维持自然界的平衡方面扮演着重要的角色。

balcony [ˈbælkəni]

n. platform with a wall or rail built onto the outside wall of a building and reached from an upstairs room 阳台

All bedrooms are double with private bathroom; some with a *balcony*. 所有的卧室都是双人房并有独立的浴室；其中一些还有阳台。

capture [ˈkæptʃə(r)]　　　　　　　　　　　　　　　　　　　[同] ② catch

v. ① to take control of a place, building, etc. using force 用武力夺取；攻占 ② to succeed in recording, showing, or describing a situation or feeling, using words or pictures 捕捉住，（用照片等）留存

A still picture could only imply the existence of time, while time in a novel passed at the whim of the reader. But in cinema, the real, objective flow of time was *captured*. 一张静止的图片只能表明时间的存在，一部小说中时间的流逝是由读者的一时念头决定的，但电影可以记录时

间真实、客观的流动。

career [kəˈrɪə(r)] ✓

n. the series of jobs that a person has in a particular area of work, usu. involving more responsibility as time passes 生涯；职业

What made you decide on *career* as a vet? 是什么驱使你选择兽医这门职业的？

carve [kɑːv] [同] sculpture

v. to make objects, pattern, etc. by cutting away material from wood or stone 雕刻

The statue was *carved* out of a single piece of stone. 这座雕像是用一整块石料雕成的。

cashier [kæˈʃɪə(r)] ✓

n. a person whose job is to receive and pay out money in a bank, shop, hotel, etc. 出纳员

She worked as a petrol station *cashier*. 她以前在加油站做收银员。

dawn [dɔːn] [反] sunset

n. the time at the beginning of the day when light first appears 黎明

The boats set off at *dawn*. 小船天一亮就出发。We reached harbour at sunset

the *dawn* of civilisation/time 文明 / 时间的起始

deadline [ˈdedlaɪn] ✓

n. point in time by which sth. must be done 截止时间

You may wish to know more about essay *deadlines*, or how to use the library. 或许你想更多地了解论文的截止时间或如何使用图书馆。

dean [diːn] ✓

n. head of a university department of studies (大学的)系主任

dean of the faculty of law 法律系系主任

effect [ɪˈfekt] ✓ [同] influence [近] impact

n. a change that sb./sth. causes in sb./sth. else; a result 效应；影响；结果

Although both programs had similar *effects* on productivity, they had significantly different results in other respects. 尽管两个项目对生产力的作用相差无几，在其他方面却有着显著的不同。

efficient [ɪˈfɪʃnt] [反] inefficient

adj. doing sth. well and thoroughly with no waste of time, money, or energy 效率高的，有能力的

efficient heating equipment 效能好的供暖设备

elaborate [ɪˈlæbərət] [同] complex [反] simple

adj. very complicated and detailed; carefully prepared and organized 复杂的；详尽的；精心制作的

Archaeological traces of far more *elaborate* cultures have been dismissed as the ruins of invaders from outside the region. 那些更为复杂的文明的考古线索被当作外来侵略者留下的废墟而不被理会。

factor [ˈfæktə(r)] ✓ [同] element

n. one of several things that cause or influence sth. 因素；要素

Freight rates and cargo-handling schedules become insignificant *factors* in deciding where to make the product. 载货率和货物运送日程成为决定货物生产地点的无关紧要的因素。

faculty [ˈfæklti]

n. ①a department or group of related departments within a university (大学)系；科

the *Faculty* of Law 法律系

② any of the physical or mental abilities that a person is born with 官能；天赋

the *faculty* of sight 视觉

gap [gæp]

n. deficiency which needs to be filled 需加填补的不足、缺陷或空白

There was a terrible *gap* in her life after her husband died. 丈夫去世后，她的生活出现了一片极大的空白。

✓ **garbage** [ˈgɑːbɪdʒ] [同] junk, litter

n. (esp. AmE) waste material, esp. domestic refuse 废物；(尤指家庭的)垃圾

garbage collection/disposal 垃圾收集 / 处理

✓ **hall** [hɔːl]

n. (also hallway) space or passage on the inside of the main entrance or front door of a building 门厅；正门走廊

Leave your coat in the *hall*. 把你的大衣放在门厅。

halt [hɔːlt]

n. temporary stop; interruption of progress 暂停；停顿

It took me just seconds to start reserving a car but then the whole thing ground to a *halt* and refused all attempts to access the reservation system. 开始订车只花了我几秒钟，可之后进程慢慢地停了下来，我再也无法登录预订系统了。

ignorance [ˈɪgnərəns] [同] illiteracy

n. lack of knowledge or information (about sth.) (对某事物)无知

We are in complete *ignorance* of your plans. 我们对你的计划一无所知。

ignorant [ˈɪgnərənt] [同] empty-headed

adj. not knowing facts or information that you ought to know 无知的；愚昧的；不知道的

He's not stupid, just *ignorant*. 他并不蠢，只是无知罢了。

"We're all ignorant, just about different stuff."
— Will Rogers

✓ **ignore** [ɪgˈnɔː(r)] [同] neglect

v. to take no notice of (sb./sth.) 忽视

If you *ignore* these instructions, this medicine could affect your heart rhythm. 如果你服用时无视这些说明，这种药会影响你的心率的。

lag [læg] [同] delay

v. to go too slow; fail to keep pace with others 走得极慢；落后

Prices are rising sharply, while incomes are *lagging* far behind. 物价飞涨而收入却远远落后。

✓ **maintain** [meɪnˈteɪn] [同] keep up

v. to make sth. continue at the same level, standard, etc. 维持；保持

Creating health would help people *maintain* healthy behaviours and lifestyles. 创造健康能帮助人们保持健康的行为和生活方式。

✓ **majesty** [ˈmædʒəsti] [同] nobility

n. the impressive and attractive quality that sth. has 雄伟壮观；庄严

the sheer *majesty* of St. Peter's in Rome 罗马圣·彼得大教堂的雄伟庄严

✓ **major** [ˈmeɪdʒə(r)] [同] ①chief

① *adj.* very large or important, when compared to other things or people of a similar kind 主要

的；重要的

② *n.* the main subject that a student studies at college or university 专业

There is a *major* problem with parking in Beijing. 在北京，停车是个大问题。

✓ **majority** [mə'dʒɒrəti]	*the ~ of*	[反] minority

n. the largest part of a group of people or things 太部分；大多数

The *majority* of the victims are children. 大部分受害者是孩子。

✓ **namely** ['neɪmli]

adv. used to introduce more exact and detailed information about sth. that you have just mentioned 即；也就是

Tourism is a leisure activity which presupposes its opposite, *namely* regulated and organized work. 旅游是一种要先以其相对面做基础的休闲行为，也就是有组织有纪律的工作。

overthrow [ˌəʊvə'θrəʊ]   [同] overturn

v. to cause the downfall or defeat of (sb./sth.); put an end to 推翻，打倒（某人/某物）；使终止或结束

The rebels tried to *overthrow* the government. 叛乱者企图推翻政府。

✓ **performance** [pə'fɔːməns]

n. ①when someone performs a play or a piece of music 演出 ②how well or badly a person, company, etc. does a particular job or activity 表现；业绩

a training program to improve employees' *performance* 旨在改善员工业绩的培训项目

✓ **period** ['pɪəriəd]

n. a particular length of time with a beginning and an end 一段时间

The new taxes will be introduced over a *period* of time. 新的税种会在一段时间后开始征收。

✓ **periodical** [ˌpɪəri'ɒdɪkl]   [同] ②journal

① *adj.* published at a regular intervals of more than one day 定期出版的

② *n.* a publication issued at regular intervals of more than one day 期刊

Library requests in the field of science and technology showed that only 13 per cent were for foreign language *periodicals*. 图书馆在科学技术这个领域的需求只有13%是外文期刊。

permanent ['pɜːmənənt] ≠ perpetual 永久的；不间断的   [同] lasting, enduring

adj. lasting or expected to last for a long time or for ever 永久的；长久的

She is looking for *permanent* employment. 她正在找固定的工作。

✓ **permission** [pə'mɪʃn]   [同] allowance, consent

n. act of allowing sb. to do sth.; consent 许可；允许；同意

You must ask *permission* before taking any photographs inside the church. 在教堂内拍照得事先征得许可。

✓ **restrict** [rɪ'strɪkt]   [同] limit, confine

v. to limit the size, amount or range of sth. 限制，限定（数量、范围等）

I'd like to start by *restricting* myself to countries where English is the main language. 我愿在论述之初就限定自己只讲英语国家的情况。

✓ **result** [rɪ'zʌlt]   [同] ①effect

① *n.* the information that you get from a scientific test or piece of research 结果；成果

The attempt was made without *result*. 那尝试白费心机了。

② *v.* to happen because of sth. else that happen first（因…）发生；（随…）发生

When water levels rise, flooding *results*. 水位上升，就会发生洪水。

✓ **resume** [rɪˈzuːm]　　　　　　　　　　　　　　　　[同] continue, pick up

v. (fml.) to begin again or continue after an interruption 重新开始；（中断后）继续

She *resumed* her career after an interval of six years. 经过六年的间歇后，她又重操旧业。

shed [ʃed]　　　　　　　　　　　　　　　　　　　　　[同] fall off

v. ① if a plant sheds its leaves or if an animal sheds skin or hair, they fall off as part of a natural process 脱落；掉毛；蜕皮 ② shed light on to make something easier to understand, by providing new or better information 帮助理解；增加认识

Cross-national comparison can also *shed* light on this question. 跨国间的比较能让我们更好地理解这个问题。
照明，照亮。

shelter [ˈʃeltə(r)]

① *n.* a place to live, considered as one of the basic needs of life 住所

② *v.* to give shelter to sb./sth.; protect sb./sth. 给某人／某物提供庇护处；保护某人／某物

Is our country's industry *sheltered* from foreign competition? 我国的工业在与外国竞争时是否有足够的保障？

✓ **shift** [ʃɪft]

v. to (cause sth./sb./oneself to) change or move from one position or direction to another（使某物／某人／自己）改变位置或方向

He *shifted* his focus to designing buildings. 他把自己关注的焦点转移到了建筑设计上。

Take the Test ≫

一、英汉互译

阳台	_____	faculty	_____
出纳员	cashier	majority	大部分
最后期限	deadline	periodical	期刊
垃圾	garbage	permanent	永久的
忽视	ignore / ignorant	shelter	_____

二、翻译句子

1）我们的老师可以使用大量的材料，包括最先进的语言教学技术方面的。（access）

_____

2）或许你想更多地了解论文的截止时间或如何使用图书馆。（deadline）

_____

3）物价飞涨而收入却远远落后。（lag）

_____

4）跨国间的比较能让我们更好地理解这个问题。（shed light on）

_____

accommodate [əˈkɒmədeit]   [同]②adapt ①hold

v. ① to provide with a place to live or to be stored in 容纳，提供住宿 ② (fml.) to get used to a new situation 适应

A variety of different organizational structures have evolved over time to **accommodate** the needs of both the company and society. 各种不同的组织结构不断出现和发展以适应公司和社会的需要。

accommodation [əˌkɒməˈdeiʃn]   [同] (AmE) accommodations

n. (BrE) a place to live, work or stay in 住宿

I need to know what kind of **accommodation** you'd like, so I can get you something suitable. 我得知道你想要什么样的住宿条件，这样我才能给你找到合适的住处。

                                                                              [同] go hand in hand with

accompany [əˈkʌmpəni]

v. to happen or appear with something else 陪同；伴随

In real situations the number and words are often **accompanied** by gestures to help resolve any confusion. 在实际情况中，数字及文字往往伴随着手势来解决(交流中的)困惑。

ban [bæn]   [同]②prohibit, forbid

① n. an official order that prevents sth. from being used or done 禁令

② v. to officially forbid (sth.) 明令禁止(某事物)

The play was **banned** (by the censor). 该剧本遭(审查员)查禁。

barbecue [ˈbɑːbikjuː]

n. outdoor party at which food is cooked on metal frame over an open fire (吃烤肉等的)烧烤

a big **barbecue** lunch party 一个大型的烧烤午餐派对

catalogue [ˈkætəlɒg]   [近] list

n. a complete list of items, for example of things that people can look at or buy 目录，目录簿

to consult the library **catalogue** 查看图书馆目录

category [ˈkætəgəri]   [同] group

n. a group of people or things with particular features in common 类别，种类

The results of this survey can be divided into three main **categories**. 这次调查结果可分为三大类。

caution [ˈkɔːʃn]   *Warn*   [同]①warning

① n. the quality of being very careful to avoid danger or risks 谨慎，小心

We must proceed with extreme **caution**. 我们必须谨小慎微。

② v. to warn sb. about the possible dangers or problems of sth. 警告；告诫；提醒

I would **caution** against getting too involved. 我想告诫说，别陷得太深。

cease [siːs]   [同] stop, discontinue *v.* (fml.) to stop happening or existing; to stop sth. from happening or existing (使)停止，终止，结束

Welfare payments *cease* as soon as an individual starts a job. 一旦就业，即停发福利救济。

✓ **celebrate** [ˈselɪbreɪt] [同] commemorate

v. to show that a day or an event is important by doing sth. special on it 庆祝，庆贺

How do people *celebrate* New Year in your country? 你们国家的人怎样庆贺新年？

✓ **debate** [dɪˈbeɪt] [同] argumentation

n. a formal argument or discussion of a question, e.g. at a public meeting or in Parliament, with two or more opposing speakers, and often ending in a vote 正式的辩论，讨论

The *debate* surrounding literacy is one of the most charged in education. 在教学中，围绕文化程度的辩论气氛最为紧张。

decade [ˈdekeɪd]

n. period of ten years 十年

the first *decade* of the 20th century 20 世纪最初的十年

✓ **element** [ˈelɪmənt] [同] component

n. a necessary or typical part of sth. 要素；基本部分；典型部分

He resisted imitating architectural styles and adding design *elements* solely for ornamentation. 他坚决反对盲目模仿建筑风格以及单纯为了装饰而添加建筑材料。

✓ **elevate** [ˈelɪveɪt] [同] raise, promote

v. (fml.) to give sb./sth. a higher position or rank, often more important than they deserve 提拔；晋升(到不应有的位置)

He *elevated* many of his friends to powerful positions within the government. 他将许多朋友都提拔到政府部门的要职上。

✓ **faint** [feɪnt] [反] ①clear

① *adj.* that cannot be clearly seen, heard or smelt (光、声、味)微弱的；不清楚的

a *faint* smell of perfume 淡淡的香水味

② *v.* to become unconscious when not enough blood is going to your brain, usu. because of the heat, a shock, etc. 昏厥

to *faint* from hunger 饿昏过去

✓ **faith** [feɪθ] [同] belief

n. a strong feeling of trust or confidence in someone or something 信念，宗教信仰

People lose *faith* in their culture. 人们失去了对其文化的信仰。

✓ **garment** [ˈɡɑːmənt] [同] clothe

n. (fml.) a piece of clothing 衣服；外衣

She works in the *garment* district of Manhattan. 她在曼哈顿的服装区工作。

✓ **gather** [ˈɡæðə(r)] [同] group

v. to come together and form a group, or to make people do this 聚集；召集

At 10 o'clock, all the new students will *gather* in the Main Hall. 十点钟的时候，全部新生将聚集在中央大厅。

✓ **hamper** [ˈhæmpə(r)] [同] tie one's hands

v. to prevent the free movement or activity of (sb.); hinder (sb./sth.) 束缚(某人)；妨碍(某人/某物)

Our progress was *hampered* by the bad weather. 我们的进程受到了恶劣天气的阻碍。

handful [ˈhændfʊl]   [同] few

n. an amount that you can hold in your hand 一把

Approximately 1,500 beetles are released, a *handful* at a time, into fresh cow pats in the cow pasture. 大约 1500 只甲壳虫被一次一把地放到牧场上新鲜的牛粪里去了。

✓ **illegal** [ɪˈliːgl]   [同] unlawful

adj. against the law; not legal 不合法的; 违法的

Some may also earn income through begging, or through theft and other *illegal* activities.
一些人也可能通过乞讨或者偷窃以及其他非法行为来获得收入。

✓ **illiterate** [ɪˈlɪtərət]   [同] ignorant

adj. not able to read or write 不会读或不会写的; 不识字的

an *illiterate* child 不识字的孩子

✓ **illusion** [ɪˈluːʒn]

n. an idea or opinion that is wrong, especially about yourself 错误的观念; 幻觉; 错觉

I have no *illusions* about my ability. 我对自己的能力如何颇有自知之明。

✓ **illustrate** [ˈɪləstreɪt]   [近] clarify

v. to explain or make (sth.) clear by examples, diagrams, pictures, etc. (用示例、图表等) 说明, 阐明 (某事物)

I'd like to *illustrate* with reference to a specific event which occurred several years ago. 我想要引用一些参考资料来阐明一件发生于数年之前的具体事件。

✓ **jog** [dʒɒg]

v. (usu. go jogging) run slowly and steadily for a time, for physical exercise 慢跑

He goes *jogging* every evening. 他每天晚上都要慢跑。

✓ **joint** [dʒɔɪnt]   [近] shared

adj. involving two or more people or groups, or owned or shared by them 共同的, 联合的

The Y.S.E.I in Zambia is a *joint* program with the Red Cross Society and the Y.W.C.A. 赞比亚的 Y.S.E.I.是红十字会与 Y.W.C.A.的联合项目。

✓ **landlord** [ˈlændlɔːd]

n. a man who rents a room, building, or piece of land to someone 房东

If you have a pet, ask your previous *landlord* for a reference letter stating that your animal is well-behaved. 如果你养宠物的话, 请让先前的房东写封信, 证明你的宠物表现很好。

✓ **landscape** [ˈlændskeɪp]

n. scenery of an area of land (陆上) 风景, 景色

It may be difficult to fit trees into the local *landscape*. 在当地的风景中加上一些树可能比较困难。

✓ **mall** [mɔːl, mæl]

n. (AmE) a large, often enclosed shopping complex containing various stores, businesses, and restaurants 大型的常是封闭的综合商业区

Let's go to the *mall*. 我们去商场吧。

manifest [ˈmænɪfest]   [同] ②clear

① *v.* to show sth. clearly, esp. a feeling, an attitude or a quality 表明, 清楚显示 (尤指情感、态度或品质)

Social tensions were *manifested* in the recent political crisis. 最近的政治危机显示了社会关系

的紧张。

clear and obvious.

② *adj.* (fml.) easy to see or understand 明显的；显而易见的

His nervousness was *manifest* to all. 所有在场的人都看出了他很紧张。

---

manipulate [məˈnɪpjuleɪt]

v. to control or influence sb./sth., often in a dishonest way so that they do not realize it (暗中)控制；操纵

The history of human civilisation is entwined with the history of the ways we have learned to manipulate water resources. 人类的文明史与人类学会以各种方式来驾驭水资源的历史交织在一起。

✓ **persevere** [ˌpɜːsɪˈvɪə(r)]　　　　　　　　　　　　　　[同] persist, carry on

v. (usu. apprec.) to continue trying to do sth., esp. in spite of difficulty 坚持做某事(尤指不畏困难)

You'll need to *persevere* if you want the business to succeed. 要想事业成功，就得持之以恒。

✓ **persist** [pəˈsɪst]　　　　　　　　　　　　　　　　　　　[反] desist

v. to continue to do sth., esp. in an obstinate and determined way and in spite of opposition, argument or failure 坚持；执意

If you *persist*, you will annoy them even more. 你若执迷不悔，他们就会更为恼火。

✓ **persistence** [pəˈsɪstəns]　　　　　　　　　　　　　　[同] continuation, tenacity

n. being persistent 坚持不懈；执意；持续；存留

His *persistence* was rewarded when they finally agreed to resume discussions. 他们终于同意继续谈判，这是他坚持不懈的结果。

✓ **personality** [ˌpɜːsəˈnæləti]　　　　　　　　　　　　　[同] character

n. characteristics and qualities of a person seen as a whole 人格；性格

a likeable *personality* 讨人喜欢的性格

✓ **retain** [rɪˈteɪn]　　　　　　　　　　　　　　　　　　　[同] preserve

maintain

v. (fml.) to keep sth.; to continue to have sth. 保持；保留

He struggled to *retain* control of the situation. 他曾努力保持对局势的控制。

✓ **retreat** [rɪˈtriːt]　　　　　　　　　　　　　　　　　　[同] ②withdraw

① *n.* an act of trying to escape from a particular situation to one that you think is safer or more pleasant 逃避；退避

Is watching television a *retreat* from reality? 看电视是对现实的一种逃避吗？

② *v.* to move away or back 离开；后退

The flood waters slowly *retreated*. 洪水慢慢地消退了。

✓ **reveal** [rɪˈviːl]　　　　　　　　　　　　　　　　　　　[同] disclose

v. to make sth. known to sb. 揭示；透露

Details of the murder were *revealed* by the local paper. 地方报纸披露了谋杀的细节。

✓ **shortage** [ˈʃɔːtɪdʒ]　　　　　　　　　　　　　　　　　[同] shortfall

n. lack of sth. needed; deficiency 缺少；不足；短缺

a *shortage* of rice, funds, equipment 大米、资金、设备不足

✓ **shortly** [ˈʃɔːtli]　　　　　　　　　　　　　　　　　　[同] presently

adv. in a short time; not long; soon 马上；立刻；不久

shortly afterwards 不久以后

shrink [ʃrɪŋk]　　　　　　　　　　　　　　　　　　　　[同] contract, compress

v. to (cause sth. to) become smaller, esp. because of moisture or heat or cold（使某物）收缩（尤指因受潮、受热或受凉所致）；萎缩

Employees who had been putting in 12-hour days, six days a week, found their time on the job *shrinking* to 10 hours daily. 原来每周工作 6 天、每天 12 个小时的雇员们发现工作时间减少到了每天 10 小时。

sigh [saɪ]

v. to take a long deep breath that can be heard, expressing sadness, tiredness, relief, etc. 叹息；叹气

He *sighed* with pleasure after the excellent meal. 他美餐一顿之后，满足地叹了口气。

Take the Test ▶▶

一、英汉互译

住宿	accomodate	faith	信仰
类别	category	illiterate	
要素	element	illustrate	阐释
性格	personality	landscape	风景
揭示	reveal	manipulate	暗中控制

二、翻译句子

1）我得知道你想要什么样的住宿条件，这样我才能给你找到合适的住处。（accommodation）

2）一旦就业，即停发福利救济。（cease）

3）你们国家的人怎样庆贺新年？（celebrate）

4）看电视是对现实的一种逃避吗？（retreat）

accomplish [əˈkʌmplɪʃ] ✓   [同] achieve, attain *finish* *to do.*

v. to succeed in doing something, esp. after trying very hard 完成(尤指克服了极大困难)

People discover that, once they learn to plan their days, all the work can be ***accomplished*** and there'll still be time for leisure. 人们发现一旦自己学会了做计划，所有的工作都可以完成，而且还有时间放松一下。

accordingly [əˈkɔːdɪŋli] ✓   [同] therefore, consequently, for that reason

adv. as a result of something 因此

There aren't many jobs available. ***Accordingly***, companies receive hundreds of resumes for every opening. 目前没有太多的就业机会。因此公司一旦有空缺的职位就会收到几百份简历。

account [əˈkaʊnt] ✓

① *n.* a written or spoken description of an event 介绍，描述

I'm going to give you a brief ***account*** of the history of the museum before letting you roam about on your own. 在大家自己游览之前，我先对本博物馆的历史做一个简要介绍。

② *v.* to be a particular amount or part of sth. (数量上、比例上)占

Coal continues to ***account*** for almost 27 per cent of the world's energy needs. 煤炭依然占到整个世界能源需求的近 27%。

bare [beə(r)]   [同] naked

adj. without the usual covering or protection 缺少遮盖的；没有保护的

with one's ***bare*** hands 赤手空拳(未带工具或武器)

ceremony [ˈserəməni]

n. a public or religious occasion that includes a series of formal or traditional actions 典礼；仪式

an awards/opening ***ceremony*** 颁奖/开幕仪式

certainty [ˈsɜːtnti] ✓   [同] assurance [反] uncertainty

n. the state of being certain 确定性

The question is one that can never be answered with any degree of ***certainty***. 这个问题是不可能带任何确定性来回答的。

certificate [ˌsəˈtɪfɪkət]

n. an official document that may be used to prove that the facts it states are true 证明，证明书

When you open an account, most banks ask you to bring your ***certificate*** of enrolment. 你开户时，大多数银行都要求你出具入学证明。

chain [tʃeɪn] ✓

n./v. ① a series of connected metal rings, used for pulling or fastening things 链子；锁链

② a group of shops or hotels owned by the same company 连锁商店

international hotel/supermarket ***chains*** 国际连锁宾馆/超市

③ people or things which are connected or next to each other forming a line 一连串；山脉

Eruptions have rifted continents, raised mountain ***chains***, constructed islands and shaped the topography of the earth. 火山喷发撕裂了大陆，形成了山脉，造就了岛屿，塑造了地球的地形特征。

✓ deceive [dɪˈsiːv] [同] beguile, fool

v. to make sb. believe sth. that is not true (so as to make him do sth.); to deliberately mislead sb. 欺骗某人(去做某事); 故意使(某人)误解

We were *deceived* into believing that he could help us. 我们受骗了，还以为他能帮助我们。

decent [ˈdiːsnt]

adj. of a good enough standard or quality 相当好的，像样的

You can't get anything *decent* under £10. 10镑以下根本买不到像样的东西。

declare [dɪˈkleə(r)]

v. ①to state officially and publicly that a particular situation exists or that something is true 宣告，声称 ②to tell a customs official that you are carrying goods on which you should pay tax when you enter a country 申报

We celebrate October 1st, the day when China *declared* independence. 我们庆祝 10 月 1 日，那一天中国宣布建国。

✓ embarrass [ɪmˈbærəs]

v. to make sb. feel shy, awkward or ashamed, esp. in a social situation (尤指在社交场合)使窘迫; 使尴尬

Her questions about my private life *embarrassed* me. 她询问我的私生活使我感到很尴尬。

embrace [ɪmˈbreɪs]

v. ①to put your arms around sb. as a sign of love or friendship 拥抱 ② to eagerly accept a new idea, opinion, religion, etc. 接受; 采纳

embrace opp Drawing1

Film has never lost its unique power to *embrace* its audiences and transport them to a different world. 电影不断地以其独特力量去拥抱观众并将他们带入到一个不同寻常的世界。

emerge [iˈmɜːdʒ] [近] appear [反] fade

v. to come out of a dark, enclosed or hidden place (从暗处或隐蔽处)出现，浮现，露出

A new style of architecture *emerged* to reflect more idealistic notions for the future. 一种新的建筑风格出现了，反映了对于未来更加理想化的想法。

fake [feɪk] *false*

① *adj.* not real and seeming to be something it is not, in order to deceive people 假的

a *fake* American accent 伪装的美国口音

② *n.* a copy of a valuable object, painting, etc. that is intended to deceive people 假货; 赝品

All the paintings proved to be *fakes*. 所有这些画结果证实都是赝品。

③ *v.* to make sth. false appear to be genuine, esp. in order to deceive sb. 伪造; 冒充

She *faked* her mother's signature on the document. 她仿照母亲的笔迹在文件上签了字。

✓ familiar [fəˈmɪliə(r)]

adj. well-known to you and easy to recognize 熟知的; 熟悉的

The voice on the phone sounded *familiar*. 电话里的声音听起来很熟悉。

✓ fan [fæn]

n. ① a machine with turning blades that is used to cool the air in a room by moving it around 电扇 ② someone who likes a particular sport or performing art very much, or who admires a famous person 迷; 狂热者

He's a big *fan* of Elvis Presley. 他是猫王的狂热粉丝。

√ gay [geɪ]

① *adj.* homosexual 同性恋的

I didn't know he was *gay*. 我不知道他是同性恋。

② *n.* sb. who is homosexual, esp. a man 同性恋者

handicapped [ˈhændikæpt]

adj. suffering from a serious physical or mental disability 有生理缺陷的；弱智的；残疾的

a school for the severely *handicapped* 残疾人学校

√ handle [ˈhændl]

① *n.* the part of an object that you use for holding it 把手；柄

It works by squeezing the *handle* to generate the power. 它是通过挤压把手产生能量而工作的。

② *v.* to deal with a situation or problem by behaving in a particular way and making particular decisions 处理

Most customers were satisfied with the way their complaints were *handled*. 绝大多数的客户对他们的投诉被处理的方式感到满意。

√ illustration [ˌɪləˈstreɪʃ(ə)n]   [近] example

n. drawing, diagram or picture in a book, magazine, etc. 书或杂志上的图画、图表或照片

colour *illustrations* 彩色插图

√ image [ˈɪmɪdʒ]

n. mental picture or idea 心目中的形象或概念

I have this *image* of you as always being cheerful. 在我的心目中，你的样子总是兴高采烈的。

√ imaginative [ɪˈmædʒɪnətiv]

adj. containing new and interesting ideas; good at thinking of new and interesting ideas 富有想象力的

an *imaginative* solution to the litter problem 一个解决乱扔弃问题的有创意的方法

imitate [ˈɪmɪteɪt]   [同] copy, reproduce

v. to copy the behaviour of (sb./sth.); take or follow as an example 学(某人／某物)的样子；仿效

Decide what you want to do; don't just *imitate* others. 想做什么自己决定，不要一味学别人。

√ journal [ˈdʒɜːnl]

n. newspaper or periodical, esp. one that is serious and deals with a specialized subject 报纸；定期刊物(尤指涉及某一学科的) 日记

Have you checked out the *journal* articles in the list? 你查看了列表上的那些刊物文章吗？

lane [leɪn]

n. strip of road marked out for a single line of traffic (有标志的)单行车道

bus *lane* 公交车道

mansion [ˈmænʃ(ə)n]

n. a large impressive house 公馆；宅第

Once a private *mansion*, it is a classic hotel in the best tradition. 这曾经是一处私人寓所，现在成为极具传统色彩的经典酒店。

manual [ˈmænjuəl]   [同] ②handbook

① *adj.* manual work involves using your hands or your physical strength rather than your mind 动手的；使用体力的

manual dexterity 心灵手巧

② *n.* a book that tells you how to do or operate sth. (handbook) 手册；指南

Bookstores now abound with *manuals* describing how to manage time and cope with stress.

现在书店里满是讲解如何利用时间和应对压力的手册。

✓ musical [ˈmjuːzɪkl]

adj. connected with music; containing music 音乐的；有音乐的

musical talent/ability/skill 音乐天赋 / 才能 / 技巧

naughty [ˈnɔːti]

adj. (BrE) (esp. of children) behaving badly; not willing to obey 顽皮的；淘气的

I don't believe in hitting children, no matter how ***naughty*** they've been. 我觉得打孩子是不对的，不管他们有多调皮。

✓ overwhelming [ˌəʊvəˈwelmɪŋ]

adj. too great to resist or overcome; very great 压倒一切的；无法抗拒的；巨大的

an ***overwhelming*** urge to smoke 不可遏止的吸烟冲动

✓ personnel [ˌpɜːsəˈnel]   [同] staff

n. people employed in one of the armed forces, a firm or a public office; staff 人员；职员

trained ***personnel*** 经过培训的职员

✓ perspective [pəˈspektɪv]   [同] vista, outlook

n. subjective evaluation of relative significance; a point of view 客观的观点，看法

We have to look at everything from an international ***perspective***. 任何问题我们都要从全球的角度来看待。

✓ persuade [pəˈsweɪd]   [同] induce
                                                                    convince

v. to make someone decide to do something 说服；劝服

After this accident, it will be difficult for the government to ***persuade*** people that nuclear power stations are safe. 这次事件后，政府将很难让人们相信核电站的安全性。

pessimistic [ˌpesɪˈmɪstɪk]   *fz : optimistic*

adj. influenced by or showing pessimism 悲观的；悲观主义的

Many people in our era are drawn to the ***pessimistic*** view that the new media are destroying old skills. 我们时代的很多人都悲观地认为新的媒体将会破坏旧的技术。

✓ revenue [ˈrevənjuː]   [近] income

n. the money that a government receives from taxes or that an organization, etc. receives from its business 财政收入；税收收入；收益

Advertising ***revenue*** finances the commercial television channels. 广告收入给商业电视频道提供资金支持。

✓ reverse [rɪˈvɜːs]   [同] ②overturn

① *n.* the opposite of what has just been mentioned 相反的情况（或事物）

Although I expected to enjoy living in the country, in fact the ***reverse*** is true. 尽管我以为会喜欢乡村生活，但实际情况正好相反。

② *v.* to change sth. completely so that it is the opposite of what it was before 颠倒；彻底转变

It is sometimes possible to arrest or ***reverse*** the disease. 有时候可以阻止病情发展或使病情彻底好转。

✓ significant [sɪɡˈnɪfɪkənt]   [同] important, expressive

adj. important; considerable 重要的；重大的；可观的

a ***significant*** rise in profits 利润的巨大增长

✓ similar [ˈsɪmələ]   [同] alike

adj. almost the same 相似的；类似的

To my mind they are remarkably ***similar***. 在我看来他们惊人地相似。

simulate ['sɪmjuleɪt]　　　　　　　　　　　　　　　　[同] imitate, copy

v. to reproduce (certain conditions) by means of a model, etc., e.g. for study or training purposes (用模型等)模拟(某环境)(如用于研究或训练)

The computer *simulates* conditions on the sea bed. 这个计算机能模拟海底环境。

tab [tæb]

n. small projecting flap or strip of cloth, metal, paper, etc., esp. one by which sth. can be grasped, hung, fastened or identified 小片，小条，小带(尤指用以抓住、悬挂、固定或识别某物的)

open the can by pulling the *tab* 拉环开罐

tabloid ['tæblɔɪd]

n. popular newspaper with pages that are half the size of those of larger newspapers 小型报纸；小报

You need to compare the *tabloid* newspapers of today with those of 50 years ago. 你需要比较一下现在的小报和五十年前的。

Take the Test >>

一、英汉互译

完成　accomplish　　　handicapped

仪式　ceremony　　　musical　音乐的

证明　　　　　personnel　职员

出现　appear　　　perspective　客观的观点

假的　fake　　　pessimistic　悲观的

二、翻译句子

1)煤炭依然占到整个世界能源需求的近27%。(account)

2)任何问题我们都要从全球的角度来看待。(perspective)

3)广告收入给商业电视频道提供资金支持。(revenue)

4)你需要比较一下现在的小报和五十年前的。(tabloid)

Word List 6

accumulate [əˈkjuːmjuleɪt]　　　　　　　　　　　　[同] amass　[反] dissipate

v. to gradually get more and more of sth. over a period of time 积累；增加

Fat tends to ***accumulate*** around the hips and thighs. 脂肪容易在臀部和大腿部堆积。

accuracy [ˈækjərəsi]

n. the state of being exact or correct 准确性；精确程度

This type of work can easily be carried out on an out-dated computer, with the same degree of ***accuracy*** as any modern computer. 这样的工作在过时的计算机上也能轻易完成，而且其准确率和任何现代的计算机都相同。

accustom [əˈkʌstəm]　　　　　　　　　　　　　　　　　　　[同] familiarize

v. to make yourself/sb. familiar with sth. or become used to it 使习惯于

It took a while for me to ***accustom*** myself to all the new rules and regulations. 我过了一段时间才适应了所有新的规定。

achieve [əˈtʃiːv]　　　　　　　　　　　[同] accomplish [反] fail (in or to do)

v. to succeed in reaching a particular goal, status or standard, esp. by making an effort for a long time 达到（某目标、地位、标准）（尤指经过长期的努力）

There is clear-cut evidence that supervision can ***achieve*** significant increases in production. 有确凿的证据表明监督的确可以带来产量的显著增加。

bargain [ˈbɑːgɪn]　　　　　　　　　　　　　　　　　　　[同] ②haggle

① *n.* sth. you buy cheaply or for less than its usual price 便宜货

② *v.* to discuss（with sb.）prices, terms of trade, etc. with the aim of buying or selling goods, or changing conditions, on terms that are favourable to oneself 讨价还价；洽谈成交条件；谈判

The unions ***bargained***（with management）for a shorter working week. 工会为缩短工作周而（与资方）谈判。

barrier [ˈbærɪə]　ticket barrier　　　　　　　　[同] bar, block

n. thing that prevents or controls progress or movement 阻碍进步或控制活动的事物

Bringing these trade ***barriers*** down would help the world's economies grow even closer. 打破这些贸易壁垒会让全球经济的联系更加密切。

challenge [ˈtʃælɪndʒ]　　　　　　　　　　　　　[同] ②question

① *n.* a new or difficult task that tests sb.'s ability and skill 挑战

② *v.* to question whether a statement or an action is right, legal, etc.; to refuse to accept sth. 对…怀疑（或质疑）；拒绝接受

In Western society today, notions of health and health promotion are being ***challenged*** and expanded in new ways. 在现代西方社会，关于何为健康和促进健康的观念受到了挑战，并从新的角度被加以阐述。

champion [ˈtʃæmpiən]

n. ① a person, team, etc. that has won a competition, esp. in a sport 冠军；优胜者

the champion tennis player 获得冠军的网球运动员

②someone who publicly fights for and defends an aim or principle, such as the rights of a group of people 带头人，支持者

a *champion* of women's rights 女权主义的拥护者

channel [ˈtʃænəl]

① *n.* a television station 电视台

We are doing a market research for a new television *channel* starting in two year's time. 我们正在为一个两年后将要开播的电视频道做市场调查。

② *v.* to direct money, feelings, ideas, etc. towards a particular thing or purpose 为…引资；引导；贯注

channel the efforts 集中精力（做某事）

character [ˈkærəktə]

n. ①a person in a book, play, film, etc. 角色 ②the particular combination of qualities that makes someone a particular type of person 性格

A person's *character* is very important to me when I decide who I want to work with. 当我决定跟谁共事时，我很看重对方的性格。

③the particular combination of features and qualities that makes a thing or place different from all others 特点，本质

Hypotheses are imaginative and inspirational in *character*. 科学假想在本质上来讲具有很强的想象力和启发性。

characteristic [ˌkærəktəˈrɪstɪk]   [同] feature, attribute

adj. typical 典型的，特有的 *n.* a typical feature or quality that sth./sb. has 特征；特点

Indeed acting as a tourist is one of the defining *characteristics* of being 'modern'. 事实上，像旅行家那样四处旅游正是"时髦"的一个重要特征。

decline [dɪˈklaɪn]   [同]①②drop, decrease [反]①②rise

① *n.* a decrease in the quality, quantity, or importance of something 下降

the *decline* in world commodity prices 世界商品价格的下降

② *v.* to become smaller, weaker, fewer, etc.; diminish 变小；变弱；变少

Across species, play tends to peak about halfway through the suckling stage and then *decline*. 无论什么物种，玩耍都倾向于在哺乳期的中期达到顶峰，然后开始下降。

decoration [ˌdekəˈreɪʃ(ə)n]

n. thing used for decorating 装饰物，装饰品

the carved *decoration* around the doorway 门口周围的雕刻装饰

decrease [dɪˈkriːs]   [同]①reduce [反]①②increase

① *v.* (cause sth.) to become smaller or fewer; diminish (使某物)变小或变少；减少

The size of the population begins to *decrease*. 人口规模减小了。

②[ˈdiːkriːs]*n.* decreasing; reduction 减少；降低

some *decrease* in the crime rate 犯罪率的少许下降

emit [iˈmɪt]   [同] give off

v. to send out sth. such as light, heat, sound, gas, etc. 发出，散发(光、热、声音、气等)

City streets and motorways *emit* excessive levels of smoke and fumes. 城市的街道和高速公路上产生了过多的废气和烟。

emotion [ɪˈməʊʃn]   [同] feeling

n. a strong feeling such as love, fear or anger; the part of a person's character that consists of feelings 强烈的感情；情绪

It also reveals the power of the pauses and noises we use to play for time, convey *emotion*, doubt and irony. 这也体现了我们(在演讲中)用来拖延时间所使用的停顿和声音是很有功效的，可以传达情绪、疑虑和讽刺之意。

fancy [ˈfænsi]   *V.想像+doing*   [反] disapprove

v. (BrE, infml.) to want sth. or want to do sth. 想要；想做

Do you *fancy* a drink? 想喝一杯吗？   *fancy oneself 顿十…自以为…*

fantastic [fænˈtæstɪk]   [同] excellent [反] common

adj. (infml.) extremely good; excellent 极好的；了不起的

Great to see so many of you here this morning for the opening of our *fantastic* exhibition on spiders! 非常高兴今早能有这么多人参加我们盛大的蜘蛛展览开幕式！

gear [giə]   [同] equipment

n. equipment, clothing, etc. needed for an expedition, a sport, etc. (远征、运动等需用的)设备、装备、衣物等

All his camping *gear* was packed in the rucksack. 他的野营物品全都放在背囊里了。

handout [ˈhændaʊt]

n. duplicated sheet containing examples, etc. distributed by a teacher 教师分发给学生的讲义等

I have a *handout* here with references on the subject. 我这儿有关于这个题目的参考讲义。

harbour [ˈhɑːbə]   [同] ①shelter

① *n.* place of shelter for ships 港；港口；港湾

Several boats lay at anchor in the *harbour*. 港湾里停泊着几只船。

② *v.* to contain something, especially something hidden and dangerous 包含；包庇

Sinks and draining boards can *harbour* germs. 水槽和排水板能隐藏细菌。

immature [ˌɪməˈtjʊə(r)]   [同] childish

adj. someone who is immature behaves or thinks in a way that is typical of someone much younger—used to show disapproval (行为或思想)不成熟的，不够老练的

He's very *immature* for his age. 就他的年龄来说，他很不成熟。

immense [ɪˈmens]   [同] enormous

adj. extremely large 巨大的；广大的

The annual value of these subsidies is *immense*. 这些津贴每年的数额是非常庞大的。

immediately [ɪˈmiːdiətli]   [同] at once

adv. without delay; very soon before or after something 立即；马上

This does not mean that it was *immediately* used to propel rockets. 这并不意味着它马上就被用来推动火箭。

immigrate [ˈɪmɪgreɪt]

v. to come into a country in order to live there permanently 移入(外国定居)

About 6.6 million people *immigrated* to the United States in the 1970s. 20世纪70年代大约有660万人移居美国。

imminent [ˈɪmɪnənt]   [同] impending

adj. (esp. of unpleasant events) about to happen very soon (尤指不愉快的事件)即将发生的；临近的；逼近的

no warning of *imminent* danger 没有即将发生危险的警告

knit [nɪt]

knit ... out of 材料 用材料原来… *knit sb sth* 为某人织某物

v. to make (a garment or fabric) by forming wool, silk, yarn, etc. into connecting loops, either by hand (using long needles) or on a machine 编织，针织(衣物等)

She *knitted* her son a sweater. 她给儿子织了一件毛衣。

last [lɑːst]　　　　　　　　　　　　　　　　　　　　　　　　　　　　[同] continue

v. to continue for a period of time; endure 延续；持续；维持；持久

The Principal's talk will *last* about fifteen minutes. 校长的谈话将持续大约 15 分钟。

manufacture [ˌmænjuˈfæktʃə(r)]　　　　　　　　　　　　　　　　　　　[同] produce

v. to make or produce goods in large quantities, using machinery (用机器)大量生产；成批制造

Today, it is finished *manufactured* products that dominate the flow of trade. 今天，在贸易流程中占主导地位的是制成品。

manuscript [ˈmænjuskrɪpt]

n. a copy of a book, piece of music, etc. before it has been printed 手稿；原稿

I read her poems in *manuscript*. 我读过她的诗作的手稿。

marble [ˈmɑːbl]

n. a type of hard stone that is usu. white and often has coloured lines in it and it can be polished and is used in building and for making statues, etc. 大理石

The columns were made of white *marble*. 柱子由白色大理石制成。

pest [pest]

n. ①a small animal or insect that destroys crops or food supplies 害虫 ②（infml.）annoying person or thing 讨厌的人；害人、坑人的事物

That child is an absolute *pest*—he keeps ringing the doorbell and then running away! 那孩子讨厌极了——老是来按门铃，按完就跑！

phase [feɪz]

phase in　*phase out*

n. one of the stages of a process of development or change 阶段；时期

There are three *phases* in the lifecycle of a butterfly. 蝴蝶的生命周期分为三个阶段。

phenomenon [fəˈnɒmɪnən]

n. fact or occurrence, esp. in nature or society, that can be perceived by the senses 现象

Moreover, as unemployment becomes a global *phenomenon* people are forced to be more willing to uproot and move to where the work is. 此外，随着失业变成一个全球化的现象，人们被迫更加倾向于背井离乡到那些有工作的地方。

review [rɪˈvjuː]

① *n.* an examination of sth., with the intention of changing it if necessary 评审；检查

The terms of the contract are under *review*. 合同条文正在审议。

② *v.* to think about past events, for example to try to understand why they happened 回顾；反思

She had been *reviewing* the previous week on her way home. 她在回家的路上对前一个星期进行了回顾。

revise [rɪˈvaɪz]　　　　　　　　　　　　　　　　　　　　　　　　　　[同] amend

v. to change sth., such as a book or an estimate, in order to correct or improve it 修改，修订(书刊、估算等)

revised edition 修订版

I'll prepare a *revised* estimate for you. 我将为你准备一份经过修正的评估报告。

revolution [ˌrevəˈluːʃn]

n. a great change in conditions, ways of working, beliefs, etc. that affects large numbers of

people 巨变；大变革；革命

A ***revolution*** in information technology is taking place. 信息技术革命正在发生。

signpost [ˈsaɪnpəʊst]

① *n.* post at a road junction, etc. with arms pointing to places along the roads, and often showing the distances to them 路标

②*v.* （usu. passive）provide （a road）with signposts; indicate （a route or place）with signposts 为(路)设置路标；用路标指示(路 径或地方)

Our village is so small that it's not even ***signposted***. 我们的村子很 小，连路标都没有。

sincere [sɪnˈsɪə(r)]　　　　　　　　　　　　　　　　[同] hearty

adj. a feeling, belief, or statement that is sincere is honest and true, and based on what you really feel and believe 真诚的；诚挚的

I would like to say a ***sincere*** thank you to everyone who has helped and supported me. 我想对所 有帮助过我、支持过我的人表示诚挚的感谢。

sink [sɪŋk]　　　　　　　　　　　　　　　　　　　　[同] ②go down

① *n.* a large open container that you fill with water and use for washing yourself, washing dishes, etc. 洗碗池；洗涤槽

② *v.* to go down under the surface of a liquid or soft substance 下沉；沉没

Wood does not ***sink*** in water; it floats. 木头在水中不沉，而是漂在水面。

✓ **taboo** [təˈbuː, təˈbu]　　　　　　　　　　　　　　[近] forbiddance

n. （in certain cultures）ban or prohibition on sth. that is regarded for religious or other reasons as not to be done, touched, used, etc. (某些文化的)禁忌，忌讳

Until a few years ago, there was a ***taboo*** around the subject of divorce. 就在几年前离婚还是一 个人们所忌讳的话题。

tackle [ˈtækl]

v. to deal with or overcome （an awkward problem, a difficult piece of work, etc.）应付，对付， 处理(棘手的问题、困难的工作等)

The introduction to the essay should explain to the reader how you are going to ***tackle*** the question. 你在这篇论文的引言部分应该向读者说明将如何解决这个问题。

Take the Test ≫

一、英汉互译

积累	*accumulate*	accuracy	
达到	*achieve*	bargain	
挑战	*challenge*	gear	
性格	*character*	immigrate	
不成熟的	*immature*	imminent	

二、翻译句子

1）我过了一段时间才适应了所有新的规定。（accustom）

_____

2）在现代西方社会，关于健康和保健的观念受到了挑战，并从新的角度被加以阐述。（challenge）

_____

3）当我决定跟谁共事时，我很看重对方的性格。（character）

_____

4）我想对所有帮助过我、支持过我的人表示诚挚的感谢。（sincere）

_____

My fellow Americans, ask not what your country can do for you, ask what you can do for your country. My fellow citizens of the world: ask not what American will do for you, but what together we can do for the freedom of man.

美国同胞们，不要问国家能为你们做些什么，而要问你们能为国家做些什么。全世界的公民们，不要问美国将为你们做些什么，而要问我们共同能为人类的自由做些什么。

——美国总统 肯尼迪（John Kennedy, American president）

Word List 7

acid [ˈæsɪd]

n. a chemical substance that has a PH of less than 7 酸

Acid rain is a problem facing many countries at the moment, and a global solution is required. 目前酸雨困扰着很多国家，因此我们需要一个全球范围内的解决方案。

acknowledge [əkˈnɒlɪdʒ]　　　　　　　　　　　　　　　[同] admit [反] deny

v. to accept that sth. is true 承认

The government must *acknowledge* what is happening and do something about it. 政府必须承认现状并采取一些措施。

acquaintance [əˈkweɪntəns]　　　　　　　　　　　　　　　　　　[近] friend

n. a person you know but who is not a close friend 泛泛之交；熟人

Mathew has a wide circle of friends and *acquaintances*. 马修交友很广。

acquire [əˈkwaɪə(r)]　　　　　　　　　　　　　　　　　　[同] gain, obtain

v. to gain sth. by your own efforts, ability or behaviour 获得，得到

University is not about getting a degree, but about *acquiring* skills for life. 上大学不是为了拿个文凭，而是为了获得各种生活的技能。

basement [ˈbeɪsmənt]

n. lowest room or rooms in a building, partly or wholly below ground level 地下室

bargain *basement*（设在大商店地下室的）廉价部

battery [ˈbætri]

n. portable container of a cell or cells for supplying electricity 电池；电池组；电瓶

a car *battery* 汽车用的蓄电池

charge [tʃɑːdʒ]

① *n.* a position of having control over sb./sth.; responsibility for sb./sth. 主管；掌管；责任

A recent survey tried to find out who usually takes *charge* of the quality control function. 最近的一次调查试图找出是谁通常掌管质量控制。

② *v.* to ask an amount of money for goods or a service 收费；要价

Interest will be *charged* after the initial 60-day interest-free period. 最初 60 天的免息期过后就要开始收取利息了。

charity [ˈtʃærəti]

n. the aim of giving money, food, help, etc. to people who are in need 慈善；赈济；施舍

The race is to help raise money for *charity*. 这次赛跑是为了给慈善事业募集资金。

charming [ˈtʃɑːmɪŋ]　　　　　　　　　　　　[同] attractive, glamorous

adj. very pleasing or attractive 迷人的，有魅力的

He is *charming*, good-looking and in his early forties. 他四十出头，长相英俊，富有魅力。

chart [tʃɑːt]　　　　　　　　　　　　　　　　　　　　　[同] ①graph

① *n.* a page of sheet of information in the form of diagrams, lists of figure, etc. 图表

a weather ***chart*** 气象图

② *v.* to record or follow the progress or development of sb./sth. 记录，跟踪(进展或发展)

The exhibition ***charts*** the history of the palace. 展览记载了这座王宫的历史。

| ✓ **dedicate** | [ˈdedɪkeɪt] | [同] devote |

v. to give or devote (oneself, time, effort, etc.) to (a noble cause or purpose) 将(自己、时间、精力等)奉献给(崇高的事业或目的)

She ***dedicated*** her life to helping the poor. 她毕生致力于帮助穷人。

| ✓ **deduce** | [dɪˈdjuːs] |

v. to arrive at (facts, a theory, etc.) by reasoning; infer sth. 用推理的方法获知(实情、理论等)；演绎；推断

Detectives ***deduced*** from the clues who had committed the crime. 侦探根据所掌握的线索推断出作案的人。

| ✓ **defeat** | [diˈfiːt] | [同] ①failure ②conquer |

① *n.* failure to win or succeed 失败

I never consider the possibility of ***defeat***. 我从未考虑过失败的可能性。

② *v.* to win a victory over (sb.); overcome 战胜(某人)；击败

The enemy was ***defeated*** in a decisive battle. 敌人在一场具有决定性的战斗中被击败了。

| ✓ **emphasis** | [ˈemfəsɪs] | [同] stress |

n. special attention or importance 重视

In some countries like Japan, there is a lot of ***emphasis*** on politeness. 在日本之类的国家，(人们)非常注重礼貌。

| ✓ **emphasize** | [ˈemfəsaɪz] | [同] stress |

v. to give special importance to sth. 强调；重视

This report ***emphasizes*** that cancer is not caused by a single element in cigarette smoke; harmful effects to health are caused by many components. 这个报告着重指出癌症不单是因为吸烟这么一个因素而导致的，很多原因都会对健康造成有害的影响。

| ✓ **empire** | [ˈempaɪə(r)] |

n. a group of countries or states that are controlled by one ruler or government 帝国

the Roman ***Empire*** 罗马帝国

| ✓ **far-reaching** | [fɑːˈriːtʃɪŋ] |

adj. likely to have a lot of influence or many effects 影响深远的；广泛的

far-reaching consequences/implications 影响深远的后果/意味深长

| **fascinate** | [ˈfæsɪneɪt] | [同] attract, appeal [反] offend |

v. to attract or interest sb. very much 深深吸引；迷住

The human heart has ***fascinated*** mankind since ancient times. 自古以来，人类就被人的内心世界所深深吸引。

| ✓ **gender** | [ˈdʒendə(r)] | [同] sex |

n. the fact of being male or female 性别

Why are there such ***gender*** differences? 为什么会有这些性别差异？

| ✓ **gene** | [dʒiːn] |

n. unit in a chromosome which controls heredity 基因

a dominant/recessive ***gene*** 显性/隐性基因

| ✓ **immoral** | [iˈmɒrəl] | [近] wrong |

adj. not following accepted standards of morality; not moral 不道德的；邪恶的

It's *immoral* to steal. 盗窃是不道德的。

✓ **immune** [iˈmjuːn]

adj. ① someone who is immune to a particular disease cannot catch it 有免疫力的

I'm *immune* to smallpox as a result of vaccination. 我种过牛痘了，所以对天花有免疫力。

② not affected by something that happens or is done 不受影响的

The Labour Party is not *immune* to new ideas. 工党并非不会接受新观点。

✓ **impact** [ˈimpækt]   [近] effect

n. the effect or influence that an event, situation, etc. has on someone or something 巨大的影响

Cigarette smoke has the same *impact* on smokers as it does on non-smokers. 香烟的烟雾对吸烟者与非吸烟者有着相同的影响。

✓ **implement** [ˈimplimənt]   [同] fulfill

v. to take action or make changes that you have officially decided should happen 使(某事物)生效；贯彻；实施

These systems were *implemented* with varying degrees of success and criticism. 这些体制的执行伴随着各种各样的成功和批评。

✓ **journalist** [ˈdʒɜːnəlist]

n. someone who writes news reports for newspapers, magazines, television, or radio 记者；新闻工作者

She worked as a *journalist* on the *New York Times*. 她是《纽约时报》的记者。

✓ **lasting** [ˈlɑːstiŋ]   [同] long-lasting

adj. continuing for a long time 持续很长一段时间的

The committee's decision could have a *lasting* effect on the community. 委员会的决定将对社区产生深远的影响。

✓ **latitude** [ˈlætitjuːd]

n. distance of a place north or south of the equator, measured in degrees 纬度

The birds breed in northern *latitudes*. 鸟儿们在北方繁殖。

✓ **margin** [ˈmɑːdʒin]

n. the difference between the cost and the selling price of securities or commodities 盈余；利润；证券或商品的成本与销售价之间的差额

They have always had to make do with relatively small profit *margins*. 他们不得不经常设法应付较少的利润额。

✓ **marked** [mɑːkt]   [同] noticeable

remarkable
conspicuous

adj. very easy to notice 显著的

Europe's railways have shown *marked* productivity improvements. 欧洲的铁路已经显示出生产效率的明显提高。

marine [məˈriːn]

adj. connected with the sea and the creatures and plants that live there *海的；海产的*

the enormous variety of *marine* life 海洋生物的多样性

✓ **navigate** [ˈnævigeit]

v. to sail along, over or through a sea, river, etc. 航行；航海；横渡

The river became too narrow and shallow to *navigate*. 河道变得又窄又浅，无法航行。

✓ **philosophy** [fəˈlɒsəfi]

n. ① search for knowledge and understanding of the nature and meaning of the universe and of human life 哲学 ② the attitude or set of ideas that guides the behaviour of a person or organization 人生观；处世哲学

My *philosophy* is, I leave work at 5 o'clock and forget all about it till the next day. 我的行为哲学是 5 点下班后就把工作忘得干干净净，直到第二天上班。

pillar [ˈpɪlə(r)]   [同] column

n. ①a tall upright round post used as a support for a roof or bridge 柱子；支柱 ② strong supporter of sth. (某事物的)强大支持者；支柱

One of the *pillars* of a civilized society must be that everyone has equal access to the legal system. 支撑一个文明社会的支柱之一就是法律面前人人平等。

reward [rɪˈwɔːd]

① *n.* something that you get because you have done something good or helpful or have worked hard 回报；奖励

② *v.* to give something to someone because they have done something good or helpful or have worked for it 奖赏；回报

The job is difficult, but the financial *rewards* are great. 工作很艰巨，但经济上的回报很可观。

rhythm [ˈrɪðəm]

n. a strong regular repeated pattern of sounds or movements 节奏；韵律；律动

If you ignore these instructions, this medicine could affect your heart *rhythm*. 如果你不看这些说明，这种药可能会影响到你的心率。

riddle [ˈrɪdl]   [同] mystery

n. a question that is difficult to understand, and that has a surprising answer, that you ask sb. as a game 谜；谜语

Stop talking in *riddles*—say what you mean. 不要再拐弯抹角了，有什么话你就直说。

site [saɪt]   [近] place

n. place where a building, town, etc. was, is, or will be situated (建筑物、城镇等的)地方，位置；遗址；地基

I picked a sheltered *site* for the tent. 我选了个有遮蔽的地方搭帐篷。

situate [ˈsɪtʃueɪt]

v. (esp. passive)place or locate (e.g. a building or town) in a certain position 使(如建筑物或城镇)建于或坐落在某处

Situated at the heart of West London, West Thames College is ideally placed to serve the training and education needs of local industry and local people. 坐落于西伦敦的中心，西泰晤士大学理想的地理位置非常利于它提供服务来满足当地工业与居民对培训和教育的需要。

sketch [sketʃ]   [同] ①②outline

① *n.* a simple, quickly-made drawing that does not show much detail 素描

② *v.* to give a general description or account of sth.; outline sth. 概述（ 某事 ）；草拟

Once you have collected your source material you should then *sketch* out a plan. 一旦收集好你的原始材料，你就应该草拟一份计划了。

skim [skɪm]   [同] glance

v. to read sth. quickly, noting only the main points 略读；浏览

My approach is to *skim* the book first to see what's important and what isn't. 我的方法是先浏览全书，看看哪些重要，哪些不重要。

tag [tæɡ]   [同] ticket, label *n.* label fastened to or stuck into sth. to identify it, show its price, etc. 标签

put a name *tag* on it 附上名字标签

tailor [ˈteɪlə]

[同]②adapt

① *n.* maker of men's clothes, esp. one who makes coats, jackets, etc. for individual customers（男装）裁缝，成衣匠

② *v.* to make something so that it is exactly right for someone's particular needs or for a particular purpose 定制

The classes are *tailored* to suit learners' needs. 这些课程是为了满足学习者的需求而量身定制的。

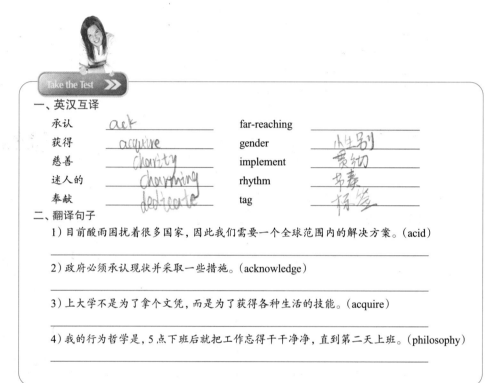

Take the Test >>>

一、英汉互译

承认	ack	far-reaching	
获得	acquire	gender	性别
慈善	charity	implement	贯彻
迷人的	charming	rhythm	节奏
奉献	dedicate	tag	标签

二、翻译句子

1）目前酸雨困扰着很多国家，因此我们需要一个全球范围内的解决方案。（acid）
_____

2）政府必须承认现状并采取一些措施。（acknowledge）
_____

3）上大学不是为了拿个文凭，而是为了获得各种生活的技能。（acquire）
_____

4）我的行为哲学是，5点下班后就把工作忘得干干净净，直到第二天上班。（philosophy）
_____

You never know what you can do till you try.

除非你亲自尝试一下，否则你永远不知道你能够做什么。

——英国小说家 马里亚特（Frederick Marryat, British novelist）

✓ **activate** [ˈæktɪveɪt] [同] vitalize

v. to make an electrical system or chemical process start working 激活；使活化

The burglar alarm is **activated** by movement. 这防盗警报器一动就响。

✓ **adapt** [əˈdæpt] [同] adjust, fit

v. to gradually change your behaviour and attitudes in order to be successful in a new situation 适应

Different styles of leadership have evolved in order to **adapt** to these changes. 人们为适应这些变化而发展了多种不同的领导风格。

✓ **address** [əˈdres] *n.* 地址；演讲

v. try to solve 设法解决；处理

The creation of health must include **addressing** issues such as poverty, pollution and poor working conditions. 要实现健康，必须解决贫穷、污染和恶劣的工作环境等问题。

✓ **bear** [beə(r)] [同] endure 忍耐

v. to bravely accept or deal with a painful, difficult, or upsetting situation 忍受

Overcrowding makes prison life even harder to **bear**. 人满为患使得监狱生活更加难以忍受。

behalf [bɪˈhɑːf] in ~ of / in sb's ~ 为某人 | on ~ of / on sb's ~ 代表某人

n. on behalf of somebody, instead of someone, or as their representative 代表某人

He speaks on **behalf** of millions of poor and disadvantaged people. 他为上百万的穷人和弱势群体代言。

✓ **chemical** [ˈkemɪkl]

n./adj. a substance used in chemistry or produced by a chemical process 化学物品（的）

Chemical and pesticides may contaminate water supplies. 化学物品和杀虫剂会污染水源。

cherish [ˈtʃerɪʃ] [同] appreciate, treasure

v. to love sb./sth. very much and want to protect them or it 珍爱；爱护

Children need to be **cherished**. 儿童需要无微不至的爱护。

chill [tʃɪl] ~ + of [同] ①cold

① *n.* a feeling of being cold 寒冷；寒意

There's a **chill** in the air this morning. 今天早晨寒气袭人。

② *v.* to make sb. very cold 使很冷，使冰冷

They were **chilled** by the icy wind. 凛冽的寒风吹得他们遍体冰凉。

chip [tʃɪp]

① *n.* a long thin piece of potato fried in oil or fat 油炸土豆条；炸薯条

fish and **chips** 炸鱼和土豆条

② *v.* to damage sth. by breaking a small piece off it; to become damaged in this way 打破，弄缺；被损坏

These plates **chip** easily. 这些盘子容易破损。

defect [dɪˈfekt, ˈdiːfekt] [同] flaw

drawback.

n. fault or lack that spoils a person or thing 缺点；不足之处

a *defect* of character 性格上的缺陷   V. 逃跑，判变.

✓ **defence** [dɪˈfens]   [反] attack

n. the act of protecting something or someone from attack 防御；防护；保卫

The immune system is the body's *defence* against infection. 免疫系统是人体对感染的防线。

define [dɪˈfaɪn]   限制；确定；明界试 规定；限定

v. to state precisely the meaning of（e.g. words）给（词语等）下定义

Health in this sense has been *defined* as the absence of disease or illness. 在这个意义上，健康就是指没有疾病。

✓ **employ** [ɪmˈplɔɪ]   [同] hire

v. to give sb. a job to do for payment 雇用

For the past three years he has been *employed* as a firefighter. 过去这三年来他一直在当消防员。

✓ **enclose** [ɪnˈkləuz]   [同] surround

v. to build a wall, fence, etc. around sth.（用墙、篱笆等）把…围起来

The yard had been *enclosed* with iron railings. 院子用铁栅栏围了起来。

✓ **encounter** [ɪnˈkauntə(r)] have ~ 与...见面   [同] ②confront

① *n.* a meeting, esp. one that is sudden, unexpected or violent（突然、意外或暴力的）相遇

I've had a number of close *encounters* with bad drivers. 我好几次都险些与技术不佳的司机相撞。

② *v.* to experience sth., esp. sth. unpleasant or difficult, while you are trying to do sth. else 遭遇；遇到（尤指令人不快或困难的事）

fascinate I had never *encountered* such resistance before. 我以前从未遇到过这么大的阻力。

✓ **fascinating** [ˈfæsɪneɪtɪŋ]   [同] charming

adj. extremely interesting and attractive 极有吸引力的；迷人的

The results of the survey made *fascinating* reading. 调查结果令人读起来饶有兴趣。

✓ **fashion** [ˈfæʃn]

n. a popular style of clothes, hair, etc. at a particular time or place; the state of being popular（衣服、发式等的）流行款式；时兴式样

Later, feather fans and big, decorated hats went out of *fashion*. 后来，羽毛扇子和装饰华丽的宽边帽子就过时了。

✓ **generalize** [ˈdʒenrəlaɪz]

v. to draw （a general conclusion）from particular examples or evidence（从某些事例或证据中）归纳，概括出（一般性结论）

You cannot *generalize* about the effects of the drug from one or two cases. 你不能根据一两个病例就得出该药是否有效的结论。

✓ **generate** [ˈdʒenəreɪt]   [同] create

n. to cause （sth.）to exist or occur; produce 使（某物）存在或发生；产生

It works by squeezing the handle to *generate* the power. 它是通过按压手柄以产生能量而工作的。

harmony [ˈhɑːməni]   [同] accord

n. agreement （of feelings, interests, opinions, etc.）（感情、兴趣、意见等）相符，一致

和睦；融洽.

working towards **harmony** in international affairs 致力使国际事务协调一致

implicit [ɪmˈplɪsɪt]

have ~ confidence in sb 对某人绝对信任 [反] explicit

adj. suggested or understood without being stated directly 含蓄的；不明确的

Her words contained an **implicit** threat. 她的言语中含着一丝威胁的意味。

imply [ɪmˈplaɪ]

simply imply 直接意味着，strongly imply 强烈地暗示 [同] hint

generally / normally ~
in no way ~ 决不意味 *usually ~ 通常意味着*

v. to suggest that something is true, without saying this directly 含有…的意思；暗示

A still picture could only **imply** the existence of time. 一幅静止的图画仅仅意味着时间的存在。

impose [ɪmˈpəʊz]

v. 征税；加(负担)，惩罚于 (on, upon)

v. to try to make sb. accept (an opinion or a belief); inflict sth. 使某人接受(意见或信仰)；将某事物强加于

Standards **imposed** vary greatly from country to country and industry to industry. 加诸于各个国家各个产业的标准都极为不同。

knob [nɒb]

n. round handle (of a door, drawer, etc.) (门、抽屉等的)圆形拉手

Turn the door **knob** to open the door. 拧门把手开门。

launch [lɔːntʃ]

使开始从事；使投入；发射 [近] throw

v. to put (sth.) into motion; send on its course 使(某事物)运动；送上轨道

The company hopes to **launch** the new drug by next October. 公司打算明年十月份前推出一种新药。

✓ **laundry** [ˈlɔːndri]

n. clothes, sheets, etc. that need to be washed or have just been washed 要洗或已经洗过的衣服

She did the **laundry** and hung it out to dry in the back yard. 她把衣服洗了，然后挂在后院晾干。

marvel [ˈmɑːvl]

do marvels 创造奇迹 [同] ①miracle ①②wonder

① *n.* a wonderful and surprising person or thing 令人惊异的人(或事)；奇迹

The bridge is an engineering **marvel**. 这座桥是建筑工程的奇迹。

② *v.* to be very surprised or impressed by sth. 感到惊奇；大为赞叹

Everyone **marveled** at his courage. 人人都对他的勇气惊叹不已。

✓ **massive** [ˈmæsɪv] [同] huge

adj. extremely large or serious 巨大的；非常严重的

Over the past seventy years or so, there has been a **massive** increase in one type of crime. 在过去的七十多年里，有一种形式的犯罪增加显著。

✓ **mate** [meɪt] [同] partner

n. (BrE, infml.) a friend 朋友；伙伴

They've been best **mates** since school. 他们从上学时起就是最要好的朋友。

✓ **necessity** [nɪˈsesəti] [同] need

n. a thing that you must have and cannot manage without 必需的事物；必需品

Many people cannot even afford basic **necessities** such as food and clothing. 许多人甚至买不起食物和衣服之类的基本必需品。

pioneer [ˌpaɪəˈnɪə]

① *n.* one who opens up new areas of thought, research, or development 开拓者，先锋 *开路者*

He is a **pioneer** in aviation. 他是航空业的先驱者。

② *v.* to open up (a way, etc.) 开辟(道路等)

pioneer a new route to the coast 开辟通往海岸的新路线

pitch [pɪtʃ] [近] put in

v. to erect and fix in place (a tent or camp), esp. for a short time 搭(帐篷), 扎(营)(尤指临时)

It's only $10 a day to *pitch* a tent. 搭帐篷一天才 10 美元。

✓ **placement** [ˈpleɪsmənt]

n. action of placing or state of being placed 放置；安置；定名次；就业安排

The course includes a *placement* in Year 3. 本课程在第三年有实习课。

✓ **ridiculous** [rɪˈdɪkjələs]　　　　　　　　　　　　　　　　　　[同] foolish

adj. very silly or unreasonable 愚蠢的；荒唐的

I look *ridiculous* in this hat. 我戴这顶帽子看上去很可笑。

rigid [ˈrɪdʒɪd]　　　　　　　　　　　　　　　　　　　　　　[同] stiff

adj. (of rules, methods, etc.) very strict and difficult to change 死板的；僵硬的

You have a *rigid* format to follow. 你要遵循严格的格式。

✓ **risk** [rɪsk]　　　　　　　　　　　　　　　　　　　　　　　[同] danger

n. the possibility that something bad, unpleasant, or dangerous may happen 风险；危险

Healthy eating can help reduce the *risk* of heart disease. 健康的饮食可以帮助减少患心脏病的风险。

✓ **skip** [skɪp]　　　　　　　　　　　　　　　　　　　　　[同] ①②hop

v. ① to move lightly and quickly, esp. by taking two steps with each foot in turn 轻快地跳；跳绳 ② to not do something that you usually do or that you should do 跳过；略过

He *skipped* chemistry class three times last month. 上个月他翘了三次化学课。

✓ **slam** [slæm]

v. to (cause sth. to) shut forcefully and loudly (使某物)猛然关闭并发出巨响

The door *slammed*. 门砰的一声关上了。

✓ **slender** [ˈslendə]　　　　　　　　　　　　　　　　　　　[同] slim

adj. (approv.) not very wide but comparatively long or high 细长的；纤细的

a wineglass with a *slender* stem 高脚杯

✓ **slice** [slaɪs]　　　　　　　　　　　　　　　[同] ①piece

① *n.* thin wide flat piece cut off from an item of food (从食物上切下的)薄片

② *v.* to cut sth. into thin flat pieces 切片

a *slice* of pizza 一块比萨

✓ **talent** [ˈtælənt]　　　　　　　　　　　[同] gift

n. (instance of) special or very great ability 特殊的能力；才能；才干；天才

The amateurs, he says, provide enthusiasm and *talent*, while the professionals provide guidance. 他说业余爱好者有热情和天分，而专业人员则提供指导。

✓ **tame** [teɪm]　　　　　　　　　　　　　　　[同] ①domestic

① *adj.* (of animals) gentle and unafraid of human beings; not wild or fierce (指动物)驯服的，不怕人的，不凶猛的

a *tame* monkey 驯服的猴子

② *v.* to make (sth.) tame or manageable 使(某物)驯服或顺从

tame wild birds 调教野鸟

Take the Test >>

一、英汉互译

设法解决	_____	implicit	_____
代表某人	_____	imply	_____
珍爱	_____	laundry	_____
遇到	_____	necessity	_____
归纳，概括	_____	placement	_____

二、翻译句子

1）他为上百万的穷人和弱势群体代言。（on behalf of）

_____

2）许多人甚至买不起食物和衣服之类的基本必需品。（necessity）

_____

3）健康的饮食可以帮助减少患心脏病的风险。（risk）

_____

4）上个月他翘了三次化学课。（skip）

_____

Victory won't come to me unless I go to it.

胜利是不会向我走来的,我必须自己走向胜利。

——美国女诗人 穆尔（M. Moore, American poetess）

✓ **adequate** [ˈædɪkwɪt]　　　　　　　　　　　[同] sufficient　[反] inadequate

adj. enough in quantity or of a good enough quality for a particular purpose 足够的；合格的

The traditional distinction between the old and new media is no longer *adequate* for understanding the world. 新旧媒体间的传统区分已不足以解释这个世界了。

✓ **adjacent** [əˈdʒeɪsənt]　　　　　　　　　　[同] neighboring　[反] remote

adj. situated next to or near sth. 邻近的

The houses *adjacent* to the highway or nearest to the airport require high density insulation materials in the roof. 邻近高速公路或者距离机场最近的房屋都需要在屋顶上安装高密度隔音材料。

✓ **adjust** [əˈdʒʌst]　　　　　　　　　　　　　　　　　　[同] adapt

v. to change or move sth. slightly to improve it or make it more suitable for a particular purpose 调整；调节

This button is for *adjusting* the volume. 这个按钮是调节音量的。

✓ **behaviour** [bɪˈheɪvjə(r)]

n. way of acting or functioning 行为方式；活动方式

Children may take the heroes of TV programs as role models and copy their *behaviour*. 孩子们可能会将电视节目中的英雄当作自己的行为榜样并模仿他们的言行举止。

✓ **chop** [tʃɒp]　　　　　　　　　　　　　　　　　　　　[近] ②cut

① *n.* a thick slice of meat with a bone attached to it, esp. from a pig or sheep 猪（或羊等）排

a lamb *chop* 羊排

② *v.* to cut sth. into pieces with a sharp tool such as a knife 切碎；剁碎；砍

Chop the carrots into small pieces. 把胡萝卜切成小块。

✓ **chore** [tʃɔː]　　　　　　　　　　　　　　　　　　　[近] task

n. a task that you do regularly 日常事务；例行工作

doing the household/domestic *chores* 干家务杂活

✓ **circulate** [ˈsɜːkjəleɪt]　　　　　　　　　　　　　[同] spread

v. when a liquid, gas, or air circulates or is circulated, it moves continuously around a place or system （液体或气体）环流，循环

Swimming helps to get the blood *circulating* through the muscles. 游泳有助于血液循环。

✓ **circumstance** [ˈsɜːkəmstəns]　　　　　　　　　[同] occurrence

n. the conditions that affect a situation, action, event, etc. 境况；境遇

The services that banks will offer you depend on your individual *circumstances* and on the discretion of the bank manager involved. 银行给你提供的服务取决于你的个人经济状况和银行管理者的判断。

✓ **circus** [ˈsɜːkəs]

n. a group of people and animals who travel to different places performing skillful tricks as

entertainment 马戏团

A few of the students here quite like the idea of running away with a *circus*. 这儿还真有些学生想跟着马戏团云游四海。

definite ['defɪnət]　　　　　　　　　　　　　　　　　　　　　　[同] fixed

adj. clearly known, seen, or stated 明确的

It's impossible for me to give you a *definite* answer. 我不可能给你个很明确的答案。

definitely ['defɪnətli]　　　　　　　　　　　　　　　　　　　　[同] certainly

adv. in a clear, not doubtful manner 明确地；清楚地

She states her views very *definitely*. 她非常明确地阐述自己的观点。

delay [dɪ'leɪ]

① *n.* delaying or being delayed 耽搁；延期

We must leave without *delay*. 我们必须立即离开。

② *v.* (cause sb. to) be slow or late 使(某人)慢或迟到；耽搁；延误

She *delayed* (for) two hours and missed the train. 她耽搁了两个小时，结果误了火车。

encyclopedia [ɪnˌsaɪklə'pi:diə]

n. a book or set of books giving information about all areas of knowledge or about different areas of one particular subject 百科全书；(某一学科的)专科全书

"Does anyone know when Mozart was born?" "Look it up in the *encyclopedia*." "有人知道莫扎特是什么时候出生的吗？""查查百科全书吧。"

endanger [ɪn'deɪndʒə]　　　　　　　　　　　　　　　　　　　[同] hazard

v. to put sb./sth. in a situation in which they could be harmed or damaged 使遭受危险；危及

The health of our children is being *endangered* by exhaust fumes. 我们的孩子们的健康正受到排放出的废气的损害。

fasten ['fɑ:sn]　　　　　　　　　　　　　　　　　　　　　　　[近] attach

v. to close or join together the two parts of sth.; to become closed or joined together (使两部分)系牢，扣紧

Fasten your seat belts, please. 请系好安全带。

fatal ['feɪtl]　　　　　　　　　　　　　　　　　　　　　　　　[同] deadly

adj. causing or ending in death 致命的

The majority of them are *fatal*. 它们中的绝大部分是致命的。

generous ['dʒenərəs]　　　　　　　　　　　　　　　　　　　　[反] mean

adj. giving or ready to give freely 慷慨的；大方的

She's always very *generous* to the kids. 她对孩子总是很慷慨。

harsh [hɑ:ʃ]　　　　　　　　　　　　　　　　　　　　　　　　[同] severe

adj. stern; cruel; severe 严酷的；无情的；严厉的

His theory met with *harsh* criticism from colleagues. 他的理论遭到同事无情的批判。

harvest ['hɑ:vɪst]

n. the time or season of gathering 收获季节；收获期

Farmers are very busy during (the) *harvest*. 在收获季节农民非常忙碌。

impress [ɪm'pres]　　　　　　　　　　　　　[同] make/leave one's mark

v. to make someone feel admiration and respect 给予某人深刻印象；使某人钦佩

The sights of the city never fail to *impress* foreign tourists. 外国游客无一不对该市的景象留有深刻印象。

✓ impression [ɪmˈpreʃn]

n. the opinion or feeling you have about someone or something because of the way they seem 印象；看法

Could you tell us something about your first *impressions* of the town when you arrived? 你能给我们讲讲你刚来时对这个小城的第一印象吗？

✓ imprison [ɪmˈprɪzən]　　　　　　　　　　　　　　　　　[同] jail

v. to put someone in prison or to keep them somewhere and prevent them from leaving 监禁；关押

The government *imprisoned* all opposition leaders. 政府监禁了所有反对派领导人。

✓ impulse [ˈɪmpʌls]　　　　　　　　　　　　　　　　　　[同] urge

n. a sudden strong desire to do something without thinking about whether it is a sensible thing to do 冲动（未顾及后果）；突如其来的念头

Impulse shopping can take a heavy toll on consumers. 冲动购物会让消费者付出沉重代价。

✓ inaccessible [ˌɪnækˈsesəbl]　　　　　　　　　　　　[反] accessible

adj. difficult or impossible to reach; difficult or impossible to understand or afford 达不到的；难以理解的

In winter, the villages are *inaccessible* by road. 在冬季，这些村庄都无法通过道路来到达。

✓ journey [ˈdʒɜːni]

n. a time spent travelling from one place to another, especially over a long distance 旅行，旅程

Her work involves a lot of travelling. 她的工作包括大量的旅行。

✓ layer [ˈleɪə(r)]

n. thickness of material （esp. one of several）laid over a surface or forming a horizontal division 层

Two *layers* of plasterboard will be needed for the interior bedroom walls. 卧室的内墙将需要两层石膏板。

mutual [ˈmjuːtʃuəl]

adj. used to describe feelings that two or more people have for each other equally, or actions that affect two or more people equally 相互的；彼此的

mutual respect/understanding 相互的尊敬/理解

✓ plantation [plɑːnˈteɪʃn]

n. large piece of land, esp. in a tropical country, where tea, cotton, sugar, tobacco, etc. are grown （茶、棉、甘蔗、烟草等的）大种植园，大农场（尤指热带国家的）

This period is greatly reduced with modern growing methods, particularly in *plantations* where you have perfect tropical conditions. 得力于现代种植技术，尤其是在那些具备完全热带环境的大种植园，这个过程大大缩短了。

plateau [ˈplætəʊ]

n. large area of fairly level land that is high above sea-level 高原

The *plateau* was a far cry from the workaday cottages by the harbour. 这个高原距离港口旁的普通住宅区很远。

platform [ˈplætfɔːm]

n. level surface raised above the surrounding ground or floor, esp. one from which public speakers, performers, etc. can be seen by their audience 台；平台；（尤指）讲台，舞台，戏台

the concert *platform* 钢琴演奏台

rival [ˈraɪvl] [同] ①competitor

① *n.* a person, company, or thing that competes with another in sport, business, etc. 竞争对手

The Japanese are our biggest economic *rivals*. 日本人是我们最大的经济竞争对手。

② *v.* to be as good, impressive, etc. as sb./sth. else 与…相匹敌；比得上

You will find scenery to *rival* anything you can see in the Alps. 你能看到的景色可与你在阿尔卑斯山所见的景色相媲美。

roar [rɔː(r)]

① *n.* a loud deep sound made by an animal, esp. a lion, or by sb.'s voice 咆哮；吼叫

His speech was greeted by a *roar* of applause. 他的讲话引来了雷鸣般的掌声。

② *v.* to make a very loud, deep sound 吼叫；咆哮

The wind was *roaring* in my ears. 风在我的耳边咆哮。

robust [rəʊˈbʌst] [同] strong

adj. (of a system or an organization) strong and not likely to fail or become weak 强劲的；富有活力的

It was very strong and *robust* in appearance. 它看上去是强劲有力的。

slide [slaɪd]

n. picture, diagram, etc. on photographic film, usu. held in a small frame and shown on a screen using a projector; transparency 幻灯片（有框的透明软片）

If you take a look at this *slide* I've prepared, you'll see there are a number of distinct advantages with this type of system. 如果你看看我准备的幻灯片，你将能了解到这类系统的一些独特优势。

slim [slɪm] [同] thin

adj. not fat or thick; slender 纤细的；修长的；苗条的

It also helps control body weight, so it's a perfect way to keep *slim*. 这对控制体重也会有帮助，因此不失为保持身材的好办法。

slippery [ˈslɪpəri]

adj. something that is slippery is difficult to hold, walk on, etc. because it is wet or greasy 滑的；光滑的

Be careful—the floor is very *slippery*. 小心，地面很滑。

slogan [ˈsləʊgən] [同] catchword

n. word or phrase that is easy to remember, used as a motto e.g. by a political party, or in advertising 标语；口号

'You can stop corruption' is their *slogan*. "一切权力归人民"是他们的口号。

smash [smæʃ] [同] shatter

v. (cause sth. to) be broken violently into pieces (使某物)粉碎，破碎

smashed potatoes 土豆泥

tap [tæp]

n. device for controlling the flow of liquid or gas out of a pipe or container (控制液体或气体流出的)龙头，旋塞

Don't leave the *taps* running, i.e. turn them off. 要把龙头关上。

tape [teɪp]

v. to record sound or pictures onto a tape 录音，录像

Would you mind if I *taped* this conversation? 你不介意我把这段对话录下来吧？

✓ **target** [ˈtɑːgɪt]

n. ① something that you are trying to achieve, such as a total, an amount, or a time 目标 ② on target [习语]likely to achieve 可以实现的

The company says that growth of 10% is on ***target***. 该公司称可以实现 10% 的增长。

v. to make something have an effect on a particular limited group or area 针对；对准

The program is ***targeted*** at improving the health of women of all ages. 这个项目旨在改善各年龄段女性的健康状况。

✓ **task** [tɑːsk]

n. a piece of work that must be done, especially one that is difficult or unpleasant or that must be done regularly 任务；工作

Our first ***task*** is to gather information. 我们的第一个任务就是搜集信息。

Take the Test ➤➤

一、英汉互译

调节	_____	adjacent	邻近的
日常杂务	~~chorm~~ chore	circulate	循环
境况	_____	impulse	冲动
百科全书	_____	plateau	_____
印象	impression	slogan	_____

二、翻译句子

1）新旧媒体间的传统区分已不足以解释这个世界了。（adequate）

_____

2）你能给我们讲讲你刚来时对这个小城的第一印象吗？（impression）

_____

3）冲动购物会让消费者付出沉重代价。（impulse）

_____

4）日本人是我们最大的经济竞争对手。（rival）

_____

You never know what you can do till you try.

除非你亲自尝试一下, 否则你永远不知道你能够做什么。

——英国小说家 马里亚特（Frederick Marryat, British novelist）

administration [ədˌmɪnɪsˈtreɪʃn]

n. (also BrE infml. admin) the activities that are involved in managing the work of a company or organization 管理，行政

The *administration* office is opposite the car park. 办公楼在停车场对面。

√ **admire** [ədˈmaɪə]　　　　　　　　　　　　[同] appreciate　[反] abhor

v. to respect sb. for what they are or for what they have done 钦佩；赞赏

I don't quite agree with her, but I *admire* her for sticking to her principle. 我不同意她的意见，但是我赞赏她坚持原则的精神。

[习语] think highly of 高度评价

Your boss must think highly of you if she gives you so much responsibility. 如果你的老板把这么重要的事交给你，那说明她一定特别器重你。

√ **admit** [ədˈmɪt]　　　　　　　　　　　　　　　　　　[反] deny

v. to agree unwillingly that something is true (不情愿地)认可，承认

You may not like her, but you have to *admit* that she's good at her job. 你可以不喜欢她，但你不得不承认她的确工作出色。

√ **bend** [bend]　　　　　　　　　　　　　　　　　　[同] curve

n./v. curve or turn, esp. in a road, racecourse, river, etc. 弯，拐角（尤指道路、赛场跑道、河流等）

a gentle *bend* 一个平缓的弯

cite [saɪt]　　　　　　　　　　　　　　　　　　[同] quote

v. to speak or write the exact words from a book, an author, etc. 引用；引述；援引

They *cited* some previous research in support of their recent findings. 为了支持最近的发现，他们引用了一些以前的研究成果。

√ **civil** [ˈsɪvl]　　　　　　　　　　　　　公民的 [近] uncivil

adj. connected with the state rather than with religion or with the armed forces 国家的，政府的

Personality questionnaires were used by the ancient Chinese for picking out clerks and *civil* servants. 在古代，中国人就已使用性格问卷来选拔职员和国家公务员了。

√ **claim** [kleɪm]　　　　　　　　　　　　　　　　[同] maintain, argue

v. to say that sth. is true although it has not been proved and other people may not believe it 宣称；声称；断言

Some Russian scientists *claim* that children learn better after being exposed to ultraviolet light. 一些俄罗斯科学家宣称处于紫外线照射下的孩子学东西会快些。

√ **clarify** [ˈklærɪfaɪ]　　　　　　　　　　　　[同] explain, elucidate

v. (cause sth. to) become clear or easier to understand (使某事物)清楚易懂，澄清

I hope that what I say will *clarify* the situation. 我希望我说的话能澄清这一情况。

[习语] make plain

Let me make it plain. We do not want you here. 明白告诉你吧，我们这里不需要你。

classic [ˈklæsɪk] [同] ①typical ②masterpiece

① *adj.* very typical 典型的

classic engineering problems 典型的工程问题

② *n.* a book, play, or film that is important and has been admired for a long time 名著，经典

The play has become a Chinese *classic*. 这部戏剧成了中国经典名剧。

delete [dɪˈliːt] [同] erase

v. to cross out or deliberately omit (sth. written or printed) 删除或删略(文字)

The editor *deleted* the last paragraph (from the article). 编辑删除了(文章的)最后一段。

deliberate [dɪˈlɪbərət] [同] intentional

adj. done on purpose; intentional 故意的；有意的；蓄意的

a *deliberate* insult/lie/act 蓄意的侮辱/存心编造的谎言/故意的行为

endure [ɪnˈdjʊə(r)] [同] bear, continue

v. to experience and deal with sth. that is painful or unpleasant, esp. without complaining 忍耐；忍受

They had to *endure* a long wait before the case came to trial. 在此案审理前他们只得忍受长时间的等待。

energetic [ˌenəˈdʒetɪk] [同] vigorous

adj. having or needing a lot of energy and enthusiasm 精力充沛的；充满活力的；积极的

He knew I was *energetic* and dynamic and would get things done. 他知道我精力充沛，富有活力，会把事情办成的。

energy [ˈenədʒi] [同] power

n. the physical and mental strength that makes you able to do things 能量；活力

She was full of *energy* after her vacation. 她在休假结束后充满了活力。

fault [fɔːlt] [同] imperfection

n. the responsibility for sth. wrong that has happened or been done 责任；过错；过失

Why should I say sorry when it's not my *fault*? 不是我的错为什么要我道歉？

feasible [ˈfiːzəbl] [同] possible

adj. that is possible and likely to be achieved 可行的；行得通的

a *feasible* plan 可行计划

generation [ˌdʒenəˈreɪʃn]

n. all people of about the same age 一代

generation gap 代沟

genius [ˈdʒiːniəs] [同] gift

n. exceptionally great mental or creative ability 天才；创造力

Mozart did not view himself as a *genius*. 莫扎特并不把自己当天才看。

hatch [hætʃ] [近] generate

v. (of a young bird or fish, etc.) emerge from an egg (指小鸟、小鱼等)(从卵中)孵出

Hatched chicks are nourished well and protected from danger. 孵出来的小鸡被照看得很好，而且远离危险。

haunt [hɔːnt] [同] ①hang around

① *v.* to visit (a place) regularly (指鬼魂)常出没于(某处)

a *haunted* house 经常闹鬼的房子

② *n.* place visited frequently by the person or people named (某人)常去之处

This pub is a favourite *haunt* of artists. 这家小酒店是艺术家们喜欢光顾的地方。

incentive [ɪnˈsentɪv]　　　　　　　　　　　　　　　　[同] stimulus

n. thing that encourages sb. to do sth.; stimulus 激励某人做某事的事物；刺激；奖励

I was an enthusiastic student and I never found it difficult to find the *incentive* to paint. 我是一个充满激情的学生，我从来都能毫不费力地找到画画的动力。

incidence [ˈɪnsɪdəns]

n. the number of times something happens, especially crime, disease, etc. 发生率（尤指罪行、疾病等）

There's a high *incidence* of depression in this area. 该地区低气压发生率很高。

incident [ˈɪnsɪdənt]

n. event or happening, often of minor importance 事情，发生的事情（常指小事）

He could remember every trivial *incident* in great detail. 每件小事他都可以记得很清楚。

inclination [ˌɪnklɪˈneɪʃn]

n. feeling that makes sb. want to behave in a particular way; disposition 倾向；意向；意愿

I have little *inclination* to listen to you all evening. 我可不愿意一晚上都听你说话。

lay-off [ˈleɪɒf]

n. dismissal of a worker, usu. for a short time 解雇（工人）（通常为短期）

more *lay-offs* in the car industry 在汽车工业有更多的人失业

layout [ˈleɪaʊt]

n. the way in which the parts of sth. are arranged according to a plan 安排；设计；布局

The noise factor will have to be taken into consideration with the *layout* of the houses. 噪声因素将与房屋的布局同时被考虑到。

✓ **material** [məˈtɪəriəl]

n. the things that are used for making or doing something 材料，原料

The water and the availability of raw *materials* in the area made this site suitable for industry from a very early time. 该地区的水源和丰富的原材料使得这里在很早以前就已经适于工业生产。

✓ **mattress** [ˈmætrɪs]

n. the soft part of a bed, that you lie on 床垫

We sat on the *mattress* because that was all the furniture I had. 我们坐在床垫上，因为那是我仅有的家具。

✓ **mature** [məˈtjʊ(r)]　　　　　　　　　　　　　　　　[同] grown-up

v. to become fully grown or developed 成熟；长成

Brains *mature* at different rates. 每个人的大脑成熟的速度是不一样的。

✓ **negative** [ˈnegətɪv]　　　　　　　　　　　　　　　　[同] adverse

adj. considering only the bad side of sth./sb.; lacking enthusiasm or hope 消极的；负面的；缺乏热情的

Scientists have a *negative* attitude to the theory. 科学家们对这个理论的态度是否定的。

✓ **ownership** [ˈəʊnəʃɪp]

n. state of being an owner; (right of) possession 物主的身份；所有权

This sense of *ownership* exists in many forms: the home, the street, the village, town, city, province, and eventually country. 这种主人翁精神存在于多种形式上，包括家、街道、村庄、城镇、城市、省份以至于国家。

plot [plɒt]

n. (plan or outline of the) events in the story of a play or novel (戏剧或小说的)故事情节

The **plot** was a little confusing. 情节有点让人搞不懂。

plunge [plʌndʒ]

v. to (cause sb./sth. to) move suddenly forwards and/or downwards (使某人/某物)突然前移或跌落

The unemployment rate **plunged** sharply. 失业率大幅下降。

plus [plʌs]

① *conj.* used to add more information 此外；另外

He's really cute, **plus** he's got a good job. 他人很乖巧，工作也不错。

② *prep.* with the addition of 加；加上

Two **plus** five is seven. 二加五等于七。

romantic [rəʊˈmæntɪk]

① *adj.* connected or concerned with love or a sexual relationship 浪漫的；爱情的

a **romantic** candlelight dinner 浪漫的烛光晚餐

② *n.* a person who is very imaginative and emotional and who has ideas and hopes that may not be realistic 浪漫的人；耽于幻想的人

He was a **romantic** at heart and longed for adventure. 他骨子里是个浪漫的人，渴望历险。

rouse [raʊz]   [同] wake

v. (fml.) to wake sth. up, esp. when they are sleeping deeply 唤醒；使醒来

The telephone **roused** me from my sleep at 6 a.m. 早晨六点，电话铃声就把我从睡梦中吵醒了。

smog [smɒg]

n. mixture of fog and smoke 雾和烟的混合物；烟雾

It's the stationary cars that cause the pollution and **smog**. 污染与烟雾是由那些开着发动机却未行驶的汽车造成的。

snack [snæk]

n. small meal, usu. eaten in a hurry, esp. between main meals 小吃，点心(通常指匆匆食用，尤指两正餐之间的)

Usually I only have a **snack** at lunchtime. 我中午通常只吃点心。

tease [tiːz]   [近] give a bad time

v. to laugh at someone and make jokes in order to have fun by embarrassing them, either in a friendly way or in an unkind way 取笑；调侃

Don't get upset. I was only **teasing**. 别在意，我只是开个玩笑。

technical [ˈteknɪkl]

adj. connected with knowledge of how machines work 技术的

Our staff will be available to give you **technical** support. 我们的员工可以随时给你们提供技术支持。

technique [tekˈniːk]   [同] method

n. method of doing or performing sth., esp. in the arts or sciences 技术；方法；手段；(尤指艺术或科学方面的)技法，手法，技巧

I found this to be a really effective *technique* because it saved lots of time. 我发现这种技术非常有效，因为其大大节省了时间。

✓ **technology** [tekˈnɒlədʒi]

n. new machines, equipment, and ways of doing things that are based on modern knowledge about science and computers 技术

Many people are unwilling to embrace new *technologies*. 很多人并不接受新科技。

Take the Test ≫

一、英汉互译

行政	_____	civil	_____
故意的	*deliberate*	incentive	_____
精力充沛的	*energetic*	inclination	_____
可行的	*feasible*	plunge	_____
布局	_____	snack	小吃

二、翻译句子

1) 我不同意她的意见，但是我赞赏她坚持原则的精神。(admire)

_____

2) 这部戏剧成了中国(经典名剧)。(classic)

_____

3) 他骨子里是个浪漫的人，渴望历险。(romantic)

_____

4) 很多人并不接受新科技。(technology)

_____

You have to believe in yourself. That's the secret of success.
人必须相信自己，这是成功的秘诀。

——美国演员 卓别林(Charles Chaplin, American actor)

admission [əd'mɪʃn]

n. the act of accepting sb. into an institution, organization, etc. 准许加入，入学

The ***admissions*** office is open Monday to Friday. 招生办公室周一至周五办公。

adopt [ə'dɒpt]　　　　　　　　　　　　　　[同] embrace [反] discard

v. to start to deal with or think about something in a particular way 采用

The Braille's system was not officially ***adopted*** until 1854. 布莱叶盲文系统直到 1854 年才被正式采用。

adore [ə'dɔː(r)]　　　　　　　　　　　　　[同] dote (on) [反] detest

v. to love someone very much and feel very proud of them 热爱

It is obvious that she ***adores*** him. 她显然深深地爱着他。

beneficial [ˌbenɪ'fɪʃl]　　　　　　[同] advantageous [反] detrimental, harmful

adj. having a helpful or useful effect; advantageous 有益的；有用的；有好处的

Classical music is ***beneficial*** to learning and mind relaxation. 古典音乐对学习与头脑放松很有好处。

classical ['klæsɪkl]

adj. widely accepted and used for a long time 古典的；经典的；传统的

classical tradition 经典的传统

classify ['klæsɪfaɪ]　　　　　　　　　　　[同] assort, categorize

v. to arrange (sth.) systematically in classes or groups 将（某事物）编排，分类

The books in the library are ***classified*** by/according to subject. 图书馆的书是按照 / 根据科目分类的。

client ['klaɪənt]　　　　　　　　　　　　　[同] customer, patron

n. the person who receives help or advice from a professional person （e.g. a lawyer, an accountant, a social worker, an architect, etc.） 委托人，当事人

The instructors prepare routine of exercises to suit the individual ***client's*** age and level of fitness. 教员针对每个客户的年龄以及健康状况安排了训练计划。

delicate ['delɪkət]

adj. soft or tender when touched; made of sth. fine or thin 柔软的；柔和的；娇嫩的

The eye is one of the most ***delicate*** organs of the body. 眼睛是人体最娇贵的器官之一。

delicious [dɪ'lɪʃəs]　　　　　　　　　　　　[同] delightful

adj. giving pleasure, esp. to the senses of taste and smell 美味的；可口的

a ***delicious*** meal/cake/flavour 可口的饭菜 / 糕点 / 味道

enforce [ɪn'fɔːs]

v. to make sth. happen or force sb. to do sth. 强迫；迫使

You can't ***enforce*** cooperation between the players. 队员间的配合并非强迫命令而成。

engage [ɪn'geɪdʒ]　　　　　　　　　　　　[同] hire, involve

v. (fml.) to employ sb. to do a particular job 雇用；聘用

Most of any city's population is ***engaged*** in providing goods and services for the city itself. 任何城市的大部分人都在为该市本身提供物品和服务。

feat [fi:t]

n. an action or piece of work that needs skill, strength or courage 技艺；武艺；业绩

The tunnel is a brilliant ***feat*** of engineering. 这条隧道是工程方面的光辉业绩。

genuine ['dʒenjuɪn]   [同] real

adj. real; truly what it is said to be; not fake or artificial 真的；名副其实的；非人工的

For years people thought the picture was a ***genuine*** Van Gogh, but in fact it's a fake. 多年来人们以为这幅画是梵高的真迹，但事实上它是赝品。

hazard ['hæzəd]   [同] danger

n. (thing that can cause) danger; risk 危险；有危险的事物；风险

In Mexico City, vehicle pollution is a major health ***hazard***. 在墨西哥城，汽车污染是主要的健康隐患。

incline [ɪn'klaɪn]   [同] tend

v. to think that a particular belief or opinion is most likely to be correct 倾向于

I ***incline*** to accept the official version of events. 我倾向于接受事件的官方版本。

inclusive [ɪn'klu:sɪv]   [反] exclusive

adj. including all or a wide variety 包括许多或全部的

Prices are fully ***inclusive*** of insurance. 价格中已经包括了保险费。

✓ **intermediate** [ˌɪntə'mi:diət]

adj. situated or coming between two people, things, etc. in time, space, degree, etc. （时间、空间、程度等）介于（两人、物等）之间的，居间的

The pupa is at an ***intermediate*** stage of development; it is ***intermediate*** between the egg and the adult butterfly. 蛹是蝴蝶发育的中间阶段，介于卵和成虫之间。

✓ **internal** [ɪn'tɜ:nl]   [反] external

adj. of or on the inside 内部的；在内部的

A tree has got an ***internal*** mechanism to keep the temperature regulated. 树有一种内部机制来保持其温度正常。

✓ **judgement** ['dʒʌdʒmənt]   [同] inference

n. an opinion that you form, especially after thinking carefully about something 判断

A linguist's personal ***judgements*** are often uncertain, or disagree with the ***judgements*** of other linguists. 语言学家的个人判断往往是不确定的，或是反对其他语言学家的判断的。

junction ['dʒʌŋkʃn]   [近] joint

n. place where roads or railway lines meet 公路或铁路的交叉点；交叉路口

The accident happened at one of the country's busiest railway ***junctions***. 事故发生在该国极为繁忙的铁路交叉点之一。

✓ **leaflet** ['li:flɪt]

n. printed sheet of paper, usu. folded and free of charge, containing information 散页印刷品；（通常指）传单

Students were handing out election ***leaflets*** at the station. 学生在车站分发选举传单。

leak [li:k]

n. hole, crack, etc. through which liquid or gas may wrongly get in or out 漏洞；裂隙

A gas ***leak*** caused the explosion. 天然气泄露导致了爆炸。

✓ **maximize** ['mæksɪmaɪz]   [反] minimize *v.* to increase something such as profit or income as much as possible 使最大化；使增加到最大限度

The company's main function is to ***maximize*** profit. 该公司的主要任务就是使利润最大化。

√ **maximum** ［'mæksɪməm］ ［反］minimum

adj. as large, fast, etc. as is possible, or the most that is possible or allowed 最高的；最多的；最大极限的

For ***maximum*** effect do the exercises every day. 每天锻炼以取得最佳效果。

√ **neglect** ［nɪ'glekt］ ［同］②ignore

① *n.* the act of not giving enough care or attention to sth./sb.; the state of not receiving enough care or attention 忽略；未被重视

After years of ***neglect*** they still manage to function, though. 尽管它们已经好几年无人照管，却仍在运作。

② *v.* to fail to take care of sb./sth. 疏于照顾；未予看管

The buildings had been ***neglected*** for years. 这些大楼多年来一直无人看管。

polar ［'pəʊlə］

adj. of or near the North or South Pole（南、北）极的；地极的；近地极的

The largest bear existing today is either the ***Polar*** Bear or the Brown Bear. 现存最大的熊不是北极熊就是灰熊。

√ **polish** ［'pɒlɪʃ］ ［近］②refine

v. ①to（cause sth. to）become smooth and shiny by rubbing 磨光，擦亮（某物）②to improve a piece of writing, a speech, etc. by making slight changes to it before it is completely finished 润色

Your essay is good, you just need to ***polish*** it a bit. 你的文章不错，最后再润色一下即可。

poll ［pəʊl］ ［同］survey

n. voting at an election; counting of votes 选举投票；计票

be successful at the ***poll*** 选举投票中获胜

√ **popularity** ［'pɒpju'lærəti］

n. when something or someone is liked or supported by a lot of people 普及，受欢迎程度

Campus ballads are growing in ***popularity***. 校园民谣日益盛行。

√ **route** ［ruːt］ ［同］way

n. a way that you follow to get from one place to another 路线；路途

We came by a longer ***route*** than usual. 我们走了一条比通常要长的路来的。

routine ［ruː'tiːn］

n. the normal order and way in which you regularly do things 常规；正常顺序

Make exercise a part of your daily ***routine***. 让锻炼成为你日常生活的一部分。

√ **soar** ［sɔː］ ［近］rise

v. ①go up high in the air quickly 急速升入高空 ②to increase quickly to a high level 迅速增长

Consequently, company's profits ***soar*** ever higher at the expense of the workers. 结果，以牺牲工人利益为代价，公司利润进一步激增。

sole ［səʊl］ ［同］single, only

adj. one and only; single 惟一的；单独的

NASA's ***sole*** concern was the safety of the astronauts. NASA 惟一关注的是宇航员的安全。

√ **solid** ［'sɒlɪd］ ［同］firm

adj. not in the form of a liquid or gas; keeping its shape; firm 固体的；保持形状的；密实的

When water freezes it becomes ***solid*** and we call it ice. 水遇冷凝结，我们称之为冰。

√ **solution** ［sə'luːʃn］ ［同］answer

n.（action or way of finding an）answer to a problem, question, difficulty, etc. 解决；解答；解

决方法

Technical *solutions* can reduce the pollution problem. 技术解决方案可以减轻污染问题。

sorrow [ˈsɒrəʊ]   [同] heartache

n. a feeling of great sadness 悲痛；忧伤

It is my great *sorrow*, and it makes my life very unhappy. 那是一种巨大的伤痛，我的生活也随之不快。

tedious [ˈtiːdɪəs]   [同] boring

adj. tiresome because of being too long, slow or dull; boring（因过长、过慢或单调）令人厌倦的；烦人的

The work is *tedious*. 这工作令人厌倦。

✓ **temper** [ˈtempə]   [同] mood

n. state of the mind as regards anger or calmness 心情；脾气；性情

It is generally believed that *tempers* grow shorter in hot, muggy weather. 通常认为在闷热的天气里人更加烦躁。

temperate [ˈtempərɪt]   [同] moderate

adj. showing self-control（行为）有节制的；克制的

Please be more *temperate* in your language. 在言语上请再克制一些。

temporary [ˈtempərəri]

adj. lasting or meant to last for a limited time only; not permanent 暂时的；临时的；一时的

temporary employment 临时工作

✓ **ultimate** [ˈʌltɪmət]   [同] ①last

adj. ①the ultimate result of a long process is what happens at the end of it 最终的；最后的 ②main and most important 最主要的；最重要的

Human welfare is the *ultimate* goal of economic activity. 人类的福祉是经济活动的最终目标。

✓ **ultimately** [ˈʌltɪmətli]   [同] eventually, finally

adv. in the end; finally 最终；最后；终归

A poor diet will *ultimately* lead to illness. 不均衡的饮食终将导致疾病。

Take the Test ▶▶

一、英汉互译

有益的	~~beneticial~~	intermediate	
真的	~~fett~~ genuine	leaflet	传单
交叉路口		poll	
最多的		tedious	
常规		ultimate	最终的

二、翻译句子

1) 招生办公室周一至周五办公。（admission）

_____

2) 在墨西哥城，汽车污染是主要的健康隐患。（hazard）

_____

3) 校园民谣日益盛行。（popularity）

_____

4) 技术解决方案可以减轻污染问题。（solution）

_____

✓ **adult** ['ædʌlt]   [同] grown-up

adj./n. a person or animal that has grown to full size and strength 成年(的)

Adults and children are frequently confronted with statements about the alarming rate of loss of tropical rainforests. 无论是成人还是孩子都经常会发现一些关于热带雨林如何以惊人的速度消失的言论。

✓ **advance** [əd'vɑːns]   [同] advancement, progress [反] recession

n./v. a change, discovery, or invention that brings progress 进步；发展

Clearly, certain diseases are beating a retreat in the face of medical ***advances***. 很明显，由于医学研究的进步，某些疾病正逐渐退出人们的视线。

in ***advance*** 提前

We do ask that you sign up three days in ***advance***. 我们要求您至少提前三天报名。

✓ **advantage** [əd'vɑːntidʒ]   [同] edge [反] disadvantage

n. a condition giving a greater chance of success 优势，优点

There are tremendous ***advantages*** to involving parents in the program. 将家长融入到这个活动中来的好处非常多。

✓ **clerical** ['klerɪkl]

adj. relating to office work, especially work such as keeping records or accounts 办公室的，文职的

clerical workers 文员

✓ **clue** [kluː]   [同] hint, cue

n. fact or piece of evidence that helps to solve a problem or reveal the truth in an investigation 线索；端倪

After analysing the timbers, they have uncovered a vital ***clue*** as to why the ship sank. 在分析了船骨之后，他们找到了船只失事的一个重要线索。

clumsy ['klʌmzi]   [同] awkward, bumbling

adj. awkward and ungraceful in movement or shape (行动或形状)笨拙而难看的

You ***clumsy*** oaf — that's the second glass you've broken today! 你这个笨家伙——这是你今天打碎的第二个玻璃杯!

✓ **deliver** [dɪ'lɪvə]

v. to take (letters, parcels, goods, etc.) to the places or people they are addressed to 递送，传送(信件、包裹、货物等)

The heart is responsible for ***delivering*** blood to every part of the body. 心脏负责将血液送往全身的每一个部分。

✓ **demand** [dɪ'mɑːnd]   [同] ①requirement, need

① *n.* the need or desire that people have for particular goods and services 需求

There is a huge ***demand*** for new cars. 对新车的需求量很大。

② *v.* to ask for something very firmly, especially because you think you have a right to do this 要求

People were **demanding** that their fundamental right to health-care be satisfied by the state. 人们要求国家满足他们享有卫生保健这一基本权利。

✓ **enhance** [ɪnˈhɑːns]　　　　　　　　　　　　　　　　　[同] heighten

v. to increase or further improve the quality, value or status of sb./sth. 提高；增强；增进

These organizations provide a range of opportunities for women to **enhance** their skills and contacts. 这些组织为妇女提供了一系列的机会以提高她们的技术和增进交流。

✓ **enlarge** [ɪnˈlɑːdʒ]　　　　　　　　　　　　　　　　　[同] increase

v. to make sth. bigger, to become bigger 扩大；增大

Reading will **enlarge** your vocabulary. 阅读能扩大词汇量。

✓ **feature** [ˈfiːtʃə(r)]　　　　　　　　　　　　　　　　　[同] characteristic

n. something important, interesting or typical of a place or thing 特色；特征

One of the main **features** is satisfying the customer's needs and expectations. 其中的一个主要特征就是要满足顾客的需要和期望。

✓ **geographical** [ˌdʒiːəˈgræfɪkl]

adj. (also geographic) relating to the place in an area, country, etc. where something or someone is 地理的；地理学的

The second question concerned the **geographical** location of rain forests. 第二个问题关系到热带雨林的地理位置。

✓ **headline** [ˈhedlaɪn]

n. line of words printed in large type at the top of a page, esp. in a newspaper 书刊(尤指报纸)页首的大字标题

headline news 头版头条新闻

inconsistent [ˌɪnkənˈsɪstənt]　　　　　　　　　　　　[同] contradictory

adj. not right according to a particular set of principles or standards 不协调的；矛盾的

High achievers should not be put into jobs that are **inconsistent** with their needs. 有高成就的人不应该被置于与他们需求相矛盾的职位上。

✓ **incorporate** [ɪnˈkɔːpəreɪt]　　　　　　　　　　　　　[近] absorb

v. to include something as part of a group, system, plan, etc. 将某事包括进去；包含

Many of your suggestions have been **incorporated** in the new plan. 你的建议多已纳入新计划中。

interpret [ɪnˈtɜːprɪt]　　　　　　　　　　　　　　　　[同] explain

v. to explain (sth. which is not easily understandable) 解释；说明

Thus, we concluded that the blind **interpret** abstract shapes as sighted people do. 因此，我们得出盲人和视力正常的人在解释抽象的形状时是一样的结论。

✓ **interrupt** [ˌɪntəˈrʌpt]

v. to stop (sb.) speaking, etc. or (sth.) happening by speaking oneself or by causing some other sort of disturbance 打断(某人)讲话；打岔；打扰

The lecture was **interrupted** by accident. 讲座意外地被打断了。

✓ **knot** [nɒt]

n. ① fastening made by tying a piece or pieces of string, rope, etc. (线、绳等的)结 ② a part where one or more pieces of string, rope, cloth, etc. have been tied or twisted together 结打结，结(绳索等)

v. to make sth. together with a knot 打结

Two basic skills are needed—**knotting** and weaving. 这需要两个基本技巧——打结和编织。

√ **knowledgeable** [ˈnɒlidʒəbl]   [同] bright

adj. well-informed 消息灵通的；在行的

There is nothing wrong with talking to *knowledgeable* people about your project; in fact, this shows initiative. 和懂行的人谈论你的方案并没有什么错；事实上，这正体现出主动性。

√ **leap** [li:p]   [同] jump

v. to jump vigorously 跳；跳跃

He *leapt* across the room to answer the door.

他冲出房间去开门。

learned [ˈlɜːnid]

adj. having much knowledge acquired by study 有学问的；博学的

He's very *learned* but rather absent-minded. 他很有学问，可是好忘事。

meadow [ˈmedəʊ]

n. a field covered in grass 草地；牧场

The country subsequently converted 11 per cent of its cropped land to *meadow* or forest. 政府随之就将其 11%的农业用地改造成了牧场或森林。

√ **mean** [mi:n]   [同] stingy

adj. (BrE) not willing to give or share things, esp. money 吝啬的；小气的

She's always been *mean* with money. 她在花钱方面总是非常吝啬。

√ **means** [mi:nz]   [同] method

n. an action, an object or a system by which a result is achieved; a way of achieving or doing sth. 方式；方法；途径

The provision of small loans to support ambitions of youth can be an effective *means* to help them change their lives. 为支持年轻人的抱负而提供小额贷款是一种有效的帮助他们改变生活的方法。

by no *means* 绝不

negotiate [nɪˈɡəʊʃieɪt]   [近] settle

v. to discuss something in order to reach an agreement, especially in business or politics 协商；谈判

They continue to refuse to come to the *negotiating* table. 他们依然拒绝坐到谈判桌前。

√ **neighbouring** [ˈneɪbərɪŋ]   [同] close-by

adj. near the place where you are or the place you are talking about 临近的；附近的

It's surprising how little most teachers know about *neighbouring* schools. 大部分老师对临近的学校知之甚少，这很让人惊讶。

portion [ˈpɔːʃn]   [同] section

n. part or share into which sth. is divided 部分；（分事物时的）一份

He divided up his property and gave a *portion* to each of his children. 他把财产分给了子女，每人一份。

pose [pəʊz]

v. ①to sit or stand in a particular position in order to be painted, drawn or photographed 摆姿势 ②to exist in a way that may cause a problem, danger, difficulty, etc. 造成；提出

The advance of science has *posed* a challenge for theology. 科学的进步对神学提出了挑战。

√ **positive** [ˈpɒzətɪv]

adj. ①if you are positive about things, you are hopeful and confident, and think about what is good in a situation rather than what is bad 积极的；正面的 ②providing help; constructive 有助

的；有益的；建设性的 ③very sure, with no doubt at all that something is right or true 确信的

Customer comments, both *positive* and negative, are recorded by staff. 消费者的评价，无论是正面的还是负面的，都被员工记录下来。

TODAY, I TRIED TO THINK POSITIVE BUT IT DIDN'T WORK.

✓ **qualified** [ˈkwɒlɪˌfaɪd] [同] able

adj. having completed the relevant training or examination 经过训练或考试的；有资格的；合格的

a *qualified* doctor 合格的医生

✓ **qualify** [ˈkwɒlɪfaɪ] [同] entitle

v. to have the right to have or do something, or to give someone this right 取得资格；使有资格

You may *qualify* for unemployment benefit. 你也许有资格领取失业救济。

✓ **row** [rəʊ] [同] line

①*n.* a number of people standing or sitting next to each other in a line; a number of objects arranged in a line 一排；一列

The vegetables were planted in neat *rows*. 蔬菜种得整整齐齐。

②*v.* to move a boat through water using oars 划(船)

We *rowed* around the island. 我们绕着岛划船。

rub [rʌb]

v. to move your hand, or sth. such as a cloth, backwards and forwards over a surface while pressing firmly 擦；磨；搓

The cat *rubbed* itself against my legs. 猫在我腿上蹭来蹭去。

ruin [ˈruːin] [同] destroy

①*n.* the part of a building that is left after the rest has been destroyed 遗迹；废墟

We visited the *ruins* of the old temple. 我们参观了老寺庙的遗址。

②*v.* to spoil or destroy something completely 毁灭；破坏

sound [saʊnd] [反] unsound

adj. sensible and likely to produce the right results 合理的；明智的

The book is full of *sound* advice. 这本书里有很多合理的建议。

✓ **source** [sɔːs]

n. ①a thing, place, activity, etc. that you get something from 来源；源头 ②a person, book, or document that supplies you with information 原始资料

the country's main *source* of income 国家的主要收入来源

✓ **souvenir** [ˌsuːvəˈnɪə(r)] [同] memento

n. thing taken, bought or received as a gift, and kept to remind one of a person, a place or an event 纪念品；纪念物

Remember to visit the *souvenir* stalls in the car park in front of the main entrance to the stadium. 记得去体育场主入口前停车场里的纪念品商店看看。

spacious [ˈspeɪʃəs] [同] roomy

adj. having or providing much space; roomy 宽敞的；宽广的

a very *spacious* kitchen 非常宽敞的厨房

✓ **tempt** [tempt] [同] lure

v. to try to persuade someone to do sth. by making it seem attractive 诱惑，引诱

The new program is designed to *tempt* young people into studying engineering. 新的方案旨在吸引年轻人学习工程。

temptation [temp'teɪʃn]

n. tempting or being tempted 劝诱；诱惑

It is equally important to avoid the ***temptation*** to pad your essay with unwanted information. 避免在论文里加入不必要的信息同等重要。

✓ **unbiased** [ʌn'baɪəst]　　　　　　　　　　　　　　　　　　[近] just, fair

bias

adj. fair, not influenced by one's own or other people's opinions 没有偏见的；公正的

There is no such thing as ***unbiased*** news report. 这世界上就没有绝对公正的新闻报道。

uncertainty [ʌn'sɜːtənti]

n. something that you cannot be sure about; a situation that causes you to be or feel uncertain 拿不定的事；令人无法把握的局面

life's ***uncertainty*** 人生的不可知因素

Take the Test ≫

一、英汉互译

线索	clue	clumsy	
特征	feature	incorporate	包括
大字标题	headline	knowledgeable	
不协调的		learned	
打断	interrupt	neighbouring	邻近的

二、翻译句子

1）将家长融入到这个活动中来的好处非常多。（advantage）

＿＿＿＿＿＿＿＿＿＿＿＿＿＿＿＿＿＿＿＿＿＿＿＿＿＿＿

2）这些组织为妇女提供了一系列的机会以提高她们的技术和增进交流。（enhance）

＿＿＿＿＿＿＿＿＿＿＿＿＿＿＿＿＿＿＿＿＿＿＿＿＿＿＿

3）你的建议多已纳入新计划中。（incorporate）

＿＿＿＿＿＿＿＿＿＿＿＿＿＿＿＿＿＿＿＿＿＿＿＿＿＿＿

4）科学的进步对神学提出了挑战。（pose）

＿＿＿＿＿＿＿＿＿＿＿＿＿＿＿＿＿＿＿＿＿＿＿＿＿＿＿

Word List 13

✓ adventure [əd'ventʃə(r)]

n. an exciting experience in which dangerous or unusual things happen 冒险；奇遇

a spirit of **adventure** 冒险精神

adverse ['ædvɜːs]　　　　　　　　　　　[同] detrimental, negative

adj. not good or favourable 不利的，有害的

Lack of money will have an **adverse** effect on our research programme. 缺少资金将对我们的研究项目有不利影响。

✓ advertise ['ædvətaɪz]

v. to tell the public about a product or service in order to persuade them to buy it 做广告

They no longer **advertise** alcohol or cigarettes at sporting events. 他们不在体育赛事上做烟酒广告了。

✓ beverage ['bevərɪdʒ]　　　　　　　　　　　　　　　[同] drink

n. (fml.) any type of drink except water, e.g. milk, tea, wine, beer (除水以外的)饮料(如牛奶、茶、葡萄酒、啤酒)

food and **beverage** 食物与饮料

✓ coach [kəʊtʃ]

n. ① bus(usu. with a single deck) for carrying passengers over long distances 长途公共汽车(通常指单层的)② somebody who trains a person or team in sport (体育运动的)教练

travel by overnight **coach** to Scotland 乘坐夜间长途汽车去苏格兰

Italy's national **coach** 意大利国家队教练

✓ code [kəʊd]

n. ① (system of) words, letters, symbols, etc. that represent others, used for secret messages or for presenting or recording information briefly 密码；暗号

bar **codes** 条形码

② set of moral principles accepted by society or a group of people 道德准则

code of practice 行为准则

coherent [kəʊ'hɪərənt]

adj. (of ideas, thoughts, speech, reasoning, etc.) connected logically or consistent; easy to understand; clear (指看法、思想、言语、推理等)有条理的，前后一致的

The government lacks a **coherent** economic policy. 政府的经济政策缺乏一致性。

demonstrate ['demənstreɪt]　　　　　　　　　　　　[同] prove, show

v. to be an example of (sth.); show 是(某事物)的实例；表明；表示

A new study conducted for the World Bank by Murdoch University's Institute for Science and Technology Policy has **demonstrated** that public transport is more efficient than cars. 默多克大学的科技政策研究所为世界银行所做的最新研究表明，公共交通的效率高于小汽车。

enlightened [ɪnˈlaɪtənd]

adj. someone with enlightened attitudes has sensible, modern views and treats people fairly and kind 开通的；开明的；进步的

In less ***enlightened*** countries, the trend has been to reduce rather than eliminate farming subsidies, and to introduce new payments to encourage farmers to treat their land in environmentally friendlier ways. 在一些不太进步的国家，发展趋势是减少而不是取消农业补助，并且通过引入新的补偿来鼓励农民以更环保的方式耕作土地。

✓ **enormous** [ɪˈnɔːməs]   [同] huge

adj. extremely large 巨大的；庞大的

On the same note, the ***enormous*** cost of the war left much of Europe financially vulnerable. 同样地，战争的巨大成本使欧洲大多数国家的财政都变得很脆弱。

federal [ˈfedərəl]

adj. a federal country or system of government consists of a group of states which control their own affairs, but which are also controlled by a single national government 联邦的

Some years ago, ***federal*** money was granted to build a new road. 数年以前，联邦储备被准予用于修建一条新公路。

✓ **gesture** [ˈdʒestʃə(r)]

n. expressive movement of a part of the body, esp. the hand or head 姿势；手势

with a ***gesture*** of despair 用表示绝望的姿势

headquarters [ˈhedˌkwɔːtəz]

n. a place from which an organization or a military operation is controlled 总部；指挥部

The daily paper is compiled at the editorial ***headquarters***, known as the pre-press centre. 日报在编辑总部，也就是通常所说的出版中心编排。

increasingly [ɪnˈkriːsɪŋli]

adv. more and more all the time 日益；越发

Modern economies are ***increasingly*** interdependent. 现代经济变得越来越相互依赖。

incredible [ɪnˈkredəbl]   [同] unbelievable

adj. very difficult to believe; extremely good, large, or great 难以置信的

What an ***incredible*** story! 这件事真让人难以置信！

isolate [ˈaɪsəleɪt]   [近] separate

v. to put or keep sb./sth. entirely apart from other people or things; separate sb./sth. 使(某人／某物与他人／他物)完全隔离；孤立(某人／某物)

When a person has an infectious disease, he is usually ***isolated*** (from other people). 人患传染病时通常要(与他人)隔离。

isolated [ˈaɪsəleɪtɪd]   [同] alone

adj. feeling alone and unable to meet or speak to other people 孤独的

Seeman found that elderly people who felt emotionally ***isolated*** maintained higher levels of stress hormones even when asleep. Seeman 发现那些在情感上觉得孤独的年长人群即使在睡觉的时候也能维持较高的压力荷尔蒙水平。

jungle [ˈdʒʌŋgl]

n. area of land, usu. in a tropical country, that is covered with a thick growth of trees and tangled plants (通常指热带国家的)丛林地带

the dense *jungles* of Africa and South America 非洲和南美洲的茂密丛林

✓ **lecture** ['lektʃə(r)]　　　　　　　　　　　　　　　　　　　　　[同] speech

n. a long talk on a particular subject that someone gives to a group of people, especially to students in a university 讲座

I am giving you the *lectures* on Environmental Noise this term. 我这个学期会做一些关于环境噪音的讲座。

✓ **measure** ['meʒə(r)]　　　　　　　　　　　　　　　　　　　　　[同] step

n. an official action that is done in order to achieve a particular aim 措施；方法

take positive *measures* 采取积极措施

mechanism ['mekənɪzəm]

n. a set of moving parts in a machine that performs a task 机械装置；机件

The *mechanism* behind the idea of propelling an object into the air has been around for well over two thousand years. 向空中发射物体的背后机理已经存在两千多年了。

✓ **media** ['miːdɪə]

n. the main ways that large numbers of people receive information and entertainment, that is television, radio and the newspaper 大众传播媒介；大众传播工具(指电视、广播、报纸等)

The nuclear disaster in Chernobyl continued to receive high *media* exposure. 切尔诺贝利的核泄漏事件仍然被媒体广泛曝光。

nerve [nɜːv]

n. the feelings of worry or anxiety 神经质；神经紧张

Everyone's *nerves* were on edge. 人人都觉得紧张。

possession [pə'zeʃn]　　　　　　　　　　　　　　　　　　　　　[同] belongings

n. thing that is possessed; property 所有物；财产

I was told by the landlord that it would be a good idea to get some insurance for the furniture and other personal *possessions*. 房东告诉我最好给家具及其他私人财产上保险。

✓ **possibility** [ˌpɒsə'bɪləti]　　　　　　　　　　　　　　　　　　[同] ①potential

n. ①if there is a possibility that something is true or that something will happen, it might be true or it might happen 可能性 ②an opportunity to do something, or something that can be done or tried 可以做的事；可行性

Computers have opened up many exciting *possibilities*. 计算机开启了一片令人兴奋的新天地。

✓ **poster** ['pəʊstə]

n. large placard displayed in a public place 招贴；海报

posters of old movie stars 旧日影星的海报

✓ **postpone** [pə'spəʊn]　　　　　　　　　　　　　　　　　　　　[同] defer

v. to arrange sth. at a later time; defer sth. 使某事物延期；推迟某事物

The match was *postponed* to the following Saturday because of bad weather. 比赛因天气不好而延期到下星期六进行。

✓ **potential** [pə'tenʃl]　　　　　　　　　　　　　　　　[同] ①possible

①*adj.* that can or may come into existence; possible 可能存在或出现的；可能的

potential customers 潜在客户

②*n.* possibility of being developed or used 潜能；潜力

a young player with great *potential* 大有潜力的年轻运动员

✓ **quality** ['kwɒləti]

n. degree of goodness or worth 质量；品质

The *quality* of education should take priority over profitability. 教育质量应该优于盈利程度。

questionnaire [ˌkwestʃə'neə(r)]

n. written or printed list of questions to be answered by a number of people, esp. to collect statistics or as part of a survey 问卷；(尤指为做统计或调查用的)问题单，调查表

Please complete and return the enclosed *questionnaire*. 所附问卷请填妥交回。

queue [kjuː]   [同] line

n. line of people, vehicles, etc. waiting for sth. or to do sth. (人或车辆等的)长列，行列

By 7 o'clock a long *queue* had formed outside the cinema. 到七点钟时，电影院门外已经排起了长队。

rumour ['ruːmə(r)]   [近] report

n. a piece of information, or a story, that people talk about, but that may not be true 谣言；传闻

Some malicious *rumours* are circulation about his past. 有人别有用心地散布谣言，说他过去如何如何。

✓ **rural** ['rʊərəl]   [近] country

adj. connected with or like the countryside 乡村的；农村的

Technological advances also helped bring about the decline of *rural* industries. 科技的进步也导致了乡村工业的衰落。

spare [speə(r)]   [同] superfluous

adj. in addition to what is usu. needed or used; kept in reserve for use when needed 多余的；剩余的；备用的

In fact, it's a very good idea to bring some *spare* clothes. 事实上，带一些备用的衣物是个相当明智的想法。

✓ **specialize** ['speʃəlaɪz]

v. to be or become a specialist 成为专家；专门从事；专攻

He *specializes* in oriental history. 他专门研究东方史。

tenant ['tenənt]

n. person who pays rent to a landlord for the use of a room, a building, land, etc. 房客；租户

Tenants are not allowed to keep pets. 房客不得饲养宠物。

✓ **tendency** ['tendənsi]   [同] trend

n. way a person or thing tends to be or behave (人或物呈现的)倾向，趋势

The effort to clean up cars may do little to cut pollution if nothing is done about the *tendency* to drive them more. 如果不设法改变更多地使用汽车的趋势，净化汽车的努力可能对减少污染作用甚微。

tender ['tendə(r)]

① *adj.* gentle and careful in a way that shows love 亲切的，关心的

Her voice was *tender* and soft. 她的声音温柔亲切。

② *n.* person who looks after or tends sth. 照管、照料或照看某事物者

a bar *tender* 酒吧服务员

✓ **uncover** [ʌn'kʌvə(r)]   [同] reveal, expose, disclose

v. to discover sth. that was previously hidden or secret 发现；揭露

Over the past few years their observations have *uncovered* previously unknown trends and cycles in bird. 在过去几年中，他们的观察发现了他们以前所不知的鸟类的动向和生活周期。

underestimate [ˌʌndərˈestɪmeɪt]

v. to think or guess that the amount, cost or size of sth. is smaller than it really is 低估；对…估计不足

We **underestimated** the time it would take to get there. 我们低估了抵达那里所需的时间。

undergo [ˌʌndəˈgəʊ]　　　　　　　　　　　　　　　　　　　　[同] experience

v. to experience sth., especially a change or sth. unpleasant 经历；经受（变化、不快的事等）

For a relatively new industry it is not surprising that ecotourism has **undergone** teething pains. 生态旅行作为一个相对新兴的产业已经历了开始的痛苦时期，这不足为奇。

√ **underground** [ˌʌndəˈgraʊnd]　　　　　　　　　　　　　　　　　[同] underearth

adj. under the surface of the ground 地下的；地面以下的

There is an **underground** room in the old house. 在老房子里有一个地下室。

Take the Test ▶▶

一、英汉互译

冒险	*adventure*	beverage	饮料
巨大的	*enormous*	coherent	
总部	*headquarters*	enlightened	开明的
难以置信的		mechanism	
孤独的		poster	海报

二、翻译句子

1）缺少资金将对我们的研究项目有不利影响。（adverse）

_____

2）现代经济变得越来越相互依赖。（increasingly）

_____

3）房东告诉我最好给家具及其他私人财产上保险。（possession）

_____

4）科技的进步也导致了乡村工业的衰落。（rural）

_____

advocate ['ædvəkət]   [同] ②back ①②champion

① *n.* a person who supports sth. 拥护者；支持者

['ædvəkeɪt]

② *v.* to support sth. publicly 拥护；提倡

The proposal *advocated* the creation of hundreds of urban villages. 该提议呼吁建立上百个城市卫星村。

affect [ə'fect]   [同] influence

v. to have an influence on sb. or sth. 影响

No activity *affects* more of the earth's surface than farming. 没有哪个活动能像耕作那样影响到如此大面积的地球表面。

agency ['eɪdʒənsi]

n. a business that provides a particular service for people or organizations 服务机构；代理机构

The travel *agency* is at the Smith Street's end of the building. 旅行社在那座楼靠近史密斯街的那一侧。

bias ['baɪəs]   [同] prejudice

n. opinion or feeling that strongly favours one side in an argument or one item in a group or series; predisposition; prejudice 偏见；成见；偏心

political *bias* in the press 报业中的政治偏见

collapse [kə'læps]   [同] fall to pieces

v. (of prices, currencies, etc.) to suddenly decrease in value 突然降价；暴跌；倒塌

The whole market *collapsed*. 整个市场崩溃了。

colleague ['kɒliːg]   [同] associate, co-worker

n. a person with whom one works, esp. in a profession or business 同事；同僚

David is a *colleague* of mine. 戴维是我的同事。

collective [kə'lektɪv]

adj. of, by or relating to a group or society as a whole; joint; shared 集体的；整个社会的；共同的；共有的

collective action/effort/guilt/responsibility/wisdom 集体的行动/努力/罪责/责任/智慧

deny [dɪ'naɪ]   [反] acknowledge, admit

v. say that (sth.) is not true 否认，否定（某事）

No one is *denying* that books are competing with other forms of entertainment for children's attention. 没有人否认书本正和其他形式的娱乐争夺着孩子们的注意力。

departure [dɪ'pɑːtʃə(r)]   [同] exit

n. an act of leaving a place 离开；离去

Any extra costs incurred must be paid to the hotel by yourself before *departure* from the hotel. 在离开之前必须由本人向宾馆付清所有额外的费用。

enquiry [ɪnˈkwaɪəri]

n. the act of asking questions or collecting information about sb./sth. 查询; 探究; 探索

Research has been conducted in this field of *enquiry*. 在这个研究领域也进行了调查。

Enquiry

enrich [ɪnˈrɪtʃ]

v. to improve the quality of sth. often by adding sth. to it 充实; 使丰富

Most breakfast cereals are *enriched* with vitamins. 多数谷类早餐食物都添加了维生素。

fee [fiː]

n. an amount of money that you pay to do sth. or that you pay to a professional person for their work 费用

The insurance company paid all my medical *fees*. 保险公司支付了我的全部医疗费用。

giant [ˈdʒaɪənt]

n. usu. a large person, animal, plant, business organization, etc. 巨人(异常大的动植物、商业组织等)

a cabbage of *giant* size 巨大的洋白菜

heal [hiːl]   [近] cure

v. (cause sth. to) become healthy again (使某物)康复

The wound *healed* slowly. 伤口愈合得很慢。

indefinite [ɪnˈdefɪnət]   [同] vague

adj. without definite end arranged in advance; not clear or exact 不确定的; 不明确的; 模糊的

He has rather *indefinite* views on the question. 他对该问题的看法颇为模糊。

index [ˈɪndeks]

① *n.* figure showing the relative level of prices or wages compared with that of a previous date (物价或工资的)指数

the cost-of-living *index* 生活费用指数

② *v.* make an index for (sth.) 为(某事物)编索引

The book is not well *indexed*. 这部书的索引做得不好。

issue [ˈɪʃuː, ˈɪsjuː]   [同] problem

n. a subject or problem that is often discussed or argued about, esp. a social or political matter that affects the interests of a lot of people 讨论或争议中的问题、争论点等

This is surprising considering the high level of media coverage on this *issue*. 考虑到在这个问题上的媒体高曝光率, 这很令人惊讶。

item [ˈaɪtəm]

n. single piece of news 一则或一条新闻

Items placed here just don't attract people. 放在这里的新闻根本不吸引人。

legal [ˈliːgl]   [反] illegal

adj. of or based on the law 法律的; 依照法律的; 法定的

The role definitions of lawyers and doctors are fairly clearly defined both in *legal* and in cultural terms. 在法律和文化层面, 律师和医生在角色上的定义都是非常清楚的。

lessen [ˈlesn]   [同] reduce

v. to become less 变少

The pain was already *lessening*. 疼痛已有所减轻。

√ **medium** [ˈmiːdɪəm]

adj. in the middle between two sizes, amounts, lengths, temperatures, etc. 中等的；中号的

There are three sizes—small, *medium* and large. 有三种尺寸——小号、中号和大号。

melody [ˈmelədi]

n. a tune, esp. the main tune in a piece of music written for several instruments or voices 旋律；曲调

The song has a simple *melody* and beautiful lyrics. 这首歌曲调简单，歌词优美。

√ **network** [ˈnetwɜːk]

n. ①a system of lines, tubes, wires, roads, etc. that cross each other and are connected to each other 网络 ②a group of people, organizations, etc. that are connected or that work together 人脉；圈子

Melbourne's large tram *network* has made car use in the inner city much lower. 墨尔本庞大的有轨电车网极大地减少了市中心区的汽车使用。

√ **pottery** [ˈpɒtəri]

n. pots, dishes made with clay that is baked in an oven, esp. when they are made by hand 陶器（尤指手工制的）

Roman *pottery* 罗马时期的陶器

√ **poverty** [ˈpɒvəti]　　　　　　　　　　　　　　　　　　　　［同］destitution

n. state of being poor 贫穷；贫困

live in *poverty* 过着穷困的生活

√ **practitioner** [prækˈtɪʃənə]

n. ①someone who works as a doctor or a lawyer 执业律师；执业医生 ②someone who regularly does a particular activity 实践者；从事者

Well, the first thing you have to do is find a family doctor—sometimes we call them general *practitioners* as well—and register with him or her. 你要做的第一件事就是去找个家庭医生——有时候我们也称他们为"全科医生"，然后在他或她那儿登记。

precede [prɪˈsiːd]　　　　　　　　　　　　　　　　　　　　　［同］forerun

v. to happen or exist before sth. or sb., or to come before sth. else in a series 领先于；

On vehicle license plates in the UK, the numbers are *preceded* by a single letter. 在英国的汽车牌照上，一个字母后跟着一些数字。

precise [prɪˈsaɪs]　　　　　　　　　　　　　　　　　　　　　［同］accurate

adj. exact, clear, and correct 精准的；精确的

"She's a lot older than you, isn't she?" "Fifteen years, to be *precise*." "她比你年长不少吧？" "15岁，准确地讲。"

√ **quit** [kwɪt]

v. to go away from (a place); leave 从（某处）离开；离去

He got his present job when he *quit* the army. 他退伍后得到现在这份工作。

√ **quiz** [kwɪz]

n. competition, esp. on TV or radio, in which people try to answer questions to test their knowledge 竞赛，比赛（尤指电视或电台中人们竞相回答问题以测验其知识）

take part in a *quiz* 参加知识竞赛

✓ **quote** [kwəʊt]

① *n.* a sentence or phrase from a book, speech, etc. which you repeat in a speech or piece of writing 引用

② *v.* to repeat exactly what sb. else has said or written 引述；引用

Corporate crime been defined as, *quote*, 'crime which is committed for the corporate organization, not against it', unquote. 公司犯罪被定义为 "为了公司机构的利益而进行的犯罪，而不是伤害它"。

species [ˈspiːʃiːz]   [同] type

n. (pl. unchanged) group of animals or plants within a genus differing only in minor details from the others, and able to breed with each other but not with other groups 物种；种

endangered *species* 濒危物种

✓ **specific** [spəˈsɪfɪk]   [近] special

adj. detailed, precise and exact 详细而精确的；确切的

specific instructions 明确的指示   *precise, exat.*

specify [ˈspesɪfaɪ]

v. to state sth. in an exact and detailed way 详细说明

The regulations *specify* that you may use a dictionary in the examination. 规则规定考试时可使用字典。

tense [tens]   [同] ①tight

① *adj.* feeling worried, uncomfortable, and unable to relax 紧张；无法放松的

② *n.* any of the forms of a verb that show the time, continuance, or completion of an action 时态

③ *v.* to make your muscles tight and stiff, or to become tight and stiff 拉紧；紧绷

Relax, and try not to *tense* up so much. 放松点，试着别那么紧张。

tension [ˈtenʃn]   [同] ①②strain ①stress

n. ① mental, emotional or nervous strain; tenseness 心理、情绪或神经方面的紧张 ②the feeling that exists when people or countries do not trust each other and may suddenly attack each other or start arguing 关系紧张

That generation knows only too well what political *tension* can mean. 那一代人最清楚政治紧张意味着什么。

✓ **term** [tɜːm]

in terms of…
就…而言 ☆

n. ①one of the three periods of time that the school or university year is divided into 学期 ②a word or expression with a particular meaning 叫法；说法 ③[习语]in terms of if you explain or describe something in terms of a particular fact or event, you are explaining or describing it only in relation to that fact or event 就…而言；从…角度来讲

In *terms* of quality ingredients, this is the best ice cream you can buy. 就原料的优劣而言，这是你能买到的最好的冰激凌。

underlie [ˌʌndəˈlaɪ]

v. to be the cause of sth., or be the basic thing from which sth. develops 成为…的依据；支撑

We have looked at some of the key principles that *underlie* microeconomics. 我们已经看过了一些支撑微观经济学的主要原理。

✓ **underline** [ˌʌndəˈlaɪn]   [同] emphasize

v. to draw a line under a word, sentence, etc. 在(词语等下)画线；画底线标出

You can *underline* or highlight new words. 你可以在新词底下画线或标出重点符号。

undertake [ˌʌndəˈteɪk]   [同] take on *v.* (fml.) to make yourself responsible for sth. and start doing it 承担；从事；负责

These tiny, unassuming insects spend their lives engaged in the task that they are genetically programmed to **undertake**. 这种小而朴实的昆虫尽其一生完成它们生来既定的任务。

underway [ˌʌndəˈweɪ]

adj. happening now 正在进行中的

The project is already well **underway**. 这个项目已经开始实施了。

✓ **zone** [zəʊn]   [同] area

n. an area or a region with a particular feature or use (有某种特色或作用的)地区，地带

The system wouldn't overcome the problem of different time **zones**. 这个系统不能解决时区不同所带来的问题。

Take the Test ▶▶

一、英汉互译

提倡 _____   bias _____

服务机构 _____   departure _____

查询 _____   index _____

贫困 _____   practitioner _____

承担 _____   underlie _____

二、翻译句子

1）有三种尺寸——小号、中号和大号。（medium）

_____

2）这首歌曲调简单，歌词优美。（melody）

_____

3）你要做的第一件事就是去找个家庭医生——有时候我们也称他们为"全科医生"，然后在他或她那儿登记。（practitioner）

_____

4）那一代人最清楚政治紧张意味着什么。（tension）

_____

Trouble is only opportunity in work clothes.
困难只是穿上工作服的机遇。

——美国实业家 凯泽（H.J. Kaiser, American businessman）

agenda ✓ [əˈdʒendə] [同] programme

n. a list of the subjects to be discussed at a meeting 议程表，议事日程

Many consumers feel that government and business have taken on the environmental *agenda*.

很多消费者感觉到政府和企业已经把环境问题提上了议程。

aggregate [ˈægrɪɡeɪt] [同] amount

n./v. the total after a lot of different figures or points have been added together 总数；总计

Manchester United won 2-1 on *aggregate*. 曼联队以总分 2 比 1 获胜。

aggressive [əˈɡresɪv] [同] assertive [反] submissive

adj. ①behaving in an angry, threatening way, as if you want to fight or attack someone 进攻性的 ②very determined to succeed or get what you want 积极进取的

Kids who play violent video games show much more *aggressive* behaviour than those who don't.

经常玩暴力电游的孩子要比那些不玩的孩子表现出更多的攻击性行为。

bibliography ✓ [ˌbɪbliˈɒɡrəfi]

n. list of books or articles about a particular subject or by a particular author（有关某一专题或某一作者的著作的）书目，索引，文献

In coursework and assessment essays, don't forget to acknowledge your sources in a *bibliography*. 在写学期论文与评估作业时，别忘记在书目中列出你引用的文献来源。

colossal [kəˈlɒsl] [同] huge, gigantic

adj. very large; immense; huge 巨大的；广大的；庞大的

a *colossal* building/man/price/amount 巨大的建筑 / 巨人 / 高价 / 庞大的数量

combine ✓ [kəmˈbaɪn] [同] join, unite

v. to join or mix together to form a whole（使物件）结合或混合形成一整体；组合；合并

Circumstances have *combined* to ruin our plans for a holiday. 各种情况凑在一起破坏了我们的休假计划。

comedy ✓ [ˈkɒmədi]

n. light or amusing plays or films, usu. with a happy ending 喜剧；喜剧片

I prefer *comedy* to tragedy. 我喜欢喜剧，不喜欢悲剧。

deposit [dɪˈpɒzɪt] [近] ②bank

① *n.* the sum paid into an account, e.g. at a bank 存款

She made two *deposits* of £500 last month. 她上月存了两笔 500 英镑的款。

② *v.* to put（money）into a bank, esp. to earn interest, etc. 将（钱）存入银行

The cheque was only *deposited* yesterday, so it hasn't been cleared yet. 这张支票昨天才存入银行，所以尚未兑现。

depressed [dɪˈprest] [同] downcast

adj. sad and without enthusiasm 忧愁的；消沉的

They become so ***depressed*** and lacking in energy that their work and social life are affected. 他们变得如此无精打采，以致工作和社会生活都受到了影响。

enrol [ɪnˈrəʊl] [近] register

v. （AmE enroll）to arrange for yourself or for sb. else to officially join a course, school, etc. (使)加入；注册

You need to ***enrol*** before the end of August. 你必须在八月底前注册。

en suite [ɒnˈswiːt]

n. a bathroom that is joined onto a bedroom, especially in a hotel 独立卫生间

Each room has an ***en suite*** and a balcony. 每个房间都有独立卫生间和阳台。

feedback [ˈfiːdbæk]

n. advice, criticism or information about how good or useful sth. or sb.'s work is 反馈的意见（或信息）

I'd appreciate some ***feedback*** on my work. 如果有人对我的工作提出意见，我将感激不尽。

gifted [ˈɡɪftɪd] [同] intelligent

adj. having a great deal of natural ability or talent 有天才的；有天赋的

She was an extremely ***gifted*** poet. 她是一个极具才华的诗人。

gigantic [dʒaɪˈɡæntɪk] [同] huge

adj. of very great size or extent; immense 巨大的；庞大的

a problem of ***gigantic*** proportions 重大的问题

hectare [ˈhektɑː]

n. （abbr. ha）measure of area in the metric system, equal to 10,000 square metres 公顷

The rich soils in the west provide excellent pasture, and the farms there are quite large, typically around 800 ***hectares***. 西部肥沃的土地提供了优良的牧场，因而那里的农场非常大，一般为800公顷。

indicate [ˈɪndɪkeɪt] [同] show

v. to show that a particular situation exists, or that something is likely to be true 表明；显示

Pupils' responses ***indicate*** some misconceptions in basic scientific knowledge of rainforests' ecosystems. 小学生的反馈显示出了在热带雨林生态系统的基础科学知识方面的一些错误认识。

indicator [ˈɪndɪkeɪtə]

n. one of the lights on a car that flash to show which way the car is turning (车辆的)方向指示装置(尤指闪动的灯光)

His left-hand/right-hand ***indicator*** is flashing. 他的左／右信号灯在闪动。

indigestion [ˌɪndɪˈdʒestʃn]

n. pain that you get when your stomach cannot break down food that you have eaten 消化不良

Other side effects are dizziness or headaches, and ***indigestion*** or stomachache. 其他副作用包括头昏、头痛、消化不良或者胃疼。

junior [ˈdʒuːnɪə] [反] ①②senior

① *adj.* lower in rank or standing（than sb.）(较某人)地位或身份低的

The most ***junior*** officers wore a red stripe on their sleeves. 最下级的职员在袖口处配有红色带子。

② *n.* (AmE) student in his third year of a four-year course at college or high school (四年制的大学或中学的)三年级学生

junk [dʒʌŋk]

n. (infml.) things that are considered useless or of little value 无用的或无价值的东西

I must clean out this cupboard—it's absolutely full of *junk*. 我必须得打扫一下橱柜，里面尽是没用的东西。

melt [melt]　　　　　　　　　　　　　　　　　　　　　　　　　　[同] liquefy

v. to become or make sth. become liquid as a result of heating (使)融化; (使)熔化

The ice *melted* when the sun shone on it. 冰块在太阳的炙烤下很快就融化了。

mentality [menˈtæləti]

n. the particular attitude or way of thinking of a person or group 心态; 思想状况

I cannot understand the *mentality* of football hooligan. 我无法理解足球流氓的心态。

✓**merchandise** [ˈmɜːtʃəndaɪz]

n. (fml.) goods that are bought or sold; goods that are for sale in a shop 商品; 货物

a wide selection of *merchandise* 品种丰富的商品

neutral [ˈnjuːtrəl]　　　　　　　　　　　　　　　　　　　　　[近]①abstract

adj. ①not supporting any of the people or groups involved in an argument or in a war 中立的 ②
a neutral colour is a colour such as grey, light brown, or cream 中性色

Switzerland remained *neutral* during World War II. 瑞士在二战时期保持中立。

nevertheless [ˌnevəðəˈles]

adv. (fml.) in spite of sth. that you have just mentioned 尽管如此; 然而

There is little chance that we will succeed in changing the law. *Nevertheless*, it is important that we try. 我们几乎没有可能成功地改变法律，不过，重要的是我们努力过了。

✓**precious** [ˈpreʃəs]　　　　　　　　　　　　　　　　　　　　　[同] costly

adj. of great value (and beauty) 贵重的; 宝贵的

For Australia, water is a *precious* resource and its wise management is of the greatest importance. 在澳大利亚，水是非常宝贵的资源，合理运用水资源是最重要的。

✓**predict** [prɪˈdɪkt]　　　　　　　　　　　　　　　　　　　　　[同] foretell

v. to say that something will happen, before it happens 预计; 预测

Some scientists *predict* that the Earth's temperature will rise by as much as 5℃ over the next 20 years. 有些科学家预测在未来 20 年全球气温会上升多达 5℃。

✓**prediction** [prɪˈdɪkʃn]

n. a statement about what you think is going to happen, or the act of making this statement 预测; 预言

It's a bit early to make *predictions*. 现在就做预测还有点为时过早。

predominant [prɪˈdɒmɪnənt]　　　　　　　　　　　　　　　　　[近] chief

adj. more powerful, more common, or more easily noticed than others 主要的; 占优势的; 最显著的

Housing is the *predominant* social issue of the day. 住房是如今的主要社会话题。

✓**quotation** [kwəʊˈteɪʃn]

n. a group of words taken from a book, play, speech, etc. and used again, usu. by sb. other than the original author 语录; 引文; 引用语

a dictionary of *quotations* 语录汇编

specimen [ˈspesɪmən]　　　　　　　　　　　　　　　　　　　　[同] sample

n. thing or part of a thing taken as an example of its group or class（esp. for scientific research or for a collection）样品，标本（尤用于科研或作收藏品）

There were some fine *specimens* of rocks and ores in the museum. 博物馆里有些很好的岩石和矿石标本。

spectacle ［ˈspektəkl］

n. grand public display, procession, performance, etc. 大场面（壮观的公开展示、队列、表演等）

The ceremonial opening of Parliament was a fine *spectacle*. 该议会的开幕式场面隆重。

spectacular ［spekˈtækjələ(r)］　　［同］sensational

adj. making a very fine display or show 壮观的；精彩的

a *spectacular* display of fireworks 壮观的烟火会

speculate ［ˈspekjuleɪt］　　［同］ponder

v. to form opinions without having definite or complete knowledge or evidence; guess 思考；推断；推测

Instead all we can do is hypothesize about the causes and *speculate* upon the future. 换言之，我们所能做的只是猜测起因与推测未来。

terminate ［ˈtɜːmɪneɪt］　　［同］end

v. (fml.) to come to an end or bring (sth.) to an end 结束；使（某事）终止，终结

The company had the right to *terminate* his employment at any time. 公司有权在任何时候解聘他。

terminology ［ˌtɜːmɪˈnɒlədʒi］

n. technical terms of a particular subject（某学科的）专门用语，术语

a word not used except in medical *terminology* 仅用于医学的专业词

unfold ［ˌʌnˈfəʊld］　　［近］open

v. ①to spread open or flat 展开；打开　②if a series of events unfold, they happen 发展；展开

We discover that Jack isn't as innocent as he seems, as the plot *unfolds*. 随着剧情的展开，我们发现杰克并非像他看上去那样单纯。

✓ unfortunate ［ʌnˈfɔːtʃənət］　　［同］unlucky

adj. having bad luck; caused by bad luck 不幸的；倒霉的

He was *unfortunate* to lose in the final round. 他不幸在最后一轮输了。

✓ uniform ［ˈjuːnɪfɔːm］

n. a particular type of clothing worn by all the members of a group or organization such as the police, the army, etc. 制服；工作服

I used to hate wearing a school *uniform*. 我曾经讨厌穿校服。

vacant ［ˈveɪkənt］　　［近］empty

adj. (of a seat, hotel room, house, etc.) empty; not being used 空着的；未被占用的

The seat next to him was *vacant*. 他旁边的座位空着。

✓ vacation ［vəˈkeɪʃn, veɪˈkeɪʃn］　　［同］holiday

n. esp. AmE a holiday, or time spent not working 假期

the Christmas/Easter/summer *vacation* 圣诞节假期 / 复活节假期 / 暑假

vacuum ［ˈvækjuəm］

① *n.* a space that is completely empty of all substances, including all air or other gas 真空

② *v.* to clean using a vacuum cleaner 用吸尘器打扫

Have you *vacuumed* the carpets? 你有没有拿吸尘器吸过地毯？

一、英汉互译

存款	_____	aggregate	_____
表明	_____	en suite	_____
心态	_____	merchandize	_____
大场面	_____	neutral	_____
空着的	_____	terminology	_____

二、翻译句子

1) 很多消费者感觉到政府和企业已经把环境问题提上了议程。(agenda)

_____

2) 在写学期论文与评估作业时, 别忘记在书目中列出你引用的文献来源。
(bibliography)

_____

3) 如果有人对我的工作提出意见, 我将感激不尽。(feedback)

_____

4) 住房是如今的主要社会话题。(predominant)

_____

The supreme happiness of life is the conviction that we are loved.
生活中最大的幸福是坚信有人爱我们。

——法国小说家 雨果(Victor Hugo, French novelist)

agony [ˈæɡəni] [同] distress, misery

n. extreme physical or mental pain 极度痛苦

The worst *agonies* of the war were now beginning. 战争最深重的苦难现在开始了。

✓ **aid** [eɪd] [同] assistance [反] impediment

n. /v. money, food, etc. that is sent to help countries in difficult situations 援助

First *Aid* boxes and fully-trained First Aiders are also on hand at various locations around the college. 学校里很多地点都设有急救箱，并随时有训练有素的急救人员提供帮助。

aisle [aɪl]

n. a long passage between rows of seats in a church, plane, theatre, etc., or between rows of shelves in a supermarket 过道

Here is a diagram of one supermarket *aisle* and two rows of shelves. 这幅图上画着超市里的两排货架和中间的过道。

✓ **bind** [baɪnd] [同] tie

v. tie or fasten, e.g. with rope 捆绑或系紧（如用绳）

the feelings that *bind* him to her 把他与她结合在一起的感情

✓ **comfort** [ˈkʌmfət]

n. state of being free from suffering, pain or anxiety; state of physical or mental well-being 舒适；身心健康

live in *comfort* 生活舒适

commence [kəˈmens] [同] begin, start

v. (fml.) begin (sth.); start 开始（某事物）

The course *commences* with a one week introduction to Art Theory. 课程的第一周是艺术理论概述。

✓ **comment** [ˈkɒment] [同] ①②remark

① *n.* written or spoken remark giving an opinion on, explaining or criticizing （an event, a person, a situation, etc.) 意见；解释；评论；批评

Have you any *comment*(s) to make on the recent developments? 你对最近的事态发展有什么评论吗？

② *v.* to express an opinion about sb. or sth. 评价

The discovery is hardly *commented* by the press. 对于这一发现新闻界几乎没有加以评价。

deputy [ˈdepjuti]

n. person who is immediately below the head of a business, school, etc. （企业、学校等领导人的）副手

deputy directors 副主管

descend [dɪˈsend]

v. (of properties, qualities, rights) to pass from father to son; be inherited by sb. from sb. （指财产、气质、权利）由父传子，传下，遗传

If there are only 20 individuals of a species and only one is a male, all future individuals in the species must be **descended** from that one male. 如果一个物种只剩下 20 个个体而且其中只有一个是雄性，那么该物种所有的后代都将是那个雄性个体的后代。

ensure [ɪnˈʃʊə(r)] [同] assure

v. to make sure that sth. happens or is definite 保证；确保

The book **ensured** his success. 这本书保证了他的成功。

enterprise [ˈentəpraɪz] [同] company, business

n. a company or business 公司；企业单位；事业单位

state-owned **enterprises** 国有企业

fertile [ˈfɜːtaɪl] [同] productive

adj. (of land or soil) that plants grow well in 肥沃的；富饶的

If we contrast the region with the Eastern region, the east is flatter and with **fertile** soils. 如果把这个地区和东部比，东部地区要平坦些，土壤也很肥沃。

fund [fʌnd]

① *n.* sum of money saved or made available for a particular purpose 专款；基金

a disaster/relief **fund** 赈灾／救济款

② *v.* to provide money for an activity, organization, event, etc. 资助；投资

The project is jointly **funded** by several local companies. 这个项目由几家本地公司共同资助。

fundamental [ˌfʌndəˈmentl] [同] basic

adj. of or forming the basis or foundation of sth.; essential 基本的；构成基础的；根本的

There are **fundamental** differences between your religious beliefs and mine. 你我的宗教信仰有着根本的不同。

[记] found a 馒头 (民以食为天)

gist [dʒɪst] [近] core

n. main point or general meaning (of sth. spoken or written) 主旨；要点；大意

get the **gist** of an argument/a conversation/a book 理解一场辩论／一次谈话／一部书的主旨

heighten [ˈhaɪtn] [同] increase

v. (cause sth. to) become higher or more intense (使某事物)提高，加强

The case has **heightened** public awareness of the problem of sexual harassment. 这个案件提高了老百姓对性骚扰问题的认识。

indispensable [ˌɪndɪˈspensəbl] [同] essential

反: dispensable.

adj. that cannot be dispensed with; absolutely essential 不可缺少的；必需的

In a liberal society basic health is seen as one of the **indispensable** conditions. 在自由社会，基础健康被视作必需条件之一。

individual [ˌɪndɪˈvɪdʒuəl] [同] being

n. single human being 个人

Culture is a reflection of how the group, rather than the **individual** thinks and behaves. 文化是一个群体的想法和行为的反映，而不是个人的。

justice [ˈdʒʌstɪs] [同] ① judge ② equity

n. ① the system by which people are judged in courts of law and criminals are punished 司法 ② fairness in the way people are treated 公平；正义

Many people no longer have confidence in the criminal *justice* system. 很多人不再对司法系统抱有信任。

✓ justify ['dʒʌstɪfaɪ]

v. to show that (sb./sth.) is right, reasonable or just 表明或证明(某人／某事)是正当的、有理的或公正的

Such action can be *justified* on the grounds of greater efficiency. 以提高功效为依据可以证明采取这种措施是正确的。

levy ['levi]

v. to collect (a payment, etc.) by authority or force; impose sth. 征收，征集(款额等)；强加某事物

Today, these taxes are still *levied* by many Third World governments because they are straightforward to collect and hard to evade. 今天，很多第三世界国家依然征收这些税种，因为它们易于征收，很难逃匿。

mere [mɪə(r)]   [同] bare

adj. used to emphasize how small or unimportant something or someone is 仅仅的，起码的

Humans first settled in the Arctic a *mere* 4,500 years ago. 人类仅仅是在4500年前才在北极圈安家。

merely ['mɪəli]   [同] only, just

adv. used to emphasize how small or unimportant sth. or sb. is; used to emphasize that nothing more than what you say is involved 只；仅仅

Some scientists argue that trouble starts more often in hot weather *merely* because there are more people in the street. 一些科学家认为炎热的天气里故障发生更加频繁仅仅是因为路上人更多。

merit ['merɪt]   [同] ①virtue

① *n.* (fml.) the quality of being good and of deserving praise, reward or admiration 优点；美德；价值

I want to get the job on *merit*. 我想凭才能得到这份工作。

② *v.* to do sth. to deserve praise, attention, etc. 应得；值得

He claimed that their success was not *merited*. 他声称他们不应该获得成功。

✓ nickname ['nɪkneɪm]   [同] ①byname

① *n.* an informal, often humorous name for a person that is connected with their real name, their personality or appearance, or with sth. they have done 绰号；外号

② *v.* to give a nickname to sb./sth. 给…起绰号

She was *nicknamed* Sunny because of her happy nature. 由于她天性快乐，大家送她外号叫"阳光"。

nightmare ['naɪtmeə(r)]

n. an experience that is very frightening and unpleasant, or very difficult to deal with 可怕的经历；难以处理的事；噩梦

The trip turned into a *nightmare* when they both got sick. 当他们俩都病了时，这次旅行成了一场噩梦。

nominate ['nɒmɪneɪt]   [同] appoint

v. to formally suggest that sb. should be chosen for an important role, prize, position, etc. 提名；推荐

You're asked to *nominate* your preference. 你可以推荐你选中的人。

✓ **preference** [ˈprefərəns] [同] inclination

n. liking for sth. (more than sth. else) (与他物相较之)喜爱；偏爱

There is milk and cream—do you have a *preference*? 有牛奶也有奶油——你喜欢哪样？

✓ **prejudice** [ˈpredʒʊdɪs] [同] bias

n. opinion, or like or dislike of sb./sth., that is not founded on experience or reason 偏见；成见

The reader is at liberty to bring his or her own experiences, reflections and even *prejudices* to bear on the understanding of the message. 读者可以自由地把自己的经历、想法甚至偏见带入对这一信息的理解。

preliminary [prɪˈlɪmɪnəri] [同] introductory

adj. happening before sth. that is more important, often in order to prepare for it 初步的；预备的

The architect's plans are still in the *preliminary* stages. 建筑师的设计还处在初级阶段。

rack [ræk]

n. type of shelf for light luggage, coats, etc. over the seats of a bus, train, plane, etc. 行李架

a luggage *rack* 行李架

radiation [ˌreɪdɪˈeɪʃn]

n. (the sending out of) rays and atomic particles from radioactive substances 放射；放射现象

a low/high level of *radiation* 低 / 高强度辐射

sphere [sfɪə(r)] [同] globe

n. solid figure that is entirely round (i.e. with every point on the surface at an equal distance from the centre) 球体；球形

the *sphere* of the heavens 天球

spill [spɪl]

v. to (allow or cause liquid, etc. to) run or fall over the edge of a container 流出；溢出

Neatness can suggest efficiency but, if it is overdone, it can *spill* over and indicate an obsession with power. 整洁是效率的表现，但若是过分强调整洁，则过犹不及，还暗示着对这种能力的迷恋。

spin [spɪn]

v. to make sth. turn round and round rapidly 使某物快速旋转

The wheels where *spinning* in the mud, but the car wouldn't move. 车轮在泥里打转，但车就是不动。

terrific [təˈrɪfɪk] [近] wonderful

adj. excellent; wonderful 极好的；了不起的

doing a *terrific* job 干得很棒

terrify [ˈterɪfaɪ] [同] frighten

v. to fill (sb.) with terror; make very frightened 使(某人)感到恐怖；使害怕

A thousand years ago, a total eclipse of the sun was a *terrifying* religious experience. 一千年前，一次日全食是一次可怕的宗教经历。

territory [ˈterɪtəri]

n. (area of) land under the control of a ruler, country, city, etc. 领土(的范围)

Turkish *territory* in Europe 土耳其在欧洲部分的领土

✓ **universal** [ˌjuːnɪˈvɜːsl] [同] general

adj. done by or involving all the people in the world or in a particular group 普遍的；全体的；共同的

Such problems are a *universal* feature of old age. 这类问题是老年人的通

病。

✓ **universe** [ˈjuːnɪvɜːs]   [同] cosmos

n. a system of stars, planets, etc. in space outside our own 宇宙

He lives in a little *universe* of his own. 他生活在自己的小天地里。

vague [veɪg]   [同] obscure

adj. not clear in a person's mind（思想上）不清楚的；含糊的

They had only a *vague* idea where the place was. 他们只是大概知道那个地方的位置。

vain [veɪn]

adj. that does not produce the result you want 徒劳的；枉然的

Notwithstanding the disappointing results, it is our contention that the strategies were not in *vain*. 尽管结果令人失望，但我们认为这些策略并非没用。

Take the Test

一、英汉互译

企业	_____	aisle	_____
根本的	_____	fertile	_____
不可缺少的	_____	levy	_____
个人	_____	merit	_____
绰号	_____	preliminary	_____

二、翻译句子

1）这个项目是由几家本地公司共同资助的。（fund）

_____

2）你我的宗教信仰有着根本的不同。（fundamental）

_____

3）这个案件提高了老百姓对性骚扰问题的认识。（heighten）

_____

4）建筑师的设计还处在初级阶段。（preliminary）

_____

And gladly would learn, and gladly teach.
勤于学习的人才能乐于施教。

——英国诗人 乔叟（Chaucer, British poet）

✓ **alarm** [əˈlɑːm]　　　　　　　　　　　　　　　　　　　　　　　[同] alert

n. a device that warns people of a particular danger 警报器

Set the burglar *alarm* when you leave the house. 出门的时候打开防盗警报器。

alcohol [ˈælkəhɒl]

n. drinks such as beer or wine that contain a substance which can make you drunk 酒精饮料

The number of *alcohol*-related deaths has more than doubled in the past few years. 在过去的几年里，由于酗酒导致的死亡人数翻了一倍多。

blame [bleɪm]　　　　　　　　　　　　　　　　　　　[同] criticize

v./n. to consider or say that sb. is responsible for sth. done（badly or wrongly）or not done 责备；指责；归咎于

（saying）A bad workman *blames* his tools, i.e. refuses to accept the responsibility for his own mistakes. 拙匠埋怨工具差（不承认错在自己）。

[习语] lay the blame on

The President seemed to lay the *blame* for the shootings on video games and TV shows. 总统似乎把枪击事件归罪于电子游戏和电视。

✓ **commerce** [ˈkɒmɜːs]

n. trade（esp. between countries）; buying and selling of goods 商业；（尤指国际间的）贸易

We must promote *commerce* with neighbouring countries. 我们必须促进与邻国的贸易。

commercial [kəˈmɜːʃl]

adj. of or for commerce 商业的；贸易的

commercial law, activity, art 商业法规、活动、技巧

commit [kəˈmɪt]

v. do（sth. illegal, wrong or foolish）做（不合法的、错的或愚蠢的事）；犯

Corporate crime is defined as crime which is *committed* for the corporate organisation, not against it. 企业犯罪被定义为了企业的利益而进行犯罪，而不是损害企业利益。

committee [kəˈmɪti]

n. group of people appointed（usu. by a larger group）to deal with a particular matter（通常由较大团体所委派以处理某事务的）委员会

On behalf of the organizing *committee*, I like to welcome you all. 我代表组委会欢迎你们每个人。

✓ **deserve** [dɪˈzɜːv]　　　　　　　　　　　　　　　　　　　　[近] earn

v. to be sth. or have done sth. for which one should receive（a reward, special treatment, etc.）; be entitled to 应受（奖赏、特殊待遇等）；值得

The article *deserves* careful study. 这篇文章值得仔细研究。

despair [dɪˈspeə(r)]　　　　　[同] desperation, hopelessness [反] hope, hopefulness

n. a feeling that you have no hope at all 绝望

To the ***despair*** of the workers, the company announced the closure of the factory. 让工人们感到绝望的是，公司宣布了要关闭车间。

desperate [ˈdespərət]

adj. ①feeling or showing great despair and ready to do anything regardless of danger 感到绝望而不惜冒险的；拼命的；不顾一切的

Time was running out and we were getting ***desperate***. 时间越来越少，我们要孤注一掷了。

②needing or wanting sth. very much 极想得到的

The team is ***desperate*** for a win. 球队现在太需要一场胜利了。

✓ **entertain** [ˌentəˈteɪn]   [同] amuse

v. to amuse or interest people in a way that gives them pleasure 娱乐；招待

A museum should aim to ***entertain*** as well as educate. 博物馆应该致力于娱乐和教育并重。

enthusiastic [ɪnˌθjuːzɪˈæstɪk]

adj. feeling or showing a lot of excitement and interest about sb./sth. 热情的；满腔热忱的

an ***enthusiastic*** welcome 热烈的欢迎

fertilizer [ˈfɜːtɪlaɪzə]

n. a substance that is put on the soil to make plants grow 化肥

Fertilizer use doubled in Denmark in the period 1960－1985. 1960 至 1985 年间，丹麦的化肥使用量翻了一番。

glance [glɑːns]

① *n.* quick look 一瞥

I think what we do need is one of those big wall calendars that shows the whole year at a ***glance***. 我认为我们确实需要一幅大挂历，这样我们只要一瞥就可以看到一年的情况。

② *v.* to quickly look at sb. or sth. 扫视，匆匆一看

heir [eə(r)]

n. person with the legal right to receive property, etc. when the owner dies 继承人

She made her stepson (her) ***heir***. 她让继子做自己的继承人。

induce [ɪnˈdjuːs]   [同] bring around

v. to persuade sb. to do sth., especially sth. that does not seem wise 劝诱（某人）做某事（尤指不明智的事）

When the next generation reaches their teens, they might not want to be ***induced*** into the old traditions. 当下一代进入青春期时，他们可能就不会愿意遵从旧传统。

indulge [ɪnˈdʌldʒ]   [同] cater to

v. to let oneself/someone have or do whatever they want, even if it is bad for them 放纵自己 / 某人

They ***indulge*** their child too much; it's bad for his character. 他们过分纵容孩子，这对孩子的性格有不良影响。

liberal [ˈlɪbərəl]   [近] generous

adj. tolerant and open-minded; free from prejudice 宽容忍耐的；心胸宽广的；无偏见的

I was fortunate enough to have very ***liberal*** parents. 我很幸运，有这么开明的父母。

license [ˈlaɪsns]   [同] authorise

v. to give sb. official permission to do, own, or use sth. 批准；许可

The new drug has not yet been ***licensed*** in the UK. 种新药尚未在英国获得许可。

messy [ˈmesi]   [同] sloppy

adj. dirty and/or untidy 肮脏的；凌乱的

The house was always *messy*. 这房子总是乱糟糟的。

method ['meθəd] [同] manner

n. a well-organized and well-planned way of doing sth. 方法；方式
You can choose whichever *method* of payment you prefer. 你可以选择任何一种你喜欢的支付方式。

migrate [maɪ'greɪt]

v. to move from one town, country, etc. to go and live and/or work in another 移居；迁移
The beekeeper's family will *migrate* with them to their summer location. 养蜂人一家也会随着蜜蜂迁到它们夏季的生活地区。

mileage ['maɪlɪdʒ]

n. the distance that a vehicle has travelled, measured in miles 英里；里程
My annual *mileage* is about 10,000 miles. 我一年的行驶里程大约是 1 万英里。

nonetheless [ˌnʌnðə'les]

adv. (fml) in spite of the fact that has just been mentioned 但是；尽管如此
The region was extremely beautiful. *Nonetheless* I could not imagine spending the rest of my life there. 这个地区美极了，但我从没想过在这里度过余生。

norm [nɔːm] [同] standard

n. standards of behaviour that are typical of or accepted within a particular group or society 规范；行为标准
social/cultural *norms* 社会 / 文化规范

prescribe [prɪ'skraɪb]

v. (fml.) to advise or order the use of (esp. a medicine, remedy, etc.) 建议或吩咐采用（尤指药物、疗法等）；开（药方）
She *prescribed* some pills to help me to sleep. 她让我吃些药片以利睡眠。

prescription [prɪ'skrɪpʃn]

n. doctor's written instruction for the composition and use of a medicine 处方；药方
The doctor gave me a *prescription* for pain-killers. 医生给我开了个止痛药方。

presence ['prezəns]

n. when sb. or sth. is present in a particular place 存在；出席
Sharks have a very acute sense of smell and can sense the *presence* of food long before they can see it. 鲨鱼有很敏锐的嗅觉，在看到食物之前很早就能闻到食物的存在。

✓ **presentation** [ˌprezn'teɪʃn]

n. an event at which you describe or explain a new product or idea 展示；说明；介绍
Vivien is going to do a *presentation* on the hat-making project. Vivien 将要做一个关于帽子制作项目的说明。

preserve [prɪ'zɜːv] [近] save

v. keep or maintain (sth.) in an unchanged or perfect condition 保护，维护（某物）
Preserving historic buildings or keeping only their facades (or fronts) grew common. 保护历史建筑或者仅仅保留它们的正面的这种做法变得比较普遍。

radical ['rædɪkl] [同] drastic

adj. ①a radical change or difference is very big and important 重大的；重要的；剧烈的 ②radical ideas are very new and different, and are against what most people think or believe 激进的；标新立异的

In the next decade, the Internet will stimulate *radical* changes in every part of the educational system. 在下个 10 年里，互联网会在教育体系的每一个角落引发剧烈变化。

rage [reɪdʒ] 　　　　　　　　　　　　　　　　　　　　　　　[同] ①②anger

① *n.* (fit of) violent anger (一阵)狂怒；盛怒(之爆发)

trembling with *rage* 气得直哆嗦

② *v.* show violent anger 大发脾气；动怒

He *raged* against me for disagreeing. 他因我有异议而对我大发雷霆。

ragged [ˈrægɪd]

adj. (of clothes) old and torn 破旧的，褴褛的

a *ragged* jacket 破旧的夹克衫

✓ **random** [ˈrændəm] 　　　　　　　　　　　　　　　　　　　　　　[同] aimless

adj. done, chosen, etc. without method or conscious choice; haphazard 随便的；任意的；胡乱的

a *random* sample 随意抽取的样品

spiritual [ˈspɪrɪtʃuəl] 　　　　　　　　　　　　　　　　　　　　　[反] physical

adj. of the human spirit or soul; not of physical things 精神的；心灵的；非物质的

The moral, *spiritual* and intellectual shaping of social structures often escape observation. 道德上、精神上和智力上的社会结构的形成常常不被人们所察觉。

spoil [spɔil]

v. ①to have a bad effect on sth. so that it is no longer attractive, enjoyable, useful, etc. 破坏；损坏 ②to give a child everything they want, or let them do whatever they want, often with the result that they behave badly 宠坏；溺爱；娇惯

She's an only child, but her parents didn't really *spoil* her. 她是个独生女，但父母并没有太娇惯她。

sponsor [ˈspɒnsə] 　　　　　　　　　　　　　　　　　　　　　　[同] ①patron

① *n.* a person or company that pays for a show, broadcast, sports event, etc. especially in exchange for the right to advertise at that event 赞助商

② *v.* to give money to a sports event, theatre, institution, etc. especially in exchange for the right to advertise 赞助；资助

an athlete *sponsored* by a bank 由某银行资助的运动员

spot [spɒt] 　　　　　　　　　　　　　　　　　　　　　　　　[同] ②pinpoint

① *n.* small (usu. round) mark different in colour, texture, etc. from the surface it is on 斑点(通常指圆的)

a white skirt with red *spots* 白底红点儿的裙子

② *v.* to pick out (one person or thing from many); to catch sight of; recognize; discover (从许多人或事物中)找出，认出；发现

She *spotted* her friend in the crowd. 她在人群中认出了她的朋友。

unlikely [ˌʌnˈlaɪkli] 　　　　　　　　　　　　　　　　　　　　　[同] improbable

adj. not likely to happen; not probable 不大可能发生的

The project seemed *unlikely* to succeed. 这个项目似乎难以成功。

unplug [ʌnˈplʌg]

v. to remove the plug of a piece of electrical equipment from the electricity supply 拔掉电源插头

If I'm very busy, I **unplug** the phone. 我要是特别忙就会把电话拔掉。

update [ʌpˈdeɪt]   [同] ①renew

① *v.* to make sth. more modern by adding new parts, etc. 使现代化；更新

It's about time we **updated** our software. 我们的软件应该更新了。

② [ˌʌpdeɪt] *n.* information that updates 更新的信息

The newsletter gives an **update** on current activities. 时事通讯刊登了近期活动的最新情况。

uphold [ʌpˈhəʊld]   [同] support

v. to support sth. that you think is right, fair, etc. and make sure that it continues to exist 支持；维护(正义等)

We have a duty to **uphold** the law. 维护法律是我们的责任。

Take the Test >>

一、英汉互译

委员会	_____	enthusiastic	_____
值得，应得	_____	liberal	_____
放纵	_____	mileage	_____
许可	_____	random	_____
剧烈的	_____	sponsor	_____

二、翻译句子

1) 我们必须促进与邻国的贸易。(commerce)

_____

2) 球队现在太需要一场胜利了。(desperate)

_____

3) 你可以选择任何一种你喜欢的支付方式。(method)

_____

4) Vivien 将要做一个关于帽子制作项目的说明。(presentation)

_____

Genius only means hard-working all one's life.
天才只意味着终身不懈地努力。

——俄国化学家 门捷列夫(Mendeleyev, Russian chemist)

Word List 18

alien [ˈeɪliən]　　　　　　　　　　　　　　　　　　　　[同] ①foreign

① *adj.* strange and frightening; different from what you are used to 陌生的; 不熟悉的

a way of life that is totally *alien* to us 一种对我们来说完全陌生的生活方式

② *n.* a foreigner 外来者

allocate [ˈæləkeɪt]　　　　　　　　　　　　　　　　　　　[同] allot

v. to give sth. officially to sb./sth. for a particular purpose 拨给; 分配给

The world-wide coal industry *allocates* extensive resources to researching and developing new technologies. 全球煤矿产业将大量资源投入到新技术的研发上。

blank [blæŋk]

① *adj.* without writing or print; unmarked 空白的; 无痕迹的

a *blank* form 空白的表格

② *n.* an empty space 空白处

commodity [kəˈmɒdəti]　　　　　　　　　　　　　　[同] merchandise, goods

n. thing bought in a shop and put to use, esp. in the home 商品;（尤指）日用品

household *commodities* 家庭日用品

commonplace [ˈkɒmənpleɪs]　　　　　　　　　[同] ①common ①②ordinary

① *adj.*（often derog.）ordinary; not interesting 平常的; 平凡的; 不引起兴趣的

He's not at all exciting, in fact he's really rather *commonplace*. 他毫不出奇, 实际上平庸得很。

② *n.* sth. that happens or exists in many places, so that it is not unusual 平常事, 司空见惯的事

They are talking over the *commonplaces* of the day. 他们在谈论眼下的日常琐事。

convey [kənˈveɪ]　　　　　　　　　　　　　　　　[同] communicate

v. to make（ideas, feelings, etc.）known to another person 表达或传达（思想、感情等）

Words cannot *convey* how delighted I was. 言辞无法表达我内心的喜悦。

convince [kənˈvɪns]　　　　　　　　　　　　　　　　[同] assure

v. to make sb. feel certain; cause sb. to realize 使某人确信; 使某人明白

What she said *convinced* me that I was mistaken. 她的一番话使我认识到我错了。

communicate [kəˈmjuːnɪkeɪt]

v. ①to exchange information or conversation with other people, using words, signs, writing, etc. 交流②to make sth. known; convey sth. 使某事物被人知晓; 传送某事物

This poem *communicates* the author's despair. 这首诗流露出作者的绝望心情。

despite [dɪˈspaɪt]　　　　　　　　　　　[同] notwithstanding, in spite of

prep. without being affected by（the factors mentioned）尽管; 不管; 不顾

Despite linguists' best efforts, many languages will disappear over the next 50 years. 尽管语言学家已竭尽全力, 但很多语言在 50 年后还是要消失。

destiny [ˈdestɪnɪ]　　　　　　　　　　　　　　　　　　[同] fate

n. power believed to control events 命运

Destiny drew us together. 命运把我们连在一起了。

entire [ɪn'taɪə(r)] [同] whole

adj. (used when you are emphasizing that the whole of sth. is involved) including everything, everyone or every part 全部的；完全的

I wasted an *entire* day on it! 我为此浪费了整整一天！

entitle [ɪn'taɪtl] [同] authorise

v. to give sb. the right to have or to do sth. 使享有权利；使符合资格

Membership *entitles* you to use the various facilities of the library. 如果是会员，你可以使用图书馆里各种各样的设备。

festival ['festəvl]

n. a day or period of the year when people stop working to celebrate a special event, often a religious one 节日；喜庆日

Christmas and Easter are the main Christian *festivals*. 圣诞节和复活节是基督教的主要节日。

hence [hens] [同] therefore

adv. for this reason 因此

The cost of transport is a major expense for an industry. *Hence* factory location is an important consideration. 对工业而言运费是个比较大的支出，因此工厂的位置是个很重要的考虑因素。

industrious [ɪn'dʌstriəs] [同] hard-working

adj. hard-working; diligent 勤劳的；勤奋的；勤勉的

an *industrious* student 勤勉的学生

ineffective [ˌɪnɪ'fektɪv] [反] effective

adj. not producing the required effect(s) 不起作用的；无效果的；效果不佳的

Various drugs have proved *ineffective* against the virus. 多种药物都已证明对这种病毒无效。

inefficient [ˌɪnə'fɪʃənt] [近] efficient

adj. not using time, money, energy, etc. in the best way 无效率的；效率低下的；不经济的

Local government in this area is *inefficient*. 当地政府效率低下。

juvenile ['dʒuːvənaɪl] [同] young

adj. (fml.) characteristic of or suitable for young people who are not yet adults 未成年的；少年的；少年特有的

Juvenile crime is an increasing problem in big cities. 青少年犯罪成为大城市里日趋严重的问题。

lifespan ['laɪfspæn]

n. the length of time that sth. or sb. is likely to live, continue or function 寿命；有效期

Only approaches that slow the body's rate of aging will increase the maximum *lifespan*. 只有那些减缓身体变老速度的方法才能延长寿命。

lifestyle ['laɪfstaɪl]

n. the way a person or group of people live 生活方式

In the last 14 years, the survey has gathered data on the health and *lifestyles* of more than 20,000 men. 在过去的 14 年中，该调查收集到了超过两万名男性的健康及生活方式的数据。

mild [maɪld] [同] gentle

adj. not serious; not very strong 温和的，适度的，轻微的

The recession in Germany has been comparatively *mild*. 德国的经济衰退相对而言不太严重。

military ['mɪlɪtəri] [同] martial

adj. used by, involving, or relating to the army, navy, or airforce 军事的；军队的

The third gizmo was developed initially for *military* use. 第三个小发明最初是用于军事的。

mimic ['mɪmɪk]   [同] imitate

v. to copy the way sb. speaks, moves, behaves, etc. esp. in order to make other people laugh 模仿(人的言行举止);(尤指)做滑稽模仿

She's always *mimicking* the teachers. 她总喜欢模仿老师们的言谈举止。

mineral ['mɪnərəl]

n. a substance that is naturally present in the earth and is not formed from animal or vegetable matter, for example, gold and salt 矿物;矿物质

the recommended intake of vitamins and *minerals* 维生素和矿物质的建议摄入量

normal ['nɔ:ml]   [近] general

adj. usual, typical, or expected 正常的;普遍的

All I want is to lead a *normal* life. 我所要的只是过上正常人的生活。

nostalgia [nɒ'stældʒə]

n. a feeling of sadness mixed with pleasure and affection when you think of happy times in the past 怀旧;念旧

She is filled with *nostalgia* for her own college days. 她对自己的大学时代充满了怀念之情。

press [pres]

n. business for printing (and publishing) books or periodicals 印刷业;出版业;出版社

Oxford University *Press* 牛津大学出版社

prestige [pre'sti:ʒ]

n. the respect and admiration that sth./sb. has because of their social position, or what they have done 威信;声望

The old universities of Oxford and Cambridge still have a lot of *prestige*. 历史悠久的牛津大学和剑桥大学仍然享有很高的声望。

presume [prɪ'zju:m]   [同] assume

v. to suppose that sth. is true, although you do not have actual proof 假设;假定

I *presumed* that he understood the rules. 我假定他已经明白这些规则。

previous ['pri:viəs]   [同] past

adj. happening or existing before the event or object that you are talking about 先前的;以往的

No *previous* experience is necessary for this job. 这一工作无需相关的经验。

raid [reɪd]

① *n.* sudden surprise attack and withdrawal by troops, ships or aircraft (部队、舰艇或飞机的)突袭,突击

make/launch a bombing *raid* on enemy bases 对敌方基地进行突然的空袭

② *v.* to make a raid on (a place) 对(某处)进行突然袭击、抢劫或搜查

Customs men *raided* the house. 海关人员突然搜查了这所房子。

range [reɪndʒ]

n. limits between which sth. varies; extent (种类或变化的)范围;幅度

The chosen words spanned a *range* of pitches, to force the speakers to raise and lower their voices considerably. 选择的词语覆盖了一定范围的音高,这样说话者不得不大幅度地升高和降低他们的声音。

ranking ['ræŋkɪŋ]

n. the position of sb./sth. on a scale that shows how good or important they are in relation to other similar people or things, esp. in sport 地位，排名（尤指在体育运动中）

He has improved his *ranking* this season from 67th to 30th. 本赛季他将自己的排名从第 67 位提高到第 30 位。

spouse [spauz] [近] mate

n. (fml) husband or wife 配偶

Your family, friends, or *spouse* all have their goals for you, but what do you want? 你的家人、朋友、配偶对你都有所期望，但你想要什么呢？

spray [spreɪ] [同] ②sprinkle

① *n.* liquid sent through the air in tiny drops（by the wind or through an apparatus）雾状液体；水花

Most farmers use pesticide *sprays*. 大部分农场主都用杀虫喷剂。

② *v.* send out（liquid）onto sb./sth. in tiny drops; wet sb./sth. with liquid in this way 向某人 / 某物喷（雾状的液体）

spraying paint on her car 给她的汽车喷漆

spring [sprɪŋ] [同] arise

v. jump quickly or suddenly, esp. from the ground in a single movement; move suddenly（e.g. from a hiding place or a position of relaxation）蹦；跃起；突然活动（如从隐藏处或松弛状态）

spring out of bed/into action/to one's feet 一跃下床 / 立即投入行动 / 突然站起

squeeze [skwiːz] [同] crush

v. to press on（sth.）from opposite sides or all sides 挤；捏；向内收紧（某物）

a company *squeezed* by（i.e. under financial pressure because of）reduced sales 因销售量下降而处境困难的公司

texture [ˈtekstʃə(r)]

n. the way a surface, substance or fabric looks or feels to the touch, i.e. its thickness, firmness, roughness, etc. 质地，外观，手感

the delicate *texture* of her skin 她细嫩的皮肤

theft [θeft] [同] burglary

n.（act or instance of）stealing 偷；行窃；偷窃

A number of *thefts* have been reported recently. 近来有些偷窃案的报道。

valid [ˈvælɪd] [近] solid

adj. a valid ticket, document, or agreement is legally or officially acceptable 有效的；有法律效力的

Your return ticket is *valid* for three months. 你的返程票三个月内有效。

validate [ˈvælɪdeɪt] [同] confirm

v. to prove that sth. is true or correct, or to make a document or agreement officially and legally acceptable 验证；确认；使生效

This is an interesting hypothesis, but all attempts to *validate* it have so far failed. 这是个很有意思的假设，但迄今为止所有验证它的尝试都失败了。

vanish [ˈvænɪʃ]

v. to disappear suddenly and/or in a way that you cannot explain（莫名其妙地）突然消失

The magician *vanished* in a puff of smoke. 魔术师在一股烟雾中突然不见了。

Take the Test >>

一、英汉互译

分配	_____	entire	_____
平常的	_____	industrious	_____
青少年的	_____	mimic	_____
生活方式	_____	nostalgia	_____
威望	_____	texture	_____

二、翻译句子

1) 尽管语言学家已竭尽全力，但很多语言在50年后还是要消失。（despite）

_____

2) 青少年犯罪成为大城市日趋严重的问题。（juvenile）

_____

3) 这一工作无需相关的经验。（previous）

_____

4) 你的返程票三个月内有效。（valid）

_____

The ideals which have lighted my way, and time after time have given me new courage to face life cheerfully have been kindness, beauty and truth.

有些理想曾为我指引过道路，并不断给我新的勇气以欣然面对人生，那些理想就是——真、善、美。

——美国科学家 爱因斯坦（Albert Einstein, American scientist）

Word List 19

amateur [ˈæmətə, ˌæməˈtəː] 　　　　　　　　　　　　　　[反] professional, expert

n. a person who takes part in a sport or other activity for enjoyment or interest, not as a job 业余爱好者

There is a long tradition of collaboration between *amateur* and professional sky watchers.
业余天文爱好者和专业研究人员之间很久以来就存在着合作的传统。

amazing [əˈmeɪzɪŋ] 　　　　　　　　　　　　　　　　　[同] marvelous, astonishing

adj. very surprising, esp. in a way that makes you feel pleasure or admiration 令人大为惊奇的；令人惊喜的

an *amazing* achievement/discovery 惊人的成就/发现

athlete [ˈæθlɪt, ˈæθliːt]

n. person who trains to compete in physical exercises and sports, esp. running and jumping 运动员（尤指跑和跳项目）

Sports psychologists spend time with professional *athletes* helping them approach competition with a positive mental attitude. 运动心理学家花时间与职业运动员相处，帮助他们以一个积极的精神状态迎接比赛。

blend [blend] 　　　　　　　　　　　　　　　　　　　　[同] mix

v. to combine sth. in an attractive or effective way（使）调和，协调，融合

The entertainment and information industries must work with the educational institutions to determine how best to *blend* new technologies into the classroom. 娱乐和信息产业需要和教育机构共同努力，以决定怎样能最好地把新技术融合到课堂教学中。

community [kəˈmjuːnəti] 　　　　　　　　　　　　　　　[同] people, public

n. the people living in one place, district or country, considered as a whole 社区；团体；集体；社会

work for the good of the *community* 为集体利益服务

commute [kəˈmjuːt]

v. to regularly travel a long distance to get to work 通勤

Many may eventually be able to work from home rather than *commute* to an office. 以后很多人都可以在家办公，而不必每天往返于办公室。

destroy [dɪˈstrɔɪ]

v. to damage sth. so badly that it no longer exists or cannot be used or repaired 毁坏，破坏

Developing countries can advance their economies without *destroying* their natural resources.
发展中国家可以在不破坏自然资源的条件下发展经济。

detail [ˈdiːteɪl]

n. a single feature, fact, or piece of information about sth. 细节

Let me give you some *details* so that you know where to go and who to see if you want to pay us a visit. 我给大家讲一些细节信息，这样如果你们来我们这儿参观的话就知道该去哪儿、去

找谁了。

detect [dɪˈtekt] [近] find

v. to discover or recognize that (sth.) is present 发现、察觉或查出（某物）

The robot is designed to **detect** emotions in the person by sensing changes in the spatial arrangement of the person's eyes, nose, eyebrows, and mouth. 这种机器人被设计用于通过感知被测人眼睛、鼻子、眉毛和嘴的位置的变化来检测人的情绪。

entity [ˈentəti]

n. (fml.) sth. that exists separately from other things and has its own identity 独立存在物；实体

The unit has become part of a larger department and no longer exists as a separate **entity**. 这个单位已附属于一个大的部门，不再作为一个实体独立存在。

environment [ɪnˈvaɪrənmənt] [近] atmosphere

n. the conditions that affect the behaviour and development of sb./sth.; the physical conditions that sb./sth. exists in（影响个体或事物的行为和发展的）环境；客观环境

An unhappy home **environment** can affect a child's behaviour. 不幸的家庭环境会对孩子的行为造成影响。

fetch [fetʃ]

v. to go to where sb./sth. is and bring them/it back 去拿来；去请来

She's gone to **fetch** the kids from school. 她去学校接孩子了。

fiction [ˈfɪkʃn] [反] non-fiction

n. a type of literature that describes imaginary people and events; not real ones 小说

works of popular **fiction** 通俗小说作品

framework [ˈfreɪmwɜːk] [同] structure

n. structure giving shape and support 框架；结构

a bridge with a steel **framework** 钢铁结构的桥梁

fraud [frɔːd] [同] deception, cheat

n. (act of) deceiving sb. illegally in order to make money or obtain goods 欺骗（行为）；诈骗

The best way to fight Internet **fraud** is to learn how to avoid becoming a victim. 对付网络诈骗的最好办法就是学会如何不成为它的受害者。

herd [hɜːd]

n. a number of animals, esp. the same type 兽群；牧群

a **herd** of cows/deer/elephants, etc. 一群牛／鹿／象等

inevitable [ɪnˈevɪtəbl] [同] certain

adj. certain to happen and impossible to avoid 不可避免的；必然发生的

A further escalation of the crisis now seems **inevitable**. 该危机的进一步扩大现在看来是在所难免了。

infant [ˈɪnfənt]

n. a baby or very young child 婴儿；幼儿

infant mortality rate 婴儿死亡率

lift [lɪft] [同] rise; elevator

n. a machine that you can ride in, that moves up and down between the floors in a tall building 电梯

v. to raise sb./sth. or be raised to a higher position or level（被）提起；举起

The nets on New South Wales beaches are *lifted* and taken out to sea on the next day. 第二天，在新南威尔士海滩上的渔网会被提起并带到海上。

minimal ['mɪnɪməl] [同] least, slightest [反] maximal

adj. very small in size or amount; as small as possible 极小的；极少的；最少的

The work was carried out at a *minimal* cost. 这项工作是以最少的开销完成的。

minimum ['minɪməm] [反] ①②maximum

① *adj.* the minimum number, degree, or amount of sth. is the smallest or least that is possible, allowed, or needed 最小的；最低的

② *n.* the smallest amount of sth. or number of things that is possible or necessary 最小值

The *minimum* age for retirement is 55. 退休的最低年龄是 55 岁。

ministry ['mɪnɪstri] [近] agency

n. a government department that is responsible for one of the areas of government work, such as education or health 部委

the *Ministry* of Education 教育部

notable ['nəʊtəbl] [同] famous

adj. deserving to be noticed or to receive attention; important 值得注意的；显著的；重要的

Helping to create inherent economic value in wilderness environments and threatened cultures has undoubtedly been one of the ecotourism movement's most *notable* achievements. 毫无疑问地，帮助荒野地区和受到威胁的文化区创造其与生俱来的经济价值已经成为生态旅行运动最显著的成就之一。

note [nəʊt]

v. to notice or pay careful attention to sth. 注意；留意；记录

Employees are requested to *note* down their own suggestions for improvement. 员工们被要求把自己的改进建议都记下来。

primary ['praɪməri] [同] ①②elementary

adj. ①most important 最重要的；首要的 ② (BrE) connected with the education of children between the ages of about five and eleven 初等教育的；小学教育的

This degree course is designed for preparing students to teach in *primary* and secondary schools. 这个学位的课程是为培养小学和中学教师而设计的。

prime [praɪm] [同] principal

adj. main, most important, basic 主要的；首要的；基本的

The care of the environment is of *prime* importance. 保护环境是最重要的。

primitive ['prɪmətɪv] [反] advanced

adj. belonging to a very simple society with no industry, etc. 原始的；远古的

Studies of *primitive* societies suggest that the earliest method of making fire was through friction. 对原始社会的研究表明最早的取火方式是通过摩擦。

principal ['prɪnsəpl] [同] ①chief

① *adj.* most important; main 最重要的；主要的

New roads will link the *principal* cities of the area. 新建道路将连通这个地区的主要城市。

② *n.* (BrE) the person who is in charge of a college or a university 大学校长；学院院长

Peter Brown, *principal* of St John's college 圣约翰学院院长彼得·布朗

rash [ræʃ] [同] ①hasty

① *adj.* acting or done without careful consideration of the possible consequences; impetuous 未仔细虑及后果的；轻率的

a *rash* young student 鲁莽的年轻学生

② *n.* (fig.) sudden widespread appearance of sth. unpleasant 令人不快的事情突然大量出现

a *rash* of ugly new houses 一下子冒出来的一大片难看的新房子

rating [ˈreɪtɪŋ]

n. a level on a scale that shows how good, important, popular, etc. sb. or sth. is 等级；排行；排名

The new comedy had the highest television *rating* this season. 新推出的喜剧在本季收视率最高。

G	GENERAL AUDIENCES
	All Ages Admitted

PG	PARENTAL GUIDANCE SUGGESTED
	SOME MATERIAL MAY NOT BE SUITABLE FOR CHILDREN

PG-13	PARENTS STRONGLY CAUTIONED
	Some Material May Be Inappropriate for Children Under 13

R	RESTRICTED
	UNDER 17 REQUIRES ACCOMPANYING PARENT OR ADULT GUARDIAN

NC-17	NO ONE 17 AND UNDER ADMITTED

ratio [ˈreɪʃɪəʊ] [同] proportion

n. relation between two amounts determined by the number of times one contains the other 比；比率

The *ratios* of 1 to 5 and 20 to 100 are the same. 1 与 5 之比和 20 与 100 之比相同。

stability [stəˈbɪlɪti] [同] firmness

n. the condition of being steady and not changing 稳定性

Our aims must be: To achieve price *stability*. 我们的目标必须是：实现价格稳定。

stable [ˈsteɪbl] [同] steadfast

adj. firmly established or fixed; not likely to move or change 稳定的；稳固的；牢固的

Nevertheless, supermarkets offered people *stable* employment. 不过，超级市场给人们提供了稳定的就业机会。

stadium [ˈsteɪdɪəm]

n. enclosed area of land for games, athletic contests, etc., usu. with seats for spectators 体育场，运动场

Toilets are to be found in all four corners of the *stadium*. 在体育场的四角都能找到厕所。

staff [stɑːf] [同] personnel

n. (usu. sing.) group of assistants working together in a business, etc. responsible to a manager or person in authority 全体职工；全体雇员

We need more *staff* in the office. 我们办公室需要增加人手。

theme [θiːm] [同] subject

n. subject of a talk, a piece of writing or a person's thoughts; topic（谈话或写作的）主题；（某人观念的）核心；题目

The *theme* of our discussion was 'Europe in the 1980's'. 我们讨论的题目是"二十世纪八十年代的欧洲"。

theoretical [θɪəˈretɪkl] [反] applied

adj. concerned with the theory of a subject 理论的；理论上的

She has *theoretical* knowledge of teaching, but no practical experience. 关于教学她有理论知识，但没有实践经验。

urban [ˈɜːbən]

adj. connected with a town or city 城市的；都市的

damage to both *urban* and rural environments 对城乡环境的破坏

urge [ɜːdʒ]

v. to advise or try hard to persuade sb. to do sth. 敦促，力劝

The report *urged* that all children be taught to swim. 这份报告呼吁向所有的儿童教授游泳。

urgent [ˈɜːdʒənt] [同] pressing

adj. very important and needing to be dealt with immediately 紧急的；急迫的

Half the nation's schools are in *urgent* need of physical improvement.

整个国家一半的学校急需硬件上的改善。

vapour [ˈveɪpə(r)] [同] steam

n. (BrE)a mass of very small drops of liquid in the air, for example, steam；（AmE）vapor 蒸汽；雾气

water *vapour* 水蒸气

variety [vəˈraɪəti] [同] diversity

n. several different sorts of the same thing (同一事物的)不同种类；多种样式

There is a wide *variety* of patterns to choose from. 有种类繁多的图案可供选择。

Take the Test >>

一、英汉互译

业余爱好者 _____   commute _____

运动员 _____   entity _____

不可避免的 _____   fiction _____

稳定性 _____   minimal _____

紧急的 _____   primitive _____

二、翻译句子

1）不幸的家庭环境会对孩子的行为造成影响。（environment）

_____

2）对付网络诈骗的最好办法就是学会如何不成为它的受害者。（fraud）

_____

3）退休的最低年龄是 55 岁。（minimum）

_____

4）新推出的喜剧在本季收视率最高。（rating）

_____

Histories make men wise; poems witty; the mathematics subtle; natural philosophy deep; moral grave; logic and rhetoric able to contend.

历史使人明智；诗词使人灵秀；数学使人周密；自然哲学使人深刻；伦理使人庄重；逻辑修辞学使人善辩。

——英国哲学家 培根（Francis Bacon, British philosopher）

alter [ˈɔːltə(r)]　　　　　　　　　　　　　　　　　　　　　　　　　　[同] change, modify

v. to make sb./sth. different 改变，更改

Whether you like it or not you're going to have to change your ways and *alter* your lifestyle.
不管你喜不喜欢，你都将不得不改变自己的习惯和生活方式。

alternative [ɔːlˈtɜːnətɪv]　　　　　　　　　　　　　　　　　　　　[同] ②substitute, option

① *adj.* that can be used instead of sth. else 可供替代的

A possible *alternative* solution to the growing problem of global communication may be the virtual office. 全球交流问题日益显著，而解决它的一个可能方案就是"虚拟办公室"。

② *n.* a thing that you can choose to do or have out of two or more possibilities 可供选择的事物

compare [kəmˈpeə(r)]

v. to examine or judge two or more things in order to show how they are similar to or different from each other 比较

a 20% reduction in burglary *compared* with last year 入室行窃比去年减少 20%

comparison [kəmˈpærɪsn]

n. an act of comparing 比较

By *comparison* with other European countries, car prices in the UK are very high. 与其他欧洲国家相比，英国的汽车价格相当高。

compensate [ˈkɒmpenseɪt]　　　　　　　　　　　　　　　　[同] indemnify

v. to give（sb.）sth. good to balance or lessen the bad effect of damage, loss, injury, etc.; recompense 补偿；赔偿

Nothing can *compensate* for the loss of one's health. 失去健康是无法补偿的。

competition [ˌkɒmpəˈtɪʃn]　　　　　　　　　　　　　　　　　　　　[同] contest

n. competing; activity in which people compete 竞争；角逐

We're in *competition* with several other companies for the contract. 我们与另几家公司角逐争取这项合同。

determine [dɪˈtɜːmɪn]　　　　　　　　　　　　　　　　　　　　　　[同] decide

v.（fml.）to fix（sth.）precisely; decide 确定（某事物）；决定

The Chinese think a name may somehow *determine* the future of a child. 中国人认为名字能够以某种方式决定孩子的未来。

device [dɪˈvaɪs]

n. thing made or adapted for a special purpose（为某种用途而制作或改装的）装置，器具

a *device* for measuring pressure 测压装置

devil [ˈdevl]　　　　　　　　　　　　　　　　　　　　　　　　　　[同] demon

n. wicked spirit 魔鬼；鬼怪

He believes in *devils* and witches. 他相信魔鬼、巫婆这类事。

envy [ˈenvi]

① *n.* the feeling of wanting to be in the same situation as sb. else; the feeling of wanting sth. that

sb. else has 羡慕，忌妒

She felt a pang of *envy* at the thought of his success. 她一想到他的成功便感到一阵忌妒的痛苦。

② *v.* to wish you had the same qualities, possessions, opportunities, etc. as sb. else 羡慕；忌妒

I *envy* you having such a close family. 我羡慕你有这么一个亲密的家庭。

episode ［ˈepɪsəʊd］

n. ①a television or radio programme that is one of a series of programmes in which the same story is continued each week（电视或电台节目的）集；期 ②an event, a situation, or a period of time in sb.'s life, a novel, etc. that is important or interesting in some way（人生的）一段经历；（小说的）片段；插曲

the first *episode* of a new drama series 新电视连续剧的第一集

fierce ［fɪəs］ ［同］desperate

adj. showing strong feelings or a lot of activity, often in a way that is violent 狂热的；猛烈的

Despite *fierce* competition within the real estate industry, prices are unlikely to drop any further. 尽管房地产业竞争激烈，但房价不太可能再降了。

file ［faɪl］

n. a box or folded piece of card, often with a wire or mental rod, for keeping loose papers together and in order 文件箱；文件夹；卷宗

A stack of *files* are awaiting me on my desk. 我桌上有一堆文件正待我去处理。

glimpse ［glɪmps］ ［同］glance

n. short look 一瞥；一看

a quick *glimpse* at the newspaper headlines 对报纸大标题匆匆地看一遍

hesitate ［ˈhezɪteɪt］

v. be slow to speak or act because one feels uncertain or unwilling; pause in doubt 犹豫；迟疑

She replied without *hesitating*. 她毫不犹豫地做了回答。

hesitation ［ˌhezɪˈteɪʃn］

n. state of hesitating 犹豫；迟疑

She agreed without the slightest *hesitation*. 她毫不犹豫地同意了。

infect ［ɪnˈfekt］

v. to make sth./sb. contain sth. harmful that gives people a disease 传染；感染

People with the virus may feel perfectly well, but they can still *infect* others. 病毒携带者可能没有任何感觉，但他们仍然会传染别人。

infection ［ɪnˈfekʃn］

n. becoming ill through contact with bacteria, etc. 传染；感染；侵染

The antibiotic ointment will prevent *infection*. 抗生素膏可以预防感染。

infer ［ɪnˈfɜː］ ［同］deduce

v. to form an opinion that sth. is probably true because of information that you have（根据事实或推理）推断，推定

It is possible to *infer* two completely opposite conclusions from this set of facts. 从这些事实中可能推断出两种截然相反的结论。

light-hearted ［ˈlaɪt ˈhɑːtɪd］ ［同］free-minded

adj. not being burdened by trouble, worry, or care; happy and carefree 快乐的；心情愉快的

He is not so *light-hearted* now as he used to be—too much responsibility. 他不再像以前那样无忧无虑了——承担了太多责任。

minor ['maɪnə] [反] major

① *adj.* not very large, important or serious 较小的；次要的；轻微的

There may be some *minor* changes to the schedule. 时间安排也许会有些小小的变动。

② *n.* a person who is under the age at which he/she legally becomes an adult and is responsible for his/her actions 未成年人

It is an offence to serve alcohol to *minors*. 向未成年人提供含酒精的饮料是违法的。

minority [maɪ'nɒrəti] [反] majority

n. the smaller part of a group; less than half of the people or things in a large group 少数派；少数人

Many *minority* languages are on the danger list. 很多少数民族的语言都即将消失。

minus ['maɪnəs] [反] ②plus

① *n.* (infml.) a negative quality; a disadvantage 负值；缺点

Let's consider the pluses and *minuses* of changing the system. 我们来考虑一下改变系统的利弊吧。

② *prep.* used when you subtract one number or thing from another one 减；减去

Seven *minus* three is four. 七减去三等于四。

notion ['nəʊʃn] [同] idea

n. an idea, a belief or an understanding of sth. 观念；信念

A new style of architecture emerged to reflect more idealistic *notions* for the future. 一种新的建筑风格出现了，反映了对于未来更加理想化的想法。

principle ['prɪnsɪpəl] [同] rule

n. ①the basic idea that a plan or system is based on 原则；原理 ②a moral rule or belief about what is right and wrong, that influences how you behave 原则；道义

the basic *principles* of business management 商业管理的基本原则

prior ['praɪə(r)] [同] preceding

adj. happening or existing before sth. else or before a particular time 先前的；较早的；在前的

This information must not be disclosed without *prior* written consent. 未事先征得书面许可前，此消息不得泄露。

privacy ['praɪvəsi, 'prɪvəsi]

n. the state of being alone and not watched or disturbed by other people 隐私；私密

Not surprisingly, biometrics raise thorny questions about *privacy* and the potential for abuse. 并不奇怪，生物测定学引发了关于隐私和潜在的滥用情况等棘手问题。

privilege ['prɪvəlɪdʒ] [同] prerogative

n. a special right or advantage that a particular person or group of people has 特殊利益；优惠待遇

Education should be a universal right and not a *privilege*. 教育应当是全民的权利而非某部分人特别享有的。

procedure [prə'siːdʒə(r)] [同] process

n. a way of doing sth., esp. in the usual or correct way (正常)程序，手续

Making a complaint is quite a simple *procedure*. 投诉的程序相当简单。

rational ['ræʃnəl] [同] reasonable

adj. not foolish or absurd; sensible; reasonable 出于理性的；理智的；明事理的；讲道理的

Paper recycling must be carried out in a *rational* and viable manner for it to be useful to both industry and the community. 为了使废纸循环有用于工业生产和社区生活，我们必须采取一种合理可行的方式。

raw [rɔ:]　　　　　　　　　　　　　　　　　　　　　　　　　　[同] uncooked

adj. raw substances are in a natural state and not treated or prepared for use 未加工的；生的

The cost of our *raw* materials has risen significantly. 原材料成本涨幅很大。

react [rɪˈækt]

v. to behave differently or change as a result of sth.; respond 做出反应；回应

Local residents have *reacted* angrily to the news. 当地居民对这一消息表示愤怒。

stage [steɪdʒ]

n. ①a particular time or state that sth. reaches as it grows or develops 阶段；时期 ②the raised area in a theatre which actors or singers stand on when they perform 舞台

the early *stages* of a child's development 儿童成长的早期阶段

stain [steɪn]　　　　　　　　　　　　　　　　　　　　　　　　　[同] blot

n. a mark that is difficult to remove 污点；染污

I can't get this *stain* out of the carpet. 我没法把这个污点从地毯上除掉。

stake [steɪk]　　　　　　　　　　　　　　　　　　　　　　　　　[同] bet

n. money, etc. invested by sb. in an enterprise so that he has an interest or share in it 投资；投放的本钱

She has a *stake* in the future success of the business. 她在这项生意上投了资以期将来获利。

standard [ˈstændəd]　　　　　　　　　　　　　　　　　　　　　　[同] criteria

adj. accepted as normal or usual 标准的

n. thing used as a test or measure for weights, lengths, quality, purity, etc. 标准；水准；规格；规范

These figures clearly show the difference in world living *standards*. 这些图表清晰地表明世界各国间生活水平的差异。

thereby [ˈðeəbaɪ]　　　　　　　　　　　　　　　　　　　　　　　[同] thus

adv. (fml.) by that means 借以；从而；由此

They paid cash, *thereby* avoiding interest charges. 他们付的是现金，以免付利息。

thesis [ˈθiːsɪs]　　　　　　　　　　　　　　　　　　　　　　　[同] dissertation

n. (BrE) long written essay submitted by a candidate for a university degree; dissertation 毕业论文；学位论文

a doctoral *thesis* 博士论文

utilize [ˈjuːtɪlaɪz]　　　　　　　　　　　　　　　　　　　　　[同] use, employ

v. (fml.) to use sth., esp. for a practical purpose 使用；利用

The Romans first *utilized* concrete as a building material. 罗马人首先使用混凝土做建筑材料。

utmost [ˈʌtməʊst]　　　　　　　　　　　　　　　　　　　　　　[同] extreme

adj. greatest; most extreme 最大的；极度的

This is a matter of the *utmost* importance. 这是个极其重要的问题。

vary [ˈveəri]　　　　　　　　　　　　　　　　　　　　　　　[同] change, differ

v. (of a group of similar things) to be different from each other in size, shape, etc. (大小、形状等)相异；不同

The students' work *varies* considerably in quality. 学生作业的质量参差不齐。

vast [vɑːst] [同] huge

adj. extremely large in area, size, amount, etc. 巨大的；庞大的

The logistics of transporting such *vast* quantities of water would be insurmountable. 安排运送如此大量的水资源所面临的困难将是难以克服的。

Take the Test »

一、英汉互译

可替代的	_____	episode	_____
装置	_____	infection	_____
犹豫	_____	infer	_____
少数派	_____	prior	_____
隐私	_____	stake	_____

二、翻译句子

1）失去健康是无法补偿的。（compensate）

_____

2）中国人认为名字能够以某种方式决定孩子的未来。（determine）

_____

3）这些图表清晰地表明世界各国间生活水平的差异。（standard）

_____

4）学生作业的质量参差不齐。（vary）

_____

The people who get on in this world are the people who get up and look for circumstances they want, and if they cannot find them, they make them.

在这个世界上，取得成功的人是那些努力寻找他们想要机会的人，如果找不到机会，他们就去创造机会。

——英国剧作家 肖伯纳（George Bernard Shaw, British dramatist）

ambition [æmˈbɪʃn]   [同] aspiration, drive

n. sth. you want to do or achieve very much 追求的目标；抱负；干劲

His burning *ambition* was to study medicine. 他梦寐以求的是学医。

amend [əˈmend]   [同] correct

v. to change a law, statement, etc. slightly in order to correct a mistake
or to improve it 修正；修订

You can *amend* or add to the plan as you proceed. 在实施过程中你可以
修正或补充这个方案。

block [blɒk]   [同] hinder

n. ① a large building divided into separate parts 大型建筑的一部分；单元 ② the four city
streets that form a square around an area of buildings 街区

v. to make movement or flow difficult or impossible on or in sth.; obstruct sth. 阻碍；堵塞

The heavy snow *blocks* the mountain passes, so you have to make considerable detours.
大雪阻住了山路，你得绕很大的弯才行。

compile [kəmˈpaɪl]

v. collect (information) and arrange it in a book, list, report, etc. 收集（资料）并编辑（成书、
表、报告等）

The tests are *compiled* by experts and they believe the answers can provide a few simple
indicators as to roughly the type of person you are. 这套测试由专家编写，他们认为测试结果
能提供一些信息，大致地反映你是何种类型的人。

complement [ˌkɒplɪmənt]   [同] ①supplement

n. ①sb. or sth. that emphasizes the good qualities of another person or thing 补充，互为补充的
东西

This wine would be a nice *complement* to grilled dishes. 这种酒配烤肉再好不过了。

②the number or quantity needed to make a group complete 整套，足额

With increasing global participation in athletics it is more likely that individuals possessing the
unique complement of genes for athletic performance can be identified early. 随着全球各国越
来越多地参与体育运动，那些有着独特运动基因的个人有可能更早地被挖掘出来。

complex [ˈkɒmpleks]   [同] complicated [反] simple

adj. difficult to understand or explain because there are many different parts（因有很多部分）难
于理解或解释的；复杂的

a *complex* argument/theory/subject 复杂的论证／理论／学科

couple [ˈkʌpl]   [近] pair

n. two people or things that are seen together or associated, esp. a man and woman together 一
对，一双（尤指男女）

Several *couples* were on the dance floor. 有几对舞伴在舞池中。

coverage [ˈkʌvərɪdʒ]   [同] content *n.* reporting of events, etc. 新闻报道

There's little coverage of foreign news in the newspaper. 报纸上几乎没有对国外新闻的报道。

devote [dɪ'vəʊt]　　　　　　　　　　　　　　　　　　　[同] allocate, set aside

v. to give (one's time, energy, etc.) to sb./sth.; dedicate 为某人 / 某事物付出 (时间、精力等);
献身于某事物

The amount of time and effort you *devote* to writing an essay will depend on how it fits into the overall scheme of assessment. 写议论文所花费的全部时间和精力的多少取决于这些时间和精力是否符合评估的总体计划。

diabetes [ˌdaɪə'biːtiːz]

n. a serious disease in which there is too much sugar in your blood 糖尿病

Obesity, heart disease and *diabetes* are beginning to appear in a people for whom these have never before been problems. 肥胖、心脏病和糖尿病开始在这些人群中出现，而此前他们从来没有面对过此类问题。

equip [ɪ'kwɪp]　　　　　　　　　　　　　　　　　　　　　　　[同] furnish

v. to provide yourself/sb./sth. with the things that are needed for a particular purpose or activity
配备；装备

IIe got a bank loan to rent and *equip* a small workshop. 他取得一笔银行贷款来租用和装备一个小车间。

era ['ɪərə]　　　　　　　　　　　　　　　　　　　　　　　　　　[同] period

n. a period of time, usu. in history, that is different from other periods because of particular characteristics or events 时代；年代；纪元

the post-war *era* 战后时代

fin [fɪn]

n. a thin flat part that sticks out from the body of a fish, used for swimming and keeping balance
(鱼的)鳍

When stocking a pool with fish, take care to select healthy individuals with firm, meaty bodies and erect dorsal *fins*. 往水池里放鱼时，要注意选择那些躯体结实多肉、背鳍直立的健康的鱼。

finance [fɪ'næns]　　　　　　　　　　　　　　　　　　　　[同] ①②fund

① *n.* the management of money by governments, large organizations, etc. 财政；金融

Russia's finance minister 俄罗斯财政大臣

② *v.* to provide money, especially a lot of money, to pay for sth. 为···提供资金

The concerts are *financed* by the Arts Council. 该演奏会是被艺术委员会资助的。

freight [freɪt]　　　　　　　　　　　　　　　　　　　　　　　[同] load

n. goods transported by ships, aeroplanes, or trains (水运、空运、陆运的)货物

send goods by air *freight* 空运发货

global ['gləʊbl]　　　　　　　　　　　　　　　　　　　　　[同] ①universal

adj. ①covering or affecting the whole world; world-wide 全球性的，全世界的 ②considering all the parts of a problem or situation together 整体的，全局的

Global car use is increasing at a faster rate. 全世界的汽车使用正加速增长。

inferior [ɪn'fɪəriə(r)]　　　　　　　　　　　　　　　　　　[反] ①②superior

① *n.* sb. who has a lower position or rank than you in an organisation 下属；下级

② *adj.* low(er) in rank (较)低的，次要的；差的

Their performance was *inferior* to that of other teams. 他们的表现比其他队都要差一些。

inflation [ɪnˈfleɪʃn]

n. a continuing increase in prices, or the rate at which prices increase 通货膨胀；物价上涨

Inflation is now running at over 16%. 通胀率现在达到了 16% 以上。

lightweight [ˈlaɪtweɪt]　　　　　　　　[反] heavyweight

n. sb. who has no importance or influence, or who does not have the ability to think deeply 无足轻重者；不能胜任者

an intellectual ***lightweight*** 一个无足轻重的知识分子

minute [maɪˈnjuːt]　　　　　　　　　　　　　　　[同] tiny

adj. extremely small; very detailed, careful and thorough 细小的；细致入微的，详细的

A rocket motor's 'bullets' are ***minute***, high-speed particles produced by burning propellants. 火箭马达的"子弹"是由燃烧推进物产生的细小高速颗粒。

miracle [ˈmɪrəkl]　　　　　　　　　　　　　　　[同] marvel

n. (infml.) a lucky thing that happens that you did not expect or think to be possible 奇迹；不平凡的事

It's a ***miracle*** that nobody was killed in the crash. 撞车事故中竟然没有一人丧生，这真是个奇迹。

mirror [ˈmɪrə]

① *n.* a piece of special flat glass that reflects images, so that you can see yourself when you look in it 镜子

a rear-view mirror（车内的）后视镜

② *v.* to have features that are similar to sth. else and which show what it is like 反映

The music of the time ***mirrored*** the feeling of optimism in the country. 这个时期的音乐反映出了这个国家的乐观精神。

notorious [nəʊˈtɔːriəs]　　　　　　[同] disreputable; infamous

adj. well-known for being bad 声名狼藉的；臭名昭著的

The country is ***notorious*** for its appalling prison conditions. 这个国家因监狱状况恶劣而臭名远扬。

notwithstanding [ˌnɒtwɪðˈstændɪŋ]　　　　[同] despite, regardless of

prep. (fml.) in spite of sth. 尽管；虽然

Notwithstanding differences, there are clear similarities in all of the world's religions. 世界上的宗教虽然有差异，但也有很明显的共性。

nought [nɔːt]

n. (BrE) the figure 0（数字）零

A million is written with six ***noughts***. 一百万写出来有六个零。

[记] 音接近 not

proceed [prəˈsiːd]　　　　　　　　　　　　[同] continue

v. to continue doing sth. that has already been started; to continue being done 继续做（或从事、进行）

We are not sure whether we still want to ***proceed*** with the sale. 我们不确定是否还要继续减价促销。

process [ˈprəʊses]　　　　　　　　　　　　[同] procedure

n. a series of things that are done in order to achieve a particular result（为达到某一目标的）过

程;进程

I'm afraid getting things changed will be a slow *process*. 改变现状恐怕是个缓慢的过程。

production [prə'dʌkʃn]

n. the process of growing or making food, goods or materials, esp. in large quantities 生产;制造

Production of the new aircraft will start next year. 新飞机的生产将于明年开始。

professional [prə'feʃənl]　　　　　　　　　　　　[同]①②expert

①*adj.* connected with a job that needs special training or skill, esp. one that needs a high level of education 职业的;专业的

Without hesitation he embarked on his new career, financing it by his *professional* work as a musician. 用他做音乐家的收入作资本,他毫不犹豫地开始了新的职业生涯。

②*n.* a person who has a lot of skill and experience 内行;专门人才

This was clearly a job for a real professional. 这显然是需要一位真正的专家才能担任的工作。

realistic [ˌrɪə'lɪstɪk]　　　　　　　　　　　　　　[同] down-to-earth

adj. based on facts rather than on sentiment or illusion; practical 实事求是的

Always plan a project thoroughly before you begin it but be *realistic* about how much time you can devote to it. 开始一个项目之前一定要细致全面地计划,但也要实际地考虑你能投入多少时间。

reap [riːp]　　　　　　　　　　　　　　　　　　　[同] harvest

v. to get sth., esp. sth. good, as a result of what you have done 收获;得到报偿

Those who do take risks often *reap* the rewards. 敢冒险的人通常会有所收获。

rear [rɪə(r)]　　　　　　　　　　　　　　　　　　[同]①back

① *adj.* at or near the back of sth. 后面的,后部的

the *rear* entrance of the building 大楼后面的入口

② *v.* (esp. BrE) bring up and educate (children, etc.) 养育(子女等)

rear a family 养家

reasonable ['riːznəbl]　　　　　　　　　　　　　[近] rational

adj. (of emotions, opinions, etc.) in accordance with reason; not absurd; logical (指情感、见解等)合情理的,不荒谬的,合逻辑的

Please explain why you think there's a problem then suggest a *reasonable* solution. 请解释一下为什么你认为有问题,并且提出一个合理的解决方法。

reassure [ˌriːə'ʃʊə(r)]

v. to remove sb.'s fears or doubts; make sb. confident again 消除某人的恐惧或疑虑;恢复某人的信心;使某人放心

The police *reassured* her about her child's safety. 警方让她放心,她的孩子很安全。

starve [stɑːv]

v. (cause a person or an animal to) suffer severely or die from hunger (使人或动物)挨饿,饿死

I'm *starving*! When do we eat? 我快饿死了,什么时候吃饭?

stationary ['steɪʃənri]　　　　　　　　　　　　[同] static, immobile

adj. not moving 静止的

No form of living speech can be *stationary*. 没有一种活语言可以停滞不前。

stationery ['steɪʃənri]

n. writing materials (e.g. paper, pens, envelopes, etc.) 文具

I'd like to order some *stationery*, please. 我想订一些文具,可以吗?

statistics [stə'tɪstɪks]

n. ① science of collecting, classifying and analysing such information 统计学 ②a set of numbers which represent facts or measurements 统计数据

Statistics is a branch of mathematics that is used in the study of many disciplines from physics, through to the social sciences. 统计学作为数学的分支，在从物理到社会科学的诸多学科中都得到广泛应用。

thoughtful [ˈθɔːtfl]   [反] thoughtless

adj. thinking deeply; absorbed in thought 深思的；思考的

thoughtful looks 沉思的表情

threshold [ˈθreʃhəʊld]

n. ① the entrance to a room or building, or the area of floor or ground at the entrance 门槛，(喻)开端

As he reached the ***threshold*** of the station, he put his bag down once again and paused. 他到达车站入口的时候，再次放下包停了下来。

② the level at which sth. starts to happen 域，界限

The normal noise ***threshold*** for private housing is 55 decibels. 私人住宅的正常噪音上限为 55 分贝。

vegetarian [ˌvedʒəˈteəriən]

① *adj.* of or relating to vegetarianism or vegetarians 吃素的；素食者的

a ***vegetarian*** restaurant 素食餐厅

② *n.* a person who does not eat meat or fish 素食者

She is a ***vegetarian***. 她是个素食者。

vehicle [ˈviːəkl] [同] mean

n. sth. that can be used to express your ideas or feelings or as a way of achieving sth. (用于表达思想、感情或达到目的的)手段，工具

Language is the ***vehicle*** of human thought. 语言是人类表达思想的工具。

Take the Test »

一、英汉互译

抱负	_____	complement	_____
糖尿病	_____	finance	_____
通货膨胀	_____	inferior	_____
奇迹	_____	notorious	_____
统计数据	_____	nought	_____

二、翻译句子

1）报纸上几乎没有对国外新闻的报道。（coverage）

_____

2）改变现状恐怕是个缓慢的过程。（process）

_____

3）开始一个项目之前一定要细致全面地计划，但也要实际地考虑你能投入多少时间。

（realistic）

_____

4）请解释一下为什么你认为有问题，并且提出一个合理的解决方法。（reasonable）

_____

The tragedy of life is not so much what men suffer, but what they miss.

生活的悲剧不在于人们受到多少苦，而在于人们错过了什么。

——英国散文家、历史学家 卡莱尔

（Thomas Carlyle, British essayist and historian）

Word List 22

ample ['æmpl]   [同] sufficient, abundant [反] meager

adj. more than enough 足够的

There is *ample* car parking here and plenty of bars and restaurants. 这里有足够多的停车位和众多的酒吧和饭馆。

amusing [ə'mju:zɪŋ]

adj. funny and entertaining 有趣的，逗笑的

The book is full of *amusing* stories about his childhood. 这本书里充满了他的童年趣事。

bloom [blu:m]   [同] ①②flower

n. ① a flower or flowers 花朵 ② the best time 繁盛期

If it were not for the dung beetle, chemical fertiliser and dung would be washed by rain into streams and rivers, polluting water courses and causing *blooms* of blue-green algae. 如果没有屎壳郎，化肥和粪便就会被雨水冲进溪流，从而污染水道并导致蓝藻的泛滥。

[记] 形: 6100 朵玫瑰盛开——花朵

blossom ['blɒsəm]

① *n.* a flower or the flowers on a tree or bush 花朵

② *v.* to become more healthy, confident or successful 变得更加健康、自信或成功

The idea *blossomed* into a successful mail order business. 这个创意成功地发展成为邮购业务。

complicated ['kɒmplɪkeɪtɪd]   [同] complex, elaborate

adj. difficult to understand or deal with, because many parts or details are involved（因复杂而）难于理解或解释的

In an increasingly crowded and *complicated* world, biometrics may well be a technology whose time has come. 在这个越来越拥挤复杂的世界里，生物测定学这门技术的时代已到来。

component [kəm'pəʊnənt]   [同] element, constituent

n. any of the parts of which sth. is made（某事物的）组成部分；成分；零部件

the *components* of an engine/a camera 发动机 / 照相机的部件

compose [kəm'pəʊz]   [同] create

v. write (music, opera, etc.) 写，创作(乐曲、歌剧等)

She began to *compose* (songs) at an early age. 她年轻时就已开始创作(歌曲)。

diagnose ['daɪəgnəʊz]   [近] identify

v. to find out the nature of esp. an illness by observing its symptoms 判断；(尤指)诊断(疾病)

The doctor *diagnosed* measles. 医生诊断出麻疹。

diagram ['daɪəgræm]

n. a drawing or plan that uses simple lines rather than realistic details to explain or illustrate a machine, structure, process, etc. 图解；图表；示意图

It is important to keep the essay relevant and to provide some examples, illustrations, *diagrams* or maps wherever appropriate. 保证文章不跑题并且在合适的地方加入一些例子、插图、示意图或者地图非常重要。

erase [ɪˈreɪz]　　　　　　　　　　　　　　　　　　　　　[同] delete, wipe out

v. to remove sth. completely 清除；消除

All doubts were suddenly *erased* from his mind. 他心中所有的疑虑突然烟消云散了。

finite [ˈfaɪnaɪt]　　　　　　　　　　　　　　　　　　　　　　　[反] infinite

adj. having a definite limit or fixed size 有限的；有限制的

The world's resources are *finite*. 世界的资源是有限的。

glorious [ˈglɔːriəs]　　　　　　　　　　　　　　　　　　　[同] ①②splendid

adj. ①having, worthy of or bringing great fame or glory 荣誉的；光荣的；显赫的 ② very beautiful or impressive 灿烂的；辉煌的

die a *glorious* death, i.e. esp. in battle for one's country 死得光荣(尤指为国捐躯)

highlight [ˈhaɪlaɪt]

v. to give special attention to (sth.); emphasize 对(某事物)予以特别的注意；强调

This observation is a useful starting point for any discussion of extinction as it *highlights* the role of luck and chance in the extinction process. 这个观察对于任何有关灭绝的讨论来说都是一个有益的开端，因为它强调了灭绝过程中侥幸与偶然的作用。

high-tech [ˌhaiˈtek]

adj. using high technology 高科技的

high-tech industries 高科技产业

influence [ˈɪnfluəns]　　　　　　　　　　　　　　　　　　[近] effect, impact

n./v. (the power) to affect the way sb. or sth. develops, behaves, or thinks without using direct force or orders 影响(力)

These factors are known to *influence* the kind of language used. 这些因素被认为影响了使用中的语言。

influenza [ˌɪnfluˈenzə]　　　　　　　　　　　　　[同] flu

n. an infectious disease that is like a very bad cold 重流感

In 1990, smoking caused more than 84,000 deaths, mainly resulting from such problems as pneumonia, bronchitis and *influenza*. 在 1990 年，吸烟导致了 8.4 万多起由肺炎、支气管炎和重流感之类问题引起的死亡。

informative [ɪnˈfɔːmətɪv]　　　　　　　　　　　　　　[反] uninformative

adj. giving much information; instructive 提供大量信息的；授予知识的

The lecture was very *informative* and helpful. 讲座的知识性很强，让人受益匪浅。

likelihood [ˈlaɪklihʊd]

n. the chance of sth. happening; how likely sth. is to happen 可能；可能性

There is some *likelihood* that all accountants will be alike. 有可能所有的会计师都相似。

miserable [ˈmɪzrəbl]　　　　　　　　　　　　　　　　　　[同] wretched

adj. very unhappy, uncomfortable 痛苦的；非常难受的

I have many women patients who say they have completely given up exercise because the pain makes them so *miserable*. 我的很多女病人都说她们彻底地放弃了锻炼，因为疼痛使她们相当痛苦。

misery [ˈmɪzəri]　　　　　　　　　　　　　　　　　　　　[近] unhappiness

n. great suffering of the mind or body 痛苦；悲惨

Fame brought her nothing but *misery*. 名声只给她带来了痛苦。

missile ['mɪsaɪl]

n. a weapon that is sent through the air and that explodes when it hits the thing that it is aimed at 导弹

a *missile* base/site 导弹基地 / 发射场

nourish ['nʌrɪʃ]　　　　　　　　　　　　　　　　　　　　　　　[同] nurture

v. to keep a person, an animal or a plant alive and healthy with food, etc. 抚养；滋养

All the children were well *nourished* and in good physical condition. 所有这些孩子都营养良好，身体健康。

novelty ['nɒvlti]　　　　　　　　　　　　　　　　　　　　　　　[同] newness

n. the quality of being new, different and interesting 新奇；新鲜

There's a certain *novelty* value in this approach. 这种方法有一定的新意。

nuclear ['nju:kliə(r)]

adj. of an atom, or the energy produced when the nucleus of an atom is either split or joined with the nucleus of another atom 原子能的；核能的

By then *nuclear* energy should be contributing more than one-fifth of the electricity generation. 到那时，核能将占发电总量的五分之一多。

proficiency [prə'fɪʃnsi]

n. a good standard of ability and skill 熟练；精通

The students' *proficiency* in speaking English is also tested. 学生的英语口语的熟练程度也得到测试。

profile ['prəʊfaɪl]　　　　　　　　　　　　　　　　　　　　　[同] outline

n. a short description that gives important details about a person, a group of people, or a place 轮廓；简要描述

When fully developed, this system will enable him to build a biomechanical *profile* for coaches to use to help budding swimmers. 该系统设计完成后，他将能够为教练们建立生物力学的模型来协助培养游泳运动员。

prohibit [prə'hɪbɪt]　　　　　　　　　　　　　　　　　　　　　[同] ban

v. (fml.) to stop sth. from being done or used esp. by law (尤指以法令)禁止

a law *prohibiting* the sale of alcohol 禁止售酒的法令

project ['prɒdʒekt]　　　　　　　　　　　　　　　　　　　　　[同] plan

n. a plan of a piece of work that is designed to find information about sth. to produce sth. new, or to improve sth. 生产(或研究等)项目；工程

It's just a pilot *project*. 这不过是个试点工程。

prolong [prə'lɒŋ]　　　　　　　　　　　　　　　　　　　　　　[同] extend

v. to make sth. last longer 延长

The operation could *prolong* his life by two or three years. 这次手术可使他多活两三年。

recall [rɪ'kɔːl]　　　　　　　　　　　　　　　　　　　　　　　[同] remember

v. bring (sth./sb.) back into the mind; recollect 回忆(某事物或某人)；记起

I can't *recall* his name. 我想不起他的名字了。

reception [rɪ'sepʃn]

n. (BrE) area in a hotel or an office building where guests or clients are received, registered, etc. (旅馆或事务所的)接待处

Wait for me at *reception*. 在接待处等我吧。

recipe ['resəpi]

n. set of instructions for preparing a food dish, including the ingredients required 烹饪法；食谱

recipe books 烹饪书

statue ['stætʃuː]   [同] sculpture

n. an image of a person or animal that is made in solid material such as stone or metal and is usually large 雕像；塑像；铸像

The committee will try to raise $20,000 to erect a commemorative *statue* on City Hall's front lawn. 委员会将努力筹措两万美元在市政厅前的草坪上建造一尊纪念雕像。

status ['steɪtəs]   [同] position

n. a person's social, legal or professional position or rank in relation to others 地位；身份；职位

Promotion offers ever-higher degrees of social *status* and material wealth. 晋升带来更高的社会地位与物质财富。

steer ['stɪə(r)]   [同] ②guide

v. ①to direct or control the course of (a boat, car, etc.) 操纵 (船、汽车等) 的行驶方向；驾驶 ②to guide sb.'s behaviour or the way a situation develops 引导；指导

Teachers should *steer* pupils away from drugs. 教师应该引导学生远离毒品。

stereo ['steriəʊ]

n. stereophonic sound or recording; broadcast in stereo 立体声；立体声录音；立体声广播

I've got a fridge and a *stereo* system which I've just bought from a friend. 我刚刚从一位朋友那里买了一台冰箱与一套立体声设备。

stimulate ['stɪmjuleɪt]   [同] motivate

v. to make sb./sth. more active or alert; arouse sb./sth. 使某人 / 某物奋发起来；刺激、激励某人 / 某物

In other words, a dull rat in a *stimulating* environment will almost do as well as a bright rat. 换句话说，在一个刺激性的环境中，一只迟钝的老鼠与一只聪明的老鼠表现得几乎一样好。

threaten ['θretn]

v. ①to say that you will cause sb. harm or trouble if they do not do what you want 恐吓；威胁 ②to be likely to harm or destroy sth. 威胁；可能会破坏

Soil erosion *threatens* the productivity of land. 水土流失会破坏土地的生产能力。

thrifty ['θrɪfti]   [反] wasteful

adj. using money carefully and wisely 节约的；节俭的

My grandma is a very *thrifty* woman who never wastes anything. 我奶奶是个很节约的人，从不浪费任何东西。

venture ['ventʃə(r)]

n. a business project or activity, esp. one that involves taking risks 企业；投机活动；经营项目 (尤指有风险的)

We have joint *ventures* with organizations around the world. 我们有和世界各地的组织的合营项目。

venue ['venjuː]   [同] locality

n. a place where people meet for an organized event, for example a concert, sporting event or conference 聚会地点 (如音乐厅、体育比赛场馆、会场)

The band will be playing at twenty different *venues* on their UK tour. 这个乐队在英国巡回演

出期间将在二十个不同的地点演出。

verge [vɜːdʒ] [同] border

n. the extreme edge or margin, a border 边沿；边缘

These events left her on the *verge* of having a nervous breakdown. 这些事使得她的精神濒于崩溃。

Take the Test ≫

一、英汉互译

组成部分	_____	diagnosis	_____
强调	_____	finite	_____
核能的	_____	nourish	_____
回忆	_____	proficiency	_____
雕像	_____	profile	_____

二、翻译句子

1）这本书里充满了他的童年趣事。（amusing）

_____

2）讲座的知识性很强，让人受益匪浅。（informative）

_____

3）这不过是个试点工程。（project）

_____

4）教师应该引导学生远离毒品。（steer）

_____

Activity is the only road to knowledge.

行动是通往知识的惟一道路。

——英国剧作家 肖伯纳（George Bernard Shaw, British dramatist）

Word List 23

analyse [ˈænəlaɪz]   [近] examine

v. to examine the nature or structure of sth. 分析

It would be pertinent to consider the realities of life for Eskimos before ***analyzing*** their language. 在分析爱斯基摩人的语言之前有必要考虑一下他们的真实生活情况。

analysis [əˈnæləsɪs]   [同] breakdown [反] synthesis

n. a careful examination of sth. in order to understand it better 分析

A representative sample of language, compiled for the purpose of linguistic ***analysis***, is known as a corpus. 为了进行语言分析而收集的具有代表性的语言样本被称为语料库。

ancestor [ˈænsestə(r)]   [同] forefather [反] descendant

n. a member of your family who lived a long time ago 祖先

The soldiers would go into battle in the same manner as their ***ancestors*** had done centuries before. 士兵们会像几个世纪前他们的祖先那样走上战场。

blueprint [ˈbluˌprɪnt]   [同] plan

n. photographic print of building plans, with white lines on a blue background 蓝图

blueprints of a new aircraft 新型飞机的蓝图

compound [ˈkɒmpaʊnd]   [同] mixture

n. substance consisting of two or more elements chemically combined 化合物

chemical ***compounds*** 化合物

comprehension [ˌkɒmprɪˈhenʃn]

n. (power of) understanding 理解(力)

a problem above/beyond sb.'s ***comprehension*** 某人不能理解的问题

crisis [ˈkraɪsɪs]   [同] turning point

n. time of great difficulty or danger; decisive moment in illness, life, history, etc. 危机; (疾病、生命、历史等的)决定性的时刻

Energy-efficient homes became popular after the oil ***crisis***. 节能型住房在石油危机后很受欢迎。

critic [ˈkrɪtɪk]

n. person who evaluates and describes the quality of sth., esp. works of art, literature, music, etc. 评论员,评论家(尤指对艺术、文学、音乐等作品)

a play praised by the ***critics*** 评论家交口称誉的剧本

dialect [ˈdaɪəlekt]

n. form of a language (grammar, vocabulary and pronunciation) used in a part of a country or by a class of people 方言; 土语; 地方话

the Yorkshire ***dialect*** 约克郡方言

diet [ˈdaɪət]

① *n.* sort of food that is usually eaten (by a person, community, etc.) (某人、共同生活的人等)通常吃的食物; 日常食物

the Japanese **diet** of rice, vegetables and fish 米、蔬菜、鱼等日本人常吃的食物

② *v.* (be allowed to) eat only some foods or a little food, especially to lose weight 只(准)吃某类食物或少量食物;(尤指为减轻体重)节食

You ought to **diet** and take more exercise. 你应该节食并多做运动。

error	[ˈerə]	[同] mistake

n. a mistake, esp. one that causes problems or affects the result of sth. 错误;差错;谬误

No payments were made last week because of a computer **error**. 由于计算机出错,上周未付任何款项。

essay [ˈeseɪ]

n. a short piece of writing by a student as part of a course of study 短论;文章,短文

an **essay** on the causes of the First World War 关于一战起因的文章

essence [ˈesns]

n. the most important quality or feature of sth. that makes it what it is 实质;本质;精髓

In **essence**, your situation isn't different from mine. 从本质上讲,你我的情况并无差别。

fitness [ˈfɪtnɪs]

n. the state of being physically healthy and strong 健壮;健康

This new science was used to improve our health and **fitness**. 这门新科学被用在提高我们的身心健康上。

glossary [ˈɡlɒsəri]

n. list of technical or special words (esp. those occurring in a particular text) explaining their meanings (注释)词汇表,术语或专门词语汇编,集注(尤指针对某篇文字的)

glossary of terms 难词 / 专业词 / 外来语词汇表

hijack [ˈhaɪdʒæk]

v. to seize control of (a vehicle, esp. an aircraft) in order to force it to go to a new destination, to take its passengers hostage or to steal its cargo 劫持(交通工具,尤指飞机)

The plane was **hijacked** while on a flight to Delhi. 该机在飞往德里的途中遭到劫持。

infrastructure [ˈinfrəˈstrʌktʃə(r)]

n. the basic systems and structures that a country or organization needs in order to work properly 基础设施

However, public **infrastructure** did not keep pace with urban sprawl. 然而,公共基础设施并没有跟上城市扩张的速度。

ingredient	[ɪnˈɡriːdiənt]	[同] element

n. any of the food that are combined to make a particular dish (烹调用的)材料,原料,成分

Ingredients	Weight
Chili Paste	
Sliced shallots	100 g
White fermented	100 g
Chopped cilantro root	10 g
Pepper	3 g
Dried chilies	2 g
Others	
Minced pork	100 g
Minced prawn	150 g
Sliced tofu	100 g
Palm sugar	140 g
Tamarind juice	80 g
Salt	13 g

The food is home-cooked using fresh **ingredients**. 这些食物是使用新鲜材料在家做的。

likewise	[ˈlaɪkwaɪz]	[近] also

adv. (fml.) the same; in a similar way 同样地;类似地

He voted for the change and he expected his colleagues to do **likewise**. 他投票赞成变革,并期望他的同事也和他一样。

mission [ˈmɪʃn]

n. the purpose or the most important aim of an organization 宗旨;使命

The **mission** of the International Office is to enable students of different cultures to live together and build life-long friendships. 国际办公室的宗旨是让来自不同文化的学生生活在一起并建立终生的友谊。

mobile ['məʊbail]　　　　　　　　　　　　　　　　　　[同] movable, unstable

adj. that is not fixed in one place and can be moved easily and quickly 非固定的；可移动的

When an organization is shrinking, the best and most *mobile* workers are prone to leave voluntarily. 当企业衰退时，流动性最强的最优秀的员工就会主动离开。

nuisance ['njuːsns]　　　　　　　　　　　　　　　　　　[同] pest

n. a thing, a person or situation that is annoying or causes trouble or problems 麻烦事；讨厌的人（或东西）

I hope you're not making a *nuisance* of yourself. 我希望你没有讨人嫌。

numerous ['njuːmərəs]　　　　　　　　　　　　　　　　[同] many

adj. (fml.) existing in large numbers 众多的；许多的

Numerous overseas visitors have come to see how the program works. 许多海外来客都来参观这项工程是如何运作的。

prominent ['prɒmɪnənt]　　　　　　　　　　　　　　　　[同] distinguished

adj. important or well-known 重要的；杰出的

He played a *prominent* part in the campaign. 他在这次运动中发挥了重要作用。

promising ['prɒmɪsɪŋ]　　　　　　　　　　　　　　　　　[同] hopeful

adj. showing signs of being good or successful 有希望的；有前途的

He was voted the most *promising* newcomer for his part in the movie. 他因在电影中扮演的角色而被评为最有前途的新人。

promote [prə'məʊt]　　　　　　　　　　　　　　　　　　[同] advance

v. to help sth. to happen or develop 促进；推动

Industrial training schemes have *promoted* an increase in linguistic and cultural awareness. 产业培训计划促进了人们语言和文化意识的提高。

prompt [prɒmpt]　　　　　　　　　　　　　　　　　　　[同] ①quick

① *adj.* done without delay 立即；迅速的；及时的

Prompt action was required as the fire spread. 由于火势蔓延，需要立即采取行动。

② *v.* to make sb. decide to do sth.; to cause sth. to happen 促使；导致

In Britain, the fact that 30 per cent of 16 year olds have a reading age of 14 or less has helped to *prompt* massive educational changes. 在英国，30%的16岁的孩子只有14年的阅龄甚至更少，这一事实促进教育领域的巨大改革。

propel [prə'pel]　　　　　　　　　　　　　　　　　　　[同] promote

v. to move, drive, or push sth. forward or in a particular direction 推动；驱动

The concept of the rocket, or rather the mechanism behind the idea of *propelling* an object into the air, has been around for well over two thousand years. 火箭的概念，或者说把一个物体发射到空中的想法的背后的机械原理，已经存在了两千多年。

recital [rɪ'saɪtl]

n. public performance of music, dance, etc. by a soloist or a small group 独唱会；独奏会；（小型团体的）音乐演奏会、舞蹈表演会等

give a piano *recital* 举行钢琴独奏会

reckon ['rekən]　　　　　　　　　　　　　　　　　　　　[同] consider

v. BrE. (infml.) to assume; to think 假定；想；认为

How long do you *reckon* it will take? 你认为得花多长时间？

recognize ['rekəgnaɪz] [同] acknowledge

v. to be able to identify（sb./sth. that one has seen, heard, etc. before）; know sb./sth. again 认出或识别某人／某物

I *recognized* her by her red hat. 根据她的红色帽子我认出了她。

stir [stɜː(r)]

v. to move a spoon, etc. round and round（in a liquid or some other substance）in order to mix it thoroughly 搅动，搅和，搅拌（液体等）

stir one's tea with a spoon 用匙搅动茶

storage ['stɔːrɪdʒ]

n. storing of goods, etc.（货物等的）储存，储藏

Our *storage* and distribution costs are reduced dramatically. 我们货物的储存和发送成本大大降低。

storey ['stɔːri]

n. section of a building with rooms all at the same level; floor 楼层

a house of two *storeys* 两层的楼房

straightforward [ˌstreɪt'fɔːwəd]

adj. ①easy to understand or do; without complications or difficulties 易懂的；易做的；简单的 ②honest about your feelings or opinions and not hiding anything 坦率的；率直的

The new networking system is fairly *straightforward* — you shouldn't have any problems. 新的网络系统简单易懂，你应该不会有什么问题的。

timely ['taɪmli]

adj. occurring at just the right time; opportune 及时的；适时的；合时宜

thanks to your *timely* intervention 多亏你及时调停

tiny ['taɪni]

adj. very small 极小的；微小的

Bad teachers are a *tiny* minority. 坏老师只是极少数。

tip [tɪp]

n. ①pointed or thin end of sth. 尖端；尖儿 ②a small amount of additional money that you give to sb. such as a waiter or a taxi driver 小费

Did you leave a *tip*? 给小费了吗？

versatile ['vɜːsətaɪl] [同]②talented

adj. ①（of food, a building, etc.）having many different uses 多用途的；多功能的 ②sb. who is versatile has many different skills 多才多艺的

Eggs are easy to cook and are an extremely *versatile* food. 鸡蛋容易烹煮，怎么做着吃都行。

version ['vɜːʃn, 'vɜːrʒn]

n. ①a copy of sth. that has been changed so that it is slightly different 版本；型号 ② a description of an event from the point of view of a particular person or a group of people（个人或群体的）说法；描述

I think I preferred the television *version*. 我觉得我还是倾向于电视版。

versus ['vɜːsəs] [同] contra

prep.（abbr. v, vs）（esp. sport or law）used to show that two teams or sides are against each other（尤指运动、诉讼中的）相对，反对

It is France *versus* Brazil in the final. 决赛是法国队对巴西队。

via ['vaɪə] [同] by

prep. through a place 经由；经过(某一地方)

We flew home *via* Dubai. 我们乘飞机经由迪拜回国。

Take the Test

一、英汉互译

分析(*n.*)	_____	blueprint	_____
本质，精髓	_____	glossary	_____
基础设施	_____	ingredient	_____
有前途的	_____	nuisance	_____
及时的	_____	propel	_____

二、翻译句子

1) 节能型住房在石油危机后很受欢迎。(crisis)

_____

2) 国际办公室的宗旨是让来自不同文化的学生生活在一起并建立终生的友谊。(mission)

_____

3) 许多海外来客都来参观这项工程是如何运作的。(numerous)

_____

4) 我觉得我还是倾向于电视版。(version)

_____

If you shed tears when you miss the sun, you also miss the stars.

如果你因错过太阳而流泪，那么你也将错过群星。

——印度诗人 泰戈尔(Ranbindranath Tagore, Indian poet)

ancient ['eɪnʃənt]   [同] age-old [反] modern

adj. belonging to a time long ago in history 古老的

Acupuncture is an *ancient* healing art. 针灸是古代的一种医术。

announcement [ə'naʊnsmənt]   [同] declaration

n. an important or official statement 通告，公告

I'd just like to make a few *announcements* before the first performances begin. 演出开始前我有几件事要通知一下。

boast [bəʊst]   [同] brag

v. talk （about one's own achievements, abilities, etc.）with too much pride and satisfaction 自夸；自吹自擂

He *boasted* of being/*boasted* that he was the best player in the team. 他自夸是队里的最佳队员。

comprise [kəm'praɪz]   [同] constitute

v. to have as parts or members; be made up of 包括；组成

a committee *comprising* people of widely differing views 由观点极不相同的成员组成的委员会

compute [kəm'pjuːt]   [近] calculate

v. calculate sth. with a computer 用计算机计算

Scientists have *computed* the probable course of the rocket. 科学家用计算机计算了火箭可能运行的轨道。

conceal [kən'siːl]   [同] hide [反] reveal

v. to keep sth./sb. from being seen or known about; hide sth./sb. 隐藏、掩盖或隐瞒某事／某人

a tape recorder *concealed* in a drawer 藏在抽屉里的录音机

differ ['dɪfə(r)]   [反] agree

v. not to be the same （as sb./sth.）; be unlike （与某人／某物）不同，不一样，有区别；不像；相异

Even among identical twins who have exactly the same genes, one in six pairs will *differ* in their handedness. 即便是一模一样的双胞胎，有着完全一样的基因，每六对中也会有一对使用左右手的习惯不同。

digest ① ['daɪdʒest] *n.* short condensed account; summary 摘要；概要

a digest of the week's news 一周新闻摘要

② [daɪ'dʒest] *v.* to change （food）in the stomach and bowels so that it can be used by the body 消化（食物）

Fish is easy to *digest* when you're ill. 生病时吃鱼容易消化。

dignity ['dɪgnəti]   [近] grace

n. quality that earns or deserves respect; true worth 高尚的品质；尊严；尊贵

the *dignity* of labour 劳动的尊严

establish [ɪ'stæblɪʃ]   [同] found

v. to start or create an organization, a system, etc. that is meant to last for a long time 建立；创立；设立

The new treaty *established* a free trade zone. 新条约设立了一个自由贸易区。

estate [ɪˈsteɪt]

n. （BrE）an area of land with a lot of houses or factories of the same type on it 住宅区；工业区；工厂区

She lives in a tower block on an *estate* in London. 她住在伦敦某住宅区的一栋高楼里。

real *estate* 房地产

fix [fɪks]

v. ① to repair sth. that is broken or not working properly 维修

The owner of the property won't help *fix* things that go wrong. 物品的主人将不帮助修理损坏了的东西。

② to attach sth. firmly to sth. else, so that it stays there permanently 装配；固定

The shelves should be *fixed* to the wall with screws. 架子需要用螺钉固定到墙上。

flame [fleɪm]

n. hot glowing portion of burning gas that comes from sth. on fire 火焰

The whole hotel went up in *flames* in minutes. 整个旅馆几分钟就烧毁了。

hike [haɪk]

① *n.* long walk, esp. in the country, taken for pleasure or exercise 远足，徒步旅行（尤指在乡间进行者）

go on a ten-mile *hike* 做一次十英里的徒步旅行

② *v.* to go for a long walk 做远足旅行；做徒步旅行

a *hiking* holiday 做远足活动的假日

inhabit [ɪnˈhæbɪt]

v. to live in (sth.); occupy 居住于（某处）；占据；栖居于

Vision is obviously more useful to species *inhabiting* clear open waters than to those living in turbid rivers and flooded plains. 很显然，视线对于栖息在清澈宽广的湖面上的物种要比对那些在湍急的河流或者洪水泛滥的平原上生活的物种作用更大。

inhabitant [ɪnˈhæbɪtənt]

n. person or animal living in a place（某地的）居民，住户，栖息的动物

The archaeological evidence shows that the natural history of Amazonia is tied to the activities of its prehistoric *inhabitants*. 考古学的证据显示亚马孙河流域的自然历史是与在那里的史前栖息者的活动联系在一起的。

limitation [ˌlɪmɪˈteɪʃn]   [近] confinement

n. condition, fact or circumstance that limits 起限制作用的条件、事实或环境；局限；限制

There are technical *limitations* to the amount of paper which can be recycled and some paper products cannot be collected for reuse. 技术的局限使对纸张的循环利用不能大量进行，一些纸制品也不能被收集并重新使用。

linguist [ˈlɪŋgwɪst]

n. a person who studies languages 语言学家

Linguists also make great use of structured sessions. 语言学家也充分利用了结构化的时间段。

mock [mɒk]   [同] ②ridicule

① *n.* (infml.)（in Britain）a practice exam that you do before the official one（英国）模拟考试

The *mocks* are in November. 模拟考试在 11 月份进行。

② *v.* to laugh at sb./sth. in an unkind way, esp. by copying what they say or do 嘲笑；（模仿）嘲弄

The other children ***mocked*** her, laughing behind their hands. 其他孩子学她的样子，用手捂着嘴笑。

mode [məʊd]

n. (fml.) a particular way of doing sth.; a particular type of sth. 方式；风格；样式

In Europe most cities are still designed for the old ***modes*** of transport. 在欧洲，大多数城市仍是依古老的运输模式设计。

moderate ['mɒdərət]   [同] temperate

adj. that is neither very good, large, hot, etc. nor very bad, small, cold, etc. 适度的；中等的

Even ***moderate*** amounts of the drug can be fatal. 这种药的用量即使不是很大也会致命。

nurture ['nɜːtʃə(r)]   [同] ②nurse

① *n.* care, encouragement and support given to sb./sth. while they are growing 养育；培养
② *v.* to help a plan, idea, feeling, etc. to develop 培育；培养

Indeed, many researchers now point to this harmony of nature and ***nurture*** to explain why musicians with absolute pitch show different levels of the talent. 事实上，现在许多学者都指出天赋和后天培养的协调性，以此解释为何有着音高辨别力的音乐家们会有不同程度的这方面的才能。

nutrition [njuː'trɪʃn]

n. the process by which living things receive the food necessary for them to grow and be healthy 营养；滋养

to study food science and ***nutrition*** 研究食物科学和营养

property ['prɒpəti]   [近] ①wealth

n. ①the thing or things that sb. owns 财产 ②a building, a piece of land, or both together 地产；房地产 ③a quality or power that a substance, plant, etc. has 特性

Property prices have shot up recently. 房地产价格最近飙升。

proportion [prə'pɔːʃn]   [同] percentage

n. a part or share of a whole 部分；份额

A substantial ***proportion*** of the population of modern societies engages in tourist practices. 现代社会的很大一部分人都旅行。

proposal [prə'pəʊzl]   [同] suggestion

n. a formal suggestion or plan; the act of making a suggestion 提议；建议

They judged that the time was right for the ***proposal*** of new terms for the trade agreement. 他们判断，提出贸易协定新条款的时机成熟了。

propose [prə'pəʊz]

v. to suggest sth. as a plan or course of action 提议；主张

In his speech he ***proposed*** that the UN should set up an emergency centre for the environment. 他在发言中提议联合国为环境成立一个紧急事务中心。

recollect [ˌrekə'lekt]   [同] remember

v. to succeed in calling (sth.) back to the mind 想起；记得；回忆起

As far as I ***recollect***, you came late. 我记得你来晚了。

recommend [ˌrekə'mend]   [同] advise

v. to suggest (a course of action, treatment, etc.); advise 建议（采取某种做法、对策等）；劝告

We do **recommend** that you buy the core books. 我们建议你买下这些核心书籍。

recover [rɪˈkʌvə(r)] [同] restore

v. to get back the control of (oneself, one's actions, one's emotions, etc.) 重新控制（自己、自己的行动、自己的情绪等）; 恢复

The skater quickly **recovered** his balance. 滑冰者很快恢复了平衡。

recreation [ˌrekrɪˈeɪʃn] [同] entertainment

n. (means of) refreshing or entertaining oneself after work; relaxation 业余消遣或娱乐（的方式）;（身心的）放松; 休憩

My favourite **recreation** is chess. 我最喜欢的娱乐是下国际象棋。

strategy [ˈstrætədʒi] [近] plan

n. plan or policy designed for a particular purpose 针对性措施; 对策; 策略

The convention presents fundamental **strategies** and approaches in achieving health. 大会提出一些实现健康的基本措施与方法。

strengthen [ˈstreŋθn] [同] reinforce

v. (cause sth./sb.) to become stronger （使某物／某人）更强

Sand was driven into the seabed to **strengthen** it. 沙被冲到了海底，进而加固了海床。

stress [stres] [同] ①strain ②emphasise

① *n.* continuous feelings of worry about your work or personal life, that prevent you from relaxing 压力; 忧虑

Yoga is excellent for relieving **stress**. 瑜伽减压效果明显。

② *v.* to put stress or emphasis on (sth.) 着重，强调（某物）; 重读（某音节）

She **stressed** the importance of a balanced diet. 她强调了均衡饮食的重要性。

stretch [stretʃ] [同] ①②extend

v. ①to make sth. bigger or looser by pulling it 拉长; 伸展 ②to straighten your arms, legs, or body to full length 伸展身体、四肢

Always **stretch** before exercising. 锻炼前一定先伸展一下四肢。

strict [strɪkt] [同] rigid

adj. expecting people to obey rules or to do what you say 严格的; 严厉的

Teachers need to be **strict**, but also fair. 老师应该严厉，但同时要公正。

toast [təʊst]

n. sliced bread made brown and crisp by heating under a grill, in a toaster, etc. 烤面包片（面包切成片后放在烤架下、面包片加热器等中烤黄、烤脆）

make some **toast** for breakfast 烤些面包片作早餐

toil [tɔɪl] [近] ①②work, labour

① *n.* (fml. or rhet.) hard or lengthy work 辛苦的或长时间的工作

after years of **toil** 辛苦地工作了多年之后

② *v.* (fml.) to work long or hard 长时间地或辛苦地工作

students **toiling** over their homework 辛辛苦苦做功课的学生

tolerance [ˈtɒlərəns] [同] endurance

n. willingness or ability to tolerate sb./sth. 容忍; 忍受; 宽容

We have to have a far greater **tolerance** of difference and a far greater respect for differences of view. 我们要对差异有更大的宽容性，要对不同的观点尤为尊重。

victim [ˈvɪktɪm]

n. sb. who suffers because of sth. bad that happens or because of an illness 受害者

victims of domestic abuse 家庭暴力的受害者

victory [ˈvɪktəri]   [同] triumph

n. the success you achieve when you win a battle, game, election, etc. 成功；胜利

The crowds were celebrating Italy's ***victory***. 人们在庆祝意大利队的胜利。

vigour [ˈvɪgə(r)]

n. physical or mental energy and determination 精力；活力

Holidays make it possible for you to return to your normal routine with renewed ***vigour*** and enthusiasm. 休假能让你带着活力和热情回到日常工作中去。

Take the Test

一、英汉互译

建立	_____	conceal	_____
居民	_____	linguist	_____
养育，培养	_____	mock	_____
营养	_____	proportion	_____
策略	_____	toil	_____

二、翻译句子

1）针灸是古代的一种医术。（ancient）

_____

2）我们建议你买下这些核心书籍。（recommend）

_____

3）我最喜欢的娱乐是下国际象棋。（recreation）

_____

4）瑜伽减压效果明显。（stress）

_____

Character cannot be developed in ease and quiet. Only through experience of trial and suffering can the soul be strengthened, vision cleared, ambition inspired, and success achieved.

要使性格有所发展并非简单之事，只有通过艰难和困苦的磨炼才能使心灵强化，视野开阔，雄心振奋，从而达到成功的目的。

——美国作家 海伦·凯勒（Helen Keller, American writer）

annoy [əˈnɔɪ]   [同] irritate [反] soothe

v. to make sb. slightly angry 使恼怒；使生气

It really *annoys* me when people forget to say thank you. 当有人连谢谢都忘记说时我确实感到不愉快。

annual [ˈænjʊəl]

adj. happening once a year 每年的；年度的

The books enable readers to calculate the daily, seasonal, and *annual* climatic conditions and predict their effects on health. 这些书能让读者计算每天、每个季度和每年的气候情况并预测这些情况对健康的影响。

bold [bəʊld]   [同] brave

adj. confident and brave; daring; enterprising 自信和勇敢的；大胆的；有进取心的

What we need is a strong leader, someone who is *bold* enough to make tough decisions. 我们所需要的是一个强势的领袖，一个可以做出大胆决策的人。

conceive [kənˈsiːv]   [同] think

v. to form (an idea, a plan, etc.) in the mind; imagine sth. 想出（主意、计划等）；构思

It was then that I *conceived* the notion of running away. 就在那时我产生了逃跑的念头。

concentrate [ˈkɒnsntreɪt]

v. to focus (one's attention, effort, etc.) exclusively and intensely on sth. 全神贯注，精神集中，专心致志（于某事物）

I can't *concentrate* (on my studies) with all that noise going on. 吵闹声不绝于耳，我无法集中注意力（学习）。

concept [ˈkɒnsept]   [同] idea

n. an idea of how sth. is, or how sth. should be done 概念

The *concept* of the rocket has been around for well over two thousand years. 火箭这个概念已经存在了两千多年。

concern [kənˈsɜːn]

① *n.* worry, anxiety 担心，焦虑

There is no cause for *concern*. 不必发愁。

② *v.* to be the business of (sb.); be important to; affect 是（某人）的事；对⋯有重要性；影响

Don't interfere in what doesn't *concern* you. 别管与自己无关的事。

diligent [ˈdɪlɪdʒənt]   [同] assiduous

adj. showing care and effort (in what one does); hard-working 认真刻苦的；勤勉的；勤奋的

a *diligent* worker 勤奋的工作者

dimension [daɪˈmenʃn]   [同] aspect

n. a part of a situation or a quality involved in it 方面；侧面

Good health is a major resource for social, economic and personal development and an important *dimension* of quality of life. 健康是社会、经济和个人发展的重要本钱，也是生活质量的一

个重要方面。

esteem [ɪˈstiːm]

n. （fml.）great respect and admiration; a good opinion of sb. 尊重；敬重；好评

She is held in high *esteem* by her colleagues. 她深受同事们的敬重。

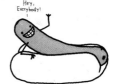

estimate [ˈestɪmət]　　　　　　　　　[同]①②value ②assess

① *n.* a judgement that you make without having the exact details or figures about the size, amount, cost, etc. of sth. (对数量、成本等的) 估计，估价

According to the best *estimates*, there are some 6,000 languages in the world. 据最准确估计，全世界大约有 6000 种语言。

② *v.* [ˈestɪmeɪt] to form an idea of the cost, size, value, etc. of sth., but without calculating it exactly 估价；估算

Police estimate the crowd at 30,000. 警方估计聚集的人有三万。

flash [flæʃ]

① *n.* a special bright light used when taking photographs indoors or when there is not much light 闪光灯

[习语] a flash in the pan 昙花一现(指成功)

② *v.* to shine suddenly and brightly for a short time, or to make sth. shine in this way 闪光；闪现

Red warning lights *flashed* on and off. 红色警报灯一闪一闪的。

flatter [ˈflætə(r)]

v. to praise (sb.) too much or insincerely, esp. in order to gain favour for oneself 恭维，奉承，讨好(某人)

If you *flatter* your mother a bit she might invite us all to dinner. 你要是奉承你母亲几句，说不定她会把我们全请去吃饭。

glue [gluː]

n. thick sticky liquid used for joining things 胶；胶水

He sticks to her like *glue*. 他如胶似漆地寸步不离开她。

goal [gəʊl]　　　　　　　　　　　　　[同]aim

n. object of one's efforts; target 努力的对象；目标

The company has set itself some stiff production *goals* for this year. 公司今年定下了很高的生产指标。

hinder [ˈhɪndə(r)]　　　　　　　　　[同]bar, block

v. to prevent the progress of sb./sth.; to obstruct or delay sb./sth. 阻碍，妨碍；阻挠或耽搁

Higher interest rates could *hinder* economic growth. 高利息率会阻碍经济增长。

hint [hɪnt]　　　　　　　　　　　　　[同]clue

n. subtle way of indicating to sb. what one is thinking or what one wants; indirect suggestion 暗示；示意；间接的提示

a strong/delicate *hint* 强烈的 / 微妙的暗示

inherit [ɪnˈherɪt]

v. to derive (qualities, etc.) from an ancestor 因遗传而获(特性等)

Research has shown that there is a genetic or *inherited* element to handedness. 研究表明有一种基因或遗传因素决定了用左手或右手的习惯。

initial [ɪˈnɪʃ(ə)l]　　　　　　　　　　[同]first

adj. of or at the beginning; first 开始的；最初的；第一个的

Initial sales figures have been very good. 最初的销售数字很不错。

link [lɪŋk] [同]①②bond, join

① *n.* a connection between two or more people or things 联系；连接

High levels of these hormones have been ***linked*** to heart disease. 心脏病与这些高含量的荷尔蒙有关。

② *v.* to connect in some way 相关联；联系

We're talking about the ***links*** between power and crime. 我们在讨论权利与犯罪间的联系。

literacy [ˈlɪtərəsi] [反] illiteracy

n. ability to read and write 读写能力

The development of ***literacy*** has far-reaching effects on general intellectual development. 读写能力的发展对一般智力发展有着深远的影响。

modest [ˈmɒdɪst] [同] humble

adj. not talking much about your own abilities or possessions 谦虚的；谦逊的

She's very ***modest*** about her success. 谈起自己的成功，她非常谦虚。

modify [ˈmɒdɪfaɪ] [同] change, alter

v. to change sth. slightly, esp. in order to make it more suitable for a particular purpose 调整；对…稍作修改；使更合适

If the predictions are not shown to be correct then you discard or ***modify*** your hypothesis. 如果预测被证实不正确，那么你需要放弃或者修正你的假设。

module [ˈmɒdjuːl]

n. a unit that can form part of a course of study, esp. at a college or university in Britain 单元（尤指英国大学课程的一部分）

The course consists of ten core ***modules*** and five optional ***modules***. 这门课程包括十个必修单元和五个选修单元。

oath [əʊθ] [同] swearword

n. a formal promise to do sth. or a formal statement that sth. is true 宣誓；誓言

Before giving evidence, witnesses in court have to take the ***oath***. 作证之前，证人必须当庭宣誓。

obedient [əˈbiːdiənt] [反] disobedient

adj. always doing what you are told to do, or what the law, a rule, etc. says you must do 服从的；顺从的

Is being faithful the same thing as being ***obedient***? 忠诚和顺从是一回事吗？

prospect [ˈprɒspekt] [同] vista

n. an idea of what might or will happen in the future 前景；展望

In business as a whole, there are a number of factors encouraging the ***prospect*** of greater equality in the workforce. 总体说来，在商业界有很多因素可以促使劳动力更为平等的前景实现。

prosper [ˈprɒspə(r)] [同] succeed

v. to develop in a successful way; to be successful, esp. financially 繁荣；成功

The economy ***prospered*** under his administration. 他主政期间经济繁荣了起来。

protein [ˈprəʊtiːn]

n. one of several natural substances that exist in food such as meat, eggs, and beans, and which your body needs in order to grow and remain strong and healthy 蛋白质

Ostrich meat is slightly higher in *protein* than beef. 鸵鸟肉的蛋白质含量略高于牛肉。

recycle [ˌriːˈsaɪkl]

v. to get（natural products）back from used material by treating it 再造；回收

As a result, industry's use of *recycled* fibres is expected to increase at twice the rate of virgin fibre over the coming years. 结果，在未来几年内工业循环纤维使用率预计将以两倍于原始纤维的速度增长。

redundant [rɪˈdʌndənt]　　　　　　　　　　　　　　　　　　　[同] wordy

adj.（usu. of language or art）not needed; superfluous; unnecessary 不必要的；冗赘的；多余的

The illustration had too much *redundant* detail. 解说中不必要的细节太多。

reference [ˈrefərəns]

n. the act of looking at sth. for information 查询；检索

For easy *reference*, the experimental changes in these two divisions will be labelled the 'participative programme'. 为了检索方便，这两个组实验性的改变将被标注为"参与程序"。

strike [straɪk]

v. to subject（sb./sth.）to an impact; hit（sb./sth.）使（某人／某物）遭受撞击；打，击，敲

She *struck* the desk with her knee. 她的膝盖撞上了桌子。

striking [ˈstraɪkɪŋ]　　　　　　　　　　　　　　　　　　　　[同] dramatic

adj. attracting attention or interest 引人注意的；显著的；饶有兴趣的

There is a *striking* contrast between the two interpretations. 这两种解释截然不同。

strip [strɪp]

n. a long narrow piece of paper, cloth, etc. 条，带

You will need a *strip* of stiff cardboard to make this hat. 做这顶帽子你需要一条硬纸板。

strive [straɪv]　　　　　　　　　　　　　　　　　　　　　　[同] endeavor

v.（fml.）to try very hard（to obtain or achieve sth.）努力，奋斗

strive to improve one's performance 努力提高演技

torch [tɔːtʃ]

n. small hand-held electric lamp powered by a battery 手电筒；电棒

Shine the *torch* on the lock while I try to get the key. 我插钥匙时，请用电筒照着锁。

total [ˈtəʊtl]　　　　　　　　　　　　　　　　　　　　　　　[同] whole

① *adj.* the number, amount, etc. that is the total 总的

② *n.* the final number or amount of things, people, etc. 总数

There were probably about 40 people there in *total*. 那儿大概总共有 40 人。

tough [tʌf]

adj. ① not easily cut, broken, or worn out 坚韧的；不易切开、打破或磨损的

as *tough* as leather 坚韧如皮革

② difficult to do or deal with 苦难的，艰难的

It was a *tough* race. 这是场艰难的比赛。

violate [ˈvaɪəleɪt]　　　　　　　　　　　　　　　　　　　　[反] obey

v. to disobey or do sth. against an official agreement, law, principle 侵犯；违反

The media regularly *violates* people's privacy. 媒体经常侵犯人们的隐私。

virtual [ˈvɜːtʃuəl]　　　　　　　　　　　　　　　　　　　　[反] ①actual

adj. ①almost or very nearly the thing described, so that any slight difference is not important 很接近的；实质上的 ②made, done, seen, etc. on the Internet or on a computer, rather than in the real world 虚拟的

The company has a *virtual* monopoly in this area of trade. 这家公司实质上已经垄断了这一领域的贸易。

virtually [ˈvɜːtʃuəli]

adv. almost; practically 几乎；实际上

Virtually all students will be exempt from the tax. 差不多所有的学生都会被豁免此税项。

Take the Test

一、英汉互译

年度的	_____	hint	_____
概念	_____	module	_____
最初的	_____	obedient	_____
读写能力	_____	prospect	_____
繁荣	_____	protein	_____

二、翻译句子

1）健康是社会、经济和个人发展的重要本钱，也是生活质量的一个重要方面。（dimension）

_____

2）据最准确估计，全世界大约有6000种语言。（estimate）

_____

3）这门课程包括十个必修单元和五个选修单元。（module）

_____

4）差不多所有的学生都会被豁免此税项。（virtually）

_____

Character cannot be developed in ease and quiet. Only through experience of trial and suffering can the soul be strengthened, vision cleared, ambition inspired, and success achieved.

要使性格有所发展并非简单之事，只有通过艰难和困苦的磨炼才能使心灵强化，视野开阔，雄心振奋，从而达到成功的目的。

——美国作家 海伦·凯勒（Helen Keller, American writer）

anticipate [ænˈtɪsɪpeɪt] 　　　　　　　　　　　　　　　　　　　　　　　　　[同]foresee

v. expect（sth.）期望，预料（某事物）

A good speaker is able to *anticipate* an audience's needs and concerns. 好的演讲者能够预料到听众的需求和他们感兴趣的话题。

antique [ænˈtiːk] 　　　　　　　　　　　　　　　　　　　　　　　　　　[近]①ancient

① *adj.* made in the ancient time and often valuable 古董的；古时的

② *n.* object that is old and valuable, esp. one that is of interest to collectors 文物；古董；古玩

an *antique* shop 古玩店

bond [bɒnd] 　　　　　　　　　　　　　　　　　　　　　　　　　　　　[近]contract

n. sth. that unites two or more people or groups, such as love, or a shared interest or idea 联系

The trade agreement helped to strengthen the *bonds* between the two countries. 这项贸易协定有助于加强两国之间的联系。

concise [kənˈsaɪs] 　　　　　　　　　　　　　　　[同]brief [反]redundant

adj. （of speech or writing）giving a lot of information in few words; brief（指语言或文字）简明的；言简意赅的

a *concise* summary/account 简明的摘要/报道

conclude [kənˈkluːd] 　　　　　　　　　[同]close, complete

v. come or bring（sth.）to an end（使某事物）结束

She *concluded* her talk with a funny story. 她以一个有趣的故事结束了演讲。

conclusion [kənˈkluːʒn] 　　　　　　　　　　　　　　　　　　　　　　[同]end

n. end 结束；结尾

There are perhaps two main *conclusions* to be drawn from the above discussion. 从上述讨论中或许可以得出两个主要结论。

diminish [dɪˈmɪnɪʃ] 　　　　　　　　　　　　　　　　　　　　　　　[同]reduce

v. （cause sth. to）become smaller or less; decrease 变小；变少

Heritage studies constitute a developing field, where it is realised that the world's cultural heritage is a *diminishing* resource which holds different meanings for different people. 文化遗产研究构成了一个不断发展的领域，在这一领域里，人们认识到世界的文化遗产是一个正在减少的资源，而这一资源对不同的民族有着不同的意义。

diploma [dɪˈpləʊmə]

n. certificate awarded for passing an examination, completing a course of study, etc. 毕业证书；毕业文凭

a one-year *diploma* course 一年制的文凭课程

disable [dɪsˈeɪbl] 　　　　　　　　　　　　　　　　　　　　　　　　[近]weaken

v. to make（sb.）unable to do sth., esp. by making a limb or limbs useless 使（某人）丧失能力；使残疾，使（某人）残废

a *disabled* child in a wheelchair 坐轮椅的残疾儿童

ethic [ˈeθɪk]

n. a general idea or belief that influences people's behaviour and attitudes 道德规范；伦理
Our professional ethic enjoins us to stay uncommitted and report the facts. 我们的职业道德要求我们要保持中立，报道事实真相。

ethnic [ˈeθnɪk]　　　　　　　　　　　　　　　　　　　　　　[同] racial

adj. connected with or belong to a nation, race or tribe that shares a cultural tradition 民族的；种族的；部落的
The students are from a variety of *ethnic* backgrounds. 学生们来自不同的民族背景。

evaluate [ɪˈvæljueɪt]　　　　　　　　　　　　　　　　　　　　[同] assess

v. to form an opinion of the amount, value or quality of sth. after thinking about it carefully 估值；评价；评估
The worth of the output is *evaluated* independently. 产出的价值需要独立评估。

flavour [ˈfleɪvə(r)]　　　　　　　　　　　　　　　　　　　　　[同] taste

n. taste and smell, esp. of food 味道与气味（尤指食物的）
Adding salt to food improves the *flavour*. 食物中加盐可以提味。

flaw [flɔː]　　　　　　　　　　　　　　　　　　　　　　　　[同] defect

v. cause (sth.) to have a crack or fault (in an object or in material); make sth. imperfect 使（某物）有缺陷
If Whorf was correct in his assumption then any experiments designed to support or disprove his theory will be *flawed*. 如果沃尔夫的假设正确，那么为证实或反驳他的理论所做的任何试验都是有漏洞的。

historian [hɪˈstɔːriən]

n. sb. who studies history, or the history of a particular thing 历史学家
Most *historians* of technology credit the Chinese with its discovery. 大部分技术史学家都将此发明归于中国人。

historic [hɪˈstɒrɪk]

adj. famous or important in history 历史上著名的或重要的
Today is a *historic* occasion for our country. 在我国，今天是具有历史意义的日子。

initiate [ɪˈnɪʃieɪt]　　　　　　　　　　　　　　　　　　　　　[同] begin

v. (fml.) to put (a scheme, etc.) into operation; cause (sth.) to begin 开始实施（计划等）；发起，创始，开始（某事物）
The article *initiated* a debate on the task of medicine, its professional obligations, social position and moral justification. 这篇文章引发了一场关于药物的作用、专业义务、社会地位以及道德合理性的辩论。

injection [ɪnˈdʒekʃən]

n. an act of putting a drug into sb.'s body using a special needle 注射；打针
The only sure treatment is antibiotics, preferably by *injection*. 唯一保险的治疗法就是抗生素，而且最好是注射。

injury [ˈɪndʒəri]　　　　　　　　　　　　　　　　　　　　　[同] damage

n. physical harm to a living being（对生物体的）伤害，损害
The body's response to back *injury* can be very negative. 身体对于背部伤害的反应会非常严重。

literal [ˈlɪtərəl]

adj. being the basic or usual meaning of a word or phrase 字面意义的

Pictures are more than *literal* representations. 图片远远超过了文字的表达。

literally ['lɪtərəli]　　　　　　　　　　　　　　　　　[同] word for word

adv. in a literal manner; exactly 照原文地; 精确地

It is impossible to translate all proverbs *literally*. 谚语不可能都逐字直译。

moist [mɔɪst]　　　　　　　　　　　　　　　　　　　[同] damp

adj. slightly wet 微湿的; 湿润的

Water the plants regularly to keep the soil *moist*. 定时浇灌植物以保持土壤湿润。

monitor ['mɒnɪtə(r)]　　　　　　　　　　　　　　　[同] ②observe

① *n.* a piece of equipment used to check or record sth. 监控器; 监测器

a heart *monitor* 心脏监测器

② *v.* to watch and check sth. over a period of time in order to see how it develops, so that you can make any necessary changes 监视; 检测

Each student's progress is closely *monitored*. 每一位同学的学习情况都受到密切的关注。

obesity [əʊ'biːsəti]

n. being obese 过度肥胖

Obesity is a problem for many people in western countries. 西方国家很多人都有过度肥胖的问题。

object [əb'dʒekt]　　　　　　　　　　　　　　　　　[同] oppose

v. to say that you disagree with; disapprove of or oppose sth. 不同意; 反对

Many local people *object* to the building of the new airport. 许多当地的居民都反对兴建新机场。

objection [əb'dʒekʃn]　　　　　　　　　　　　　　[同] opposition

n. a reason why you do not like or are opposed to sth.; a statement about this 反对的理由; 异议

I have no *objection* to him coming to stay. 我不反对他来小住。

protest ['prəʊtest]　　　　　　　　　　　　　　　　[同] object to

n. the expression of strong disagreement with or opposition to sth.; a statement or an action that shows this 抗议; 抗议书(或行动)

Thousands of ordinary workers marched on the streets in *protest* of low wages and poor working conditions. 数以千计的普通工人上街游行, 抗议过低的工资和过差的工作条件。

proverb ['prɒvɜːb]　　　　　　　　　　　　　　　　[同] saying

n. a well-known phrase or sentence that gives advice or says sth. that is generally true 格言; 谚语

'Don't put all your eggs in one basket' is a *proverb*. "不要把全部鸡蛋放在同一个篮子里"(切勿孤注一掷)是一句谚语。

refine [rɪ'faɪn]　　　　　　　　　　　　　　　　　　[同] purify

v. to remove impurities from (sth.); purify 从(某物)中除去杂质; 精炼; 提纯

refine sugar/oil/ore 制糖/炼油/提炼矿石

reflect [rɪ'flekt]　　　　　　　　　　　　　　　　　[同] mirror

v. to show or be a sign of a particular situation or feeling 表现; 反映; 代表

A building *reflects* the scientific and technological achievements of the age. 一座大楼反映出一个时代的科学与技术成就。

reform [rɪ'fɔːm]

n. a change or changes made to a system or organization in order to improve it 改革; 改造

The government announced a much-needed program of economic *reform*. 政府宣布了一项急

需的经济改革计划。

refreshing [rɪ'freʃɪŋ]

adj. giving new strength or vigour; restoring or reviving 给人以新的力量或活力的；提神的

This breeze is very *refreshing*. 这微风使人心旷神怡。

stroke [strəʊk]

n. (medical) sudden attack of illness in the brain that can cause loss of the power to move, speak clearly, etc. 中风

Stress has been linked with many so-called modern diseases such as heart disease, *strokes* and even cancer. 压力与许多所谓的现代病，如心脏病、中风、甚至癌症有联系。

structure ['strʌktʃə(r)]　　　　　　　　　　　　　　　　　　　　[近] building

n. the way in which the parts of sth. are connected with each other and form a whole 结构；组织

They also study the economic and social *structures*, institutions and culture of the relevant countries. 他们还研究相关国家的经济和社会结构、制度和文化。

studio ['stjuːdiəʊ]

n. ①workroom of a painter, sculptor, photographer, etc. (画家、雕塑家、摄影师等的) 工作室，画室，雕塑室，摄影室 ②a small apartment with one main room 单间公寓

art *studio* 美术工作室

stuff [stʌf]　　　　　　　　　　　　　　　　　　　　　　　　　　[同] ①thing

n. ①material of which sth. is made 原料；材料 ②used when talking about different activities, subjects, or ideas, when you do not say exactly what these are …之类的；等等

Real life is the *stuff* (i.e. subject matter) of all good novels. 现实生活是所有优秀小说的题材。

I've got so much *stuff* to do this weekend. 这个周末有太多事儿要做了。

towel ['taʊəl]

n. piece of absorbent cloth or paper for drying oneself or wiping things dry 毛巾；手巾；巾

a paper *towel* 纸巾

toxic ['tɒksɪk]　　　　　　　　　　　　　　　　　　　　　　　　[同] poisonous

adj. poisonous 有毒的

a highly *toxic* pesticide 毒性很强的杀虫剂

trace [treɪs]　　　　　　　　　　　　　　　　　　　　　　　　[同] ①②track

① *n*. mark, track, sign, etc. showing what has existed or happened 踪迹；痕迹；形迹

traces of prehistoric habitation 史前居民的遗迹

② *v*. to find or discover sb./sth. by looking carefully for them 查出，找到

I have been unable to *trace* the letter you mentioned. 我没能查到你提到的那封信。

track [træk]

① *n*. a line or series of marks left by a moving vehicle, person, animal, etc. 踪迹；足迹；痕迹

② *v*. to search for a person or animal by following the marks they leave behind them on the ground, their smell, etc. 追踪；跟踪

Baleen whales can *track* objects with vision underwater. 须鲸可以在水下凭视觉追踪物体。

virtue ['vɜːtʃuː]　　　　　　　　　　　　　　　　　　　　　　　[同] merit

n. an attractive or useful quality 优点；长处

The *virtue* of job descriptions is that they lessen role ambiguity. 对工作的描述好处在于可以减少任务的不明确性。

visa ['viːzə]

n. a stamp or mark put in your passport by officials of a foreign country that gives you

permission to enter, pass through or leave their country（护照的）
签证

entry/tourist/transit *visa* 入境 / 旅游 / 过境签证

Take the Test >>

一、英汉互译

古玩	_____	concise	_____
文凭	_____	ethic	_____
味道	_____	initiate	_____
照原文的	_____	obesity	_____
格言	_____	toxic	_____

二、翻译句子

1）好的演讲者能够预料到听众的需求和他们感兴趣的话题。（anticipate）

_____

2）学生们来自不同的民族背景。（ethnic）

_____

3）在我国，今天是具有历史意义的日子。（historic）

_____

4）这个周末有太多事儿要做了。（stuff）

_____

Character cannot be developed in ease and quiet. Only through experience of trial and suffering can the soul be strengthened, vision cleared, ambition inspired, and success achieved.

要使性格有所发展并非简单之事，只有通过艰难和困苦的磨炼才能使心灵强化，视野开阔，雄心振奋，从而达到成功的目的。

——美国作家 海伦·凯勒（Helen Keller, American writer）

anxiety [æŋˈzaɪəti]　　　　　　　　　[同] concern, unease [反] security

n. the feeling of being very worried about sth. 焦虑

It can help if you discuss your *anxieties* with someone. 把你的焦虑跟别人聊聊或许会管用。

anyway [ˈeniweɪ]

adv. whatever the facts may be 无论如何；即使如此；至少

Anyway, you can try. 至少你可以试试。

apologize [əˈpɒlədʒaɪz]

v. make an apology; say one is sorry 道歉；赔不是

I don't know why I *apologized*, because I didn't do anything wrong. 真不知道当时为什么要道歉，我没做错任何事。

bonus [ˈbəʊnəs]

n. payment added to what is usual or expected, e.g. an extra dividend paid to shareholders in a company or to holders of an insurance policy 额外津贴；奖金；红利

Company employees received a £25 Christmas *bonus*. 公司雇员得到 25 英镑的圣诞节礼金。

conduct [kənˈdʌkt]　　　　　　　　　　　　　　　　　[近] direct

v. to carry out a particular activity or process, especially in order to get information or prove facts 实施，进行

Psychologists have *conducted* studies showing that people become less sceptical and more optimistic when the weather is sunny. 心理学家们开展的研究表明当天气晴朗时，人们会少些不信任，更为乐观。

conference [ˈkɒnfərəns]

n. discussion or exchange of views 讨论（会）；会议

Many international *conferences* are held in Geneva. 许多国际会议在日内瓦举行。

confidence [ˈkɒnfɪdəns]　　　　　　　　　　　[同] ①trust ②faith

n. ①the feeling that you can trust sb. or sth. to be good, work well, or produce good results 信任；信赖 ②the belief that you have the ability to do things well or deal with situations successfully 信心

She's a good student, but she lacks *confidence*. 她是个好学生，但缺乏自信。

disaster [dɪˈzɑːstə(r)]

n. event that causes great harm or damage, e.g. a fire, a serious defeat, the loss of a large sum of money 灾难；灾祸

natural *disasters* 自然灾害

discipline [ˈdɪsɪplɪn]

n. ①branch of knowledge; subject of instruction 学科；教学科目 ②the ability to control your own behaviour, so that you do what you are expected to do 纪律

Statistics is a branch of mathematics that is used in the study of many *disciplines* from physics, through to the social sciences. 统计学是广泛应用于从物理学到社会科学的各种学科的数学分支。

even [ˈiːvn]   [同] equal

adj. equal or the same for each person, team, place, etc. 相等的；均等的

Our scores are now *even*. 我们的比分现在相等。

eventually [ɪˈventʃuəli]   [同] yet, finally

adv. at the end of a period of time or a series of events 最后，终于

She hopes to get a job on the local newspaper and *eventually* work for *China Daily*. 她希望先在当地报纸找到一份工作，最终在《中国日报》工作。

flee [fliː]   [同] escape

v. to run or hurry away; escape (esp. from danger, threat, etc.) 逃跑；(尤指遇到危险、威胁等)逃离

The customers *fled* （from the bank） when the alarm sounded. 警铃响起，顾客纷纷(从银行)逃走。

flexible [ˈfleksəbl]   [反] inflexible

adj. easily changed to suit new conditions 易适应新情况的；可变通的；灵活的

Our plans are quite *flexible*. 我们的计划十分灵活。

gossip [ˈɡɒsɪp]

n. （derog.） casual talk about the affairs of other people, typically including rumour and critical comments 闲言碎语；八卦

She's too fond of idle *gossip*. 她太爱听飞短流长的话了。

govern [ˈɡʌvən]   [同] rule

v. to officially and legally control a country and make all the decisions about taxes, laws, public services, etc. 统治；治理

The *governing* party controls two-thirds of the parliament. 执政党控制了议会三分之二的席位。

holistic [həʊˈlɪstɪk]

adj. considering a whole thing or being to be more than a collection of parts 整体的；全面的

a *holistic* approach to life 对生命的整体分析

hollow [ˈhɒləʊ]

① *adj.* sunken; deeply set 凹的；凹陷的

He was short and thin, with a sharp nose and *hollow* eyes. 他又矮又瘦，高鼻梁，两眼深陷下去。

② *v.* to make a hole or empty space by removing the inside part of sth. 掏空；挖空

innocent [ˈɪnəsnt]   [同] guiltless

adj. not guilty （of wrongdoing） 无辜的；无罪的；清白的

Nobody would believe that I was *innocent*. 没人相信我是无罪的。

innovate [ˈɪnəveɪt]

v. to start to use new ideas, methods, or inventions 创新

The company has successfully *innovated* new products and services. 公司成功地推出了新的产品和服务。

input [ˈɪnpʊt]

n. ideas, advice, money, or effort that you put into a job or activity in order to help it succeed 放入；投入；输入

Employees will perceive that rewards or outcomes are equitable and equal to the *inputs* given.

雇员会察觉到回报或者产出是公平的并且与投入持平。

monopoly [mə'nɒpəli]

n. the complete control of trade in particular goods or the supply of a particular service; a type of goods or a service that is controlled in this way 垄断；专营服务

In the past central government had a ***monopoly*** on television broadcasting. 过去，中央政府对电视节目播放实行垄断。

monster ['mɒnstə(r)] [同] freak

n. an imaginary creature that is very large, ugly and frightening 怪兽；怪物

a ***monster*** with three heads 三只头的怪兽

mood [muːd]

n. the way you are feeling at a particular time 情绪；心情

She's in a good ***mood*** today. 她今天心情很好。

objective [əb'dʒektɪv] [同] ①goal

① *n.* sth. that you are trying to achieve 目标；目的

The prime ***objective*** of the benchmarking process was to compare a range of service delivery processes. 定一个标准流程的最初目的是为了比较一系列的服务流程。

② *adj.* based on facts, or making a decision that is based on facts rather than on your feelings or beliefs 客观的

Is there such a thing as '***objective***' reporting? 天底下有所谓的"客观"报道吗？

oblige [ə'blaɪdʒ] [同] compel

v. to force sb. to do sth., by law, because it is a duty, etc. (以法律、义务等)强迫，迫使

Parents are ***obliged*** by law to send their children to school. 法律规定父母必须送子女入学。

provoke [prə'vəʊk] [同] irritate

v. to say or do sth. that you know will annoy sb. so that they react in an angry way 挑衅；激怒

The lawyer claimed his client was ***provoked*** into acts of violence by the defendant. 律师声称，他的当事人是受到被告的挑衅才采取暴力行动的。

psychology [saɪ'kɒlədʒi]

n. ① the study of the mind and how it influences people's behaviour 心理学 ② the mental processes involved in believing in sth. or doing a certain activity 心理；心理过程

People who study ***psychology*** never seem able to apply it to real life. 好像研究心理学的人从来没能把这门学问用到实际生活中来。

pulse [pʌls]

n. (usu. sing.) regular beating of the arteries as blood is pumped through them by the heart, esp. as felt at the wrist 脉搏

The doctor listened to his breathing and checked his ***pulse***. 大夫听了他的呼吸并测了脉搏。

refreshment [rɪ'freʃmənt]

n. (pl.) snacks 小吃；点心

Light ***refreshments*** (e.g. ice-cream, crisps, chocolate) are available during the interval. 中间休息时有些点心(如冰激凌、炸土豆片、巧克力)。

refund [rɪ'fʌnd]

① *n.* ['riːfʌnd] an amount of money that is given back to you if you are not satisfied with the goods or services that you have paid for 退款；退费

② *v.* to pay back (money received); reimburse (expenses incurred) 退还(所收的钱); 偿付(花去的费用)

Postage costs will be *refunded* to you. 邮费将退还给你。

regarding [rɪ'gɑːdɪŋ]　　　　　　　　　　　　　　　　　　　　[同] about

prep. with reference to (sb./sth.); concerning 对于(某人/某事物); 关于; 至于

You can make an appointment to see your tutors if you need any advice *regarding* your studies. 如果你需要关于学习的建议, 你可以约见你的指导老师。

subjective [səb'dʒektɪv]　　　　　　　　　　　　　　　　　　[反] objective

adj. (of ideas, feelings, etc.) existing in the mind and not produced by things outside the mind (指思想、感情等)主观的(属于自我意识方面的)

Talent is as *subjective* as intelligence. 才干与智力同样是主观的。

submit [səb'mɪt]

v. to give sth. (to sb./sth.) so that it may be considered, decided on, etc. (向某人/某事物)提交或呈递某事物(以供考虑、裁决等)

Employees are invited to *submit* their ideas for discussion. 员工被邀请提出他们的建议以供讨论。

subscribe [səb'skraɪb]

① *n.* subscription 订阅; 订购

② *v.* (agree to) buy (a newspaper, periodical, etc.) regularly over a period of time 订阅; 订购(报刊等)

The magazine is trying to get more readers to *subscribe*. 该杂志正大力发展新订户。

subsequent ['sʌbsɪkwənt]　　　　　　　　　　　　　　　[同] succedent, ensuing

adj. later; following 后来的; 随后的

Tang civilization left a rich legacy to *subsequent* centuries. 唐代的文明为后来的几个世纪留下了丰富的遗产。

subsidize ['sʌbsɪdaɪz]　　　　　　　　　　　　　　　　　[同] finance

v. to give a subsidy to (sth./sb.) 给(某事物/某人)津贴或补贴; 资助或补助(某人/某事物)

They *subsidize* the exploitation and consumption of natural resources. 他们给开发与消费自然资源以补贴。

tradition [trə'dɪʃn]　　　　　　　　　　　　　　　　　　　　[近] heritage

n. passing of beliefs or customs from one generation to the next, esp. without writing 信仰或风俗的世代相传(尤指无文字记载的); 传统

By *tradition*, people play practical jokes on 1 April. 按照传统风俗, 四月一日可以搞恶作剧。

tragedy ['trædʒɪdi]　　　　　　　　　　　　　　　　　　　[近] misfortune

n. serious play with a sad ending 悲剧

Shakespeare's *tragedies* and comedies 莎士比亚的悲剧和喜剧

tragic ['trædʒɪk]

adj. causing great sadness, esp. because extremely unfortunate; having terrible consequences 悲惨的; 悲痛的; 可悲的

Hers is a *tragic* story. 她的经历十分悲惨。

visible ['vɪzəbl]

adj. that can be seen 看得见的; 可见的

Most stars are not *visible* to the naked eye. 大多数星星肉眼看不见。

vision [ˈvɪʒn]　　　　　　　　　　　　　　　　　　　　　　　[同] sight

n. the ability to see; the area that you can see from a particular position 视力；视野

Cats have good night *vision*. 猫在夜间视力好。

visual [ˈvɪʒuəl]

adj. of or connected with seeing or sight 视力的；视觉的

The building makes a tremendous *visual* impact. 这栋建筑物给人以极其深刻的视觉印象。

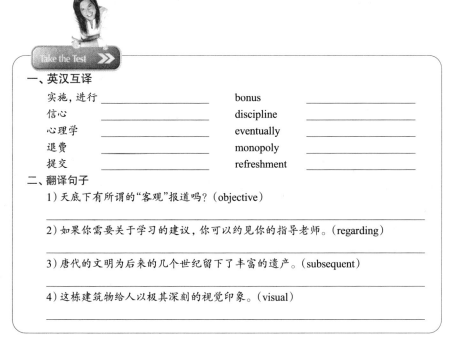

一、英汉互译

实施，进行	_____	bonus	_____
信心	_____	discipline	_____
心理学	_____	eventually	_____
退费	_____	monopoly	_____
提交	_____	refreshment	_____

二、翻译句子

1）天底下有所谓的"客观"报道吗？（objective）

_____

2）如果你需要关于学习的建议，你可以约见你的指导老师。（regarding）

_____

3）唐代的文明为后来的几个世纪留下了丰富的遗产。（subsequent）

_____

4）这栋建筑物给人以极其深刻的视觉印象。（visual）

_____

Character cannot be developed in ease and quiet. Only through experience of trial and suffering can the soul be strengthened, vision cleared, ambition inspired, and success achieved.

要使性格有所发展并非简单之事，只有通过艰难和困苦的磨炼才能使心灵强化，视野开阔，雄心振奋，从而达到成功的目的。

——美国作家 海伦·凯勒（Helen Keller, American writer）

apparent [ə'pærənt]   [同] obvious, evident

adj. clearly seen or understood; obvious 清楚易见的；明显的；显然的

This phenomenon has become increasingly *apparent* in modern industrialized societies. 这个现象在现代工业社会里变得越来越明显。

appeal [ə'piːl]   [同] attract, fascinate

v. be attractive or interesting（to sb.）有吸引力；（使某人）感兴趣

You should read things of general interest that *appeal* to you. 你应该读一些吸引你的大家都感兴趣的东西。

booking ['bʊkɪŋ]

n. （esp. BrE）an arrangement that you make in advance to buy a ticket to travel somewhere, go to the theatre, etc. 预订

Can I make a *booking* for Friday afternoon? 我可以订星期五下午的票吗？

confine [kən'faɪn]   [同] restrict, imprison

v. to keep（a person or an animal）in a restricted space 限制在某空间以内

Is it cruel to *confine* a bird in a cage? 把鸟关在笼子里残忍吗？

confirm [kən'fɜːm]   [同] verify [反] deny

v. ①to show that sth. is definitely true, especially by providing more proof 证实；证明正确性
②to tell sb. that a possible arrangement, date, or situation is now definite or official 确认

I'll call the hotel and *confirm* our reservations. 我会打电话给酒店确认我们的预订。

conflict ['kɒnflɪkt]

① *n.* a state of disagreement or argument between people, groups, countries, etc. 矛盾；分歧

the *conflict* between tradition and innovation 传统和创新间的矛盾
② *v.* [kən'flikt] to be in opposition or disagreement 不合；不一致；冲突

The results of the studies about environmental issues suggest that older children seem to acquire the ability to appreciate, value and evaluate *conflicting* views. 关于环境问题的研究结果显示年龄大点的儿童好像具备了理解、尊重和评估相互矛盾的观点的能力。

discount ['dɪskaʊnt]   [近] deduction

n. amount of money taken off the cost of sth. 从某物的价格中扣去的数目；折扣

We give a 10% *discount* for cash, i.e. for immediate payment. 即刻付款，我们予以九折优惠。

evidence ['evɪdəns]

n. facts or signs that show clearly that sth. exists or is true 证据

At present we have no *evidence* of life on other planets. 现今我们没有任何证据证明在其他星球上存在着生命。

evident ['evɪdənt]   [同] obvious

adj. easy to see, notice, or understand 明显的

It was *evident* that she was unhappy. 很明显，她不开心。

float [fləʊt]　　　　　　　　　　　　　　　　　　　　　　　[同] drift

v. to stay or move on the surface of a liquid or in the air without sinking 漂浮；飘浮

She spent the whole afternoon *floating* on her back in the pool. 她整个下午都在游泳池里漂着。

grab [græb]　　　　　　　　　　　　　　　　　　　　　　　[同] seize

v. to grasp sth. suddenly or roughly; snatch sth. selfishly or rudely 抢；抓；抢夺

When I gave him the chance, he *grabbed* it at once. 我给他这一机会，他立刻抓住不放。

holy [ˈhəʊli]

adj. associated with God or with religion; of God 与神或宗教有关的；神的；上帝的

the *Holy* Bible/Scriptures 圣经

homestay [ˈhəʊmsteɪ]

n. the period abroad while living in local resident's home（在国外的访问者）在当地居民家居住的时期

The exchange student is looking for *homestay*. 这个交换生在找寄宿家庭。

inquire [ɪnˈkwaɪə(r)]　　　　　　　　　　　　　　　　　　[同] ask

(= enquire) *v.* (fml.) to ask to be told sth. (by sb.) 讯问

She *inquired* of me most politely whether I wished to continue. 她非常有礼貌地问我是否想继续下去。

inquiry [ɪnˈkwaɪəri]

n. investigation 调查；查究

Hypotheses provide the initiative and incentive for the *inquiry* and influence the method. 众多的假设为调查提供了主动性与鼓励，并影响着调查的方法。

insane [ɪnˈseɪn]　　　　　　　　　　　　　　　　　　　　　[反] sane

adj. not sane; mad; senseless 精神失常的；疯狂的；愚蠢的

The whole idea sounds absolutely *insane* to me. 整个想法在我看来完全不可理喻。

literature [ˈlɪtrətʃə(r)]

n. ①writings that are valued as works of art, esp. fiction, drama and poetry (as contrasted with technical books and journalism) 文学；文学作品

She taught English *Literature* at my old high school and we've kept in touch through letters over the years. 她在我原来的高中教英国文学，这些年来我们一直保持通信。

②all the books, articles, etc. on a particular subject 文献

literature on the history of science 有关科学历史的文献

monument [ˈmɒnjumənt]

n. a building, column, status, etc. built to remind people of a famous person or event 纪念碑（或馆、堂、像等）

A *monument* to him was erected in St. Paul's Cathedral. (人们)在圣保罗大教堂为他修了一块纪念碑。

morality [məˈræləti]

n. principles concerning right and wrong or good and bad behaviour 道德；道德准则

Standards of *morality* seem to be dropping. 道德标准似乎在下降。

motivation [ˌməʊtɪˈveɪʃn]　　　　　　　　　　　　　　　　[同] stimulus

n. sth. that motivates; an inducement or incentive 动力；提供动机的事物

He's intelligent enough but he lacks *motivation*. 他很聪明，但缺乏积极性。

observation [ˌɒbzə'veɪʃn] [同] notice

n. the act of watching sb./sth. carefully for a period of time, esp. to learn sth. 观察；观测

But further *observation* revealed two curious facts. 进一步观察会发现两个有趣的事实。

observe [əb'zɜːv]

v. to watch sb./sth. carefully, esp. to learn sth. 观察；注视

We asked them questions about what they'd *observed* or experienced. 我们就他们观察到或经历的事情向他们提问。

obsess [əb'ses]

v. to completely fill your mind so that you cannot think of anything else 使痴迷；使迷恋

The need to produce the most exciting newspaper story *obsesses* most journalists. 大多数记者梦寐以求的就是写出最撼动人心的新闻报道来。

obtain [əb'teɪn] [同] acquire

v. (fml.) to get sth., esp. by making an effort (尤指经过努力)获得；赢得

I finally managed to *obtain* a copy of the report. 我终于设法弄到了这份报告的一个副本。

punctual ['pʌŋktʃuəl]

adj. happening or doing sth. at the agreed or proper time 按时的；准时的；守时的

Dinner is served at seven; please try to be *punctual*. 晚饭七点开始，请尽量准时。

purity ['pjʊərəti]

n. state or quality of being pure 纯净；纯洁；纯度

test the *purity* of the water 检测水的纯度

regardless [rɪ'gɑːdləs] [同] despite

adv. (infml.) paying no attention to sb./sth. 不加理会；不顾

Some researchers even claim that we could all develop the skill, *regardless* of our musical talent. 一些研究者甚至声称不管是否有音乐才能，我们都能够发展这项技能。

region ['riːdʒən] [同] area

n. a large area of a country or of the world, usually without exact limits 区域；地区

Evidence gathered in recent years from anthropology and archaeology indicates that the *region* has supported a series of indigenous cultures for eleven thousand years. 据最近几年收集的人类学和考古学证据显示，这个地区在一万一千年里孕育了一系列的本土文化。

register ['redʒɪstə(r)] [同] enroll

v. formally record (a name, an event, a sale, etc.) in a list 登记；注册；记录

Population surveys are based on how many people are *registered* as being resident in the city. 人口数量普查是基于登记的城镇居民的数量。

regular ['regjələ(r)] [同] orderly [反] irregular

adj. happening, coming or done repeatedly at times or places which are the same distance apart 有规律的；定期的；定时的

You will also be expected to write essays on a *regular* basis. 你们将被要求定期写一些文章。

regulate ['regjuleɪt] [同] arrange

v. to control an activity or process, especially by rules 管理；调控

strict rules *regulating* the use of chemicals in food 限制食品中化学成分使用的严格规定

subsidy ['sʌbsɪdi]

n. money that is paid by a government or organization to make prices lower 补助金；补贴

Without state *subsidies*, the railways couldn't survive. 没有政府的补贴，铁路系统难以为继。

substance ['sʌbstəns]

n. a particular type of solid, liquid, or gas 物质；物品

cancer causing *substances* 致癌物质

substitute ［ˈsʌbstɪtjuːt］

n. person or thing that replaces, acts for or serves as sb. or sth. else 代替、替换或代理的人或事物；代理人；代用品

The manager was unable to attend but sent his deputy as a *substitute*. 经理不能出席，但是派了个副手作代表。

subtitle ［ˈsʌbˌtaɪtl］

n. words printed on a film that translate the dialogue of a foreign film, give those of a silent film or（on television）supply dialogue for deaf viewers 字幕

This TV programme has *subtitles* in your own language. 这个电视节目有你母语的字幕。

subtract ［səbˈtrækt］ ［同］reduce

v. to take（a number or quantity）away from（another number, etc.）从（某数等）中减去（某数或量）

subtract 6 from 99 99 减 6

trait ［treɪt］ ［同］quality, characteristic

n. element in sb.'s personality; distinguishing characteristic 人的个性；显著的特点；特征

His greatest character *trait* is his honesty. 他最大的性格特征就是诚实。

tram ［træm］

n. public passenger vehicle, usu. driven by electricity, running on rails laid along the streets of a town（有轨的）电车

That special *tram* was run to enable people to view a solar eclipse? 那辆特别的电车是为人们观察日食而运行的吗？

vital ［ˈvaɪtl］ ［同］essential

adj. necessary or essential in order for sth. to succeed or exist 必不可少的；对…极其重要的

Reading is of *vital* importance in language learning. 阅读在语言学习中至关重要。

vivid ［ˈvɪvɪd］

adj.（of memories, a description, etc.）producing very clear pictures in your mind 清晰的；生动的；逼真的

He gave a *vivid* account of his life as a fighter pilot. 他生动地描述了他当战斗机飞行员的生活。

vocational ［vəʊˈkeɪʃənl］ ［同］professional

adj. connected with the skills, knowledge, etc. that you need to have in order to do a particular job 职业的；职业技术的

a *vocational* training institute 一个职业培训学院

volcano ［vɒlˈkeɪnəʊ］

n. a mountain with a large opening at the top through which gases and lava are forced out into the air, or have been in the past 火山

An active *volcano* may erupt at any time. 活火山会随时喷发。

Take the Test ≫

一、英汉互译

明显的 _____ confine _____

矛盾,分歧 _____ inquiry _____

证据 _____ literature _____

准时的 _____ substitute _____

补贴 _____ vocational _____

二、翻译句子

1) 道德标准似乎在下降。(morality)

_____

2) 晚饭七点开始,请尽量准时。(punctual)

_____

3) 你们将被要求定期写一些文章。(regular)

_____

4) 阅读在语言学习中至关重要。(vital)

_____

Only those who have the patience to do simple things perfectly ever acquire the skill to do difficult things easily.

只有有耐心圆满完成简单工作的人,才能够轻而易举地完成困难的事。

——德国剧作家、诗人 席勒(Friedrich Schiller, German dramatist and poet)

appearance [əˈpɪərəns] [同] look

n. the way sb. or sth. looks to other people 外观；容貌

You shouldn't judge by *appearances*. 你不应该以貌取人。

appetite [ˈæpɪtaɪt] [近] desire

n. a desire for food 胃口；食欲

Until recently, research and treatment for obesity had concentrated on drugs to decrease *appetite*.

直到最近，对肥胖的研究与治疗都集中于用药物降低食欲。

boom [buːm]

v. to have a period of rapid growth; to become bigger, more successful, etc. 迅速发展；激增；繁荣昌盛

The use of glass as art is *booming*. 玻璃艺术品行业的发展欣欣向荣。

boost [buːst] [同] ①②raise, increase

① *v.* to increase the strength or value of (sth.); help or encourage (sb./sth.) 增强（某事物）的力量；促进（某人／某事物）

The unexpected win *boosted* the team's morale. 意外的胜利鼓舞了全队的士气。

② *n.* increase; help; encouragement 增加；帮助；鼓励

give sb.'s confidence a *boost* 增强某人的信心

conform [kənˈfɔːm] [同] comply, obey

v. to keep to or comply with (generally accepted rules, standards, etc.) 符合或遵守（公认的规则、准则等）

Students can be expelled for refusing to *conform* to school rules. 如果拒不服从学校的规章，学生会被开除。

confront [kənˈfrʌnt] [同] face, encounter

v. to make sb. face or consider sb./sth. unpleasant, difficult, etc. 使某人面对或正视令人不快、令人头疼等的人／事物

Adults and children are frequently *confronted* with statements about the alarming rate of loss of tropical rainforests. 无论大人还是孩子都经常会遇到关于热带雨林正以惊人的速度消失的报道。

confuse [kənˈfjuːz]

v. to make (sb.) unable to think clearly; puzzle; bewilder 把（某人）弄糊涂；使迷惑；使为难

They *confused* me by asking so many questions. 他们提了一大堆问题，把我都弄糊涂了。

discourage [dɪsˈkʌrɪdʒ] [同] deter, dishearten [反] encourage

v. to persuade sb. not to do sth., especially by making it seem difficult or bad 劝阻，使气馁

In cities that developed later, the World Bank and Asian Development Bank *discouraged* the building of public transport and people have been forced to rely on cars, creating the massive traffic jams that characterize those cities. 在后来发展起来的城市里，世界银行和亚洲发展银行不鼓励修建公共交通系统，因此人们不得不依赖汽车作为交通工具，从而导致了这些城市中典型的交通堵塞现象。

discriminate [dɪˈskrɪmɪneɪt]　　　　　　　　　　　　　　　　　[同]②differentiate

v. ①to treat a person or group differently from another in an unfair way 歧视 ②to make a difference（between two things）分辨，区别，区分（两事物）

discriminate between two cases/one case from another 区分两件事 / 将一件事与另一件事区分开

evolve [ɪˈvɒlv]

v. to develop gradually, esp. from a simple to a more complicated form 逐渐形成；逐步发展

The company has *evolved* into a major chemical manufacturer. 这家公司已逐步发展成一个主要的化工厂。

exceed [ɪkˈsiːd]　　　　　　　　　　　　　　　　　　　　[同] surpass, excel

v. to be greater than a particular number or amount 超过（数量）

His achievements have *exceeded* expectations. 他的成就已超过期望值。

excess [ɪkˈses]　　　　　　　　　　　　　　　　　　　　　　　[同] over

n. more than is necessary, reasonable or acceptable 超过；过度；过分

Are you suffering from an *excess* of stress in your life? 你生活中的压力过大吗?

flourish [ˈflʌrɪʃ]　　　　　　　　　　　　　　　　　　　　　[同] thrive

v. to be successful, very active, or widespread; prosper 旺盛；兴旺；繁荣

No new business can *flourish* in the present economic climate. 在目前的经济气候中，任何新产业都兴旺不起来。

flu [fluː]

n. (infml.) = influenza; infectious virus disease causing fever, muscular pain and catarrh 流行性感冒；流感

Flu shots are recommended for people aged 55 and older. 建议 55 岁及以上老人注射流感疫苗。

[记] Bird Flu 禽流感

graceful [ˈɡreɪsfl]　　　　　　　　　　　　　　　　　　　　[近] elegant

adj. showing a pleasing beauty of form, movement or manner（形式、动作或举止）优雅的，优美的

the *graceful* curves of the new bridge 新桥的优美曲线

gracious [ˈɡreɪʃəs]

adj. kind, polite and generous（esp. to sb. who is socially inferior）（指人及其行为）和善的，有礼貌的，大方的，亲切的

It was *gracious* of the Queen to speak to the elderly patients. 女王能慰问年老的病人让大家倍感亲切。

hopefully [ˈhəʊpfli]

adv. in a hopeful way 抱有希望地

Hopefully we can find a way of solving this problem. 我们有望找到解决这一问题的办法。

horizon [həˈraɪzn]　　　　　　　　　　　　　　　　　　　　　[同] ken

n. (usu. pl.) limit of a person's knowledge, experience, interest, etc.（知识、经验、兴趣等的）范围，见识，眼界

broaden one's *horizons* 拓宽眼界

insecure [ˌɪnsɪˈkjʊə(r)]　　　　　　　　　　　　　　　　[反] secure

adj. not secure or safe; not providing good support; that cannot be relied on 不保险的；不安全的；不稳定的

She felt lonely and *insecure* away from her family. 出门在外，她感到孤孤单单，无依无靠。

insecurity [ˌɪnsɪˈkjʊərəti]　　　　　　　　　　　　　　　[反] security

n. feeling of being insecure 不安全感

a feeling of *insecurity* 不安全感

insert [ɪnˈsɜːt]　　　　　　　　　　　　　　　　　　　　[反] extract

v. to put, fit, place sth. into sth. or between two things 插入，放入，置入

Insert the correct coins, then select the drink you want and press the button. 投入足量的硬币，然后选择你要的饮料，按键即可。

litter [ˈlɪtə]

① *n.* small pieces of rubbish such as paper, cans and bottles, that people have left lying in a public place （在公共场所乱扔的）垃圾；废弃物；杂物

There will be fines for people who drop *litter*. 乱扔垃圾的人将被罚款。

② *v.* to leave things in a place, making it look untidy 乱扔

The floor was *littered* with papers. 地板上乱七八糟地扔了许多纸。

NO LITTERING PLEASE USE A TRASH CAN

motion [ˈməʊʃn]　　　　　　　　　　　　　　　　　　　[同] movement

n. ①the process of moving or the way that sb. or sth. moves 动作；运动

One of the most important new methodologies is biomechanics, the study of the body in *motion*. 最重要的新方法之一就是生物力学，即对运动中的身体的研究。

②a proposal that is made formally at a meeting, and then is usually decided on by voting 动议；提议

motivate [ˈməʊtɪveɪt]　　　　　　　　　　　　　　　[同] prompt, stimulate

v. to be the reason why sb. does sth. or behaves in a particular way 成为…做事的动机（或原因）

It is a great deal easier to *motivate* employees in a growing organization than a declining one. 在不断壮大的企业中激励员工要比在日益衰落的企业中容易得多。

obstacle [ˈɒbstəkl]　　　　　　　　　　　　　　　　　　[同] obstruction

n. a situation, an event, etc. that makes it difficult for you to do or achieve sth. 障碍；绊脚石

A lack of qualifications can be a major *obstacle* to finding a job. 学历不足可能成为谋职的主要障碍。

obstruct [əbˈstrʌkt]　　　　　　　　　　　　　　　　　　[同] block, fill

v. to block a road, an entrance, a passage, etc. so that people cannot get through, see past, etc. 阻挡；阻塞

You can't park here; you're *obstructing* my driveway. 你不能在这里停车，你挡住了我家的车道。

pursue [pəˈsjuː]　　　　　　　　　　　　　　　　　　　　[同] seek

v. to continue doing an activity or trying to achieve sth. over a long period of time 追寻；追求

He is *pursuing* his studies at the university. 他在大学继续求学。

pursuit [pəˈsjuːt]　　　　　　　　　　　　　　　　　　　[同] seeking

n. (fml.) action of pursuing sth. 追求；寻求

The *pursuit* of profit was the main reason for the changes. 做出这些改变主要是为了追求利润。

rehearsal [rɪˈhɜːsl]

n. a time when all the people in a play, concert, etc. practise before a public performance 排练；排演；训练

put a play into *rehearsal* 排练一出戏

reinforce [ˌriːɪnˈfɔːs]

v. to give more support to (sth.); emphasize 给(某事物)更多的支持；加强

The film *reinforces* the idea that women should be pretty and dumb. 这部电影再次强调了女人应该美丽而愚蠢这样一个想法。

reject [rɪˈdʒekt]   [同] refuse

v. to put (sth.) aside or throw (sth.) away as not to be used, chosen, done, etc.; discard 抛弃(某事物)；摈弃；剔除

He *rejected* the complex mathematical analysis. 他抛弃了复杂的数学分析。

suburb [ˈsʌbɜːb]

n. (esp. residential) district outside the central part of a town or city (城镇的)郊区；(尤指)城郊住宅区

an industrial *suburb* 城郊工业区

successor [səkˈsesə]

n. sb. who takes a job or position previously held by sb. else 继任者；继承人；接班人

I'm sure she will be a worthy *successor*. 我相信她将会是个优秀的接班人。

suck [sʌk]

v. to draw (liquid or air, etc.) into the mouth by using the lip muscles (用嘴)吸(液体或气体等)；吮吸；嘬；啜

Across species, play tends to peak about halfway through the *suckling* stage and then decline. 无论什么种群的动物，玩耍都倾向于在哺乳期的中期达到顶峰，然后则开始走下坡路。

sufficient [səˈfɪʃnt]   [同] adequate

adj. enough 足够的；充足的

Merchandising activities alone did not provide *sufficient* funds for the organization. 销售活动一项并不足以为组织提供足够的资金。

suicide [ˈsuːɪsaɪd]

n. killing oneself intentionally 自杀

commit *suicide* 自杀

transaction [trænˈzækʃn]   [同] contract

n. transacting 办理；处理

real estate *transactions* 房地产交易

transcribe [trænˈskraɪb]

v. to copy sth. in writing 抄写，誊写，打印

Teams of audio typists *transcribed* the tapes to produce a computerized database of ten million words. 一组组的打字员把录音带上的内容记录下来，做成一个一千万字的数据库。

transcript [ˈtrænskrɪpt]

n. written or recorded copy of what has been said or written 抄本；打字本；副本

academic *transcript* 成绩单

transfer [trænsˈfɜː]   [同] ①divert

① *v.* to move sth./sb. from one place to another 将某物 / 某人由一处转移到另一处
The head office has been ***transferred*** from London to Cardiff. 总部已由伦敦迁至卡迪夫。
② [ˈtrænsfɜː] *n.* (instance of) transferring or being transferred 转移；转让；调动
The club's goalkeeper isn't happy here, and has asked for a ***transfer*** (to another club). 该足球俱乐部的守门员在此不愉快，已要求转会(去其他俱乐部)。

volume [ˈvɒljuːm]

n. ①the amount of sound produced by a television, radio, etc. 音量 ②the total amount of sth., especially when it is large or increasing 量；额
the ***volume*** of trade 贸易量

voluntary [ˈvɒləntəri]   [同] willing

adj. done willingly, not because you are forced 自愿的；志愿的
She is a ***voluntary*** worker at the hospital. 她在这家医院做义工。

一、英汉互译

胃口	_____	boost	_____
遵守，符合	_____	discriminate	_____
眼界	_____	flourish	_____
排练	_____	litter	_____
郊区	_____	obstruct	_____

二、翻译句子

1) 他的成就已超过期望值。(exceed)

_____

2) 我们有望找到解决这一问题的办法。(hopefully)

_____

3) 学历不足可能成为谋职的主要障碍。(obstacle)

_____

4) 她在这家医院做义工。(voluntary)

_____

A novel is a mirror walking along a main road.
一部小说犹如一面在大街上走的镜子。

——法国作家 司汤达(Stendhal, French writer)

applaud [əˈplɔːd] [同] cheer, clap [反] boo

v. show approval of (sb./sth.) by clapping the hands 向(某人/某事物)鼓掌表示欢迎或赞赏

The crowd *applauded* the performance for five minutes. 群众为演出鼓掌五分钟。

application [ˌæplɪˈkeɪʃn]

n. (to sb.) (for sth.) formal request 申请；请求

They will help you with job *applications* and interview techniques. 他们将在工作申请和面试技巧方面帮助你。

apply [əˈplaɪ]

v. ① (to sb.) (for sth.) make a formal request 申请；请求

Women tend to research thoroughly before *applying* for positions or attending interviews. 女性往往在申请职位与参加面试之前做细致的调查。

② to make use of sth. 使用，应用

There is evidence that the reaction principle was *applied* practically well before the rocket was invented. 有证据表明反作用原理在火箭被发明之前就已经得到了较好的应用。

booth [buːð]

n. a small enclosed place where you can do sth. privately, for example make a telephone call or vote 不受妨碍的封闭空间(如电话亭、投票间等)

a phone *booth* 电话亭

border [ˈbɔːdə(r)] [同] edge

n. the official line that separates two countries, states, or areas 边界

Securing our nation's *borders* is an immense task. 保证国家边界安全是个巨大的任务。

congratulate [kənˈɡrætʃuleɪt]

v. to tell sb. that one is pleased about his good fortune or achievements 祝贺；庆贺；道喜

congratulate sb. on his marriage 祝贺某人结婚

congratulation [kənˌɡrætʃuˈleɪʃn]

n. an act of congratulating or being congratulated 祝贺或受到祝贺

a speech of *congratulation* for the winner 对获胜者的贺词

congress [ˈkɒŋɡres] [近] association

n. (fml.) meeting or series of meetings for discussion between representatives 代表大会

a medical/international *congress* 医学/国际会议

conquer [ˈkɒŋkə(r)] [同] subdue, master

v. to gain control over sth. that is difficult, using a lot of effort 战胜，征服

Beyond the practical need to make order out of chaos, the rise of dictionaries is associated with the rise of the English middle class, who were anxious to define and circumscribe the various worlds to *conquer*—lexical as well as social and commercial. 除了规范英语混乱状态的实际需要外，英语词典的兴盛也与英国中产阶级的兴起有关，他们急于定义和约束要征服的

各个领域——除了社会和商业以外, 还有词汇。

dismay [dɪsˈmeɪ]　　　　　　　　　　　　　　　　　　　　[同] ①②fear

① *n.* feeling of shock and discouragement 惊愕; 气馁; 灰心

be filled/struck with ***dismay*** (at the news, etc.) (得到这消息等)极为震惊

② *v.* to fill (sb.) with dismay 使(某人)惊愕或气馁

We were all ***dismayed*** at his refusal to cooperate. 他不肯合作使我们感到非常失望。

dismiss [dɪsˈmɪs]　　　　　　　　　　　　　　　　　　　[近] decline

v. to consider sb./sth. not worth thinking or talking about 对某人/某事物不予理会或不屑一提

Archaeological traces of far more elaborate cultures have been ***dismissed*** as the ruins of invaders from outside the region. 那些更复杂文明的考古线索被当作外来入侵者留下的废墟而不被理会。

exclude [ɪkˈskluːd]　　　　　　　　　　　　　　　　　　[反] include

v. to deliberately not include sth. in what you are doing or considering 不包括; 不放在考虑之列

The cost of borrowing has been ***excluded*** from the inflation figures. 通胀数字未包括借贷成本。

excursion [ɪkˈskɜːʃn]

n. a short journey made for pleasure, esp. one that has been organized for a group of people (尤指集体)远足; 短途旅行

They've gone on an ***excursion*** to York. 他们到约克旅游去了。

fluctuate [ˈflʌktʃueɪt]　　　　　　　　　　　　　　　　　[同] vary

v. (of a price, number, rate, etc.) to rise and fall; change irregularly (指价格、数量、比率、费用等)涨落, 波动

The price ***fluctuates*** between £5 and £6. 价格在五英镑与六英镑之间波动。

Market price fluctuates

Fixed Price: With a fixed price, you lock in a set price for the duration of the heating season.

flush [flʌʃ]　　　　　　　　　　　　　　　　　　　　　　[同] bloom, blush

① *n.* sudden rush of emotions, excitement, etc. 感情、激情等的突发; 激动

a ***flush*** of enthusiasm 一阵热情

② *v.* (of a person's face) become red because of a rush of blood to the skin; blush (指人的面部)变红, 发红

Mary ***flushed*** red with embarrassment. 玛丽羞得脸红了。

grade [greɪd]　　　　　　　　　　　　　　　　　　　　　[同] class

n. a particular level of quality that a product, material, etc. has 等级; 级别

The best ***grades*** of tea are expensive. 顶级茶叶的价格很高。

gradual [ˈɡrædʒuəl]　　　　　　　　　　　　　　　　　　[反] sudden

adj. taking place by a series of small changes over a long period; not sudden 逐渐的; 渐变的

gradual decline/progress 逐渐的衰落/进步

horrible [ˈhɒrəbl]　　　　　　　　　　　　　　　　　　　[同] fearful

adj. very unpleasant and often frightening, worrying, or upsetting 可怕的; 令人恐惧的

a ***horrible*** crime 骇人听闻的罪行

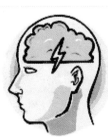

insight [ˈɪnsaɪt]

n. ability to see into the true nature (of sth.); deep understanding 洞察力; 深刻的了解

On a macro scale people work in teams which allow them to pitch their abilities, *insights* and capabilities for the betterment of the group. 从宏观上看，人们在不同的团队中工作。他们以自己的能力、才干和洞察力来优化所在的团队。

insist [ɪnˈsɪst]

v. to demand (sth.) forcefully, not accepting a refusal 坚持或坚决要求(某事物)

I *insist* that you take immediate action to put this right. 我坚决要求你立刻采取行动把事情处理好。

inspect [ɪnˈspekt]

v. to examine (sth.) closely 仔细检查(某事物)

The customs officer *inspected* my passport suspiciously. 海关官员颇为怀疑地检查了我的护照。

interact [ˌɪntərˈækt]

v. to act or have an effect on each other 相互作用；相互影响

Many factors must be considered when selecting informants, whether one is working with single speakers or two people *interacting*. 在选择调查对象时，无论他是与单独演讲人还是与两个互相影响的人一起工作，很多因素都必须被考虑到。

interdependent [ˌɪntədɪˈpendənt]

adj. depending on each other 互相依赖的；互相依存的

All nations are *interdependent* in the modern world. 当今世界上所有国家都是互相依存的。

lively [ˈlaɪvli]　　　　　　　　　　　　　　　　　　　　　[同] energetic

adj. full of life and energy; active and enthusiastic 精力充沛的；活跃热情的

a *lively* and enquiring mind 思维活跃、善于探索的头脑

load [ləʊd]　　　　　　　　　　　　　　　　　　　　　　[反] ②unload

① *n.* sth. that is being carried (usu. in large amounts) by a person, vehicle, etc. 负载；负荷

The trucks waited at the warehouse to pick up their *loads*. 货车在仓库等着装载货物。

② *v.* to put a large quantity of sth. onto or into sth. (把大量的⋯)装上；装入

Men were *loading* up a truck with timber. 工人正在把木料装上卡车。

motive [ˈməʊtɪv]

n. ①the reason that makes sb. do sth., especially when this reason is kept hidden 动机；目的 ②the power or force for a machine, vehicle, etc. makes it move 运动的；开动的

The reaction to the discharging steam provided the bird with *motive* power. 排放蒸汽时所产生的反作用为鸟提供了动力。

motto [ˈmɒtəʊ]

n. a short sentence or phrase that expresses the aims and beliefs of a person, a group, an institution, etc. and is used as a rule of behaviour 座右铭；格言

The school's *motto* is: Duty, Honour, Country. 这所学校的校训是：责任、荣誉、国家。

mount [maʊnt]　　　　　　　　　　　　　　　　　　　　[近] ②ascend

① *n.* a mountain or hill (used esp. as part of a proper name) 山峰或丘陵(尤其用在山名的专有名称中)

Mount Everest 珠穆朗玛峰

② *v.* (fml.) to go up sth., or up on to sth. that is raised 登上；爬上；攀登

She slowly *mounted* the steps. 她慢慢地爬上台阶。

obvious [ˈɒbviəs]　　　　　　　　　　　　　　　　　　　[同] apparent

adj. easy to notice or understand 明显的；显而易见的

The most *obvious* example of an information source is a dictionary. 信息来源最显而易见的例子就是字典。

occupy [ˈɒkjupaɪ]

v. to fill or use a space, an area or an amount of time 使用；占用（空间、面积、时间等）

Administrative work *occupies* half of my time. 行政事务占用了我一半的时间。

occur [əˈkɜː]　　　　　　　　　　　　　　　　　　　　　[同] happen

v. to happen 发生；出现

I'd like to illustrate with reference to a specific event which *occurred* several years ago. 我想通过几年前发生的一件具体事情加以说明。

relate [rɪˈleɪt]　　　　　　　　　　　　　　　[同] ①describe ②join

v. (fml.) ① to give an account of (facts, experiences, etc.); tell (a story, etc.) 叙述（事实、经历等）

Even if we are able to return to life to *relate* what we know, the chances of being believed are very slim. 即便我们能够回到现实生活中讲述所知道的一切，也没有人会相信我们。

② to bring into or link in logical or natural association 使有联系

to relate the two ideas 把两种观点关联起来

relative [ˈrelətɪv]　　　　　　　　　　　　　　　　[同] ①comparative

① *adj.* having a particular quality when compared with sth. else 相对的；相比较的

It's all *relative*, isn't it? Someone who is poor in this country might be considered well off in another. 一切都是相对的，不是吗？这个国家的穷人在另一个国家可能就被看做是富人了。

② *n.* a member of your family 亲戚

release [rɪˈliːs]　　　　　　　　　　　　　　　　　　[同] liberate

v. ①to let sb. go free, after having kept them somewhere 放走；释放

Approximately 1,500 beetles are *released*, a handful at a time, into fresh cow pats in the cow pasture. 大约1500只屎壳郎被投放到牧场中的新鲜牛粪中，每次放一些。

②to make a CD, video, film, etc. available for people to buy or see 发行；投放

sum [sʌm]　　　　　　　　　　　　　　　　　　　　　[同] whole

n. the whole of an amount 总数；量

He owes me a large *sum* of money. 他欠我很多钱。

summary [ˈsʌməri]

n. a short statement that gives the main information about sth., without giving all the details 总结；概述

Write a two-page *summary* of the results of your research. 就你的研究结果写一篇两页纸的总结。

summit [ˈsʌmɪt]　　　　　　　　　　　　　　　　　　[同]①top

n. ①highest point; top, esp. of a mountain 最高点；顶点；（尤指）山顶

the *summit* of her career, ambition, etc. 她事业的巅峰、最大的抱负等

②an important meeting or set of meetings between the leaders of several governments 峰会

superficial [ˌsuːpəˈfɪʃl]　　　　　　　　　　　　　[同] shallow

adj. of or on the surface only 表面的；在表面上的；肤浅的

At a *superficial* level, things seem to have remained the same. 表面看来，情况好像保持没变。

transform [trænsˈfɔːm]　　　　　　　　　　　　　[同] convert

v. to completely change the appearance or character of sth./sb. 完全改变某事物／某人的外观或特性

In the last 30 years, China has been ***transformed*** into a major industrial nation. 最近 30 年来，中国已经变为一个工业大国。

volunteer [ˌvɒlənˈtɪə(r)]

① *n.* a person who does a job without being paid for it 义务工作者；志愿者

Schools need ***volunteers*** to help children to read. 学校需要义务工作者来帮助孩子们阅读。

② *v.* to offer to do sth. without being forced to do it or without being paid for it 自愿做；义务做

Several staff members ***volunteered*** for early retirement. 几位职员自愿提前退休。

voyage [ˈvɔɪɪdʒ]   [同] cruise

n. a long journey, especially by sea or in space 航行；(尤指)航海，航天

The Titanic sank on its maiden ***voyage***. 泰坦尼克号首航便沉没了。

vulnerable [ˈvʌlnərəbl]

adj. weak and easily hurt physically or emotionally 脆弱的；易受伤害的

We work mainly with the elderly and other ***vulnerable*** groups. 我们的工作对象主要是老人和其他一些弱势群体。

Take the Test »

一、英汉互译

边界	_____	excursion	_____
波动	_____	motto	_____
洞察力	_____	occur	_____
亲戚	_____	superficial	_____
义工	_____	vulnerable	_____

二、翻译句子

1）他们将在工作申请和面试技巧方面帮助你。（application）

_____

2）当今世界上所有国家都是互相依存的。（interdependent）

_____

3）一切都是相对的，不是吗？这个国家的穷人在另一个国家可能就被看做是富人了。（relative）

_____

4）最近 30 年来，中国已经变为一个工业大国。（transform）

_____

appointment [əˈpɔɪntmənt]

n. (with sb.) arrangement to meet or visit sb. at a particular time 约会；预约

If you want to make an *appointment* you can phone or call at the office in person. 如果你想预约的话，你可以打电话或亲自登门。

appreciate [əˈpriːʃɪeɪt]　　　　　　　　　　[同] cherish, realize [反] despise

v. ① to understand and enjoy (sth.); to value highly 理解并欣赏（某事物）；高度评价

You can't fully *appreciate* foreign literature in translation. 看翻译作品很难完全欣赏到外国文学的精髓。

② to understand how serious or important a situation or problem is 理解

The results of this study suggest that pupils did not *appreciate* the complexity of causes of rainforest destruction. 研究结果表明，孩子们并不理解雨林被破坏原因的复杂性。

bore [bɔː]

① *n.* a situation or thing that is boring or that annoys you 烦人的状况或事情

It's such a *bore* having to stay up late tonight. 今天晚上得熬夜，真是烦人。

② *v.* to make (sb.) feel tired and uninterested by being dull or tedious 使（某人）感到厌烦（因单调或乏味）

I've heard all his stories before; they *bore* me. 他的事我以前都听说过了，真使我厌烦。

conscious [ˈkɒnʃəs]　　　　　　　　　　　　[同] aware [反] unconscious

adj. knowing what is going on around one because one is able to use bodily senses and mental powers; awake 意识到的；清醒的

He was in a coma for days, but now he's (fully) *conscious* again. 他昏迷了几天，但现在又（完全）清醒了。

consequence [ˈkɒnsɪkwəns]　　　　　　　　　　　　　　　　[同] effect

n. thing that is a result or an effect of sth. else 结果；后果；影响

Dust storms have numerous *consequences* beyond their effects on climate. 除了对气候的影响，沙尘暴还造成了很多后果。

conservative [kənˈsɜːvətɪv]

adj. opposed to great or sudden change 保守的；守旧的

Old people are usually more *conservative* than young people. 老年人通常比年轻人保守。

display [dɪˈspleɪ]　　　　　　　　　　　　　　　　　　　　[同] show

n. an arrangement of things for people to look at or buy 陈列；展出；展示

Samples of all the tools that were made through the ages are on *display*. 各个时代制作的工具样本都展出来了。

disposal [dɪˈspəʊzl]

n. the act of getting rid of sth. 去掉；清除；处理

sewage *disposal* systems 污水处理系统

execute [ˈeksɪkjuːt]　　　　　　　　　　　　　　　　　　　　　　　[同] implement

v. (fml.) to do a piece of work, perform a duty, put a plan into action, etc. 实行，执行，实施
Check that the computer has *executed* your commands. 检查一下计算机是否已执行指令。

exert [ɪgˈzɜːt]

v. to use power or influence to affect sb./sth. 运用；行使；施加
The moon *exerts* a force on the earth that causes the tides. 月球对地球的吸引力引起潮汐。

focus [ˈfəʊkəs]　　　　　　　　　　　　　　　　　　　　　　　[同] ②concentrate

① *n.* the thing, person, situation, etc. that people pay special attention to 焦点
The *focus* of recent research has been on environmental issues. 近期研究的焦点在环境问题上。
② *v.* to concentrate (one's attention, etc.) on (sth.) 将(注意力等)集中于(某事物)
American culture is highly *focused* on personal success, on business and on the acquisition of personal wealth. 美国文化高度关注个人成功，商业行为和个人财富的获取。

fold [fəʊld]　　　　　　　　　　　　　　　　　　[近] double [反] unfold

v. to bend or turn sth. so that one part of it lies on another; close or flatten sth. by pressing two parts of it together 折叠；折叠收拢
fold clothes (up) neatly 把衣服叠整齐

graduate [ˈgrædʒuət]

① *n.* person who holds a degree (esp. the first or bachelor's) from a university or polytechnic 有学位(尤指学士学位)的人；大学毕业生
There are many other job opportunities which our *graduates* can look forward to. 还有许多其他的工作机会值得我们大学毕业生去期待。
② *v.* [ˈgrædʒueɪt] to obtain a degree from a college or university 毕业
He *graduated* in physics from Cambridge University. 他毕业于剑桥大学的物理系。

grand [grænd]　　　　　　　　　　　　　　　　　　　　　　　[反] humble

adj. magnificent; splendid; big; of great importance (also in names of places, buildings, etc.) 宏伟的；壮丽的；大的；伟大的
These days, the *grand* old names of entertainment have more resonance than power. 如今娱乐业的老字号已经有些名不副实了。

host [həʊst]

n. sb. at a party, meal, etc. who has invited the guests and who provides the food, drink, etc. 主人
Our *host* greeted us at the door. 主人在门口迎接我们。

hostel [ˈhɒstl]　　　　　　　　　　　　　　[近] hotel

n. building in which food and lodging are provided for students, certain groups of workers, the homeless, travellers, etc. (为学生、某些工人、无家者、旅客等提供膳宿的)寄宿舍，招待所(通常收费低廉)
Youth *Hostel* 青年旅舍

inspection [ɪnˈspekʃn]　　　　　　　　　　　　　　　　　　　[同] examination

n. inspecting or being inspected 检查；视察；调查
A closer *inspection* reveals this interpretation as too simple. 进一步的调查揭示出这个解释太简单了。

install [ɪnˈstɔːl]　　　　　　　　　　　　　　　　　　　　　　[同] settle

v. to fix equipment, furniture, etc. in position for use, esp. by making the necessary connections with the supply of electricity, water, etc. 安装，设置(设备、家具等)
In the noisiest areas, mechanical ventilation will have to be *installed* in the exterior walls. 在最

嘈杂的地段，机械通风设备将要安装在外墙上。

instance [ˈɪnstəns] [同] case

n. particular occurrence of sth. that happens generally or several times; example; case 例子；实例；事例

In most *instances* the pain soon goes away. 在多数情况下，这种疼痛很快就消失。

loan [ləʊn] [近] lend

n. money that an organization such as a bank lends and sb. borrows 贷款；借款

The *loan* amounts in S.K.I. programs have generally ranged from $30－$100. S.K.I. 项目的贷款总额大致为 30 到 100 美元。

multiple [ˈmʌltɪpl]

adj. many in number, involving many different people or things 数量多的；多种多样的

multiple choice 多项选择

multiply [ˈmʌltɪplaɪ] [近] increase

v. to increase or make sth. increase very much in number or amount 成倍增加；迅速增加

In time they *multiply* and within three or four years the benefits to the pasture are obvious. 一段时间后它们成倍增加，三、四年内对草场的作用便十分明显。

murmur [ˈmɜːmə]

v. to say sth. in a soft quiet voice that is difficult to hear or understand 低语；喃喃细语

She *murmured* her agreement. 她低声表示同意。

odd [ɒd] [同] ①strange, unusual

① *adj.* strange or unusual 奇怪的；反常的

It seemed *odd* that he wanted a picture of me. 真奇怪他想要我的照片。

② *n.* a number that cannot be divided exactly by two, for example 1, 3, 5, 7, etc. 奇数

officious [əˈfɪʃəs]

adj. too ready to tell people what to do or to use the power you have to give orders 爱指手画脚的；爱发号施令的

The people at the tax department were very *officious*, and kept everyone waiting for hours while they checked their papers. 税务部门的人员好用权威了，检查文件时要让人们等上很久。

offset [ˈɒfset] [同] compensate

v. to use one cost, payment or situation in order to cancel or reduce the effect of another 抵消；弥补

Prices have risen in order to *offset* the increased cost of materials. 为补偿原料成本的增加而提高了价格。

pyramid [ˈpɪrəmɪd]

n. ①structure with a flat square or triangular base and sloping sides that meet in a point at the top, esp. one of those built of stone by the ancient Egyptians as tombs 金字塔（尤指古埃及的）②a system, society, company, etc. that is organized in different levels 像金字塔一样的层级

families at the base of a socioeconomic *pyramid* 位于社会经济结构底层的家庭

relevant [ˈrelɪvənt] [同] related, pertinent

adj. connected with what is being discussed, what is happening, what is being done, etc. 有关的；切题的

Children's books are surprisingly *relevant* to contemporary life. 儿童读物与当代生活有着惊人的相关性。

reliable [rɪˈlaɪəbl] [同] dependable

adj. consistently good in quality or performance, and so deserving trust; dependable 可信赖的；可靠的

My grandfather is a quiet and *reliable* man. 我祖父是个安静而可靠的人。

religious [rɪˈlɪdʒəs] [反] irreligious

adj. ①of religion 宗教的；宗教上的 ②believing strongly in your religion and obeying its rules carefully 虔诚的

He's always been a *religious* man, and I think that has helped him. 他一直是个笃信宗教的人，我觉得这一点帮了他。

superior [suːˈpɪərɪə(r), sjuː-] [反] ①②inferior

① *adj.* better, more powerful, more effective, etc. than a similar person or thing 比…好的，比…优越的

② *n.* person of higher rank, position, etc. 级别、地位…高的人；上级

Some people insist on blindly following the directions of their *superiors*. 有些人坚持盲从他们的上级。

supervise [ˈsjuːpəvaɪz] [同] administer

v. to watch or otherwise keep a check on （sb. doing sth. or sth. being done）to make sure it is done properly 监督(某人做某事)；察看并指导

The chief clerk *supervises* the work of the department. 书记长负责监督该部门的工作。

supplement [ˈsʌplɪmənt, ˈsʌplɪment] [同] complement

n. thing added to sth. else to improve or complete it 增补的事物；补充

The money I get from teaching the piano is a useful *supplement* to my ordinary income. 我教钢琴挣的钱是一笔很管用的外快。

supplementary [ˌsʌplɪˈmentrɪ] [同] complementary

adj. additional; extra 增补的；补充的；附加的

a *supplementary* payment/lecture/item 额外的付款 / 讲座 / 项目

suppose [səˈpəʊz]

v. to accept as true or probable; believe; imagine; assume 认定；认为，以为；猜想；料想；假定

I *suppose* the biggest industries are electronics and tourism. 我认为最大的产业是电子业与旅游业。

transit [ˈtrænzɪt]

n. process of going or being taken or transported from one place to another 搬运；载运；运输

goods delayed or lost in *transit* 在运输中延误或遗失的货物

translate [trænsˈleɪt]

v. to change written or spoken words into another language 翻译

Translate the text from Spanish into English. 把这些西班牙文字翻译成英文。

transmit [trænzˈmɪt] [同] convey

v. to send out （a signal, programme, etc.）electronically by radio waves, along a telegraph wire, etc.（借无线电波、沿电报线路等）传输，传播(信号、节目等)

The World Cup Final is being *transmitted* live to over fifty countries. 世界杯决赛现正向五十多个国家作实况转播。

transparent [trænsˈpærənt] [同] translucent

adj. allowing light to pass through so that objects behind can be seen clearly 透明的

a type of plastic that is as *transparent* as glass but stronger 一种透明如玻璃且比玻璃坚固的塑料

wander [ˈwɒndə(r)]

v. to walk slowly across or around an area, usually without a clear direction or purpose 漫步；游荡
After dinner the three of us *wandered* around the hotel. 吃过晚饭后我们三个在酒店附近闲逛。

wardrobe ['wɔːdrəʊb]

n. （BrE）a piece of furniture like a large cupboard that you hang clothes in 衣柜
Can you hang these in the *wardrobe*, please? 请问你能把这些衣服挂在衣柜里吗？

weave [wiːv]   [同] knit

v. to make fabric, a carpet, a basket, etc. by crossing threads or strips across, over and under each other by hand or on a machine called a loom（用手或机器）编；编制
The baskets are *woven* from strips of willow. 这些篮子是用柳条编的。

Take the Test >>

一、英汉互译

理解；欣赏	_____	disposal	_____
结果	_____	exert	_____
安装	_____	hostel	_____
抵消	_____	multiply	_____
透明的	_____	officious	_____

二、翻译句子

1）如果你想预约的话，你可以打电话或亲自登门。（appointment）
_____

2）老年人通常比年轻人保守。（conservative）
_____

3）儿童读物与当代生活有着惊人的相关性。（relevant）
_____

4）请问你能把这些衣服挂在衣柜里吗？（wardrobe）
_____

The important thing in life is to have a great aim, and the determination to attain it.
人生重要的事情就是确定一个伟大的目标，并决心实现它。
——德国诗人、戏剧家 歌德（Johan Goethe, German poet and dramatist）

approach [əˈprəʊtʃ]

① *n.* way of dealing with a person or thing 方法；手段

We take a cooperative *approach* to the assessment of your work. 我们采取了一种合作的方式来评价你的工作。

② *v.* to come near or nearer to (sb./sth.) in space or time（在空间或时间上）接近；靠近（某人/某事物）

As autumn *approaches*, the beekeepers pack up their hives and go south. 秋天临近，养蜂人收拾好他们的蜂箱前往南方。

appropriate [əˈprəʊpriət]   [反] inappropriate

adj. (for/to sth.) suitable; right and proper 适当的；合适的

His formal style of speaking was *appropriate* to the occasion. 他郑重其事的讲话方式适合于那个场合。

bother [ˈbɒðə(r)]   [同] ①annoy

① *n.* trouble; inconvenience 麻烦；不便

Did you have much *bother* finding the house? 你找到这所房子费劲吗？

② *v.* to cause trouble or annoyance to sb. 打扰或烦扰某人

I'm sorry to *bother* you, but could you tell me the way to the station? 对不起打扰一下，请问去车站怎么走？

considerable [kənˈsɪdərəbl]   [同] big, significant

adj. great in amount or size 相当多的；相当大的

Publishing houses are now making *considerable* profits on the back of new children's books. 现在出版社通过新的儿童书籍获得了可观的利润。

consist [kənˈsɪst]

v. to be formed from two or more things or people 包括，包含

My control group *consisted* of eighteen sighted undergraduates from the University of Toronto. 我的对照组包括18位来自多伦多大学的视力正常的本科生。

constant [ˈkɒnstənt]   [同] continual, steady

adj. going on all the time; happening again and again 经常的；不断发生的

This entrance is in *constant* use; do not block it. 这个入口经常使用，不要挡住。

constitute [ˈkɒnstɪtjuːt]   [同] comprise, make

v. (fml.)to make up or form (a whole); to be considered to be sth. 组成，构成（某整体）

Copying words from another writer's work without acknowledging the source *constitutes* the serious crime of plagiarism. 照搬其他作者的原话而不标明出处是一种非常可耻的剽窃行为。

dispute [dɪˈspjuːt]   [同] ②argue ①②question

① *n.* a disagreement between two people, groups or countries; discussion about a subject where there is disagreement 争论；辩论；争端

Exactly which field of study has benefited most from the contributions of amateurs is a matter of some **dispute**. 确切地说哪门学科中业余爱好者的贡献最大是有些争议的。

② *v.* to question whether sth. is true and valid 对…提出质疑；对…表示异议（或怀疑）

These figures have been **disputed**. 有人对这些数字提出了质疑。

disregard [ˌdɪsrɪˈɡɑːd]　　　　　　　　　　　[同] ①②neglect

① *n.* the act of treating sb./sth. as unimportant and not caring about them/it 漠视；忽视

She shows a total **disregard** for other people's feelings. 她丝毫不顾及别人的感受。

② *v.* to not consider sth.; to treat sth. as unimportant 不理会；漠视

Safety rules were **disregarded**. 安全规定被忽视了。

dissertation [ˌdɪsəˈteɪʃn]

n. a long piece of writing on a particular subject, esp. one written for a university degree 专题论文；学位论文

When shall we submit our **dissertations**? 我们什么时间交论文呀？

exhale [eksˈheɪl]　　　　　　　　　　　　　　　　[反] inhale

v. to breathe air, smoke, etc. out of your mouth 呼气

Take a deep breath, then **exhale** slowly. 深吸气，然后慢慢呼出。

exhaust [ɪɡˈzɔːst]

n. waste gases that come out of a vehicle, an engine or a machine（车辆、发动机或机器排出的）废气

car **exhaust** fumes 汽车排出的废气

forecast [ˈfɔːkɑːst]　　　　　　　　　　　　　　[同] foretell

v. to tell in advance （what is expected to happen）; predict with the help of information 预报；预测

forecast a fall in unemployment 预测失业人数将下降

forbid [fəˈbɪd]　　　　　　　　　　　　　　　　[反] allow

v. to tell sb. that they are not allowed to do sth., or that sth. is not allowed 禁止

The law strictly **forbids** racial or sexual discrimination. 该法律严厉禁止种族和性别歧视。

forgive [fəˈɡɪv]

v. to stop being angry with sb. and stop blaming them, although they have done sth. wrong 原谅；宽恕

I could never, never, never **forgive** myself for that. 那件事我绝不会原谅我自己。

graphic [ˈɡræfɪk]　　　　　　　　　　　　　　[同] ②vivid

adj. ①of visual symbols （e.g. lettering, diagrams, drawings）文字的；图表的 ②a graphic account or description of an event is very clear and gives a lot of details 栩栩如生的；生动的

graphic displays 图表展示

hostile [ˈhɒstaɪl]

adj. showing strong dislike or enmity; very unfriendly 表示极厌恶的；含敌意的；极不友好的

She found his manner towards her distinctly **hostile**. 她发现他对她极不友好。

instinct [ˈɪnstɪŋkt]

n. natural feeling that makes one choose to act in a particular way 直觉；本能

Birds have an *instinct* to build nests. 鸟儿有筑巢的天性。

institute ［ˈɪnstɪtjuːt］

n.（building that contains a）society or organization for a special purpose 学会；协会；会址

The following is a description of an important study conducted by the *Institute* for Social Research designed to answer these questions. 以下是社会研究协会为回答这些问题而进行的一项重要研究的说明。

instruct ［ɪnˈstrʌkt］ ［近］command

v. to give orders or directions to sb. 向某人下命令或指示；指导

I've *instructed* them to keep the room locked. 我已吩咐他们那房间要上锁。

locality ［ləʊˈkæləti］ ［同］district

n. the area that surrounds the place you are in or are talking about（围绕所处或提及的）地区

His job is asking older informants about how times have changed in their *locality*. 他的工作是问年长的被调查者一些关于他们所在地区的变迁的问题。

locate ［ləʊˈkeɪt］

v. to establish（sth.）in a place; situate 将（某物）设置在某处；使坐落于

Businesses can *locate* based on other considerations, such as the availability of labour. 商业还能基于其他考虑来选择位置，比如说劳动力状况。

mushroom ［ˈmʌʃruːm］ ［同］②explode

① *n.* a fungus with a round flat head and short stem 蘑菇；伞菌

cream of *mushroom* soup 奶油蘑菇汤

② *v.* to rapidly grow or increase in number 快速生长；快速增长

We expect the market to *mushroom* in the next two years. 我们期望未来两年内市场会迅速发展。

myriad ［ˈmɪriəd］

n. an extremely large number of sth. 无数；大量

Designs are available in a *myriad* of colours. 各种色彩的款式应有尽有。

offspring ［ˈɒfˌsprɪŋ］ ［同］descendant

n.（fml.）child or children of a particular person or couple（某人或某夫妇的）孩子，子女

With one right and one left-handed parent, 15 to 20 per cent of the *offspring* will be left-handed. 当父母一方习惯用左手、一方习惯用右手时，有百分之十五到二十的子女习惯用左手。

omit ［əˈmɪt］ ［同］neglect

v. to fail or neglect to do sth.; leave sth. not done 未做某事物；忽略；疏忽

omit to do/doing a piece of work 未做一件工作

ongoing ［ˈɒnˌɡəʊɪŋ］

adj. continuing to exist or progress 继续存在的；进行中的

an *ongoing* debate 持续的辩论

relief ［rɪˈliːf］ ［同］ease

n. lessening or removing of pain, distress, anxiety, etc.（痛苦、困苦、忧虑等的）减轻或解除

Marijuana can provide pain *relief* for some cancer patients. 大麻可以为某些癌症患者减轻病痛。

reluctant ［rɪˈlʌktənt］ ［同］disinclined

adj. unwilling and therefore slow to cooperate, agree, etc. 不情愿的；勉强的

She was very *reluctant* to admit the truth. 她很不情愿地承认了这事实。

sack ［sæk］ ［同］②dismiss

① *n.* a large bag with no handles, made of strong rough material or strong paper or plastic 麻布（或厚纸、塑料）大袋

They got through a sack of potatoes. 他们把一麻袋土豆都吃完了。

② *v.* (infml.) to dismiss sb. from a job 解雇；炒鱿鱼

She was *sacked* for refusing to work on Sundays. 她因拒绝在星期天上班而被解雇了。

sacred [ˈseɪkrɪd]　　　　　　　　　　　　　　　　　　[同] holy, divine

adj. connected with or dedicated to God or a god; connected with religion 神圣的；宗教的

The Japanese regard Mount Fuji as a *sacred* mountain. 日本人认为富士山是座圣山。

sacrifice [ˈsækrɪfaɪs]

① *n.* giving up of sth., usu. in return for sth. more important or valuable 放弃某事物（通常指为获得更重要或更有价值的东西）

Getting rich isn't worth the *sacrifice* of your principles. 为致富而牺牲原则是不值得的。

② *v.* to give up sth. as a sacrifice 牺牲某事物

She *sacrificed* her career to look after her kids. 她为了照顾孩子而牺牲了自己的事业。

safeguard [ˈseɪfɡɑːd]　　　　　　　　　　　　　[同] ①defense ②defend

① *n.* thing that serves as a protection from harm, risk or danger 安全设施；保护性措施

We make copies of our computer disks as a *safeguard* against accidents. 我们复制了计算机磁盘以防意外。

② *v.* to protect or guard sb./sth. 保护或保卫某人／某物

We have found a way of *safeguarding* our money. 我们已有了保护钱财的办法。

salty [ˈsɔːlti, ˈsɒlti]

adj. containing or tasting of salt 含盐的；咸的

salty sea air 海边带咸味的空气

supreme [sjuːˈpriːm]　　　　　　　　　　　　　　　　　　[同] superior

adj. highest in authority, rank or degree（权力、级别或地位）最高的；至高无上的

the *supreme* ruler of a vast empire 一个庞大帝国的最高统治者

surge [sɜːdʒ]　　　　　　　　　　　　　　　　　　　　　[同] outburst

n. sudden occurrence or increase 突然发生；激增

The term first surfaced in the early 1980s reflecting a *surge* in environmental awareness. 这个术语于 20 世纪 80 年代早期首次出现，反映了人们迅速增强的环境意识。

surgery [ˈsɜːdʒəri]

n. treatment of injuries or diseases by cutting or removing parts of the body 外科；手术

Research for obesity had concentrated on behavior modification, drugs to decrease appetite and *surgery*. 对肥胖的研究集中在行为修正、降低食欲的药物以及外科手术。

surpass [səˈpɑːs]　　　　　　　　　　[同] exceed

v. (fml.) to do or be better than sb./sth.; exceed sb./sth. 优于或超过某人／某物

The beauty of the scenery *surpassed* all my expectations. 我万万没想到风景会那么漂亮。

transplant [trænsˈplɑːnt]　　　　　　　　　　　　　　　　[同] graft

v. to take (tissue or an organ) from one person, animal or part of the body and put it into another 移植（组织或器官）

transplant a kidney from one twin to another 把孪生儿之一的肾脏移植到另一人身上

transport [ˈtrænspɔːt]

n. a system or method for carrying passengers or goods from one place to another 运送；运输；

交通

In Europe most cities are still designed for the old modes of *transport*. 欧洲的大部分城市仍然是按照老式的交通方式设计的。

trap [træp]

① *n.* device for catching animals, etc. 捕动物等的器具；陷阱

a mouse *trap* 老鼠夹

② *v.* to keep (sb.) in a place from which he wants to move but cannot 使(某人)陷入困境

Thirty miners were *trapped* underground. 30 个矿工被困在了地下。

treasure ['treʒə(r)]

n. ① a group of valuable things such as gold, silver, jewels, etc. 财宝 ② a very valuable and important object 宝贝；珍品

A husband that cooks and cleans is a real *treasure*. 一个能做饭洗衣的丈夫可真是块宝。

Take the Test ➤➤

一、英汉互译

方法，手段	_____	considerable	_____
学位论文	_____	constitute	_____
坐落于	_____	offspring	_____
不情愿的	_____	surpass	_____
外科手术	_____	transplant	_____

二、翻译句子

1) 他郑重其事的讲话方式适合于那个场合。(appropriate)

_____

2) 她因拒绝在星期天上班而被解雇了。(sack)

_____

3) 她为了照顾孩子而牺牲了自己的事业。(sacrifice)

_____

4) 这个术语于 20 世纪 80 年代早期首次出现，反映了人们迅速增强的环境意识。(surge)

_____

If you want to understand today, you have to search yesterday.

想要懂得今天，就必须研究昨天。

——美国女作家 赛珍珠 (Pearl Buck, American female writer)

Word List 33

approve [əˈpruːv] [同] accept, endorse, be in favor of [反] disapprove

v. (of sb./sth.) to say, show or feel that sth. is good or acceptable or satisfactory 赞成；同意

I *approve* of your trying to earn some money, but please don't neglect your studies. 我同意你去挣一些钱，可是请不要误了功课。

approximate [əˈprɒksɪmɪt] [同] rough [反] exact

adj. almost correct or exact but not completely so 大约的；大概的

the *approximate* time of the accident 事故的大致时间

archaeology [ˌɑːkɪˈɒlədʒi]

n. study of ancient civilizations by scientific analysis of physical remains found in the ground 考古学

Archaeology is both a physical activity out in the field and an intellectual pursuit in the study or laboratory. 考古学既是一种野外的体力活动，又是一种在书房或实验室里进行的智慧的探索。

boundary [ˈbaʊndri]

n. a real or imagined line that marks the limits or edges of sth. and separates it from other things or places; a dividing line 边界；界限；分界线

On a macro level cultures tend to follow geographical *boundaries*. 宏观上讲，文化是趋向于以地理界限来划分的。

constrain [kənˈstreɪn] [同] restrain, confine, curb

v. (fml.) to make (sb.) do sth. by strong (moral) persuasion or by force 力劝，强迫(某人)做某事

As an artist he didn't consider himself *constrained* by the same rules of social conduct as other people. 作为艺术家，他认为自己不必像一般人那样要受社会行为准则的束缚。

construct [kənˈstrʌkt] [同] build, form

v. to build (sth.); put or fit together; form 建造(某物)；构成；形成

a well-*constructed* novel 一部结构周密的小说

consult [kənˈsʌlt]

v. to discuss matters with sb.; confer with sb. 与某人商量(事情)；与某人磋商

Do not take the tablets before *consulting* your doctor. 在咨询过医生后再服药。

consume [kənˈsjuːm]

v. to use time, energy, goods, etc. 消耗，花费

I think we should use a questionnaire. It'll be so much less time-*consuming* than organising interviews. 我认为我们应该使用调查问卷，这比组织面谈省时多了。

dissolve [dɪˈzɒlv] [近] liquefy

v. to make (a solid) become part of a liquid 使(固体)溶解

to *dissolve* the tablet in water 把药片溶于水中

distinct [dɪˈstɪŋkt]

adj. clearly different or of a different kind 截然不同的；有区别的；不同种类的

There are three distinct strands to Sports Studies and you would need to choose fairly early on which *direction* you wanted to follow. 对运动的研究有三种截然不同的方向，你需要尽早选择你的研究方向。

exhibit [ɪɡˈzɪbɪt]

① *n.* an object or a work of art put in a public place, for example a museum, so that people can see it (一件)展览品；陈列品

② *v.* to show sth. in a public place for people to enjoy or to give them information 展览；展出

They will be *exhibiting* their new designs at the trade fairs this spring. 他们将于今年春季在商品交易会上展出他们的新设计。

exhibition [ˌeksɪˈbɪʃn]

n. a collection of things, for example works of art, that are shown to the public (一批)展览品

an *exhibition* of old photographs 老照片展

format [ˈfɔːmæt]

n. the way in which sth. is organized or arranged 版式

It's the same book, but a new *format*. 还是那本书，但这是新的版式。

grant [ɡrɑːnt]　　　　　　　　　　　　　　[同] ②acknowledge

① *n.* an amount of money given to sb., esp. by the government, for a particular purpose. (政府给的)拨款资助

② *v.* to agree to give or allow (what is asked for) 同意给予或允许(所求)

The minister *granted* journalists an interview. 部长答应接见记者。

instrument [ˈɪnstrumənt]　　　　　　　　　[反] implement, tool

n. implement or apparatus used in performing an action, esp. for delicate or scientific work 器具；器械；仪器

They are backed up by technicians who design *instruments* to collect data from athletes. 他们得到技术人员的支持，这些技术人员为运动员们设计了采集数据的仪器。

insufficient [ˌɪnsəˈfɪʃnt]　　　　　　　　　[同] deficient

adj. not sufficient 不充足的；不充分的；不够的

In some California housing estates, a key alone is *insufficient* to get someone in the door. 在加州的一些居住区，只有一把钥匙是不足以让人进屋的。

insulate [ˈɪnsjuleɪt]

v. to cover (sth.) to prevent sth. from getting in or out 绝缘

Not only will all the roofs need *insulating*, the exterior walls will be required to be double brick. 不仅全部的屋顶都需要绝缘，外墙也被要求使用双层砖。

interfere [ˌɪntəˈfɪə(r)]　　　　　　　　　　[同] meddle

v. to concern oneself with or take action affecting sb. else's affairs without the right to do so or being invited to do so 干涉；介入；干预

Carbon monoxide competes with oxygen in red blood cells and *interferes* with the blood's ability to deliver life-giving oxygen to the heart. 一氧化碳在红血球中与氧气竞争，从而扰乱了血液向心脏输运生命所需氧气的能力。

interior [ɪnˈtɪəriə(r)]　　　　　　　　　　　[反] exterior

n. inner part; inside 内部；里面

Two layers of plasterboard will be needed for the *interior* bedroom walls. 卧室内墙需要装两层石膏板。

lump [lʌmp]   [同] bump

n. a small piece of sth. solid, without a particular shape 小块

Melt a *lump* of butter in your frying-pan. 在煎锅里融化一小块黄油。

luxurious [lʌɡˈʒʊəriəs]   [同] grand

adj. very expensive, beautiful, and comfortable 奢侈的；极舒适的

The Duesenberg is a fantastically expensive, *luxurious* car which was built in the early part of the 20th century. Duesenberg 是于 20 世纪初生产的一款极其昂贵奢侈的车。

mysterious [mɪˈstɪəriəs]

adj. difficult to understand or explain; strange 神秘的；奇怪的

The rocket was generally ignored by writers of fiction to transport their heroes to *mysterious* realms beyond the Earth. 小说家一般都忽略了将主人公运送到地球之外神秘领域的火箭。

myth [mɪθ]

n. ①a story from ancient times, esp. one that was told to explain natural events or to describe the early history of a race 神话；神话故事 ②an idea or story that many people believe, but which is not true 错误的说法；谬论

Contrary to popular *myth*, the majority of accidents are not caused by speeding or drunkenness. 跟流行的错误观点相反的是，大部分的交通事故都不是由超速或者酗酒引起的。

mythology [mɪˈθɒlədʒi]

n. ancient myths in general; the ancient myths of a particular culture, society, etc. (统称)神话；某文化(或社会等)的神话

a study of the religions and *mythologies* of ancient Rome 关于古罗马的宗教和神话的研究

operate [ˈɒpəreɪt]   [同] work

v. (fml.) to work; be in action 工作；运转

A simple analogy can help us to understand how a rocket *operates*. 简单的类比有助于我们理解火箭的工作原理。

operation [ˌɒpəˈreɪʃn]

n. way in which sth. works; working 运转；操作；工作

I can use a word processor but I don't understand its *operation*. 我能使用文字处理机，但不了解其运转机制。

opponent [əˈpəʊnənt]   [同] adversary

n. person who is against another person in a fight, a struggle, a game or an argument 对手；敌手；(争论的)对方

our *opponents* in Saturday's game 我们星期六的比赛对手

rely [rɪˈlaɪ]

v. to trust or depend on sb. or sth. to do what you need or expect them to do 依赖；依靠

Many people now *rely* on the Internet for news. 很多人现在依靠网络获取新闻。

remarkable [rɪˈmɑːkəbl]   [同] outstanding

adj. worth noticing or unusual; exceptional 值得注意的；不寻常的；独特的

a *remarkable* person/feat/event/book 出类拔萃的人 / 非凡的业绩 / 引人瞩目的事件 / 特别优秀的书

remedy [ˈremədi]   [近] cure

n. treatment, medicine, etc. that cures or relieves a disease or pain 减轻病痛的治疗(法)、药物等

The *remedy* seems worse than the disease. 这种疗法比疾病本身更让人难受。

sample ['sɑːmpl]   [反] instance

n. one of a number of things, or part of a whole, that can be looked at to see what the rest is like; specimen 货样; 样品; 标本

My *sample* should be reasonably representative. 我的样本应该相当具有代表性。

sanction ['sæŋkʃn]

n. ①permission or approval for an action, a change, etc. (对某种行动、变化等的)认可, 批准

The book was translated without the *sanction* of the author. 这本书未经作者许可就被翻译了。

② (pl.) official orders or laws stopping trade, communication, etc. with another country, as a way of forcing its leaders to make political changes 制裁

The UN Security Council may impose economic *sanctions*. 联合国安理会可能会实施制裁。

sanitary ['sænɪtri]   [同] hygienic

adj. free from dirt or substances that may cause disease; hygienic 清洁的; 卫生的; 保健的

Conditions in the kitchen were not very *sanitary*. 厨房环境不太卫生。

scale [skeɪl]   [近] range

n. relative size, extent, etc. 规模; 程度; 范围

Large *scale* population movement was significantly reduced. 大规模的人口迁徙大大减少。

scan [skæn]   [同] scrutinize

v. look at every part of (sth.) carefully; examine (sth.) with great attention 细看(某物)的各部; 仔细检查(某物)

All luggage has to be *scanned* at the airport. 所有行李在机场都要接受检查。

scar [skɑː]

n. mark left on the skin by a wound, sore, etc. 伤痕; 疤

Will the cut leave a *scar*? 这伤口会留下疤痕吗?

surplus ['sɜːpləs]   [同] excess

n. amount left over after one has used all that one needs; amount by which money received is greater than money spent 剩余(额); 过剩; 盈余; 顺差

We have a trade *surplus* of 400 million pounds. 我们有四亿英镑的贸易顺差。

surrender [sɜ'rendə(r)]

v. to stop resisting an enemy, etc.; yield; give up 停止抵抗; 投降; 屈服; 放弃

The hijackers finally *surrendered* themselves to the police. 劫机者终于向警方投降了。

survey ['sɜːveɪ]

n. the act of surveying (investigate the behaviour, opinions, etc. of a group of people), usu. by questioning them; investigation (对部分人的行为、意见等的)调查

treatment ['triːtmənt]

n. process or manner of treating sb. or sth. 对待的方法或态度; 待遇; 处理; 治疗

These effects are often mild and usually wear off after a few days' *treatment*. 这些影响通常很弱, 而且在一段时间的治疗之后就会消失。

treaty ['triːti]   [同] agreement

n. (fml.) agreement between two or more countries (国家之间的)条约, 协定

the *Treaty* of Rome 罗马条约

tremble ['trembl]   [同] shake

v. to shake involuntarily (from fear, cold, weakness, etc.); quiver (因恐惧、寒冷、虚弱等)颤抖, 战栗, 哆嗦

Her hands were *trembling* with anger. 她气得双手直哆嗦。

Take the Test »

一、英汉互译

大约的	_____	archaeology	_____
咨询	_____	dissolve	_____
展品	_____	insulating	_____
神秘的	_____	mythology	_____
不寻常的	_____	remedy	_____

二、翻译句子

1) 宏观上讲，文化是趋向于以地理界限来划分的。（boundary）

_____

2) 跟流行的错误观点相反的是，大部分的交通事故都不是由超速或者酗酒引起的。（myth）

_____

3) 很多人现在依靠网络获取新闻。（rely）

_____

4) 我们有四亿英镑的贸易顺差。（surplus）

_____

I have nothing to offer but blood, toil, tears and sweat.

我能奉献的没有其他，只有热血、辛劳、眼泪与汗水。

——英国政治家 丘吉尔（Winston Churchill, British politician）

Word List 34

arise [əˈraɪz]

v. to become evident; appear; originate 呈现；出现；发生

Greenhouse gases *arise* from a wide range of sources. 温室气体有多种来源。

arouse [əˈraʊz]　　　　　　　　　　　　　　　　　　　　　　[同] stir

v. to cause（sth.）to appear; awaken 引起（某事物）；激发

The bridge *aroused* strong aesthetic objections from public officials. 这座桥梁在审美方面引发了政府官员们的强烈反对。

bow [baʊ]

① *n.* an act of bending the head or body 鞠躬

② *v./n.* to bend the head or body as a sign of respect or as a greeting 鞠躬；点头（表示尊敬或打招呼）

The cast *bowed* as the audience applauded. 演员们向鼓掌的观众鞠躬。

consumer [kənˈsjuːmə(r)]

n. person who buys goods or uses services 消费者；顾客

Consumers are encouraged to complain about faulty goods. 要鼓励消费者对劣质商品投诉。

consumption [kənˈsʌmpʃn]

n. the act of buying and using products 购买，消费，使用

The role of governments in environmental management is difficult but inescapable. Often, however, governments actually subsidise the exploitation and *consumption* of natural resources. 政府在环境治理方面的任务艰巨但不可推卸。然而，很多时候政府却是在资助对自然资源掠夺和使用的行为。

contact [ˈkɒntækt]　　　　　　　　　　　　　　　　　　　　　[同] ①touch

① *n.* communication 通讯；联系；交往

She's lost *contact* with her son. 她跟儿子失去了联系。

② *v.* to write to or telephone sb. 联系

I must *contact* my lawyer before I made my final decisions. 在做出最后决定之前，我必须先同我的律师联系一下。

contain [kənˈteɪn]　　　　　　　　　　　　　　　　　　　　[同] hold, include

v. to have within; to be made up of 盛放；包含

Nicotine *contains* more than 4,700 chemical compounds. 尼古丁含有 4700 多种化学物质。

distinguish [dɪˈstɪŋgwɪʃ]　　　　　　　　　　　　　　　　　[同] differentiate

v. to recognize the difference between two people or things 区分；辨别；分清

Sometimes reality and fantasy are hard to *distinguish*. 有时候现实和幻想很难区分。

distort [dɪˈstɔːt]　　　　　　　　　　　　　　　　　　　　[同] misrepresent

v. to twist or change facts, ideas, etc. so that they are no longer correct or true 扭曲；曲解

Newspapers are often guilty of *distorting* the truth. 报纸常犯扭曲事实的错误。

existence [ɪɡˈzɪstəns]　　　　　　　　　　[同] being

n. the state of existing 存在的状态

It is impossible to prove the **existence** of God. 证明上帝的存在是不可能的。

exit [ˈeksɪt]　　　　　　　　　　　　　[同] departure

n. a way out of a public building or vehicle 出口，通道

To make **exit** and re-entry simpler, could everyone leaving the site use the main entrance at the other side of the car park? 为使进出更为便利，如您要离开请走停车场另一边的主要出口。

formula [ˈfɔːmjələ]

n. list of ingredients or set of instructions for making sth., esp. medicines and fuels 配方；药方；处方

a **formula** for a new drug 新药的配方

grasp [ɡrɑːsp]　　　　　　　　　　　[同] apprehend

v. to understand (sth.) fully 全面理解(某事)；全面领会

Even very tiny babies are capable of **grasping** and remembering a concept. 即使婴儿都有能力理解并记忆一个概念。

grateful [ˈɡreɪtfʊl]　　　　　　　　　[反] ungrateful

adj. feeling or showing appreciation for sth. good done to one, for sth. fortunate that happens, etc.; thankful 感激的；感谢的

I am **grateful** to you for your help. 我感谢你的帮助。

hug [hʌg]　　　　　　　　　　　　　　[同] embrace

v. to put the arms round (sb./sth.) tightly, esp. to show love 紧紧抱住；(尤指示爱)拥抱，搂抱

They **hugged** each other. 他们相互拥抱。

insurance [ɪnˈʃʊərəns]

n. (contract made by a company or society, or by the state, to provide a) guarantee of compensation for loss, damage, sickness, death, etc. in return for regular payment 保险(契约)

You would need to take out your own personal accident **insurance**. 你需要申请你自己的个人意外保险。

intake [ˈɪnteɪk]

n. the amount of food, drink, etc. that you take into your body 纳入量

People would probably have to reduce their caloric **intake** by roughly thirty per cent. 人们很有可能被迫减少他们的热量摄入量的百分之三十左右。

integral [ˈɪntɪɡrəl]　　　　　　　　　[近] whole

adj. having or containing all parts that are necessary for completeness; whole 构成整体所需的；完整的；必备的

Dung beetles have become an **integral** part of the successful management of dairy farms in Australia. 屎壳郎已经成为了澳大利亚奶牛农场成功管理的一个不可或缺的部分。

location [ləʊˈkeɪʃn]　　　　　　　　　[同] place

n. a place where sth. happens or exists; the position of sth. 地方；地点；位置

They use a change of **location** to indicate a change in role from boss to friend. 他们利用位置的变化来暗示老板到朋友的角色转换。

opt [ɒpt]　　　　　　　　　　　　　　[同] choose

v. to decide to do sth.; choose 决定做某事；选择

He *opted* to go to Paris rather than London. 他决定去巴黎，不去伦敦。

optimistic [ˌɒptɪˈmɪstɪk] [反] pessimistic

adj. expecting the best; confident 乐观的；有信心的

Psychologists have conducted studies showing that people become less sceptical and more *optimistic* when the weather is sunny. 心理学家的研究表明当天气晴朗时，人们会更乐观而且不那么多疑。

pace [peɪs]

n. (length of a) single step in walking or running (走或跑的)一步，一步的距离

pace of life 生活节奏

pacific [pəˈsɪfɪk] [同] peaceful

adj. (fml.) making or loving peace; peaceful 和解的；爱和平的；和平的

Do we want to create a restless mood, or a calm, *pacific* one? 我们是要创造一种不安定的气氛，还是一种宁静、平和的气氛？

packed [pækt] [同] full, crowded

adj. extremely full of people 拥挤的；充满的

The island was *packed* with tourists. 岛上到处都是游客。

remind [rɪˈmaɪnd]

v. to inform (sb.) of a fact or tell (sb.) to do sth. he may have forgotten 提醒(某人)注意某事或做某事

Do I have to *remind* you again? 还需要我再次提醒你吗？

remote [rɪˈməʊt] [同] faraway

adj. far away from other communities, houses, etc.; isolated (与其他社区、房子等)远离的，遥远的；隔离的

one of the *remotest* areas of the world 世界上最荒僻的地区之一

remove [rɪˈmuːv] [同] clear away

v. to take sth. away from, out of, or off the place where it is 移动；除去

Please do not *remove* this notice. 请不要拿掉这个通知。

render [ˈrendə(r)]

v. to cause (sb./sth.) to be in a certain condition 使(某人／某物)处于某种状况

We are now in a new era whereby the teacher student ratio once again *renders* the system of education ineffective. 我们已身处新时期，而师生比例不协调再次使教育系统陷入效率低的境地。

scarce [skeəs] [同] rare

adj. not easily obtained and much less than is needed 难获得而不足的

scarce resources 资源不足

scarcely [ˈskeəsli] [同] just barely

adv. only just; hardly 仅仅；几乎不

There were *scarcely* a hundred people present. 出席的不足一百人。

scatter [ˈskætə(r)] [同] spread

v. to throw (sth.) in different directions; to put here and there 撒(某物)；散播

We *scattered* plates of food around the room before the party. 我们在聚会前把一盘盘食物摆放在屋中各处。

scenario [sɪˈnɑːrɪəʊ]

n. a situation that could possibly happen 可能的情况；场景；方案

A common *scenario* is that a woman marries and sacrifices her career for her husband. 一个很常见的情况就是女人结了婚，并为丈夫牺牲了自己的事业。

scene [siːn]

n. view as seen by a spectator 景色；景象；景致

The fighting *scenes* are remarkable. 打斗的场面棒极了。

survival [səˈvaɪvl]

n. state of continuing to live or exist; surviving 继续生存或存在；存活；幸存

A lot of small companies have to fight for *survival*. 很多小公司为了生存拼得你死我活。

survive [səˈvaɪv]

v. to continue to live or exist 继续生存或存在

If you remove the water the microorganisms simply can't *survive*. 如果去除了水，这些微生物将无法存活。

suspect [səˈspekt]　　　　　　　　　　　　　　　　　　　　　　　　　［同］②distrust

v. ①to think that sth. is probably true, especially sth. bad 猜想；觉得；估摸 ②to think that sth. is not honest or true 怀疑

I *suspect* that 10 years after the book is published, nobody will even remember the name of the author. 我估摸着这本书出版 10 年后，甚至没有人会再记得作者的名字。

suspend [səˈspend]　　　　　　　　　　　　　　　　　　　　　　　　　　［同］postpone

v. to prevent（sth.）from being in effect for a time; to stop（sth.）temporarily 暂不实行（某事物）；使（某事物）暂停

suspend a rule 暂不实行一项规定

tremendous [trəˈmendəs]　　　　　　　　　　　　　　　　　　　　　　　　［同］enormous

adj. very great; immense 极大的；巨大的

The 1970s and 1980s were a time of *tremendous* social change. 二十世纪七八十年代发生了巨大的社会变革。

trend [trend]　　　　　　　　　　　　　　　　　　　　　　　　　　　　　［同］tendency

n. general tendency or direction 趋势；趋向；动向

In fact the figures for Japan start to show a reverse *trend*. 事实上有关日本的数据开始显示出一种相反的趋势。

trial [ˈtraɪəl]

n. examination of evidence in a lawcourt, by a judge and often a jury, to decide if sb. accused of a crime is innocent or guilty 审问；审讯；审理；审判

The *trial* lasted a week. 审讯持续了一个星期。

weight [weɪt]

① *n.* how heavy sb./sth. is, which can be measured in, for example, kilogram or pounds 重量；分量

It is about 76 kilos in *weight*. 这东西重约 76 千克。

② *v.* to give different values to things to show how important you think each of them is compared with the others 使加权

The results of the survey were *weighted* to allow for variations in the sample. 这次调查的结果进行了加权处理，以备样本中出现变化。

welfare [ˈwelfeə(r)]

n. practical or financial help that is provided, often by government, for people or animals that

need it (政府给予的)福利

The Language Institute provides student support, *welfare* and activities services. 语言学院为学生提供支持、福利和各种活动服务。

"First, I'm going to wipe out poverty."

Take the Test ≫

一、英汉互译

消费者	_____	distort	_____
区分	_____	formula	_____
必备的	_____	intake	_____
乐观的	_____	packed	_____
生存(n.)	_____	render	_____

二、翻译句子

1) 一个很常见的情况就是女人结了婚, 并为丈夫牺牲了自己的事业。(scenario)

_____

2) 打斗的场面棒极了。(scene)

_____

3) 很多小公司为了生存拼得你死我活。(survival)

_____

4) 二十世纪七八十年代发生了巨大的社会变革。(tremendous)

_____

Hew out of the mountain of despair a stone of hope and you can make your life a splendid one.
追求卓越, 挑战极限, 从绝望中寻找希望, 人生终将辉煌。

——新东方校训

artificial [ˌɑːtɪ'fɪʃl]　　　　　　　　　　　　　　[同] false [反] natural, genuine

adj. made or produced by man in imitation of sth. natural; not real 人造的；人工的；假的

The quest for true ***artificial*** intelligence has produced very mixed results. 对人工智能的探索产生了多种不同的结果。

aspect ['æspekt]

n. particular part or feature of sth. being considered 方面

Literacy is declining because it is less central to some ***aspects*** of everyday life. 读写能力对于日常生活的一些方面来说不那么重要，因此正逐步退化。

brag [bræg]　　　　　　　　　　　　　　　　　　　[同] boast

v. to talk with too much pride (about sth.) 吹嘘(某事物)；自夸

Not to ***brag***, I could draw anything. 不是瞎吹，我什么都能画。

contemporary [kən'temprəri]　　　　　　　　　[近] present

adj. ①belonging to the present time 现代的；当代的 ②of the time or period being referred to; belonging to the same time 属于同一时代的

Children's books are surprisingly relevant to ***contemporary*** life. 儿童读物与当代的社会生活有着惊人的联系。

contest ['kɒntest]　　　　　　　　　　　　　　　[同] compete

n. event in which people compete against each other for a prize; competition 比赛；竞赛

The election was so one-sided that it was really no ***contest***. 选举呈现一边倒的局面，实际上毫无竞争可言。

context ['kɒntekst]

n. circumstances in which sth. happens or in which sth. is to be considered (某事物产生的或应考虑到的)环境，背景

Health is now being viewed in terms of the social and economic ***context*** in which people live. 如今，健康这个概念被放到了一个人们赖以生存的社会和经济大环境中加以考虑。

contract [kən'trækt]　　　　　　　　　　　　　　[同] compress, constrict

v. (cause sth.) to become tighter or narrower (使某物)紧缩或收缩

The heart is simply a muscle that expands and ***contracts***. 心脏只不过是一块会张开和收缩的肌肉而已。

distract [dɪ'strækt]　　　　　　　　　　　　　　　[近] confuse

v. to take sb.'s attention away from what they are trying to do 转移(注意力)；分散(思想)；使分心

Try not to ***distract*** other students. 尽量不要干扰到其他学生。

distress [dɪ'stres]　　　　　　　　　　　　　　　[同] ①suffering

① *n.* a feeling of great worry or unhappiness; great suffering 忧虑；悲伤；痛苦

She was obviously in ***distress*** after the attack. 她受到打击后显然很痛苦。

② *v.* to make sb. feel very worried or unhappy 使忧虑；使悲伤；使苦恼

Don't *distress* yourself. 你别自寻烦恼了。

distribute [dɪˈstrɪbjuːt]

v. to give things to a large number of people; to share sth. between a number of people 分发；分配

The organization *distributed* food and blankets to the earthquake victims. 这个机构向地震灾民分发了食品和毯子。

expand [ɪkˈspænd]　　　　　　　　　　　　　　　　[反] contract

v. to become greater in size, number or importance; to make sth. greater in size, number or importance 扩大，增加，增强(尺码、数量或重要性)

Sydney's population *expanded* rapidly in the 1960s. 20 世纪 60 年代，悉尼的人口迅速增加了。

expansion [ɪkˈspænʃn]　　　　　　　　　　　　　[同] growth

n. when sth. increases in size, range, amount, etc. 膨胀；扩充

The rapid *expansion* of cities can cause social and economic problems. 城市的迅速膨胀会导致社会和经济问题。

expert [ˈekspɜːt]

n. sb. who has a special skill or special knowledge of a subject, gained as a result of training or experience 专家；行家

He's a world *expert* on marine mammals. 他是世界级的海洋哺乳动物专家。

formulate [ˈfɔːmjuleɪt]

v. to create (sth.) in a precise form 将(某事物)形式固定；制定

formulate a rule/policy/theory 制定规则 / 制定政策 / 创立理论

forthcoming [ˌfɔːθˈkʌmɪŋ]

adj. about to happen or appear in the near future 即将发生或出现的

a list of *forthcoming* books 即将出版的图书目录

gratitude [ˈɡrætɪtjuːd]　　　　　　　　　　　　　[反] ingratitude

n. being grateful; thankfulness 感激；感谢

I felt a deep sense of *gratitude* to the teacher who had encouraged me to go on to university. 我深深感激那个鼓励我继续读大学的老师。

humanity [hjuːˈmænəti]　　　　　　　　　　　　　[同] mankind

n. human beings collectively; the human race; people 人(总称)；人类

Thirty per cent of *humanity* live in conditions of terrible poverty. 30%的人口生活在极度贫困中。

integrate [ˈɪntɪɡreɪt]

v. to combine sth. in such a way that it becomes fully a part of sth. else　(将某事物与另一事物结合)构成整体

Twenty-six species of dung beetles are known to have become successfully *integrated* into the local environment. 据知，26 种屎壳郎成功地融入到当地的环境中去了。

intellectual [ˌɪntəˈlektʃuəl]

adj. relating to the ability to understand things and think intelligently 智力的；理智的

One of the first great *intellectual* feats of a young child is learning how to talk. 年幼孩子智慧的一个重要表现就是学会如何讲话。

intelligence [ɪnˈtelɪdʒəns]

n. power of learning, understanding and reasoning; mental ability 学习、理解和推理的能力；

智力；脑力

The most important inputs were ***intelligence*** and personal involvement with task accomplishment. 最重要的投入就是智力和完成任务所需的个人参与。

"Oh, brother — and they say that *television* insults your intelligence!

logic [ˈlɒdʒɪck]

n. a way of thinking or explaining sth. 思维方式；逻辑

I fail to see the ***logic*** behind his argument. 我不明白支持他论据的是什么逻辑。

option [ˈɒpʃn]   [同] alternative

n. a choice you can make in a particular situation 选择；可选性

These people have no ***option*** but to take low paid unattractive work. 这些人没有其他选择，只能从事收入低、条件差的工作。

orbit [ˈɔːbɪt]

n. path followed by a planet, star, moon, etc. round another body（天体运行的）轨道

the earth's ***orbit*** round the sun 地球绕行太阳的轨道

organ [ˈɔːgən]

n. ①a part of the body, such as the heart or lungs, that has a particular purpose 器官 ②large musical instrument from which sounds are produced by air forced through pipes 风琴；管风琴

Today, most ***organ*** transplants are relatively safe procedures. 今天，大部分的器官移植手术都是比较安全的医疗程序。

organism [ˈɔːgənɪzəm]

n.（usu. small）living being with parts that work together（通常指微小的）生物，有机体

study the minute ***organisms*** in water 研究水中的微生物

panel [ˈpænl]

n. ①a group of people with skills or specialist knowledge who have been chosen to give advice or opinions on a particular subject 咨询小组；顾问小组

A ***panel*** of experts has looked at the proposal. 专家组看过了提议。

②a board on which the controls and instruments of an aircraft, a car, etc. are mounted（飞行器、汽车等的）控制面板，仪表板

panic [ˈpænɪk]   [同] fear

n. sudden irrational feeling of great fear 恐慌；惊慌

Small business owners are in a ***panic*** over whether they will survive. 小型企业主处于恐慌之中，不知道自己的企业能否生存下去。

[记] 原指由潘神（Pan）的出现所引起的大恐慌

panorama [ˌpænəˈrɑːmə]

n. a view of a wide area of land 全景

There is a superb ***panorama*** of the mountains from the hotel. 从旅馆可饱览层峦叠嶂的雄伟景观。

renew [rɪˈnjuː]   [同] restore

v. replace (sth.) with sth. new of the same kind 更将（某物）换成新的；更新（某物）

There will be a buffet reception afterwards—a chance to ***renew*** acquaintance with old friends. 之后会有个自助酒会，这是个跟老朋友叙旧的好机会。

renowned [rɪˈnaʊnd]   [同] famous

adj. famous; celebrated 著名的；有声望的

renowned as an actress/for her acting 出名的女演员 / 因演技而出名

rental ['rentl]

n. renting 租赁

In addition, some uniform companies also offer **rental** services. 另外，一些制服公司还提供租赁服务。

scent [sent]　　　　　　　　　　　　　　　　　　　　　　　　　[同] odor

n. characteristic smell of sth., esp. a pleasant one (某物特有的)气味；(尤指)香味

Modern roses have no **scent**. 现在的玫瑰不香。

schedule ['ʃedjuːl]

n. programme of work to be done or of planned events 进度表；预定计划表

If you see your timetable for this semester you will see that you have regular report writing workshops built into your **schedule**. 看一下你们本学期的时间表，可以发现你们的时间表里加入了定期的报告写作研讨会。

Daily Schedule

scholarship [ˌskɒləʃɪp]

n. (award of a) grant of money to a scholar 奖学金；获得奖学金的资格

The Foundation's goals include providing **scholarships** for gifted young students. 基金会的目标包括为那些有才华的年轻学生提供奖学金。

scientific [ˌsaɪən'tɪfɪk]

adj. about or related to science, or using its methods 科学的；与科学相关的

There is no **scientific** basis for such policies. 这些政策根本就没有科学依据。

suspicious [sə'spɪʃəs]　　　　　　　　　　　　　　　　　　[同] doubtful

adj. having or showing suspicion 有疑心的；表示怀疑的

a **suspicious** look/attitude 怀疑的样子 / 态度

sustain [sə'steɪn]　　　　　　　　　　　　　　　　　　　　[同] maintain

v. to keep (sb./sth.) alive or in existence 维持(某人 / 某物)的生命或存在

Experiments have already shown that enough oxygen can be produced by plants to **sustain** human life. 实验表明植物能制造足够的氧气来维持人的生命。

tricky ['trɪki]

adj. sth. that is difficult to deal with or do because it is complicated and full of problems 麻烦的；复杂困难的

Getting everyone to use the new technology will be **tricky**. 让每个人都用新科技有点困难。

trifle ['traɪfl]

n. thing, question or activity that has little value or importance 无多大价值或重要性的事物、问题或活动

I bought a few **trifles** as souvenirs. 我买了些小玩意儿作纪念品。

trigger ['trɪɡə(r)]　　　　　　　　　　　　　　　　　　　　[同] initiate

v. to make sth. happen very quickly, especially a series of events 成为突然发生的 (常为激烈的)反应的原因；引发

Studying overseas can **trigger** a personal crisis. 出国留学可能会引发一场个人危机。

whereas [ˌweər'æz]　　　　　　　　　　　　　　　　　　　　[同] though

conj. used to compare or contract two facts (用以比较或对比两个事实)然而；尽管；但是

Some of the studies show positive results, **whereas** others do not. 有一些研究结果令人满意，然而另一些则不然。

whereby [weəˈbaɪ]

adv. (fml.) by which; because of which 凭此；借以；由于

They have introduced a new system **whereby** all employees must undergo regular training. 他们采用了新的制度，那就是所有的雇员都必须接受常规的培训。

Take the Test

一、英汉互译

方面	_____	artificial	_____
现代的	_____	distract	_____
分发	_____	forthcoming	_____
感激	_____	intelligence	_____
进度表	_____	organism	_____

二、翻译句子

1）如今，健康这个概念被放到了一个人们赖以生存的社会和经济大环境中加以考虑。（context）

_____

2）城市的迅速膨胀能导致社会和经济问题。（expansion）

_____

3）出国留学可能会引发一场个人危机。（trigger）

_____

4）有一些研究结果令人满意，然而另一些则不然。（whereas）

_____

Today is the first day of the rest of my life, I wake as a child to see the world begin. On monarch wings and birthday wonderings, want to put on faces, walk in the wet and cold. And look forward to my growing old, to grow is to change, to change is to be new, to be new is to be young again, I barely remember when.

——美国乡村歌手 约翰·丹佛（John Denver）

assemble [ə'sembl] [同] ①gather [反] ②disperse

v. ① (cause people or things) to come together; collect 集合；收集

assemble evidence 收集证据

② to put all the parts of sth. together 装配

It was easy to *assemble* the bookcase myself. 我自己轻易地就把书架安装好了。

assess [ə'ses] [同] evaluate, appraise

v. estimate the quality of sth. 估计，评定(某事物的质量)

The testing must *assess* the impact of both the product itself and the manufacturing process. 测试必须评估产品本身与生产流程的影响。

branch [brɑːntʃ]

n. subdivision of a family, a subject of knowledge, or a group of languages (家族的)分支；(知识的)分科；(语言的)分系

Statistics is a *branch* of mathematics that is used in the studies of many disciplines from physics, through to the social sciences. 统计学是数学的一个分支，应用于从物理学到社会学的很多学科。

brand [brænd] [近] trademark

n. particular make of goods or their trade mark 商品的牌子；商标

Which *brand* of toothpaste do you prefer? 你爱用什么牌子的牙膏？

contract ['kɒntrækt] [同] agreement

n. an official agreement between two or more people, stating what each will do 合同

Read the *contract* carefully before you sign it. 签合同前仔细读一读。

contrary ['kɒntrəri] [同] opposite

adj. opposite in nature, tendency or direction (在性质、倾向或方向等上)相反的，相违的

Contrary to popular belief, a desert can be very cold. 与普遍看法相反的是，沙漠可以是个很寒冷的地方。

contrast [kən'trɑːst] [同] compare

v. to compare (two different people or things) so that difference are made clear 对比；相比

The poem *contrasts* youth and age. 这首诗对比了青春与年老。

contribute [kən'trɪbjuːt]

v. to increase sth.; to add to sth. 增加某事物；添加到某事物中

Her work has *contributed* enormously to our understanding of this difficult subject. 她的工作大大帮助了我们对这个困难问题的了解。

district ['dɪstrɪkt] [同] locality

n. an area of a country or town, esp. one that has particular features 地区；区域

the city of London's financial *district* 伦敦的金融区

disturb [dɪ'stɜːb] [同] bother [反] calm

v. to make sb. worry 使焦虑；使不安；使烦恼

Research being conducted in two countries is reaching similarly ***disturbing*** conclusions concerning this little-understood pollutant. 在两个国家所做的研究得出的关于这种人们不太了解的污染物的结论很相似，这一结论很让人不安。

expire [ɪk'spaɪə(r)] [反] inspire

v. (of a document, an agreement, etc.) to be no longer valid because the period of time for which it could be used has ended (因到期而)失效；终止

When does your driving licence ***expire***? 你的驾照什么时候到期？

explode [ɪk'spləʊd] [同] ①rocket

v. ①to increase suddenly and very quickly in number 突增；激增 ②to burst, or to make sth. burst, into small pieces 爆炸

The world's population has ***exploded***. 世界人口迅猛增长。

explicit [ɪk'splɪsɪt] [反] indefinite

adj. (of a statement or piece of writing) clear and easy to understand 清楚明白的；易于理解的

He gave me very ***explicit*** directions on how to get there. 他清楚地向我说明了去那儿的路线。

fortnight ['fɔːtnaɪt]

n. (esp. BrE) two weeks 两星期(的时间)

I spent about a ***fortnight*** in bed, and then felt fine again. 我在床上躺了大约俩礼拜，然后又感觉好了。

forum ['fɔːrəm]

n. place where important public issues can be discussed (讨论公共问题的)场所，论坛

The letters page serves as a useful ***forum*** for the exchange of readers' views. 读者来信版是读者们交流想法的有益园地。

grave [greɪv] [近] ①serious

① *adj.* grave problems, situations, or worries are very great or bad 严肃的；庄重的

It is a matter of ***grave*** concern. 这件事很让人担忧。

② *n.* the place in the ground where a dead body is buried 坟墓

gravity ['grævɪti]

n. ①importance (of a worrying kind); seriousness (令人忧虑的)重要性；严重性

For an offence of this ***gravity***, imprisonment is the usual punishment. 对这种重大罪行通常处以监禁。

②the force that causes sth. to fall to the ground or to be attracted to another planet 重力

humble ['hʌmbl] [反] ignoble

adj. (of a thing) not large or elaborate; poor (指事物)简陋的，低劣的

The modern day space programs owe their success to the ***humble*** beginnings of those in previous centuries who developed the foundations of the reaction principle. 现代空间项目的成功源于过去几个世纪里那些建立反作用力原理的人们最初简单的开端。

humidity [hjuː'mɪdəti]

n. degree of moisture, esp. in the air; dampness 湿度(尤指空气中的)；潮湿

Some plants need warmth and high ***humidity***. 有些植物需要温暖和高湿度的环境。

intend [ɪn'tend] [同] aim

v. to have (a particular purpose or plan) in mind; mean 打算；意欲；想要

The owners of the tanker certainly did not **intend** it to explode. 当然，油轮的所有者们并没想过要让它爆炸。

intense [ɪnˈtens]

adj. (of sensations) very great or severe; extreme (指感觉)强烈的，剧烈的；极度的

Large thunderclouds are generating the **intense** electrical fields that can cause lightning flashes. 巨大的雷雨云正形成能产生闪电的强电场。

intention [ɪnˈtenʃn]

n. purpose or aim; meaning 意图；目的；意思

What do you think was the author's **intention** in this passage? 你认为作者写这一段的用意是什么？

logo [ˈləʊɡəʊ]

n. a printed design or symbol that a company or an organization uses as its special sign (公司或机构的)标志；徽标

The baseball team has a new **logo**. 棒球队有了个新队徽。

longitude [ˈlɒŋɡɪtjuːd]

n. the distance of a place east or west of Greenwich Meridian, measured in degrees 经度

The **longitude** of New York is 74 degrees west of Greenwich. 纽约的经度是西经 74 度。

orient [ˈɔːrient]

v. (AmE orientate) to direct the interest of sb. (to sth.) 对某人的兴趣(朝向某事物)进行引导

In the late 1940s the World Health Organization challenged this physically and medically **oriented** view of health. 20 世纪 40 年代末，世界卫生组织对这一生理以及医学意义上的健康概念提出了挑战。

orientation [ˌɔːriənˈteɪʃn]

n. activity of orientating oneself; state of being orientated 熟悉情况；认识环境；确定方位

Welcome to the student **orientation** program! 欢迎参加新生指南活动！

originate [əˈrɪdʒɪneɪt]　　　　　　　　　　　　　　　　　　　[同] generate

v. (fml.) to have sth./sb. as a cause or beginning 始自某事物 / 某人；起源；发端

This style of architecture **originated** from/with the ancient Greeks. 这种建筑风格起源于古希腊。

paradise [ˈpærədaɪs]　　　　　　　　　　　　　　　　　　　　[同] heaven

n. ideal or perfect place 理想的或完美的地方；乐园；乐土

This island is a **paradise** for bird-watchers. 这个岛是鸟类观察者的乐土。

paradox [ˈpærədɒks]

n. statement that seems to be absurd or contradictory but is or may be true 似非而是的隽语；看似矛盾而实际(或可能)正确的说法

'More haste, less speed' is a well-known **paradox**. "欲速则不达"是人所熟知的隽语。

parallel [ˈpærəlel]　　　　　　　　　　　　　　　　[反] ①nonparallel, unparallel

① *adj.* two lines, paths, etc. that are parallel to each other are the same distance apart along their whole length 平行的

② *n.* a relationship or similarity between two things, especially things that exist or happen in different places or at different times 相似之处

There are many **parallels** between politics and acting. 政治和表演之间有很多相似之处。

repeal [rɪˈpiːl]　　　　　　　　　　　　　　　　　　　　　　[同] abrogate

v. to withdraw (a law, etc.) officially; revoke 废止(法规等)；撤销；取消

In America, laws preventing television broadcasters from owning programme companies were *repealed* earlier this decade. 在美国，限制电视广播公司拥有节目制作公司的法律在这个年代的早期已被废止了。

replace [rɪˈpleɪs]

v. to take the place of（sb./sth.）代替，取代（某人/某事物）

Robots are *replacing* people on assembly lines. 机器人正逐渐取替流水线上的工人。

replicate [ˈreplɪkeɪt]　　　　　　　　　　　　　　　　　　　　　　　[近] copy

v. if you replicate sb.'s work, a scientific study, etc, you do it again, or try to get the same result again 复制

Other scientists were unable to *replicate* the experiment. 其他科学家无法复制该试验。

represent [ˌreprɪˈzent]　　　　　　　　　　　　　　　　　　　　　　[同] body

v. ①to be a symbol of sth. 代表；象征 ②to officially speak or take action for another person or group of people 代表

In Chinese culture peony *represents* fortune and prosperity. 在中国文化中牡丹代表富贵。

scope [skəʊp]　　　　　　　　　　　　　　　　　　　　　　　　　　[同] range

n. the range of things that a subject, activity, book, etc. deals with 范围；幅度

Let us extend the *scope* of the study to examine more factors. 让我们把研究的范围拓宽些，考察更多的因素。

score [skɔː(r)]

① *n.* the number of marks in a game（比赛中的）得分

② *v.* to win a point in a sport, game, competition, or test 得分

He has *scored* 12 goals so far this season. 这个赛季迄今为止他已经进了 12 个球。

scramble [ˈskræmbl]

v. ① to climb or crawl quickly, usu. over rough ground or with difficulty; clamber 攀登；爬 ② to mix words, ideas, sentences, etc. so that they are not in the right order and do not make sense 打散；搅乱

She *scrambled* down the tree as quickly as she could. 她以最快的速度从树上爬了下来。

swear [sweə(r)]　　　　　　　　　　　　　　　　　　　　　[同] ①vow, pledge

v. ①to promise that you will do sth. 发誓 ②to use rude and offensive language 骂人；说脏话

Don't *swear* in front of the children. 不要在孩子面前说脏话。

sweep [swiːp]

v. to remove（dust, dirt, etc.）with or as if with a broom or brush 扫，掸，打扫（灰尘、污垢等）

sweep the dust from the carpets 清扫地毯上的灰尘

triple [ˈtrɪpl]

adj. three times as much or as many 三倍的；三重的

travelling at *triple* the speed 以三倍的速度前进

triumph [ˈtraɪəmf]　　　　　　　　　　　　　　　　　　　　　　[同] ①victory

n. ①an important victory or success after a difficult struggle 成功；胜利 ②（joy or satisfaction at）being successful or victorious 成功或胜利的喜悦

The dam represents man's *triumph* over nature. 这个大坝象征着人定胜天。

trivial [ˈtrɪvɪəl]　　　　　　　　　　　　　　　　　　　　　　[同] insignificant

adj.（derog.）that has little importance 不重要的；琐碎的

Why waste time watching *trivial* TV programs? 为什么要浪费时间看那些无聊的电视节目？

Take the Test >>

一、英汉互译

分支	_____	expire	_____
品牌	_____	explicit	_____
强烈的	_____	intention	_____
起源	_____	longitude	_____
琐碎的	_____	paradox	_____

二、翻译句子

1) 与普遍看法相反的是, 沙漠可以是个很寒冷的地方。(contrary)

_____

2) 她的工作大大帮助了我们对这个困难问题的了解。(contribute)

_____

3) 欢迎参加新生指南活动!(orientation)

_____

4) 在中国文化中牡丹代表富贵。(represent)

_____

Every day I remind myself that my inner and outer life are based on the labors of other men, living and dead, and that I must exert myself in order to give in the same measure as I have received and am still receiving.

每天我都提醒着自己:我的精神生活和物质生活都是以别人的劳动为基础的,我必须尽力以同样的分量来报偿我所获得的和至今仍在接受着的东西。

————美国科学家 爱因斯坦(Albert Einstein, American scientist)

assignment [əˈsaɪnmənt] [同] task

n. task or duty that is assigned to sb. 指定给某人的任务或职责；作业

You should hand your *assignments* in on time and turn up for all the tutorials. 你应该及时交作业并参加所有的辅导课。

assist [əˈsɪst] [同] help [反] hamper, impede

v. (in/with sth.) help 帮助；援助；协助

The number of young people who work, and therefore *assist* in the creation of wealth, are fewer in number than the older, retired generation. 参加工作因而能帮助创造财富的年轻人在数量上少于年老退休的那代人。

associate [əˈsəʊʃɪeɪt] [同] connect, relate

v. join (people or things) together; connect (ideas, etc.) in one's mind 将(人或事物)联系起来；在头脑中联想

The 9 to 5 working day has traditionally been *associated* with office work. 朝九晚五工作制传统上总与办公室工作相联系。

association [əˌsəʊsɪˈeɪʃn]

n. ①group of people joined together for a common purpose; organization 社团；协会；学会

The American Medical *Association* represents about half of all the US doctors. 美国医师学会代表着近半数的美国医生。

②mental connection between ideas 联想

Association is a very powerful yet little understood psychological phenomenon. 联想这种心理现象力量很强大，却还很少被人们所了解。

breed [briːd] [同] ①type ②generate

① *n.* a type of animal that is kept as a pet or on a farm 品种

Sharks vary in weight with size and *breed*. 鲨鱼的体重因大小和品种的不同而不同。

② *v.* (of animals) to have sex and produce young (指动物)生育，繁殖

Ted Hunter is here to tell us about the possibilities of *breeding* and rearing ostrich here in this country. 泰德·亨特来到这里是为了给我们介绍在这个国家繁殖和饲养鸵鸟的可能性。

brief [briːf] [同] ①②short ②concise

adj. ①continuing for a short time 短暂的 ② using very few words or including few details 简要的

I'm going to give you a *brief* account of the history of the museum. 我将给大家简要地介绍一下本博物馆的历史。

convenient [kənˈviːniənt] [同] handy [反] inconvenient

adj. fitting in well with people's needs or plans; giving no trouble or difficulty; suitable 适合需要的；方便的

Cars easily surpass trains or buses as a flexible and *convenient* mode of personal transport. 汽车作为一种方便灵活的个人交通工具，轻而易举地超过火车与公共汽车。

convention [kən'venʃn]

n. ①a large formal meeting for people who belong to the same profession or organization or who have the same interests 会议，大会 ②general, usu. unspoken, agreement about how people should act or behave in certain circumstances（某种情况下的）习俗，惯例

The handshake is a social *convention*. 握手是一种社会习俗。

converse ['kɒnvɜːs]　　　　　　　　　　　　　　　　　　　　[同] opposite

n. the opposite 相反的事物

He says she is satisfied, but I believe the *converse* to be true: she is very dissatisfied. 他说她已心满意足了，不过我认为实际情况相反：她很不满意。

convert [kən'vɜːt]　　　　　　　　　　　　　　　　　　　　[同] transform

v. to change（sth.）from one form or use to another 改变（某事物）的形式或用途

The original house was *converted* into a residential college for the university. 原来的房子被改造为大学的一所寄宿学院。

diverse [daɪ'vɜːs]　　　　　　　　　　　　　　　　　　　　[同] different

adj. very different from each other and of various kinds 不同的；多种多样的

If properly applied, the new knowledge generated by the project may free humanity from the terrible scourge of *diverse* diseases. 如果被合理使用，这项工程所产生的新知识将把人类从各种疾病的痛苦折磨中解脱出来。

divorce [dɪ'vɔːs]　　　　　　　　　　　　　　　　　　　　[同] ①separation

n. ①a separation; the ending of a relationship between two things 分离；脱离 ②the legal ending of a marriage 离婚

The word literacy is a 19th-century coinage to describe the *divorce* of reading and writing from a full knowledge of literature. "读写能力"这个词是 19 世纪的新词，它表现了读和写从文学这个整体里分离了出来。

document ['dɒkjumənt]

n. an official paper or book that gives information about sth., or that can be used as evidence or proof of sth. 文件；公文；文献；证件

Copies of the relevant *documents* must be filed at court. 有关文件副本必须送交法院备案。

domestic [də'mestɪk]　　　　　　　　　　　　　　　　　　　　[近] home

adj. of or inside a particular country; not foreign or international 本国的；国内的

domestic flights 国内航班

exploit [ɪk'splɔɪt]　　　　　　　　　　　　　　　　　　　　[同] use

v. to treat a person or situation as an opportunity to gain an advantage for yourself 利用（…为自己谋利）

He *exploited* his father's name to get himself a job. 他利用他父亲的名声为自己找到了一份工作。

fossil ['fɒsl]

n. remains of a prehistoric animal or plant preserved by being buried in earth and now hardened like rock 化石

This helps save *fossil* fuels, such as coal, oil and gas, which are argued to be in short supply.

这将帮助节约据称会出现供应短缺的化石燃料，如煤、石油和天然气。

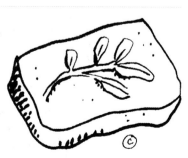

foster ['fɒstə(r)]　　　　　　　　　　[同] encourage; promote

v. to help the growth or development of（sth.）; encourage or promote 培养，培育（某物）; 鼓励；促进

foster the growth of local industries 扶植地方产业

found [faʊnd] [同] ①establish

v. ① to start sth. such as an organization, company, school, or city, often by providing the necessary money 建立；创办

New Oriental School was ***founded*** in the year 1995. 新东方学校创办于 1995 年。

② to be the solid layer of cement, stones, etc. that a building is built on 建造

The castle is ***founded*** on solid rock. 这座城堡建造在坚硬的岩石上。

foundation [faʊnˈdeɪʃn] [同] basis

n. layer of bricks, concrete, etc. forming the solid base of a building underground 地基；房基；基础

The ***foundations*** had yet to be dug, but customers queued up to buy the unusual part-submerged houses. 地基还未开挖，顾客就排起长龙购买这种与众不同的部分浸在水中的房子。

fraction [ˈfrækʃn]

n. small part, bit, amount, or proportion（of sth.）（某物的）小部分；片断

The car stopped within a ***fraction*** of an inch of the wall. 汽车在离墙不到一英寸的地方停住了。

greedy [ˈgriːdi]

adj. filled with greed or desire 贪吃的；贪心的；热望的

greedy for power 贪图权力的

greet [griːt]

v. to give a conventional sign or word of welcome or pleasure when meeting sb. or receiving a guest 欢迎；迎接；问候

When you arrive at an airport here in Australia, you may be ***greeted*** in the baggage hall by a detector dog. 当你到达澳大利亚的机场时，在行李厅迎接你的可能是一只缉毒犬。

hygiene [ˈhaɪdʒiːn]

n. study and practice of cleanliness as a way of maintaining good health and preventing disease 卫生（学）

Wash regularly to ensure personal ***hygiene***. 要经常洗澡以保证个人卫生。

hypothesis [haɪˈpɒθəsɪs] [同] speculation

n. idea or suggestion that is based on known facts and is used as a basis for reasoning or further investigation 假说，假设

The results of our experiment confirmed this ***hypothesis***. 我们实验的结果证明了这一假设。

intersection [ˌɪntəˈsekʃn]

n. （=BrE junction）a place where roads, lines, etc. cross each other, esp. where two roads meet 交叉口

Turn left at the ***intersection*** onto Mohawken Avenue. 在交叉路口左转，进入莫霍肯（Mohawken）大街。

interview [ˈɪntəvjuː]

① *n.* meeting at which sb.（e.g. sb. applying for a job）is asked questions to find out if he/she is suitable 面试；面谈；采访

It'll be so much less time-consuming than organizing ***interviews***. 这将比组织一些采访要节约更多时间。

② *v.* to ask sb questions during an interview 面试

intimate [ˈɪntəmət]   [近] familiar

adj. having or being a very close and friendly relationship 亲密的；密切的

This provides a smaller, more ***intimate*** space, which we use for ballet, modern dance and martial arts. 这为我们的芭蕾、现代舞以及武术提供了一个更小的、更为亲密的空间。

otherwise [ˈʌðəwaɪz]   [反] likewise

adv. in other or different respects; apart from that 在其他方面；除此以外

Every act of observation we make is a function of what we have seen or ***otherwise*** experienced in the past. 我们每一次的观察行为都是我们过去所见及所经历而导致的。

outcome [ˈaʊtkʌm]   [同] effect, result

n. the final result of a meeting, discussion, war, etc.—used especially when no one knows what it will be until it actually happens 结果

Whatever the ***outcome***, I hope we remain friends. 不管结果如何，我希望我们依然是朋友。

paralyse [ˈpærəlaɪz]

v. to affect (sb.) with paralysis 使(某人)瘫痪或麻痹

The accident left her ***paralysed*** from the waist down. 事故后她腰部以下瘫痪了。

paraphrase [ˈpærəfreɪz]

v. to express in a shorter, clearer, or different way what sb. has said or written. 改写；换个说法

Let me ***paraphrase*** what he said like this. 让我把他说过的话这样来解释一下。

participate [pɑːˈtɪsɪpeɪt]   [同] partake

v. to take part or become involved (in an activity) 参加，参与(某活动)

When students are weary from study and want the chance to relax, they can ***participate*** in a number of recreational activities. 当学生们学习疲倦了想要找机会放松一下，他们可以参加许多休闲活动。

particle [ˈpɑːtɪkl]

n. very small bit or piece (of sth.) 微粒；粒子

particles of dust 尘埃

reproduce [ˌriːprəˈdjuːs]

v. to cause sth. to be seen or heard again, or to occur again 再现某事物的形象或声音；放映或播放某事物

a portrait that ***reproduces*** every detail of the sitter's face 把被画人的容貌表现得惟妙惟肖的画像

reputation [ˌrepjuˈteɪʃn]   [同] fame

n. what is generally said or believed about the abilities, qualities, etc. of sb./sth. 名声；名誉；名气

The restaurant certainly lived up to its ***reputation***; the food was delicious. 这个餐馆名副其实，饭菜很好吃。

script [skrɪpt]   [同] handwriting

n. text of a play, film, broadcast, talk, etc. (戏剧、电影、广播、讲话等的)剧本；脚本；讲稿

That line isn't in the ***script***. 脚本上没有那句台词。

swift [swɪft]   [同] fast

adj. quick or rapid; prompt 快的；迅速的；敏捷的

a ***swift*** reply/reaction/revenge 迅速的回答 / 反应 / 报复

switch [swɪtʃ]

① *v.* (cause sth.) to shift or change, esp. suddenly (使某事物)转变或改变(尤指突然)

switch to modern methods 改用现代方法

② *n.* device for completing or breaking an electric circuit（电路的）开关，转换器，闸

syllabus [ˈsɪləbəs]

n. list of subjects, topics, texts, etc. included in a course of study 教学大纲

Hamlet is on this year's English literature *syllabus*.《哈姆雷特》是本学年英国文学教学大纲中规定的作品。

trunk [trʌŋk]

n. main stem of a tree, from which the branches grow 树干

He left his bicycle leaning against a tree *trunk*. 他把他的自行车靠在树干上。

trustworthy [ˈtrʌstˌwɜːði]   [同] dependable

adj. worthy of trust; reliable 值得信任的；可信赖的；可靠的

Most of our employees are pretty *trustworthy*, I think. 我认为我们的大多数员工都很可靠。

tuition [tjuˈɪʃn]

n. ①teaching or instruction, esp. that given to individuals or small groups（尤作文雅语）教学，讲授（尤指对个人或小组的）②the money you pay for being taught 学费

Each hour consists of 50 minutes' *tuition* and a 10-minute break. 每个小时包括 50 分钟的授课时间和 10 分钟的休息时间。

Take the Test ≫

一、英汉互译

作业	_____	association	_____
习俗	_____	convert	_____
培养	_____	exploit	_____
假说	_____	fossil	_____
交叉口	_____	hygiene	_____

二、翻译句子

1）朝九晚五工作制在传统上总与办公室工作相联系。（associate）

_____

2）汽车作为一种方便灵活的个人交通工具，轻而易举地超过火车与公共汽车。（convenient）

_____

3）不管结果如何，我希望我们依然是朋友。（outcome）

_____

4）这个餐馆名副其实，饭菜很好吃。（reputation）

_____

assume [əˈsjuːm]　　　　　　　　　　　　　　　　[同] presume

v. to accept（sth.）as true before there is proof 假定；假设；设想

One would *assume* that the present situation was going to continue. 有人会认为目前的情况将会继续下去。

assumption [əˈsʌmpʃn]　　　　　　　　　　　　[同] presumption

n. thing accepted as true or as sure to happen, but not proved 假定；假设

British industry has often been criticized for its *assumption* that foreign buyers will be happy to communicate in English. 英国企业对外国顾客乐于用英语交流的假定时常招来批评。

astonishing [əˈstɒnɪʃɪŋ]　　　　　　　　　　　[同] amazing

adj. so surprising that it is difficult to believe 令人惊讶的

The Internet in China is developing at an *astonishing* speed. 中国的互联网正以惊人的速度发展着。

astronaut [ˈæstrənɔːt]

n. person who travels in a spacecraft 宇航员

Within a few weeks of being in space *astronauts* can lose up to 40% of their bone mass. 在太空中，宇航员会在几周之内丧失他们近40%的骨骼重量。

bruise [bruːz]

v. ①to get hit or hurt and a bruise appears 使受瘀伤 ②（usu. passive）
to affect sb. badly and make them feel unhappy and less confident 打击；挫伤

My skin *bruises* quite easily. 我的皮肤很容易青一块紫一块的。

budget [ˈbʌdʒɪt]

① *n.* the money that is available to a person or an organization and a plan of how it will be spent over a period of time 预算

The share of the family *budget* spent on leisure now rises much less sharply than it used to.
现在，家庭预算中用于休闲的支出比例的增长速度较以前显著减缓。

② *v.* to be careful about the amount of money you spend; to plan to spend an amount of money for a particular purpose 谨慎花钱；把…编入预算

If we *budget* carefully we'll be able to afford the trip. 我们精打细算一点就能够负担这次旅行。

crucial [ˈkruːʃl]　　　　　　　　　　　　　　　[同] critical, key, vital

adj. very important; decisive 至关重要的；决定性的

Getting this contract is *crucial* to the future of our company. 签订此份合同对本公司的前途至关重要。

crude [kruːd]　　　　　　　　　　　　　　　　[同] unrefined

adj. not developed to a high standard, or made with little skill 粗糙的

a *crude* wooden bridge 一座手艺粗糙的木桥；*crude* oil 原油

crush [krʌʃ]　　　　　　　　　　　　　　　　　　　　　　　　[同] press

v. to press or squeeze(sth./sb.) hard so that there is breakage or injury 压(或挤)坏,压(或挤)伤(某物 / 某人)

Several people were *crushed* to death by the falling rocks. 有几个人被落下来的岩石压死了。

crystal [ˈkrɪstl]

n. ①transparent colourless mineral, such as quartz 无色透明的矿物(如石英); 水晶 ②a small regular-shaped piece of a substance, formed naturally when this substance becomes solid 晶体

copper sulphate *crystals* 硫酸铜晶体

cube [kjuːb]

n. solid body with six equal square sides 立方体; 立方形物

an ice *cube* 冰块儿; Water *Cube* 水立方

dominate [ˈdɒmɪneɪt]　　　　　　　　　　　　　　　　　　　　[同] govern

v. to control or have a lot of influence over sb./sth., esp. in an unpleasant way 支配; 统治; 左右

The task of 'prompting' means making sure that participants who tend to *dominate* allow the quieter members a chance to speak. "激励"的任务就是确保那些意欲控制(讨论)的参加者能让保持沉默的成员有机会发言。

donate [dəʊˈneɪt]　　　　　　　　　　　　　　　　　　　　　　[同] give

v. to give money, food, clothes, etc. to sb./sth., esp. a charity (尤指向慈善机构)捐赠; 赠送

He *donated* thousands of pounds to charity. 他向慈善事业捐款数千英镑。

dormitory [ˈdɔːmɪtri]

n. a room for several people to sleep in, esp. in a school or other institution (有多张床位的)寝室; 学生宿舍

Children sleep in *dormitories* when they live at school. 孩子们住校时, 在宿舍睡觉。

dose [dəʊs]

n. the amount of a medicine or a drug that you should take 剂量

At high *doses*, alcohol slows down the central nervous system. 如果饮酒过量, 酒精会减慢中枢神经(的反应速度)。

downside [ˈdaʊnsaɪd]

n. the disadvantages or less positive aspects of sth. 缺点; 不利方面

Living in big cities has its *downside*—the cost of living is so expensive and most people can't really afford to go out very often. 住在大城市里也有不利的方面: 生活费用太高, 以至于大多数人不能经常外出娱乐。

explore [ɪkˈsplɔː]　　　　　　　　　　　　　　　　　　　　[同] look into

v. to examine sth. completely or carefully in order to find out more about it 探究; 调查研究; 探索

Instead of using timber, stone and traditional building techniques, architects began to *explore* ways of creating buildings. 建筑师们开始探求新的建筑方法而不是采用木头、石料和传统的建筑技术。

export [ɪkˈspɔːt]　　　　　　　　　　　　　　　　　[反] ①②import

① *v.* to sell and send goods to another country 出口; 输出

The islands *export* sugar and fruit. 这些岛屿出口糖和水果。

② *n.* [ˈekspɔːt] the selling and transporting of goods to another country 出口; 输出

a ban on the *export* of live cattle 禁止活牛出口

expose [ɪkˈspəʊz]　　　　　　　　　　　　　　　[同] show [反] hide

v. to put sb./sth. in a place or situation where they are not protected from sth. harmful or unpleasant 使面临，使遭受(危险或不快)

Some Russian scientists claim that children learn better after being *exposed* to ultraviolet light.
一些俄罗斯科学家宣称被紫外线照射过的孩子学东西会快些。

fragment ['frægmənt]   [同] particle

n. separate or incomplete part (of sth.) (某事物的)片断或不完整部分

I heard only a *fragment* of their conversation. 我只听到他们谈话的只言片语。

fragrant ['freɪgrənt]   [反] fetid

adj. having a pleasant or sweet smell 有香味的；芳香的

The honey produced here is *fragrant* and sweet and can be sold by the beekeepers. 这儿出产的
蜂蜜甜美芳香，可向养蜂人购买。

freeze [friːz]

v. to change or be changed from liquid to solid by extreme cold 结冰；凝固

Water *freezes* at 0℃. 水在 0℃时结冰。

grief [griːf]   [同] sorrow

n. deep or violent sorrow 忧伤；悲伤

driven almost insane by *grief* over his death 因他的死去而悲伤得几乎发狂

gross [grəʊs]

adj. clearly wrong and unacceptable 显然恶劣的

California has developed a scheme to get these *gross* polluters off the streets. 加州提出一项计
划，旨在将恶劣的污染源迁离街道。

intrigue [ɪn'triːg]   [同] interest

v. to rouse sb.'s interest or curiosity 激起某人的兴趣或好奇心

It solved a problem that had *intrigued* man for ages. 它解决了多
年来让人一直好奇的一个问题。

intrinsic [ɪn'trɪnsɪk]   [同] inherent

adj. (of a value or quality) belonging naturally; existing within, not
coming from outside (指价值或性质)固有的，内在的，本质的

views which seem to place an *intrinsic* value on non-human animal life 看似在非人类的动物
生活中赋予了固有价值的观点

outlet ['aʊtlet]   [同] opening

n. way out (for water, steam, etc.) (水、蒸汽等的)出口，出路，排放口

an *outlet* for water 排水孔

outline ['aʊtlaɪn]   [同] summarize

v. to give a short general description of (sth.) 概述(某事物)

At the Ottawa Conference in 1986, a charter was developed which *outlined* new directions for
health promotion. 1986 年的渥太华会议制定了新的宪章，简明扼要地指出了促进健康发展
的新方向。

particular [pə'tɪkjələ(r)]   [同] ①special

① *adj.* [only before noun] used to emphasize that you are referring to one individual person,
thing or type of thing and not others 特定的；个别的；特殊的

It is common for supporters of road networks to reject the models of cities with good public
transport by arguing that such systems would not work in their *particular* city. 公路网络的拥护
者们普遍反对以发达的公共交通系统为标志的城市发展模式，他们认为该系统在他们所
在的特定城市并不适用。

② *n.* (usu. pl.) a fact or detail especially one that is officially written down(正式记下的)细节，详情

partner [ˈpɑːtnə(r)] [同] associate

n. person who takes part in an activity with another or others, esp. one of several owners of a business 伙伴；同伙；(尤指)合伙人，股东

The income of your parents, spouse, *partner* or other relatives is not taken into account. 你父母、配偶、伴侣或者其他亲戚的收入并没有计算在内。

passion [ˈpæʃn] [同] fervour

n. strong feeling (e.g. of hate, love or anger) 强烈的情感(如恨、爱、怒)

She argued with great *passion*. 她争论时情绪很激动。

blogging requires passion and authority. Which leaves out most people.

request [rɪˈkwest] [同] ask

n. act of asking for sth. in speech or writing, esp. politely (口头或书面的)要求；(尤指)请求

Evening appointments are available on *request*. 如有要求，可以晚间约见。

require [rɪˈkwaɪə(r)] [同] demand

v. to need sth. 需要；要求

The job *requires* a college degree and a knowledge of computers. 这份工作要求本科学历，且对计算机有所了解。

requirement [rɪˈkwaɪəmənt] [同] essential, must

n. thing depended on or needed 要求

Our latest model should meet your *requirements* exactly, i.e. be just what you want. 我们的最新型号会恰好满足您的需要，即如您所愿。

sculpture [ˈskʌlptʃə(r)]

n. art of making figures, objects, etc. by carving wood or stone, shaping clay, making metal casts, etc. 雕塑；雕刻

the techniques of *sculpture* in stone 石雕技术

seal [siːl]

n. substance or device used to fill a gap, crack, etc. so that gas or fluid cannot enter or escape (用以填充的)密封物质或装置

a rubber *seal* in the lid of a jar 罐子盖儿的橡皮密封圈

symbol [ˈsɪmbl]

n. image, object, etc. that suggests or refers to sth. else; emblem 象征；标志

The lion is the *symbol* of courage. 狮子是勇武的象征。

symbolize [ˈsɪmblaɪz] [同] represent

v. to be a symbol of (sth.) 作为(某事物)的符号或标志；象征(某事物)

In Europe, the colour white *symbolizes* purity but in Asia it is often the symbol of deep mourning. 在欧洲白色象征着纯洁，但在亚洲它却经常代表着哀悼。

sympathetic [ˌsɪmpəˈθetɪk] [反] unsympathetic

adj. caring and feeling sorry about sb.'s problems 有同情心的；怜悯的

He is such a *sympathetic* person. 他是个非常有同情心的人。

tunnel [ˈtʌnl]

n. a passage that has been dug under the ground for cars, trains, etc. to go through 隧道；坑道

The *tunnels* abandoned by the beetles provide excellent aeration and water channels for root systems. 这些甲壳虫遗弃的穴道为植物根系提供了良好的通风和供水通道。

tutor ['tjuːtə(r)]

n. (BrE) a teacher whose job is to pay special attention to the studies or health, etc. of a student or a group of students 导师；指导教师

DON'T BE EMBARRASSED TO ASK FOR HELP DAD.

The *tutors* here at Bedford College are all very experienced in their field of teaching. 贝德福德学院的教师们在他们任教的领域上都富有经验。

tutorial [tjuː'tɔːriəl]

n. a period of teaching in a university that involves of students and a tutor (大学导师的)个别辅导时间，辅导课

Whereas previously lecturers were holding *tutorials*, their time is now spent marking hundreds of essays. 以前讲师们都会上很多辅导课，现在却把时间都花在给成百上千的论文打分上。

Take the Test ≫

一、英汉互译

假定(n.)	_____	crucial	_____
预算	_____	expose	_____
捐赠	_____	intrinsic	_____
雕塑	_____	symbolize	_____
辅导课	_____	tunnel	_____

二、翻译句子

1）中国的互联网正以惊人的速度发展着。(astonishing)

_____

2）孩子们住校时，在宿舍睡觉。(dormitory)

_____

3）住在大城市里也有不利的方面：生活费用太高，以至于大多数人不能经常外出娱乐。(downside)

_____

4）狮子是勇武的象征。(symbol)

_____

Word List 39

atmosphere [ˈætməsfɪə(r)]   [同]①ambience

n. ① feeling in the mind that is created by a group of people or a place; mood 气氛；情绪

All interviews are confidential and conducted in a relaxed and friendly *atmosphere*. 所有的访问都保密，并且在一种轻松而友好的气氛下进行。

② the mixture of gases that surrounds the earth 大气，大气层(包围地球的气体)

We could help the situation by reducing the amount of chemical pollutant we release into the *atmosphere*. 我们可以通过减少向大气排放化学污染物来缓解这种局面。

atom [ˈætəm]   [近] particle

n. the smallest part of an element that can exist chemically 原子

an *atom* scientist 原子能专家

attach [əˈtætʃ]   [同] fix, affix [反] detach

v. to fasten or join sth. (to sth.) 将某物系在、缚在或附在(另一物)上

When you get your sticker, you must *attach* it to the front windscreen of your car. 当拿到你的标签时，你必须把它贴在车前的挡风玻璃上。

attack [əˈtæk]   [近]①②strike

① *n.* strong criticism in speech or writing 抨击；非难

② *v.* to deliberately use violence to hurt a person or damage a place 攻击

Since the average American spends 18 hours indoors for every hour outside, it looks as though many environmentalists may be *attacking* the wrong target. 普通的美国民众每花 1 个小时待在户外，就会花 18 个小时待在屋里。这使得许多的环保主义者看上去仿佛抨击了一个错误的目标。

bulk [bʌlk]   [同] mass

n. the main part of sth.; most of sth. 主体；大部分

The *bulk* of the population lives in cities. 大多数人口居住在城市里。

cosmetic [kɒzˈmetɪk]

n. (usu. pl.)substance for putting on the body, esp. the face, to make it beautiful 化妆品(尤指用于面部的)

Lipstick and hair conditioner are *cosmetics*. 口红和护发素都是化妆品。

cost-effective [ˈkɒst ɪˈfektɪv]

adj. bringing the best possible profits or advantages for the lowest possible costs 高性价比的，划算的

The simplest and most *cost-effective* action needed against passive smoking is to establish smoke-free work places, schools and public places. 对付被动吸烟最简单也是最划算的办法就是在办公室、学校等公共场所禁烟。

costly [ˈkɒstli]   [同] expensive [反] inexpensive, cheap

adj. costing much; expensive 费钱的；昂贵的

a *costly* mistake 造成重大损失的错误

costume ['kɒstjuːm]　　　　　　　　　　　　　　　　　　　　[同] dress, outfit

n. garment or style of dress, esp. of a particular period or group or for a particular activity 服装，服装式样（尤指用于某时期、某团体或某活动的服装）

People wore historical *costumes* for the parade. 人们穿着古装参加游行。

cosy ['kəʊzi]

adj. (warm and) comfortable（暖和而）舒适的

I felt all *cosy* tucked up in bed. 我钻进被窝，暖暖和和，舒服极了。

counter ['kaʊntə(r)]

① *adv.* in the opposite direction to sth; in opposition to sth; contrary to sth. 与某事物的方向相反；相反地

Economic trends are running *counter* to the forecasts. 经济发展趋势与预测的结果截然相反。

② *n.* long narrow flat surface over which goods are sold or served or business done in a shop, bank, etc.（商店、银行等的）柜台

OTC = over the *counter*（指药品）非处方药

doze [dəʊz]

① *n.* the short period of sleep, usu. during the day（通常日间的）瞌睡；小睡

I had a *doze* on the train. 我在火车上打了个盹儿。

② *v.* to sleep lightly for a short time 打瞌睡；打盹儿

I *dozed* fitfully until dawn. 我断断续续打瞌睡直到黎明。

draft [drɑːft]

n. a rough written version of sth. that is not yet in its final form 草稿；草案；草图

You must read the question carefully and give it a great deal of thought before you even start planning or writing your first *draft*. 你开始计划写初稿之前一定要仔细地阅读问题并做大量的思考。

drama [drɑːmə]

n. a play for the theatre, television, radio, etc. 戏剧

a lavish costume *drama* 奢华的古装戏

dramatic [drə'mætɪk]

adj. (of a change, an event, etc.) sudden, very great and often surprising 突然的；巨大的；令人吃惊的

The changes in China's Pearl River delta, however, are more *dramatic* than these natural fluctuations. 然而，中国珠江三角洲的变化比这些自然的波动更为巨大。

extend [ɪk'stend]　　　　　　　　　　　　　　　　　　　　[同] expand

v. to make a business, an idea, an influence, etc. cover more areas or operate in more places 扩大…的范围（或影响）

The importance of these discoveries *extends* beyond the objects themselves. 这些发现的重要性已经不局限于他们原来的目标本身了。

extension [ɪk'stenʃn]　　　　　　　　　　　　　　　　　　　[同] expansion

n. the act of increasing the area of an activity, a group of people, etc. that is affected by sth. 扩大；延伸

the *extension* of new technology into developing countries 新技术向发展中国家的传播

extent [ɪk'stent]　　　　　　　　　　　　　　　　　　　　　[近] size

n. length; area; range 长度；面积；范围

I was amazed at the *extent* of his knowledge. 他知识之渊博令我惊奇。

frequent [ˈfriːkwənt]　　　　　　　　　　　　　　[反] infrequent

adj. happening often; habitual 时常发生的；惯常的

The most *frequent* reason stated for absence was minor illness. 最常用来做缺席借口的是微不足道的小病。

friction [ˈfrɪkʃn]　　　　　　　　　　　　　[同] tension

n. ① disagreement, angry feelings, or unfriendliness between people 摩擦；冲突

Having my mother living with us causes *friction* at home. 让我妈跟我们一起住在家里造成了小摩擦。

② resistance of one surface to another surface or substance that moves over it 摩擦力

The force of *friction* affects the speed at which spacecraft can reenter the earth's atmosphere. 摩擦力能影响航天器返回地球大气层的速度。

fridge [frɪdʒ]

n. (infml.) refrigerator 冰箱

I had been saving up to buy a cooker and *fridge*. 我一直在攒钱买锅和冰箱。

guilty [ˈɡɪlti]　　　　　　　　　　　　　　　　[反] guiltless

adj. having done wrong; being to blame (for sth.) 有罪的；犯罪的；(对某事)有罪责的

I feel really *guilty* at forgetting her birthday again. 又忘记了她的生日，我觉得很内疚。

gust [ɡʌst]　　　　　　　　　　　　　　　[同] outburst

n. a sudden violent rush of wind (突然的)一阵狂风

A sudden *gust* of wind blew the door shut. 忽然的一阵风把门关上了。

introduce [ˌɪntrəˈdjuːs]

v. to bring a plan, system, or product into use for the first time 引进，传入

Shark-meshing was *introduced* to the state of Queensland around 1970. 鲨鱼网捞技术于 1970 年左右被引入昆士兰州。

invade [ɪnˈveɪd]

v. to enter (a country or territory) with armed forces in order to attack, damage or occupy it 武装进入(一国或一领地)，侵犯，侵入，侵略

The Romans *invaded* Britain 2,000 years ago. 罗马人曾在两千年前侵略过英国。

invent [ɪnˈvent]

v. to make, design, or think of a new type of thing 发明，创造

The steam engine was *invented* and then the railways came and the centres of industry were able to move away from the rivers and the countryside and into the towns. 随着蒸汽机的发明，铁路出现了，这使得工业中心得以从乡村、河畔移到城镇中来。

long-term [ˌlɒŋˈtɜːm]　　　　　　　　　　　　[反] short-term

adj. that will last or have an effect over a long period of time 长期的；长远的；长期有效的

a *long-term* strategy/solution 长期战略 / 解决方案

outlook [ˈaʊtlʊk]　　　　　　　　　　　　　[同] ②③vista

n. ①your general attitude to life and the world 世界观；心态 ②view on which one looks out 景色；景致 ③the probable future for sb./sth.; what is likely to happen 前景，展望

She still has an optimistic *outlook* for the future. 展望将来，她依然态度乐观。

outnumber [ˌaʊtˈnʌmbə(r)]

v. to be more in number than (sb.) 在数量上超过（某人）

The demonstrators were *outnumbered* by the police. 警方的人数多于示威者。

output [ˈaʊtpʊt] [同] production

n. quantity of goods, etc. produced (by a machine, worker, etc.) (机器、工人等的)产量

The average *output* of the factory is 20 cars a day. 该工厂的平均产量是每天 20 辆汽车。

passive [ˈpæsɪv] [反] ①inactive

① *adj.* not active; submissive 被动的；消极的

play a *passive* role in a marriage 在婚姻中扮演被动的角色

② *n.* (grammar) passive form of a verb (phrase) or sentence 动词被动形式；被动句；被动语态

In the sentence 'He was seen there', 'was seen' is in the *passive*. 在"He was seen there"句中的"was seen"是被动形式。

pastime [ˈpɑːstaɪm] [同] recreation

n. thing done to pass the time pleasantly 消遣；娱乐

Photography is her favourite *pastime*. 摄影是她最喜爱的消遣。

patent [ˈpeɪtnt]

① *adj.* obvious; clear; evident 显著的；清楚的；明显的

a *patent* lie 明显的谎言

② *n.* a grant made by a government that confers upon the creator of an invention the sole right to make, use, and sell that invention for a set period of time, and an invention protected by such a grant 专利权，专利品

He had a *patent* and had earned millions of dollars in royalties. 他有一个专利，并已经从专利使用费中赚取了数百万美元。

rescue [ˈreskjuː] [同] save

v. to save or bring away sb./sth. from danger, captivity, etc. (从危险、囚禁等中)搭救或救出某人(某物)

Firefighters worked for two hours to *rescue* people who were trapped in the bus. 消防员花了两个小时来营救困在巴士里的乘客。

research [rɪˈsɜːtʃ] [同] enquiry

n. serious study of a subject, in order to discover new facts or test new ideas 调查；研究

I'm still doing *research* for my thesis. 我还在为论文做研究。

resemble [rɪˈzembl]

v. to look like or be similar to sb. or sth. 长相与…相似

a small object *resembling* a pin 像大头针的小物件

section [ˈsekʃn] [同] segment

n. any of the parts into which sth. may be or has been divided 部分

This *section* of the road is closed. 这段路已经封闭。

sector [ˈsektə(r)] [同] field

n. the part or branch of a particular area of activity, esp. of a country's economy (活动领域的)部门；(尤指)经济领域

the manufacturing *sector*, i.e. all the manufacturing industries of a country 制造业

secure [sɪˈkjʊə(r)] [同] ①safe ②defend

① *adj.* (fml.) safe; protected 安全的；受保护的

The strong-room is as *secure* as we can make it. 我们的保险库建造得十分安全。

② *v.* make sth. safe; protect 使某事物安全；保护

It was possible to *secure* incentives from local businesses. 保护本地商家的动机是可能的。

seek [si:k] [同] search (for or out)

v. to look (for sth.); try to find or obtain (sth.) 寻找；找到或得到(某事物)

Nevertheless, public opinion forces governments to *seek* alternative ways of disposing of their unwanted byproducts. 不过，公众的意见迫使政府去寻求其他去除多余副产品的方法。

twilight ['twaɪlaɪt] [近] evening

n. the faint light or the period of time at the end of the day after the sun has gone down 暮色；黄昏

It was hard to see him clearly in the *twilight*. 在朦胧的暮色中很难看清他。

twin [twɪn] [同] ①double

① *adj.* used to describe two things that are used as a pair 成双的；成对的

All the *twin* rooms have private bathrooms. 所有的标准间都有独立卫浴。

② *n.* one of two children born at the same time to the same mother 双胞胎之一

She's expecting *twins*. 她怀着双胞胎。

Take the Test »

一、英汉互译

气氛	_____	bulk	_____
高性价比的	_____	costume	_____
巨大的	_____	counter	_____
长期的	_____	pastime	_____
部门，领域	_____	patent	_____

二、翻译句子

1) 所有的访问都保密，并且在一种轻松而友好的气氛下进行。(atmosphere)

_____

2) 你开始计划写初稿之前一定要仔细地阅读问题并做大量的思考。(draft)

_____

3) 展望将来，她依然态度乐观。(outlook)

_____

4) 我还在为论文做研究。(research)

_____

attain [əˈteɪn]　　　　　　　　　　　　　　　　　　　　　　　　　　[同] achieve, gain

v. to succeed in getting (sth.); achieve 获得（某事物）；达到；实现

The challenge is to *attain* a sustainable balance between population, economic growth and the environment. 挑战在于实现人口、经济增长与环境之间可持续的平衡。

attempt [əˈtempt]　　　　　　　　　　　　　　　　　　　　　　　　[同] ①②endeavor

① *n.* act of making an effort to accomplish (sth.); try (to do sth.) 尝试；努力；试图

In an *attempt* to reduce the level of absenteeism the management introduced three different strategies. 管理层提出三条不同的策略以期减少旷工现象。

② *v.* to try (to do sth.) 尝试；努力

attend [əˈtend]

v. to go to an event such as a meeting or a class 参加

Please let us know if you are unable to *attend*. 如果你不能参加请通知我们。

attitude [ˈætɪtjuːd]　　　　　　　　　　　　　　　　　　　　　　　　[同] position

n. (to/towards sb./sth.) way of thinking or behaving 看法；态度

Since meeting him, my *attitude* towards life and other people has changed dramatically. 自从认识了他以后，我对人生和其他人的态度发生了巨变。

attract [əˈtrækt]　　　　　　　　　　　　　　　　　　　　　　[同] appeal [反] repel

v. to arouse interest or pleasure in (sb./sth.) 引起兴趣或快感；激发；引诱

It is the culture of this part of the island that *attracts* so many tourists to Hornchurch. 正是岛上这一地区的文化吸引着众多游客来到 Hornchurch。

bump [bʌmp]　　　　　　　　　　　　　　　　　　　　　　　[同] clash, collide

v. to hit sb./sth. accidentally (无意地)碰；撞

In the dark I *bumped* into a chair. 我在黑暗中撞上了一把椅子。

crack [kræk]　　　　　　　　　　　　　　　　　　　　　　　　　[同] ②break

① *n.* a very narrow space between two things or two parts of sth. 缝隙

② *v.* to break (sth.) open or into pieces 砸开或砸碎(某物)

crack a safe 砸开保险箱

cradle [ˈkreɪdl]

n. small bed for a baby, usu. shaped like a box with curved parts underneath so that it can move from side to side 摇篮

Greece, the *cradle* of Western culture. 希腊，西方文明的发源地。

craft [krɑːft]　　　　　　　　　　　　　　　　　　　　　　　　[同] handicraft

n. occupation, esp. one that needs skill in the use of the hands; a skill or technique 行业；（尤指）手工业；工艺

The region is a diverse agricultural area, rich in historic sites, arts and *crafts*, mountains and rivers. 该地区是一个丰富多彩的农业区，有着大量的历史遗迹、艺术作品和丰富的手工工艺，并且有山有水。

create [kri'eɪt]　　　　　　　　　　　　　　　　　　[同] generate, compose

v. to make sth. exist that did not exist before 创造，创作

The Department of Ethnography was *created* as a separate department within the British Museum in 1946. 民族志部作为大英博物馆下属的一个独立部门在 1946 年得以创立。

creature ['kriːtʃə(r)]

n. living being, esp. an animal 生物；(尤指)动物

creatures from Mars 来自火星的生物

credit ['kredɪt]　　　　　　　　　　　　　　　　　　[反]①②discredit

① *n.* an arrangement with a shop, bank, etc. that allows you to buy sth. and pay for it later 信用制，赊账

Small-scale business training and *credit* programs have become more common throughout the world. 小规模的商业培训和贷款项目在世界范围内越来越普遍。

② *v.* to believe that sb./sth. has sth.; to attribute sth. to sb./sth. 认为某人 / 某事物有某事物；把某事物归功于某人 / 某事物

Most historians of technology *credit* the Chinese with the discovery of gunpowder. 大部分历史学家都把火药的发明归功于中国。

drift [drɪft]　　　　　　　　　　　　　　　　　　[同]①②flow

① *n.* a slow steady movement from one place to another; a gradual change or development from one situation to another, esp. to sth. bad 流动；趋势；逐渐变化(尤指向坏的方向)

a population *drift* away from rural areas 农村地区的人口外流

② *v.* to move along smoothly and slowly in water or air 漂流；漂移

Clouds *drifted* across the sky. 朵朵浮云在空中飘过。

drill [drɪl]

① *n.* a tool or machine with a pointed end for making holes 钻；钻头；钻床

a hand *drill* 手钻

② *v.* to make a hole in sth., using a drill 钻(孔)，打(眼)

The original granite island which had hills up to 120 meters high was *drilled* and blasted into boulders no bigger than two meters in diameter. 那个花岗岩质岛屿上原本有一些高达 120 米的小山，现在岛被钻了很多孔甚至被炸成许多直径不超过两米的石块。

drip [drɪp]　　　　　　　　　　　　　　　　　　[同]①②drop

① *n.* a small drop of liquid that falls from sth. 水滴；滴液

We put a bucket under the hole in the roof to catch the *drips*. 我们在屋顶漏洞下放了一个水桶来接水滴。

② *v.* to fall in small drops 滴下

She was hot and sweat *dripped* into her eyes. 她很热，汗水滴入了双眼。

dual ['djuːəl]　　　　　　　　　　　　　　　　　　[同] double

adj. having two parts or aspects 两部分的；双重的；双的

She has *dual* nationality. 她有双重国籍。

extinct [ɪk'stɪŋkt]　　　　　　　　　　　　　　　　　　[同] dead, vanished

adj. no longer in existence 不再存在的；已灭绝的；绝种的

This language had been *extinct* for about a century, but had been quite well documented. 这种语言已经绝迹差不多一个世纪了，不过相关的文字资料倒是很多。

extinguish [ɪkˈstɪŋgwɪʃ] [反] ignite

v. to make a fire stop burning or a light stop shining; to destroy sth. 熄灭；扑灭；消灭

Firefighters tried to *extinguish* the flames. 消防队员奋力救火。

News of the bombing *extinguished* all hope of peace. 轰炸的消息使和平的希望全部破灭。

frustrate [frʌˈstreɪt] [反] ①②fulfill

v. ① if sth. frustrates you, it makes you feel annoyed or angry because you are unable to do what you want 使失望；使沮丧

The fact that he's working with amateurs really *frustrates* him. 与业余爱好者共事这一事实使他觉得很沮丧。

② to prevent (sb.) from doing or achieving sth. 阻止(某人)做成某事；妨碍

He had hoped to set a new world record, but was *frustrated* by bad weather. 他本希望能创造新的世界纪录，但因天气恶劣而落空了。

frustrating [frʌˈstreɪtɪŋ]

adj. annoying; discouraging 使人心烦的；使人灰心的；使人沮丧的

I find it *frustrating* that I can't speak other languages. 我不会说别的语言，这令我感到很沮丧。

fuel [fjuəl]

n. material burned to produce heat or power, e.g. wood, coal, oil, etc. 燃料

What sort of *fuel* do these machines need? 这些机器需要哪种燃料？

growth [grəʊθ] [反] decline

n. an increase in amount, number, or size 增长；增加

The company is preparing for zero *growth* this year. 这家公司今年的业绩增长将为零。

guarantee [ˌgærənˈtiː] [同] ①warranty

① *n.* a formal written promise to repair or replace a product if it breaks within a specific period of time 保修

② *v.* to promise sth. with certainty (to sb.) (向某人)担保某事物；保证

We cannot *guarantee* the time or location of a student's course although every attempt is made to place students in the centre and at the time of their choice. 尽管我们尽可能以学生为中心并让他们能自主选择时间，但我们不能确保能为一位学生的课程提供时间和场地。

invest [ɪnˈvest] [反] divest

v. to use (money) to buy shares, property, etc., in order to earn interest or bring profit 投资；投资于

Supermarkets are able to *invest* millions of pounds in powerful computers which tell them what sells best and where. 超市有能力在能分析出最畅销产品和最佳销售地点的作用大的电脑上投资几百万。

investigate [ɪnˈvestɪgeɪt] [同] explore

v. to find out and examine (all the facts about sth.) in order to obtain the truth 调查；侦查

Scientists are *investigating* to find out the cause of the crash/are *investigating* how the crash occurred. 科学家们正在调查失事的原因 / 事故是如何发生的。

lotion [ˈləʊʃn]

n. a liquid used for cleaning, protection or treating the skin 护肤液；润肤乳

a body/hand *lotion* 护肤 / 手乳液

lottery [ˈlɒtəri]

n. ①a game used to make money for a state or a charity in which people buy tickets with a series of numbers on them 彩票 ②a selection made by lot from a number of applicants or competitors

（在多个应选者或竞争者中）通过抓阄来选举

To stand a chance of winning the *lottery*, you need lots of different tickets. 想中彩票，你得有足够多的有着不同号码的彩票。

outspoken [ˌaʊt ˈspəʊkən]　　　　　　　　　　　　　　　　　　　　[同] candid

adj. saying openly exactly what one thinks; frank 直言的；坦率的

an *outspoken* critic of the government 直言批评政府的人

outstanding [ˌaʊt ˈstændɪŋ]　　　　　　　　　　　　　　　　　　　[同] superb

adj. exceptionally good; excellent 杰出的；优秀的

an *outstanding* piece of work 优秀的作品

outweigh [ˌaʊt ˈweɪ]　　　　　　　　　　　　　　　　　　　　　　[同] overweigh

v. to be greater in weight, value or importance than（sth.）在重量、价值或重要性上超过（某事物）

Human genetic similarity greatly *outweighs* the variations. 人类基因的相似性远远大于其多样性。

patron [ˈpeɪtrən]　　　　　　　　　　　　　　　　　　　　　　　[同] sponsor

n. person who gives money or other support to a person, cause, activity, etc. 资助人；赞助人

a wealthy *patron* of the arts 富有的艺术赞助人

pause [pɔːz]

① *n.* temporary stop in action or speech（行为、讲话中的）暂停，临时中止

It also reveals the power of the *pauses* and noises we use to play for time, convey emotion, doubt and irony. 它也揭示了我们为拖延时间或者表达感情、疑惑以及讽刺而停顿或发出的声音的作用。

② *v.* to stop speaking or doing sth. for a short time before starting again 在短时间内停止说话或做事，然后再继续说或做

Pausing briefly at the door, Linus straightened his tie. Linus 在门前停了一小会，整理了一下领带。

reservation [ˌrezə ˈveɪʃn]

n. reserved seat or accommodation, etc.; record of this 保留的座位、住处等；（座位、住处等的）预订

make/hold *reservations*（in the name of T Hill）（以 T·希尔的名字）预订

reserve [rɪ ˈzɜːv]　　　　　　　　　　　　　　　　　　　　　　　[同] keep

v. to have or keep（a specified power）; retain 具有或保持（某种权力）；保留

After an assessment you will be able to *reserve* a place on the next available course. 在评估之后，你将可以在下一轮可选课程中保留一个位置。

segment [ˈsegmənt]　　　　　　　　　　　　　　　　　　　　　　[同] portion

n. part of sth. separated or marked off from the other parts; part of sth. that can be separated off in the mind 分出的或标出的一部分；想像中可分出的一部分

She cleaned a small *segment* of the painting. 她把画上的一小部分擦干净了。

segregate [ˈsegrɪgeɪt]　　　　　　　　　　　　　　　　　　　　　[同] separate

v. to put sb./sth. in a place away from the rest; isolate 将某人/某事物隔离、分离或分开

segregate cholera patients 把霍乱病人隔离开

seize [siːz]　　　　　　　　　　　　　　　　　　　　　　　　　　[同] catch

v. to take hold of sth. suddenly and violently 抓住

Suddenly she *seized* my hand. 她突然抓住我的手。

select [sɪˈlekt] [同] ①choose ②chosen

① *v.* to choose sb./sth., esp. as being the best or most suitable 选择；挑选；选拔（尤指最好的或最合适的）

select a gift/candidate/wine 挑选礼物 / 候选人 / 葡萄酒

② *adj.* carefully chosen, esp. as the best out of a larger group 仔细挑选的；（尤指）精选的

select passages of Milton's poetry 弥尔顿诗选

typical [ˈtɪpɪkl] [同] model

adj. having the usual features or qualities of a particular group or thing 典型的；有代表性的

This advertisement is a *typical* example of their marketing strategy. 这个广告是他们营销策略的典型代表。

wholesome [ˈhəʊlsəm] [同] healthful

adj. good for your health 有益健康的

The diet is a *wholesome* one; healthy foods such as salads, *wholemeal* bread and semi-skimmed milk are used. 这样的饮食有益于健康，它包含着像沙拉、全麦面包和半脱脂牛奶等这样的健康食品。

wicked [ˈwɪkɪd]

adj. behaving in a way that is morally wrong 邪恶的

a *wicked* witch 邪恶的巫婆

widespread [ˈwaɪdspred]

adj. existing or happening in many places or situations, or among many people 遍布的；广泛的

Whether the technology ever will gain *widespread* use is uncertain. 该科技是否能得到广泛应用还不确定。

Take the Test ▶▶

一、英汉互译

灭绝的	_____	crack	_____
使人沮丧的	_____	drift	_____
保证	_____	drip	_____
调查	_____	patron	_____
保留	_____	wholesome	_____

二、翻译句子

1）挑战在于实现人口、经济增长与环境之间可持续的平衡。（attain）

_____

2）自从认识他以后，我对人生和其他人的态度发生了巨变。（attitude）

_____

3）大部分历史学家都把火药的发明归功于中国。（credit）

_____

4）这个广告是他们营销策略的典型代表。（typical）

_____

attribute　　　　　　　　　　　　　　　　　　　　[同]②characteristic, feature

① [ə'tribjuːt] *v.* to regard sth. as belonging to, caused by or produced by sb./sth. 认为某事物属于某人(或某事物); 认为某事物由某人(或某事物)引起或产生

He ***attributes*** his physical prowess to an exercise regimen inspired by the lifestyles of our Paleolithic ancestors. 他把他的高超体能归功于从旧石器时代祖先的生活方式中得到启发的运动养生法。

② *n.* [æ'tribjuːt] a quality or feature 性质, 特点

He had all the ***attributes*** of a great leader. 他具有一个伟大领袖所有的全部特质。

audience　['ɔːdiəns]　　　　　　　　　　　　　　　　　　[近]public

n. group of people who have gathered together to hear or watch sb./sth. 听众; 观众

The ***audience*** was enthusiastic on the opening night of the play. 那出戏首次公演之夜观众非常热情。

authority　[ɔː'θɒrɪti]　　　　　　　　　　[同]expert, power

n. power to give orders and make others obey 权力; 权威

The manufacturer's target market is the wealthy social elite who are in positions of power and ***authority***. 制造商的目标市场是那些手握实权的富有的社会精英。

bunch　[bʌntʃ]　　　　　　　　　　　[同]group

n. a number of things of the same type which are growing or fastened together 串; 束; 扎

a ***bunch*** of bananas/grapes 一串香蕉/葡萄

critical　['krɪtɪkl]　　　　　　　　　　　　　　　　[反]uncritical

adj. ①saying that sb. or sth. is bad or wrong 批评的 ②very important because what happens in the future depends on it 至关重要的

develop ***critical*** life skills 培养重要的生活技能

cure　[kjʊə(r)]　　　　　　　　　　　　　　　[同]①②remedy

① *n.* a medicine or medical treatment that makes an illness go away 解药, 治疗方法

the latest anti-aging ***cure*** 最新的抗衰老药

② *v.* to make sb. healthy again 治愈某人

The doctors ***cured*** her of cancer. 医生治好了她的癌症。

curious　['kjʊəriəs]　　　　　　　　　　　　　　　　[反]inquisitive

adj. eager to know or learn 富于好奇心的; 有求知欲的

He is a ***curious*** boy who is always asking questions. 他是个有求知欲的孩子, 老是问这问那。

curl　[kɜːl]

n. thing, esp. a small bunch of hair, that curves round and round like a spiral or the thread of a screw 卷状物; 螺旋状物; (尤指)一绺卷发

the little boy's golden ***curls*** 这个小男孩的金色鬈发

current [ˈkʌrənt]   [同] ①present

① *adj.* happening or existing now 现在的

According to one economist, at the **current** growth rate, China will have the largest economy in the world by 2030. 一位经济学家认为，按现在的发展速度计算，到 2030 年中国将成为世界上最大的经济体。

② *n.* a continuous movement of water, air or electricity 水流，空气流，电流

It's dangerous to swim in the sea here because the **current** is so strong. 在这个海域游泳很危险，因为水流太急了。

curse [kɜːs]

① *n.* impolite or obscene word or words used to express violent anger 咒骂语

angrily muttering **curses** 愤怒地低声咒骂

② *v.* to swear 咒骂

curve [kɜːv]   [同] bend

n. line of which no part is straight and which changes direction without angles 曲线；弧线

a **curve** on a graph 图表上的曲线

cushion [ˈkʊʃn]

n. small bag filled with soft material, feathers, etc., used to make a seat more comfortable, to kneel on, etc. 软垫，靠垫

Jumpers land on the **cushions**. 跳高运动员落到了垫子上。

cute [kjuːt]

adj. attractive; pretty and charming 有吸引力的；逗人喜爱的

Even as a child, he was always **cute** enough to get what he wanted. 他小时候就挺机灵，想要什么，总能弄到手。

cycle [ˈsaɪkl]   [同] round

n. a number of related events that happen again and again in the same order 循环，周期

the **cycle** of the seasons 四季轮回

due [djuː]   [同] ②unpaid

adj. ① caused by sb./sth.; because of sb./sth. 由于；因为

The team's success was largely **due** to her efforts. 团队的成功在很大程度上是她努力的结果。

② expected to happen or arrive at a particular time 到期的

I'm having a bit of trouble with the second assignment, and it's **due** in twelve days. 我第二份作业遇到了点问题，而这份作业 12 天后就要交了。

dull [dʌl]

adj. ① not interesting or exciting 无聊的 ② not bright and with lots of clouds 多云的

In Britain, the **dull** weather of winter drastically cuts down the amount of sunlight which strongly affects some people. 在英国，冬天的阴霾天气极大地减少了日晒，而这强烈地影响到了一些人。

dumb [dʌm]   [同] stupid

adj. stupid 愚蠢的

What a **dumb** question! 多么愚蠢的问题！

dump [dʌmp]   [同] ①discard

① *v.* to get rid of sth. you do not want, esp. in a place which is not suitable（尤指在不合适的地方）丢弃；扔掉

Too much toxic waste is being *dumped* at sea. 太多的有毒废料正倾倒进海里。

② *n.* a place where waste or rubbish is taken and left 垃圾场；废物堆

a unclear waste *dump* 核废料堆

durable [ˈdjuərəbl]　　　　　　　　　　　　　　　　　　　　　　[同] lasting

adj. likely to last for a long time without breaking or getting weaker 耐用的；持久的

Wood is a *durable* material. 木头是种耐用的材料。

duration [djuˈreɪʃn]　　　　　　　　　　　　　　　　　　　　　[同] continuation

n. (fml.) the length of time that sth. lasts or continues 持续时间；期间

Courses of longer *duration* require a student permit which is issued for the length of study only.
(参加)长期课程需要专门为该长期课程发放的学生证。

extra [ˈekstrə]　　　　　　　　　　　　　　　　　　　　　　　　[同] additional

adj. more than is usual, expected, or than exists already 额外的；份外的；外加的

If you want your other laundry to be done by the college this can be arranged for a small *extra*
fee. 让学生公寓楼帮你洗一些其他衣物的话需要额外交点费用。

extract [ˈekstrækt]

n. a short passage from a book, piece of music, etc. that gives you an idea of what the whole
thing is like 摘录；选录

The following *extract* is taken from her new novel. 下面内容摘自她的新小说。

fulfil [fulˈfɪl]　　　　　　　　　　　　　　　　　　　　　　　　[同] complete

v. (=AmE fulfill) to perform (sth.) or bring (sth.) to completion 履行(某事)；使(某事)实现

fulfil a promise/prophecy 履行诺言 / 使预言实现

function [ˈfʌŋkʃn]　　　　　　　　　　　　　　　　　　　　　　[近] duty

n. special activity or purpose of a person or thing 作用；职能；职责

The dams store water for a variety of *functions*. 大坝储水做不同用途。

furious [ˈfjuəriəs]　　　　　　　　　　　　　　　　　　　　　　[反] intense

adj. violent; intense; unrestrained 猛烈的；强烈的

She drove off at a *furious* speed. 她飞快地把车开走了。

guardian [ˈgɑːdiən]　　　　　　　　　　　　　　　　　　　　　[近] keeper

n. sb. who is legally responsible for looking after sb. else's child 监护人

His aunt is his legal *guardian*. 他的姑妈是他的法定监护人。

guideline [ˈgaɪdlaɪn]

n. advice (usu. from sb. in authority) on policy (政策的)指导方针

draw up *guidelines* on prices and incomes 拟订物价和收入的指标

irrigation [ˌɪrɪˈgeɪʃn]

n. the act of supplying (land or crops) with water (by means of streams, reservoirs, channels,
pipes, etc.) 灌溉(田地或作物)

Higher yields have been achieved by increased *irrigation* and better crop breeding. 产量的增加
是因为增加了灌溉以及采用了更好的作物培植。

lounge [launʤ]　　　　　　　　　　　　　　　　　　　　　　　[近] bar

n. public sitting-room in a hotel, club, etc. (旅馆、俱乐部等的)休息室

As a member of the museum you would be entitled to use the members' *lounge* for refreshments.
作为博物馆的会员，你有资格在会员休息室里休息。

loyal [ˈlɔɪəl]　　　　　　　　　　　　　　　　　　　　　　　　[反] disloyal

adj. always supporting your friends, principles, country, etc. 忠诚的

The army has remained *loyal* to the government. 军队对政府保持着忠诚。

| **overall** | [ˌəʊvər'ɔːl] | [同] ②generally |

① *adj.* whole 总共的

② *adv.* generally 总体上

One obvious cause is that real income *overall* has risen. 一个明显的原因是真实收入总体上增长了。

| **overcome** | [ˌəʊvə'kʌm] |

v. to succeed in dealing with or controlling a problem that has been preventing you from achieving sth. 克服，解决

Women still have to *overcome* many obstacles to gain equality. 妇女依然要克服很多障碍才能获得平等权。

| **pave** | [peɪv] |

v. to cover (a surface) with flat stones or bricks 用石或砖铺(路)

The path is *paved* with concrete slabs. 这条路是用混凝土板铺成的。

| **payable** | ['peɪəbl] | [同] unpaid |

adj. that must or may be paid 应付的；可付的

Installments are *payable* on the last day of the month. 分期付的款可于每月最后一日交付。

| **resign** | [rɪ'zaɪn] | [同] quit |

v. to officially tell sb. that you are leaving your job, an organization, etc. 辞职；辞去(某职务)

Two members *resigned* from the board in protest. 董事会的两名成员辞职以示抗议。

| **resist** | [rɪ'zɪst] | [同] withstand |

v. to refuse to accept sth. and try to stop it from happening 抵制；阻挡

They are determined to *resist* pressure to change the law. 他们决心顶住压力来改变法律。

| **semester** | [sɪ'mestə] |

n. (esp. in U.S. universities and colleges) either of the two divisions of the academic year (尤指美国的大专院校的)学期(半学年)

the summer/winter *semester* 夏季/冬季学期

| **seminar** | ['semɪnɑː] | [近] conference |

n. small group of students at a university, etc. meeting to discuss or study a particular topic with a teacher (大学生与教师的)(专题)研讨会

Teaching is by lectures and *seminars*. 教学形式为讲座和研讨会。

| **senior** | ['siːnɪə(r)] | [同] ①superior |

① *adj.* higher in rank, authority, etc. (级别、权位等)较高的

All the *senior* managers have worked their way up from the bottom. 所有的高级经理都是从底层奋斗起来的。

② *n.* member of a senior school 高年级学生

a football match between the juniors and the *seniors* 低年级学生和高年级学生之间的足球赛

| **symptom** | ['sɪmptəm] |

n. a change in your body or mind that shows that you are not healthy 症状

flu *symptom* 流感症状

| **systematic** | [ˌsɪstə'mætɪk] | [同] orderly |

adj. organized carefully and done thoroughly 系统的；有体系的

Analysis of the data should have been more *systematic*. 对数据的分析本应更系统化一些。

| **wisdom** | ['wɪzdəm] | [同] knowledge |

n. the knowledge that a society or culture has gained over a long period of time (社会或文化长

期积累的)知识，学问

It was the responsibility of the older people to pass on their skills, knowledge and *wisdom* to the younger members of society. 老年人有责任把他们的技能、知识和智慧传递给社会中年轻的一代。

Take the Test »

一、英汉互译

观众	_____	critical	_____
丢弃	_____	cushion	_____
指导方针	_____	duration	_____
灌溉	_____	lounge	_____
智慧	_____	symptom	_____

二、翻译句子

1) 一位经济学家认为，按现在的发展速度计算，到2030年中国将成为世界上最大的经济体。（current）

_____

2) 一个明显的原因是真实收入总体上增长了。（overall）

_____

3) 妇女依然要克服很多障碍才能获得平等权。（overcome）

_____

4) 教学形式为讲座和研讨会。（seminar）

_____

A man is not old as long as he is seeking something. A man is not old until regrets take the place of dreams.

只要一个人还有所追求，他就没有老。直到后悔取代了梦想，一个人才算老。

——美国演员 巴里穆尔（J. Barrymore, American actor）

Word List 42

automatic [ˌɔːtəˈmætɪk]

adj. working by itself without direct human control; self-regulating 自动的；自动调整的
My camera is fully *automatic*. 我的相机是全自动的。

available [əˈveɪləbl]　　　　　　　　　　　　　　　[同] attainable [反] unavailable

adj. that can be used or obtained（指物）可用的；可得到的
The new media make our cultural past *available* to the whole nation. 新的媒体使我们的历史文化能够被整个国家所了解。

average [ˈævərɪdʒ]　　　　　　　　　　　　　　　[同]①medium ①②mean

① *adj.* found by calculating the result of adding several amounts together and dividing the total by the number of amounts 平均的
Without the greenhouse effect, the earth's *average* temperature would be 33－35 degrees Celsius lower. 如果没有温室效应，地球的平均气温会低 33 至 35 摄氏度。
② *n.* result of adding several amounts together and dividing the total by the number of amounts 平均数；平均水平

on *average* 平均起来

aware [əˈweə(r)]　　　　　　　　　　　　　　　　　　[反]unaware

adj. having knowledge or realization of sb./sth. 对某人／某事物知道的；察觉到的；意识到的
Since the early eighties we have been only *aware* of the devastating effects of large-scale environmental pollution. 到八十年代早期，我们才开始意识到大规模环境污染的毁灭性作用。

awkward [ˈɔːkwəd]　　　　　　　　[同] clumsy [反] graceful

adj. causing difficulty, embarrassment or inconvenience 造成困难、尴尬或不便的
You've put me in a very *awkward* position. 你将我置于了一个极其尴尬的境地。

burst [bɜːst]　　　　　　　　　　　　　　　[同]②explode

① *n.* short period of a particular activity or strong emotion that often starts suddenly 突发；猝发；迸发
Her breath was coming in short *bursts*. 她的呼吸急迫短促。
② *v.* to break open or apart, esp. because of pressure from inside; to make sth. break in this way（使）爆裂，胀开
That balloon will *burst* if you blow it up any more. 你再给气球充气的话，它就要爆了。

cooperate [kəʊˈɒpəreɪt]　　　　　　　　　　　[同] collaborate, team up

v. to work or act together with another or others（与他人）合作，协作
cooperate with one's friends in raising/to raise money 与朋友合作集资

coordinate

n. [kəʊˈɔːdɪnət]（usu. co-ordinate）either of two numbers or letters used to fix the position of a

point on a graph or map 坐标

the x and y *coordinates* on a graph 图表上的 x 和 y 坐标

v. [kəʊˈɔːdɪneɪt] to cause (different parts, limbs, etc.) to function together efficiently 使(各部分、肢体等)协调，协同动作

We must *coordinate* our efforts to help the flood victims. 我们应该同心协力来援助遭遇水灾的灾民。

cope [kəʊp]　　　　　　　　　　　　　　　　　　　　　　　[同] handle

v. to manage successfully; to be able to deal with sth. difficult 对付；(善于)处理(棘手之事)

cope with problems/difficulties/misfortune 对付问题 / 困难 / 灾祸

core [kɔː]　　　　　　　　　　　　　　[同] heart, centre

n. the most important part of sth. 核心

This concept is at the very *core* of her theory. 这个概念是她的理论的核心。

corporate [ˈkɔːpərət]

adj. of or belonging to a corporation 法人团体的；公司的

Corporate executives usually have high salaries. 公司的管理人员一般享有高薪。

corporation [ˌkɔːpəˈreɪʃn]

n. group of people authorized to act as an individual, e.g. for business purposes 法人团体(如贸易公司)

Broadcasting authorities are often public *corporations*. 广播事业机构一般为国有单位。

correspond [ˌkɒrɪˈspɒnd]　　　　　　　　　　　　　　　[同] agree, accord

v. to be in agreement; not contradict sth. or each other 相一致；相符合

The written record of our conversation doesn't *correspond* with what was actually said. 对我们的交谈所做的文字记录与我们的原话不符。

dusk [dʌsk]　　　　　　　　　　　　　　　　　　　　　　[同] evening

n. the time of day when the light has almost gone, but it is not yet dark 黄昏；傍晚

The tour leaves at sundown and lets you catch a glimpse of some of the rainforest's wildlife as it comes out at *dusk* to feed. 旅行在日落时分开始，这样你可以一览雨林中傍晚出来觅食的野生动物。

dusty [ˈdʌsti]

adj. full of dust; covered with dust 布满灰尘的

a *dusty* road 尘土飞扬的路

duty [ˈdjuːti]　　　　　　　　　　　　　　　　　　　　　[同] obligation

n. sth. that you feel you have to do because it is your moral or legal responsibility 责任；义务

I don't want you to visit me simply out of a sense of *duty*. 我希望你不只是出于责任感才来看我。

dwarf [dwɔːf]　　　　　　　　　　　　　　　　　　　　　[反] ①giant

① *n.* a person, animal or plant that is much smaller than the normal size 矮子；侏儒；短小的动物或植物

dwarf conifers 矮小的针叶树

② *v.* to make sth. seem small or unimportant compared with sth. else 使显得矮小；使相形见绌

Dinosaurs lived millions of years ago, and ranged in size from roughly the size of a small dog to beasts of enormous proportions that would *dwarf* even the largest of today's elephants. 恐龙生活在数百万年前，体形最小的只有小狗那么大，最大的如体积庞大的猛兽，即使是今天最高

大的大象在它面前也会显得很矮小。

dwell [dwel]   [同] reside

v. (fml.) to live somewhere 居住；栖身

He *dwelt* in a ruined cottage on the hillside. 他居住在山坡上破败不堪的小屋里。

dynasty [ˈdɪnəsti]

n. a series of rulers of a country who all belong to the same family 王朝；朝代

the Ming *Dynasty* 明朝

extraordinary [ɪkˈstrɔːdinəri]   [同] unusual, incredible [反] common, usual

adj. not normal or ordinary; greater or better than usual 不平凡的；卓越的

Some of her rings are quite *extraordinary* and have beautiful colored stones in them. 她的戒指
有些很特别，上面有漂亮的彩色宝石。

extreme [ɪkˈstriːm]   [同] utmost

adj. very great in degree 极度的；极大的

We are working under *extreme* pressure at the moment. 目前我们正在极大的压力下工作。

furnish [ˈfɜːnɪʃ]

v. to provide sth. with furniture; put furniture in（a place）为某物提供家具；用家具布置（某
地方）

a *furnished* flat 一套配备家具的公寓

furniture [ˈfɜːnɪtʃə(r)]

n. movable articles, e.g. tables, chairs, beds, etc. put into a house or an office to make it suitable
for living or working in 家具

In organizations, office signs and *furniture* are often used as role signs. 在公司里，办公室的标
记和家具常被当作职位的标志。

furthermore [ˈf(ɜː)ðəˈmɔː]   [同] also

adv. in addition to what has already been said 此外

He is old and unpopular. *Furthermore*, he has at best only two years of political life ahead of
him. 他上了年纪且不受欢迎。此外，他最多也只有两年的政治生涯了。

futile [ˈfjuːtaɪl]   [同] pointless

adj. producing no result; useless; pointless 无效的；无用的；无意义的

Their efforts to revive him were *futile*. 他们对他的抢救无效。

gym [dʒɪm]   [同] gymnasium

n. （infml.）a special building or room that has equipment for doing physical
exercise 体育馆；健身房

I go to the *gym* as often as I can. 我尽可能多去健身房。

investment [ɪnˈvestmənt]

n. investing of money 投资

A good mattress is a wise *investment* for people who want to avoid headaches. 要想避免头疼，
一个好的床垫是一项明智的投资。

involve [ɪnˈvɒlv]   [反] include

v. to include or affect（sb./sth.）in its operation 包括；包含；牵涉；涉及

The task I gave them *involved* some problem solving. 我给他们布置的任务里包含了一些问题
求解。

irregularity [ɪˌreɡjəˈlærəti]   [同] inequality

n. thing that is irregular 不整齐、不平坦、无规律、不规则或不合常规的事物

the *irregularities* of the earth's surface 地球表面的凹凸不平

luxury [ˈlʌkʃəri]

n. the enjoyment of special and expensive things, particularly food and drink, clothes and surroundings 奢侈的享受；奢华

Since those days, leisure has steadily become more of a *luxury*. 那些日子以来，休闲渐渐变得尤为奢侈。

overestimate [ˌəʊvərˈestɪmeɪt]　　　　　　　　　　　　　　　　　[同] overvalue

v. to think sth. is better, more important, etc. than it really is 高估；过份评价

He tends to *overestimate* his own abilities. 他往往高估自己的能力。

overlap [ˌəʊvəˈlæp]

v. part of one thing covers part of the other（物体）部分重叠

A fish's scales *overlap* each other. 鱼鳞是一片片上下交叠起来的。

overlook [ˌəʊvəˈlʊk]　　　　　　　　　　　　　　　　　　　　[同] neglect

v. to fail to see or notice sth. 忽略；未注意到

He seems to have *overlooked* one important fact. 他好像忽略了一个重要的事实。

peak [piːk]　　　　　　　　　　　　　　　　　　　　　　　　[同] apex, top

n. pointed top, esp. of a mountain 尖顶；（尤指）山峰

The plane flew over the snow-covered *peaks*. 飞机飞过了积雪的山峰。

peculiar [pɪˈkjuːliə(r)]　　　　　　　　　　　　　　　　　　　[同] bizarre

adj. odd or strange 奇怪的；奇异的；罕有的

a *peculiar* taste/smell/noise 怪异的口味／气味／噪音

resolution [ˌrezəˈluːʃn]

n. a firm decision to do or not to do sth. 决心；决定

Have you made any New Year's *resolutions*? 你制定出什么新年计划了吗？

resolve [rɪˈzɒlv]　　　　　　　　　　　　　　　　　　　　　　[同] ②solve

v. ① to make a firm decision to do sth. 决心；决定

We had *resolved* on making an early start. 我们已经决定早点动身。

② to find a satisfactory way of dealing with a problem or difficulty 解决（问题或困难）

The crisis was *resolved* by negotiations. 危机通过协商得到了解决。

sensible [ˈsensəbl]　　　　　　　　　　　　　　　　　　　　　[同] wise

adj. having or showing good sense; reasonable 识别力强的；合理的

a *sensible* person 通情达理的人

sensitive [ˈsensɪtɪv]

adj. ①easily upset or offended by events or things that people say 敏感的 ②easily affected or damaged by sth. such as a substance or temperature 易受影响的

Older people tend to be very *sensitive* to cold. 年纪大的人往往容易受到感冒的影响。

withdraw [wɪðˈdrɔː]　　　　　　　　　　　　　　　　　　　　[同] retreat

v. ① to stop taking part in an activity, belonging to an organization, etc., or to make sb. do this 退出 ② to take money out of a bank account 取款；取钱

I'd like to *withdraw* ￡500 from my current account. 我想从我的活期账户上取出 500 英镑。

witness [ˈwɪtnɪs]　　　　　　　　　　　　　　　　　　　　　[同]①beholder

① *n.* a person who sees sth. happen and is able to describe it to other people 目击者；见证人

an eye *witness* 目击证人

② *v.* to see sth. happen because you are there when it happens 当场看到；目击

She was shocked by the violent scenes she had **witnessed**. 她被亲眼目睹的暴虐场面惊呆了。

workload ['wɜːkləʊd]

n. the amount of work that has to be done by a particular person or organization(某一人或组织的)工作量，工作负担

We have taken on extra staff to cope with the increased **workload**. 我们已经额外雇用员工来应付增加了的工作量。

Take the Test ≫

一、英汉互译

自动的	_____	available	_____
意识到	_____	coordinate	_____
极度的	_____	dusk	_____
家具	_____	dwarf	_____
包括，涉及	_____	overestimate	_____

二、翻译句子

1）如果没有温室效应，地球的平均气温会低33至35摄氏度。（average）

_____

2）这个概念是她的理论的核心。（core）

_____

3）年纪大的人往往容易受到感冒的影响。（sensitive）

_____

4）她被亲眼目睹的暴虐场面惊呆了。（witness）

_____

If you would go up high, then use your own legs! Do not let yourselves carried aloft; do not seat yourselves on other people's backs and heads.

如果你想要走到高处，就要使用自己的两条腿！不要让别人把你抬到高处；不要坐在别人的背上和头上。

——德国哲学家　尼采（F. W. Nietzsche, German philosopher）

7 分词汇

abbreviation [əˌbriːvɪˈeɪʃn]
n. a short form of a word or expression 缩写形式
BBC is an *abbreviation* for British Broadcasting Corporation. BBC 是英国广播公司的缩写。

aboriginal [ˌæbəˈrɪdʒənl] [同] native, indigenous
adj. relating to the people or animals that have existed in a place or country from the earliest times 土著的
the *aboriginal* peoples of Canada 加拿大土著

abstraction [æbˈstrækʃn]
n. a general idea about a type of situation, thing, or person rather than a specific example from real life 抽象；抽象概念
This in turn could result in the development of certain superior skills such as logic, rationality and *abstraction*. 这反过来又使得某些高级的能力如逻辑、理性和抽象思维得以发展。

backbone [ˈbækbəʊn] [同] spine, mainstay
n. ① the spine 脊椎 ② (fig.) chief support 中坚；栋梁
The Ottawa Charter for Health Promotion remains as the *backbone* of health action today. 渥太华健康促进宪章在今天仍然是健康运动的支柱。

✓ **background** [ˈbækɡraʊnd]
n. person's social class, education, training, etc. 背景(人的社会阶层、学历、资历等)
a strong *background* in sport 体育方面很强的背景

calorie [ˈkæləri]
n. a unit for measuring the amount of energy that food will produce 卡路里(热量单位)
a low-*calorie* diet 低热量的饮食

calibre [ˈkælɪbə(r)] [同] quality, merit
n. the quality of sth., esp. a person's ability 质量；(尤指人的)能力
He was impressed by the high *calibre* of applicants for the job. 求职人员出色的能力给他留下了深刻印象。

campaign [kæmˈpeɪn]
n. a series of planned activities that are intended to achieve a particular social, commercial or political aim 运动(为社会、商业或政治目的而进行的一系列有计划的运动)
'Your Travel Choice Makes a Difference' is an educational *campaign* aimed at helping consumers understand the potential positive and negative impacts of their travel decisions. "旅行选择影响重大"是一次有教育意义的运动，旨在帮助消费者了解他们的旅行选择会带来的潜在的积极与消极影响。

capability [ˌkeɪpəˈbɪlɪti] [同] ability, qualification
n. the natural ability, skill, or power that makes a machine, person, or organization able to do sth., especially sth. difficult 能力，才干
the country's manufacturing *capability* 国家的生产制造能力

capricious [kəˈprɪʃəs]   [同] changeable [反] steadyfast

adj. likely to change suddenly or behave in an unexpected way 反复无常的，多变的

capricious weather 多变的天气

dairy [ˈdeəri]

n. place where milk is kept and milk products are made 牛奶场；奶品场

dairy cream 奶品场制的奶油

dazzling [ˈdæzlɪŋ]

adj. ①a light that is dazzling is very bright and makes you unable to see properly for a short time 晃眼的 ②very impressive and attractive 眼花缭乱的，吸引人的

a *dazzling* display of football skills 令人眼花缭乱的足球球技展示

decay [dɪˈkeɪ]   [同] break down, corrupt, go bad

v. (cause sth.) to become bad; rot; decompose (使某物)变坏，腐烂，变质

Sugar *decays* your teeth. 糖能腐蚀牙齿。

eccentric [ɪkˈsentrɪk]   [同] odd, weird

adj. considered by other people to be strange or unusual 古怪的；异乎寻常的

The image of green consumerism as associated in the past with the more *eccentric* members of society has virtually disappeared. 像过去那样把绿色消费者跟社会另类分子相提并论的观念已经不复存在了。

echo [ˈekəʊ]

① *n.* the reflecting of sound off a wall or inside an enclosed space so that a noise appears to be repeated; a sound that is reflected back in this way 回响，回音

The hills sent back a faint *echo*. 群山传来微弱的回声。

② *v.* to repeat an idea or opinion 重复；共鸣

Results of the study *echo* the findings of recent newspaper polls. 研究结果与最近报纸上的民意调查结果不谋而合。

✓ edge [edʒ]   [同] border

n. the outside limit of an object, a surface or an area; the part furthest from the center 边缘；边沿

California is on the cutting *edge* of trends that spread nationwide. 加利福尼亚正位于席卷全国的时尚的最前沿。

fabricate [ˈfæbrikeit]   [近] form

v. to invent false information in order to deceive people 编造；虚构

The evidence was totally *fabricated*. 这个证据纯属伪造。

gauge [geidʒ]

n. (=AmE gage) standard measure, esp. of width or thickness 标准量度(尤指宽度或厚度)

the *gauge* of a sheet of metal 金属板的厚度

hail [heɪl]   [同] ②acclaim, applaud

① *n.* frozen rain falling in a shower 雹；冰雹

hail storm 雹暴

② *v.* to describe sb. or sth. as being very good 欢呼，称赞

Zhang Yimou's first film was immediately *hailed* as a masterpiece. 张艺谋的第一部电影在上映后立即被赞誉为杰作。

ideology [ˌaɪdɪˈɒlədʒi]

n. (set of) ideas that form the basis of an economic or political theory or that are held by a particular group or person 思想(体系)；思想意识

Our *ideologies* differ. 我们的思想不同。

identity [aɪˈdentəti]

n. who or what sb./sth. is 本体；身份

There has been a crisis of *identity* as the traditional skills of hunting, trapping and preparing skins have begun to disappear. 由于打猎、围捕和兽皮工艺这些传统技术已经开始渐渐消失，(因纽特人中)出现了"身份危机"。

idiosyncratic [ˌɪdiəsɪŋˈkrætik]

adj. unusual, unique 独特的，特别的

This involves the investigation of bizarre and *idiosyncratic* social practices. 这包括了对独特的社会行为的调查研究。

jeopardize [ˈdʒepədaɪz]　　　　　　　　　　　　　　　　　[同] endanger

v. to cause (sth.) to be harmed, lost or destroyed; to put in danger 使(某事物)受到伤害、损失或破坏；使陷于险境

The security of the whole operation has been *jeopardized* by one careless person. 整个行动的安全让一个粗心大意的人给破坏了。

kin [kɪn]

n. (fml.) one's family and relatives 家人和亲戚

All his *kin* were at the wedding. 他的家人和亲戚都参加了婚礼。

laborious [ləˈbɔːriəs]　　　　　　　　　　　　　　　　　　[同] effortful

adj. needing much effort (指工作等)艰苦的，费力的

Collecting the raw materials proved a long and *laborious* task. 收集素材是一项长期而艰苦的工作。

magnitude [ˈmæɡnɪtjuːd]

n. (fml.) the great size or importance of sth.; the degree to which sth. is large or important 重大；巨大；重要性

We did not realize the *magnitude* of the problem. 我们没有意识到这个问题的重要性。

mainstream [ˈmeɪnstriːm]

n. the ideas and opinions that are thought to be normal because they are shared by most people; the people whose ideas and opinions are most accepted 主流思想；主流群体

Most disabled students are integrated into the *mainstream* educational system. 大部分残疾学生融入到了主流教育体制中。

narrative [ˈnærətɪv]

n. (fml.) a description of events, esp. in a novel (尤指小说中的)描述；叙述

Using family and friends as models, the painter composes *narratives* about birth and death, life and religion. 用家人和朋友作原型，画家创作出了关于生和死、生命和宗教的画作。

obligation [ˌɒblɪˈɡeɪʃn]　　　　　　　　　　　　　　　[同] duty, commitment

n. the state of being forced to do sth. because it is your duty, or because of a law, etc. 义务；职责

You're under no *obligation* to buy anything. 你不必非买什么东西不可。

pacify [ˈpæsɪfaɪ]　　　　　　　　　　　　　　　[同] calm [反] arouse

v. to calm or soothe the anger or distress of (sb.) 使(某人)安静，息怒；抚慰

It was no use trying to *pacify* him; he was simply too upset. 试图安慰他是没有用的，他太沮丧了。

painstaking [ˈpeɪnzteɪkɪŋ]　　　　　　　　　　　　　　　[同] arduous

adj. done with, requiring or taking great care or trouble 极小心的；辛勤的；辛苦的

a **painstaking** job/investigation 艰苦的工作 / 调查

parade [pəˈreɪd]   [同] display

v. display (sth.); show (sth.) off 展示，炫耀 (某事物)

It celebrated scientific and engineering achievements by openly **parading** the sophisticated techniques used in construction. 为了庆祝科学及工程上的成就，结构中的精密技术被公开地展示了出来。

qualification [ˌkwɒlɪfɪˈkeɪʃn]   [近] ability, capability

n. training, examination or experience that qualifies sb. for work, further training, etc. 资格；资历

Some of these courses are open to school leavers, but for some you need previous **qualifications**, or relevant employment. 其中的一些课程面向所有的离校生，还有一些则需要一定的资历或者相关的工作经历。

radiator [ˈreɪdɪˌeɪtə(r)]

n. apparatus for radiating heat into rooms, etc., esp. a metal casing through which hot water or steam is circulated (取暖用的)散热器；(尤指以热水或蒸汽循环供热的)暖气装置

The house is equipped with several high-quality **radiators**. 这幢房子里装有几台高质量的散热器。

rafting [ˈrɑːftɪŋ]

n. the activity of travelling on a raft, especially as a sport 漂流

We've got white-water **rafting**, canoeing, climbing, mountain racing, all the excitement. 我们这里提供漂流、皮划艇、攀岩和山地赛车，一切刺激活动应有尽有。

salvage [ˈsælvɪdʒ]   [近] rescue

n. rescue of a damaged ship or its cargo; rescue of property from damage caused by fire, floods, etc. 海上营救；财物抢救

Salvage of the wreck was made difficult by bad weather. 恶劣的天气使得对遇难船只的救援工作十分困难。

sanitation [ˌsænəˈteʃn, ˌsænɪˈteɪʃn]   [同] hygiene

n. systems that protect people's health, esp. those that dispose efficiently of sewage 卫生系统或设备(尤指下水道设备)

During this period, there is an emphasis on providing clean water, improved **sanitation** and housing. 在这个时期特别强调提供洁净的水、改进了的下水道设备以及住宅设施。

ubiquitous [juːˈbɪkwɪtəs]   [同] universal

adj. (fml.) seeming to be everywhere or in several places at the same time; very common 似乎无所不在的；十分普遍的

Plastic containers are **ubiquitous** nowadays. 塑料容器如今到处都是。

Take the Test ≫

词组翻译

反过来 _____	经济学方面很强的背景 _____
低热量饮食 _____	有教育意义的活动 _____
积极和消极影响 _____	最前沿 _____
身份危机 _____	主流教育体制 _____
义务 _____	资历 _____

abound [əˈbaʊnd]

v. to exist in very large numbers 大量存在，充满

Other examples *abound* in the world of commerce. 商业世界里类似的例子比比皆是。

accelerate [əkˈseləreɪt] [同] speed up [反] decelerate

v. to happen or make sth. happen faster 加速，加快

The Ferrari can *accelerate* from 0 to 60 mph in 6.3 seconds. 法拉利车可以在 6.3 秒内从静止状态加速到 60 英里 / 小时。

accessible [ækˈsesəbl] [同] usable [反] inaccessible

adj. that can be reached, entered, used, seen, etc. 可以接近的；可以使用的

The invention of the radio made music *accessible* to everyone and virtually free. 收音机的发明让每个人都能听到音乐，而且是免费的。

accessory [əkˈsesəri]

n. an extra piece of equipment that is useful but not essential 附件；配件；配饰

fashion *accessories* 时装配饰

backlash [ˈbæklæʃ] [同] backfire

n. extreme and usually violent reaction to some event 反冲；强烈反对

The 1970s saw the first *backlash* against the women's movement. 二十世纪七十年代首次出现了对女权运动的强烈反对。

badge [bædʒ] [同] ①insignia

n. ①a small piece of metal, cloth, or plastic with a picture or words on it, worn to show rank, membership of a group, support for a political idea, etc. 徽章，勋章 ②thing that shows a quality or condition 象征；标志

a *badge* of identity 身份的象征

carefree [ˈkeəfriː] [同] free-minded, happy-go-lucky

adj. having no worries or responsibilities 无忧无虑的；无牵挂的

Play may look like a *carefree* and exuberant way to pass the time before the hard work of adulthood comes along, but there's much more to it than that. 玩耍看上去像是成人世界在辛苦工作到来之前无忧无虑、精力充沛的消磨时光的方式，其实远非如此。

carnivore [ˈkɑːnɪvɔː]

n. any animal that eats meat 食肉动物

With certain *carnivores*, only the dominant male copulates with the females. 在某些食肉动物中，只有领头雄性与雌性进行交配。

casualty [ˈkæʒʊəlti]

n. a person that suffers or a thing that is destroyed when sth. else takes place 受害者；毁坏物；损坏物

Ironically, one major *casualty* of that extreme position has been the environment itself. 具有讽

刺性的是，那种极端情况的主要受害者之一就是环境本身。

catastrophe [kəˈtæstrəfi]　　　　　　　　　　　　　　　　　　　[同] disaster

n. a sudden disaster that causes many people to suffer 灾难；灾祸

Early warnings of rising water levels prevented another major *catastrophe*. 提前发出的水位上涨警报防止了又一次重大灾害。

dedicated [ˈdedikeɪtɪd]　　　　　　　　　　　　　　　　　　　　[近] devoted

adj. devoted to sth.; committed 献身于某事物的；专心致志的

a *dedicated* worker 有献身精神的工作者

dedication [ˌdedɪˈkeɪʃn]

n. devotion to a cause or an aim 对某事业或目的的忠诚；奉献

It takes time and *dedication* to be a master of a craft. 要成为一位熟练的手工艺人必须花费时间和精力。

deductive [dɪˈdʌktɪv]　　　　　　　　　　　　　　　　　　　[近] reasoned

adj. using knowledge about things that are generally true in order to think about particular situations or problems 演绎的，推理的

deductive reasoning 演绎推理

deem [diːm]　　　　　　　　　　　　　　　　　　　[同] consider, regard

v. (fml.) to consider; regard 认为；视为

He *deemed* that it was his duty to help. 他认为他有责任加以援助。

edible [ˈedɪbl]　　　　　　　　　　　　　　　　　　　[同] eatable

adj. fit or suitable to be eaten; not poisonous 适宜食用的；无毒的

The food at the hotel was bare *edible*. 这家旅馆的食物简直不能入口。

edification [ˌedɪfɪˈkeɪʃn]

n. (fml.) the improvement of sb.'s mind or character 教化；启迪；陶冶

During the 17th century, scientists were largely men of private means who pursued their interest in natural philosophy for their own *edification*. 在 17 世纪，科学家大多是富人，为陶冶自我的情操，他们将兴趣倾注于自然科学的研究。

efficiency [ɪˈfɪʃnsi]　　　　　　　　　　　　　　　　　　　[近] performance

n. the quality of doing sth. well with no waste of time or money 效率；效能；功效

Technical solutions can reduce the pollution problem and increase the fuel *efficiency* of engines. 技术解决方案可以缓解污染问题，同时提高发动机的燃油功效。

facade [fəˈsɑːd]

n. (fml.) the front of a building (建筑物的)正面

It is built into a hill and little can be seen from outside except a glass *facade*. 它(建筑物)被建在一座山体内部，除了一个玻璃的正面外，从外面什么也看不到。

generalization [ˈgenərəlaɪˈzeɪʃn]

n. a statement about all the members of a group that may be true in some or many situations but is not true in every case 概括；一概而论

In our example, the data seem too contradictory to support any clear *generalization* about gender and voting. 在我们的例子中，数据实在相差太大，以至于无法支持任何有关性别和选举行为间关系的明确概论。

hallmark [ˈhɔːlmɑːk]

n. distinctive feature, esp. of excellence 特点(尤指优良事物所具有者)

Attention to detail is the *hallmark* of a fine craftsman. 能工巧匠的特点是一丝不苟。

illiteracy [ɪˈlɪtərəsi]   [同] ignorance

n. state of being illiterate 文盲；缺乏教育；无知

Illiteracy is a major problem in some developing countries. 在一些发展中国家，文盲是个大问题。

imagery [ˈɪmɪdʒəri]

n. the use of words or pictures to describe ideas or actions in poems, books, films, etc. 画像；表述

From the earliest days of industry, Hollywood has dominated the world film market. American *imagery*—the cars, the cities, the cowboys—became the primary *imagery* of film. 从电影业发展的初期起，好莱坞电影就统治着世界电影市场。美国影像——汽车、城市、牛仔——成了电影的主要影像。

immerse [ɪˈmɜːs]   [同] dip, engage

v. to involve oneself deeply（in sth.）; absorb oneself 使自己沉浸（于某事物）；使自己深陷于或专心于

He *immersed* himself totally in his work. 他埋首于工作。

jury [ˈdʒʊəri]

n. group of people in a law court who have been chosen to listen to the facts in a case and to decide whether the accused person is guilty or not guilty 陪审团

The *jury* returned a verdict of not guilty. 陪审团做出被告无罪的裁决。

kindle [ˈkɪndl]

v. (cause sth.) to catch fire（使某物）燃烧，着火

The sparks *kindled* the dry grass. 有些火星把干草给引着了。

kindle a candle 点燃蜡烛

lament [ləˈment]   [反] rejoice

v. to feel or express great sorrow or regret for（sb./sth.）为（某人/某事物）感到悲痛；哀悼；痛惜

The nation *lamented* the death of its great leader. 整个国家为失去他们伟大的领袖而悲痛。

landfill [ˈlændfɪl]

n. the practice of burying waste under the ground, or the waste buried in this way 垃圾掩埋法

The rest is dumped in *landfill* sites. 其他的被堆放在垃圾填埋场。

WHAT WE DO WITH OUR TRASH
Burn 14%
Landfill 55%
Recycle 31%

maintenance [ˈmeɪntənəns]   [同] preservation

n. the act of keeping sth. in good condition by checking or repairing it regularly 维护；保养

The school pays for heating and the *maintenance* of the buildings. 学校负担这些大楼的供暖和维护费用。

navigation [ˌnævɪˈɡeɪʃn]

n. the movement of ships or aircraft 航海；航行

The voyage was an achievement of *navigation* and courage. 这次航程既是航海的成就，也是勇气的成就。

oblivious [əˈblɪviəs]   [同] ignorant

adj. not aware of sth. 不知道的；未注意的

You will eventually become *oblivious* to the noise. 你终究会变得不在意吵闹声的。

paradigm [ˈpærədaim]　　　　　　　　　　　　　　　　　　　　　[同] model

n. a very clear or typical example of sth. 模式；典范

The needs of today's children cannot be met by our old educational *paradigms*. 现代儿童的需求是旧的教育模式所不能满足的。

paradoxical [ˌpærəˈdɒksɪkl]

adj. of paradox 看似矛盾的

It is *paradoxical* that some of the poorest people live in some of the richest areas of the country. 某些最贫穷的人却住在这个国家最富有的地区，这似乎很矛盾。

rationale [ˌræʃəˈnɑːl]　　　　　　　　　　　　　　　　　　　　[同] explanation

n. fundamental reason for or logical basis of sth. 基本原理；理论基础

The *rationale* for using this teaching method is to encourage student's confidence. 使用这种教学方法的原理在于培养学生的信心。

rationality [ˌræʃˈnæləti]

n. quality of being rational; reasonableness 理性；合理性；理智

the *rationality* of his argument 他的论点的合理性

savage [ˈsævidʒ]　　　　　　　　　　　　　　　　　　　　　　[近] uncivilized

adj. wild and fierce 野性的；凶猛的

a *savage* attack by a big dog 大狗的凶猛攻击

scaffold [ˈskæfəld, -fəʊld]

n. frame made of long metal tubes put up next to a building so that builders, painters, etc. can work on it, or to support a platform 脚手架；建筑架

It provides a useful *scaffold* for your essay. 这给你的论文提供了很有用的框架。

unanimous [juːˈnænɪməs]　　　　　　　　　　　　　　　　　　[近] agreed

adj. sharing the same opinions or views; being in complete harmony or accord（全体）一致的；观念或见解完全和谐或一致的

The meeting was *unanimous* in adopting the proposals. 会议一致决定采用这个方案。

vacancy [ˈveɪkənsi]　　　　　　　　　　　　　　　　　　　　[反] occupancy

n. a job that is available for sb. to do（职位的）空缺；空职

fill a *vacancy* 填补空缺

Take the Test ▶▶

英汉互译

make...accessible to...　_____　　技术解决方案　_____

提高效率　_____　　关注细节　_____

大问题　_____　　垃圾填埋场　_____

维护，保养　_____　　教育模式　_____

教学方法　_____　　论点的合理性　_____

acclaim [əˈkleɪm]   [同] ②applaud [反] ②denounce

① *n.* a strong expression of praise 赞扬

② *v.* to praise sb. or sth. publicly 赞誉某人 / 某事物

a highly *acclaimed* performance 受到高度赞扬的演出

acquisition [ˌækwɪˈzɪʃn]   [同] acquirement

n. the process by which you gain knowledge or learn a skill（知识、技能等的）获得

American culture is highly focused on personal success, on business and on the *acquisition* of personal wealth. 美国文化高度强调个人成功、商业和个人财富的获得。

acupuncture [ˈækjupʌŋktʃə(r)]

n. a treatment for pain and disease that involves pushing special needles into parts of the body 针灸疗法

Acupuncture and many other healing techniques have as their basic principle the concept of energy flows in the body. 针灸和其他很多治病方法都是以体内能量流动的概念为基本原理的。

baffle [ˈbæfl]   [同] frustrate

v. to be too difficult for (sb.) to understand; puzzle 使（某人）困惑；难倒

One of the exam questions *baffled* me completely. 有一道试题把我完全难住了。

ballot [ˈbælət]   [同] vote

n. piece of paper used in secret voting 选票

Voting will be by secret *ballot*. 投票将以无记名选票方式进行。

cater [ˈkeɪtə(r)]

v. to provide food and drinks for a social event 提供饮食；承办酒席

Most of our work now involves *catering* for weddings. 我们现在的工作多半是承办婚宴。

cathedral [kəˈθiːdrl]

n. the main church of a district, under the care of a bishop 主教座堂；教区总教堂

What I really want to do at the *Cathedral* is climb the tower. The view is supposed to be spectacular. 在大教堂我最想做的事就是爬上那个塔楼。据说上面的景色相当壮观。

cautious [ˈkɔːʃəs]   [同] careful, discreet

adj. being careful about what you say or do, esp. to avoid danger or mistakes; not taking any risks 小心的；谨慎的

He was very *cautious* about committing himself to anything. 他谨小慎微，从不轻易承诺任何事。

celebrity [səˈlebrəti]   [同] big name, figure [反] nobody

n. a famous person 名人，名流

a sporting *celebrity* 体育名人

cellular [ˈseljələ(r)]

adj. connected with or consisting of the cells of plants or animals 细胞的，由细胞组成的

cellular structure/processes 细胞结构 / 变化过程

default [dɪˈfɔːlt]　　　　　　　　　　　　　　　　　　　　[同]①absence

n. ①failure to do sth., esp. to pay a debt or appear in court 不做某事, (尤指)不还债, 不出庭
②the way in which things are arranged on a computer screen unless you decide to change them
缺省设置

The bank can seize the asset in the event of a *default* in payment. 如果到期未付款, 银行可以没收该资产。

deficiency [dɪˈfɪʃnsi]　　　　　　　　　　　[同]shortage, dearth [反]abundance, sufficiency

n. state of lacking sth. essential 缺乏 ; 缺少

Deficiency in vitamins can lead to illness. 身体缺乏维生素会生病。

deforestation [diːˈfɒrɪˈsteɪʃn]

n. the cutting or burning down of all the trees in an area 砍伐树林, 植被破坏

Land clearing for agriculture is the largest single cause of *deforestation*. 农业圈地是导致森林砍伐的最大原因。

degenerate [dɪˈdʒenəreɪt]　　　　　　　　　　　　　　　　[同]deteriorate

v. to become worse 衰退 ; 恶化

Although at least some cetaceans have taste buds, the nerves serving these have *degenerated* or are rudimentary. 尽管有些鲸鱼也有味蕾, 但这些味蕾的神经要么已经退化, 要么就是相当低级。

ejection [ɪˈdʒekʃn]

n. the act of throwing out with force 驱逐 ; 喷出

The reaction to the *ejection* of these small particles causes the rocket to move forwards. 这些微小颗粒喷出时的反作用力使得火箭前行。

facet [ˈfæsɪt]　　　　　　　　　　　　　　　　　　　　　　　　[同]phase

n. a particular part or aspect of sth. (事物的)部分, 方面

Now let's look at another *facet* of the problem. 现在咱们看问题的另一面。

factual [ˈfæktʃuəl]　　　　　　　　　　　　　　　　　　　　　[同]①actual

① *adj.* based on or containing facts 根据事实的 ; 真实的

We need more *factual* programmes like news and documentaries. 我们需要更加真实的节目, 比如新闻或是纪录片。

② *n.* a factual account of events 事件的如实报道

haphazard [ˌhæpˈhæzəd]　　　　　　　　　　　　　　[同]random [反]planned

adj. without plan or order; random 无计划的 ; 无秩序的 ; 任意的

books piled on shelves in a *haphazard* fashion 乱七八糟地堆在书架上的书籍

harass [ˈhærəs]

v. to trouble and annoy (sb.) continually 不断打扰, 骚扰(某人)

Black teenagers are being constantly *harassed* by the police. 黑人青少年总是受到警察的骚扰。

impair [ɪmˈpeə(r)]　　　　　　　　　　　　　　　　[同]injure [反]improve, repair

v. to weaken or damage (sth.) 削弱或损害

Loud noise can *impair* your hearing. 巨大的噪音有损听觉。

impart [ɪmˈpɑːt]　　　　　　　　　　　　　　　　　　　　　[同]communicate

v. to give (a quality) to sth. 将(某性质)给予或赋予某事物

Her presence *imparted* an air of elegance to the ceremony. 她的出席给仪式增添了高雅的气氛。

impede [ɪmˈpiːd]　　　　　　　　　　　　　　　　　　　[反] aid, assist

v. to hinder or obstruct the progress or movement of (sb./sth.) 阻碍，妨碍，阻止

The lack of a common language can severely *impede* progress or can halt it altogether. 没有通用语言会严重阻碍进程，甚至使整个进程暂停。

justification [ˌdʒʌstɪfɪˈkeɪʃn]　　　　　　　　　　　　　[近] explanation

n. acceptable reason (for doing sth.) (做某事的)正当理由

I can see no *justification* for dividing the company into smaller units. 我认为没有理由把公司划分成更小的单位。

kiosk [ˈkiːɒsk]

n. small open structure where newspapers, refreshments, etc. are sold (出售报纸、饮料等的)小摊棚，售货亭

There must be a *kiosk* selling phone cards around here somewhere. 附近一定有一间卖电话卡的售货亭。

landmark [ˈlændmɑːk]

n. object, etc. easily seen and recognized from a distance (自远处易辨识的)陆标，地标

The Bird's Nest is a famous *landmark* on the Beijing skyline. 鸟巢是北京的高大楼厦中著名的标志性建筑。

makeshift [ˈmeɪkˌʃɪft]

adj. used temporarily for a particular purpose because the real thing is not available 临时替代的；权宜的

A few cushions formed a *makeshift* bed. 临时用几个垫子拼了一张床。

necessitate [nɪˈsesɪteɪt]　　　　　　　　　　　　　　　[近] require, call for

v. (fml.) to make sth. necessary 使成为必要

Lack of money *necessitated* a change of plan. 资金不足导致了计划的变化。

obsessive [əbˈsesɪv]

adj. thinking too much about one particular person or thing; showing this 着迷的；迷恋的

an *obsessive* attention to details 过份注重细枝末节

paramount [ˈpærəmaʊnt]　　　　　　　　　　　　　　　[同] dominant

adj. (fml.) having the greatest importance or significance; supreme 最重要的；最重大的；至上的

This matter is of *paramount* importance. 此事至关重要。

partial [ˈpɑːʃl]　　　　　　　　　　　　[同] incomplete [反] whole

adj. of or forming a part; not complete 部分的；不完全的

This attitude altered with the realization that marginal communities can survive and adopt in spite of *partial* integration into a notoriously fickle world economy. 尽管只能部分融入这变幻极其无常的世界经济，边缘团体还是能够存在并且适应；有了这样的认识，这种态度也随之改变了。

participant [pɑːˈtɪsɪpənt]

n. person or group of people who participate in sth. 参加者

All the *participants* in the debate had an opportunity to speak. 所有参加辩论的人都有机会发言。

qualitative [ˈkwɒlɪtətɪv]

adj. of or concerned with quality 性质的；质量的；与性质或质量有关的

qualitative analysis 定性分析

quantitative ['kwɒntɪtətɪv]

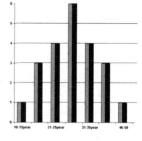

adj. of or concerned with quantity 数量的；关于数量的

quantitative research 定量研究

reaction [rɪ'ækʃn]

n. response to a situation, an act, an influence, etc. （对情况、行动、影响等做出的）反应，回应

In *reaction* to the backward discharge of bullets, the gun move forwards. 在子弹向后发射的后坐力作用下，枪支向前运动。

readily ['redɪli]   [同] ①easily

adv. ①quickly and easily 容易地，迅速地 ②quickly, willingly, and without complaining 欣然地

Evidence of early stages of arithmetic and numeration can be *readily* found. 早期算术和计数法的痕迹很容易就能被找到。

scenery ['siːnəri]   [同] scene

n. general natural features of an area, e.g. mountains, valleys, rivers, forests 景色；风光

The skiing can be excellent, the *scenery* is beautiful and the whole experience unforgettable. 滑雪很棒，景色极美，整个经历让人难以忘怀。

scheme [skiːm]   [同] plan

n. plan for doing or organizing sth. 计划；方案

pension *scheme* 养老保险；membership *scheme* 会员制

scratch [skrætʃ]   [同] scrape

v. to make marks on or in (a surface) with a sharp tool, nails, claws, etc.; make a shallow wound in (the skin) in this way 刮，划，抓（物体表面或皮肤）

The medicine relieves the itching, so the child doesn't *scratch* so much. 药物缓解了瘙痒，小孩子不再那么频繁地抓挠了。

Take the Test

句子翻译

1）美国文化高度强调个人成功、商业和个人财富的获得。（acquisition）

_____

2）在大教堂我最想做的事就是爬上那个塔楼。据说上面的景色相当壮观。（cathedral）

_____

3）我们需要更加真实的节目，比如新闻或是纪录片。（factual）

_____

4）鸟巢是北京的高楼大厦中著名的标志性建筑。（landmark）

_____

5）滑雪很棒，景色极美，整个经历让人难以忘怀。（scenery）

_____

acute [əˈkjuːt]　　　　　　　　　　　　　　　　　　　　　　[反] chronic

adj. very serious or severe 严重的；急性的

The old and ill are the most vulnerable to the *acute* effects of heavily polluted air. 老人和病人最容易受到空气重污染的影响。

adaptation [ˌædæpˈteɪʃn]

n. a film or television programme that is based on a book or play 改编本

the BBC *adaptation* of the best-selling book BBC 对畅销书的电视改编本

addicted [əˈdɪktɪd]

No I am NOT addicted!!!

adj. unable to stop taking harmful drugs, or using or doing sth. as a habit 上瘾的；成瘾的

Not only do we not notice the level of noise that surrounds us, but people actually become *addicted* to it, unable to live without it. 我们非但没有意识到周围噪音的强度，反而对此上了瘾，离开噪音反而无法生存下去了。

adhere [ədˈhɪə(r)]　　　　　　　　　　　　　　　　　　　　　　[同] stick

v. (fml.) to behave according to a particular rule, agreement, or belief 坚持，遵守

Only 23 per cent of firms have a set of standards which *adhere* to international requirements. 只有 23% 的公司有一套符合国际要求的标准。

bandwagon [ˈbændˌwægən]　　　　　　　　　　　　　　　　　[同] fashion

n. (infml.) the act of joining others in doing sth. fashionable or likely to be successful 赶时髦；随大流

The keep-fit *bandwagon* started rolling in the mid 80s. 健身风潮兴起于 80 年代中期。

banish [ˈbænɪʃ]　　　　　　　　　　　　　　　　　　[同] ①exile ①②cast out

v. ①to send sb. away, esp. out of the country, as a punishment 放逐某人(尤指驱逐出境，作为惩罚) ② to not allow sb. or sth. to stay in a particular place 开除

If the therapies resulted in the death of a patient, the healer was to be *banished* for two and a half years. 如果治疗导致病人死亡的话，医治者将被禁止在未来的两年半内行医。

Celsius [ˈselsiəs]

n. a scale of temperature in which water freezes at 0° and boils at 100°　摄氏度

It will be a mild night, around nine degrees *Celsius*. 晚间天气暖和，温度约 9 摄氏度。

censor [ˈsensə]　　　　　　　　　　　　　　　　　　　　　　[同] screen

v. to examine books, films, letters, etc. to remove anything that is considered offensive, morally harmful, or politically dangerous, etc.(书籍、电影等的)审查

Student newspapers should not be *censored* by school officials. 学生办的报纸不应被学校官员审查。

census [ˈsensəs]

n. the process of officially counting sth., esp. a country's population, and recording various facts

（官方的）统计；人口普查

When was the first *census* in China taken? 中国第一次人口普查是什么时候？

certify [ˈsɜːtɪfaɪ] [同] attest

v. to state officially, esp. in writing, that sth. is true（尤指书面）证明；证实

He handed her a piece of paper *certifying*（that）she was in good health. 他递给她一份她的健康证明书。

degradation [ˌdegrəˈdeɪʃn] [同] demotion

n. process of degrading 堕落、恶化、退化的过程

One of the foremost examples of modern human-induced environmental *degradation* is the drying up of the Aral Sea in Central Asia. 中亚地区咸海的干涸是现代人类导致的环境恶化的最主要的例子之一。

delectable [dɪˈlektəbl] [同] delightful, delicious

adj.（fml.）（esp. of food）delightful; pleasant （尤指食物）令人喜爱的，合意的，美味的

a *delectable* meal 美餐

deliberate [dɪˈlɪbəreɪt] [同] ponder

v.（fml.）to think or talk carefully 仔细考虑或谈论

We had no time to *deliberate* on the problem. 我们没有时间仔细思考这个问题。

delighted [dɪˈlaɪtɪd] [近] pleased

adj. very pleased; showing delight 非常高兴的；显示愉快的

a *delighted* smile/look/child 愉快的微笑 / 样子 / 小孩

elegant [ˈelɪgənt]

adj. tasteful in appearance or manner 优雅的，高雅的

an *elegant* woman/style of writing 优雅的女人 / 优美的写作风格

eligible [ˈelɪdʒəbl] [反] ineligible

adj. qualified or entitled to be chosen 合格的；有资格或有权力被选中的

However, it's important to note that as an international student you'll not necessarily be *eligible* for all the facilities offered to resident students. 不过，作为留学生，需要注意的是你不一定能使用为本国学生提供的所有设备。

eliminate [ɪˈlɪmɪneɪt] [同] remove

v. to remove or get rid of sth./sb. 排除；消除

We are working together to *eliminate* poverty, unemployment and social unrest. 我们正共同努力以消除贫穷、失业和社会动荡。

fade [feɪd] [同] vanish

v. to disappear gradually 逐渐消失

Hopes of reaching an agreement seem to be *fading* away. 达成协议的希望看来已逐渐渺茫。

faithful [ˈfeɪθfl] [反] faithless

adj. staying with or supporting a particular person, organization or belief 忠实的；忠诚的

He remained *faithful* to the ideas of the party until his death. 他至死都对党的信念坚贞不渝。

geometric [ˌdʒiːəˈmetrɪk]

adj.（also geometrical）of geometry; of or like the lines, figures, etc. used in geometry 几何（学）的；（似）几何线条、图形等的

a *geometric* design 几何图形设计

harness [ˈhɑːnɪs]

v. to control and use the natural force or power of sth. 控制；使用

We can ***harness*** the power of the wind to generate electricity. 我们可以利用风能发电。

imperative [ɪmˈperətɪv] 　　　　　　　　　　　　　　　[同] essential

adj. very urgent or important; needing immediate attention 紧急的；极重要的

It is ***imperative*** that we make a quick decision. 我们要尽快做出决定。

impetus [ˈɪmpɪtəs] 　　　　　　　　　　　　　　　　[同] stimulus

n. thing that encourages a process to develop more quickly 推动；刺激；促进

The treaty gave (a) fresh ***impetus*** to trade. 这个条约使双方的贸易又推进了一步。

impinge [ɪmˈpɪndʒ]

v. to have a harmful effect on sb. or sth. 妨害；影响

Personal problems experienced by students may ***impinge*** on their work. 学生的个人问题会影响他们的学业。

kit [kɪt]

n. a set of tools, equipment, etc. that you use for a particular purpose or activity 装备

first-aid ***kit*** 急救箱

managerial [ˌmænəˈdʒɪəriəl]

adj. connected with the work of a manager 经理的；管理的

Managerial skills and technical expertise are often in short supply. 管理才能和技术特长总是供不应求。

mandate [ˈmændeɪt] 　　　　　　　　　　　　　　　[同] ②command

① *n.* the authority to do sth., given to a government or other organization by the people who vote for it in an election (政府或组织等经选举而获得的)授权

The election victory gave the party a clear ***mandate*** to continue its programme of reform. 选举获胜明确给予了这个政党继续推行改革的权力。

② *v.* to order sb. to behave, do sth. or vote in a particular way 强制执行；委托办理

The law ***mandates*** that imported goods should be identified as such. 法律规定进口物品必须如实标明。

obsolete [ˈɒbsəliːt] 　　　[同] outmoded [反] current

adj. no longer used because sth. new has been invented 淘汰的；过时的

With technological changes many traditional skills have become ***obsolete***. 随着技术的革新，许多传统技艺已被淘汰。

" WOW! LOOK AT THE SIZE OF GRANDPA'S CO. "

participation [pɑːˌtɪsɪˈpeɪʃn]

n. the act of taking part in an activity or event 参与；加入

Thank you for your ***participation***. 谢谢你的参与。

passionate [ˈpæʃənət] 　　　　　　　　　[同] impassioned, ardent

adj. caused by or showing strong feelings 出于或表现强烈感情的

It's interesting how some people can be ***passionate*** about certain things while others have no interest in them at all. 有趣的是，某些人非常喜欢的东西在另外一些人看来毫无趣味。

pasture [ˈpɑːstʃə(r)]

n. (piece of) land covered with grass and similar plants, suitable for grazing animals 牧场；牧地；草原

acres of rich *pasture* 广阔富饶的牧场

realm ［relm］ ［近］②range

n. ①(fml.) kingdom 王国 ② a general area of knowledge, activity, or thought 领域

new discoveries in the *realm* of science 科学领域的新发现

reasoning ［ˈriːzənɪŋ］

n. the process of thinking about things in a logical way 推想；推理

This line of *reasoning* is faulty. 这样的思路有问题。

scrutinize ［ˈskruːtɪnaɪz］ ［同］eye, overhaul

v. to look at or examine (sth.) carefully or thoroughly 仔细或彻底检查(某事物)

He *scrutinized* all the documents. 他仔细审阅了所有文件。

secular ［ˈsekjələ(r)］ ［反］religious

adj. not concerned with spiritual or religious affairs; worldly 现世的；世俗的

secular education/art/music 世俗教育／艺术／音乐

semifinal ［ˌsemɪˈfaɪnl］

n. match or round preceding the final, e.g. in football 半决赛(如足球赛的)

He's through to the *semifinal* of the men's singles. 他已打入男子单打半决赛。

uncompromising ［ˌʌnˈkɒmprəmaɪzɪŋ］ ［同］inflexible, unbending

adj. unwilling to change your opinions or behaviour 不让步的；不妥协的

He has a reputation for being tough and *uncompromising*. 他的严厉和强硬态度是出了名的。

warehouse ［ˈweəhaʊs］ ［同］storehouse

n. a building where large quantities of goods are stored, esp. before they are sent to shops to be sold 仓库；货仓

Prices rose in April 2009, but fell again in May after an upsurge in *warehouse* copper stocks. 价格在 2009 年 4 月上涨, 但在铜库存猛涨之后, 在 5 月又下跌了。

Take the Test ≫

句子翻译

1) 学生办的报纸不应被学校官员审查。(censor)

_____

2) 不过,作为留学生,需要注意的是你不一定能使用为本国学生提供的所有设备。(eligible)

_____

3) 我们正共同努力以消除贫穷、失业和社会动荡。(eliminate)

_____

4) 随着技术的革新,许多传统技艺已被淘汰。(impinge)

_____

5) 他的严厉和强硬态度是出了名的。(uncompromising)

_____

adjoin [əˈdʒɔɪn] [同] border

v. (written) to be next to or joined to sth. 紧挨；邻接

A luxury hotel *adjoins* the convention center. 一家豪华酒店紧挨着会议中心。

administer [ədˈmɪnɪstə(r)]

v. (fml.) to give or to provide sth., esp. in a formal way 给予；提供

The test was *administered* to all 11-year-olds. 所有 11 岁的孩子都接受了测试。

admittedly [ədˈmɪtɪdli]

adv. used when you are admitting that sth. is true（尤用于句首）诚然，无可否认

Admittedly, some fields are more open to amateurs than others. 诚然，某些领域对业余爱好者来说要更开放一些。

adolescence [ˌædəˈlesns] [同] youth

n. the time, usually between the ages of 12 and 18, when a young person is developing into an adult 青春期

It has been calculated that 17 per cent of cases of lung cancer can be attributed to high levels of exposure to second-hand tobacco smoke during childhood and *adolescence*. 据计算，有 17%的肺癌病例是由幼时和青少年时经常遭遇被动吸烟而导致的。

bankrupt [ˈbæŋkrʌpt] [同] insolvent

adj. unable to pay one's debts 无力还债的

go/be *bankrupt* 破产

banquet [ˈbæŋkwɪt] [同] feast

n. elaborate formal meal, usually for a special event, at which speeches are often made 宴会，盛宴

a wedding *banquet* 婚宴

chamber [ˈtʃeɪmbə(r)] [近] ①room

n. ①a room used for the particular purpose that is mentioned 房间，室 ②an enclosed space, especially in your body or inside a machine 腔，室

brood *chamber* 育虫室；蜂巢

champion [ˈtʃæmpiən] [近] support

v. to fight for or speak in support of a group of people or a belief 为…而斗争；捍卫；声援

He has always *championed* the cause of women's rights. 他一直在为争取妇女的权利而斗争。

chaos [ˈkeɪɒs] [同] confusion, disorder [反] order

n. a state of complete confusion and disorder 混乱；杂乱；紊乱

There was no standard way of speaking or writing and no agreement as to the best way of bringing some order to the *chaos* of English spelling. Dr. Johnson provided the solution. 当时口语和书面语没有统一的标准，对于如何最好地整顿英语拼写混乱的局面也没有统一的看法。这个时候约翰逊博士提供了解决方法。

charter [ˈtʃɑːtə(r)]

n. a written statement describing the rights that a particular group of people should have (阐述某部分民众应有权利的)宪章

The Ottawa *Charter* brings practical meaning and action to this broad notion of health promotion. 渥太华宪章为健康促进统一宏观概念带来了实际意义，并促进了实际行动。

checklist [ˈtʃeklɪst]

n. a list of the things you must remember to do, to take with you or to find out (记事)清单，一览表

Here is a *checklist* of things you need to buy before travelling to Egypt. 这里是一份清单，上面写着去埃及旅行前要买的东西。

delightful [dɪˈlaɪtfl] 　　　　　[同] pleasant [反] horrid

adj. giving delight 使人快乐的；令人愉快的

All the tours offer excellent value for money and the opportunity to relax in a *delightful* rural setting. 所有线路都物有所值，而且提供了在令人愉快的乡间放松的机会。

demanding [dɪˈmɑːndɪŋ] 　　　　　　　　[近] arduous, challenging [反] undemanding

adj. needing much patience, skill, effort, etc. (指任务等)需要很大耐性、技巧、努力等的，高要求的

Climbing is physically *demanding*. 登山运动对身体素质要求很高。

demographic [ˌdeməˈɡræfɪk]

adj. of statistics of births, deaths, diseases, etc. in order to show the state of a community 人口统计学的

Demographic trends suggest that the number of women going into employment is steadily increasing. 人口发展趋势表明女性的就业人数正在稳步增长。

elite [eɪˈliːt]

n. a group of people in a society, etc. who are powerful and have a lot of influence, because they are rich, intelligent, etc. 上层集团；社会精英

In these countries, only the *elite* can afford an education for their children. 在这些国家，只有上层人士才供得起子女上学。

eloquent [ˈeləkwənt] 　　　　　　　　　　　　　　　[同] expressive

adj. able to use language and express your opinions well, esp. when you are speaking in public 雄辩的；有口才的

an *eloquent* speaker 口才很好的演讲者

elusive [ɪˈluːsɪv]

adj. difficult to find, define, or achieve 难找的；难以解释的；难以达到的

A solution to the problem of toxic waste is proving *elusive* in the extreme. 据证实，有毒废物的问题极难解决。

fallacy [ˈfæləsi] 　　　　　　　　　　　　　　　[同] misconception

n. a false idea that many people believe is true 谬见；谬论

It is a *fallacy* to say that the camera never lies. 说照相机绝不骗人，这是谬见。

germ [dʒɜːm]

n. micro-organism, esp. one capable of causing disease 微生物；细菌；病菌

Disinfectant kills *germs*. 消毒剂可杀菌。

implication [ˌɪmplɪˈkeɪʃn]

n. a possible effect or result of an action or a decision 可能的影响(作用或结果)

This has important *implications* for the learning of a foreign language. 这会对学习外语产生重要的影响。

imposing [ɪmˈpəʊzɪŋ]　　　　　　　　　　　　　　　　[同] grand [反] unimposing

adj. grand; impressive in appearance or manner 壮观的;(外表或举止)令人印象深刻的

an *imposing* facade 宏伟的外观

knack [næk]　　　　　　　　　　　　　　　　　　　　　　　　[同] ability

n. skill or ability at performing some special task 技巧;诀窍

Making an omelette is easy once you've got the *knack* (of it). 一旦你掌握了煎蛋饼的技巧,做起来就很容易了。

laud [lɔːd]　　　　　　　　　　　　　　　　　　　　　　　　　[同] praise

v. (fml.) to praise (sb./sth.); glorify 称赞(某人 / 某事物);赞美;赞扬

Once Britain was *lauded* for its education system. 英国曾一度因为其教育体制而备受推崇。

mandatory [ˈmændətəri]　　　　　　　　　　　　[同] compulsory [反] optional

adj. (fml.) required by law 强制的;法定的

It is *mandatory* for blood banks to test all the donated blood for the virus. 血库必须检查所有捐献的血液是否含有这种病毒。

maneuver [məˈnuːvə(r)]　　　　　　　　　　　　　　　　　　[近] move

n. a movement performed with care and skill 细致巧妙的移动;机动动作;操作

You will be asked to perform some standard *maneuvers* during your driving test. 驾驶测试中会要求你演示几个标准操作。

negligible [ˈneɡlɪdʒəbl]　　　　　　　　　　　　　　　　[反] significant

adj. of very little importance or size and not worth considering 微不足道的;不值一提的

The cost was *negligible*. 费用可以忽略不计。

occupation [ˌɒkjuˈpeɪʃn]　　　　　　　　　　[同] ①work ②habitation

n. ① a job or profession 工作,职业 ② when sb. lives or stays in a building or place 居住;占据

The tropical forest has been ecologically unfit for large-scale human *occupation*. 就生态环境而言,热带森林不适合大规模的人类居住。

pedestrian [pəˈdestriən]

n. person walking in the street (contrasted with people in vehicles) 行人

Banning traffic from the shopping areas has made life much more pleasant for *pedestrians*. 商业区的交通限行措施让行人的生活方便了很多。

penetrate [ˈpenɪtreɪt]

v. to make a way into or through sth. 进入或穿过某物

Few U.S. companies have successfully *penetrated* the Japanese electronics market. 几乎没有哪家美国公司能成功地打入日本的电子市场。

perceptible [pəˈseptəbl]　　　　　　　　　　　　　　　　[近] appreciable

adj. (fml.) that can be observed with the senses 可感知的;可觉察的

a small but *perceptible* change 一个很小但可以觉察出的变化

perception [pəˈsepʃn]　　　　　　　　　　　　　　　　　　[同] ①idea

n. ① way of seeing or understanding sth. 看法;理解 ② the way that you notice things with your senses of sight, hearing, etc. 感觉

There has been a sea change in the *perception* of the conventions. 人们对常规的看法发生了巨变。

receipt [rɪˈsiːt]

n. written statement that sth. (esp. money or goods) has been received 收条；收据

Keep your *receipt* in case you want to bring it back. 保存好发票，以防你想退货。

receptive [rɪˈseptɪv]　　　　　　　　　　　　　[同] open-minded [反] unreceptive

adj. able or quick to receive new ideas, suggestions, etc. (对新的思想、建议等)易于接受的，接受得快的

a *receptive* person/mind/attitude 易于接受新思想的人 / 头脑 / 态度

sensational [senˈseɪʃnl]

adj. ①very interesting, exciting, and surprising 轰动的；群情激动的 ②intended to interest, excite, or shock people—used in order to show disapproval 耸人听闻的

a *sensational* victory 令人难以置信的胜利

sentiment [ˈsentɪmənt]　　　　　　　　　　　　[同] feeling, affection

n. tender feelings of pity, nostalgia (怜悯、怀旧等的)情感

act from rational motives rather than *sentiment* 行事出于理智而非出于情感

sewage [ˈsjuːɪdʒ]

n. waste matter from human bodies, factories, towns, etc. that flows away in sewers (or sewer) (下水道的)污物

chemical treatment of *sewage* 对下水道污物的化学处理

weird [wɪəd]　　　　　　　　　　　　　　　　　　[近] strange

adj. unusual or different; not normal 不寻常的；奇异的

It's really *weird* seeing yourself on television. 看到自己上电视感觉怪怪的。

zeal [ziːl]　　　　　　　　　　　　　　　　　　　[近] passion

n. great energy or enthusiasm connected with sth. that you feel strongly about 热情；激情

He shows great *zeal* for knowledge. 他表现出极大的求知热情。

Take the Test 》》

句子翻译

1) 他一直在为争取妇女的权利而斗争。(champion)

_____

2) 这里是一份清单，上面写着去埃及旅行前要买的东西。(checklist)

_____

3) 登山运动对身体素质要求很高。(demanding)

_____

4) 人口发展趋势表明女性的就业人数正在稳步增长。(demographic)

_____

5) 几乎没有哪家美国公司能成功地打入日本的电子市场。(penetrate)

_____

adorable [əˈdɔːrəbl]　　　　　　　　　　　　　　　　　　[同] lovable

adj. used to describe a person or animal that makes you feel great affection because they are so attractive and often small 非常可爱的

We eventually found the cat in the wardrobe, surrounded by six *adorable* kittens. 我们最终在衣柜里发现了那只猫，周围围着六只极可爱的小猫咪。

advent [ˈædvent]　　　　　　　　　　　　　　　　[同] arrival [反] exit

n. the time when sth. first begins to be widely used (重要事件、人物、发明等的)到来

Even with the *advent* of industrialization in the 18th century people continued to work, live and socialize as a collective. 尽管 18 世纪工业化已经到来，人们依然在集体中工作、生活和交往。

aerobics [eəˈrəʊbiks]

n. physical exercises intended to strengthen the heart and lungs 有氧运动

do *aerobics* 做有氧运动

bar [bɑː]

n. ① a long narrow shape 柱状

The *bar* graph shows reasons why people change where they live. 柱状图显示了人们改变住处的各种原因。

② a long piece of wood or metal 条，棒

During the 1968 Olympics in Mexico City, a relatively unknown high jumper named Dick Fosbury won the gold by going over the *bar* backwards. 在 1968 年的墨西哥城奥运会上，一个当时还没有太大名气的跳高运动员迪克·弗思贝里用背跃式跳过横杆夺得了金牌。

barrel [ˈbærəl]　　　　　　　　　　　　　　　　　　　[同] cask

n. large round container with flat ends and bulging in the middle, made of wood, metal or plastic 桶

Finally the honey is poured into *barrels* for shipment. 最后蜂蜜被倒入桶中以便装船运输。

chic [ʃiːk]　　　　　　　　　　　　　　　　　　　　　[同] stylish

adj. very fashionable and elegant 时髦的；优雅的；雅致的

a *chic* restaurant 一家很时尚的餐馆

chronic [ˈkrɒnɪk]　　　　　　　　　　　　　　　　　　[同] habitual

adj. continuing for a long time and cannot easily be solved 持续时间很长的；顽固的

Los Angeles suffers from *chronic* highway blockages, despite efforts to encourage people to use public transport. 尽管洛杉矶(政府)大力鼓励人们使用公共交通设施，该市还是长期受高速公路交通堵塞的困扰。

chronological [ˌkrɒnəˈlɒdʒɪkl]

adj. arranged in the order in which they happened 按发生的时间顺序排列的

The facts should be presented clearly and in *chronological* order. 这些事实应按时间先后顺序

陈述清楚。

circulation [ˌsɜːkjəˈleɪʃn]　　　　　　　　　　　　　　　　　　[近] circuit

n. the movement of blood around the body 血液循环

blood *circulation* 血液循环

civilian [səˈvɪliən]

n. a person who is not a member of the armed forces or the police 平民；老百姓

He left the army and returned to *civilian* life. 他从军队退了役，重新过上了平民百姓的生活。

demolish [dɪˈmɒlɪʃ]　　　[同] tear down, destroy　[反] construct, rebuild

v. to pull or knock down（a building, etc.）拆毁，拆除（建筑物等）

Many of these buildings were poorly designed and constructed and have since been *demolished*.
很多房屋设计不合理、建筑不合格，已经被拆除了。

denote [dɪˈnəʊt]　　　　　　　　　　　　　　　[同] mean

v. to be the name, sign or symbol of（sth.）; refer to 作为（某事物）的名称、符号或象征；指的是

What does the term 'organic' *denote*? "organic"一词指的是什么？

density [ˈdensəti]

n. quality of being dense 浓度；密度

the *density* of a forest/the fog 森林的密度 / 雾的浓度

depict [dɪˈpɪkt]　　　　　　　　　　　　　　　[同] represent, describe

v. to describe（sth.）in words 描述，描写（某事物）

The tropical forest has been *depicted* as ecologically unfit for large-scale human occupation.
从社会生态学角度来说，热带雨林不适宜大规模的人群居住。

embark [ɪmˈbɑːk]　　　　　　　　　　　　　[同] ①board ②begin

v. ①to get onto a ship; to put sth. onto a ship 上船；装船 ②to start sth., especially sth. new, difficult, or exciting 从事；开始工作

The country *embarked* upon a program to convert 11 per cent of its cropped land to meadow or forest. 这个国家开始着手把 11% 的耕地转化为牧场和树林。

embed [ɪmˈbed]　　　　　　　　　　　　　　　[同] entrench

v. to fix sth. firmly into a substance or solid object 把…牢牢地嵌入（插入或埋入）

a clock *embed* in the wall 嵌在墙里的钟

embody [ɪmˈbɒdi]　　　　　　　　　[同] represent [反] disembody

v. to express or represent an idea or a quality 具体表现；体现（思想或品质）

She *embodies* everything I admire in a teacher. 她具有我所欣赏的教师的一切品质。

fanatical [fəˈnætɪkl]

adj. extremely enthusiastic about sth. 入迷的

a *fanatical* interest in football 对足球入迷

fanfare [ˈfænfeə(r)]　　　　　　　　　　　[近] shine

n. a large amount of activity and discussion on television, in newspapers, etc. to celebrate sb./sth.（为庆祝而在媒体上的）炫耀

The new century began amid much *fanfare* worldwide. 新世纪在全球众多欢庆活动中开始了。

ghetto [ˈɡetəʊ]

n. (often derog.)area of a town lived in by any minority national or social group, typically crowded and with poor housing conditions 少数民族居住区；贫民区

the clearance of slum *ghettos* to make way for new housing developments 为建新住宅区而对贫民区的拆除

haven [ˈheɪvn]	[同] shelter

n. place of safety or rest; refuge 安全的地方；避难所

The church is a *haven* of peace in one of London's busiest areas. 这个教堂是伦敦最繁华地区之一的一处世外桃源。

impoverished [ɪmˈpɒvərɪʃt]	[同] poor

adj. very poor; without money 赤贫的

the *impoverished* areas of the city 这个城市的贫民区

impressive [ɪmˈpresɪv]	[近] grand

adj. having a strong effect on sb., esp. through size, grandeur, or importance 给人以深刻印象的（尤指因巨大、壮观或重要）

This figure is especially *impressive*. 这个数据尤其令人印象深刻。

knock-on [ˈnɒkɒn]	

adj. started by a process in which everything that happens causes sth. else to happen 连锁反应的；连环的

These price rises will have a *knock-on* effect on the economy. 物价上涨会对经济产生一系列连锁影响。

layman [ˈleɪmən]	[反] expert

n. a man who is a nonprofessional 非专业的人士；外行

To a *layman* all these plants look pretty similar. 对一个外行来说，所有这些植物看上去都很相似。

mania [ˈmeɪniə]	[同] craziness

n. an extremely strong desire or enthusiasm for sth., often shared by a lot of people at the same time（通常指许多人共有的）强烈的欲望；狂热

He had a *mania* for fast cars. 他是个飞车狂。

manifestation [ˌmænɪfeˈsteɪʃn]	

n. an event, action or thing that is a sign that sth. exists or is happening 显示；表明

It is one *manifestation* of how work and leisure are organized as separate spheres of social practice in modern societies. 这就是工作和休闲如何在现代社会活动中分属不同社会行为领域的一个表现。

negotiate [nɪˈɡəʊʃɪeɪt]	[同] settle

v. to try to reach an agreement by formal discussion 谈判；磋商；协商

We have been *negotiating* for more pay. 我们一直在为增加工资进行协商。

occurrence [əˈkʌrəns]	

n. sth. that happens or exists 发生的事情；存在的事物

Vandalism used to be a rare *occurrence* here. 过去这里很少发生故意破坏公物的事。

perennial [pəˈreniəl]	[同] permanent, continuing

adj. lasting for a long time 长久的；持久的

a *perennial* subject of interest 关于兴趣的永恒的主题

perishable [ˈperɪʃəbl]	

adj. likely to go bad 易腐烂的

perishable goods 易腐烂变质的商品

recession [rɪˈseʃn]   [同] depression

n. temporary decline in economic activity or prosperity （经济）衰退；不景气

an industrial/a trade *recession* 工业 / 贸易的衰退

recipient [rɪˈsɪpiənt]

n. person who receives sth. 接受者

recipients of awards 领奖者

shackle [ˈʃækl]   [同] fetters

n. (fig.) conditions, circumstances, etc. that prevent one from acting or speaking freely 束缚；羁绊

the *shackles* of convention 习俗的束缚

shape [ʃeɪp]

v. to have a great influence upon (sb./sth.); to determine the nature of (sth.) 对(某人 / 某事物)有重大影响；决定(某事物)的性质

Consequently the person's thinking is *shaped* by the language he or she uses. 因此，一个人使用的语言决定着他或她的思维习惯。

shatter [ˈʃætə(r)]   [近] break

v. to (cause sth. to) break suddenly and violently into small pieces (使某物)突然而剧烈地裂成碎片，粉碎

The pot *shattered* as it hit the floor. 罐子掉在地板上摔了个粉碎。

shortsighted [ˌʃɔːtˈsaɪtɪd]   [反] longsighted

adj. having or showing an inability to foresee what will happen 目光短浅的；无远见的

a *shortsighted* person/attitude/plan 目光短浅的人 / 看法 / 计划

telling [ˈtelɪŋ]

adj. having a noticeable effect; impressive 有明显效果的；显著的

a *telling* argument 有力的论据

Take the Test ≫

句子翻译

1) 这些事实应按时间先后顺序陈述清楚。(chronological)

_____

2) 这个教堂是伦敦最繁华地区之一的一处世外桃源。(haven)

_____

3) 这个数据尤其令人印象深刻。(impressive)

_____

4) 物价上涨会对经济产生一系列连锁影响。(knock-on)

_____

5) 因此，一个人使用的语言决定着他或她的思维习惯。(shape)

affection [əˈfekʃn]   [同] love [反] coldness

n. a feeling of liking or love and caring 喜爱

Children need lots of love and **affection**. 孩子需要多加疼爱和关怀。

affiliate [əˈfɪlɪeɪt]

v. to link a group, a company, or an organization very closely with another large one 使隶属

The Society is not **affiliated** with any political party. 该协会并不隶属于任何政党。

affirm [əˈfɜːm]   [同] assert

v. (fml.) to state publicly that sth. is true 声明；确认

It might be safely **affirmed** that almost all occupations more or less affect the health. 可以肯定地讲，所有职业都会或多或少地影响健康。

beforehand [bɪˈfɔːhænd]   [同] ahead, in advance

adv. before sth. else happens or is done 预先

We were aware of the problem **beforehand**. 我们事先就知道有这个问题。

benchmark [ˈbentʃmɑːk]   [同] standard, criterion

n. standard example or point of reference for making comparisons（供比较之用的）样板或参照点；标杆

In the 1960s and 1970s the Swedish political system was regarded as a **benchmark** for other European countries. 二十世纪六七十年代，瑞典的政治体系被认为是欧洲其他国家参考的样板。

civilization [ˌsɪvəlaɪˈzeɪʃn]

n. human society with its highly developed social organizations, or the culture and way of life of a society or country at a particular period in time 文明，文化

Many Europeans made long visits to China to study its history and **civilization** in the fourteenth century. 14 世纪，众多的欧洲人长途跋涉来中国学习中国历史和文化。

clan [klæn]   [同] family

n. group of families descended from a common ancestor 宗族；家族

Most people want many sons because it means their **clan** can claim more land. 大多数人想生很多儿子，因为这意味着他们家族可以申请占有更多的土地。

clarity [ˈklærəti]   [同] clearness

n. clearness; lucidity 清楚；明晰；清澈

a lack of **clarity** in the law 缺乏法律上的明确性

clay [kleɪ]

n. stiff sticky earth that becomes hard when baked, used for making bricks and pottery 黏土

Making **clay** models is a fun, creative activity that anyone can enjoy. 捏泥人是个好玩又颇具创造性的活动，而且人人可以尝试。

conventional [kən'venʃənl] [同] current, traditional

adj. based on convention 依照惯例的；约定俗成的

The *conventional* wisdom is that high wage rises increase inflation. 人们普遍认同的看法是工资增长过快会加剧通货膨胀。

deploy [dɪ'plɔɪ]

v. to use (sth.) effectively 有效地使用（某物）

Fingerprint scanners are currently the most widely *deployed* type of biometric application. 指纹扫描是目前应用最广泛的生物计量技术。

depression [dɪ'preʃn] [同] sadness

n. being depressed; low spirits 忧愁；沮丧；消沉

Gloomy weather can cause *depression*. 阴郁的天气会导致情绪低落。

deprive [dɪ'praɪv] [反] provide

v. to take sth. away from sb./sth.; prevent sb./sth. from having sth. 剥夺；阻止某人／某事物享有或使用某事物

The loss of diversity may *deprive* us of different ways of looking at the world. 多样性的消失会让我们无法多角度地看这个世界。

emergency [ɪ'mɜːdʒənsi]

n. a sudden serious and dangerous event or situation which needs immediate action to deal with 紧急情况；突发事件

They should only be opened from the inside in case of *emergency*. （这些门）一定要而且只能从里面打开，以防有紧急情况出现。

eminent ['emɪnənt] [近] famous

adj. famous and respected, esp. in a particular profession（尤指在某专业中）卓越的；显赫的

an *eminent* architect 著名的建筑师

emission [ɪ'mɪʃn]

n. a gas or other substance that is sent into the air 排放物；排放气体

While *emissions* from new cars are far less harmful than they used to be, city streets and motorways are becoming more crowded than ever. 虽然新型汽车排放的尾气远没有以前那么有害了，但城市的街道和高速公路却变得比以前拥挤了。

exempt [ɪg'zempt]

v. (fml.) to give or get sb.'s official permission not to do sth. or not to pay sth. they would normally have to do or pay 免除；豁免

His bad eyesight *exempted* him from military service. 他因视力不好而免服兵役。

fantasy ['fæntəsi] [反] imagination

n. a pleasant situation that you imagine but that is unlikely to happen 幻想；想像

Young children sometimes can't distinguish between *fantasy* and reality. 低龄儿童有时无法分辨幻想和现实。

far-fetched [ˌfɑː'fetʃt]

adj. (infml.)very difficult to believe 难以置信的；牵强的

The whole story sounds very *far-fetched*. 整个故事听起来让人很难以置信。

havoc ['hævək] [同] ruin

n. widespread damage; great destruction（大范围的）破坏；（巨大的）毁坏

The floods created *havoc*. 洪水造成了巨大的损失。

impromptu [ɪmˈprɒmptjuː] [同] offhand

adj. (done) without preparation, rehearsal or thought in advance 事先无准备的；临时的；即兴的

an *impromptu* speech 即席讲话

improvise [ˈɪmprəvaɪz]

v. to compose or play (music), speak or act without previous preparation (即兴地或即席地)创作、演奏、讲话、表演等

The pianist forgot his music and had to *improvise* (the accompaniment). 钢琴演奏者把乐谱忘了，只好即兴伴奏。

legacy [ˈlegəsi] [同] heritage

n. thing passed to sb. by predecessors or from earlier events, etc. 先人或过去遗留下来的东西

Medicine was a most fascinating ingredient of Tang civilization and it left a rich *legacy* to subsequent centuries. 医学是唐代文明的一个令人着迷的组成部分，为后来的几个世纪留下了丰富的遗产。

legend [ˈledʒənd] [同] myth

n. story handed down from the past, esp. one that may not be true 传奇；传说

According to the *legend*, the whole castle was washed into the sea. 传说整个城堡都被冲进了大海。

manipulative [məˈnɪpjələtɪv]

adj. clever at controlling or deceiving people to get what you want—used in order to show disapproval 操纵的；工于心计的

He is selfish and *manipulative*. 他自私且工于心计。

maritime [ˈmærɪtaɪm] [近] marine

adj. connected with the sea or ships 海的；海事的；海运的

San Francisco has lost nearly all of its *maritime* industry. 旧金山丧失了几乎所有跟海洋相关的产业。

neutralize [ˈnjuːtrəlaɪz]

v. to prevent sth. from having any effect 抵消；使无效

This fertilizer *neutralizes* the salts in the soil. 这种肥料中和了土壤中的盐。

permeate [ˈpɜːmieɪt] [同] pervade

v. (fml.) to enter sth. and spread to every part 弥漫；散布；充满；遍布

Water has *permeated* (through) the soil. 水已渗遍那片土壤。

perpetuate [pəˈpetʃueɪt] [同] eternalize

v. to cause (sth.) to continue 使(某事物)永久、永存或持续

These measures will *perpetuate* the hostility between the two groups. 这些措施会使那两个集团永远对立。

perplex [pəˈpleks] [同] puzzle

v. to make (sb.) feel puzzled or confused 使(某人)困惑、糊涂或迷惑

The question *perplexed* me. 那问题把我难住了。

persistent [pəˈsɪstənt] [同] tenacious

adj. refusing to give up 坚持的；不屈不挠的

She eventually married the most *persistent* of her admirers. 她终于嫁给了最执着追求她的人。

personalize [ˈpɜːsənəlaɪz] [同] embody

v. to design or change sth. so that it is suitable for a particular person 针对个体；使个性化

All the products can be *personalized* to the client's exact requirements. 所有产品都能按照客户的具体要求进行个性化生产。

reciprocal [rɪˈsɪprəkl]

adj. given and received in return; mutual 互相给予的；互惠的；相互的

There are branches around the world and 57 *reciprocal* clubs world wide. 其分支机构遍布全世界，此外还有 57 家合作俱乐部。

recommendation [ˌrekəmenˈdeɪʃn]

n. action of recommending 推许；推荐；赞许；建议；劝告

I bought it on your *recommendation*. 我是经你推荐才买的。

sibling [ˈsɪblɪŋ]

n.（fml.）any one of two or more people with the same parents; brother or sister 兄弟姊妹

I have two brothers and a sister: three *siblings* in all. 我有两个哥哥和一个妹妹：共三个兄妹。

temperament [ˈtempərəmənt]　　　　　　　　　　　　　　[同] character, nature

n. a person's or an animal's nature as shown in the way they behave or react to situations or people（人或动物的）气质，性情，性格

have an artistic *temperament* 有艺术家气质

tempo [ˈtempəʊ]　　　　　　　　　　　　　　　　　　　　[近] pace

n. speed or rhythm of a piece of music 乐曲的速度或拍子

Your *tempo* is too slow. 你的拍子太慢了。

underlying [ˌʌndəˈlaɪɪŋ]　　　　　　　　　　　　　　　[同] fundamental

adj. important in a situation but not always easily noticed or stated clearly 根本的；潜在的

Unemployment may be an *underlying* cause of the rising crime rate. 失业可能是犯罪率攀升的潜在原因。

Take the Test ≫

句子翻译

1）二十世纪六、七十年代，瑞典的政治体系被认为是欧洲其他国家参考的样板。（benchmark）

_____

2）捏泥人是个好玩又颇具创造性的活动，而且人人都可以尝试。（clay）

_____

3）阴郁的天气会导致情绪低落。（depression）

_____

4）虽然新型汽车排放的尾气远没有以前那么有害了，但城市的街道和高速公路却变得比以前拥挤得多。（emission）

_____

5）失业可能是犯罪率攀升的潜在原因。（underlying）

_____

afflict [əˈflɪkt]   [反] comfort

v. (fml.) to affect sb./sth. in an unpleasant or harmful way 折磨；使痛苦

Even Moscow has joined the list of capitals *afflicted* by congestion and traffic fumes. 连莫斯科也成了受交通堵塞和汽车尾气之苦的首都之一。

affluent [ˈæfluənt]   [同] rich

adj. having a lot of money and a good standard of living 富裕的

As people become more *affluent*, their standard and style of living improves. 随着人们越来越富足，他们的生活水平和生活方式都得到了改善。

agent [ˈeɪdʒənt]

n. ① a person who acts for or represents another 代理人，中介

For further information, please contact your local travel *agent*. 要想获得更多信息，请与您当地的旅行社联系。

② a chemical or substance that produces a particular effect or change 药剂

a chemical *agent* 化学药剂

bet [bet]

① *n.* an action or situation that is likely to be successful 可能会成功的行动或条件

Hardly anyone looks at the cafe noticeboard. The newsletter is probably your best *bet*. 几乎是没人看咖啡厅里的留言板的。简报或许是你最好的选择。

② *v.* to risk (money) on a race or on some other events of which the result is doubtful 打赌；赌博

climax [ˈklaɪmæks]   [同] height

n. most interesting or significant event or point in time; culmination 顶点，极点，高潮（最有趣或最有意义的事件或时刻）

The *climax* of the celebration was a firework display. 庆祝会的高潮是燃放烟火。

[记] climax = climb 爬 + max 最大 = 爬到最高点 = 顶点

clinic [ˈklɪnɪk]

n. private or specialized hospital （私人的）诊所；专科医院

He holds special *clinics* for people with back trouble. 他拥有多家医治背部疾病的专科诊所。

coarse [kɔːs]   [同] rough, crude [反] smooth, fine

adj. having a rough surface that feels slightly hard 粗糙的；粗的

Australia's native dung beetles specialize in *coarse* marsupial droppings. 澳大利亚本土的屎壳郎擅长分解有袋动物的粗糙粪便。

coeducation [ˌkəʊedʒuˈkeɪʃn]

n. education of girls and boys together 男女合校的教育

Girls tend to do better academically in single-sex schools than in *coeducational* ones. 在女校里，女孩子在学习方面的表现往往要比在男女混合的学校里好。

cognitive [ˈkɒgnɪtɪv]

adj. of or relating to cognition, which is action or process of acquiring knowledge, by reasoning or by intuition or through the senses 认知的；有关认识的

a child's *cognitive* development 儿童认知能力的发展

deregulation [ˈdiːˌregjuˈleɪʃn]

n. the act of freeing from regulation (especially from governmental regulations) 解除管制，取消控制

Deregulation of the power industry was supposed to use the discipline of free markets to generate just the right amount of electricity at the right price. 对电力产业的解禁是想通过自由市场的约束达到以合理的价格生产合理电量的目的。

derive [dɪˈraɪv]　　　　　　　　　　　　　　　　　　　　　　　　　　　[近] conclude

v. (fml.) to obtain sth. from sth.; get sth. from sth. 得到；获取

He *derives* great satisfaction from his child readers. 他从他的儿童读者中得到了极大的满足感。

descendant [dɪˈsendənt]　　　　　　　　　　　　　　　　　　　　　　[同] offspring

n. sb. who is related to a person who lived a long time ago, or to a family, group of people, etc. that existed in the past 后裔；子孙

His *descendants* were to live here for the next 120 years. 他的子孙在接下来的 120 年里将一直生活于此。

desirable [dɪˈzaɪərəbl]

adj. worth having; to be wished for 值得有的；称心的

The ability to speak a foreign language is highly *desirable*. 能讲一门外语的能力非常值得拥有。

empirical [emˈpɪrɪkl]　　　　　　　　　　　　　[同] experiential [反] theoretical

adj. based on experiments or experience rather than ideas or theories 以试验（或经验）为依据的

Amazingly, there is virtually no *empirical* evidence to support the use of pictures in teaching reading. 令人惊讶的是，事实上并没有关于图片用于阅读教学的实践经验资料。

enact [ɪˈnækt]　　　　　　　　　　　　[同] constitute, establish [反] repeal

v. (fml.) to pass a law 通过（法律）

In many European countries the state took over the role traditionally played by the feudal lord by *enacting* a social welfare system. 在很多欧洲国家，政府通过制定社会福利制度取代了原来封建帝王的角色。

encompass [ɪnˈkʌmpəs]　　　　　　　　　　　　　　　　　　　　　　[同] surround

v. to include a large number or range of things 包括；包含；涉及（大量事物）

However, each type of structure is far from infallible; they all *encompass* both advantages and disadvantages. 然而任何一种结构都远不是完美的，都有其优缺点。

fastidious [fæˈstɪdiəs]　　　　　　　　　　　　　　　　　　　　　　　[反] uncritical

adj. being careful that every detail of sth. is correct 一丝不苟的；严谨的

Everything was planned in *fastidious* detail. 样样都一丝不苟地计划好了。

fatigue [fəˈtiːg]　　　　　　　　　　　　　　　　　　[同] exhaustion, tiredness

n. a feeling of being extremely tired, usu. because of hard work or exercise 疲劳；劳累

Driver *fatigue* was to blame for the accident. 这个事故是驾驶员的疲劳所致。

glamourous [ˈglæmərəs]　　　　　　　　　　　　　　　[同] attractive, charming

adj. full of glamour 富有魅力的；美丽动人的

On television, she looks so *glamourous*. 在电视上，她看上去光彩照人。

hazardous [ˈhæzədəs]　　　　　　　　　　　　　　　　　　　　　　　[同] dangerous *adj.* dangerous; risky 危险的；冒险的

hazardous work/conditions 危险的工作 / 情况

incongruous [ɪnˈkɒŋɡrʊəs]　　[同] inconsonant, conflicting [反] congruous

adj. strange because not in harmony with the surrounding features; out of place 不协调的；不和谐的；不一致的

The new theatre looks utterly ***incongruous*** in its setting. 新剧院显得与周围的环境格格不入。

increment [ˈɪnkrəmənt]　　　　　　　　　　　　[同] addition

n. increase, esp. in money paid as a salary; added amount 增加；增长；(尤指)加薪

Your salary will be ￡12,000 a year, with annual ***increments*** of ￡500. 你的年薪为 1.2 万英镑，每年增加 500 英镑。

legislation [ˌledʒɪsˈleɪʃn]

n. action of making laws 立法；法律的制定

Action is being taken along several fronts through new ***legislation***, improved enforcement and innovative technology. 人们正在制定新法、加强执法与创新科技等方面采取行动。

legitimate [lɪˈdʒɪtɪmət]　　　　　　　　　[同] lawful, legal [反] illegitimate

adj. in accordance with the law or rules; lawful 法定的；依法的；合法的

Tobacco smuggling into the UK is seriously affecting the profits of ***legitimate*** importers. 英国的烟草走私严重影响到合法进口企业的赢利。

massacre [ˈmæsəkə(r)]　　　　　　　　　　[同] slaughter, wipe out

n. the killing of a large number of people esp. in a cruel way 屠杀；残杀

the bloody ***massacre*** of innocent civilians 对无辜平民的血腥屠杀

masterpiece [ˈmɑːstəpiːs]　　　　　　　　　　　　[同] masterwork

n. a work of art such as a painting, film, book, etc. that is an excellent or the best example of the artist's work 代表作；杰作

The museum houses several of his impressionist ***masterpieces***. 博物馆收藏了他的几件印象派杰作。

nicotine [ˈnɪkətiːn]

n. a substance in tobacco which makes it difficult for people to stop smoking 尼古丁

Nicotine and other toxins in cigarette smoke activate small blood cells called platelets, which increases the likelihood of blood clots. 香烟中的尼古丁和其他有害物质会刺激被称为血小板的小型血细胞，从而增加血栓发生的几率。

offhand [ˌɒfˈhænd]

adv. without being able to check sth. or think about it 未经核实地；不假思索地；即席地

I can't remember ***offhand*** where the file is. 我一时想不起来文件放哪儿了。

pertinent [ˈpɜːtɪnənt]　　　　　　　　　　　　　　[同] relevant

adj. (fml.) relevant (to sth.); to the point 有关的；中肯的；恰当的

pertinent comments/points/questions 中肯的意见 / 观点 / 问题

pervasive [pəˈveɪsɪv]

adj. present and perceived everywhere; pervading 无处不在的；遍布的；充斥各处的

the ***pervasive*** mood of pessimism 普遍存在的悲观情绪

pesticide [ˈpestɪsaɪd]　　　　　　　　　　　　　　[反] insecticide

n. chemical substance used to kill pests, esp. insects 消灭有害动物的化学药物；(尤指)杀虫剂

The flea-infested room had to be sprayed with a strong *pesticide*. 房间里有大批跳蚤出没，得喷强力杀虫剂。

reconcile [ˈrekənsaɪl]　　　　　　　　[同] harmonize [反] estrange

v. to cause（people）to become friends again, e.g. after quarrelling 使（人）重新和好；使和解；使复交

We were finally *reconciled* when he apologized. 他道歉以后我们终于言归于好了。

reconstruct [ˌriːkənˈstrʌkt]

v. ① to create again （sth. that has existed or happened）by using evidence or imagination（根据证据或想像）重现 ② to build sth. again after it has been destroyed or damaged 重建

Mechanization, with all that it involves, is certainly able to distort, destroy and *reconstruct* many aspects of a civilization. 机械化和它所涉及的一切，肯定能够扭曲、破坏和重建文明的诸多方面。

recruit [rɪˈkruːt]

① *n.* new member of a club, society, etc.（俱乐部、会社等的）新成员，新会员

After the final interview, potential *recruits* were divided into three categories. 经过最后一轮面试，可能被聘用的候选者被分成三组。

② *v.* to find new people to work in a company, join an organization, do a job, etc. 征募新人

We're having difficulty *recruiting* enough qualified staff. 招收到足够的合格员工有困难。

simplicity [sɪmˈplɪsɪti]

n. being easy, plain or straightforward 简单；朴素；率直

a character marked by frankness and *simplicity* 爽直朴素的性格

simplistic [sɪmˈplɪstɪk]

adj. treating difficult subjects in a way that is too simple 过份简单化的

It would be *simplistic* to suggest that the Bible promotes male domination. "圣经宣扬男性的统治地位"一说有把复杂问题过份简单化之嫌。

simulation [ˌsɪmjuˈleɪʃn]

n. the activity of producing conditions which are similar to real ones, especially in order to test sth., or the conditions that are produced 模拟

Pilots receive additional training by means of computer *simulations*. 飞行员通过计算机模拟的方式得到辅助培训。

terrace [ˈterəs]

n. ① continuous row of similarly designed houses in one block 排房（设计相同的一排房屋）② one of a series of flat areas cut out of a hill like steps, and used to grow crops 梯田的一层

turning a hillside into a series of ascending *terraces* for farming 把一块山坡变成了一块块种植农作物的梯田

句子翻译

1）随着人们越来越富足，他们的生活水平和生活方式都得到了改善。（affluent）

_____

2）在女校里，女孩子在学习方面的表现往往要比在男女混合的学校里好。（coeducation）

_____

3）然而任何一种结构都远不是完美的，都有其优缺点。（encompass）

_____

4）在电视上，她看上去光彩照人。（glamourous）

_____

When an end is lawful and obligatory, the indispensable means to it are also lawful and obligatory.

如果一个目的是正当而必须做的，则达到这个目的的必要手段也是正当而必须采取的。

——美国政治家 林肯（Abraham Lincoln, American statesman）

aggravate ['ægrəveɪt]　　　　　　　　　　　　　　　　　　[近] intensify [反] improve

v. to make a bad situation, an illness, or an injury worse 使严重；使恶化

Cutting down the old forests may ***aggravate*** global warming. 砍伐年代久远的森林可能会使全球变暖更加严重。

ailment ['eɪlmənt]　　　　　　　　　　　　　　　　　　　　　　　　[近] disease

n. an illness that is not very serious 轻病；小恙

The project will open up new understanding of, and new treatments of many of the ***ailments*** that afflict humanity. 这个项目会让人们重新认识困扰人类的很多轻微疾病，并开发出新的治疗方法。

alarming [ə'lɑːmɪŋ]

adj. causing worry and fear 使人惊恐的；令人惊慌的

As globalization intensifies its grip on modern societies, traditional communities break up at an ***alarming*** rate. 随着现代社会全球化的加剧，传统社区以令人震惊的速度分崩瓦解。

bid [bɪd]

n. ①price offered in order to buy sth., esp. at an auction（为购某物的）出价（尤指拍卖时）② an offer to do work or provide services for a specific price 竞标

The U.S. Conference of Mayors on Monday passed a resolution supporting Chicago's ***bid*** to host the 2016 Olympic and Paralympic Games. 美国市长联席会议周一通过了一项决议，支持芝加哥申办 2016 年的奥运会和残奥会。

bilateral [ˌbaɪ'lætərəl]

adj. having two sides; affecting or involving two parties, countries, etc. 有两边的；（两党、两国等）双边的

a ***bilateral*** agreement/treaty 双边协议 / 条约

coincidence [kəʊ'ɪnsɪdəns]

n.（instance of the）occurrence of similar events or circumstances at the same time by chance 巧合（的事）

By a strange ***coincidence*** we happened to be traveling on the same train. 巧得出奇，我们正好坐同一列火车。

collaborate [kə'læbəreɪt]

v. to work together（with sb.）, esp. to create or produce sth.（与某人）合作；协作

She ***collaborated*** with her sister on a biography of their father. 她和姐姐合作写父亲的传记。

collide [kə'laɪd]　　　　　　　　　　　　　　　　　　　　　　　　[同] bump

v.（of moving objects or people）to strike violently against sth. or each other（指运动中的物体或人）猛撞某物或互撞

As the bus turned the corner, it ***collided*** with a van. 公共汽车转过拐角时与一辆货车相撞。

collision [kəˈlɪʒn]　　　　　　　　　　　　　　　　　　　　　　[反] impact, bump

n. one object or person striking against another; （instance of）colliding; crash （物与物或人与人）相撞，碰撞，撞坏

a（head-on）*collision* between two cars 两车（迎头）相撞

collocation [ˌkɒləˈkeɪʃn]

n. regular combination of words 经常搭配着用的词语

'Strong tea' and 'by accident' are English *collocations*. "strong tea"与"by accident"都是英语中经常搭配的词组。

destination [ˌdestɪˈneɪʃn]

n. place to which sb./sth. is going or being sent 目的地

Tokyo was our final *destination*. 东京是我们的最终目的地。

detached [dɪˈtætʃt]　　　　　　　　　　　　　　　　　　　　[同] alone, isolated

adj. not joined to another house on either side 单独的

detached house 独栋房屋

deter [dɪˈtɜː(r)]　　　　　　　　　　　　　　　　　　　　　[同] dissuade, disadvise

v. to make sb. decide not to do sth. 使人决定不做某事

We are not *deterred* from rising to the challenge of how to overcome the problem. 面对如何克服困难这一挑战，我们没有畏缩不前。

endeavour [ɪnˈdevə(r)]　　　　　　　　　　　　　　　　　　[同] ①②attempt

① *n.*（fml.）an attempt to do sth., esp. sth. new or difficult（尤指新的或艰苦的）努力；尝试

Please make every *endeavour* to arrive on time. 请尽全力按时到达。

② *v.* to try very hard to do sth. 努力；竭力

There are a few organizations that *endeavour* to educate travellers and operators about the benefits of responsible ecotourism. 一些组织竭力使旅行者和管理人员能了解到负责任的生态旅行的好处。

endorse [ɪnˈdɔːs]　　　　　　　　　　　　　　　　　　　　　　　[同] approve

v. to say publicly that you support a person, a statement or course action（公开）赞同，支持某个人、观点或举动

I wholeheartedly *endorse* his remarks. 我真诚地赞同他的话。

endurance [ɪnˈdjʊərəns]　　　　　　　　　　　　　　　　　　　[同] tolerance

n. the ability to continue doing sth. difficult or painful over a long period of time 耐力

The marathon is a test of *endurance*. 马拉松是对耐力的考验。

feasibility [ˌfiːzəˈbɪləti]

n. the possibility and the likelihood sth. to be achieved 可行性

I doubt the *feasibility* of the plan. 我怀疑这个计划的可行性。

heap [hiːp]　　　　　　　　　　　　　　　　　　　　　　　　　　　[同] pile

n. number of things or mass of material lying or piled up 堆

clothes left in *heaps* on the ground 丢弃在地上的一堆堆的衣服

incumbent [ɪnˈkʌmbənt]

adj. holding the specified official position; current 现任的；在职的

the *incumbent* president 现任总裁

incur [ɪnˈkɜː]　　　　　　　　　　　　　　　　　　　　　　　　[同] bring down on

v. to cause oneself to suffer sth. bad; to bring upon oneself 蒙受；招致；带来

The auto manufacturer *incurred* a $800 million loss in 1990. 1990 年，汽车制造商亏损了八亿

美元。

indigenous [ɪnˈdɪdʒɪnəs] [同] native [反] naturalized

adj. (fml.) belonging naturally (to a place); native 本地的；土产的；土生土长的

Kangaroos are *indigenous* to Australia. 袋鼠产于澳大利亚。

lenient [ˈliːniənt] [同] forbearing [反] exacting

adj. not severe (esp. in punishing people); merciful 宽大的(尤指惩罚人)；仁慈的

I hope the judge will be *lenient*. 我希望法官宽大为怀。

mastery [ˈmɑːstəri] [同] power

n. control or power 掌握；控制；驾驭

A host of progressives protest that literacy is much more complicated than a simple technical *mastery* of reading and writing. 许多进步论者主张文化水平远不是简单的掌握读写技巧。

maternal [məˈtɜːnl]

adj. having feelings that are typical of a caring mother towards a child 母亲的；母亲般慈爱的

Lack of *maternal* love can have a profound effect on a child's psychological development. 缺少母爱会对儿童的心理发育产生深远影响。

nil [nɪl] [同] nothing, zero

n. the number 0, esp. as the score in some games (数字)零；(体育比赛的)零分

Newcastle beat Leeds four to *nil*. 纽卡斯尔队以四比零战胜利兹队。

oligopoly [ˌɒliˈɡɒpəli]

n. a market condition in which sellers are so few that the actions of any one of them will materially affect price and have a measurable impact on competitors 求过于供的市场情况；寡头垄断

The petrol market is an *oligopoly*. 汽油市场被垄断。

petty [ˈpeti] [反] important

adj. small or trivial; unimportant 小的；琐碎的；不重要的

petty details/queries/regulations/troubles 细节 / 小问题 / 琐碎的规章 / 小麻烦

phenomenal [fɪˈnɒmɪnl] [同] exceptional

adj. very remarkable; extraordinary 非凡的；格外的；了不起的

the *phenomenal* success of the film 影片非常成功

picturesque [ˌpɪktʃəˈresk] [同] scenic

adj. forming a pretty scene; charming or quaint 优美如画的；迷人的；奇特有趣的

a *picturesque* fishing village in the bay 风景如画的海湾渔村

piercing [ˈpɪəsɪŋ]

n. a hole made through part of your body so that you can put jewellery there 穿孔

Facials, body massage, ear *piercing*—it's all on offer. 面部保养、按摩、打耳洞，这些服务全都提供。

rectangle [ˈrektæŋɡl]

n. four-sided geometric figure with four right angles, esp. one with unequal adjacent sides 方形；(尤指)长方形，矩形

A *rectangle* is subdivided into one large and two small squares. 一个长方形被分成了一个大正方形和两个小正方形。

rectify [ˈrektɪfaɪ]   [同] correct

v. to put (sth.) right; correct 改正(某事物)，纠正

rectify an error/omission 修订错处 / 疏漏处

redemption [rɪˈdempʃn]   [同] ransom

n. (fml.) redeeming or being redeemed 赎回；补救；偿清；兑现

the *redemption* of one's property/debts/shares/promises 财产的赎回 / 债务的偿清 / 股票的兑现 / 诺言的履行

simultaneous [ˌsɪmlˈteɪnɪəs]   [同] contemporary

adj. happening or done at the same time (as sth.) 同时的；同时发生的；同时做出的

The explosion was timed to be *simultaneous* with the plane's take-off. 爆炸的时间被定在了飞机起飞的那刻.

sitcom [ˈsɪtkɔm]

n. (infml.) = situation comedy 情景喜剧

Several family-oriented *sitcoms* are on in the early evening. 有几部以家庭为收视群体的情景喜剧在傍晚播出。

skeleton [ˈskelɪtn]

n. framework of bones supporting an animal or a human body （动物或人的)骨骼，骨架

the human *skeleton* 人类骨架

well-being [ˌwelˈbiːɪŋ]   [反] ill-being

n. general health and happiness 健康；安乐；康乐

Over the past 30 years Western living standards have increased dramatically, yet the sense of *well-being* has plummeted. 在过去的 30 年里，西方社会的生活水平有了巨大的提高，但富足感却不断下降。

whim [wɪm]   [同] caprice

n. a sudden feeling that you would like to do or have sth., especially when there is no important or good reason 任性；冲动；心血来潮

A still picture could only imply the existence of time, while time in a novel passed at the *whim* of the reader. But in cinema, the real, objective flow of time was captured. 静止的图画仅仅暗示了时间的存在，小说中的时间随着读者的意愿而变化。然而电影却捕捉住了真实而客观的时光流逝。

Take the Test ▷▷

词组翻译

尽全力 _____   母爱 _____

心理发育 _____   迎接挑战 _____

土生土长的 _____   风景如画的村庄 _____

句子翻译

1) 砍伐年代久远的森林可能会使全球变暖更加严重。(aggravate)

_____

2) 随着现代社会全球化的加剧，传统社区以令人震惊的速度分崩瓦解。(alarming)

_____

3) 在过去的 30 年里，西方社会的生活水平有了巨大的提高，但富足感却不断下降。(well-being)

alert [əˈlɜːt] [同] watchful

adj. watchful; vigilantly attentive 警惕的；注意的

We must be ***alert*** to the possibility of danger. 我们必须警惕危险的可能性。

alienate [ˈeɪliəneɪt] [同] estrange [反] unite

v. to make sb. feel that they do not belong to a particular group 使疏远

Very talented children may feel ***alienated*** from the others in their class. 天赋出众的孩子可能觉得与班上的同学格格不入。

align [əˈlaɪn]

v. to arrange things so that they form a line or are parallel to each other, or to be in a position that forms a line, etc. 排整齐；使一致

Domestic prices have been ***aligned*** with those in world markets. 国内价格已调整到与世界市场一致。

[记] 音: a + line= 排成直线

biodegradable [ˌbaiəʊdiˈɡreidəbl]

adj. (of substances) that can be made to rot by bacteria (指物质) 可由微生物降解的

Paper does not pose as much threat to the environment when it is ***biodegradable***. 当纸张被丢弃时并不会对环境构成什么威胁，因为纸张是可降解的。

bizarre [bɪˈzɑː(r)] [同] strange, odd

adj. strange in appearance or effect; grotesque; eccentric 奇形怪状的；古怪的

bizarre clothing 奇装异服

comic [ˈkɒmɪk] [同] ①laughable

① *adj.* causing people to laugh; funny 使人发笑的；可笑的；滑稽的

a ***comic*** song, performance, etc. 滑稽的歌曲、表演等

② *n.* a magazine for children that tells a story using comic strips 漫画；连环画

a ***comic*** book 连环画，小人书

commemorate [kəˈmeməreɪt] [同] memorialize, celebrate

v. to keep (a great person, event, etc.) in people's memories 纪念(伟人、大事件等)

We ***commemorate*** the founding of our nation with a public holiday. 我们放假以庆祝国庆。

commission [kəˈmɪʃn]

n. ①a group of people who have been given the official job of finding out about sth. or controlling sth. 调查委员会 ②an extra amount of money that is paid to a person or organization according to the value of the goods they have sold or the services they have provided 返佣，佣金

Another body, the Australian Sports ***Commission*** (ASC), finances programmes of excellence in a total of 96 sports for thousands of sportsmen and women. 另一家机构即澳大利亚体育运动委员会(ASC)，则为总计 96 项体育运动中的数千名男女运动员的卓越表现提供资助。

detergent [dɪˈtɜːdʒənt]

n. substance that removes dirt, e.g. from the surface of clothes or dishes 洗涤剂；去污剂

Most synthetic *detergents* are in the form of powder or liquid. 大多数合成洗涤剂呈粉状或液态。

deteriorate [dɪˈtɪəriəreɪt]　　　　　　　　　　　　　　　[同] disimprove, worsen

v. to become worse in quality or condition 变坏；变质；恶化

Air quality in many of the world's major cities will *deteriorate* beyond reason. 世界很多主要城市的空气质量都将无可避免地恶化。

detest [dɪˈtest]　　　　　　　　　　　　　　　　　　　　　　　　[同] hate

v. to dislike (sb./sth.) very much; hate 憎恶，憎恨(某人／某事物)

You don't understand. It's not just that I don't like cabbage—I absolutely *detest* it! 你不明白。我不仅仅是不喜欢圆白菜——我绝对憎恨这东西！

enduring [ɪnˈdjʊərɪŋ]　　　　　　　　　　　[同] lasting [反] fleeting

adj. continuing for a very long time 长期的；持久的

Cartoons have a universal and *enduring* appeal. 卡通在世界范围内有着经久不衰的魅力。

enlightenment [ɪnˈlaɪtnmənt]

n. the process of understanding sth. or making sb. understand it 启迪；开导

cultural/spiritual *enlightenment* 文化／心灵的启迪

enlist [ɪnˈlɪst]

v. to persuade sb. to help you or to join you in doing sth. 争取；谋取(帮助、支持或参与)

They hoped to *enlist* the help of the public in solving the crime. 他们希望寻求公众协助来破案。

feature [ˈfiːtʃə(r)]

v. to include a particular person or thing as a special feature 以…为特色；是…的特征

Many of the hotels *featured* in the brochure offer special deals for weekend breaks. 小册子列举的多家旅馆都有周末假日特别优惠。

feeble [ˈfiːbl]　　　　　　　　　　　　　　　　　　　　　[同] ①weak

adj. ①extremely weak 很虚弱的 ②not effective, not showing determination or energy 无效的；无力的

My grandmother's very *feeble* now and needs someone at home full-time to look after her. 我奶奶现在很虚弱，需要有个人全天候地在家照顾她。

globalization [ˌɡləʊbəlaɪˈzeɪʃn]

n. the process of making sth. such as a business operate in a lot of different countries all around the world 全球化

Distance therefore poses no obstacle to the *globalization* of the disk-drive industry. 因此距离不再是磁盘驱动器产业全球化的障碍。

hectic [ˈhektɪk]

adj. with much confused activity and excitement; very busy 忙乱的；忙碌的

hectic last-minute preparations 最后关头忙碌的准备工作

indignant [ɪnˈdɪɡnənt]　　　　　　　　　　　　　　[近] angry, mad

adj. angry and scornful, especially at injustice or because of undeserved blame, etc. 愤慨的，愤怒的

She was most *indignant* with me when I suggested she might try a little harder. 我建议她不妨再努力一些，她竟大为恼火。

indiscriminate [ˌɪndɪsˈkrɪmɪnət] [反] selective, discriminate

adj. acting without careful judgement 不加鉴别的；不加分析的

indiscriminate in his choice of friends（他）择友不慎重

individualistic [ˌɪndɪvɪdʒʊəˈlɪstɪk]

adj. of individualism or its principles 我行我素的；独特的

She has a highly *individualistic* approach to painting. 她在绘画方面很有自己的特色。

lethal [ˈliːθl] [同] deadly, fatal

adj. causing or able to cause death 致死的；能致命的

These bugs and weeds are becoming resistant to poisons, so next year's poisons must be more *lethal*. 这些虫子和野草对毒药的抵抗力越来越强，所以明年要用药性更强的毒药了。

maze [meɪz]

n. a system of paths separated by walls or hedges built in a park or garden that is designed so that it is difficult to find your way through 迷宫

We lost in the *maze*. 我们在迷宫里迷失了方向。

nobility [nəʊˈbɪləti]

n. (fml.) the quality of being noble in character 高贵的品质

the bravery and *nobility* of these men who died for their country 这些为国捐躯者的勇敢精神和高尚品格

piracy [ˈpaɪərəsi]

n. illegal copying or broadcasting 非法复制或播放，盗版

With the expansion of the Internet, *piracy* has grown more widespread. 随着互联网的扩张，盗版现象日益普遍。

plagiarism [ˈpleɪdʒəˌrɪzəm]

n. action of plagiarizing 剽窃；抄袭

be accused of *plagiarism* 被控剽窃

plausible [ˈplɔːzəbl] [同] believable [反] implausible

adj. (of a statement, an excuse, etc.) seeming to be right or reasonable; believable（指陈述、借口等）似乎正确的，似乎有理的，可信的

She could find no *plausible* explanation for its disappearance. 她无法解释清楚它何以不翼而飞。

plea [pliː] [同] prayer, appeal

n. earnest request; appeal 恳求；请求

a *plea* for forgiveness/money/more time 恳求原谅 / 给予金钱 / 多给些时间

referee [ˌrefəˈriː] [近] judge

n. (in football, boxing, etc.) official who controls matches, prevents rules being broken, etc.（足球、拳击等的）裁判员

assistant *referee* 副裁判长

referendum [ˌrefəˈrendəm]

n. when people vote in order to make a decision about a particular subject 公投

The government has promised to hold a *referendum* and let the people choose. 政府已承诺会进行公投，让人民做出选择。

refinement [rɪˈfaɪnmənt] [同] culture, breeding [反] vulgarity

n. culture or elegance of manners, taste, language, etc.（仪态、趣味、语言等的）高雅，文雅

a person of great *refinement* 温文尔雅的人

refresh [rɪˈfreʃ] [同] renew, invigorate

v. to give new strength or vigour to（sb./sth.）; restore or revive 给（某人／某事物）新的力量或活力；使恢复；使振作

refresh oneself with a cup of tea/a hot bath 喝杯茶／洗个热水澡以提神

skeptical ［ˈskeptɪkl］ ［反］incredulous

adj. marked by or given to doubt; questioning 怀疑的，有（或产生）怀疑的特征的；有问题的

a *skeptical* attitude 怀疑的态度

skyscraper ［ˈskaɪˌskreɪpə(r)］

n. very tall modern city building 摩天大楼

They also believe that building *skyscrapers* helps to solve the problem of the growing scarcity of land in the city. 他们还认为建造高楼大厦有助于解决城市里土地日趋紧张的问题。

slack ［slæk］ ［同］②relax

① *n.* slack part of a rope, etc.（绳等的）松弛的部分

too much *slack* in the tow-rope 拖缆很松

② *v.* to make less effort than usual, or to be lazy in your work 松懈，怠工

The job is to make sure workers don't *slack* from their duties. 该工作是确保工人在工作中不偷懒。

undermine ［ˌʌndəˈmaɪn］ ［同］weaken

v. to make sth., especially sb's confidence or authority, gradually weaker or less effective 逐渐削弱（信心、权威等）；使逐步减少效力

Our confidence in the team has been seriously *undermined* by their recent defeats. 他们最近的几次失败已严重动摇了我们对该队的信心。

underpin ［ˌʌndəˈpɪn］

v. to support or form the basis of an argument, a claim, etc. 加强；巩固；构成（基础等）

The report is *underpinned* by extensive research. 这份报告以广泛的研究为基础。

validity ［vəˈlɪdəti］ ［反］①invalidity

n. ① the state of being legally or officially acceptable（法律上的）有效，合法性 ② being reasonable and sensible 合理性；正确性

The period of *validity* of the agreement has expired. 本协议的有效期已过。

Take the Test

词组翻译

| 构成威胁 | _____ | 可生物降解的 | _____ |
| 连环画 | _____ | 特价 | _____ |

句子翻译

1）天赋出众的孩子可能觉得与班上的同学格格不入。（alienate）

_____

2）世界很多主要城市的空气质量都将无可避免地恶化。（deteriorate）

_____

3）卡通在世界范围内有着经久不衰的魅力。（enduring）

_____

4）随着互联网的扩张，盗版现象日益普遍。（piracy）

_____

5）他们还认为建造高楼大厦有助于解决城市里土地日趋紧张的问题。（skyscraper）

_____

If you put out your hands, you are a laborer; if you put out your hands and mind, you are a craftsperson; if you put out your hands, mind, heart and soul, you are an artist.

如果你用双手工作，你是一个劳力；如果你用双手和头脑工作，你是一个工匠；如果你用双手和头脑工作，并且全身心投入，你就是一个艺术家。

——美国电影 *American Heart and Soul*

allergy ［ˈælədʒi］

n. a medical condition that causes you to react badly or feel ill when you eat or touch a particular substance 过敏

I have an *allergy* to animal hair. 我对动物的毛过敏。

alleviate ［əˈliːvieit］ ［同］relieve, lighten ［反］aggravate

v. to make sth. less severe 减轻；缓和

A number of measures were taken to *alleviate* the problem. 采取了一系列措施来缓解这个问题。

alliance ［əˈlaiəns］ ［同］association, coalition

n. an arrangement in which two or more countries, groups, etc. agree to work together to try to change or achieve sth. 联盟；同盟

The Social Democrats are now in *alliance* with the Greens. 社会民主党现在与绿党结成联盟。

bleak ［bliːk］ ［同］②grim, gloomy

adj. ①（of a landscape）bare; exposed; wind-swept（指景物）荒凉的；裸露的；光秃秃的 ②（fig.）not hopeful or encouraging; dismal; gloomy 无望的；阴郁的；黯淡的

a *bleak* future 前途渺茫

commitment ［kəˈmitmənt］ ［同］obligation

n. the thing one has promised to do; pledge; undertaking 承诺；承担

I'm overworked at the moment—I've taken on too many *commitments*. 我现在有点劳累过度——应承的事情太多了。

THERAPY CENTRE FOR COMMITMENT PHOBICS

"I'm not sure I can make it next week."

companion ［kəmˈpæniən］ ［近］mate

n. person or animal that goes with or spends much time with another（相伴的）人或动物；同伴；伙伴

my *companions* on the journey 我的旅伴

comparable ［ˈkɒmpərəbl］ ［反］disparate

adj. able or suitable to be compared 可比较的；适合相比的

The achievements of an athlete and a writer are not *comparable*. 运动员的成就与作家的成就不能相提并论。

compatible ［kəmˈpætəbl］ ［同］consonant

adj.（of people, ideas, arguments, principles, etc.）suited; that can exist together（指人、想法、论点、原则等）适合的；能共存的；相容的

driving a car at a speed *compatible* with safety 以符合安全要求的速度驾驶

compel ［kəmˈpel］ ［同］force

v.（fml.）to make（sb.）do sth.; force 使（某人）做某事；强迫

We cannot *compel* you to do it, but we think you should. 我们不能强迫你去做，但认为你应该做。

detour ［ˈdiːtuə(r)］

n.（esp. AmE）route that avoids a blocked road, etc.; deviation（绕开受阻道路等的）绕行路线，迂回路线

We managed to keep all these dates, which is amazing considering the *detours* we made. 我们设法记下了所有的日程，令人吃惊的是，我们绕了很多的弯路。

detrimental [ˌdetrɪ'mentl]　　　　　　　　[同] harmful, adverse

adj. harmful 有害的；不利的

The measures had a *detrimental* effect. 这些措施已产生不良影响。

devastate ['devəsteɪt]　　　　　　　　　[同] ravage

v. to completely destroy (sth.); ruin 彻底毁坏(某事物)；毁灭

The country has been *devastated* by floods. 这个国家已受到洪水的严重破坏。

devastating ['devəsteɪtɪŋ]

adj. ① badly damaging or destroying sth. 毁灭性的；破坏性的 ② making sb. feel extremely sad or shocked 打击人的；重创人的

Acid rain has a *devastating* effect on the forest. 酸雨对森林有毁灭性的影响。

ensue [ɪn'sjuː]　　　　　　　　　　　　[同] follow

v. to happen after or as a result of another event 接着发生；因而产生

An argument *ensued*. 紧接着的是一场争论。

entail [ɪn'teɪl]

v. to involve sth. that cannot be avoided 牵涉；需要

The job *entails* a lot of hard work. 干这份工作需要十分努力。

enterprising ['entəpraɪzɪŋ]　　　　　　　[同] go-ahead

adj. having or showing the ability to think of new projects or new ways of doing things and make them successful 有事业心的；有创新精神的

And in the newer and flatter organization where there is little opportunity for promotion, how does an *enterprising* employee advance? 在一个更新的效益平平的公司里，几乎没有晋升的机会，一个有进取心的员工又如何获得提升呢?

gloomy ['gluːmi]　　　　　　　　　　　[同] depressing

adj. dark or unlighted, esp. in a way that is depressing or frightening 阴暗的，黑暗的(尤指使人沮丧或恐惧的)

Gloomy weather can cause depression. 阴沉的天气会让人感到沮丧。

hedonism ['hiːdənɪzəm]

n. (behaviour based on the) belief that pleasure should be the main aim in life 享乐主义；享乐主义的行为

Hedonism is the philosophy that pleasure is of ultimate importance. 享乐主义是一种快乐至上的哲学。

individuality [ˌɪndɪˌvɪdʒu'æləti]　　　　[同] distinctiveness

n. the qualities that make sb. or sth. different from other things or people 个性

We have a close working relationship while retaining our *individuality* and separate interests. 我们之间有着紧密的工作关系，但同时又保留着自己的个性和各自的兴趣。

inductive [ɪn'dʌktɪv]

adj. using known facts to produce general principles 归纳的

There're two kinds of sciences, *inductive* and deductive. 有两种科学：一种是归纳式的，一种是演绎式的。

inept [ɪˈnept] [反] capable, skilful

adj. completely unskilful（at sth.）不熟练的；不擅长的

I've never heard anyone so *inept* at making speeches. 我从未听过有如此不擅于讲话的人。

meagre [ˈmiːgə(r)]

adj. too small and is much less than you need 少量的；贫乏的

He supplements his *meagre* income by working on Saturdays. 他通过在周六工作来贴补自己微薄的收入。

medieval [ˌmedɪˈiːvl]

adj. connected with the Middle Ages （about 1000 AD to 1450 AD）中世纪的（约公元 1000 到 1450 年）

the literature of the late *medieval* period 中世纪后期的文学

notably [ˈnəʊtəbli] [同] especially

adv. used for giving a good or the most important example of sth. 尤其；特别

A similar problem was identified in other English-speaking countries, *notably* the USA, Australia and New Zealand. 在其他英语国家也出现了类似的问题，特别是美国、澳大利亚和新西兰。

pliable [ˈplaɪəbl] [反] unpliable

adj. easily bent, shaped or twisted; flexible 易弯的；可塑的；可扭曲的

Cane is *pliable* when wet. 藤条潮湿时易弯曲。

plummet [ˈplʌmɪt] [同] ②plunge

① *n.* weight attached to a plumb line 测深锤；铅锤；垂直线

② *v.* to suddenly and quickly decrease in value or amount 迅速下跌

Profits *plummeted* from £49 million to £11 million. 利润从 4900 万英镑迅速下跌到 1100 万英镑。

pointless [ˈpɔɪntlɪs] [同] senseless, insignificant

adj. with little or no sense, aim or purpose 无意义的；无目标的

make a *pointless* remark 说不相干的话

pollutant [pəˈluːtənt]

n. substance that pollutes（e.g. exhaust fumes from motor vehicles）污染物质（如机动车辆排出的废气）

release *pollutants* into the atmosphere 将污染物质排放到空气里

populate [ˈpɒpjuleɪt] [同] inhabit

v. to live in（an area）and form its population 居住于（某地区）（而构成其人口成分）

Many viruses, such as the flu, originate from hot, humid, densely *populated* areas of the world such as South East Asia. 很多病毒，像流感病毒，都起源于世界上高热、潮湿、人口密集的地区，比如东南亚。

refundable [rɪˈfʌndəbl]

adj. that can be refunded 可退还的；可偿还的

Deposits and payments are non-*refundable* and non-transferable. 保证金和已付款不可退还，也不可转让。

refute [rɪˈfjuːt] [同] ①②disprove

v. ① to prove that a statement or idea is not correct 驳斥；推翻 ② to say that a statement is wrong or unfair 否认；驳斥

There is a widespread belief that increasing wealth encourages people to live farther out where cars are the only viable transport. The example of European cities **refutes** that. 有一种广为流传的说法是：财富的不断增长促使人们到更远的地方居住，而汽车是那里惟一可行的交通工具。然而许多欧洲城市的例子可以反驳这一说法。

regime [reɪˈʒiːm]

n. prevailing method or system of administration (e.g. in a business)（如商业中的）盛行的管理方式或制度

changes made under the present **regime** 在现行的管理制度下所做的变化

regimen [reˈdʒɪmən]

n. a special plan of food, exercise, etc. that is intended to improve your health 养生法

A low protein diet is also effective, but compliance with such a **regimen** may be a problem. 低蛋白饮食同样有效，但能否坚持这样的食物疗法是个问题。

sleek [sliːk]　　　　　　　　　　　　　　　　　　　[同] glossy

adj. smooth and glossy 光滑而有光泽的

sleek hair/fur 光滑而有光泽的毛发／毛皮

slightly [ˈslaɪtli]

adv. to a slight degree 轻微地；稍稍

The patient is **slightly** better today. 病人今天稍稍好些。

sluggish [ˈslʌgɪʃ]　　　　　　　　　　　　　　　[同] lethargic

adj. slow-moving; not alert or lively; lethargic 行动迟缓的；无精打采的

a **sluggish** stream/pulse 流速缓慢的溪流／跳动缓慢的脉搏

Just a little sluggish thats all.

slump [slʌmp]　　　　　　　　　　　　　　　　　[同] plunge

v. (of prices, trade, business activity) to fall suddenly or greatly 突然或大幅度下跌或减少

What caused share values to **slump**? 股价暴跌是什么原因？

terrain [təˈreɪn]　　　　　　　　　　　　　　　[同] topography

n. stretch of land, with regard to its natural features 地形；地貌；地势；地带

For geologists who may have to negotiate rough **terrain**, the robot serves as the perfect vehicle. 对可能需要穿越险恶地势的地质学家而言，机器人成为理想的运输工具。

Take the Test ≫

词组翻译

有害影响　_____　　毁灭性影响　_____

个性　_____　　排放污染物　_____

句子翻译

1）采取了一系列措施缓解这个问题。（alleviate）

_____

2）运动员的成就与作家的成就不能相提并论。（comparable）

_____

3）干这份工作需要十分努力。（entail）

_____

4）在其他英语国家也出现了类似的问题，特别是美国、澳大利亚和新西兰。（notably）

_____

allowance [əˈlaʊəns]   ．[同] ration

n. an amount of money that is given to sb. regularly or for a particular purpose 津贴；补助

a travel *allowance* 交通补贴

all-round [ˈɔːlˈraʊnd]   [同] versatile

adj. good at doing many different things 全面的；全能的

an *all-round* education 素质教育

altitude [ˈæltɪtjuːd]

n. the height above sea level 海拔

It grows at *altitudes* of below 600 metres. 它生长在海拔 600 米以下。

[记] Attitude determines *altitude*. 态度决定高度。

compelling [kəmˈpelɪŋ]

adj. ①extremely interesting and exciting, so that one has to pay attention 有强烈吸引力的
② that makes you feel certain that sth. is true or that you must do sth. about it 令人信服的

a *compelling* novel/account/story 引人入胜的小说 / 报道 / 故事

competence [ˈkɒmpɪtəns]   [同] ability

n. being competent; ability 胜任；能力；称职

No one doubts her *competence* as a teacher. 没人对她能胜任教师工作的能力表示质疑。

competent [ˈkɒmpɪtənt]   [同] capable, able [反] incompetent

adj. having the necessary ability, authority, skill, knowledge, etc. 胜任的；能干的

a highly *competent* driver 技术高超的司机

"You're arrogant, rude, insensitive, and incompetent - just the consultant we're looking for!"

competitive [kəmˈpetətɪv]

adj. ① products or prices that are competitive are cheaper than others but still of good quality 有竞争能力的

Cheap labour makes Chinese clothing *competitive* in America. 廉价劳动力使得中国服装产品在美国颇具竞争力。
② relating to competition 竞争性的

Competitive sports encourage children to work together as a team. 竞技性体育项目鼓励孩子进行团队合作。

complaint [kəmˈpleɪnt]

n. ① a statement in which sb. complains about sth. 投诉

I want to make a *complaint*. 我要投诉。

② an illness that affects a particular part of your body 症状，病症

Researchers, now analysing the results of data gathered in 1994, say arthritis, high blood pressure and circulation problems—the major medical *complaints* in this age group—are troubling a smaller proportion every year. 研究人员在分析完 1994 年收集的数据结果后表示，困扰这一年龄段人群的主要疾病——关节炎、高血压和循环系统疾病的患病人数比

COMPLAINT DEPT.

例正在逐年降低。

deviance [ˈdiːviəns]

n. deviant tendencies or behaviour 反常的倾向或行为

a study of social *deviance* and crime 对社会反常行为和犯罪行为的研究

deviate [ˈdiːvieɪt]

v. to stop following (a course, standard, etc.) 偏离（路线、标准等）；背离

The plane *deviated* from its usual route. 飞机偏离了正常的航线。

devise [dɪˈvaɪz]

v. to think out (a plan, system, tool, etc.); invent 想出；设计；发明

The exercise programme was *devised* by a leading health expert. 这个健身计划是由一位知名的健康专家设计的。

devoted [dɪˈvəʊtɪd]　　　　　　　　　　　　　　　　　　[同] loving

adj. very loving or loyal 热爱的；非常忠实的；全心全意的

a *devoted* son/friend/supporter 孝子 / 忠实的朋友 / 不遗余力的支持者

enthusiasm [ɪnˈθjuːziæzəm]　　　　　　　　　　　　　[同] ardor

n. a strong feeling of excitement and interest in sth. and a desire to become involved in it 热情；热心；热忱

The students provide *enthusiasm* and talent while the tutors provide guidance. 学生发挥热情和才能，而老师提供指导。

entice [ɪnˈtaɪs]　　　　　　　　　　　　　　　　　　　[同] lure

v. to persuade sb. to do sth. or go somewhere, usually by offering them sth. that they want 诱使，怂恿

It is a great deal easier to motivate employees in a growing organization than a declining one. Management is able to use the growth to *entice* and encourage employees. 在不断壮大的企业中激励员工要比在日益衰落的企业中容易得多。管理层能够利用企业的发展来吸引和鼓舞员工。

entrepreneur [ˌɒntrəprəˈnɜː(r)]

n. a person who makes money by starting or running businesses, esp. when this involves taking financial risks 创业者；企业家

It is common for city *entrepreneurs* to own tour companies in country areas. 城里的企业家们在乡下开旅游公司是很平常的。

ferocious [fəˈrəʊʃəs]　　　　　　　　　　[同] fierce [反] tender

adj. very fierce, violent or aggressive; very strong 凶猛的；猛烈的

a man driven by *ferocious* determination 被强烈的决心所驱使的人

fibre [ˈfaɪbə(r)]

n. one of the many thin threads that form body tissue, such as muscle, and natural materials, such as wood and cotton (人或动物身体组织及天然物质的)纤维

Most paper products must contain some virgin *fibre*. 大多数纸制品都会含有一定量的天然纤维。

gratify [ˈɡrætɪfaɪ]　　　　　　　　　　　　　　　　　[同] please

v. (fml.) to give pleasure or satisfaction to (sb.) 使(某人)高兴或满意

I was most *gratified* at/by/with the outcome of the meeting. 我对会议的结果感到极其满意。

heed [hiːd]　　　　　　　　　　　　　　　　　　　　[同] listen

v. (fml.) to pay attention to (advice, etc.); to take notice of (sth.) 注意或听从(劝告等)；留心(某事物)

If she had only **heeded** my warnings, none of this would have happened. 如果当时她听进去了我的警告，这一切就都不会发生了。

[习语] give/pay heed to 留心，注意

herald [ˈherəld]   [同] forerunner

n. person or thing that announces or shows that sb./sth. is coming 报信者，使者；先兆

In England the cuckoo is the **herald** of spring. 在英国，杜鹃鸟是春天的使者。

inextricably [ˌɪnɪkˈstrɪkəbli]

adv. if two or more things are inextricably linked, they are very closely related and affect each other 分不开地；解不开地

Physical health is **inextricably** linked to mental health. 身体健康和心理健康密不可分。

infinity [ɪnˈfɪnəti]   [同] eternity

n. state of being endless or boundless; infinite nature 无穷；无极

the **infinity** of space 空间的无限

inflict [ɪnˈflɪkt]   [近] strike

v. to cause (a blow, penalty, etc.) to be suffered (by sb.) 使(某人)遭受(打击、惩罚等)

The strikes **inflicted** serious damage on the economy. 罢工使经济受到重创。

liability [ˌlaɪəˈbɪləti]

n. legal responsibility for sth. 法律责任或义务

Tenants have legal **liability** for any damage they cause. 房客们应对他们造成的任何破损负法律责任。

mediocre [ˌmiːdiˈəʊkə(r)]   [同] medium

adj. not very good; of only average standard 平庸的；普通的；平常的

The play was only **mediocre**. 这部戏剧只是平庸之作。

melancholy [ˈmelənkɒli]   [近] sadness, blues

n. (fml.) a deep feeling of sadness that lasts for a long time and often cannot be explained 忧郁；伤悲

A mood of **melancholy** descended on us. 一种悲伤的情绪袭上我们的心头。

onslaught [ˈɒnslɔːt]   [同] ①②attack

n. ① a large violent attack by an army 冲击；猛攻 ② strong criticism of sb. 批评；批判

There are still huge gaps in our environmental knowledge, and despite the scientific **onslaught**, many predictions are no more than best guesses. 我们的环境知识还有很多盲区，尽管科学突飞猛进，但许多预测也不过是猜测而已。

porcelain [ˈpɔːsəlɪn]   [同] china

n. hard white translucent material made from china clay, used for making cups, plates, ornaments, etc. 瓷

a **porcelain** figure 瓷像

pornography [pɔːˈnɒɡrəfi]

n. describing or showing sexual acts in order to cause sexual excitement 色情描绘；色情表演

It is now clear that there is a link between **pornography** and sex crimes. 现在，显而易见，色情表演与性犯罪之间有联系。

portable [ˈpɔːtəbl]   [同] carriageable

adj. that can be (easily) carried; not fixed permanently in place 便携式的；手提式的；轻便的

a **portable** radio 便携式收音机

portfolio [pɔːtˈfəʊliəʊ]

n. ① a large flat case used especially for carrying pictures, documents, etc. 文件夹

② a set of pictures or other pieces of work that an artist, photographer, etc. has done 作品集

You'll need to prepare a ***portfolio*** of your works. 你要准备一份自己的作品集。

registration ［ˌredʒɪˈstreɪʃn］

n. the act of recording names and details on an official list 登记；注册；挂号

The ***registration*** fee is $75. 注册费是 75 美元。

regulation ［ˌregjuˈleɪʃn］

n. regulating or being regulated; control 管理；调校；校准；调节；控制

the ***regulation*** of share prices 股票价格的管制

smother ［ˈsmʌðə(r)］ ［同］choke

v. （cause sb.）to die from lack of air, or from not being able to breathe; suffocate （使某人）窒息，闷死

Such children are not necessarily ***smothered*** with love by their parents. 这样的孩子并不一定会因为父母的溺爱而被宠坏。

sociable ［ˈsəʊʃəbl］ ［同］affable

adj. fond of the company of other people; friendly 好交际的；友好的；合群的

He has never really been the ***sociable*** type. 他从不好交际。

solely ［ˈsəʊlli］ ［同］only, exclusively

adv. alone; only 惟一地；只；仅

Scholarships are awarded ***solely*** on the basis of financial need. 奖学金的发放只基于（学生）资金方面的需求。

tertiary ［ˈtɜːʃəri］

adj. third in order, rank, importance, etc.; next after secondary 第三等的；第三位的；第三的

The only thing about ***tertiary*** education on which everyone agrees is that it is a mess. 人们对高等教育的惟一共识就是它简直一团糟。

testimony ［ˈtestɪməni］

n. ① written or spoken statement declaring that sth. is true, esp. one made under oath 证词（尤指发誓后做出的）② a fact or situation that shows or proves very clearly that sth. exists or is true 证明；证据

These results are a ***testimony*** to the coach's skill and hard work. 这些结果是对教练的技术和勤奋工作的证明。

Take the Test »

句子翻译

1）竞技性体育项目鼓励孩子进行团队合作。（competitive）

_____

2）学生发挥热情和才能，而老师提供指导。（enthusiasm）

_____

3）身体健康和心理健康密不可分。（inextricably）

_____

4）我们的环境知识还有很多盲区，尽管科学突飞猛进，但许多预测也不过是猜测而已。（onslaught）

_____

5）人们对高等教育的惟一共识就是它简直一团糟。（tertiary）

_____

Jovons saw the kettle boil and cried out with the delighted voice of a child; Marshal too had seen the kettle boil and sat down silently to build an engine.

杰文斯看见壶开了，高兴得像孩子似地叫了起来；马歇尔也看见壶开了，却悄悄地坐下来造了一部蒸气机。

——英国经济学家 凯恩斯（John Maynard Keynes, British economist）

Word List 13

amass [əˈmæs]　　　　　　　　　　　　　　　　　　[同] accumulate [反] distribute

v. to collect sth. esp. in large quantities 积累，积聚

His fame is derived from the enormous amount of personal wealth he has ***amassed*** since he founded Microsoft. 他的名气来自于他自建立微软以来所积累的巨大的个人财富。

ambiguous [æmˈbigjuəs]　　　　　　　　　　　　[同] unclear, vague [反] explicit

adj. that can be understood in more than one way 模棱两可的；含混不清的

The system enables us to categorize phenomena that are essentially ***ambiguous***. 这套体系能让我们把本质上不清晰的现象进行分类。

ameliorate [əˈmiːliəreɪt]　　　　　　　　　　　[同] improve [反] worsen, deteriorate

v. （fml.）to make sth. better 改善；改进

Steps have been taken to ***ameliorate*** the situation. 已经采取措施以改善局面。

blunt [blʌnt]　　　　　　　　　　　　　　　　[同] ①②dull [反] ①sharp

① *adj.* without a sharp edge or a point 不锋利的；不尖的；钝的

This pencil is ***blunt***! 这支铅笔不尖了！

② *v.* to make sth. weaker or less effective 使减弱，使降低效应

Age hadn't ***blunted*** his passion for adventure. 岁月没有冲淡他的冒险激情。

blur [blɜː(r)]

① *n.* sth. that is not clearly seen 模糊不清的事物

② *v.* ❶ to become difficult to see or to make sth. difficult to see, because the edges are not clear 使模糊，使看不清 ❷ to make the difference between two ideas, subjects, etc. less clear 使界限、区别模糊不清

The current trend towards ***blurring*** these role signs in dress is probably democratic, but it also makes some people very insecure. 现今，穿着打扮所体现出来的社会角色特征日益模糊不清，这种趋势可能是民主的体现，但同时也让一部分人失去了安全感。

complementary [ˌkɒmplɪˈmentri]　　　　　　　　　　　　　　[同] supplementary

adj. two people or things that are complementary are different but together form a useful or attractive combination of skills, qualities or physical feature 互补的；补充的；互相补充的

The management introduced three different, yet potentially ***complementary*** strategies. 管理层采用了三种不同但可能相互补充的策略。

complexity [kəmˈpleksəti]　　　　　　　　　　　[同] complicatedness [反] simplicity

n. state of being complex 复杂性；错综复杂的状态

a problem of great ***complexity*** 极复杂的问题

compliment [ˈkɒmplɪmənt]

n. expression of praise, admiration, approval, etc. 赞美，敬佩，恭维

One likes to hear ***compliments*** on one's appearance. 人人都爱听夸奖自己容貌的话。

compound [kəmˈpaʊnd]　　　　　　　　　　　　　　　　　　　[近] increase

v. to make a difficult situation worse by adding more problems 使恶化，加剧

Tokyo is another city with old structure problems *compounded* by a huge population. 东京是另一个面临布局陈旧加之人口众多的问题的城市。

comprehend ［ˌkɒmprɪˈhend］ ［同］understand, grasp

v. to understand（sth.）fully 全面理解、领会（某事物）

fail to *comprehend* the seriousness of the situation 未能理解形势的严重性

diameter ［daɪˈæmɪtə(r)］

n.（length of a）straight line connecting the centre of a circle or sphere, or of the base of a cylinder, to two points on its sides 直径

the *diameter* of a tree-trunk 树干的直径

differentiate ［ˌdɪfəˈrenʃieɪt］ ［同］distinguish ［反］confuse

v. to see or show（two things）to be different; show sth. to be different（from sth. else）看出或指出（两者）不同；辨别；区分

Can you *differentiate* between the two varieties? 你能辨别这两个品种吗？

dilemma ［dɪˈlemə］

n. situation in which one has to choose between two undesirable things or courses of action 进退两难的窘境；进退维谷的困境

place sb. in a *dilemma* 置某人于进退两难之境

［记］音：地雷吗 = 进退两难

epic ［ˈepɪk］

n. a long poem about the actions of great men and women or about a nation's history 叙事诗；史诗

one of the great Hindu *epics* 伟大的印度教史诗之一

epidemic ［ˌepɪˈdemɪk］

n. a large number of cases of a particular disease happening at the same time in a particular community 流行病

Fire, flood, drought or *epidemic* may reduce population sizes. 火灾、水灾、旱灾或流行病都可能使人口减少。

equation ［ɪˈkweɪʒn］

n. the act of making sth. equal or considering sth. as equal 相等；等同看待

The *equation* of wealth with happiness can be dangerous. 把财富与幸福等同起来会是危险的。

finance ［ˈfaɪnæns］

① *n.* the management of money by governments, large organizations, etc. 财务；财政

② *v.* to provide money, especially a lot of money, to pay for sth. 提供资金，资助

a nonprofit corporation to *finance* low-income housing 一个资助低收入人群住房项目的非赢利性公司

graze ［greɪz］

v.（of cattle, sheep, etc.）to eat growing grass（指牛、羊等）吃青草

Groups of cattle were grazing on the rich grass. 一群群牛在丰美的草原上吃草。

herbivore ［ˈhɜːbɪvɔː(r)］

n. animal that feeds on plants 食草动物

If the ground is covered with snow, how does this affect the *herbivores*? 如果地面被积雪覆盖，那么食草动物会受到什么影响呢？

heritage ［ˈherɪtɪdʒ］ ［近］tradition

n. things such as works of art, cultural achievements and folklore that have been passed on from earlier generations 遗产

cultural *heritage* 文化遗产

influx [ˈɪnflʌks] [同] inflow [反] outflux

n. arrival of people or things, esp. suddenly and in large numbers or quantities (人或事物的)注入，涌入，汇集

frequent *influxes* of visitors 来访的人纷至沓来

infringe [ɪnˈfrɪndʒ] [同] trespass

v. to break (a rule, an agreement, etc.) 违反，违背(规则、协议等)

If a teacher makes copies of software for students, he or she is *infringing* copyright. 如果老师将软件拷贝给学生，那么他/她就侵犯了版权。

ingenious [ɪnˈdʒiːniəs] [同] inventive, creative

adj. clever at finding new or simple solutions for complex problems (指人)善于用新颖的或简单的方法解决复杂问题的；心灵手巧的

Many fishes have *ingenious* ways of protecting their eggs from predators. 很多鱼类都有聪明的办法来保护鱼卵不受天敌的侵袭。

liaison [liˈeɪzn]

n. communication and cooperation between units of an organization 组织内各单位间的交流与合作

The project has been set up in *liaison* with the art department. 这个项目是跟艺术系联合推出的。

melodious [məˈləʊdiəs] [同] euphonic

adj. pleasant to listen to; like music 悦耳的；优美动听的

a rich *melodious* voice 圆润悦耳的声音

memorandum [ˌmeməˈrændəm] [近] note

n. (fml.) an official note from one person to another in the same organization 备忘录

an internal *memorandum* 内部备忘录

portray [pɔːˈtreɪ] [同] represent, depict

v. to make a picture of sb. 为某人画像；画某人的像

She is *portrayed* wearing her coronation robes. 给她画的是她穿着加冕礼服的像。

possess [pəˈzes] [同] have, own

v. to have (sth.) as one's belongings; own 拥有(某事物)；持有

He decided to give away everything he *possessed* and become a monk. 他决定放弃他所有的一切，出家为僧。

posture [ˈpɒstʃə(r)]

n. attitude or position of the body 姿势；姿态

PE teachers help the development of coordination, balance, *posture*, and flexibility with things like simple catching and throwing skills. 体育老师通过简单的抓和扔的技巧训练协调性、平衡力、姿态和柔韧性。

potent [ˈpəʊtnt] [同] powerful [反] impotent

adj. strongly persuasive; convincing 说服力强的；令人信服的

potent arguments/reasoning 有说服力的论据/推理

rehabilitate [ˌriːəˈbɪlɪteɪt] [同] restore, recover

v. to restore (sb.) to a normal life by retraining, medical treatment, etc., esp. after imprisonment or illness (通过重新培训、治疗等)使(某人)恢复正常生活(尤指出狱者或病愈者)

rehabilitate the mentally/physically disabled in the community 使社区中智力/身体有缺陷的人恢复正常的生活

reimburse [ˌriːɪmˈbɜːs] [同] compensate

v. to pay money back to sb. when their money has been spent or lost 偿还、补偿丢失或已花费的钱；报销

The company will ***reimburse*** you for travel expenses. 公司会给你报销差旅费。

relatively [ˈrelətɪvli]

adv. in relation or proportion to sb./sth. else; comparatively（与他人或其他事物）相对地；比较地

Considering the smallness of the car, it is ***relatively*** roomy inside. 就这辆汽车的小而言，里面还比较宽敞。

somehow [ˈsʌmhaʊ]

adv. ①in some way, or by some means, although you do not know how 以某种方式；用某种方法 ②for some reason that is not clear to you or that you do not understand 不知怎么地；莫名其妙地

The Chinese think a name may ***somehow*** determine the future of the child. 中国人认为名字会以某种方式决定孩子的未来。

somewhat [ˈsʌmwɒt]

adv. more than a little but not very 稍微

Things have changed ***somewhat*** since then. 从那时起，情况发生了些许变化。

sophisticated [səˈfɪstɪkeɪtɪd] [同] ①complex, intricate [反] ①②unsophisticated

adj. ①complicated and refined; elaborate; subtle 复杂的；精良的；尖端的 ② having a lot of experience of life, and good judgment about socially important things such as art, fashion, etc. 成熟的；有良好品味的

sophisticated modern weapons 精良的现代武器

therapy [ˈθerəpi]

n. any treatment designed to relieve or cure an illness or a disability 治疗；疗法

At our clinic, we are beginning to realize the unique benefits of relaxation ***therapy***. 我们的诊所已经开始意识到放松疗法的独特好处。

gene therapy

thorough [ˈθʌrə] [同] exhaustive, complete

adj. done completely and with great attention to details; not superficial 彻底的；完全的；深入的

The report was ***thorough*** and detailed. 报告全面而细致。

Take the Test >>

词组翻译

文化遗产 _____   侵犯版权 _____

放松疗法 _____   全面而细致 _____

句子翻译

1）这套体系能让我们把本质上不清晰的现象进行分类。（ambiguous）

_____

2）把财富与幸福等同起来会是危险的。（equation）

_____

3）这个项目是跟艺术系联合推出的。（liaison）

_____

4）从那时起，情况发生了些许变化。（somewhat）

_____

Man errs so long as he strives.

人只要奋斗就会犯错误。

——德国诗人、剧作家 歌德

（Johann Wolfgang Goethe, German poet and dramatist）

amenity [əˈmiːnəti]

n. a feature that makes a place pleasant, comfortable or easy to live in 生活便利设施

Many of the houses lacked even basic *amenities*. 很多房屋甚至缺少基本的生活设施。

analogy [əˈnælədʒi]　　　　　　　　　　　　　　　　　　　[同] likeness

n. a comparison of one thing with another that has similar features 类比；比喻

A simple *analogy* can help us understand how a rocket operates. 一个简单的类比就可以帮助我们理解火箭是怎么工作的。

botanical [bəˈtænɪkl]

adj. relating to plants or the scientific study of plants 与植物或植物研究相关的

botanical garden 植物园

comprehensive [ˌkɒmprɪˈhensɪv]　　　　　　　　　　　　　[同] all-around

adj. including all the necessary facts, details, or problems that need to be dealt with 综合性的，全面性的

a *comprehensive* overview of the subject 对该课题全面的回顾

compulsory [kəmˈpʌlsəri]　　　　　　　　　　　　　　　[同] mandatory

adj. that must be done; required by the rules, etc.; obligatory 必须做的；按规定要做的；有义务的

Is English a *compulsory* subject? 英语是必修科目吗？

conceivable [kənˈsiːvəbl]　　　　　　　　　　　　　　　[反] imaginable

adj. that can be conceived or believed; imaginable 可想到的；可相信的；可想像的

It is hardly *conceivable* that she should do such a thing. 简直难以想像她会干这种事。

concession [kənˈseʃn]　　　　　　　　　[近] allowance

n. ① sth. that you allow sb. to have in order to end an argument or a disagreement 让步；允许

The Chinese were not prepared to make any *concessions*. 中国人不准备做任何让步。

② a reduction in the price of tickets, fees, etc. for certain groups of people, for example old people or children 价格优惠，降价

"He's not 'Mr. Right', but he's definitely 'Mr. Better-than-the-other-ones!'"

The new *concession* will apply to buses only. 新的价格优惠只适用于公共汽车。

concrete [ˈkɒŋkriːt]　　　　　　　　　　　　　　　　　[反] ① abstract

① *adj.* existing in material form; that can be touched, felt, etc. 以物质形式存在的；具体的；实体的

Physics deals with the forces acting on *concrete* objects. 物理学研究作用于物体上的力。

② *n.* building material made by mixed cement with sand, gravel, etc. and water 混凝土

diplomatic [ˌdɪpləˈmætɪk]　　　　　　　　　[同] tactful [反] undiplomatic

adj. tactful; having or showing diplomacy 圆通的；灵活变通的；策略的

a *diplomatic* answer/move 很有策略的回答／一步

disapprove [ˌdɪsə'pruːv]   [反] approve

v. to consider (sb./sth.) to be bad, immoral, foolish, etc.; to not approve of sb./sth. 认为 (某人 / 某事物) 不好、不道德、不明智等；不赞成

She wants to be an actress, but her parents *disapprove* (of her intentions). 她想当演员，但她父母不赞成 (她的想法)。

discard [dɪs'kɑːd]

v. to throw (sth.) out or away 扔掉，丢弃 (某物)；放弃

It's easier to discard your work and try another approach when you don't have a lot of effort invested. 在没有投入过多的精力之前，放弃现在的工作而尝试新的方法还是比较容易的。

equivalent [ɪ'kwɪvələnt]   [同] ①same [反] ①different

① *adj.* equal in value, amount, meaning, importance, etc. (价值、数量、意义、重要性等) 相等的，相同的

Eight kilometers is roughly *equivalent* to five miles. 八公里约等于五英里。

② *n.* a thing, amount, word, etc. that is equal to sth. else 相等的东西；等量；对应词

Breathing such polluted air is the *equivalent* of smoking ten cigarettes a day. 呼吸污染如此严重的空气等于每天抽十根烟。

equivocal [ɪ'kwɪvəkl]   [同] obscure, ambiguous

adj. not having one clear or definite meaning or intention; able to be understood in more than one way 模棱两可的；意义双关的

She gave an *equivocal* answer, typical of a politician. 她的回答模棱两可，是典型的政客做法。

firework ['faɪəwɜːk]

n. a small container filled with powder that burns or explodes to produce coloured lights and noise in the sky 焰火

The climax of the celebration was a *firework* display. 庆祝活动的高潮是燃放焰火。

grid [grɪd]

n. framework of crossing or parallel metal or wooden bars; grating (金属的或木的) 格子；栅栏

a cattle-*grid* 牲口栅子 (置于沟渠上，以防牲口走上公路)

hierarchy ['haɪərɑːki]

n. system with grades of authority or status from the lowest to the highest 等级制度

She's high up in the management *hierarchy*. 她高居于管理层。

ingenuity [ˌɪndʒə'njuːəti]

n. cleverness and originality in solving problems 心灵手巧；善于发明创造

Since the dawn of human *ingenuity*, people have devised ever more cunning tools to cope with work that is dangerous, boring, or just plain nasty. 从发现自身的创造力的那一刻起，人类就设计出越来越多的巧妙工具去应付危险、乏味或仅仅是工作环境肮脏的工作。

inhale [ɪn'heɪl]   [同] breathe in [反] exhale

v. to breathe sth. in 吸入某物

It is dangerous to *inhale* the fumes produced by these chemicals. 吸入这些化学品产生的烟雾是很危险的。

inherent [ɪn'hɪərənt]   [同] built-in

adj. existing as a natural or permanent feature or quality of sb./sth. 内在的；固有的；本来的

I'm afraid the problems you mention are *inherent* in the system. 恐怕你提到的问题是这个系统所固有的。

linen [ˈlɪnɪn]

n. household articles (eg. sheets, table cloths, etc.) 日用织品（如床单、桌布等）

bed *linen* 床上用品

menace [ˈmenəs] [同] danger

n. a person or thing that will probably cause serious damage, harm or danger 威胁；危险的人（或物）

Now, let's look at some of the reasons why back pain is developing into such a unique *menace*. 现在让我们来看看背部疼痛之所以发展成为一种特殊危害的原因。

mentor [ˈmentɔː(r)]

n. an experienced person who advises and helps sb. with less experience over a period of time 导师；顾问

Second, you need a *mentor* to guide you along the way. 其次，你需要一位导师来一路直指导你。

optical [ˈɒptɪkl] [同] visual

adj. of the sense of sight 视觉的；视力的

optical effects and sound effects 视觉效果与声音效果

optimism [ˈɒptɪmɪzəm] [反] pessimism

n. tendency to expect the best in all things; confidence in success; belief that good will triumph over evil in the end 乐观；乐观主义

He was still full of *optimism* for the future despite his many problems. 他尽管有许多问题，但对未来仍十分乐观。

pragmatic [præɡˈmætɪk] [同] practical

adj. treating things in a sensible and realistic way; concerned with practical results 务实的；实事求是的；注重实效的

a politician valued for his *pragmatic* approach 因讲求实际而受人尊重的政治家

precarious [prɪˈkeəriəs] [同] doubtful, unstable

adj. depending on chance; uncertain 依靠机会的；不确定的

She makes a rather *precarious* living as a novelist. 她当小说家，过着不太稳定的生活。

relentless [rɪˈlentləs]

adj. strict or harsh 不留情的；严格的；苛刻的

He was *relentless* in questioning the suspect. 他毫不讲情面，一个劲地盘问嫌疑犯。

relevance [ˈreləvəns]

n. pertinence to the matter at hand 相关性

have/bear some *relevance* to the matter in hand 与要做的事情有一些关系

reliance [rɪˈlaɪəns] [同] dependence

n. dependence 依靠；寄托

The increasing self-*reliance* of many elderly people is probably linked to a massive increase in the use of simple home medical aids. 许多老年人自理能力的增强可能与简易家庭医疗辅助用品的广泛使用有关。

relieve [rɪˈliːv] [同] alleviate, ease [反] intensify

v. to lessen or remove (pain, distress, anxiety, etc.) 减轻或解除（痛苦、困苦、忧虑等）

This drug will *relieve* your discomfort. 这种药可减轻你的病痛。

sovereign [ˈsɒvrɪn] [近] dominant

adj. (fml.) (of power) without limit; highest (指权力)无限的，至高无上的

Who holds *sovereign* power in the state? 谁掌握着国家的最高权力？

spark [spɑːk] 　　　　　　　　　　　　　　　　　　　　　　[同] arouse

v. spark sth. off: (infml.) to be the immediate cause of (usu. sth. bad); lead to sth. 直接导致（尤指坏事）；引发某事

When Columbus discovered America in the 15th century it *sparked* off the imagination of many people. 哥伦布在 15 世纪发现新大陆，这引发了许多人的想像。

spatial [ˈspeɪʃl]

adj. (fml.) of concerning or existing in space 空间的；有关空间的；存在于空间的

the *spatial* qualities of the new concert hall 新音乐厅的空间特性

specialty [ˈspeʃəlti]

n. (esp. U.S.) (also speciality) interest, activity, skill, etc. to which a person gives particular attention or in which he/she specializes 专业；特长

His specialty is barbecued *steaks*. 烤牛排是他的拿手好菜。

specification [ˌspesɪfɪˈkeɪʃn]

n. details and instructions describing the design, materials, etc. of sth. to be made or done 规格；规格说明

specifications for (building) a garage（建造）车库的规格说明

undo [ʌnˈduː] 　　　　　　　　　　　　　　　　　　　[近] abolish, bring down/low

v. to cancel the effect of sth. 消除；废止（某事物的影响）

It's not too late to try and *undo* some of the damage. 想办法补救部分损失还为时不晚。

unilateral [ˌjuːnɪˈlætrəl]

adj. done by one member of a group or an organization without the agreement of the other member 单方的

They were forced to take *unilateral* action. 他们被迫采取单方面行动。

unique [juːˈniːk] 　　　　　　　　　　　　　　　　　　　　　　[同] peerless

adj. belonging to or connected with one particular person, place or thing（某人、某地或某物）独具的；特有的

Biometric security systems operate by storing a digitized record of some *unique* human feature. 生物安全系统是通过对一些人类独具的特征进行数字化记录来运行的。

Take the Test ▶▶

句子翻译

1）一个简单的类比就可以帮助我们理解火箭是怎么工作的。(analogy)

_____

2）中国人不准备做任何让步。(concession)

_____

3）庆祝活动的高潮是燃放焰火。(firework)

_____

4）恐怕你提到的问题是这个系统所固有的。(inherent)

_____

5）哥伦布在 15 世纪发现新大陆，这引发了许多人的想像。(spark)

_____

anatomy [ə'nætəmi]

n. the scientific study of the structure of human or animal bodies 解剖学

The project will reveal a new human *anatomy*—the complete genetic blueprint for a human.
这个项目将会揭示一个崭新的人体结构，即一个人完整的基因构成。

anecdotal [ˌænɪk'dəʊtl]

adj. based on anecdotes and possibly not true or accurate 传闻的

Anecdotal evidence clearly suggests that these practices are working. 传闻的证据清晰地表明
这些惯例正在发挥作用。

anniversary [ˌænɪ'vɜːsəri]

n. a date on which sth. special or important happened in a previous
year 周年纪念日

the theatre's 25th *anniversary* celebrations 剧院 25 周年庆祝活动

bound [baʊnd]

adj. certain or likely to happen, or to do or be sth. 一定会的，很可能会的

There is *bound* to be one course that fits in with your academic, personal or professional
commitments. 一定会有一门和你的学术、个人或是专业承诺相符的课程。

condense [kən'dens]　　　　　　　　　　　　　　　　　　　　　　　[同] contract

v. to become thicker or more concentrated (使某物)变稠或变浓；浓缩

Soup *condenses* when boiled. 汤煮过后就浓了。

condition [kən'dɪʃn]　　　　　　　　　　　　　　　　　　　　　　　[近] disease

n. an illness or health problem that affects you permanently or for a very long time 长期疾病

Scientific research has been providing evidence that years of cigarette smoking vastly increases
the risk of developing fatal medical *conditions*. 科学研究已经提供出证据表明常年吸烟极大
地增加了患致命疾病的风险。

conducive [kən'djuːsɪv]

adj. allowing or helping sth. to happen 容许或有助于某事发生的；有益的

These noisy conditions aren't really *conducive* to concentrated work. 这些嘈杂的环境实在不利
于专心工作。

confess [kən'fes]　　　　　　　　　　　　　　　　　　　　　　　　[同] acknowledge

v. to admit sth. that you feel embarrassed about 承认；坦白

I must *confess* that I do not find this to be a serious problem. 说实话我真没觉得这是个多么严
重的问题。

confidential [ˌkɒnfɪ'denʃl]　　　　　　　　　　　　　　　　　　　[近] private

adj. to be kept secret; not to be made known to others 恪守秘密的；机密的

All interviews are *confidential* and conducted in a relaxed and friendly atmosphere. 所有的面谈
都是保密的，并且在一种放松而友好的气氛下进行。

discharge [dɪs'tʃɑːdʒ]　　　　　　　　　　　　　　　　　　　　　[近] free

v. to officially allow sb. to leave somewhere, esp. the hospital or the army, navy, etc. 准许离开；获准离开

Hospitals now tend to ***discharge*** patients earlier than in the past. 如今医院准许病人比以前早出院。

| **discourse** | [ˈdɪskɔːs] | [近] speech |

n.（fml.) lengthy and serious treatment of a subject in speech or writing 论文；演讲

He was hoping for some lively political ***discourse*** at the meeting. 他希望在会上听到些生动的政治演讲。

| **discreet** | [dɪˈskriːt] | [同] cautious [反] indiscreet |

adj. careful or showing good judgement in what one says or does; not too obvious 言谈举止谨慎的；言行审慎的

We must be extremely ***discreet***; my boss suspects something. 我们必须极为小心才是，我老板已起疑了。

| **eradicate** | [ɪˈrædɪkeɪt] | [同] wipe out |

v. to destroy or get rid of sth. completely, esp. sth. bad 消灭；根除；杜绝

We are determined to ***eradicate*** racism from our sport. 我们决心要杜绝体育活动中的种族歧视现象。

| **erosion** | [ɪˈrəʊʒn] |

n. the process by which rock or soil is gradually destroyed by wind, rain, or the sea 侵蚀

the problem of soil ***erosion*** 水土流失问题

| **erroneous** | [ɪˈrəʊniəs] | [同] false [反] correct, accurate |

adj.（fml.) not correct; based on wrong information 错误的

erroneous conclusions/assumptions 错误的结论／假设

| **fledg(e)ling** | [ˈfledʒlɪŋ] | [同] beginner, freshman |

n. inexperienced person 无经验的人

a ***fledgling*** skier 滑雪新手

| **grievance** | [ˈɡriːvns] | [同] complaint |

n. real or imagined cause for complaint or protest 委屈，牢骚，不满；怨恨

invite the members to air their ***grievances*** 请成员们诉说苦衷

> We like to deal promptly with any employee grievance in this firm.

| **hilarious** | [hɪˈleəriəs] |

adj. extremely amusing; very funny 十分有趣的；非常滑稽的

a ***hilarious*** account of their camping holiday 有关他们野营度假的有趣的记述

| **initiative** | [ɪˈnɪʃətɪv] |

n. action taken to resolve a difficulty 为解决困难而采取的行动

It is hoped that the government's ***initiative*** will bring the strike to an end. 希望政府采取的行动可以结束罢工。

| **innate** | [ˌɪˈneɪt] | [同] inborn, natural [反] acquired |

adj.（of a quality, feeling, etc.）in one's nature; possessed from birth（指特质、感情等）天生的，先天的，固有的，天赋的

Children have an ***innate*** ability to learn language. 孩子天生有学习语言的能力。

| **merger** | [ˈmɜːdʒə(r)] | [同] incorporation |

n. the act of joining two or more organizations or businesses into one（机构或企业的）合并，

归并

West Thames College came into existence in 1976 following the *merger*. 1976 年经过合并，西泰晤士学院成立了。

optimum ［ˈɒptɪməm］

adj. (fml.) best or most favourable 最佳的；最适宜的；最有利的

the *optimum* temperature for the growth of plants 植物生长的最佳温度

precaution ［prɪˈkɔːʃn］ ［同］forethought

n. thing done in advance to avoid danger, prevent problems, etc. 预防措施或方法

Take an umbrella just as a *precaution* 带把伞，有备无患。

precedent ［ˈpresɪdənt］ ［近］preceding

n. earlier decision, case, event, etc. that is regarded as an example or rule for what comes later 可援为先例的判决、事例、事件等

create/establish/set a *precedent* (for sth.) (为某事物)开创先例

precipitate ［prɪˈsɪpɪteɪt］

v. (fml.) to cause sth. to happen suddenly or sooner; hasten 使(某事)突然或迅速地发生；加速

The 2008 sub-prime mortgage crisis *precipitated* the collapse of the American banking system. 2008 年的次贷危机加速了美国金融体系的崩溃。

relish ［ˈrelɪʃ］ ［同］flavour

n. great enjoyment of food, etc.; zest (美食等的)享受；滋味；乐趣

She savoured the joke with *relish*. 她对这个笑话很感兴趣。

remnant ［ˈremnənt］ ［同］remains

n. small remaining quantity or part or number of things or people (事物或人)剩余的小部分，余下的数量

remnants of a meal 残羹冷炙，剩饭

remuneration ［rɪˌmjuːnəˈreɪʃən］

n. (fml) the pay you give sb. for sth. they have done for you 报酬；酬劳

The *remuneration* system is performance-related. 薪酬体系与业绩挂钩。

rendezvous ［ˈrɒndɪvuː］ ［同］date, engagement

n. (place chosen for a) meeting at an agreed time 约会；约会地点

Boats picked us up at pre-arranged *rendezvous*. 船在事先约定的地方接我们。

spectator ［spekˈteɪtər］ ［近］observer, beholder

n. person who watches (esp. a show or game) 观看者；(尤指表演或比赛的)观众

The *spectators* go to sport to be entertained rather than out of loyalty to a team. 观众去体育场是为了娱乐而并非出于对某个队的忠诚。

spectrum ［ˈspektrəm］ ［近］① range

n. ① a complete range of opinions, people, situations, etc., going from one extreme to its opposite 范围；系列 ② the set of bands of coloured light into which a beam of light separates 光谱

a solar *spectrum* 太阳光谱

speedy ［ˈspiːdi］ ［同］fast

adj. (infml.) moving quickly; fast 快速的；迅速的

a *speedy* business operator 办事效率高的经营者

spell [spel]   [近] ①charm ②shift

n. ①words that are thought to have magical power; charm 咒语；符咒 ②a period of a particular kind of activity, weather, illness, etc., usually a short period 一段时间

After a brief *spell* in the army, I returned to teaching. 在部队待了一段时间后，我又回来教书。

spice [spais]   [同] fragrance

n. any of various types of substance obtained from plants, with a strong taste and/or smell, used, esp. in powder form, for flavouring food 香料(从植物中提取而得，尤指粉状的)

Ginger, cinnamon, pepper and cloves are common *spices*. 姜、肉桂、胡椒和丁香都是常用的香料。

thrilled [θrɪld]

adj. very excited, happy, and pleased 兴奋的；高兴的

We were *thrilled* to bits when our daughter appeared on TV. 当我们的女儿出现在电视上时，我们高兴得不得了。

thrive [θraɪv]   [同] boom, flourish

v. to grow or develop well and vigorously; prosper 茁壮成长；蓬勃发展；繁荣

It is still unclear whether dotcom companies will continue to *thrive* in the long-term future. 网络公司能否长期持续繁荣依然不得而知。

time-consuming [ˈtaɪm kənˌsjuːmɪŋ]

adj. taking or needing much time 耗费时间的

Some of the more *time-consuming* jobs can now be done by machines. 有些更费时间的工作现在可以用机器做了。

variable [ˈveəriəbl]   [同] changeable

adj. often changing; likely to change 多变的；变化无常的

variable rainfall/temperature 变化不定的雨量 / 气温

Take the Test ➤➤

句子翻译

1) 一定会有一门和你的学术、个人或是专业承诺相符的课程。(bound)

_____

2) 这些嘈杂的环境实在不利于专心工作。(conducive)

_____

3) 我们决心要杜绝体育活动中的种族歧视现象。(eradicate)

_____

4) 2008 年的次贷危机加速了美国金融体系的崩溃。(precipitate)

_____

5) 网络公司能否长期持续繁荣依然不得而知。(thrive)

_____

6) 有些更费时间的工作现在可以用机器做了。(time-consuming)

_____

appalling [əˈpɔːlɪŋ] [同] fearful, terrible

adj. (infml.) shocking; extremely bad 骇人的；极恶劣的

Jews were rounded up by the German Nazis and executed under the most **appalling** and inhuman conditions. 犹太人被德国纳粹驱赶到一起并在极为可怕与残忍的情况下被处死。

apparatus [ˌæpəˈreɪtəs] [同] equipment

n. set of instruments, etc. used esp. in scientific experiments 仪器；设备；装置

You will need a fairly flexible plan because sometimes resources, **apparatus**, and consumables may not be available when you need them. 你需要一个相当灵活的计划，因为有时当你需要资源、设备和消耗品时，你不一定能得到。

apparently [əˈpærəntli] [同] seemingly

adv. according to the way sb. looks or a situation appears, although you cannot be sure 看来，据说

However, this **apparently** does not just depend on the temperature. 不过看来这不仅仅取决于气温。

boycott [ˈbɔɪkɒt]

v. to refuse to buy, use or take part in sth. as a way of protesting 拒绝购买、使用或参加；抵制

We are asking people to **boycott** goods from companies that use child labour. 我们正呼吁大家抵制雇用童工的公司生产的产品。

congestion [kənˈdʒestʃən]

n. too blocked or crowded and causing difficulties 拥塞

The traffic **congestion** in the city gets even worse during the summer. 城里的堵车情况到了夏天更为严重。

conjunction [kənˈdʒʌŋkʃn] [同] association

n. (fml.) combination (of events, etc.) (事件等的)结合，同时发生

The next factor to be determined is whether the goals should be assigned by a manager or collectively set in **conjunction** with the employees. 下一个要决定的因素是目标应由管理者分配，还是跟员工共同设定。

conscientious [ˌkɒnʃiˈenʃəs] [同] ethical, painstaking

adj. (of people or conduct) careful to do what one ought to do, and do it as well as one can (指人或行为)认真的，尽责的

a **conscientious** worker/pupil/attitude 勤勤恳恳的工人／学生／态度

consecutive [kənˈsekjʊtɪv]

adj. coming one after another without interruption; following continuously 按顺序来的；连续不断的

on three **consecutive** days 连续三天

discrepancy [dɪˈskrepənsi] [同] difference

n. difference; failure to agree 差异；不一致

There is considerable *discrepancy* between the two versions of the affair. 这件事的两种说法有很大出入。

discrete [dɪˈskriːt]　　　　　　　　　　　　　　　　　　[反] indiscrete

adj. separate; distinct 分离的；截然分开的

discrete particles 离散颗粒

discretion [dɪˈskreʃn]　　　　　　　　　　　　[同] prudence [反] indiscretion

n. quality of being discreet; good judgement 谨慎；明智

What the banks can offer you will depend on your individual circumstances and on the *discretion* of the bank manager involved. 银行所能提供的取决于你的个人情况和相关银行经理的谨慎程度。

discrimination [dɪˌskrɪmɪˈneɪʃn]

n. treating a person or group differently （usu. worse）than others 歧视

Many women still face sex *discrimination* in the military. 在军队里很多女性依然受到性别歧视。

escalate [ˈeskəleɪt]　　　　　　　　　　[近] expand, grow

v. to become or make sth. greater, worse, more serious, etc. (使)逐步扩大，不断恶化，加剧

The fighting *escalated* into a full-scale war. 这场交战逐步扩大为全面战争。

essential [ɪˈsenʃl]　　　　　　　　　　　　[近] fundamental, vital

adj. completely necessary, extremely important in a particular situation or for a particular activity 完全必要的；必不可少的；极其重要的

Most spiders are quite harmless and play an *essential* role in maintaining the balance of nature. 大多数蜘蛛都是无毒无害的，而且它们在维持自然界的平衡中有着非常重要的作用。

established [ɪˈstæblɪʃt]　　　　　　　　　　[同] fixed, settled

adj. respected or given official status because it has existed or been used for a long time 已确立的；已获确认的

They are an *established* company with a good reputation. 他们是一家地位稳固、信誉很好的公司。

flimsy [ˈflɪmzi]　　　　　　　　　　　　　　　　　[近] weak

adj. weak or feeble; unconvincing 软弱无力的；不足信的

a *flimsy* excuse 站不住脚的借口

hindrance [ˈhɪndrəns]　　　　　　　　　　　　　　　　　[反] help

n. sth. or sb. that makes it difficult for you to do sth. 妨碍；障碍

The country's poor infrastructure is a major *hindrance* to foreign investors. 这个国家薄弱的基础设施对外国投资者来说是个很大的障碍。

inner [ˈɪnə(r)]　　　　　　　　　　　　　　　　　　[反] outer

adj. （of feelings）unexpressed (指感情)内心的，未表达出来的

Poetry serves as a window into the deep, *inner* reflective thoughts of the author. 诗歌是作者将心底的深思熟虑的想法表达出来的一种方式。

innovation [ˌɪnəˈveɪʃn]

n. a new idea, method, or invention 新方法；新技术；新思想

technical *innovations* in industry 工业中的技术革新

innumerable [ɪˈnjuːmərəbl]　　　　　　　　　[同] countless

adj. too many to be counted 无数的；数不清的

There are **innumerable** stars in the sky. 天上有无数的星星。

linguistic [lɪŋ'gwɪstɪk]

adj. connected with language or the scientific study of language 语言学的

new developments in **linguistic** theory 语言学理论的新发展

metabolism [mɪ'tæbəlɪzəm]

n. the chemical processes in living things that change food, etc. into energy and materials for growth 新陈代谢

Although the **metabolism** myth has been completely disproved, science has far from discounted our genes as responsible for making us whatever weight we are, fat or thin. 尽管新陈代谢的神话已经被完全打破，科学仍无法推翻基因决定我们的体重、决定我们是胖是瘦的论断。

metaphor ['metəfə(r)] [近] analogy

n. a way of describing sth. by referring to it as sth. different and suggesting that it has similar qualities to that thing 比喻

She uses some wonderful images and **metaphors** in her writing. 她在写作中使用了一些很美的意象和比喻。

metaphorical [ˌmetə'fɒrɪkl]

adj. connected with or containing metaphors 隐喻的；含比喻的

'They don't talk the same language' has a major **metaphorical** meaning alongside its literal one. "他们不讲同一种语言"除了其字面意思外还有一个很显著的喻义。

precision [prɪ'sɪʒn] [同] accuracy

n. exactness and clarity; quality of being precise 准确(性)；明确(性)；精确(性)

Your report lacks **precision**. 你的报告不够准确。

predator ['predətə(r)] [同] hunter

n. animal that kills and eats other animals 捕食其他动物的动物；食肉动物

predators of the African grasslands 非洲草原的食肉动物

predecessor ['priːdɪsesə(r)] [近] precursor

n. person who held an office or position before sb. else (职务或职位的)前任者

The decision was made by my **predecessor**. 那个决定是我的前任作出的。

predominate [prɪ'dɒmɪneɪt] [近] rule

v. to have control, power or influence (over sb./sth.) 支配，统治，左右(某人／某事物)

In most developing countries, old cars and old technologies continue to **predominate**. 在绝大多数发展中国家，老式汽车和旧技术仍然占据主导地位。

pregnant ['pregnənt] [同] childing

adj. (of a woman or female animal) having a baby or young animal developing in the womb (指妇女或雌性动物)怀孕的，妊娠的

She was six months **pregnant**. 她那时已怀有六个月的身孕。

renounce [rɪ'naʊns] [同] abandon

v. (fml.) to agree to give up ownership or possession of (sth.), esp. formally 同意放弃(某事物)的所有权或占有权(尤指正式地)

renounce a claim/title/right/privilege 宣布放弃要求／头衔／权利／特权

renovate ['renəveɪt] [同] renew

v. to restore (esp. old buildings) to good condition 修复(尤指旧建筑物)；整修

Recently it was completely *renovated*, and now looks brand new. 最近它被彻底整修过，现在看上去像全新的一样。

| **repel** | [rɪˈpel] | | [同] keep off |

v. ①to make sb. who is attacking you go away by fighting them 反抗；击退 ②to keep sth. or sb. away from you 驱散；赶走

The army was ready to *repel* an attack. 军队已做好击退进攻者的准备。

| **replenish** | [rɪˈplenɪʃ] |

v. to fill sth. again 再将某物充满

Let me *replenish* your glass with more wine. 我给你把杯子再斟满酒吧。

| **splash** | [splæʃ] | | [同] spray |

v. to cause (a liquid) to fly about in drops; to make sb./sth. wet in this way 使(液体)溅起；溅湿某人/某物

splash water on/over the floor 把水溅在地板上

| **spokesperson** | [ˈspəʊksˌpɜːsən] | | [同] spokesman |

n. person who speaks, or is chosen to speak, on behalf of a group 发言人

A government *spokesperson* has denied the allegations of corruption. 政府发言人否认了腐败的指控。

| **whirl** | [wɜːl] | | [同] spin |

v. to move, or make sb./sth. move, around quickly in a circle or in a particular direction (使)旋转；回旋；打转

Leaves *whirled* in the wind. 落叶在风中旋转。

| **wholesale** | [ˈhəʊlseɪl] |

adj. connected with goods that are bought and sold in large quantities, especially so they can be sold again to make a profit 批发的

wholesale goods/prices 批发货物/价格

| **wide-ranging** | [ˌwaɪd ˈreɪndʒɪŋ] |

adj. including or dealing with a large number of different subjects or areas 覆盖面广的；内容广泛的

The commission has been given *wide-ranging* powers. 委员会被授予的权限很广。

Take the Test >>

句子翻译

1) 我们正呼吁大家抵制雇用童工的公司生产的产品。(boycott)

_____

2) 城里的堵车情况到了夏天更为严重。(congestion)

_____

3) 在军队里很多女性依然受到性别歧视。(discrimination)

_____

4) 在绝大多数发展中国家，老式汽车和旧技术仍然占据主导地位。(predominate)

_____

5) 最近它被彻底整修过，现在看上去像全新的一样。(renovate)

_____

appliance [əˈplaɪəns]   [同] device

n. instrument or device for a specific purpose 工具；器具

a kitchen full of electrical *appliances* 有各种电器的厨房

appraisal [əˈpreɪzl]   [同] estimate, assessment

n. appraising sb./sth.; evaluation 评价；鉴定；评定

a critical *appraisal* of the existing facilities 一份关于现存设备的关键评估

apprentice [əˈprentɪs]   [近] beginner

n. person who has agreed to work for a skilled employer for a fixed period in return for being taught his trade or craft 学徒；徒弟

an *apprentice* plumber 见习水管工人

brainstorm [ˈbreɪnstɔːm]

① *n.* a way of finding answers in which all people in a group work together 头脑风暴

② *v.* to try to develop ideas and think of ways of solving problems 头脑风暴

Group *brainstorming* appears to inhibit creativity, not stimulate it. 集体头脑风暴看上去会限制创造力，而不是激发它。

breach [briːtʃ]   [同] ①violation

① *n.* a failure to do sth. that must be done by law (对法规等的)违背，违反

a *breach* of contract/copyright 违反合同；侵犯版权

② *v.* to break 打开；违背

[记] break = 打破, 形近记忆

consensus [kənˈsensəs]   [同] agreement

n. agreement in opinion; collective opinion 意见一致；共同看法

The two parties have reached a *consensus*. 这两个政党达成了一致意见。

consequently [ˈkɒnsɪkwəntli]   [同] therefore, accordingly

adv. as a result; therefore 所以；因而

Consequently, the effects of passive smoking are far greater on non-smokers than on smokers. 因此，被动吸烟对不吸烟者的危害远大于对吸烟者的危害。

conservation [ˌkɒnsəˈveɪʃn]   [近] saving

n. preservation of the natural environment 对自然环境的保护

Founded in 1990, the Ecotourism Society aims to make ecotourism a tool for *conservation* and sustainable development. 成立于 1990 年的"生态旅游"社团目的在于使生态旅游成为一种环境保护和可持续发展的有效方式。

considerate [kənˈsɪdərət]   [同] thoughtful

adj. careful not to hurt or inconvenience others; thoughtful 为他人着想的；考虑周到的

It was *considerate* of you not to play the piano while I was asleep. 在我睡觉时你不弹钢琴，真

是体贴入微。

dismantle [dɪsˈmæntl]   [同] strip, bare

v. to take (sth.) to pieces 将(某物)拆开；拆除(某物)

dismantle a faulty motor (for repairs) 拆开有毛病的发动机(以便修理)

disparity [dɪˈspærətɪ]   [反] parity

n. (fml.) difference or inequality 不同；不等

Comparison of the two accounts revealed numerous ***disparities***. 比较一下两本账，发现了许多出入。

dispose [dɪˈspəʊz]   [近] order, arrange

v. to get rid of sth., especially sth. that is difficult to get rid of 处理；除掉

The recycling process still creates emissions which require treatment before they can be ***disposed*** of safely. 循环过程仍然会产生排放物，这些物质经过处理后才能被安全倒掉。

etiquette [ˈetɪket]   [同] manner

n. the formal rules of correct or polite behaviour in society or among members of a particular profession (社会或行业中的)礼节，礼仪，规矩

Etiquette was considered very important in Victorian England. 英国在维多利亚时代非常注重礼仪。

evacuate [ɪˈvækjʊeɪt]

v. to move people from a place of danger to a safer place (把人从危险的地方)疏散，转移，撤离

Police ***evacuated*** nearby buildings. 警方已将附近大楼的居民疏散。

everlasting [ˌevəˈlɑːstɪŋ]   [同] eternal, unending

adj. continuing for ever; never changing 永恒的；永久不变的

an ***everlasting*** memory of her smile 她的微笑留下的永久回忆

flip [flɪp]

① *n.* an action in which you make a flat object such as a coin go upwards and turn over in the air 抛；扔

In the end the decision was made by the ***flip*** of a coin. 最后还是通过抛硬币的方式做出了决定。

② *v.* to move (sth.) with a quick sharp movement; flick 快速猛然移动(某物)

hindsight [ˈhaɪndsaɪt]

n. wisdom about an event after it has occurred 事后的觉悟；事后的聪明

We failed, and with ***hindsight*** I now see where we went wrong. 我们失利了，事后一想，我现在明白了错在哪里。

inspiration [ˌɪnspəˈreɪʃn]

n. stimulation of the mind, feelings, etc. to do sth. beyond a person's usual ability, esp. creative ability in art, literature, music, etc. 灵感

Wordsworth found ***inspiration*** in the Lake District scenery. It was a great source of ***inspiration*** to him. 华兹华斯从风景优美的英格兰湖区获得灵感，那里是他灵感的巨大源泉。

inspire [ɪnˈspaɪə]

v. to fill sb. with thoughts, feelings or aims 激励或鼓舞某人

The lecture today really ***inspired*** me to read more poetry. 今天的讲座激励着我去读更多的诗。

livelihood [ˈlaɪvlɪhʊd] 　　　　　　　　　　　　　　　　　[同] bread and butter

n. (usu. sing.) means of living; income 生活的手段；生计；收入

We understand a port as a centre of land-sea exchange, and as a major source of *livelihood* and a major force for cultural mixing. 我们将港口看作是海陆交流的中心，同时，它也是一种重要的收入来源和一种促进文化融合的力量。

methodology [ˌmeθəˈdɒlədʒi]

n. the set of methods and principles that you use when studying a particular subject or doing a particular kind of work 方法学；方法论

There are some differences in *methodology* between the two studies. 两项研究中所使用的方法有些不同。

meticulous [mɪˈtɪkjʊləs] 　　　　　　　　　　　　　　　　[同] careful, scrupulous

adj. paying careful attention to every detail 细心的；小心翼翼的

He's always *meticulous* in keeping the records up to date. 他总是十分细心地补充最新的资料。

preliminary [prɪˈlɪminəri] 　　　　　　　　　　　　　　　[同] ①introductory

① *adj.* coming before a more important action or event; preparatory （作为某一重要行动或事情的）开端的；预备性的

after a few *preliminary* remarks 在几句开场白之后

② *n.* preliminary action, event, measure, etc. 初步的行动、事件、措施等

the necessary *preliminaries* to a peace conference 为召开和平会议而做的必要的准备工作

premier [ˈpremiə] 　　　　　　　　　　　　　　　　　　[同] ①foremost

① *adj.* (fml.) best or most important 首要的；最好的

The Super Bowl is America's *premier* sporting event. "超级碗"是美国最重要的体育赛事。

② *n.* a prime minister 总理

premise [ˈpremɪs] 　　　　　　　　　　　　　　　　　　[同] assumption

n. statement or idea on which reasoning is based; hypothesis（推理所依据的）前提；假定

Advice to investors was based on the *premise* that interest rates would continue to fall. 给予投资者的建议是以利率将继续下降这一点为前提的。

prerequisite [ˌpriːˈrekwɪzɪt] 　　　　　　　　　　　　　[同] essential, necessary

adj. (infml.) required as a condition (for sth.) 必备的；作为先决条件的

A degree is *prerequisite* for employment at this level. 必须具备大学学位才能从事这一级的工作。

preservation [ˌprezəˈveɪʃn]

n. the act of keeping sth. in its original state or in good condition 保存；保护；维护

the *preservation* of our cultural heritage 对文化遗产的保护

representative [ˌreprɪˈzentətɪv] 　　　　　　　　　　　[同] ①typical, ②delegate

① *adj.* serving to show or portray a class or group 有代表性的；典型的

② *n.* sb. who has been chosen to speak, vote, or make decisions for sb. else 代表；代理

Is a questionnaire answered by 500 people truly *representative* of national opinion? 一份由五百人作答的调查问卷是否能真正代表全国人民的意见？

reproduction [ˌriːprəˈdʌkʃn] 　　　　　　　　　　　　　[反] ②original

n. ①the act or process of producing babies, young animals, or plants 繁殖

Scientists studied the *reproduction*, diet, and health of the dolphins. 科学家们研究了海豚的繁殖、饮食和健康情况。

②the act of producing a copy of a book, picture, piece of music, etc. 复制

resent [rɪˈzent]　　　　　　　　　　　　　　　　　　　　[同] hate

v. to feel bitter, indignant or angry about（sth. hurtful, insulting, etc.）对（某事物）感到愤恨、怨恨或气愤

I bitterly *resent* your criticism. 我对你的批评十分反感。

reservoir [ˈrezəvwɑː(r)]

n. ① a lake, especially an artificial one, where water is stored before it is supplied to people's houses 水库 ②（fig.）large supply or collection of sth. 储藏；汇集

The show is a *reservoir* of new talent. 这次演出真是新秀荟萃。

resident [ˈrezɪdənt]　　　　　　　　　　　　　　　　　　[同] ①inhabitant

① *n.* a person who lives in a particular place or who has their home there 居民；住户

② *adj.* living in a particular place（在某地）居住的

There were confrontations between local *residents* and the police. 当地居民和警察之间有过冲突。

residential [ˌrezɪˈdenʃ(ə)l]

adj.（of an area of a town）suitable for living in; consisting of houses rather than factories or offices 适合居住的；住宅的

Their *residential* building is located next to the park. 他们的住宅大楼坐落于公园旁。

spot-on [ˈspɒtɒn]

adj.（infml.）exactly right; accurate 一点不错；对极了；准确

His assessment of the situation was *spot-on*. 他对形势判断得很准确。

sprawl [sprɔːl]

v. to sit, lie or fall with the arms and legs spread out loosely 四肢摊开着坐、卧或倒下

He was *sprawling* in an armchair in front of the TV. 他四肢摊开坐在电视机前的扶手椅上。

squander [ˈskwɒndə(r)]　　　　　　　　　　　　　　　　　[同] waste

v. to waste（time, money, etc.）; to use sth. wastefully 浪费（时间、金钱等）；挥霍

England *squandered* a golden opportunity to score, seconds before the final whistle. 英格兰队在全场结束前几秒钟浪费了一次绝佳的破门机会。

unparalleled [ˌʌnˈpærəleld]　　　　　　　　　　　　　　　[同] matchless

adj.（fml.）used to emphasize that sth. is bigger, better or worse than anything else like it 无比的；绝无仅有的

The book has enjoyed a success *unparalleled* in recent publishing history. 这本书在近期出版史上是空前的成功。

unprecedented [ˌʌnˈpresɪdentɪd]

adj. that has never happened, been done or been known before 前所未有的；史无前例的

The situation is *unprecedented* in modern times. 这种情况在现代还没有出现过。

Take the Test >>

句子翻译

1) 集体头脑风暴看上去会限制创造力，而不是激发它。（brainstorm）

_____

2) 英国在维多利亚时代非常注重礼仪。（etiquette）

_____

3) 最后还是通过抛硬币的方式做出了决定。（flip）

_____

4) 两项研究中所使用的方法有些不同。（methodology）

_____

5) 一份由五百人作答的调查问卷，是否能真正代表全国人民的意见？（representative）

_____

Ordinary people merely think how they shall spend their time; a man of talent tries to use it. 普通人只想到如何度过时间，有才能的人设法利用时间。

——德国哲学家 叔本华（Arthur Schopenhauer, German philosopher）

approval [əˈpruːvl]　　　　　　　　　　　　　　　　　　[同] approbation [反] disapproval

n. feeling or showing that one thinks sth. is good or acceptable or satisfactory 赞同；同意

give one's ***approval*** 表示同意

apt [æpt]　　　　　　　　　　　　　　　　　　　　[同] fit, appropriate [反] inapt, inept

adj. exactly right for a particular situation or purpose 合适的

The punishment should be ***apt*** for the crime. 罪与罚应相当。

aptitude [ˈæptɪtjuːd]

n. (for sth./doing sth.) natural ability or skill 天资；天赋

aptitude test 能力倾向测验(用以确定某人是否适宜从事某种工作或参加某种训练课程)

breakthrough [ˈbreɪkθruː]　　　　　　　　　　　　　　　　　　　　　　[同] rise

n. an important development that may lead to an agreement or achievement 重大进展；突破

a significant ***breakthrough*** in negotiations 谈判中的重大突破

breakup [ˈbreɪkʌp]　　　　　　　　　　　　　[同] breakdown

n. the ending of a relationship or an association （关系、联系、交往的）破裂，中断

He did nothing to stop the ***breakup*** of their marriage. 他丝毫没有尝试挽救破裂的婚姻。

consideration [kənˌsɪdəˈreɪʃən]　　　　　　　　[近] concern

n. careful thought and attention, especially before making an official or important decision 考虑，认真思考

In the past, the case for public transport has been made on the basis of environmental and social justice ***considerations*** rather than economics. 过去在考虑公共交通问题时，人们更关心的是环境和社会公平方面的因素，而不是基于经济因素。

consistent [kənˈsɪstənt]　　　　　　　　　　[同] congruous [反] conflicting, inconsistent

adj. in agreement 一致的；相符的

The research results are clear and ***consistent***. 这些研究结果条理清楚且相互符合。

consolidate [kənˈsɒlɪdeɪt]　　　　　　　　　　　　　　　　　　　　[同] unify

v. to become more solid, secure, or strong 使某事物巩固；加固；加强

The time has come for the firm to ***consolidate*** after several years of rapid expansion. 经过几年的迅速发展，是公司该巩固自身实力的时候了。

conspicuous [kənˈspɪkjuəs]　　　　　　　　　　[同] noticeable [反] inconspicuous

adj. easily seen; noticeable; remarkable 显而易见的；明显的；惹人注目的

If you're walking along a badly-lit road at night you should wear ***conspicuous*** clothes. 晚上在照明很差的路上行走，应该穿显眼的衣物。

disillusion [ˌdɪsɪˈluːʒn]

v. to destroy the pleasant but mistaken beliefs or ideals of (sb.) 使(某人)醒悟；理想或幻想破灭

She still believes in Santa Claus and it would be cruel to ***disillusion*** her. 她仍然相信有圣诞老

人，要使她这一幻想破灭有点残忍。

disintegrate [dɪsˈɪntɪɡreɪt]　　　　　　　　　　　　　　　　[同] ②decay

*v.*① (cause sth.) to break into small parts or pieces (使某物)碎裂，崩裂 ② to become weaker or less united and be gradually destroyed 瓦解；分化

a society *disintegrating* under economic pressures 一个在经济压力下日渐瓦解的社会

establishment [ɪsˈtæblɪʃmənt]　　　　　　　　　　　　　　　　[近] enterprise

n. (fml.) an organization, a large institution or a hotel 机构；大型机关；旅馆

an educational *establishment* 教育机构

eternal [ɪˈtɜːnəl]　　　　　　　　　　　　　　　　[同] everlasting

adj. without an end; existing or continuing for ever 不朽的；永久的；永恒的

eternal truth 永恒的真理

ethical [ˈeθɪkl]　　　　　　　　　　　[同] moral

adj. connected with beliefs and principles about what is right and wrong (有关)道德的；伦理的

The use of animals in scientific tests raises difficult *ethical* questions. 用动物来做科学实验为我们提出了伦理难题。

fluffy [ˈflʌfi]

adj. like fluff; covered with fluff 似绒毛的；有绒毛的

Most animals are soft and *fluffy* when first born. 大多数动物刚出生时都很软，身上有绒毛。

groan [ɡrəʊn]

v. to make a deep sad sound when in pain, or to express despair, disapproval or distress 呻吟；叹息；嘘(某人)

The audience *groaned* at his terrible jokes. 他讲的笑话很糟，听众发出了不满的嘘声。

inspirational [ˌɪnspəˈreɪʃnl]

adj. providing encouragement or new ideas for what you should do 有启发性的；鼓舞人心的

an *inspirational* speech 鼓舞人心的演讲

instalment [ɪnˈstɔːlmənt]

n. (AmE installment) one of a series of regular payments that you make until you have paid all the money you owe 分期付款

They're letting me pay for the washing machine by monthly *instalments*. 他们答应让我用分月付款的方式购买这台洗衣机。

livestock [ˈlaɪvstɒk]

n. the animals kept on a farm, for example cows or sheep 牲畜；家畜

There is a *livestock* auction this afternoon. 今天下午有一个家畜拍卖会。

metropolitan [ˌmetrəˈpɒlɪtən]

adj. connected with a large or capital city 大城市的；大都会的

metropolitan districts 都市区

milestone [ˈmaɪlstəʊn]　　　　　　　　[近] event, milepost

n. a very important stage or event in the development of sth. 重要事件；转折点；里程碑

The invention of the computer was a *milestone* in the history of man. 计算机的发明是人类历史上的一件大事。

prestigious [preˈstɪdʒəs]　　　　　　[同] famous, renowned

adj. admired as one of the best and most important 有威望的；声誉高的

a highly *prestigious* university 一所声誉极高的大学

prevail [prɪˈveɪl] 　　　　　　　　　　　　　　　[同] dominate

v. to exist or be very common at a particular time or in a particular place 普遍存在；流行

Those beliefs still *prevail* among certain social groups. 这些信念在某些社会群体中仍很盛行。

prevailing [prɪˈveɪlɪŋ] 　　　　　　　　　　　　　[同] predominant

adj. existing or most common at a particular time 普遍的；盛行的

the *prevailing* attitude towards science at the time 当时对科学的普遍看法

prevalent [ˈprevələnt] 　　　　　　　　　　　　　[同] prevailing

adj. (fml.) that exists or is very common at a particular time or in a particular place 流行的；普遍存在的

These prejudices are particularly *prevalent* among people living in the North. 这些偏见在北方人中尤为常见。

prey [preɪ] 　　　　　　　　　　　　　　[同] ①victim, bottom dog

① *n.* a person who is harmed or deceived by sb., esp. for dishonest purposes 受害者；受骗者

Elderly people are easy *prey* for dishonest salesmen. 老年人容易上狡诈推销员的当。

② *v.* to harm sb. who is weaker than you, or make use of them in a dishonest way to get what you want 欺凌；敲诈(弱者)

Bogus social workers have been *preying* on old people living alone. 冒牌社会福利工作人员不断坑害独居老人。

resistance [rɪˈzɪstəns]

n. the act of using force to oppose sb./sth. 抵抗；反抗

The demonstrators offered little or no *resistance* to the police. 示威者们几乎没有对警察进行任何反抗。

resonance [ˈrezənəns]

n. ①the sound or other vibration produced in an object by sound or vibration of a similar frequency from another object 回响；共振 ②the special meaning or importance that sth. has for you because it relates to your own experiences 共鸣

The movie had a special emotional *resonance* for me. 这部电影引起了我的情感共鸣。

respectable [rɪˈspektəbl] 　　　　　　　　　　　[同] decent

adj. considered by society to be acceptable, good, or correct 体面的；得体的；值得尊敬的

a highly *respectable* neighbourhood 非常体面的社区

stack [stæk] 　　　　　　　　　　　　　　[同] pile

v. to make sth. into a pile or piles; to pile sth. up 将某物堆起或摞起

People worked in the warehouses, *stacked* and replenished the shelves, cleaned the floors and fridges. 在仓库工作的人要堆叠货物并补充货架，还要清洗地板与冰箱。

stagnant [ˈstægnənt] 　　　　　　　　　　　　[近] static, immobile

adj. (of water) not flowing and therefore dirty and smelling unpleasant; still and stale (指水)因不流动而污浊、腐臭的，静止而不新鲜的

The old and ill are the most vulnerable to the acute effects of heavily polluted *stagnant* air. 年老体弱的人对严重污染的污浊空气所产生的剧烈作用的抵抗力最为脆弱。

staple [ˈsteɪpl] 　　　　　　　　　　　　　　[同] basic

adj. main or principal; standard 主要的；基本的；标准的

Once television became widespread, film and radio stopped being the *staple* form of entertainment. 一旦电视普及，电影和广播就不再是娱乐的主要形式了。

stark [stɑːk]　　　　　　　　　　　　　　　　　　　　[近] utter

adj. clearly obvious to the eye or the mind 显而易见的；明摆着的；鲜明的

The language barrier presents itself in *stark* form to firms who wish to market their products in other countries. 对那些希望在其他国家营销自己产品的公司来说，语言不通是最为明显的障碍。

startle [ˈstɑːtl]　　　　　　　　　　　　　　　　[同] astound, frighten

v. to give a sudden shock or surprise to （a person or an animal）; to cause to move or jump suddenly (from surprise) 使(人或动物)惊吓或吓一跳

I was *startled* to hear his news/by his news. 我听到他的消息大吃了一惊。

token [ˈtəʊkən]　　　　　　　　　　　　　　　　　　　[同] indication

n. sign, symbol or evidence of sth. 表征；标志；证据

A white flag is used as a *token* of surrender. 白旗是投降的标志。

unravel [ʌnˈrævəl]　　　　　　　　　　　　　[同] expound, figure out

v. to explain sth. that is difficult to understand or is mysterious; to become clearer or easier to understand 阐释；说明

Since then a massive research program has taken place to *unravel* the mystery of why the ship sank. 从那之后展开了一项重大的研究项目以解释沉船之谜。

unrealistic [ˌʌnrɪəˈlɪstɪk]　　　　　　　　　　　　　[反] inpractical

adj. not showing or accepting things as they are 不切实际的；不实事求是的

It is *unrealistic* to expect them to be able to solve the problem immediately. 指望他们能够立即解决问题是不现实的。

unveil [ʌnˈveɪl]　　　　　　　[同] ①②disclose [反] ①②veil

v. ① to show or tell people about a new product or plan for the first time 首次公布 ② to remove the cover from sth., especially as part of a formal ceremony 揭幕；揭牌

The government has *unveiled* its plans for low-income housing. 政府已公布了经济适用房的开发计划。

Take the Test

词组翻译

重大突破 _____ 鼓舞人心的演讲 _____
月供 _____ 声誉极高的大学 _____
情感共鸣 _____ 经济适用房 _____

句子翻译

1）用动物来做科学实验为我们提出了伦理难题。（ethical）
_____

2）计算机的发明是人类历史上的一件大事。（milestone）
_____

3）这些信念在某些社会群体中仍很盛行。（prevail）
_____

4）这些偏见在北方人中尤为常见。（prevalent）
_____

5）指望他们能够立即解决问题是不现实的。（unrealistic）
_____

The man who has made up his mind to win will never say "impossible".

凡是决心取得胜利的人是从来不说"不可能的"。

——法国皇帝 拿破仑（Bonaparte Napoleon, French emperor）

arable [ˈærəbl] [同] cultivable

adj. suitable for ploughing and for growing crops (土地)适于耕作的

arable land 可耕的土地

arbitrary [ˈɑːbɪtrərɪ] [同] capricious

adj. based on personal opinion or impulse, not on reason 任意的；任性的；主观的

The choice of players for the team seems completely *arbitrary*. 队员的挑选似乎完全是主观决定的。

arch [ɑːtʃ]

n. curved structure forming a passageway or an ornamental gateway 拱道；拱门

Go through the *arch* and follow the path. 穿过拱门，沿着那条路走。

breeding [ˈbriːdɪŋ] [同] procreation

n. producing of young by animals (动物的)生育，繁殖，生殖

the *breeding* season 繁殖季节

brink [brɪŋk] [同] edge, border

n. if you are on the brink of sth., you are almost in a very new, dangerous or exciting situation (…的)边缘；(…的)初始状态

A language can be brought back from the very *brink* of extinction. 一种语言可以从消失的边缘被挽救回来。

constraint [kənˈstreɪnt] [同] restriction

n. thing that limits or restricts 限制性或约束性的事物

There are no *constraints* on your choice of subject for the essay. 文章题材不限。

consultant [kənˈsʌltənt]

n. person who gives expert advice (in business, law, etc.) (商业、法律等方面的)顾问

the President's *consultant* on economic affairs 总统的经济事务顾问

consumerism [kənˈsjuːmərɪzəm]

n. the belief that it is good to buy and use a lot of goods and services—often used to show disapproval 消费至上主义

But the growth in consumer debt should not be simply seen and condemned as a complete descent into mindless *consumerism*. 但是消费者负债的增加不应该被简单看作或谴责为一种向盲目的消费至上主义沦陷的彻底堕落。

container [kənˈteɪnə(r)]

n. box, bottle, etc. in which sth. is kept, transported, etc. 容器(如箱、瓶等)

The radioactive material is stored in a special radiation-proof *container*. 放射性材料被贮存在防辐射的特殊容器内。

contaminate [kənˈtæmɪneɪt] [同] pollute [反] purify

v. to make sth./sb. impure by adding dangerous or disease-carrying substances 使某物／某人受污染

Pesticides may *contaminate* water supplies. 杀虫剂可能会污染供水系统。

disproportionate [ˌdɪsprəˈpɔːʃənət]

adj. too large or too small when compared with sth. else 不成比例的；不相称的

Clearly in simple population terms the older age groups account for a *disproportionate* amount of health care expenditure. 很明显，就单纯的人口数字而言，老年人占用了过多的医疗开支。

disseminate [dɪˈsemɪneɪt] [同] spread

v. (fml.) to spread information, knowledge, etc., so that it reaches many people 散布，传播（信息、知识等）

Their findings have been widely *disseminated*. 他们的研究成果已经广为传播。

distinction [dɪˈstɪŋkʃn] [同] difference, dissimilarity

n. a clear difference or contrast esp. between people or things that are similar or related 差别；区别；对比

distinctions between traditional and modern societies 传统社会和现代社会的差别

distinctive [dɪˈstɪŋktɪv] [同] characteristic

adj. having a quality or characteristic that makes sth. different and easily noticed 独特的；有特色的

distinctive feature 明显的特征

evoke [ɪˈvəʊk] [近] extract

v. to bring a feeling, a memory or an image into sb.'s mind 引起，唤起（感情、记忆或形象）

His case is unlikely to *evoke* public sympathy. 他的情况不大可能引起公众的同情。

evolution [ˌiːvəˈluːʃn] [近] development

n. the gradual development of plants, animals, etc. over many years, from simple to more complicated forms 进化

Darwin's theory of *evolution* 达尔文的进化论

exacerbate [ɪɡˈzæsəbeɪt] [反] assuage

v. to make sth. worse, esp. a disease or problem 使恶化；使加剧

His aggressive reaction only *exacerbated* the situation. 他挑衅性的反应只能使情况更糟。

groundbreaking [ˈɡraʊndˌbreɪkɪŋ]

adj. characterized by originality and innovation 有创造力的；以创造力和创新为特征的

a *groundbreaking* technology 极富创造力的技术

homemade [ˌhəʊmˈmeɪd] [反] shop-bought

adj. made at home, rather than produced in a factory and bought in a shop 家里制作的

Try one of these *homemade* cookies. 尝尝这些自制的点心吧。

institution [ˌɪnstɪˈtjuːʃn]

n. ① a large organization that has a particular kind of work or purpose 机构，组织

the government and other political *institutions* 政府和其他的政治机构

② an important system of organization in society that has existed for a long time 制度；风俗

social *institutions* such as the family and religion 诸如家庭、宗教之类的社会体系

insurmountable [ˌɪnsəˈmaʊntəbl] [反] insuperable

adj. (fml.) (of obstacles, difficulties, etc.) that cannot be overcome（指障碍、困难等）无法超越的，不能克服的

The problems are not *insurmountable*. 问题不是无法解决的。

lobby [ˈlɒbɪ]

n. ①a wide passage or large hall just inside the entrance to a public building 大厅；门廊 ②a group of people who try to persuade a government that a particular law or situation should be changed 游说群体

a powerful environmental *lobby* group 一个强大的环保游说团体

millennium [mɪˈlenɪəm]

n. a period of 1, 000 years, esp. as calculated before or after the birth of Christ 一千年；千年期（尤指公元纪年）

the second *millennium* AD 公元第二个千年

miniature [ˈmɪnɪtʃə(r)]　　　　　　　　　　　　　　　　　[同] ②pocket edition

① *adj.* very small; much smaller than usual 很小的；微型的

a rare breed of *miniature* horses 一种罕见的小矮马

② *n.* a very small copy or model of sth.; a very small version of sth. 微缩模型；微型复制品

miscellaneous [ˌmɪsəˈleɪnɪəs]　　　　　　　　　　　　　　[同] mixed, assorted

adj. consisting of many different kinds of things that are not connected and do not easily form a group 混杂的；多种多样的

a sale of *miscellaneous* household items 各种生活用品大减价

priority [praɪˈɒrəti]

n. sth. that you think is more important than other things and should be dealt with first 优先事项；首要事情

You need to get your *priorities* right. 你需要把轻重缓急分清楚。

privileged [ˈprɪvəlɪdʒd]

adj. having special rights or advantages that most people do not have 有特权的；受特别优待的

Only the *privileged* few can afford private education. 只有极少数的特权阶层才能支付得起私立教育。

probation [prəˈbeɪʃn]

n. ①a system that allows some criminals not to go to prison 缓刑 ②a time of training and testing when you start a new job to see if you are suitable for the work 试用期；见习期

a three month *probation* period 三个月的试用期

respondent [rɪˈspɒndənt]

n. a person who answers questions, esp. in a survey 回答问题的人；（尤指）调查对象

Only 53 per cent of the *respondents* felt that every effort was made to schedule staff fairly. 只有53%的调查对象认为（公司）在尽最大努力使员工工作时间公平合理。

responsive [rɪˈspɒnsɪv]

adj. reacting quickly and in a positive way 反应敏捷的；反应积极的

Firms have to be *responsive* to consumer's demand. 公司必须对顾客的需求迅速做出反应。

restless [ˈrestlɪs]　　　　　　　　　　　　　　　　　　　　[近] uneasy, unpeaceful

adj. unable to stay still or be happy where you are, because you are bored or need a change 坐立不安的；不耐烦的

After five years in the job, he was beginning to feel *restless*. 这份工作干了五年以后，他开始厌烦了。

static [ˈstætɪk]　　　　　　　　　　　　　　　　　　　　　[同] immobile, stationary *adj.* not moving or changing; stationary 静止的；稳定的；静态的

House prices, which have been *static* for several months, are now rising again. 房价稳定了几个月，现在又上涨了。

stem [stem]

① *n.* the long thin part of a plant, from which leaves, flowers, or fruit grow 茎；干

② *v.* to stop sth. from happening, spreading or developing 阻止；遏制

The measures are meant to *stem* the tide of obesity. 这些措施旨在控制日渐严重的肥胖问题。

stem from: to develop as a result of sth. else 出自；源于

stereotype ['steriətaɪp]

n. image, idea, character, etc. that has become fixed or standardized in a conventional form without individuality (and is therefore perhaps false) 模式化的形象、思想、人物等；老一套

Old *stereotypes* and perceptions die hard. 旧的想法和观念很顽固。

tournament ['tɔːnəmənt]   [同] contest

n. series of contests of skill between a number of competitors, often on a knock-out basis 联赛，比赛，竞赛，锦标赛（常为淘汰制）

a tennis *tournament* 网球锦标赛

toxin ['tɒksɪn]

n. a poisonous substance 毒素

These bacteria can produce powerful *toxins*. 这些细菌可以产生剧毒。

trail [treɪl]   [同] ①track ②drag

① *n.* mark or sign in the form of a long line left by sth. or sb. passing by 痕迹；足迹；踪迹

vapour *trails*, e.g. those left in the sky by high-flying aircraft 蒸汽尾迹（如飞机在高空飞行留下的）

② *v.* (cause sth.) to be dragged behind (使某物)被拖在后面

Her long skirt was *trailing* along the floor. 她的长裙拖在了地板上。

wilderness ['wɪldənəs]   [同] wasteland

n. a large area of land that has never been developed or used for growing crops because it is difficult to live there 未开发的地区；荒无人烟的地区

The Antarctic is the world's last great *wilderness*. 南极地区是世界上最后一块巨大的未开发地区。

Take the Test ▶▶

词组翻译

明显的特征 _____   自制的点心 _____

社会体系 _____   游说团体 _____

句子翻译

1）杀虫剂可能会污染供水系统。（contaminate）

_____

2）你需要把轻重缓急分清楚。（priority）

_____

3）只有极少数的特权阶层才能支付得起私立教育。（privileged）

_____

4）公司必须对顾客的需求迅速做出反应。（responsive）

_____

5）旧的想法和观念很顽固。（stereotype）

_____

Lying disguises our mortality, our inadequacies, our fears and anxieties, our loneliness in the midst of the crowd. We yearn for the comfort of familiar lies to create a more amenable reality.

说谎掩盖了人死的必然性、缺陷、恐惧、焦虑和在熙熙攘攘的人群中所感到的孤独。 耳熟能详的谎言会创造一个较易应付的现实。 人渴望从这些谎言中得到安慰。

——美国作家 梅尔．*H.*（*Howards Mel, USAwriter*）

arena [əˈriːnə]

n. (fig.) place or scene of activity or conflict 活动或斗争的场所或场面

More and more graduates flood the job market *arena* on a yearly basis and chase an ever-diminishing number of jobs. 每一年都有越来越多的毕业生涌入就业市场去竞争日益减少的工作。

arguably [ˈɑːgjuəbli]

adv. possibly 可能，大概

Techniques like these have transformed Australia into *arguably* the world's most successful sporting nation. 这些技术已使得澳大利亚成为世界上大概最成功的体育强国。

artistic [ɑːˈtɪstɪk]

adj. ①good at painting, drawing, or producing beautiful things 有艺术天赋的 ②relating to art or culture 艺术的

She described her mother as 'very intelligent and *artistic*'. 她说她母亲"智慧过人而且有艺术天赋"。

brochure [ˈbrəʊʃə(r)]

n. a magazine or book containing information about sth. or advertising sth. （作介绍或宣传用的）小册子

a travel/holiday *brochure* 旅游／度假指南

contemplate [ˈkɒntempleɪt]　　　　　　　　　　　　　　　[同] consider

v. to look at or consider (sth.) thoughtfully 凝视，打量，沉思（某事物）

She stood *contemplating* the painting. 她站着审视那幅图画。

contempt [kənˈtempt]　　　　　　　　[同] scorn　　　　[反] esteem, respect

n. feeling that sb./sth. is completely worthless and cannot be respected 轻视；蔑视

I shall treat that suggestion with the *contempt* it deserves. 我对那项建议理所当然应嗤之以鼻。

contend [kənˈtend]　　　　　　　　　　　　　　　[同] ①compete, rival

v. ① to struggle in order to overcome a rival, competitor or difficulty （与对手）竞争；（与他人）争夺

She's had a lot of problems to *contend* with. 她有许多问题要解决。

② to argue or state that sth. is true 宣称

Some astronomers *contend* that the universe may be younger than previously thought. 有些天文学家宣称宇宙可能比我们之前想像的年轻。

contention [kənˈtenʃn]　　　　　　　　　　　　　　　[同] argument

n. a strong opinion that sb. expresses 争论；观点

Her main *contention* is that doctors should do more to encourage healthy eating. 她的主要观点是医生应该在鼓励健康饮食方面做得更多。

contingent [kənˈtɪndʒənt]　　　　　　　　　　　　　　　[同] dependent

adj. (fml.) depending on sth. that may happen in the future 取决于的，与…相关的

Managers need to make rewards *contingent* on performance. 管理者应该把奖励和业绩挂钩。

distraction [dɪˈstrækʃn]

n. a thing that takes your attention away from what you are doing or thinking about 分散注意力的事；使人分心的事

The valley is a place to unwind and appreciate the world without a lot of interruptions and *distractions*. 这个山谷可以让人彻底放松并享受没有太多干扰的世界。

WEAPON OF MASS DISTRACTION

distribution [ˌdɪstrɪˈbjuːʃn]　　　　　　　　　　[同] arrangement

n. the way that sth. is shared or exists over a particular area or among a particular group of people 分配；分布

the unfair *distribution* of wealth 财富分配不公

diversify [daɪˈvɜːsɪfaɪ]

v. to increase the range of goods or services 使多样化

As a singer, she began to *diversify*, performing songs in many languages. 作为一名歌手，她开始用多种语言演唱，以拓宽演唱的风格。

diversity [daɪˈvɜːsɪti]　　　　　　　　　[同] variety [反] uniformity

n. a range of many people or things that are very different from each other 差异(性)；不同(点)

the biological *diversity* of the rainforests 热带雨林的生物多样性

exception [ɪkˈsepʃn]

n. a person or a thing that is not included in a general statement 不包括在内的人(或物)；例外

The processes involved in producing language are no *exception*. 产生语言的过程也不例外。

exceptional [ɪkˈsepʃənl]　　　　　　　[同] outstanding [反] unexceptional

adj. unusually good 杰出的；优秀的

At the age of five he showed *exceptional* talent as a musician. 他五岁时就表现出了非凡的音乐才能。

flux [flʌks]

n. continuous change or succession of changes; unsettled state 连续的改变；不稳定的状态

Organization of the company was then in a state of *flux*. 当时公司的内部组织正处于不稳定状态。

grudge [grʌdʒ]

v. to feel resentful about sth.; to do or give sth. very unwillingly 怨恨某事物；勉强做某事或给某事物

I *grudge* paying so much for such inferior goods. 我不愿花这么多钱买这样的次品。

homogeneous [ˌhɒməˈdʒiːniəs]

adj. formed of parts that are all of the same type 由同类部分组成的

a *homogeneous* society 相同成分组成的社会

integrity [ɪnˈtegrəti]　　　　　　　　　　　　　　[同] honesty

n. quality of being honest and morally upright 诚实而正直

Even in modern times love is associated with the heart, as all other positive emotions such as honesty, *integrity* and kindness. 即便是在现代社会，爱与诚实、正直、友善这类积极情感一样，都与"心"联系在一起。

intelligent [ɪnˈtelɪdʒənt]　　　　　　　　　　　[同] brilliant

adj. having or showing intelligence 聪明的；有才智的；有头脑的

Some scientists claim that dolphins are more ***intelligent*** than humans. 有些科学家声称海豚比人类还要聪明。

mitigate ['mɪtɪgeɪt]   [同] alleviate, relieve

v. (*fml.*) to make sth. less harmful, serious, etc. 减轻；缓和

Soil erosion was ***mitigated*** by the planting of trees. 植树造林减轻了土壤流失。

modification [ˌmɒdɪfɪ'keɪʃn]   [同] change

n. the act or process of changing sth. in order to improve it or make it more acceptable 修改；改进

Until recently, research and treatment for obesity had concentrated on behaviour ***modification***, drugs to decrease appetite and surgery. 直到最近，对肥胖症的研究和治疗仍集中于对行为的调整、抑制食欲的药物以及外科手术。

orchestra ['ɔːkɪstrə]   [近] band

n. a large group of musicians playing many different kinds of instruments and led by a conductor 交响乐团

the school ***orchestra*** 学校交响乐团

probe [prəʊb]   [同] ①enquiry ②detect

① *n.* (used esp. in newspapers) a thorough and careful investigation of sth. 探究；详尽调查

a police ***probe*** into the financial affairs of the company 警方对这家公司的财务进行的详细调查

② *v.* to ask questions in order to find out secret or hidden information about sb./sth. 盘问；探究

He didn't like the media ***probing*** into his past. 他不喜欢媒体追问他的过去。

prodigious [prə'dɪdʒəs]   [同] marvelous

adj. very large or powerful and causing surprise or admiration 巨大的；伟大的

the young Mozart's ***prodigious*** talents 小莫扎特惊人的天赋

productivity [ˌprɒdʌk'tɪvəti]

n. the rate at which a worker, a company or a country produces goods, and the amount produced, compared with how much time, work and money is needed to produce them 生产率；生产效率

This process resulted in performance measures that greatly enhanced the ability to improve ***productivity*** and quality. 这一过程产生了些生产指标，这些生产指标大大促进了提高生产率和质量的能力。

restriction [rɪ'strɪkʃn]   [同] ball and chain, limitation

n. a rule or law that limits or controls what people can do 限制；限定

There are ***restrictions*** on what you can bring into the country. Alcohol, for example, is totally forbidden. 对可以带入境的物品是有限制的，比如说酒就绝对不可以。

retard [rɪ'tɑːd]   [同] decelerate [反] advance

v. to delay the development of sth., or to make sth. happen more slowly than expected 减缓；减慢

Cold weather ***retards*** the growth of many plants. 寒冷的天气会减缓很多植物的生长。

stiff [stɪf]   [同] rigid [反] flexible

adj. not easily bent, folded, moved, changed in shape, etc. 不易弯曲、打褶、移动、变形等的；坚硬的；僵直的

Sand was dredged from the waters and piled on top of the layer of ***stiff*** clay. 沙从水中挖出，堆积在坚硬的泥土表层上。

stifle ['staɪfəl] [近] suppress

n. to stop sth. from happening or developing 扼杀；阻止

rules and regulations that *stifle* innovation 扼杀创新的规章制度

stimulus ['stɪmjʊləs] [同] incentive

n. thing that produces a reaction in living things 使生物体产生反应之物；刺激物

The nutrient in the soil acts as a *stimulus* to make the plants grow. 土壤中的养分能促进植物生长。

stipulate ['stɪpjʊleɪt] [同] specify

v. (fml.) to state (sth.) clearly and firmly as a requirement 讲明，规定(某要求)

It was *stipulated* that the goods should be delivered within three days. 按规定货物须在三日内送交。

strain [streɪn] [同] ②stress

n. ①injury to a part of the body caused by twisting a muscle, etc.; sprain 劳损；扭伤

The bones show signs of very heavy *strain* from hard work. 由于工作艰苦，骨头已经显出严重的劳损。

②a difficulty or problem that is caused when a person, relationship, organization, or system has too much to do or too many problems to deal with 压力；困境；紧张

tranquil ['træŋkwɪl] [同] calm [反] agitated

adj. pleasantly calm, quiet, and peaceful 安静的

a small *tranquil* village 一个宁静的小村子

transcend [træn'send] [同] surpass

v. to be or go beyond the range of (human experience, belief, powers, or description, etc.) 超出或超越 (经验、信念、力量或描绘等的) 范围

Such matters *transcend* man's knowledge. 这些问题超出了人类所掌握的知识的范围。

unwind [ˌʌn'waɪnd] [同] relax, ease off

v. to stop worrying or thinking about problems and start to relax 放松；轻松

Listening to music helps me *unwind* after a busy day. 听音乐使我在一天的忙碌后得到了放松。

unyielding [ˌʌn'jiːldɪŋ] [反] yielding

adj. be not easily influenced and unlikely to change 坚定的；固执的

severe *unyielding* parents 严厉固执的父母

urbanisation [ˌɜːbənaɪ'zeɪʃn]

n. (AmE urbanization) the process of being urbanized 都市化，文雅化

In the past 30 years China has speeded up *urbanisation*. 在过去的 30 年间，中国加快了城市化进程。

"A high-rise block of flats would give many people a chance to enjoy a rural life..."

Take the Test ▶▶

句子翻译

1）她说她母亲"智慧过人而且有艺术天赋"。（artistic）

_____

2）她的主要观点是医生应该在鼓励健康饮食方面做得更多。（contention）

_____

3）这个山谷可以让人彻底放松并享受没有太多干扰的世界。（distraction）

_____

4）听音乐使我在一天的忙碌后得到了放松。（unwind）

_____

Morality is not really the doctrine of how to make ourselves happy but of how we are to be worthy of happiness.

道德确实不是指导人们如何使自己幸福的教条，而是指导人们如何配享有幸福的学说。

——德国哲学家 康德. *I.*（*Immanuel Kant, German Philosopher*）

array [əˈreɪ]   [同] display

n. impressive display or series 展示；显示；一系列

From a disorderly *array* of factual information an orderly, relevant theory will somehow emerge. 从一些混乱的事实性信息中，一个有条理的相关理论可能会以某种方式浮现出来。

arrogant [ˈærəgənt]   [同] proud, pompous

adj. behaving in a proud and superior manner; showing too much pride in oneself and too little consideration for others 傲慢的；自大的

an *arrogant* tone of voice 傲慢的口气

artefact [ˈɑːtɪfækt]

n. (also artifact) thing made by man, especially a tool or weapon of archaeological interest 人工制品（尤指有考古价值的工具或武器）

The collections of the Department of Ethnography include approximately 300,000 *artefacts*. 人类学部的收藏品中包含了约 30 万件人工制品。

browse [braʊz]   [同] flip through, run through [反] pore over

v. to look through the pages of a book, newspaper, etc. without reading everything 浏览，翻阅

I found the article while I was *browsing* through some old magazines. 我在翻阅一些旧杂志时找到了这篇文章。

brunt [brʌnt]

n. bear, take, etc. the brunt of sth. means to receive the main force of sth. unpleasant 承受某事的主要压力；首当其冲

Schools will bear the *brunt* of cuts in government spending. 政府削减开支，学校将首当其冲受到影响。

continuous [kənˈtɪnjʊəs]   [同] constant, ceaseless

adj. going on without stopping or being interrupted 继续不停的；不间断的

Our political institutions are in *continuous* evolution. 我们的政治制度正在不断发展中。

contradict [ˌkɒntrəˈdɪkt]   [同] disagree [反] agree with

v. (of facts, evidence, etc.) to be contrary to (sth.); to conflict with（指事实、证据等）与（某事物）相反，相矛盾

The two statements *contradict* each other. 两种说法互相矛盾。

contributing [kənˈtrɪbjuːtɪŋ]

adj. helping to make sth. happen 成为因素的，导致的

Stress is a *contributing* factor in many illnesses. 压力是众多疾病的诱因。

contribution [ˌkɒntrɪˈbjuːʃn]   [同] donation

n. action of contributing 捐款；捐助；贡献

The signing of such a treaty would be a major *contribution* towards world peace. 签订这样一项

条约是对世界和平的重大贡献。

contrive [kənˈtraɪv] [同] ②plot

v. ① (*fml.*) to succeed in doing sth. in spite of difficulties 设法完成 ②to plan (sth.) cleverly or deceitfully; invent; design 谋划或策划(某事); 发明; 设计

contrive a device/an experiment/a means of escape 设计一个装置 / 筹划一项实验 / 谋划一个逃跑方法

control group [kənˈtrəʊlˈgruːp]

a person, group, etc. against which you compare another person or group that is very similar, in order to see if a particular quality is caused by sth. or happens by chance 对照组

A ***control group*** of non-smoking women were compared to four groups of women smokers. 一组不吸烟的女性作为对照组与四组吸烟女性进行了比照。

divert [daɪˈvɜːt] [同] turn

v. to make sb./sth. change direction 使转向; 使绕道; 转移

Northbound traffic will have to be ***diverted*** onto minor roads. 北行车辆将不得不绕上辅路行驶。

divine [dɪˈvaɪn] [近] deific, godlike

adj. coming from or connected with God or a god 天赐的; 上帝的; 神的

To early man, fire was a ***divine*** gift randomly delivered in the form of lightning, forest fire or burning lava. 对古人来说, 火是上天以闪电、林火或是熔岩的形式赐给他们的礼物。

division [dɪˈvɪʒn] [同] separation

n. the process or result of dividing into separate parts; the process or result of dividing sth. or sharing it out 分开; 分隔; 分配

the ***division*** of labour between the sexes 男女分工

dizzy [ˈdɪzi] [同] giddy, light-headed

adj. feeling as if everything is spinning around you and that you are not able to balance 头晕目眩的; 眩晕的

Climbing so high made me feel ***dizzy***. 爬那么高使我感到头晕目眩。

excessive [ɪkˈsesɪv] [反] deficient

adj. greater than what seems reasonable or appropriate; extreme 过分的; 过度的; 极度的

They complained about the ***excessive*** noise coming from the upstairs flat. 他们抱怨楼上发出的噪音太大。

exclusive [ɪkˈskluːsɪv] [反] inclusive

adj. not very willing to allow new people to become members, esp. if they are from a lower social class 排外的; 不愿接受新成员的

At the same time it's an ***exclusive*** club belonging to privileged, international companies. 同时它还是一家有特权的国际公司的俱乐部, 不轻易接纳新会员。

executive [ɪgˈzekjʊtɪv] [同] administrator

n. a person who has an important job as a manager of a company or an organization (公司或机构的)经理; 主管领导; 管理人员

sales ***executives*** 销售主管

[记] CEO = Chief Executive Officer 执行总裁

foresee [fɔːˈsiː] [同] anticipate, predict

v. to see or know that sth. is going to happen in the future; predict 预见; 预知; 预料

The difficulties could not have been *foreseen*. 这些困难是无法预见的。

grumble [ˈɡrʌmbl]　　　　　　　　　　　　　　　[同] moan

v. to complain or protest in a bad-tempered way 发怨言；鸣不平

Why *grumble* at me about your own stupid mistakes? 你自己犯了愚蠢的错误，为什么向我抱怨？

ARE YOU READY TO GRUMBLE?

honourable [ˈɒnərəbl]　　　　　　　　　　　　[同] estimable

adj. deserving, bringing or showing honour 光荣的；荣耀的

an *honourable* person/deed 享有声誉的人 / 光荣的事迹

intelligible [ɪnˈtelɪdʒəbl]　　　　　　[同] understandable [反] unintelligible

adj. that can be understood 可理解的

Her English was strongly accented but quite *intelligible*. 她的英语口音很重，但可以听懂。

intensify [ɪnˈtensɪfaɪ]　　　　　　　　　　　　[同] enhance

v. to increase in degree or strength 加强；强化

Relationships with the global trading and financial systems have continued to *intensify*. 与全球贸易和金融体系的关系继续深化。

intent [ɪnˈtent]　　　　　　　　　　　　　　　[反] accident

n. (fml.) intention; purpose 意图；意向；目的

It is not my *intent* to deny the value of university education. 我并不试图否定大学教育的价值。

logistics [ləˈdʒɪstɪks]

n. organization of supplies and services, etc. for any complex operation 物流，后勤

The *logistics* of transporting such vast quantities of water would be insurmountable. 运输如此大量的水简直比登天还难。

momentous [məʊˈmentəs]　　　　　　　　[同] important [反] trivial

adj. very important or serious, esp. because there may be important results 关键的；重要的

a *momentous* decision/occasion 重大决定 / 重要场合

momentum [məʊˈmentəm]

n. the ability to keep increasing or developing 推动力；动力

The program's losing *momentum* and finally ceasing. 这个项目失去了推动力，最后停办了。

original [əˈrɪdʒənl]　　　　　　　　　[同] initial, [反] unoriginal

adj. existing from the beginning; first or earliest 原始的；最初的；原先的；最早的

The Indians were the *original* inhabitants of North America. 印第安人是北美最早的居民。

profound [prəˈfaʊnd]　　　　　　　　　　　　　[同] deep

adj. very great; felt or experienced very strongly 巨大的；深远的

But few democratic communities are blessed with the vision and the capital to make such *profound* changes in modern lifestyles. 然而很少有民主团体具备足够的远见和资金，可以使现代生活方式发生巨大的变化。

promotion [prəˈməʊʃn]　　　　　　　　　　　[同] advancement

n. a move to a more important job or rank in a company or an organization 提升；晋升

Others will want to learn new skills purely out of interest, or out of a desire to improve their *promotion* chances. 其他人可能纯粹是出于兴趣才学习新技术，或是想增加他们升职的机会。

retention [rɪˈtenʃn]

n. (fml.) the action of keeping sth. rather than losing it or stopping it 保持；维持

The company needs to improve its training and *retention* of staff. 公司需要改进对员工的培训

和留用。

retrenchment [rɪˈtrentʃmnt]

n. the act of spending less money 紧缩；节省

The challenge to management is how to motivate employees under such ***retrenchment*** conditions. 管理层所面对的挑战是如何在企业紧缩期激励员工。

streamline [ˈstriːmlaɪn]　　　　　　　　　　　　　　　　　　　　　　[近] simplify

v. to make (sth.) more efficient and effective, e.g. by improving or simplifying working methods 使(某事物)效率更高、作用更大(如通过改进或简化工作方法)；精简

We must ***streamline*** our production procedures. 我们必须精简生产程序以提高效率。

strenuous [ˈstrenjʊəs]　　　　　　　　　　　　　　　　　　　　　　[同] arduous

adj. making great efforts; energetic 努力的；精力充沛的

make a ***strenuous*** attempt to reach the top of the mountain 力求登上山顶

stubborn [ˈstʌbən]　　　　　　　　　　　　　　[同] obstinate

adj. determined not to give way; strong-willed; obstinate 不退让的；倔强的；固执的；顽固的

show ***stubborn*** resistance to change 对改革采取顽抗态度

stunt [stʌnt]　　　　　　　　　　　　　　　　[近] trick

n. dangerous or difficult thing done as entertainment 特技表演

Her latest ***stunt*** is riding a motor cycle through a ring of flames. 她的最新特技表演是骑摩托车钻火圈。

transition [trænˈzɪʃn]　　　　　　　　　　　　　　　　　　　　　　[同] shift

n. (instance of) changing from one state or condition to another 过渡；转变；变迁

the ***transition*** from childhood to adult life 从童年到成年的过渡阶段

utensil [juːˈtensl]　　　　　　　　　　　　　　　　　　　　　　[同] implement

n. a tool that is used in the house (家庭)用具；器皿

cooking/kitchen ***utensils*** 炊具／厨房用具

Take the Test >>

句子翻译

1)政府削减开支，学校将首当其冲受到影响。(brunt)

_____

2)压力是众多疾病的诱因。(contributing)

_____

3)一组不吸烟的女性作为对照组与四组吸烟女性进行了比照。(control group)

_____

4)我们必须精简生产程序以提高效率。(streamline)

_____

articulate [ɑːˈtɪkjʊleɪt]

① *adj.* able to talk easily and effectively about things, especially difficult subjects 善于表达的；口齿伶俐的

You have to be ***articulate*** to be good at debating. 善辩者得口齿伶俐。

② *v.* speak clearly and distinctly 清楚明白地说(某事)

ascertain [ˌæsəˈteɪn]　　　　　　　　　　　　　　　　　　　　[同] discover, find out

v. (fml.) to discover (sth.) so that one is certain; to get to know 查明；弄清

ascertain the true facts 查明事实真相

aspiring [əsˈpaɪrɪŋ]　　　　　　　　　　　　　　　　　　　　　　[同] ambitious

adj. hoping to be successful in a particular job, activity, or way of life 有抱负的

Aspiring musicians must practice many hours a day. 有抱负的音乐家每天必须练习很多个小时。

bulky [ˈbʌlki]

adj. large and difficult to move or carry 庞大的；笨重的

Bulky items will be collected separately. 大件物品将分开收集。

bungalow [ˈbʌŋɡələʊ]

n. a house built all on one level, without stairs 平房

Developers no longer build the tiny ***bungalows*** that served the first postwar generation of home buyers. 开发商不再盖那种提供给战后第一代买房者的小平房了。

[记] 音：半个楼(两层楼去一半) = 平房

controversial [ˌkɒntrəˈvɜːʃl]　　　　　　　　[同] contentious

adj. causing or likely to cause controversy 引起或可能引起争论的

a ***controversial*** decision 有争议的决定

controversy [ˈkɒntrəvɜːsi]　　　　　　　　[同] argument

n. public discussion or argument, often rather angry, about sth. which many people disagree with 公开辩论；论战；争议

The appointment of the new director aroused a lot of ***controversy***. 新负责人的任命引起了很大的争议。

convenience [kənˈviːniəns]

n. the quality of being suitable or useful for a particular purpose 便利

Ready meals sell well because of their ***convenience***. 即食食品卖得很好，因为它们很方便。

conviction [kənˈvɪkʃn]　　　　　　　　　　　　　　　　　　　　[同] ①belief

n. ①a very strong belief or opinion 信念，观点 ②the convicting of a person for a crime 定罪；判刑

Careful consideration of our system of numeration leads to the ***conviction*** that, rather than being a facility that comes naturally to a person, it is one of the great and remarkable achievements of the human race. 对计数方法经过深思熟虑之后，我们确信它不是人类与生俱来的技能，而是

人类伟大的成就之一。

coordination [kəʊˌɔːdɪ'neɪʃn]

n. the organization of people or things so that they work together well 协调

coordination between central and local governments 中央政府和地方政府间的协调

documentary [ˌdɒkjʊ'ment(ə)ri]

① *adj.* consisting of documents 文件的；文献的；由文件(或文献)组成的

documentary evidence/sources 书面证据 / 文件来源

② *n.* a film or a radio or television programme giving facts about sth. 纪录影片；纪实广播（或电视）节目

a television *documentary* about/on the future of nuclear power 关于核能前景的纪实电视片

documentation [ˌdɒkjʊmen'teɪʃn]　　　　　　　　　　　　　　　[近] certification

n. the documents that are required for sth., or that give evidence or proof of sth. 必备资料；证明文件

I couldn't enter the country because I didn't have all the necessary *documentation*. 因为证明文件不齐全，我不能入境。

domain [dəʊ'meɪn, də'meɪn]　　　　　　　　　　　　　　　　　　[同] field

n. an area of knowledge or activity; esp. one that sb. is responsible for (知识、活动的)领域，范围，范畴

Physics used to be very much a male *domain*. 物理学曾在很大程度上是男人的天下。

dominant ['dɒmɪnənt]　　　　　　　　　　　　　　　　　　　　[近] chief

adj. more important, powerful or noticeable than other things 首要的；占支配地位的；占优势的

This very same attitude exists on national scales when nations compete to be the strongest, and the most *dominant*. 当各个国家相互竞争以取得最强和最具统治性的地位时，在国家的规模方面也有非常相似的观点。

exemplify [ɪg'zemplɪfaɪ]　　　　　　　　　　　　　　　　　　[近] illustrate

v. to be a typical example of sth. 是…的典型(或典范、榜样)

His food *exemplifies* Italian cooking at its best. 他的菜肴代表了意大利烹饪的最高水平。

exorbitant [ɪg'zɔːbɪtənt]　　　　　　　　　　　　　　[同] astronomical, excessive

adj. (fml.) (of a price) much too high 过高的；高得离谱的

exorbitant costs 过高的花费

foreseeable [fɔː'siːəbl]

adj. that can be foreseen 可以预见的

This problem can be solved in the *foreseeable* future. 这个问题在可预见的将来能获得解决。

horde [hɔːd]　　　　　　　　　　　　　　　　　　　　　　　[同] crowd

n. very large group (esp. of people); huge crowd; throng 大群，大帮(尤指人)；人群

hordes of fans/tourists/football supporters/shoppers 大群的狂热爱好者 / 旅游者 / 足球迷 / 购物者

interchangeable [ˌɪntə'tʃeɪndʒəbl]　　　　　　　　　　　　　[同] commutable

adj. things that are interchangeable can be used instead of each other 可互换的

These two words are almost *interchangeable*. 这两个字差不多可以相互替换。

intermittent [ˌɪntə'mɪtnt]　　　　　　　　　　　　　　　　[同] sporadic

adj. continually stopping and then starting again; not constant 断续的；间歇的

The weather forecast is for sun, with *intermittent* showers. 天气预报说晴天，时有阵雨。

interpretation [ɪnˌtɜːprɪ'teɪʃn]　　　　　　　　　　　　　　[同] explanation *n.* result of interpreting; explanation or meaning 解释；翻译；含义

the conductor's controversial ***interpretation*** of the symphony 该指挥对那支交响乐曲颇有争议的理解

longevity [lɒnˈdʒevəti]

n. ① the amount of time that sb. or sth. lives 寿命 ② long life or the long time that sth. lasts 长寿

Consumption of low calorie yet nutritionally balanced diet increases ***longevity*** and prolongs good health. 低热量且营养均衡的饮食可以延年益寿。

monotonous [məˈnɒtənəs]　　　　　　　　　　　　　　　[同] boring

adj. never changing and therefore boring 单调乏味的

New secretaries came and went with ***monotonous*** regularity. 秘书不停地更换，令人厌烦。

morale [məˈrɑːl]　　　　　　　　　　　　　　　　　　[同] spirit

n. the amount of confidence and enthusiasm, etc. that a person or a group has at a particular time 士气

Morale amongst the players is very high at the moment. 此刻选手们士气很高。

ornament [ˈɔːnəmənt]　　　　　　　　　　　　　　　　[同] ②adorn

① *n.* (fml.) decoration; adornment 装饰；点缀

The palace was rich in ***ornament***. 宫殿装饰得金碧辉煌。

② *v.* to add ornament to sth.; to decorate sth. 装饰、点缀或美化某物

a dress ***ornamented*** with lace 带花边的连衣裙

prone [prəʊn]　　　　　　　　　　　　　　　　　　　[同] ②inclined

adj. likely to suffer from sth. or to do sth. 易于遭受的；有做(坏事)的倾向的

Working without a break makes you more ***prone*** to error. 连续工作不停歇使人更容易出错。

proofread [ˈpruːfˌriːd]

v. to read and correct a piece of written or printed work 校阅；校对

Has this document been ***proofread***? 这份文件校对过没有？

prophet [ˈprɒfɪt]　　　　　　　　　　　　　　　　　[同] foreteller

n. a person who claims to know what will happen in the future 预言家；预言者

Mohammed is the ***prophet*** of the Muslims. 穆罕默德是穆斯林的先知。

retrieve [rɪˈtriːv]　　　　　　　　　　　　　　[同] recover, get back

v. (fml.) to bring or get sth. back, esp. from a place where it should not be 取回；索回

The police have managed to ***retrieve*** some of the stolen money. 警方已经追回了部分被盗钱款。

retrospect [ˈretrəspekt]　　　　　　　　　　　　　　[同] review

n. thinking about a past event or situation, often with a different opinion of it from the one you had at the time 回顾；追溯往事

In ***retrospect***, it's easy to see the futility of such actions. 回顾起来，很容易看出这些行动是没用的。

style [staɪl]　　　　　　　　　　　　　　　　　[近] manner, way

n. a particular way of doing, designing, or producing sth. 风格；方式

Car ***styles*** have changed radically in the past 20 years. 汽车款式在过去的 20 年间发生了根本性的变化。

| **sublime** | [sə'blaɪm] | [同] lofty, exalted |

adj. of the greatest, most admirable kind; causing awe and reverence 伟大的；崇高的；令人崇敬的

This man could write ***sublime*** music at will. 这个人可以任意写出令人赞叹的音乐。

| **subordinate** | [sə'bɔːdɪnət] | [近] secondary |

adj. lower in rank or position 级别或职位较低的；下级的

He was always friendly to his ***subordinate*** officers. 他对下级官员一向和蔼可亲。

| **subtle** | ['sʌtl] | [同] delicate |

adj. (esp. approv.) not easy to detect or describe; fine; delicate 难以察觉或描述的；细微的；精细的

a ***subtle*** distinction 细微的差别

| **succinct** | [sək'sɪŋkt] | [同] terse |

adj. expressed briefly and clearly; concise 简明的；简洁的；简要的

a ***succinct*** summary of the argument 论点的概要

| **treasury** | ['treʒəri] | |

n. government department that controls public revenue (英国及其他一些国家的)财政部

The ***Treasury*** is the part of the government which collects and pays out the government money. 财政部是政府的一个部门，负责政府的财政收支。

| **wildlife** | ['waɪldlaɪf] | |

n. animals, birds, insects, etc. that are wild and live in a natural environment 野生动物；野生生物

Development of the area would endanger ***wildlife***. 开发这一地区将会危及野生生物。

| **withstand** | [wɪð'stænd] | [同] sustain |

v. (fml.) to be strong enough not to be hurt or damaged by extreme conditions, the use of force, etc. 承受；经受住

They had ***withstood*** siege, hunger and deprivation. 他们经受了围困、饥饿和贫穷。

Take the Test ▶▶

句子翻译

1) 新负责人的任命引起了很大的争议。(controversy)

_____

2) 即食食品卖得很好，因为它们很方便。(convenience)

_____

3) 这个问题在可预见的将来能获得解决。(foreseeable)

_____

4) 低热量且营养均衡的饮食可以延年益寿。(longevity)

_____

5) 回顾起来，很容易看出这种行动是没用的。(retrospect)

_____

assert [əˈsɜːt]   [同] maintain

v. to make others recognize（sth.）by behaving firmly and confidently 坚定而有信心地使别人认识到(某事物)；坚持

An autocratic leader is a manager who *asserts* his or her authority in an autocratic manner. 一个专制的领导是以一种专制的方式维持着他(或她)的权威的管理者。

assertive [əˈsɜːtɪv]   [反] acquiescent

adj. showing a strong and confident personality; asserting oneself 坚定而有信心的

an *assertive* young man 有自信心的年轻人

asset [ˈæset]

n. a valuable or useful quality, skill or person 有价值的或有用的特性、技能或人物

Good health is a great *asset*. 健康就是莫大的财富。

buoyant [ˈbɔɪənt]

adj.（of prices, business activity, etc.）tending to increase or stay at a high level, usually showing financial success（价格、商业活动等）看涨的, 保持高价的；繁荣的

a *buoyant* economy/market 繁荣的经济 / 市场

bureaucracy [bjʊˈrɒkrəsi]

n. the system of official rules and ways of doing things that a government or an organization has, esp. when these seem to be too complicated 官僚主义；官僚作风

The company's huge *bureaucracy* limits creativity and independent thinking. 公司内盛行的官僚作风限制了员工的创造力和独立思考能力。

coordinator [kəʊˈɔːdɪneɪtə]

n. person who coordinates 协调人

The campaign needs an effective *coordinator*. 该运动需要一个有能力的协调人。

correlate [ˈkɒrəleɪt]

v. to have a mutual relation or connection, esp. of affecting or depending on each other 相关或相互关联

Being well educated is positively *correlated* with a decline in birth rate. 接受良好的教育与出生率的降低之间存在着相关性。

corridor [ˈkɒrɪdɔː(r)]   [同] passage

n. long narrow passage, from which doors open into rooms or compartments 过道；走廊

A *corridor* led from the old schoolrooms to a modern building. 一条走廊从旧教室通向一座现代化的大楼。

corrupt [kəˈrʌpt]

v. to have a bad effect on sb. and make them behave in an immoral or dishonest way 使堕落，腐化；贿赂

young people whose morals have been *corrupted* 道德败坏的年轻人

cosmopolitan [ˌkɒzmə'pɒlɪtən]　　　　　　　　　　　　　　　　　[同] universal

adj. containing people from all over the world 世界性的；有各国人的
a vibrant, *cosmopolitan* city 一个生机盎然的国际化都市

counterpart ['kaʊntəpɑːt]　　　　　　　　　　　　　　　　　　[近] correlate

n. person or thing that corresponds to or has the same function as sb. or sth. else 相对应或具有相同功能的人或物
The sales director phoned her *counterpart* in the other firm. 销售部的女经理给另一家公司的销售部经理打了电话。

doom [duːm]　　　　　　　　　　　　　　　　　　　　　　[近] fate, destiny

n. death or destruction; any terrible event that you cannot avoid 死亡；毁灭；劫数
Less than three years ago, *doom* merchants were predicting that the growth in video games and the rise of the Internet would sound the death knell for children's literature. 不到三年前，悲观的预言家们预言说电视游戏的发展和网络的兴起将为儿童文学敲响丧钟。

drastic ['dræstɪk]

adj. extreme in a way that has a sudden, serious or violent effect on sth. 极端的；急剧的；严厉的
The government is keen on taking a *drastic* step to curb the use of plastics. 政府急切地采取严格措施以限制塑料袋的使用。

dreadful ['dredful]

adj. very bad or unpleasant 糟糕透顶的；讨厌的
What *dreadful* weather! 多么讨厌的天气！

exotic [ig'zɒtɪk]　　　　　　　　　　　　　　　　　　　　　　[近] foreign

adj. from or in another country, esp. a tropical one; seeming exciting and unusual because it is connected with foreign countries 来自异国的(尤指热带国家的)；奇异的；异国情调的
She travels to all kinds of *exotic* locations all over the world. 她走遍了全世界所有具有奇异风情的地方。

expatriate [ˌeks'pætriət]　　　　　　　　　　　　　　　　　　[反] repatriate

n. a person living in a country that is not their own 居住在国外的人；侨民
American *expatriates* in Paris 居住在巴黎的美国人

life expectancy [laɪfɪk'spektənsi]

n. the length of time that a person or animal is expected to live 预计寿命；平均寿命
The research establishes a link between levels of education and *life expectancy*. 研究确立了受教育水平和平均寿命间的关系。

formidable ['fɔːmɪdəbl]　　　　　　　　[同] fearful [反] comforting

adj. causing fear or great anxiety; frightening; awesome 引起恐慌或不安的；可怕的；可畏的
a *formidable* appearance/look/prospect 可怕的外表 / 神情 / 景象

horizontal [ˌhɒrɪ'zɒntl]

adj. parallel to the horizon; flat; level 与地平线平行的；平的；水平的
The wine bottles should be kept in a *horizontal* position. 盛有酒的瓶子应该水平放置。

interval ['ɪntəvl]　　　　　　　　　　　　　　　　　[同] break, interlude

n. time between two events (两件事中的)间隔时间
the *interval* between a flash of lightning and the sound of thunder 闪电和雷声之间的间隙

intervene [ˌɪntə'viːn]　　　　　　　　　　　　　　　[同] step in, interpose *v.* (fml.) to come or be between (指时间)进入，介入，在其间

Although the lives of the Siriono have changed in the ***intervening*** decades, the image of them as Stone Age relics has endured. 尽管在这期间的数十年里，西里奥诺人的生活改变了很多，但他们作为石器时代遗迹的形象始终如一。

intervention [ˌɪntəˈvenʃn]

n. (instance of) interfering or becoming involved, e.g. to prevent sth. happening 干涉，干预，介入(如阻止某事发生)

Early ***intervention*** can save the lives of many women who get breast cancer. 如果早点采取行动，可以挽救很多患乳腺癌的妇女的生命。

mortgage [ˈmɔːɡɪdʒ]

n. a legal agreement by which a bank or similar organization lends you money to buy a house, etc., and you pay the money back over a particular number of years; the sum of money that you borrow 按揭(由银行等提供房产抵押借款)；按揭贷款

monthly ***mortgage*** repayments 每月偿还的按揭贷款

motif [məʊˈtiːf]　　　　　　　　　　　　　　　　　　[同] leitmotiv, subject

n. a subject, an idea or a phrase that is repeated and developed in a work of literature or a piece of music (文学作品或音乐的)主题；主旨；动机

colour ***motif*** 色彩基调

notation [nəʊˈteɪʃn]　　　　　　　　　　　　　　　　　　　　　　[同] note

n. a system of signs or symbols used to represent information, esp. in mathematics, science, and music (数学、科学和音乐等中的)符号；记号；谱号

scientific ***notation*** 科学记号

orthodox [ˈɔːθədɒks]　　　　　　　　　　　　[同] accepted [反] unorthodox

adj. (having beliefs, opinions, etc. that are) generally accepted or approved 持普遍赞同的信仰、见解等的；规范的；公认的

orthodox behaviour 合乎传统的行为

proponent [prəˈpəʊnənt]　　　　　　　　[同] exponent, supporter [反] opponent

n. (fml.) a person who supports an idea or course of action 倡导者；支持者

one of the leading ***proponents*** of the Channel Tunnel 修建英吉利海峡隧道的主要倡议者之一

proposition [ˌprɒpəˈzɪʃn]　　　　　　　　　　　　　　　　　[同] proposal

n. a statement that expresses an opinion 见解；主张；观点

Her assessment is based on the ***proposition*** that power corrupts. 她的分析是建立在权力使人腐化的观点上的。

revision [rɪˈvɪʒn]

n. a change or set of changes to sth. (一项、一轮等)修订；修改

He made some minor ***revisions*** to the report before printing it out. 在将报告打印出来之前，他做了一些小小的修改。

revival [rɪˈvaɪvl]　　　　　　　　　　　　　　　　　　　　　　[同] rebirth

n. an improvement in the condition or strength of sth. (状况或力量的)进步；复苏

the patient's speedy ***revival*** after her operation 病人在手术后的迅速康复

revive [rɪˈvaɪv]　　　　　　　　　　　　　　　　　　　　　　　[同] recover

v. to make sth. start being used or done again 重新使用；使重做

It is too soon to predict the future of these ***revived*** languages. 现在对这些恢复使用的语言的未

来做预言还为时过早。

substantial [səbˈstænʃl]　　　　　　　　　　　　　　　　　　　[同] significant

adj. large in amount; considerable 数目大的；可观的

Her contribution to the discussion was ***substantial***. 她在讨论中做了很多工作。

suffice [səˈfaɪs]　　　　　　　　　　　　　　　　　　　　　　[同] serve

v.（fml.）to be enough 满足；足够用

These few examples should ***suffice*** to illustrate how social attitudes are changing. 这几个例子应该足以说明人们的态度正在发生什么样的变化。

suntan [ˈsʌntæn]

n. browning of the skin from exposing it to the sun（皮肤的）晒黑

We need to bring ***suntan*** lotion and something to protect our head from the sun. 我们需要带防晒霜和一些其他东西以防止头部晒伤。

trespass [ˈtrespəs]　　　　　　　　　　　　　　　　　　[同] encroach, invade

v. to enter sb.'s land or property without his/her permission or other authority 非法侵入某人地界

He accused me of ***trespassing*** on his estate. 他控告我擅自闯入他的庄园。

triangle [ˈtraɪæŋgl]

n. geometric figure with three straight sides and three angles 三角形

His nose was a small ***triangle*** on his wide face. 他的鼻子在宽大的脸庞上如同一个小三角形。

utility [juːˈtɪləti]　　　　　　　　　　　　　　　　　　　　　　[同] use

n.（fml.）the quality of being useful 实用；效用

I have severe doubts about the ***utility*** of examinations on subjects which have been learned parrot-fashion. 我很怀疑对那些通过鹦鹉学舌一样机械模仿学来的科目进行考试到底有什么用。

variation [ˌveərɪˈeɪʃn]　　　　　　　　　　　　　　　　[同] change, alteration

n. the act, process, or result of varying 变化，变更

Human genetic similarity greatly outweighs the ***variations***. 人类遗传的相似性远远大于其变异性。

Take the Test ≫

句子翻译

1）公司内盛行的官僚作风限制了员工的创造力和独立思考能力。（bureaucracy）

_____

2）接受良好的教育与出生率的降低之间存在着相关性。（correlate）

_____

3）政府急切地要采取严格措施以限制塑料袋的使用。（drastic）

_____

4）现在对这些恢复使用的语言的未来做预言还为时过早。（revive）

_____

5）这几个例子应该足以说明人们的态度正在发生什么样的变化。（suffice）

assimilate [əˈsɪməleɪt]　　　　　　　　　　　　　　　　　　　　　　　[同] absorb

v. (cause sth.) to become absorbed into the body after digestion（使某物）经消化而吸收

Some foods *assimilate*/are *assimilated* more easily than others. 有些食物比另一些食物更容易吸收。

assure [əˈʃʊə(r)]　　　　　　　　　　　　　　　　　　　　　　　[同] reassure, ensure

v. to tell (sb.) positively or confidently 明确地或有信心地告诉（某人）；向（某人）保证

If you buy a Japanese car or motor bike you can rest *assured* that it will rarely, if ever, go wrong. 如果你买的是一辆日本的汽车或摩托车，你完全可以高枕无忧，因为它几乎从来不会发生故障。

astronomer [əˈstrɒnəmə(r)]

n. a person who studies or is an expert in astronomy 天文学家

Some *astronomers* suggested that there might be an undiscovered planet. 一些天文学家提出可能存在一颗尚未被发现的行星。

burgeon [ˈbɜːdʒən]　　　　　　　　　　　　　　　　　　　　　　[反] increase, blossom

v. to begin to grow or develop rapidly 激增；发展

An array of professionals have developed to service the *burgeoning* tourist industry. 一批专职人员已经涌现出来服务于蓬勃发展的旅游业。

counter-productive [ˌkaʊtəprəˈdʌktɪv]

adj. having the opposite effect to that intended 产生相反效果的；适得其反的；事与愿违的

It's *counter-productive* to be too tough: It just makes the staff resentful. 过于严厉则适得其反：使全体工作人员愤愤不平。

coupon [ˈkuːpɒn]

n. small, usu. detachable, piece of paper that gives the holder the right to do or receive sth. 证明持有人有做某事或获得某物之权利的票据（通常可撕下）；优惠券

10p off if you use this *coupon* 凭此券可优惠 10 便士

courageous [kəˈreɪdʒəs]　　　　　　　　　　　　　　　　　　　　　　[同] brave

adj. brave; fearless 勇敢的；无畏的

a *courageous* decision 一个勇敢的决定

courteous [ˈkɜːtiəs]　　　　　　　　　　　　[同] civil, genteel [反] discourteous

adj. having or showing good manners; polite 彬彬有礼的；客气的

Airline staff must be *courteous* at all times, even when passengers are not. 航空公司职员必须时刻对乘客彬彬有礼，即便有时一些乘客可能会很无礼。

craftsman [ˈkrɑːftsmən]

n. skilled workman, esp. one who makes things by hand 匠人；能工巧匠（尤指手艺人）

The original designs were made by highly skilled *craftsmen*. 最初的设计是由技术高超的工匠完成的。

crash [kræʃ]

adj. done intensively to achieve quick results 突击式的；速成的

We have a 12-week intensive course, three hours three nights a week—that's our *crash* course! 我们的精读课程每晚上 3 小时，一周上 3 次，一直持续 12 周——那是我们的速成课程。

dropout ['drɒpaʊt]

n. a person who leaves school or college before they have finished their studies 辍学者；退学者

They spend ever more on public education, yet test scores and *dropout* rates barely budge. 他们在公立教育上花了更多的钱，但考试成绩和辍学率基本没什么变化。

drought [draʊt]

n. a long period of time when there is little or no rain 久旱；旱灾

one of the worst *droughts* on record 有记载以来最严重的旱灾之一

expedient [ɪk'spiːdiənt]   [同] resource

n. an action that is useful or necessary for a particular purpose, but not always fair or right 权宜之计；应急办法

The disease was controlled by the simple *expedient* of not allowing anyone to leave the city. 通过禁止任何人出城的简单应急办法使疾病得到了控制。

expedition [ˌekspɪ'dɪʃn]   [近] journey

n. an organized journey with a particular purpose, esp. to find out about a place that is not well known 远征；探险；考察

go on an *expedition* to the North Pole 去北极探险

expenditure [ɪk'spendɪtʃə(r)]   [同] expense, cost

n. the act of spending or using money; an amount of money spent 花销；消费；开支

plans to increase *expenditure* on health and education 增加健康和教育费用的计划

hormone ['hɔːməʊn]

n. substance produced within the body of an animal and carried by the blood to an organ which it stimulates to assist growth 激素；荷尔蒙

hormone deficiency/imbalance 激素缺乏 / 失调

intricate ['ɪntrɪkət]   [同] complex, complicated

adj. made up of many small parts put together in a complex way, and therefore difficult to follow or understand 错综复杂的

a novel with an *intricate* plot 情节错综复杂的小说

intuition [ˌɪntjuˈɪʃn]

n. (power of) understanding things (e.g. a situation, sb.'s feelings) immediately, without the need for conscious reasoning or study 直觉；直觉力

Nobody told me where to find you. It was sheer *intuition*. 没有人告诉我到哪儿去找你，我纯粹是凭直觉找到你的。

intuitively [ɪn'tjuːɪtɪvli]

adv. coming from intuition 直觉；来自直觉地

If you look at the word 'like', you may *intuitively* think that the first and most frequent meaning is the verb. 当你看到 like 这个词时，你会直接想到这个词最直接以及最常用的意思是用作动词。

lease [liːs]

n. contract by which the owner of land, a building, etc. allows another person to use it for a specified time, usu. in return for rent（土地、房屋等的）租约

When does the *lease* expire? 租约什么时候期满?

lucrative [ˈluːkrətɪv]   [同] advantageous, profitable

adj. producing a large amount of money; making a large profit 赚大钱的; 获利的

Catering is a very *lucrative* business if you succeed in it. 如果你能做起来的话, 餐饮业绝对有利可图。

mould [məʊld]

n. a container that you pour a soft liquid or substance into, which then becomes solid in the same shape as the container 模具; 铸模

The glass sags through the holes and into waiting *moulds*. 玻璃从洞里落下来, 掉入接在下面的模具里。

muddle [ˈmʌdl]   [同] disorder

v. to put things in the wrong order or mix them up 弄乱; 搅混

Their letters were all *muddled* up together in a drawer. 他们的信都乱七八糟地放在一个抽屉里。

nourishing [ˈnʌrɪʃɪŋ]   [同] nutritious

adj. of or providing nourishment 有营养的; 滋养多的

A simple chicken soup is both *nourishing* and delicious. 简简单单的一份鸡汤既营养又美味。

outcry [ˈaʊtkraɪ]   [同] protest, commotion

n. strong public protest 公开的强烈抗议

There was a public *outcry* about the building of a new airport. 公众强烈反对修建新机场。

prose [prəʊz]

n. writing that is not poetry 散文

the author's clear elegant *prose* 那个作家清雅的散文

prospective [prəˈspektɪv]

adj. expected to do sth. or to become sth. 有望的; 预期的

a *prospective* buyer/client 潜在的买主 / 客户

prosperity [prɒˈsperəti]   [同] boom, abundance [反] adversity

n. the state of being successful, esp. financially 兴旺; 繁荣

The country is enjoying a period of peace and *prosperity*. 国家正值国泰民安、繁荣昌盛的时期。

rewarding [rɪˈwɔːdɪŋ]

adj. (of an activity, etc.) worth doing; that makes you happy because you think it is useful or important 值得做的; 有益的

Teaching is not very financially *rewarding*. 教书不会有很高的经济报酬。

rhetoric [ˈretərɪk]

n. (fml.) speech or writing that is intended to influence people, but that is not completely honest or sincere 华而不实的言语; 花言巧语

Whether they can live up to their campaign *rhetoric* remains to be seen. 他们能否实践竞选时发表的冠冕堂皇的诺言尚待日后分晓。

rigorous [ˈrɪgərəs]   [同] strict

adj. (fml.) demanding that particular rules, processes, etc. should be strictly followed 严格的; 严厉的

The work failed to meet their *rigorous* standards. 工作没有达到他们的严格标准。

superb [sjuːˈpɜːb]   [同] outstanding

adj. excellent; splendid 卓越的；杰出的；极好的

The sports facilities are *superb*. 运动设施是第一流的。

superfluous [sjuːˈpɜːfluəs]   [同] excess

adj. more than is needed or wanted 过多的；多余的；不必要的

The crowd was so well-behaved that the police presence was *superfluous*. 群众秩序良好，警方并无必要在场。

superstitious [ˌsuːpəˈstɪʃəs]

adj. of, based on or caused by superstition 迷信的；无充分根据的说法的

superstitious beliefs/ideas/practices 迷信的说法 / 想法 / 做法

"I'm not superstitious either, but those were the three days Harris wore his lucky socks."

supervisor [ˈsuːpəvaɪzə(r)]

n. person who supervises 监督人；管理人；指导人

This type of system requires *supervisors* to watch over the workers. 这种系统要求有管理者监督工人。

trim [trɪm]   [近] cut, crop

v. to make (sth.) neat or smooth by cutting away irregular parts 使(某物)整齐或光滑；整修，修剪

trim the top of a hedge 修剪树篱

turbulent [ˈtɜːbjʊlənt]   [同] disorderly

adj. in which there is a lot of sudden change, confusion, disagreement and sometimes violence 动乱的；混乱的

a *turbulent* part of the world 世界上动荡不安的地区

vegetation [ˌvedʒɪˈteɪʃn]

n. plants in general, esp. the plants that are found in a particular area or environment （统称）植物；(尤指某地或环境的)植被，植物群落

The samples are also analyzed to assess the ability of the soil or subsoil material to support *vegetation*. 这些样本的分析也是为了评估表层土壤和下层土壤保护植被的能力。

Take the Test ≫

词组翻译

辍学率 _____ 严格标准 _____

句子翻译

1) 过于严厉则适得其反：使全体工作人员愤愤不平。(counter-productive)

_____

2) 如果你能做起来的话，餐饮业绝对有利可图。(lucrative)

_____

3) 国家正值国泰民安、繁荣昌盛的时期。(prosperity)

_____

4) 教书不会有很高的经济报酬。(rewarding)

_____

asymmetry [ˌeɪ'sɪmətri]   [反] symmetry

n. state of not having parts that correspond to each other in size, shape, etc.; lacking symmetry 不对称

Two American researchers studied the brains of human embryos and discovered that the left-right *asymmetry* exists before birth. 两位美国研究人员研究了人类胚胎的大脑，发现了脑部的左右不对称现象在出生前就已经存在。

athletic [æθ'letɪk]   [近] ①muscular

adj. ①physically strong and good at sport 强壮的，有运动细胞的 ②relating to athletics 运动的

To date, however, biomechanics has made only a small difference to *athletic* performance. 然而，到目前为止，生物机械学在改善（运动员的）竞技表现方面的作用还很有限。

attainment [ə'teɪnmənt]   [同] acquirement, achievement

n. success in achieving sth. or reaching a particular level 获得，成就

Key rewards such as pay increases and promotions should be allocated for the *attainment* of the employee's specific goals. 像涨薪和晋升这样的重要奖励应该给那些完成了特定目标的员工。

buzzword ['bʌzwɜːd]

n. a word or phrase, esp. one connected with a particular subject, that has become fashionable and popular and is used a lot in newspapers, etc. (报刊等的)时髦术语；流行行话

Flexibility became another corporate *buzzword*. 灵活性成了商界的又一个时髦术语。

creativity [ˌkriːeɪ'tɪvəti]

n. the ability to use your imagination to produce new ideas, make things, etc. 创造力

Teachers have been attacked for stifling *creativity* in their pupils. 教师已被指责扼杀学生的创造力。

credibility [ˌkred'bɪləti]

n. the quality of deserving to be believed and trusted 可信度

'Inuit Qaujimajatuqangit' has had much more *credibility* and weight in recent years. "因纽特人智慧"近年来日益受到人们的信任和重视。

crew [kruː]   [同] group

n. group of people working together 一套工作班子；队；组

a camera *crew* 电影(或电视)摄制组

cripple ['krɪpl]   [同] ①maim ②weaken

v. ①to hurt sb. badly so that they cannot walk properly 致残 ②to damage sth. badly so that it no longer works or is no longer effective 破坏，损坏(通常用于被动语态)

a ship *crippled* by a storm 在暴风雨中受到毁坏的船只

criterion [kraɪ'tɪəriən]   [同] standard

n. standard by which sth. is judged（评判的）标准，尺度

Success in making money is not always a good *criterion* of success in life. 能挣钱并不一定是衡量人生是否成功的好标准。

dub [dʌb]　　　　　　　　　　　　　　　　　　　　　　　[近] name, title

v. to give sb./sth. a particular name, often in a humorous or critical way 把…戏称为；给…起绰号

The Belgian actor Jean Claude Van Damme has been *dubbed* 'muscles from Brussels'. 比利时演员让·克劳德·范·达默一直被戏称为"布鲁塞尔的肌肉"。

dubious [ˈdjuːbiəs]　　　　　　　　　　　　　　　　　　[同] doubtful

adj. not certain and slightly suspicious about sth.; not knowing whether sth. is good or bad 怀疑的；无把握的；拿不准的

I was rather *dubious* about the whole idea. 我对这整个想法持怀疑态度。

experimentation [ɪkˌsperɪmenˈteɪʃn]　　　　　　　　　[同] experiment

n. the process of testing various ideas, methods, etc. to find out how good or effective they are 试验；检验

Many people object to *experimentation* on animals. 很多人反对拿动物做试验。

expertise [ˌekspɜːˈtiːz]　　　　　　　　　　　　　　　　[同] know-how

n. expert knowledge or skill in a particular subject, activity or job 专门知识；专门技能；专长

We have the *expertise* to help you run your business. 我们有专门知识来帮助你经营自己业务。

fragile [ˈfrædʒaɪl]　　　　　　　　　　　　　　　　　　[同] delicate

adj. easily damaged or broken; delicate 易受伤害的；易碎的；易损的

Human happiness is so *fragile*. 人生幸福易逝。

frail [freɪl]　　　　　　　　　　　　　　　　　　　　　[同] weak, feeble

adj. (of a person) physically weak or delicate（指人）体弱的，虚弱的

At 90, she's getting very old and *frail*. 她90岁时变得非常衰老、虚弱。

hospitality [ˌhɒspɪˈtæləti]

n. friendly and generous reception and entertainment of guests or strangers, esp. in one's own home 殷勤待客；好客

Thank you for your kind *hospitality*. 谢谢你的盛情款待。

invalid [ɪnˈvælɪd]　　　　　　　　[同] null, void [反] valid

adj. not legally or officially acceptable 无效的

This passport is *invalid*. Look at the expiry date. 这个护照是无效的。看看它的有效期。

invalidate [ɪnˈvælɪdeɪt]　　　　　　　　　　　　　　　[同] nullify

v. to make (sth.) invalid 使（某事物）无效或作废

The Educational Testing Service *invalidated* the scores of 18 students. 教育考试中心取消了18名学生的成绩。

invaluable [ɪnˈvæljuəbl]　　　　　　　　　　　　　　　[同] precious

adj. of value too high to be measured; extremely valuable 价值高得无法估量的；极宝贵的

It is an *invaluable* way of informing the latest news. 这是个能提供最新消息的宝贵渠道。

luminary [ˈluːmɪnəri]　　　　　　　　　　　　　[同] notable, big name

n. a person who is an expert or a great influence in a special area or activity 专家；权威

leading *luminary* of the arts 艺术上最杰出的人物

multifaceted [ˌmʌltɪˈfæsɪtɪd]

adj. having many different aspects to be considered 多方面的；要从多方面考虑的

a complex and ***multifaceted*** problem 一个复杂的需从多方面考虑的问题

novice [ˈnɒvɪs]　　　　　　　　　　　　　[同] beginner, freshman [反] old hand

n. a person who is new and has little experience in a skill, job or situation 新手；初学者

I'm a complete ***novice*** at skiing. 滑雪我完全是新手。

outfit [ˈaʊtˌfɪt]　　　　　　　　　　　　　　　　　　[同] equipment

n. all the equipment or articles needed for a particular purpose; kit 全套装备；全套工具；全部用品

a complete car-repair ***outfit*** 修理汽车用的整套工具

prosperous [ˈprɒspərəs]　　　　　　　　　　　　　　　[同] thriving

adj. rich and successful 成功的；繁荣的

Farmers are more ***prosperous*** in the south of the country. 这个国家南部的农民较富裕。

prototype [ˈprəʊtətaɪp]　　　　　　　　　　　　　　　[同] original

n. the first design of sth. from which other forms are copied or developed 原型；雏形

a ***prototype*** of modern bicycle 现代自行车的雏形

provided [prəˈvaɪdɪd]

conj. used to say what must happen or be done to make it possible for sth. else to happen 假如；在…条件下

We'll buy everything you produce, ***provided*** of course the price is right. 当然，倘若价格合适，我们将采购你们的全部产品。

ripen [ˈraɪpən]　　　　　　　　　　　　　　　　　　[同] mature

v. to become ripe; to make sth. ripe (使)成熟

Once you cut the bunch, the bananas stop growing but they do continue to ***ripen***. 一旦你把一串香蕉割开，它们就会停止生长，不过仍会成熟。

spur [spə:(r)]　　　　　　　　　　　　　[同] stimulation

n. thing that urges a person on to greater activity; incentive 激励因素；刺激；鞭策

This book is a ***spur*** to the child's imagination. 这本书能促进孩子的想像力。

on the ***spur*** of the moment 当场；临时

suppress [səˈpres]　　　　　　　　　　　　　　　　[同] restrain

v. to prevent (sth.) from being known or seen 防止(某事物)被人知道或看到；禁止发表(某事物)

suppress the truth about sth. 隐瞒某事的真相

surmount [səˈmaʊnt]　　　　　　　　　　　　　　　[同] overcome

v. to deal with (a difficulty, etc.); overcome 克服(困难等)；战胜

We had many problems to ***surmount*** before we could start the project. 在我们着手做这项工作前得克服许多困难。

surrounding [səˈraʊndɪŋ]

adj. that is around and nearby 周围附近的

York and the ***surrounding*** countryside 约克城及其近郊

susceptible [səˈseptəbl]　　　　　　　　　　　[同] sentient, impressible

adj. easily influenced or harmed by sth. 易受某事物影响或损害的

highly ***susceptible*** to flattery 听几句好话就忘乎所以的

turmoil [ˈtɜːmɔɪl] [同] commotion

n. a state of great anxiety, confusion and uncertainty 动乱；混乱；焦虑

His statement threw the court into *turmoil*. 他的陈述使得法庭陷入一片混乱。

tweak [twiːk]

v. ① to suddenly pull or twist sth. 拧；捏；揪 ② to make small changes to a machine, vehicle, or system in order to improve the way it works 改进；微调

This focus is on individuals, *tweaking* performances to squeeze an extra hundredth of a second here, an extra millimetre there. 工作核心以人为本，其目的在于改善工作表现来提高哪怕是百分之一秒的速度或者一毫米的成绩。

ventilation [ˌventɪˈleɪʃn]

n. the act of allowing the fresh air to enter the room to make the bad air, etc. out 通风；流通空气

Make sure that there is adequate *ventilation* in the room before using the paint. 在使用油漆前确保室内通风充足。

verbal [ˈvɜːbl] [同] spoken

adj. relating to words 文字的；词语的

The job applicant must have good *verbal* skills. 这份工作的应征者必须具有良好的语言表达能力。

womb [wuːm]

n. the organ in women and female animals in which babies develop before they are born 子宫

from the *womb* to the tomb 从生到死

VERBAL 35%

NONVERBAL 65%
Facial Expressions
Tone of Voice
Movement
Appearance
Eye Contact
Gestures
Posture

wording [ˈwɜːdɪŋ] [同] diction

n. the words that are used in a piece of writing or speech, esp. when they have been carefully chosen 措辞；用词

The *wording* was deliberately ambiguous. 这里的措辞故意模棱两可。

Take the Test

句子翻译

1）灵活性成了商界的又一个时髦术语。（buzzword）

_____

2）能挣钱并不一定是衡量人生是否成功的好标准。（criterion）

_____

3）很多人反对拿动物做试验。（object）

_____

4）当然，倘若价格合适，我们将采购你们的全部产品。（provided）

_____

auction [ˈɔːkʃn]

n. method of selling things in which each item is sold to the person who offers the most money for it 拍卖(方式)

The house will be sold by *auction*. 这所房子将要拍卖。

audacious [ɔːˈdeɪʃəs]　　　　　　　　　　　　　　　　　　　[同] adventurous, brave

adj. showing a willingness to take risks; daring; fearless 有冒险精神的；大胆的

an *audacious* scheme 大胆的计划

audio-visual [ˌɔːdiəʊ ˈviʒʊəl]

adj. involving the use of recorded pictures and sound 视听的

audio-visual media 视听媒体

by and large used when making a general statement 总的来说　　　[同] generally, on the whole

National governments, *by and large*, kept a much firmer hand on truck and railroad tariffs than on charges for ocean freight. 总的来说，各国政府对公路和铁路运输关税的控制要比海运严格得多。

crown [kraʊn]　　　　　　　　　　　　　　　　　　　　　　　　　　　[近] top

n. ornamental headdress made of gold, jewels, etc. worn by a king or queen on official occasions 王冠；皇冠

crown land/property 国王的土地 / 财产

cue [kjuː]　　　　　　　　　　　　　　　　　　　　　　　　　　　　[同] hint

n. thing said or done to signal sb.'s turn to say or do sth., esp. in a theatrical or other performance 提示，暗示

When I nod my head, that's your *cue* to interrupt the meeting. 我一点头, 就是暗示你把会议中断。

cuisine [kwɪˈziːn]

n. (style of) cooking 烹饪(风味)

a restaurant where the *cuisine* is excellent 饭菜精美的餐馆

duplicate [ˈdjuːplɪkeit]　　　　　　　　　　　[同] ①②copy, double

① *v.* to make an exact copy of sth. 复制；复印

a *duplicated* form 复制的表格

② *n.* [ˈdjuːplɪkət] one of two or more things that are the same in every detail 完全一样的东西；复制品；副本

Is this a *duplicate* or the original? 这是副本还是正本？

dweller [ˈdwelə(r)]　　　　　　　　　　　　　　　　　　　　[反] inhabitant

n. a person or an animal that lives in the particular place that is mentioned 居民；居住者

apartment *dwellers* 公寓房客

exploration [ˌekspləˈreɪʃn]

n. the act of travelling through a place in order to find out about it 探究；研究；探测

the *exploration* of space 太空探索

exposure [ɪkˈspəʊʒə(r)]   [近] openness

n. the state of being in a place or situation where there is no protection from sth. harmful or unpleasant 面临，遭受（危险或不快）

prolonged *exposure* to harmful radiation 长时间接触有害辐射

exquisite [ˈekskwɪzɪt]   [同] choice

adj. extremely beautiful or carefully made 精美的；精致的

Her wedding dress was absolutely *exquisite*. 她的婚纱真是漂亮极了。

forge [fɔːdʒ]   [同] make, build

v. ① to shape（sth.）by heating it in a fire and hammering 锻造；打铁 ② to develop sth. new, especially a strong relationship with other people, groups, or countries 形成

forge ahead 进展良好

Growing environmental fears have made climate research all the more important, and Europe is *forging* ahead in this field. 对环境的日益担心使得气候研究更为重要，欧洲在这个领域进展顺利。

fraught [frɔːt]

adj. filled with sth.; charged with sth. 充满某事物的；注入某事物的

a silence *fraught* with meaning 意味深长的沉默

freelance [ˈfriːlɑːns]

n. independent artist, writer, etc. who earns his living by selling work to several employers（靠出卖作品为生的）自由艺术家、作家等

a *freelance* journalist 自由新闻工作者

frequency [ˈfriːkwənsi]

n. the number of times that sth. happens within a particular period of time or within a particular group of people 频率

the *frequency* of serious road accidents 重大交通事故的频率

humiliate [hjuːˈmɪlieɪt]

v. to make（sb.）feel ashamed or disgraced; to lower the dignity or self-respect of 使（某人）感到耻辱或不光彩；使丧失尊严或自尊

He felt *humiliated* by her scornful remarks. 他听到她那些嘲讽的话而感到屈辱。

invariable [ɪnˈveəriəbl]   [同] fixed [反] variable

adj. never changing; always the same; constant 永久不变的；始终如一的

His *invariable* answer was ‘Wait and see.’ 他的回答总是“等等看”。

inventive [ɪnˈventɪv]   [同] creative, ingenious

adj. having or showing the ability to invent things and think originally 善于发明创造的；具有创造性思考能力的

The Spoken Corpus computer shows how *inventive* and humorous people are when they are using language by twisting familiar phrases for effect. 口语语料库电脑显示出人们为达到某种效果而扭曲常用词组时所展现的创造力和幽默感。

inventory [ˈɪnvəntri]   [近] reserve

n. detailed list, e.g. of goods, furniture, jobs to be done 详细目录，清单

We made an *inventory* of everything in the apartment. 我们列了一份公寓物品清单。

multitude [ˈmʌltɪtjuːd]   [同] crowd [反] none

n. an extremely large number of things or people 众多；大量

One of the **multitudes** of problems faced by engineers of artificial hearts is regulating the blood flow. 人造心脏专家面临的大量问题之一是如何调节血液流动。

nuance [ˈnjuːɑːns]   [近] gradation

n. a very slight difference in meaning, sound, colour or sb.'s feelings that is not usually very obvious 细微差别

subtle **nuances** of meaning 意思的细微差别

overdraft [ˈəʊvədrɑːft]

n. the amount of money that you owe to a bank when you have spent more money than the money in your bank account 透支额

pay off an **overdraft** 偿还透支款

provision [prəˈvɪʒn]   [同] condition, supply

n. the act of supplying sb. with sth. that they need or want; sth. that is supplied 供给；供给品

The government is responsible for the **provision** of health care. 政府负责提供医疗服务。

proximity [prɒkˈsɪməti]   [反] distance

n. (fml.) the state of being near sb./sth. in distance or time (时间或空间)接近；靠近

The **proximity** of the college to London makes it very popular. 这所学院因靠近伦敦而备受欢迎。

prudent [ˈpruːdnt]   [同] wise, wary [反] imprudent

adj. sensible and careful when you make judgements and decisions; avoiding unnecessary risks 谨慎的；慎重的

It might be more **prudent** to get a second opinion before going ahead. 行动之前再征求一下意见也许更为慎重。

query [ˈkwɪəri]   [同] question, uncertainty

n. question 疑问；问题

answer readers' **queries** 答读者问

quest [kwest]   [同] search, pursuit

n. (fml.) act of seeking sth.; search or pursuit 寻求；寻找；搜索；追求

the **quest** for gold/knowledge/happiness 勘探黄金 / 寻求知识 / 追求幸福

ritual [ˈrɪtʃuəl]   [同] ②rite

① *adj.* associated with or performed according to a rite 仪式上的；庆典的

② *n.* a series of actions that are always carried out in the same way, esp. as part of a religious ceremony 程序；(尤指)宗教仪式

She objects to the **ritual** of organized religion. 她反对严密宗教组织里的仪式。

sustainable [səˈsteɪnəbl]   [同] bearable

adj. that can continue or be continued for a long time 可持续的

It could go a long way to shifting consumers as well as farmers towards a more sustainable system of agriculture. 将消费者和农业经营者引向一个更有可持续性的农业系统可能要花很长的时间。

swap [swɒp]   [同] exchange

v. (infml.) to give sth. in exchange for sth. else; to substitute sth. for sth. else 以某物交换他物；以此物代替彼物

Your book looks more interesting than mine, do you want to **swap** (with me)? 你的书好像比我的有意思，你愿意(和我)交换吗？

swarm [swɔːm]　　　　　　　　　　　　　　　　　　　　　　　　　　[同] ②gather like bees

① *n.* (usu. pl.) (unpleasantly) large number of people; crowd (令人反感的)大群人；人群

Many experts are now investigating whether ***swarms*** of semi-smart robots can generate a collective intelligence. 很多专家目前在研究一群半智能机器人能否产生一种集体智慧。

② *v.* to move in large numbers (in the specified direction) 大群地(朝某方向)移动

The guests ***swarmed*** round the tables where the food was set out. 客人聚集到摆好饭菜的餐桌周围。

twist [twɪst]　　　　　　　　　　　　　　　　　　　　　　　　　　　　[同] wrench

v. to bend or turn sth. into a particular shape 使弯曲；使扭曲

Her hair was ***twisted*** into a knot on top of her head. 她把头发在头顶上挽成了一个髻。

verify ['verɪfaɪ]　　　　　　　　　　　　　　　　　　　　　　　　　　　[同] confirm

v. to check that sth. is true or accurate 核实；查对

We have no way of ***verifying*** his story. 我们无法核实他所说的情况。

vertical ['vɜːtɪkl]　　　　　　　　　　　　　　　　　　[同] upright [反] horizontal

adj. going straight up or down from a level surface or from top to bottom in a picture, etc. 竖的；垂直的

It is possible to use this iron in a ***vertical*** position so that you can remove creases from clothes on coat hangers. 这个熨斗可以在垂直位置使用，这样你可以在衣架上把衣服的褶皱熨平整。

vessel ['vesl]

n. a tube that carries blood through the body of a person or an animal, or liquid through the parts of a plant (人或动物的)血管，脉管；(植物的)导管

a blood ***vessel*** 血管

wretched ['retʃɪd]

adj. extremely bad or unpleasant 极坏的；恶劣的

The animals are kept in the most ***wretched*** conditions. 这些动物的饲养条件极其恶劣。

yoga ['jəʊgə]

n. a system of exercises for your body and for controlling or to relax 瑜伽术(健体和控制呼吸的锻炼)

And ***yoga***, they argue, can contribute to a healthy and more successful life. 他们认为，瑜伽术可以带来一个健康的、更加成功的生活。

Take the Test ≫

词组翻译

总的来说　＿＿＿＿＿＿＿＿＿＿　　　医疗服务　＿＿＿＿＿＿＿＿＿＿

偿还透支款　＿＿＿＿＿＿＿＿＿＿　　可持续发展　＿＿＿＿＿＿＿＿＿＿

句子翻译

1) 对环境的日益担心使得气候研究更为重要，欧洲在这个领域进展顺利。(forge)

＿＿＿＿＿＿＿＿＿＿＿＿＿＿＿＿＿＿＿＿＿＿＿＿＿＿＿＿＿＿＿＿＿＿＿＿

2) 行动之前再征求一下意见也许更为慎重。(prudent)

＿＿＿＿＿＿＿＿＿＿＿＿＿＿＿＿＿＿＿＿＿＿＿＿＿＿＿＿＿＿＿＿＿＿＿＿

Word List 27

audition [ɔːˈdɪʃn]   [近] hearing

n. trial hearing of a person who wants to perform as an actor, a singer, a musician, etc. 试听，试音

I'm going to the *audition* but I don't expect I'll get a part. 我要去试镜，但不指望能得到什么角色。

authentic [ɔːˈθentɪk]   [同] genuine [反] inauthentic

adj. known to be true or genuine 真实的；真正的

an *authentic* signature 亲笔签字

authoritative [ɔːˈθɒrɪtətɪv]   [同] official

adj. having authority; that can be trusted; reliable 有权力的；有权威的；可靠的

information from an *authoritative* source 来自权威方面的消息

byproduct [ˈbaɪˌprɒdʌkt]   [同] spin-off

n. a thing that happens, often unexpectedly, as the result of sth. else 意外结果，副作用

Public opinion forces governments to seek alternative ways of disposing of their unwanted *byproducts*. 民众的意见迫使政府寻求另外的方法来处理他们不希望看到的结果。

culminate [ˈkʌlmɪneɪt]   [同] climax

v. (fml.) to have the specified final conclusion or result 终于获得某种结局或结果

A series of events for teachers and students will *culminate* in a Shakespeare festival next year. 一系列的师生活动最终会以明年的莎士比亚戏剧节而收尾。

cultivate [ˈkʌltɪveɪt]   [同] ①②grow ②develop, foster

v. ①to grow (crops) 种植(庄稼)

cultivate bananas 种香蕉

② to work hard to develop a particular skill, attitude, or quality 培养

cultivate an enduring interest in learning 培养对学习的长期兴趣

curb [kɜːb]   [同] control, hamper

v. to control or limit sth. in order to prevent it from having a harmful effect 防止(某事物)失控；约束

Government is taking a drastic step to *curb* the use of plastics. 政府正采取严格措施限制塑料制品的使用。

curriculum [kəˈrɪkjʊləm]

n. subjects included in a course of study or taught at a particular school, college, etc. (全部的)课程

Is German on your school's *curriculum*? 你们学校有德语课吗？

curtail [kɜːˈteɪl]   [同] shorten

v. (fml.) to reduce or limit sth. 减少，限制

Budget cuts forced schools to *curtail* after-school programs. 预算削减使得学校不得不减少课外活动项目。

dynamic [daɪˈnæmɪk]   [同] vigorous *adj.* forceful, and having a lot of energy 强有力的；充满活力的；精力充沛的

a *dynamic* personality 充满活力的个性

dysfunction [dɪsˈfʌŋkʃn]

n. abnormal or impaired functioning, esp. of a bodily system or organ 机能障碍：不正常的或受到损伤的机能(尤指身体系统或器官的)

Mental *dysfunction*—such as schizophrenia—can be passed on from parent to child. 像精神分裂症这样的神经功能紊乱疾病能够由父母遗传给子女。

ecotourism [ˈiːkəʊˌtʊərɪzəm]

n. the business of organizing holidays to natural areas, where people can visit and learn about the area in a way that will not hurt the environment 生态旅行

If there were awards for tourism phrases that have been hijacked and misused then '*ecotourism*' would earn top prize. 如果给被窃用和滥用的旅行词语设个奖项，"生态旅行"这个词一定会得头奖。

extensive [ɪkˈstensɪv]   [同] wide, broad

adj. covering a large area; great in amount 广阔的；广大的；大量的

The fire caused *extensive* damage. 火灾造成了巨大的损失。

exterior [ɪkˈstɪəriə(r)]   [反] interior

adj. on the outside of sth.; done or happening outdoors 外表的；外面的

The *exterior* walls will be required to be double brick. 外墙需要两层砖。

fringe [frɪndʒ]   [同] border

n. outer edge of an area, group or activity (地方、群体或活动的)外围

on the *fringes* of society 在社会的边缘

fulfilling [fʊlˈfɪlɪŋ]

adj. making you feel happy and satisfied because you are doing interesting, useful, or important things 有满足感的；充实的

Teaching is still one of the most *fulfilling* careers. 教书依然是最能带来满足感的职业之一。

guesswork [ˈgeswɜːk]

n. the method of trying to find the answer to sth. by guessing 猜测；推测

It's important to find out what consumers want to buy, rather than relying on *guesswork*. 调查发现顾客想买什么，而不是依赖猜测，这一点很重要。

hurdle [ˈhɜːdl]   [同] obstacle

n. difficulty to be overcome; obstacle 难关；障碍

It's still so hard for women to even get on to shortlists—there are so many *hurdles* and barriers. 女性要想进入候选名单仍然很困难，她们要面临很多的困难和阻碍。

inverse [ɪnˈvɜːs]   [同] reverse

adj. reversed in position, direction or relation (位置、方向或关系)相反的，反向的

The number of copies the paper sells seems to be in *inverse* ratio/proportion to the amount of news it contains. 这种报纸的销售量似乎与刊登的新闻多寡成反比。

invisible [ɪnˈvɪzəbl]   [反] visible

adj. that cannot be seen; not visible 看不见的；不可见的

Could there be another planet there, essentially similar to our own, but always *invisible*? 那里会存在一颗与我们的星球极其相似却总看不见的行星吗？

invoice ['ɪnvɔɪs]

n. list of goods sold or services provided with the price(s) charged, esp. sent as a bill 发票；发货清单；服务费用清单

make out an *invoice* for the goods 开份商品发货清单

irresistible [ˌɪrɪ'zɪstəbl]

adj. too strong to be resisted (强大得)不可抵抗的

The invention of the automobile created an *irresistible* demand for paved roads and vehicular bridges throughout the developed world. 汽车的发明在发达国家内引发了一种对铺设的道路和公路桥的不可抗拒的需求。

lyrics ['lɪrɪks]

n. the words of a song 歌词

He wrote some great music, but the *lyrics* weren't that good. 他写的曲子很棒，但歌词一般般。

municipal [mju:'nɪsɪpl]   [同] domestic

adj. connected with or belonging to a town, city or district that has its own local government 市政的；地方政府的

municipal election 地方政府选举

muscular ['mʌskjʊlə(r)]

adj. having large strong muscles 强壮的；肌肉发达的

a *muscular* body 强壮的身体

overdue [ˌəʊvə'dju:]   [近] unpaid

adj. not paid, done, returned by required or expected time (到期)未付的，未做的

an *overdue* payment 逾期的付款

puberty ['pju:bəti]   [近] youth

n. the stage of physical development during which you change from a child to an adult and are able to have children 青春期

A variety of physical and emotional changes take place during *puberty*. 青春期会产生一系列的身体和情感变化。

publication [ˌpʌblɪ'keɪʃn]

n. the act of printing a book, a magazine, etc. and making it available to the public; a book, a magazine, etc. that has been published (书刊等的)出版；发行；出版物

Studies of the sources cited in *publications* lead to a similar conclusion. 经过对出版物中资料来源的研究，得出了相似的结论。

rosy ['rəʊzi]   [同] ②hopeful

adj. ① pink and pleasant in appearance 粉红色的；红润的 ② seeming to offer hope of success or happiness 乐观的；有希望的

And that figure paints a misleadingly *rosy* picture. 那个数字描绘出一派乐观的景象，但这是有误导性的。

rotate [rəʊ'teɪt]   [同] alternate

v. to move or turn around a central fixed point; to make sth. do this (使)旋转；转动

Rotate the steering wheel through 180 degrees. 将方向盘转动 180 度。

symmetry ['sɪmətri]   [反] asymmetry

n. exact match in size and shape between the two halves of sth. 对称

the perfect *symmetry* of the building 这座建筑物完美的对称格局

symphony ['sɪmfəni]   [近] orchestra *n.* long complex musical composition, usu. in three or four parts（or movements）for a large orchestra 交响曲；交响乐

Beethoven's Fifth *Symphony* 贝多芬的第五交响乐

veto ['viːtəʊ]

n. the right to refuse to allow sth. to be done, esp. the right to stop a law from being passed or a decision from being taken 否决权

The British government used its *veto* to block the proposal. 英国政府行使否决权阻止了这项提案。

viable ['vaɪəbl] [同]possible, feasible

adj. that can be done; that will be successful 可实施的；切实可行的

There is no *viable* alternative. 没有其他可行的措施。

vibrant ['vaɪbrənt] [同]energetic

adj. full of life and energy 充满生机的；精力充沛的

Thailand is at its most *vibrant* during the New Year celebrations. 在欢度新年期间，泰国举国欢腾。

vibrate [vaɪ'breɪt]

v. to move or make sth. move from side to side very quickly and with small movements （使）振动；（使）颤动

Every time a train went past the walls *vibrated*. 每当火车驶过，这些墙都会震动。

vicinity [vɪ'sɪnətɪ] [同]neighbourhood

n. the area around a particular place 周围地区；附近

There is no hospital in the immediate *vicinity*. 附近没有医院。

zest [zest] [同]enthusiasm

n. enjoyment and enthusiasm 热情；狂热

He had a great *zest* for life. 他对生活有着极大的热情。

Take the Test ≫

词组翻译

成反比 _____   乐观的景象 _____

句子翻译

1）预算削减使得学校不得不减少课外活动项目。（curtail）

_____

2）教书依然是最能带来满足感的职业之一。（fulfilling）

_____

3）他写的曲子很棒，但歌词一般般。（lyrics）

_____

4）没有其他可行的措施。（viable）

authorize [ˈɔːθəraɪz] [同] commission, accredit

v. to give authority to (sb.) 授权；委任；委托

I have ***authorized*** him to act for me while I am away. 我已经委托他当我不在时代我处理事务。

autonomy [ɔːˈtɒnəmi] [同] independence

n. self-government; independence 自治；自主；独立

In education, teachers are responsible for managing the learning of their students, and as such have a high degree of ***autonomy*** in the classroom. 在教育中，老师担负着管理学生学习的责任，也因此在课堂内享有高度的自主权。

awareness [əˈweənəs]

n. knowledge or understanding of a particular subject or situation 意识；注意

By raising people's ***awareness*** generally we can reduce conflict between humans and animals. 我们可以通过普遍提高人们的意识来减少人与动物间的冲突。

cutlery [ˈkʌtləri]

n. knives, forks and spoons used for eating and serving food (刀、叉等)餐具

a ***cutlery*** box/set 餐具盒／一套餐具

[记] 形：cut 切 cutlery 切东西的器具 = 刀、叉等

cynical [ˈsɪnɪkl] [同] pessimistic

adj. unwilling to believe that people have good, honest, or sincere reasons for doing sth. 愤世嫉俗的

They've grown rather ***cynical*** about democracy. 他们已逐渐感到所谓民主制度也不过尔尔。

external [ɪkˈstɜːnl] [同] outer [反] internal

adj. happening or coming from outside a place, an organization, sb.'s particular situation, etc. 外界的；外来的；在外的

Many ***external*** influences can affect your state of mind. 许多外在因素都会影响你的内心状态。

extravagant [ɪkˈstrævəgənt] [反] restrained

adj. spending a lot more money or using a lot more of sth. than you can afford or than is necessary 奢侈的；挥霍的；铺张浪费的

I felt very ***extravagant*** spending £100 on a dress. 我觉得花 100 英镑买一条连衣裙太奢侈了。

exuberant [ɪgˈzjuːbərənt] [同] high-spirited

adj. full of energy, excitement and happiness 精力充沛的；热情洋溢的

She gave an ***exuberant*** performance. 她的表演热情洋溢。

functional [ˈfʌŋkʃənl] [同] ②practical

adj. ①designed to be useful rather than beautiful or attractive 从实用性的角度设计的 ②sth. that is functional is working correctly 可使用的；运行正常的

The buildings are beautifully designed, not purely ***functional***. 这些楼设计美观，并不仅仅实用。

fury [ˈfjʊəri] [同] anger

n. state or condition of extreme emotion, esp. anger or excitement 愤怒；激动

She flew into a *fury* when I wouldn't lend her any money. 我不再借给她钱，她顿时勃然大怒。

fuss [fʌs]

n. (esp. unnecessary) nervous excitement or activity (尤指不必要的)神经质的激动或活动

Stop all this *fuss* and get on with your work. 别大惊小怪地闹了，继续干你的活儿吧。

hysterical [hɪ'sterɪkl]

adj. in a state of extreme, and crying, laughing, etc.; in an uncontrolled way 歇斯底里的；情绪狂暴不可抑止的

Everyone in the studio bursts into *hysterical* laughter. 演播室内每个人都突然大笑起来。

irrespective [ˌɪrɪ'spektɪv]

adj. not taking account of or considering (sth./sb.) 不顾或不考虑的

The laws apply to everyone *irrespective* of race, creed or colour. 法律适用于所有的人，不分种族、信仰或肤色。

irreversible [ˌɪrɪ'vɜːsəbl]　　　　　　　　　　　　　　　[同] irrevocable [反] reversible

adj. that cannot be reversed or revoked; unalterable 不能反转的；不能撤销的；不能更改的

He suffered *irreversible* brain damage in the crash. 他在事故中大脑受伤，无法治愈。

irritation [ˌɪrɪ'teɪʃn]

n. the feeling of being annoyed about sth., esp. sth. that happens repeatedly or for a long time 愤怒；烦恼；刺激；发炎

One of London Zoo's recent advertisements caused me some *irritation*. 伦敦动物园近来的一则广告给我带来一些不快。

itinerary [aɪ'tɪnərəri]

n. plan for, or record of a journey; route 旅行的计划或记录；旅行路线

Again she went over the first few days of their *itinerary* in her mind. 她又一次在头脑中把他们头几天的行程过了一下。

mutation [mjuː'teɪʃn]　　　　　　　　　　　　　　　[近] change

n. a process in which the genetic material of a person, a plant or an animal changed in structure when it is passed on to children, etc., causing different physical characteristics to develop; a change of this kind (生物物种的)变异；突变

genetic/colour *mutation* 基因/颜色突变

nutrient ['njuːtriənt]

n. (fml.) a substance that is needed to keep a living thing alive and to help it to grow 营养素；营养物

Plants draw minerals and other *nutrients* from the soil. 植物从土壤中吸取矿物质和其他养分。

overshadow [ˌəʊvə'ʃædəʊ]　　　　　　　　　　　　　　　[同] obscure

v. to cause (sth.) to be shaded or to have little light 使(某物)被遮暗；使阴暗

a village *overshadowed* by mountains 被山影笼罩的村庄

publicity [pʌb'lɪsəti]

n. the attention that is given to sb./sth. by newspapers, television, etc. (媒体的)关注，宣传，报道

The criticism and *publicity* given to this problem since the 1960s seems to have greatly improved the situation. 自 20 世纪 60 年代以来，对这个问题的批判和报道看来大为改观了实际情况。

puppet [ˈpʌpɪt]　　　　　　　　　　　　　　　　　　　　　　[近] tool

n. (usu. derog.) person or group whose actions are controlled by another 傀儡

The union representative was accused of being a ***puppet*** of the management. 那名工会代表受到了指责，说他是资方的傀儡。

purchase [ˈpɜːtʃəs]　　　　　　　　　　　　　　　　　　　　[同] buy

n. (fml.) (action of) buying sth. 购买

It will be helpful if they can give information about the place of ***purchase*** of the product. 如果他们能提供购买该商品地点的信息，那将会很有用。

quota [ˈkwəʊtə]　　　　　　　　　　　　　　　　　　　　　　[同] ration

n. maximum number or amount of people or things allowed, e.g. to enter a country （人或事物的）最高限额（如准予入境者）

Grain imports are controlled by strict ***quotas***. 谷物进口量受最高限额的严格控制。

roughly [ˈrʌfli]　　　　　　　　　　　　　　　　　　　　[同] nearly, about

adv. not exactly 大约；大概

Roughly speaking, I'd say we need about $500. 我们大概需要 500 美金吧。

ruthless [ˈruːθlɪs]　　　　　　　　　　　　　　　　　　　　[同] grim

adj. (of people or their behaviour) hard and cruel; determined to get what you want and not caring if you hurt other people 残忍的；残酷无情的

We'll have to be ***ruthless*** if we want to make this company more efficient. 如果想提高本公司的工作效率，我们必须不留情面。

sensitivity [ˌsensəˈtɪvəti]

n. ①the ability to understand other people's feelings and problems 敏感细心

a teacher with great ***sensitivity*** 极细心的老师

② the ability to react to very small changes in light, heat, movement, etc. 灵敏度

sequel [ˈsiːkwəl]　　　　　　　　　　　　　　　　　　　　[同] succession

n. a book, film, play, etc. that continues the story of an earlier one, usually written or made by the same person 续集

I heard they've been working on a ***sequel***. 听说他们一直在拍续集呢。

simplify [ˈsɪmplɪfaɪ]　　　　　　　　　　　　　[同] streamline [反] complicate

v. to make (sth.) easy to do or understand; to make simple 使（某事）简单或简明；简化

The response of educators has been to extend the use of pictures in books and to ***simplify*** the language, even at senior levels. 教育者的反应是在书本中使用更多的图片并简化语言，即便在高年级也是如此。

specialization [ˌspeʃəlaɪˈzeɪʃn]

n. the act of giving particular attention to (a subject, product, etc.); being well-known for 专门化的行为或特殊化的过程；专门

There will be an increasing ***specialization*** in the marketplace. 市场上会有越来越多的专卖店。

symposium [sɪmˈpəʊziəm]

n. ① a formal meeting in which people who know a lot about a particular subject have discussions about it 专题研讨会 ② collection of essays by several people on a particular subject, published as a book 专题论文集

contribute to a ***symposium*** on environmental issues 为环境问题论文集撰稿

synthesis [ˈsɪnθəsɪs]

n. ① sth. that has been made by combining different things, or the process of combining things

综合；综合体 ② the act of making a chemical or biological substance 合成

a *synthesis* of scientific knowledge and religious faith 科学知识和宗教信仰的综合

tangible ［ˈtændʒəbl］

adj. clear and definite; real 明确的；确切的；真实的

the company's *tangible* assets, e.g. its buildings, machinery, etc., but not its reputation, etc. 公司的有形资产（如其建筑物、机器等，但不包括其信誉）

unconditional ［ˌʌnkənˈdɪʃənl］

adj. without any conditions or limits 无条件的；无限制的；绝对的

The role of grandparents is to give time and *unconditional* love. 祖父母的角色就意味着付出时间和无私的爱。

virgin ［ˈvɜːdʒɪn］   ［同］①untouched

① *adj.* in its original pure or natural condition and not changed, touched or spoiled 未开发的；天然的

Most paper products must contain some *virgin* fiber as well as recycled fibers. 大部分的纸制品除了含有循环利用的纤维，都一定会含有一些天然的纤维。

② *n.* sb. who has never had sex 处女

visibility ［ˌvɪzəˈbɪləti］

n. ①the situation of being noticed by people 明显可见 ②the distance it is possible to see, especially when this is affected by weather conditions 视程；能见度

The exhibition helped increase the *visibility* of women artists. 此次展览增加了人们对女性艺术家们的关注度。

vogue ［vəʊg］   ［同］fashion

n. a fashion for sth. 流行；风尚

Black is in *vogue* again. 黑色又成了流行色。

vulgar ［ˈvʌlgə(r)］

adj. not having or showing good taste; not polite, elegant or well behaved 庸俗的；粗野的

vulgar language 粗俗的语言

warranty ［ˈwɒrənti］   ［同］guarantee

n. a written agreement in which a company selling sth. promises to repair or replace it if there is a problem within a particular period of time（商品）保用单；保证书

The television comes with a full two-year *warranty*. 这台电视机有整整两年的保修期。

Take the Test >>

句子翻译

1）我们可以通过普遍提高人们的意识来减少人与动物间的冲突。（awareness）

_____

2）许多外在因素都可能影响你的内心状态。（external）

_____

3）这些楼设计美观，并不仅仅实用。（functional）

_____

4）法律适用于所有的人，不分种族、信仰或肤色。（irrespective）

_____

5）听说他们一直在拍续集呢。（sequel）

_____

We know the good, we apprehend it clearly, but we can't bring it to achievement. To persevere, trusting in what hopes he has, is courage in a man.

我们懂得善，我们理解善，但是我们无法实现善。 人的勇气就是坚信自己的希望能够实现，并为之进行不屈不挠的努力。

——法国作家　赖奇特 _J. P_（_Euripides, ancient Creek dramatist._）

附 录 1: 2000个最常用词汇

a *art.* 一(个，张，块，…)
ability *n.* 能力
about *prep.* 关于
above *prep.* 在…上面 *adv.* 在上面 *adj.* 上面的
abroad *adv.* 在国外，到国外
absence *n.* 缺席
absent *adj.* 缺席的
accept *v.* 接受
acceptable *adj.* 可接受的
accident *n.* 事故
accordance *n.* 符合，一致
according *adj.* 符合的
according to *prep.* 根据
account *n.* 账目
ache *v.* 痛
acid *adj.* 酸的
across *prep.* 穿过
act *v.* 表演
action *n.* 动作，表演
active *adj.* 积极的
activity *n.* 活动
actor *n.* 男演员
actress *n.* 女演员
actual *adj.* 真的
add *v.* 增加
addition *n.* 添加
address *n.* 地址
adjective *n.* 形容词
admiration *n.* 仰慕
admire *v.* 崇敬
admit *v.* 承认
adult *n.* 成年人
advance *n.* 前进 *v.* 推进，促进
advantage *n.* 优势
adventure *n.* 冒险

adverb *n.* 副词
advertise *v.* 做广告
advertisement *n.* 广告
advice *n.* 建议
advise *v.* 建议
affair *n.* 事情
afford *v.* 承担
afraid *adj.* 害怕的
after *prep.* 在…以后 *conj.* 在…以后
afternoon *n.* 下午
afterwards *adv.* 之后
again *adv.* 再一次
against *prep.* 与…相对
age *n.* 年龄
ago *adv.* 之前
agree *v.* 同意
agreement *n.* 同意
ahead *adv.* 在前
aim *n.* 目标
air *n.* 空气
aircraft *n.* 飞机
airforce *n.* 空军
airport *n.* 机场
alcohol *n.* 酒精
alike *adv.* 相像
alive *adj.* 活的
all *adj.* 全部的 *pron.* 全体
allow *v.* 允许
almost *adv.* 几乎
alone *adj.* 单独的
along *adv.* 沿着
aloud *adv.* 大声地
alphabet *n.* 字母表
already *adv.* 已经
also *adv.* 也
although *conj.* 虽然
altogether *adv.* 总共
always *adv.* 总是

among *prep.* 在…之中
amount *n.* 数量
amuse *v.* 使愉快
amusement *n.* 娱乐
amusing *adj.* 有趣的
an *art.* 一(个，张，块，…)
ancient *adj.* 古老的
and *conj.* 和
anger *n.* 生气
angle *n.* 角度
angry *adj.* 生气的
animal *n.* 动物
ankle *n.* 脚踝
annoy *v.* 惹恼
annoyance *n.* 恼怒
another *adj.* 另一的
answer *n.* 答案 *v.* 回答
ant *n.* 蚂蚁
anxiety *n.* 焦虑
anxious *adj.* 焦虑的
any *adj.* 任何
anyhow *adv.* 无论如何
anyone *pron.* 任何人
anything *pron.* 任何事
anywhere *pron.* 任何地方
apart *adv.* 分开
apparatus *n.* 器械
appear *v.* 出现
appearance *n.* 模样
apple *n.* 苹果
appoint *v.* 指定
approval *n.* 同意
approve *v.* 同意
arch *n.* 拱形
area *n.* 地域
argue *v.* 争论
argument *n.* 争论
arm *n.* 胳膊

armor *n.* 盔甲

arms *n.* 武器

army *n.* 军队

around *prep.* 在…周围

arrange *v.* 安排

arrangement *n.* 安排

arrival *n.* 到达

arrive *v.* 到达

art *n.* 艺术

article *n.* 文章

as *adv.* 就像

    conj. 因为，当…时

ash *n.* 灰尘

ashamed *adj.* 羞愧的

aside *adv.* 在旁边

ask *v.* 问

asleep *adv.* 睡着地

association *n.* 联合

at *prep.* 在

atom *n.* 原子

attack *v.* 攻击

attempt *v.* 试图

attend *v.* 参加

attendance *n.* 参加

attention *n.* 注意

attract *v.* 吸引

attractive *adj.* 有吸引力的

aunt *n.* 阿姨

autumn *n.* 秋季

average *adj.* 平均的 *n.* 平均

avoid *v.* 避免

awake *adj.* 醒着的

away *adv.* 离开

awkward *adj.* 尴尬的

B

baby *n.* 婴儿

back *adj.* 后面的 *adv.* 在后面 *n.* 后背

background *n.* 背景

backward *adv.* 向后

backwards *adv.* 向后

bacterial *adj.* 细菌的

bad *adj.* 坏的

bag *n.* 书包

bake *v.* 烘烤

balance *n.* 平衡

ball *n.* 球

banana *n.* 香蕉

band *n.* 品牌

bank *n.* 银行；河岸

bar *n.* 木棒 *v.* 拴住

bare *adj.* 秃的

barrel *n.* 桶

base *n.* 基础 *v.* 以…为基础

basket *n.* 篮子

bath *n.* 洗澡

bathe *v.* 洗澡

battle *n.* 战役

be *v.* 是

beak *n.* 喙

beam *n.* 梁

bean *n.* 豆子

bear *v.* 忍受

beard *n.* 胡子

beat *n.* 敲打 *v.* 敲打

beautiful *adj.* 美丽的

beauty *n.* 美人

because *conj.* 因为

become *v.* 成为

bed *n.* 床

bee *n.* 蜜蜂

beer *n.* 啤酒

before *prep.* 在…之前

beg *v.* 乞求

begin *v.* 开始

beginning *n.* 开始

behave *v.* 表现

behavior *n.* 行为

behind *adv.* 在后面较远处 *prep.* 在…后面

belief *n.* 信仰

believe *v.* 相信

bell *n.* 铃声

belong *v.* 属于

below *adv.* 在下面 *prep.* 在…下面

belt *n.* 带子

bend *v.* 弯折

beneath *prep.* 在…下面

berry *n.* 浆果

beside *prep.* 在…旁边

besides *conj.* 另外

best *adj.* 最好的

better *adj.* 较好的

between *prep.* 在…之间

beyond *adv.* 在更远处

bicycle *n.* 自行车

big *adj.* 大的

bill *n.* 账单

bind *v.* 捆绑

bird *n.* 鸟

birth *n.* 出生

birthday *n.* 生日

bit *n.* 一点儿

bite *v.* 咬

bitter *adj.* 苦的

black *adj.* 黑的 *n.* 黑色

blade *n.* 刀片

blame *v.* 责怪

bleed *v.* 流血

bless *v.* 祝福

blind *adj.* 盲的

block *v.* 阻塞

blood *n.* 血

blow *v.* 吹

blue *adj.* 蓝色的

board *n.* 木板

boat *n.* 船

body *n.* 身体

boil *v.* 煮

bomb *n.* 炸弹

bone *n.* 骨头

book *n.* 书

boot *n.* 靴子

border *n.* 边境

born *adj.* 出生的

borrow *v.* 借

both *pron.* 两者

bottle *n.* 瓶子

bottom *n.* 底部

bowel *n.* 肠子

bowl *n.* 碗

box *n.* 盒子

boy *n.* 男孩

brain *n.* 脑子

branch *n.* 分支

brass *n.* 铜

brave *adj.* 勇敢的

bread *n.* 面包

breadth *n.* 宽度

break *v.* 打破

breakfast *n.* 早餐

breast *n.* 胸

breath *n.* 呼吸

breathe *v.* 呼吸

breed *v.* 教养 繁殖、养育.

brick *n.* 砖

bridge *n.* 桥

bright *adj.* 明亮的

bring *v.* 带来

broad *adj.* 宽的

broadcast *v.* 广播

brother *n.* 兄弟

brown *adj.* 棕色的 *n.* 棕色

brush *n.* 刷子

bucket *n.* 木桶

build *v.* 建筑

building *n.* 建筑物

bullet *n.* 子弹

bunch *n.* 许多

burial *n.* 埋葬 葬礼

burn *v.* 燃烧

burst *v.* 爆发

bury *v.* 埋葬

bus *n.* 公共汽车

bush *n.* 灌木丛

business *n.* 生意

busy *adj.* 忙的

but *conj.* 但是

butter *n.* 黄油

button *n.* 按钮

buy *v.* 买

by *prep.* 通过

C

cage *n.* 笼子

cake *n.* 蛋糕

calculate *v.* 计算

calculator *n.* 计算器

call *v.* 叫

calm *adj.* 冷静的

camera *n.* 摄像机

camp *n.* 营地 *v.* 扎营

can *n.* 容器 *v.* 能，会

candle *n.* 蜡烛

cap *n.* 帽子

capital *n.* 资金；首都

captain *n.* 船长

car *n.* 汽车

card *n.* 卡片

cardboard *n.* 纸板

care *v.* 关心

careful *adj.* 细心的

careless *adj.* 粗心的

carriage *n.* 车辆

carry *v.* 携带

cart *n.* 大车

case *n.* 案子

castle *n.* 城堡

cat *n.* 猫

catch *v.* 抓住

cattle *n.* 牛 不可数

cause *n.* 原因

cell *n.* 细胞

cement *n.* 水泥

cent *n.* 分

center *n.* 中心

centimeter *n.* 厘米

central *adj.* 中心的

century *n.* 世纪

ceremony *n.* 庆祝

certain *adj.* 确定的

chain *n.* 链子

chair *n.* 椅子

chairperson *n.* 主席

chalk *n.* 粉笔

chance *n.* 机会

change *v.* 改变

character *n.* 性格

charge *v.* 索取

charm *n.* 魅力

chase *v.* 追逐

cheap *adj.* 便宜的

cheat *v.* 欺骗

check/cheque *n.* 支票

cheek *n.* 面颊

cheer *v.* 欢呼

cheerful *adj.* 高兴的

cheese *n.* 奶酪

chemical *adj.* 化学的

chemistry *n.* 化学

chest *n.* 胸

chicken *n.* 鸡

chief *adj.* 主要的

child *n.* 孩子

childhood *n.* 童年

children *n.* 孩子

chimney *n.* 烟囱

chin *n.* 下巴

chocolate *n.* 巧克力

choice *n.* 选择

choose *v.* 选择

church *n.* 教堂

cigarette *n.* 香烟

cinema *n.* 影院

circle *n.* 圆圈

circular *adj.* 圆的

citizen *n.* 市民

city *n.* 城市

civilization *n.* 文明

claim *n.* 声明

class *n.* 班级

clay *n.* 泥土

clean *adj.* 清洁的 *v.* 清洁

clear *adj.* 清楚地 *v.* 弄清楚

clerk *n.* 书记员

clever *adj.* 聪明的

cliff *n.* 悬崖

climb *v.* 爬

clock *n.* 钟

close *adj.* 紧密的，关着的 *adv.* 紧密地 *v.* 关闭

cloth *n.* 布
clothes *n.* 衣服
clothing *n.* 服装
cloud *n.* 云
club *n.* 俱乐部
coal *n.* 煤
coast *n.* 海岸
coat *n.* 外套
coffee *n.* 咖啡
coin *n.* 硬币
cold *adj.* 寒冷的
collar *n.* 衣领
collect *v.* 收集
college *n.* 大学
color *n.* 颜色
comb *n.* 梳子
combination *n.* 结合
combine *v.* 结合
come *v.* 来
comfort *v.* 安慰
comfortable *adj.* 舒服的
command *v.* 要求
committee *n.* 委员会
common *adj.* 平常的
companion *n.* 同伴
company *n.* 公司
compare *v.* 比较
comparison *n.* 比较
compete *v.* 竞争
competition *n.* 竞争
competitor *n.* 竞争者
complain *v.* 抱怨
complaint *n.* 抱怨
complete *adj.* 完全的
computer *n.* 计算机
concern *v.* 关于
concerning *prep.* 关于
concert *n.* 音乐会
condition *n.* 条件
confidence *n.* 信心
confident *adj.* 有信心的
confuse *v.* 使糊涂
connect *v.* 连接
conscience *n.* 良心

conscious *adj.* 有意识的
consider *v.* 考虑
consist *v.* 组成
contain *v.* 包括
content *n.* 内容
continue *v.* 继续
contract *n.* 合同
control *v.* 控制
convenient *adj.* 方便的
conversation *n.* 谈话
cook *v.* 烹饪
cool *adj.* 凉快的
copper *n.* 紫铜
copy *v.* 复制
cord *n.* 绳索
corn *n.* 玉米
corner *n.* 拐角
correct *adj.* 正确的
cost *n.* 成本
cotton *n.* 棉花
cough *v.* 咳嗽
could *v.* 能，会
council *n.* 委员会
count *v.* 计算
country *n.* 国家
courage *n.* 勇气
course *n.* 课程
court *n.* 法院
cover *v.* 覆盖
cow *n.* 奶牛
coward *n.* 胆小鬼
cowardly *adj.* 胆小的
crash *n.* 碰撞 *v.* 碰撞
cream *n.* 奶油
creature *n.* 生物
creep *v.* 爬行
cricket *n.* 蟋蟀
crime *n.* 罪行 *v.* 犯罪
criminal *adj.* 有罪的
crop *n.* 庄稼
cross *n.* 十字架 *v.* 穿过
crowd *n.* 人群
cruel *adj.* 残忍的
cruelty *n.* 残忍

crush *v.* 压碎
cry *v.* 哭
cup *n.* 杯子
cupboard *n.* 橱柜
cure *v.* 治愈
curl *n.* 卷发
current *adj.* 最近的
curse *v.* 诅咒
curtain *n.* 窗帘
curve *v.* 雕刻
custom *n.* 风俗
customer *n.* 顾客
cut *v.* 切割
cycle *v.* 循环

D

daily *adj.* 每天的 *adv.* 每天
damage *v.* 破坏
dance *v.* 跳舞 *n.* 舞蹈
danger *n.* 危险
dangerous *adj.* 有危险的
dare *v.* 敢
daring *adj.* 大胆的
dark *adj.* 黑的
date *n.* 日期
daughter *n.* 女儿
day *n.* 白天
dead *adj.* 死的
deal *n.* 事情
dear *adj.* 亲爱的
death *n.* 死亡
debt *n.* 债务
decay *v.* 腐朽 /dɪˈkeɪ/
deceit *n.* 欺骗
deceive *v.* 欺骗
decide *v.* 决定
decimal *n.* 小数
decision *n.* 决定
declaration *n.* 声明
declare *v.* 声明
decorate *v.* 装饰
decoration *n.* 装饰
decrease *v.* 减少

deep *adj.* 深的

deer *n.* 鹿

defeat *v.* 打败

defend *v.* 防御

defense *n.* 防御

degree *n.* 程度

delay *v.* 推迟

delicate *adj.* 精细的

delight *n.* 高兴

deliver *v.* 传送

demand *v.* 要求

department *n.* 部门

depend *v.* 取决于

dependent *adj.* 依赖的

depth *n.* 深度

descend *v.* 下降

describe *v.* 描写

description *n.* 描写

desert *n.* 沙漠

deserve *v.* 应得

desirable *adj.* 想要的

desire *v.* 想要

desk *n.* 书桌

destroy *v.* 破坏

destruction *n.* 破坏

detail *n.* 细节

determination *n.* 决定

determined *adj.* 决定的

develop *v.* 发展

devil *n.* 魔鬼

diamond *n.* 钻石

dictionary *n.* 字典

die *v.* 死

difference *n.* 不同

different *adj.* 不同的

difficult *adj.* 困难的

difficulty *n.* 困难

dig *v.* 挖掘

dinner *n.* 正餐

dip *v.* 舀，汲取

direct *adj.* 直接的 *v.* 指导

direction *n.* 方向

dirt *n.* 灰尘

dirty *adj.* 脏的

disappoint *v.* 使失望

discourage *v.* 使气馁

discouragement *n.* 气馁

discover *v.* 发现

discovery *n.* 发现

dish *n.* 菜肴

dismiss *v.* 解除

distance *n.* 距离

distant *adj.* 遥远的

ditch *n.* 沟

divide *v.* 分开

division *n.* 分开

do *v.* 做

draw *v.* 拖，拉

drawer *n.* 抽屉

dream *v.* 做梦 *n.* 梦想

dress *n.* 衣服 *v.* 穿衣

drink *v.* 喝

drive *v.* 驾驶

drop *v.* 掉落

drown *v.* 溺死

drug *n.* 药物；毒品

drum *n.* 鼓

drunk *adj.* 喝醉的

dry *adj.* 干燥的

duck *n.* 鸭子

dull *adj.* 阴暗的

during *prep.* 在…期间

dust *n.* 灰尘

duty *n.* 责任

each *adj.* 每一个的 *pron.* 每一个

eager *adj.* 热切的

ear *n.* 耳朵

early *adj.* 早的

earn *v.* 赢得

earth *n.* 地球

east *n.* 东方

eastern *adj.* 东方的

easy *adj.* 容易的

eat *v.* 吃

edge *n.* 边缘

educate *v.* 教育

education *n.* 教育

effect *n.* 影响

effective *adj.* 有效的

effort *n.* 努力

egg *n.* 蛋

eight *num.* 八

eighth *num.* 第八

either *pron.* (两者)任一个

elbow *n.* 肘

elect *v.* 选举

election *n.* 选举

electric *adj.* 电的

electricity *n.* 电

elephant *n.* 大象

else *adj.* 另外的

employ *v.* 雇用

employer *n.* 雇主

employment *n.* 雇佣

empty *adj.* 空的 *v.* 清空

enclose *v.* 包围

enclosure *n.* 包围

encourage *v.* 鼓励

encouragement *n.* 鼓励

end *n.* 结局

enemy *n.* 敌人

engine *n.* 发动机

engineer *n.* 工程师

English *n.* 英语

enjoy *v.* 享受

enjoyment *n.* 享受

enough *adj.* 足够的

enter *v.* 进入

entertain *v.* 给…娱乐

entertainment *n.* 娱乐

entrance *n.* 入口

envelope *n.* 信封

equal *adj.* 平等的 *n.* 同等的人 *v.* 使平等

equality *n.* 平等

escape *v.* 逃跑

especially *adv.* 特别地

establish *v.* 建立

establishment *n.* 建立

even *adj.* 平坦的 *adv.* 即使

evening *n.* 晚上

event *n.* 事件

ever *adv.* 永远

every *adj.* 每一个的

everyone *pron.* 每个人

everything *pron.* 每件事

everywhere *pron.* 每个地方

evil *adj.* 邪恶的 /i:vol/

exact *adj.* 准确的

examination *n.* 考试

examine *v.* 考察

example *n.* 例子

excellent *adj.* 优秀的

except *conj.* 除了

exchange *v.* 交换

excite *v.* 使兴奋

excited *adj.* 兴奋的

exciting *adj.* 使人兴奋的

excuse *v.* 原谅

exercise *v.* 练习

exist *v.* 存在

existence *n.* 存在

expect *v.* 期望

expensive *adj.* 昂贵的

experience *n.* 经历

explain *v.* 解释

explanation *n.* 解释

explode *v.* 爆炸

explosion *n.* 爆炸

explosive *adj.* 爆炸的

express *v.* 表达

expression *n.* 表达

extreme *adj.* 极其的

eye *n.* 眼睛

eyelid *n.* 眼睑

F

face *n.* 脸

fact *n.* 事实

factory *n.* 工厂

fail *v.* 失败

failure *n.* 失败

Herrl

faint *adj.* 晕的 *v.* 晕倒

fair *adj.* 公平的

fairy *n.* 仙女

faith *n.* 信仰

faithful *adj.* 忠实的；虔诚的

fall *v.* 掉落

false *adj.* 错误的

fame *n.* 声誉 信誉

familiar *adj.* 熟悉的

family *n.* 家庭

famous *adj.* 著名的

fancy *n.* 想像力

far *adj.* 遥远的

farm *n.* 农场

farmer *n.* 农民

fashion *n.* 时髦

fashionable *adj.* 时髦的

fast *adj.* 快的 *adv.* 快地

fasten *v.* 加快

fat *adj.* 肥胖的

fate *n.* 命运 *destiny* 宿命（献身精神）

father *n.* 父亲

fault *n.* 错误

favor *n.* 喜爱

favorable *adj.* 喜爱的

favorite *adj.* 最爱的

fear *v.* 害怕

feather *n.* 羽毛

feed *v.* 喂养

feel *v.* 感觉

feeling *n.* 感受

fellow *n.* 伙伴

female *n.* 女性

fence *n.* 栅栏

fever *n.* 发烧

few *adj.* 很少的

field *n.* 土地

fierce *adj.* 凶猛的

fifth *num.* 第五

fight *v.* 战斗

figure *n.* 数字

fill *v.* 填补

film *n.* 电影

find *v.* 找到

fine *adj.* 好的

finger *n.* 手指

finish *v.* 结束

fire *n.* 火

fireplace *n.* 壁炉

firm *adj.* 坚定的 *n.* 公司

first *num.* 第一

fish *n.* 鱼

fisherman *n.* 渔夫

fit *adj.* 合适的 *v.* 使适合

five *num.* 五，五个

fix *v.* 安装

flag *n.* 旗帜

flame *n.* 火焰

flash *n.* 闪光 *v.* 闪光

flat *adj.* 平的，平坦的

flesh *n.* 肉

flight *n.* 飞

float *v.* 漂流

flood *n.* 洪水

floor *n.* 地板

flour *n.* 面粉

flow *v.* 流动

flower *n.* 花

fly *n.* 苍蝇 *v.* 飞

fold *v.* 折叠

follow *v.* 跟随

fond *adj.* 喜爱的

food *n.* 食物

fool *n.* 傻瓜

foolish *adj.* 愚蠢的

foot *n.* 脚

football *n.* 足球

footpath *n.* 小路

footstep *n.* 脚步

for *prep.* 为了

forbid *v.* 禁止

force *n.* 力量

forehead *n.* 额头

foreign *adj.* 外国的

foreigner *n.* 外国人

forest *n.* 森林

forget *v.* 忘记

forgive *v.* 原谅

fork *n.* 叉子

form *v.* 形成

formal *adj.* 正式的

former *adj.* 以前的

formerly *adv.* 以前

fort *n.* 堡垒

fortunate *adj.* 幸运的

fortune *n.* 财富

forward *adv.* 向前

forwards *adv.* 向前

four *num.* 四

fourth *num.* 第四

fox *n.* 狐狸

frame *n.* 框架

free *adj.* 自由的；免费的

freedom *n.* 自由

freeze *v.* 冰冻

frequent *adj.* 频繁的

fresh *adj.* 新鲜的

friend *n.* 朋友

friendly *adj.* 友好的

frighten *v.* 使惊吓

frightening *adj.* 吓人的

from *prep.* 从

front *adj.* 前面的 *n.* 前面

fruit *n.* 水果

fulfill *v.* 履行

full *adj.* 满的

fun *n.* 乐趣

funeral *n.* 葬礼 (通常的字数的)

funny *adj.* 有趣的

fur *n.* 皮毛

furnish *v.* 装饰

furniture *n.* 家具

further *adj.* 更远的

　　adv. 更远地 比较

future *n.* 未来

G

gain *v.* 得到

game *n.* 游戏

garage *n.* 车库

garden *n.* 花园

garment *n.* 衣服

gas *n.* 气体

gasoline/petrol *n.* 汽油

gate *n.* 大门

gather *v.* 收集

general *adj.* 一般的

generous *adj.* 慷慨的

gentle *adj.* 温柔的

gentleman *n.* 绅士

get *v.* 得到

gift *n.* 礼物

girl *n.* 女孩

give *v.* 给

glad *adj.* 高兴的

glass *n.* 玻璃

glory *n.* 荣誉

glue *n.* 胶水

go *v.* 去

goat *n.* 山羊

god *n.* 神

God *n.* 上帝

gold *n.* 金子

golden *adj.* 金的

good *adj.* 好的

good-bye *n.* 再见

goods *n.* 货物

govern *v.* 统治，管理

government *n.* 政府

grace *n.* 优雅

graceful *adj.* 优雅的

gradual *adj.* 逐渐的

grain *n.* 谷物

gram *n.* 电报

grammar *n.* 语法

grand *adj.* 宏伟的

grandfather *n.* 祖父

grandmother *n.* 祖母

grass *n.* 草

grateful *adj.* 感激的

grave *n.* 坟墓

gray *adj.* 灰色的 *n.* 灰色

great *adj.* 伟大的

green *adj.* 绿色的 *n.* 绿色

greet *v.* 问候

greeting *n.* 问候

grief *n.* 痛苦

grieve *v.* 感到悲痛，伤心

ground *n.* 土地

group *n.* 小组

grow *v.* 生长

growth *n.* 生长

guard *v.* 保卫

guess *v.* 猜想

guest *n.* 客人

guidance *n.* 指导

guide *v.* 指导

guilt *n.* 罪行

gun *n.* 枪

H

habit *n.* 习惯

hair *n.* 头发

hairy *adj.* 毛的，多毛的

half *n.* 一半

hall *n.* 大厅

hammer *n.* 鼓槌；铁锤

hand *n.* 手

handkerchief *n.* 手绢

handle *v.* 处理，解决

hang *v.* 悬挂

happen *v.* 发生

happy *adj.* 高兴的

hard *adj.* 坚硬的

harden *v.* 变硬

hardly *adv.* 几乎不

hardship *n.* 辛苦

harm *n.* 害处

harmful *adj.* 有害的

harmless *adj.* 无害的

hasty *adj.* 匆忙的

hat *n.* 帽子

hate *v.* 憎恨

hatred *n.* 憎恨

have *v.* 有

he *pron.* 他

head *adj.* 头部的 *n.* 头

health *n.* 健康

healthy *adj.* 健康的

hear *v.* 听

heart *n.* 心

heat *n.* 热量

heaven *n.* 天堂

heavy *adj.* 重的

heel *n.* 脚后跟

height *n.* 高度

help *v.* 帮助

helpful *adj.* 有益的

hen *n.* 母鸡

her *pron.* 她

here *adv.* 这里，在这里

hers *pron.* 她的

herself *pron.* 她自己

hide *v.* 躲藏

high *adj.* 高的 *adv.* 高

hill *n.* 小山

him *pron.* 他

himself *pron.* 他自己

hire *v.* 雇用

his *pron.* 他的

historical *adj.* 历史的

history *n.* 历史

hit *v.* 打击

hold *v.* 抓住，持有

holiday *n.* 假期

hollow *adj.* 空的

holy *adj.* 神圣的

home *adv.* 在家 *n.* 家

honest *adj.* 诚实的

honesty *n.* 诚实

honor *n.* 荣誉

honorable *adj.* 光荣的

hook *n.* 钩子

hope *v.* 希望 *n.* 希望

hopeful *adj.* 有希望的

hopeless *adj.* 没希望的

horizon *n.* 地平(线)

horn *n.* 角

horse *n.* 马

hospital *n.* 医院

host *n.* 主人

hot *adj.* 热的

hotel *n.* 旅店

hour *n.* 小时

hourly *adj.* 小时的

house *n.* 房子

how *adv.* 怎样

human *n.* 人类

humor *n.* 幽默

humorous *adj.* 幽默的

hundred *num.* 百

hundredth *num.* 第一百

hunger *n.* 饥饿 *starvation*

hungry *adj.* 饥饿的

hunt *v.* 打猎

hurry *v.* 匆忙

hurt *v.* 伤害

husband *n.* 丈夫

hut *n.* 小屋

I

I *pron.* 我

ice *n.* 冰

icy *adj.* 冰的

idea *n.* 主意

if *conj.* 如果

ill *adj.* 生病的

image *n.* 形象

imaginary *adj.* 想像的

imagination *n.* 想像

imagine *v.* 想像

importance *n.* 重要性

important *adj.* 重要的

improve *v.* 提高

improvement *n.* 提高

in *adv.* 进入 *prep.* 在里面

include *v.* 包括

income *n.* 收入

increase *v.* 增加

indoor *adj.* 室内的

indoors *adv.* 室内

industrial *adj.* 工业的

industry *n.* 工业

infect *v.* 传染

infection *n.* 传染

influence *v.* 影响

inform *v.* 通知

information *n.* 信息

ink *n.* 墨水

inner *adj.* 内部的

inquire *v.* 询问

inquiry *n.* 询问

insect *n.* 昆虫

inside *n.* 里面

instead *adv.* 作为替代

instruct *v.* 说明

instruction *n.* 说明

instrument *n.* 器具

insurance *n.* 保险

insure *v.* 保险

intend *v.* 想要

intention *n.* 目的，意图

interest *n.* 兴趣

interesting *adj.* 有趣的

international *adj.* 国际的

interrupt *v.* 打扰

interruption *n.* 打扰

into *prep.* 到里面

introduce *v.* 介绍

introduction *n.* 介绍

invent *v.* 发明

invention *n.* 发明

invitation *n.* 邀请

invite *v.* 邀请

inwards *adv.* 向内

iron *adj.* 铁的 *n.* 铁

island *n.* 岛

it *pron.* 它

its *pron.* 它的

itself *pron.* 它自己

J

jaw *n.* 下巴

jealous *adj.* 妒忌的

jealousy *n.* 妒忌

jelly *n.* 果冻

jewel *n.* 珠宝

jewelry *n.* [总称]珠宝

job *n.* 工作
join *v.* 加入
joint *n.* 关节
joke *n.* 笑话
journey *n.* 旅行
joy *n.* 高兴
judge *v.* 判断
judgment *n.* 判断
juice *n.* 果汁
jump *v.* 跳跃
just *adj.* 公平的
justice *n.* 公平

keen *adj.* 热切的
keep *v.* 保持
key *n.* 答案
kick *v.* 踢
kill *v.* 杀
kilo *n.* 千
kilogram *n.* 千克
kilometer *n.* 千米
kind *n.* 种类
king *n.* 国王
kingdom *n.* 王国
kiss *v.* 吻
kitchen *n.* 厨房
knee *n.* 膝盖
kneel *v.* 跪下
knife *n.* 刀子
knock *v.* 敲
knot *n.* 结
know *v.* 知道
knowledge *n.* 知识

labor *n.* 劳动力
lack *v.* 缺少
ladder *n.* 梯子
lady *n.* 女士
lake *n.* 湖

lamb *n.* 羔羊
lamp *n.* 灯
land *n.* 土地
language *n.* 语言
large *adj.* 大的
last *adv.* 最后 *adj.* 最后的 *v.* 持续
late *adj.* 晚的
lately *adv.* 最近
laugh *v.* 笑
laughter *n.* 笑，笑声
law *n.* 法律
lawyer *n.* 律师
lay *v.* 放
lazy *adj.* 懒惰的
lead *n.* 领导；榜样 *v.* 领导
leaf *n.* 树叶
lean *v.* 倾斜 /lɪːn/
learn *v.* 学习
least *adj.* 最少的
leather *n.* 皮子
leave *v.* 离开
left *adj.* 左边的 *n.* 左边
leg *n.* 腿
legal *adj.* 合法的
lend *v.* 出借
length *n.* 长度
less *adv.* 更少 *adj.* 更少的
lesson *n.* 课程；教训
let *v.* 让
letter *n.* 信；字母
level *adj.* 水平的 *adv.* 水平地 *n.* 水平
library *n.* 图书馆
lid *n.* 盖子
lie *v.* 放；躺下
life *n.* 生活
lift *v.* 举起
light *n.* 灯光 *adj.* 轻的 *v.* 点亮
lightning *n.* 闪电
like *prep.* 像 *v.* 喜欢
likely *adj.* 可能的
limb *n.* 四肢
limit *v.* 限制 *n.* 限制
line *n.* 线

lion *n.* 狮子
lip *n.* 嘴唇
liquid *n.* 液体
list *n.* 名单
listen *v.* 听
liter *n.* 升
literature *n.* 文学
little *adj.* 很少的
live *v.* 居住
load *n.* 担子
loaf *n.* 面包
local *adj.* 当地的
lock *v.* 锁住
lodging *n.* 寄宿
log *n.* 原木
lonely *adj.* 孤独的
long *adj.* 长的 *adv.* 长
look *v.* 看
loose *adj.* 松散的
lord *n.* 地主
lose *v.* 失去
loss *n.* 损失
lot *n.* 一批
loud *adj.* 大声的
love *v.* 爱 *n.* 爱
low *adj.* 低的
lower *v.* 降低
loyal *adj.* 忠诚的 *royal*
loyalty *n.* 忠诚
luck *n.* 运气
lump *n.* 大量，多数
lung *n.* 肺

machine *n.* 机器
machinery *n.* ［总称］机器
mad *adj.* 疯的
magazine *n.* 杂志
magic *adj.* 神奇的
magician *n.* 魔术师
mail *v.* 邮寄 *n.* 信件
main *adj.* 主要的
make *v.* 做

male *n.* 男性

man *n.* 人；男人

manage *v.* 管理

manager *n.* 经理

manner *n.* 礼貌

many *adj.* 许多的

map *n.* 地图

march *v.* 前进

mark *n.* 记号

market *n.* 市场

marriage *n.* 婚姻

marry *v.* 结婚

mass *n.* 大量

master *n.* 主人；硕士

mat *n.* 席子

match *n.* 比赛

material *n.* 物质，材料

matter *n.* 事情

may *v.* 可以

me *pron.* 我

meal *n.* 一顿饭

mean *v.* 意思是

meaning *n.* 意思

means *n.* 方法

measure *n.* 措施，方法

meat *n.* 肉

medical *adj.* 药物的；医学的

medicine *n.* 药物

meet *v.* 会面

meeting *n.* 会议

melt *v.* 融化

member *n.* 成员

memory *n.* 记忆

mend *v.* 修理

mention *v.* 提到

merry *adj.* 快乐的

message *n.* 信息

messenger *n.* 信使

metal *n.* 金属

meter *n.* 米

method *n.* 方法

metric *adj.* 公制的

microscope *n.* 显微镜

middle *adj.* 中间的 *n.* 中间

might *v.* 可能

mile *n.* 英里

military *adj.* 军队的

milk *n.* 牛奶

million *num.* 百万

millionth *num.* 第一百万

mind *n.* 思想 *v.* 介意

mine *n.* 矿山 *pron.* 我的

mineral *adj.* 矿物的

minister *n.* 部长

minute *n.* 分钟

mirror *n.* 镜子

miss *v.* 错过，想念

mist *n.* 薄雾

mistake *n.* 错误

mix *v.* 混合

mixture *n.* 混合物

model *n.* 模特

modern *adj.* 现代的

moment *n.* 时刻

money *n.* 钱

monkey *n.* 猴子

month *n.* 月

monthly *adj.* 每月的 *adv.* 每月

moon *n.* 月亮

moral *adj.* 道德的

morals *n.* 道德

more *adj.* 更多的

morning *n.* 早晨

most *adj.* 最多的

mother *n.* 母亲

motor *v.* 驾驶汽车 *n.* 汽车

mountain *n.* 山

mouse *n.* 老鼠

mouth *n.* 嘴

move *v.* 运动

much *adj.* 很多的

mud *n.* 泥土

multiply *v.* 增加

murder *v.* 谋杀

muscle *n.* 肌肉

music *n.* 音乐

musician *n.* 音乐家

must *v.* 必须

my *pron.* 我的

myself *pron.* 我自己

mysterious *adj.* 神秘的

mystery *n.* 神秘性；谜

N

nail *n.* 指甲

name *n.* 名字

narrow *adj.* 狭窄的

nasty *adj.* 肮脏的

nation *n.* 国家；民族

national *adj.* 国家的；民族的

nature *n.* 自然

naval *adj.* 海军的

navy *n.* 海军

near *adj.* 近的 *adv.* 近 *prep.* 在附近

nearly *adv.* 几乎

neat *adj.* 整洁的

necessary *adj.* 必须的

neck *n.* 脖子

need *v.* 需要

needle *n.* 针

neighbor *n.* 邻居

neighborhood *n.* 邻里

neither *adj.* 两者都不的

nerve *n.* 神经

nervous *adj.* 紧张的

nest *n.* 巢

net *n.* 网

network *n.* 网络

never *adv.* 从来不

new *adj.* 新的

news *n.* 新闻

newspaper *n.* 报纸

next *adj.* 下一个的 *adv.* 下一个

nice *adj.* 美好的，漂亮的

night *adv.* 夜晚

nine *num.* 九

ninth *num.* 第九

no *adv.* 不

no one 没有人

noble *adj.* 贵族的 *n.* 贵族

nobleman *n.* 贵族

noise *n.* 噪音

none *pron.* 没有人

nonsense *n.* 废话

nor *conj.* 也不

north *n.* 北方

northern *adj.* 北方的

nose *n.* 鼻子

not *adv.* 不

nothing *pron.* 没有任何事

notice *n.* 通知 *v.* 注意

noun *n.* 名词

now *adv.* 现在

nowhere *adv.* 没有任何地方

number *n.* 数字

nurse *n.* 护士

nut *n.* 坚果

nylon *n.* 尼龙

o'clock *adv.* …点钟

obedience *n.* 顺从

obedient *adj.* 顺从的

obey *v.* 遵从

object *n.* 物体

obtain *v.* 获得

occasion *n.* 场合

ocean *n.* 海洋

odd *adj.* 奇数的

of *prep.* …的

off *adv.* 离开

　　prep. 从…离开

offend *v.* 冒犯

offense *n.* 冒犯

offensive *adj.* 冒犯的

offer *v.* 提供

office *n.* 办公室

officer *n.* 官员

official *adj.* 官方的

often *adv.* 经常

oil *n.* 油

old *adj.* 老的

old-fashioned *adj.* 过时的

on *adv.* 在上面 *prep.* 在…上面

once *adv.* 曾经

one *num.* 一个

oneself *pron.* 某人自己

onion *n.* 洋葱

only *adv.* 只有

open *adj.* 开着的 *v.* 打开

operate *v.* 经营；做手术

operation *n.* 经营；手术

opinion *n.* 主意

opponent *n.* 对手

oppose *v.* 反对

opposite *adj.* 相反的

opposition *n.* 反面

or *conj.* 或者

orange *n.* 柑橘；橙汁

order *v.* 命令 *n.* 秩序

ordinary *adj.* 普通的

organ *n.* 器官

organization *n.* 组织

origin *n.* 来源

other *adj.* 其他的

otherwise *adv.* 否则

ought *v.* 应该

our *pron.* 我们的

ours *pron.* 我们的

ourselves *pron.* 我们自己

out *adj.* 外面的 *adv.* 外面

outdoor *adj.* 户外的

outdoors *adv.* 户外

outer *adj.* 外部的

outside *adv.* 外面

over *adv.* 在上面 *prep.* 在…上面

owe *v.* 亏欠

owing to 由于

own *adj.* 自己的 *v.* 拥有

oxygen *n.* 氧气

pack *v.* 包裹

packet *n.* 包裹

page *n.* 页

pain *n.* 疼痛

painful *adj.* 疼痛的

paint *v.* 绘画

painting *n.* 绘画

pair *n.* 一对

palace *n.* 宫殿

pale *adj.* 苍白的

pan *n.* 平底锅

paper *n.* 纸张

parcel *n.* 包裹

parent *n.* 父（母）亲

park *n.* 公园

parliament *n.* 议会

part *n.* 部分

participle *n.* 分词

particular *adj.* 特别的

partner *n.* 搭档

party *n.* 党；聚会

pass *v.* 路过

passage *n.* 段落

passenger *n.* 过路人

past *adj.* 过去的

pastry *n.* 糕点

path *n.* 道路

patience *n.* 耐心

patient *adj.* 耐心的

pattern *n.* 形式

pause *v.* 暂停

pay *v.* 支付

payment *n.* 支付

peace *n.* 和平

peaceful *adj.* 和平的

pen *n.* 钢笔

pence *n.* 分

pencil *n.* 铅笔

people *n.* 人

pepper *n.* 辣椒

per *prep.* 每，每一

perfect *adj.* 完美的

perform *v.* 表演；表现

perhaps *adv.* 可能

period *n.* 时期，阶段

permission *n.* 允许

permit *v.* 允许

person *n.* 人

personal *adj.* 私人的

persuade *v.* 劝说

pet *n.* 宠物

photograph *n.* 照片

photography *n.* 摄影

phrase *n.* 词组，短语

physical *adj.* 物质的

piano *n.* 钢琴

pick *v.* 采摘；拾起

picture *n.* 照片

piece *n.* 片断

pig *n.* 猪

pile *n.* 一堆

pilot *n.* 飞行员

pin *n.* 别针

pink *adj.* 粉红色的 *n.* 粉红色

pipe *n.* 管子

pity *n.* 可惜

place *n.* 地方

plain *adj.* 平坦的；朴素的 *n.* 平原

plan *n.* 计划 *v.* 计划

plane *n.* 飞机

plant *v.* 种植 *n.* 植物

plastic *n.* 塑料 *adj.* 塑料的

plate *n.* 盘子

play *v.* 演奏；玩

pleasant *adj.* 愉快的

please *v.* 使高兴 *adv.* 请

pleased *adj.* 高兴的

pleasure *n.* 愉快

plenty *adj.* 许多的

plural *adj.* 复数的

pocket *n.* 口袋

poem *n.* 诗

poet *n.* 诗人

poetry *n.* 诗

point *n.* 点 *v.* 指出

pointed *adj.* 显著的，突出的

poison *n.* 毒药

poisonous *adj.* 有毒的

pole *n.* 竿

police *n.* 警察

polish *v.* 擦亮

polite *adj.* 有礼貌的

political *adj.* 政治的

politician *n.* 政治家

politics *n.* 政治

pool *n.* 水池

poor *adj.* 贫穷的

popular *adj.* 受欢迎的

popularity *n.* 受欢迎度

population *n.* 人口

port *n.* 港口

position *n.* 位置

possess *v.* 拥有

possession *n.* 财产，所有物

possibility *n.* 可能性

possible *adj.* 可能的

possibly *adv.* 可能地

post *n.* 邮政

pot *n.* 锅；罐；壶

potato *n.* 土豆，马铃薯

pound *n.* 英镑

pour *v.* 倾泻，倒

powder *n.* 粉末

power *n.* 力量

powerful *adj.* 强大的

practical *adj.* 实际的

practice *n.* 练习

praise *v.* 夸奖

pray *v.* 祈祷

prayer *n.* 祈祷者

precious *adj.* 宝贵的

preparation *n.* 准备

prepare *v.* 准备

presence *n.* 存在

present *adj.* 当前的 *n.* 礼物

preserve *v.* 维护，保留

president *n.* 主席，总统

press *v.* 按，压

pressure *n.* 压力

pretend *v.* 假装

pretty *adj.* 漂亮的

prevent *v.* 防止

price *n.* 价格

prickly *adj.* 多刺的

pride *n.* 骄傲

priest *n.* 牧师

prince *n.* 王子

principle *n.* 原则，准则

print *v.* 印刷

prison *n.* 监狱

prisoner *n.* 囚犯

private *adj.* 私人的

prize *n.* 奖励

probability *n.* 可能性

probable *adj.* 可能的

problem *n.* 问题

process *n.* 过程

procession *n.* 列队

produce *v.* 生产

product *n.* 产品

production *n.* 生产

profession *n.* 专业

profit *n.* 利润

promise *v.* 承诺 *n.* 承诺

pronounce *v.* 发音

pronunciation *n.* 发音

proof *n.* 证明

proper *adj.* 适当的

property *n.* 财产

protect *v.* 保护

protection *n.* 保护

protective *adj.* 保护的

proud *adj.* 骄傲的

prove *v.* 证明

provide *v.* 提供

public *adj.* 公共的

pull *v.* 拉

pump *v.* 用泵汲水

punish *v.* 惩罚

punishment *n.* 惩罚

pupil *n.* 小学生

pure *adj.* 纯正的

purple *n.* 紫色

purpose *n.* 目的

push *v.* 推

put *v.* 放

quality *n.* 质量

quantity *n.* 数量

quarrel *v.* 吵架

quarter *n.* 四分之一

queen *n.* 王后

question *n.* 问题

quick *adj.* 迅速的

quiet *adj.* 安静的 *n.* 安静

quite *adv.* 非常

##

rabbit *n.* 兔子

race *n.* 竞赛

radio *n.* 收音机

railway *n.* 铁路

rain *n.* 雨

raise *v.* 举起

range *n.* 范围

rank *n.* 阶级

rapid *adj.* 迅速的

rare *adj.* 稀少的

rat *n.* 老鼠

rate *n.* 比率

rather *adv.* 很，非常

raw *adj.* 生的；未加工的

reach *v.* 到达

read *v.* 读书

ready *adj.* 准备好的

real *adj.* 正确的；真实的

really *adv.* 真正地

reason *n.* 原因

reasonable *adj.* 合理的

receive *v.* 收到

recent *adj.* 最近的

recently *adv.* 最近

recognition *n.* 确认，认识

recognize *v.* 确认，认识

record *n.* 纪录 *v.* 纪录

red *adj.* 红的

reduce *v.* 减少

reduction *n.* 减少

refusal *n.* 拒绝

refuse *v.* 拒绝

regard *v.* 认为

regular *adj.* 有规律的

related *adj.* 有关的

relation *n.* 关系

relative *adj.* 相对的

religion *n.* 宗教

religious *adj.* 宗教的

remain *v.* 留下

remark *n.* 评论

remember *v.* 记住

remind *v.* 提醒

remove *v.* 移动

rent *v.* 租住

repair *v.* 修理

repeat *v.* 重复

reply *v.* 回答

report *v.* 报告

represent *v.* 代表

representative *adj.* 代表的

republic *adj.* 共和的

request *v.* 要求

respect *v.* 尊重

respectful *adj.* 尊重的

responsible *adj.* 负责的

rest *n.* 休息

restaurant *n.* 饭店

result *n.* 结果

return *n.* 收益 *v.* 回来

reward *n.* 奖励

rice *n.* 大米

rich *adj.* 富有的

rid *v.* 摆脱

ride *v.* 骑

right *adj.* 正确的 *n.* 正确 *adv.* 向右

ring *n.* 铃声；戒指

ripe *adj.* 成熟的

rise *v.* 升起

risk *n.* 风险

river *n.* 小河

road *n.* 道路

rob *v.* 抢劫

rock *n.* 岩石

rod *n.* 竿；棒

roll *v.* 滚动

roof *n.* 屋顶

room *n.* 房间

root *n.* 根源

rope *n.* 绳子

rose *n.* 玫瑰

rough *adj.* 粗糙的

round *adj.* 圆的 *adv.* 在周围 *prep.* 在…周围

row *n.* 排
   v. 使排成排

royal *adj.* 皇室的

rub *v.* 摩擦

rubber *n.* 橡胶

rude *adj.* 粗鲁的

ruin *v.* 毁灭

rule *n.* 规则 *v.* 统治

ruler *n.* 统治者

run *v.* 跑

rush *v.* 冲

##

sad *adj.* 伤心的

safe *adj.* 平安的，安全的

safety *n.* 平安，安全

sail *v.* 航海

sale *n.* 出售

salt *adj.* 咸的 *n.* 盐

same *adj.* 同样的

sand *n.* 沙子

satisfaction *n.* 满意

satisfactory *adj.* 令人满意的

satisfy *v.* 使人满意

save *v.* 储蓄

say *v.* 说

scale *n.* 规模

scatter *v.* 散布

scene *n.* 风景

scenery *n.* 景色

school *n.* 学校

science *n.* 科学

scientific *adj.* 科学的

scientist *n.* 科学家

scissors *n.* 剪刀

screw *n.* 螺钉

sea *n.* 海洋

search v. 搜寻
season n. 季节
seat n. 座位
second num. 第二 n. 秒
secrecy n. 秘密
secret adj. 秘密的
secretary n. 秘书
see v. 看
seed n. 种子
seem v. 好像
seize v. 抓住
sell v. 出售
send v. 发送
sensation n. 感觉
sense n. 感觉
senseless adj. 没有感觉的
sensible adj. 合理的
sensitive adj. 敏感的
sentence n. 句子
separate adj. 分开的，独立的
　　　v. 分开
serious adj. 严重的
servant n. 仆人
serve v. 服务
service n. 服务
set n. 套，副，批 v. 设置
settle v. 安排；解决
seven num. 七
seventh num. 第七
several adj. 几个的
severe adj. 严重的
sew v. 缝
sex n. 性
sexual adj. 性的
shade n. 阴凉处
shadow n. 影子
shake v. 震撼，摇动
shall v. 应该
shame n. 羞耻
shape n. 形状
share v. 分享
sharp adj. 尖锐的
she pron. 她
sheep n. 羊

sheet n. 纸张
shelf n. 架子
shell n. 壳
shelter v. 遮蔽，防护
shield n. 保护物
shine v. 闪光
ship n. 船
shirt n. 衬衫 ← 易混
shock n. 震撼 v. 震撼
shoe n. 鞋
shoot v. 射击
shop n. 商店
shopkeeper n. 店主
shore n. 海岸
short adj. 短的；矮的
shot n. 射击
should v. 应该
shoulder n. 肩膀
shout v. 叫喊
show n. 展览 v. 展示，指出
shut v. 关闭
sick adj. 生病的
side adj. 旁边的 n. 旁边
sideways n. 旁边
sight n. 视力
sign n. 符号
signal v. 指示
signature n. 签名
silence n. 安静
silent adj. 安静的
silk n. 丝
silly adj. 傻的
silver n. 银子
similar adj. 相似的
similarity n. 相似性
simple adj. 简单的
since conj. 从…以来
sincere adj. 真诚的
sing v. 唱
single adj. 单身的
singular adj. 单一的
sink v. 下沉
sister n. 姐妹
sit v. 坐

situation n. 形势
six num. 六
sixth num. 第六
size n. 尺寸
skill n. 技术
skillful adj. 熟练的
skin n. 皮肤
skirt n. 短裙
sky n. 天空
slave n. 奴隶
sleep v. 睡觉
slide v. 滑行
slight adj. 轻微的
slip v. 滑行
slippery adj. 滑的
slope n. 斜坡
slow adj. 缓慢的
small adj. 小的
smell v. 闻，嗅
smile v. 笑
smoke n. 烟
smooth adj. 平滑的
snake n. 蛇
snow n. 雪
so conj. 所以
soap n. 肥皂
social adj. 社会的
society n. 社会
sock n. 短袜
soft adj. 柔软的
soil n. 泥土
soldier n. 士兵
solemn adj. 庄严的，肃穆的
solid n. 固体
some adj. 有些的 pron. 一些
somehow adv. 以某种方法
someone pron. 有的人
something pron. 有的事
sometimes adv. 有时
somewhere pron. 有的地方
son n. 儿子
song n. 歌曲
soon adv. 很快
sore adj. 痛的

sorrow *n.* 悲伤

sorry *adj.* 抱歉的

sort *n.* 种类

soul *n.* 灵魂

sound *n.* 声音 *v.* 听起来

soup *n.* 汤

sour *adj.* 酸的

south *n.* 南方

southern *adj.* 南方的

space *n.* 空间

spacecraft *n.* 宇宙飞船

spade *n.* 铲，锹

speak *v.* 说

spear *n.* 矛，枪

special *adj.* 特别的

specialist *n.* 专家

speech *n.* 演讲

speed *n.* 速度

spell *v.* 拼写

spend *v.* 花费

spin *v.* 纺纱，纺线

spirit *n.* 精神

spite *n.* 怨恨

splendid *adj.* 美好的

split *v.* 劈开

spoil *v.* 损坏，溺爱

spoon *n.* 汤匙

sport *n.* 体育

spot *n.* 斑点

spread *v.* 传播

spring *n.* 春季

square *adj.* 平方的 *n.* 平方；广场

stage *n.* 舞台

stair *n.* 楼梯

stamp *n.* 邮票

stand *v.* 站立

standard *n.* 标准

star *n.* 星星

start *v.* 开始

state *n.* 国家

station *n.* 车站

stay *v.* 停留

steady *adj.* 稳定的

steal *v.* 偷窃

steam *n.* 蒸汽

steel *n.* 钢铁

steep *adj.* 陡峭的

stem *n.* 树干

step *n.* 台阶

stick *v.* 粘贴

sticky *adj.* 粘性的

stiff *adj.* 硬的

still *adj.* 静止的 *adv.* 仍然

sting *v.* 刺

stitch *v.* 缝

stomach *n.* 胃

stone *n.* 石头

stop *v.* 停止

store *n.* 商店

storm *n.* 暴风雨

story *n.* 故事

straight *adj.* 直的，直接的 *adv.* 直地，直接地

strange *adj.* 奇怪的，陌生的

stranger *n.* 陌生人

stream *n.* 小溪

street *n.* 街道

strength *n.* 优势

stretch *v.* 伸展

strike *v.* 打击

string *n.* 细绳

stroke *n.* 打，击

strong *adj.* 强壮的

structure *n.* 结构

struggle *v.* 挣扎

student *n.* 学生

study *v.* 学习

stupid *adj.* 愚笨的

style *n.* 形式

subject *n.* 学科

substance *n.* 物质

subtract *v.* 减去

succeed *v.* 成功

success *n.* 成功

successful *adj.* 成功的

such *adv.* 这样地 *pron.* 这样的人 *adj.* 这样的

suck *v.* 吮吸

sudden *adj.* 突然的

suffer *v.* 遭受

sugar *n.* 糖

suggest *v.* 建议

suit *n.* 衣服

suitable *adj.* 合适的

sum *n.* 数量

summer *n.* 夏季

sun *n.* 太阳

supper *n.* 晚饭

supply *n.* 供给 *v.* 供给

support *v.* 支持

suppose *v.* 猜想

sure *adj.* 肯定的

surface *n.* 表面

surprise *v.* 使吃惊

surround *v.* 包围

swallow *v.* 吞咽

swear *v.* 发誓

sweep *v.* 打扫

sweet *adj.* 甜的 *n.* 糖果

swell *v.* 膨胀

swim *v.* 游泳

swing *v.* 摇摆

sword *n.* 剑

sympathetic *adj.* 有同情心的

sympathy *n.* 同情

system *n.* 体系

table *n.* 桌子

tail *n.* 尾巴

take *v.* 带走，拿去

talk *v.* 讲话

tall *adj.* 高的

taste *v.* 品尝

tax *n.* 税收

taxi *n.* 出租车

tea *n.* 茶

teach *v.* 教

team *n.* 小组

tear *v.* 撕毁

telephone *n.* 电话

television n. 电视

tell v. 告诉

temper n. 性情，脾气

temperature n. 温度

temple n. 塔

tend v. 照料

tendency n. 趋势，倾向

tender adj. 纤弱的

tennis n. 网球

tense n. 时态

tent n. 帐篷

terrible adj. 可怕的

terror n. 恐惧

test n. 测验

than conj. 比

thank v. 感谢

that conj. 因为，由于
  pron. 那个

the art. 这

theater n. 戏院

their pron. 他们的

theirs pron. 他们的

them pron. 他们

themselves pron. 他们自己

then adv. 那时

there adv. 那里

therefore conj. 所以

these pron. 这些

they pron. 他们

thick adj. 厚的

thief n. 小偷

thin adj. 瘦的

thing n. 事情

think v. 想，思考

third num. 第三

thirst n. 渴

thirsty adj. 口渴的

this adj. 这
  pron. 这个

thorough adj. 彻底的

those pron. 那些

though conj. 虽然

thought n. 思想

thousand num. 千

thread n. 线

threat n. 威胁

threaten v. 威胁

three num. 三

throat n. 咽喉

through adv. 通过 prep. 通过

throw v. 扔

thumb n. 大拇指

thunder n. 雷

thus conj. 所以

ticket n. 票

tidy adj. 整洁的 v. 打扫

tie n. 领带 v. 绑，系，拴

tiger n. 老虎

tight adj. 紧的

time n. 时间

timetable n. 时刻表

tin n. 罐头

tire/tyre n. 轮胎

tire v. 感到劳累

title n. 称呼

to prep. 到

tobacco n. 烟草

today adv. 在今天 n. 今天

toe n. 脚趾

together adv. 一起

tomorrow n. 明天

tongue n. 舌头

tonight adv. 今晚

too adv. 也

tool n. 工具

tooth n. 牙齿

top adj. 一流的 n. 顶部

total adj. 总共的 n. 总共

touch v. 触摸

tour v. 旅游 n. 旅游

tourist n. 旅行者

towards prep. 向着

tower n. 塔

town n. 城镇

toy n. 玩具

track n. 轨迹

trade n. 贸易

traffic n. 交通

train n. 火车

translate v. 翻译

transparent adj. 透明的

trap n. 陷阱

travel v. 旅行

treat v. 对待；治疗

treatment n. 治疗

tree n. 树木

tremble v. 颤抖

tribe n. 部落

trick n. 诡计，恶作剧 v. 欺骗，哄骗

trip n. 旅行

tropical adj. 热带的

trouble n. 麻烦

trousers n. 裤子

true adj. 真实的

trunk n. 树干

trust v. 信任

truth n. 事实

try v. 试图，努力

tube n. 试管

tune n. 语调

turn v. 转动

twice adv. 两倍

twist v. 扭转

type n. 类型

typical adj. 典型的

ugly adj. 丑陋的

uncle n. 叔叔

under prep. 在…下面

understand v. 明白

undo v. 消除

uniform n. 制服

union n. 联合

unit n. 单位

unite v. 团结，联合

universal adj. 普遍的

universe n. 宇宙

university n. 大学

until adv. 直到

up adj. 向上的 adv. 在上面 prep.

在…上面
upper *adj.* 上面的
upright *adj.* 垂直的 *adv.* 直立地
upset *v.* 颠覆
upside down 颠覆
upstairs *adj.* 楼上的 *adv.* 到楼上
urge *v.* 敦促
urgent *adj.* 紧急的
us *pron.* 我们
use *v.* 使用
useful *adj.* 有用的
useless *adj.* 无用的
usual *adj.* 通常的

valley *n.* 山谷
valuable *adj.* 有价值的
value *n.* 价值
variety *n.* 多样性
various *adj.* 多样的
vary *v.* 改变
vegetable *n.* 蔬菜
vehicle *n.* 车辆
verb *n.* 动词
very *adv.* 非常
victory *n.* 胜利
view *n.* 观点
village *n.* 村庄
violence *n.* 暴力
violent *adj.* 暴力的
visit *v.* 参观，拜访
voice *n.* 嗓音
vote *v.* 选举
vowel *n.* 元音
voyage *n.* 航海

wage *n.* 薪水
waist *n.* 腰
wait *v.* 等候
waiter *n.* 服务员

wake *v.* 叫醒
walk *v.* 步行
wall *n.* 墙
wander *v.* 漫游
want *v.* 想要
war *n.* 战争
warm *adj.* 暖和的 *v.* 温暖
warmth *n.* 温暖
warn *v.* 警告
wash *v.* 洗
waste *v.* 浪费
watch *v.* 观看
water *n.* 水
wave *n.* 波浪
way *n.* 道路
we *pron.* 我们
weak *adj.* 弱的
wealth *n.* 财富
weapon *n.* 武器
wear *v.* 穿着
weather *n.* 天气
weave *v.* 编织
wedding *n.* 婚礼
week *n.* 星期
weekly *adj.* 每周的 *adv.* 每周
weigh *v.* 重
weight *n.* 重量
welcome *v.* 欢迎
well *adv.* 好的 *n.* 井
west *n.* 西方
western *adj.* 西方的
wet *adj.* 湿的
what *pron.* 什么
whatever *adv.* 无论什么
wheat *n.* 小麦
wheel *n.* 车轮
when *adv.* 何时 *conj.* 在…时
whenever *adv.* 无论何时
where *adv.* 哪里
whether *conj.* 是否
which *pron.* 哪个
whichever *adv.* 无论哪个
while *conj.* 当
whip *n.* 鞭子

whisper *v.* 小声说话
whistle *n.* 口哨
white *adj.* 白的
who *pron.* 谁
whoever *pron.* 无论是谁
whole *adj.* 整体的
why *adv.* 为什么
wicked *adj.* 坏的
wide *adj.* 宽广的 *adv.* 广大地
widespread *adj.* 广泛传播的
width *n.* 宽度
wife *n.* 妻子
wild *adj.* 野的
will *v.* 将要
willing *n.* 意愿
win *v.* 赢得
wind *v.* 蜿蜒
wind *n.* 风
window *n.* 窗子
wine *n.* 酒
wing *n.* 翅膀
winter *n.* 冬季
wire *n.* 电线
wisdom *n.* 智慧
wise *adj.* 明智的
wish *n.* 愿望
with *prep.* 与…一起
within *prep.* 在…之内
without *prep.* 没有…
witness *n.* 证人
woman *n.* 女人
wonder *n.* 奇迹 *v.* 想知道
wood *n.* 木头
wooden *adj.* 木质的
wool *n.* 羊毛
woolen *adj.* 羊毛的
word *n.* 单词
work *n.* 工作
world *n.* 世界
worm *n.* 虫子
worry *v.* 担心
worse *adj.* 更坏的
worship *n.* 尊敬
worst *adj.* 最坏的

worth *prep.* 值…钱
worthy *adj.* 值得的
worthy of 值得
would *v.* 愿意
wound *v.* 受伤
wrap *v.* 缠绕
wreck *v.* 失事　wreckage 残骸
wrist *n.* 手腕
write *v.* 写
wrong *adj.* 错的 *adv.* 错误地 *n.* 错误
wrongdoing *n.* 坏事

yard *n.* 场院
year *n.* 年
yearly *adj.* 每年的
yellow *adj.* 黄色的 *n.* 黄色
yes *adv.* 是
yesterday *n.* 昨天
yet *conj.* 然而
you *pron.* 你
young *adj.* 年轻的

your *pron.* 你的
yours *pron.* 你的
yourself *pron.* 你自己
youth *n.* 青年

zero *n.* 零

Any one who conducts an argument by appealing to authourity is not using his intelligence; he is just using his memory.
一个借着引经据典来辩论的人，不是在运用自己的才智，他是在运用自己的记忆力。
——意大利画家　达·芬奇(*Da Vinci, Italian painter*)

附 录 2：听力真题场景词汇

剑桥雅思考试听力场景

（一）住宿

剑2 Test 2 Section 2 场景：校园住宿介绍

剑2 Test 4 Section 1 场景：咨询住房维修服务

剑3 Test 1 Section 1 场景：电话交谈——咨询租房事宜

剑4 Test 3 Section 1场景：租房

剑5 Test 4 Section 1 场景：寄宿家庭咨询与申请

剑7 Test 4 Section 1 场景：租房

（二）生活杂事

剑2 Test 2 Section 1 场景：家具和个人财物投保咨询

剑3 Test 1 Section 2 场景：家庭主妇交谈——关于英国医疗体制

剑3 Test 4 Section 2 场景：电视导购——家用器具

剑4 Test 4 Section 1 场景：准备一个告别晚会

剑5 Test 3 Section 1 场景：买车

剑6 Test 2 Section 2 场景：电话咨询火车运营时间

剑6 Test 3 Section 1 场景：银行开户

剑6 Test 4 Section 1 场景：预订会议室

剑5 Test 1 Section 2 场景：儿童床介绍

剑3 Test 1 Section 3 场景：求职面试

剑7 Test 2 Section 1 场景：关于购买汽车保险的问询

剑7 Test 3 Section 1 场景：找兼职工作

（三）旅游度假

剑2 Test 4 Section 2 场景：旅游观光地介绍

剑4 Test 1 Section 1 场景：旅游+咨询

剑4 Test 1 Section 2 场景：导游介绍游览地点

剑4 Test 2 Section 1 场景：讨论旅游行程

剑4 Test 4 Section 2 场景：旅游信息——自动电话咨询

剑5 Test 1 Section 1 场景：旅游度假咨询

剑6 Test 3 Section 2 场景：景点介绍

剑7 Test 1 Section 1 场景：行程路线咨询

剑7 Test 1 Section 2 场景：旅行社介绍

剑7 Test 2 Section 2 场景：景点介绍

剑7 Test 4 Section 2 场景：公园介绍

（四）社会和文化活动

剑2 Test 1 Section 1 场景：申请登记加入视频图书馆

剑2 Test 1 Section 2 场景：探险游历访谈

剑2 Test 3 Section 1 场景：新开电视频道问卷调查

剑3 Test 3 Section 1 场景：活动日程安排——同事间讨论预定圣诞大餐

剑3 Test 3 Section 3 场景：课外讨论——申报参加青年电子工程师大赛

剑3 Test 4 Section 1 场景：礼物选择——庆祝婴儿诞生

剑4 Test 3 Section 2 场景：节目及文艺活动介绍——一个Summer Festival及其中的表演项目

剑5 Test 2 Section 2 场景：介绍一个慈善机构

剑5 Test 4 Section 2 场景：足球俱乐部会议上的发言

剑6 Test 1 Section 1 场景：健身中心入会咨询

剑6 Test 1 Section 2 场景：剧场重开营业的采访

剑6 Test 2 Section 1 场景：关于博物馆营业时间及服务范围的电话咨询

剑6 Test 4 Section 2 场景：展览中心的准备活动

剑7 Test 3 Section 2 场景：关于徒步募捐的介绍

（五）课程介绍

剑2 Test 1 Section 4 场景：大学职业培训教育信息专题介绍

剑4 Test 3 Section 3 场景：选课

剑5 Test 1 Section 3 场景：选课

剑5 Test 3 Section 3 场景：课程评价

剑6 Test 1 Section 3 场景：课程咨询

（六）学校设施和服务介绍

剑2 Test 3 Section 2 场景：校园公共设施及服务介绍

剑3 Test 2 Section 1 场景：新生报到——入校后首日活动安排

剑3 Test 2 Section 2 场景：大学新生热线求助电话

剑3 Test 3 Section 2 场景：校园运动设施介绍

剑4 Test 2 Section 2 场景：介绍学校咨询服务的讲座

剑4 Test 3 Section 4 场景：报告——关于学生会活动中心选址问题

剑5 Test 2 Section 1 场景：图书馆信息咨询

剑5 Test 3 Section 2 场景：介绍学校

剑5 Test 4 Section 4 场景：对大学图书馆的介绍

剑6 Test 4 Section 3 场景：图书馆

（七）学习与研究

剑2 Test 1 Section 3 场景：大学学习生活及课程学习策略

剑2 Test 2 Section 3 场景：教学媒体的种类和作用

剑2 Test 3 Section 3 场景：课程论文指导

剑2 Test 4 Section 3 场景：学习技巧咨询与指导

剑3 Test 2 Section 3 场景：导师指导的讨论课——讨论员工招聘策略和方法

剑3 Test 2 Section 4 场景：课堂报告——关于手工艺品帽子的制作

剑3 Test 4 Section 3 场景：课外研讨——论文撰写与修改

剑4 Test 1 Section 3 场景：师生间就作业展开的讨论

剑4 Test 2 Section 3 场景：课外研讨场景

剑4 Test 4 Section 3 场景：研究——讨论5个实验

剑5 Test 2 Section 3 场景：讨论作业

剑5 Test 4 Section 3 场景：师生讨论商业案例

剑6 Test 3 Section 3 场景：作业——市场调查

剑6 Test 2 Section 3 场景：论文写作

剑7 Test 1 Section 3 场景：关于管理学调研的讨论

剑7 Test 2 Section 3 场景：关于南极科考的采访

剑7 Test 3 Section 3 场景：关于海洋研究的讨论

剑7 Test 4 Section 3 场景：老师布置展示作业

（八）各类讲座

剑2 Test 2 Section 4 场景：英国农业介绍

剑2 Test 3 Section 4 场景：关于澳大利亚水资源的讲座

剑2 Test 4 Section 4 场景：关于用车安全的调查报告

剑3 Test 1 Section 4 场景：健康讲座——关于背痛的起因与防治

剑3 Test 3 Section 4 场景：专题报告——鸵鸟的实用价值与驯养

剑3 Test 4 Section 4 场景：学术讲座——关于噪音污染

剑4 Test 1 Section 4 场景：关于树木对城市地貌影响的讲座

剑4 Test 2 Section 4 场景：关于企业犯罪的讲座

剑4 Test 4 Section 4 场景：讲座——澳大利亚的鲨鱼与捕鲨网

剑5 Test 1 Section 4 场景：关于不同性别省钱的讲座

剑5 Test 3 Section 4 场景：废物回收

剑6 Test 1 Section 4 场景：伦敦东部历史的讲座

剑6 Test 2 Section 4 场景：关于电影发展史的讲座

剑6 Test 4 Section 4 场景：介绍亚洲狮

剑6 Test 3 Section 4 场景：新石器时代讲座

剑5 Test 2 Section 4 场景：南极洲科研讲座

剑7 Test 1 Section 4 场景：关于纳米比亚考古的讲座

剑7 Test 2 Section 4 场景：用手习惯对人在音乐和体育方面的影响

剑7 Test 3 Section 4 场景：有关旅馆设施和服务的发言

剑7 Test 4 Section 4 场景：关于味精的介绍

剑桥雅思考试全真试题解析 2

Test 1

Section 1 场景：申请登记加入录像带图书馆

video library 录像带图书馆

application form 申请表

at the bottom 在底部

full name 全名

avenue *n.* 大街；林荫道；林荫小路

around the corner 在拐角处

driver's licence number 驾驶证编号

conduct a survey 进行调查

funny punch lines 有趣的妙语

be keen on... 热衷于…

softie *n.*（=softy）多愁善感的人

documentary *n.* 纪录片

membership fee 会员费

refundable *adj.* 可偿还的

action *n.* 动作片

comedy *n.* 喜剧片

musical *n.* 音乐剧

romance *n.* 爱情片

western *n.* 西部片

wildlife *n.* 野生生物；野生生物片

Section 2 场景：探险游历访谈

amazing *adj.* 惊人的

undertake *v.* 承担；担任

end-to-end 从头到尾

beforehand *adv.* 预先

bad moment 艰难的时刻

behave unpredictably 表现（行为）异常

block the mountain passes 挡住山口

bypass *n.* 旁道

collect maps and data 收集地图和资料

demanding *adj.* 高难度的；高要求的

expedition *n.* 探险；远征

huge gorge 大峡谷

keep dates 坚持赴约

link with... 与…相联系

make detours 绕道；迂回

outside the major visitor area 在人烟稀少的地区

out of character 失常

route book（游览）路线图

summit n. 山顶；顶峰

break record 打破纪录

take aback 惊讶

take diversion 走弯路；绕道

transport tool 交通工具

outset n. 开端；开始

considerable adj. 相当大的；相当可观的

meadow n. 草地；牧场

snow-capped mountain 积雪覆盖的山

scenery n. 风景；景色

continuously adv. 不断地；连续地

assume v. 假定；设想

Section 3 场景：大学学习生活及课程学习策略

challenge n. /v. 挑战

class schedule 课程表

day of arrival 到达日期

field research 野外调查（研究）

get through 通过（考试）；做完

reading strategy 阅读策略

stay ahead of lectures and seminars 在讲座和讨论课前
阅读相关书目

study strategy 学习策略

use a cassette recorder/ record 录音

writing assignment 写作练习

run into 撞上；偶遇

take a look around 到处看看

opt for 选择

amazingly adv. 令人惊讶地

take notes 做笔记

approach n. 方式

skim v. 浏览；略读

French Revolution 法国大革命

animal behavior 动物行为

Section 4 场景：大学职业培训教育信息专题介绍

achieve personal best 取得个人最佳成绩

arrange matches and venues 安排比赛日程和场地

be designed for... 为…而设计的

catching and throwing skill 抓举和投掷动作技巧

community health 社区健康

competition n. 竞赛；竞争

concentration n. 专注；专心致志

degree in psychology 心理学学位

diploma course 文凭课程

duration of the course 课程学习时限

four-year degree 四年学位课程

further education 继续教育

general fitness 大众健身活动

health and fitness centre 健身中心

improve general fitness 增进大众健康

information week 信息咨询周

personal fitness 个人健身

physical fitness instructor 健身教练

positive mental attitude 积极的精神状态

prerequisite n. 先决条件

professional athlete 职业运动员

recreational activity 文娱活动

relevant successful employment 相关工作经历

rounded development 全面发展

schedule of games and events 比赛日程

six-month certificate 6个月的课程证书

sports administration 体育管理

sports psychologist 运动心理学

stress management 应对压力

training programme 培训项目

vocational training 职业培训

entry requirement 入学要求

elite n. 精华；精锐

guidance n. 指导；领导

faculty n. 全体教员

qualification n. 资格；条件

component n. 成分

a wide range of 很大范围的

routine n. 日常事务

co-ordination n. 调和

balance n. 平衡

posture n. 姿势；体态

flexibility n. 弹性；适应性

Test 2

Section 1 场景：家具和个人财物投保咨询

apartment n. 公寓

break-in *n.* 入室行窃

contents of one's home 家用物品

ground floor 底层

insurance *n.* 保险

insurance application form *n.* 保险申请表

insurance cost 保险费用

personal possessions 个人财物

private contents insurance 私人财物保险

policy *n.* 保险单

recommend *v.* 推荐

stereo system 立体声音响

total annual cost 每年(保险)总费用

two-bedroom apartment 两室一厅的公寓

rent *n.* 房租

divide by 用…除；做除法

contact number 联系电话

Section 2 场景：校园住宿介绍

convert *v.* 改建

emergency fire door 紧急消防门

family house 家庭住宅

laundry fee 洗衣费

main lounge 休息大厅

north wing of building 大楼北部侧楼

office block 办公区域

recreation room 娱乐室

residential college 住宿式学院

room allocation 房间分配

dining room 餐厅

add on 附加

modernize *v.* 使现代化

indicate *v.* 指出；显示

individual room number 独立房间号

orientation pack 装有各种介绍资料的袋子

front door 正门

corridor *n.* 廊

emboss *v.* 装饰；饰以浮雕

identifiable *adj.* 可以确认的

floor senior 楼层学长

extra fee 额外的费用

Section 3 场景：教学媒体的种类和作用

audio *adj.* 音频的；声频的

audio-visual *adj.* 视听的；视听教学的

bar & pie chart 柱状图和饼状图

best suited to... 最适合于…

electronic media 电子媒体

focus one's mind on... 集中注意力于…

let imagination run wild 让想象力驰骋

plan group work 安排小组活动

print media 平面媒体

video *n.* 录像

approach *v.* 提议；着手

draw up a table 画一张表

pictorial form 图示表格

category *n.* 种类

so-called *adj.* 所谓的；号称的

isolated *adj.* 隔离的；孤立的；单独的

interact *v.* 互相作用；互相影响

share ideas 交流想法

Section 4 场景：英国农业介绍

account for 解释；说明；占据

agricultural training college 农业培训学院

agricultural workforce 农业劳动力

British agriculture 英国农业

cereal-producing region 生产谷类产品的地区

close cooperation 紧密合作

commercial farm 商业农场

contribute *v.* 贡献

country's economy 国家经济

efficiency *n.* 效率

excellent pasture 优良牧场

family-run *adj.* 家庭经营的；家庭耕作的

Farmers' Union 农民联合会

farming community 农业社团

flat and low lying land 平坦低洼的地区

geology and climate 地质环境和气候

gross national product(GNP) 国民生产总值

hilly land 丘陵地带

important portion 重要比例；重要份额

impressive figure 庞大的数字

intelligent support of the state 国家明智的支持

middle of the century 世纪中叶

plan ahead 预先计划

post-industrial *adj.* 后工业(时代)的

sense of solidarity 团体意识

supporting industry 辅助性产业

typical farm 普通农场

wool *n.* 羊毛

timber *n.* 木材

emphasize *v.* 强调

bear in mind 记住

percentage *n.* 百分比

a majority of 大多数

owe to 归功于

a good deal 许多；大量

fertile soil 肥沃的土地

increasingly *adv.* 日益；愈加

significant *adj.* 有意义的；重大的；重要的

interest group 利益集团

virtually *adv.* 事实上；实质上

Test 3

Section 1 场景：新开电视频道问卷调查

comedy show 喜剧影片

commercial channel 商业频道

complain about 抱怨；投诉

director *n.* 导演

documentary *n.* 纪录片

factual programme 纪实节目

good quality staff 高质量（水准）的东西

help relax and unwind 有助于放松和休息大脑

local information 地方消息；当地新闻

mailing list 邮寄单

make a note of 记下，记录

news bulletin 新闻快报

occupation *n.* 职业

potential customers 潜在客户

professional *n.* 专业人士

provide a service of the community 提供社区服务

respondent *n.* 被访者

set up the channel 新开频道

sound system 音响系统

special promotion 特别促销活动

specific advice 具体建议

start with some personal background information 从个人背景信息开始

tolerable to have adverts 容忍插播广告

relaxation *n.* 休闲

entertainment *n.* 娱乐

market research 市场调查

in two years' time 在两年内

system analyst 系统分析员

on average 平均

promotion *n.* 宣传；促销

as long as 只要

Section 2 场景：校园公共设施及服务介绍

advice service 咨询服务

an interesting range of shops 各种有趣的商店

Assistant Welfare Officer 助理福利官

charity 慈善（事业、活动）

charter flight 包机

cinema with six screens 六屏幕影院

get a good deal 划算的买卖

hi-tech fitness centre 高科技健身中心

ice-skating facilities 滑冰设施

indoor sports 室内运动

legal problems 法律问题

main centre of social life 社会活动中心

main square 主广场

outskirts 郊区

parking lot 停车场

pop group 流行乐队

provide catering services 提供膳食服务

raise money 筹集资金

social facilities available on the campus 校园公共设施

squash *n.* 壁球

stationary *n.* 文具

taste *n.* 爱好；口味

Theatre Royal 皇家大剧院

ticket shop 售票代理店

weekly programme of events 每周活动计划

good cause 善举

political campaign 政治竞选活动

newsagent *n.* 报刊亭

accommodation *n.* 食宿

immigration *n.* 移民

grant *n. /v.* 认可；赠予

Student Union 学生会

papershop *n.* 报刊亭

venue *n.* 地点

financial problem 财政问题

medical service 医疗服务

counseling centre 顾问咨询中心

leisure facility 休闲设施

in the centre of... 在…的中心

Olympic-size *adj.* 奥林匹克标准尺寸的

badminton *n.* 羽毛球

Section 3 场景：课程论文指导

ask for an extension 要求延期

biology *n.* 生物；生物学

confirmed *adj.* 证实的；确认的

duration of presentation 做专题报告的时间

fixed hand-in date 规定的上交日期

given tutorial topics 指定的讨论课题目

journal articles 学术文章

mountain building 山上建筑

research method 研究方法

dissertation *n.* 论文；专题；论述

questionnaire *n.* 调查表；问卷

look forward to 期待；盼望

requirement *n.* 要求

milestone *n.* 里程碑；转折点

flexible *adj.* 柔软的；可变通的

deadline *n.* 最终期限

bibliography *n.* 参考书目

get a move on... 赶快做…

draft plan 草稿计划

be of great benefit 有很大好处

second-hand *adj.* 二手的

end up 结束

to be frank 坦白地说

sort out 解决

Section 4 场景：关于澳大利亚水资源的讲座

be of great importance 有很大重要性

dryness *n.* 干旱

extensive underground water resources 丰富的地下水资源

household water consumption 家庭用水

natural problems 自然灾害

precious resource 宝贵资源

rainy water 雨水

shortage *n.* 缺乏

stream *n.* 溪流；溪水

subterranean water 地下水

tapped water 自来水

underground water 地下水

water resource 水资源

wise management 明智的管理

evaporation rate 蒸发率

penetrate *v.* 渗透

use up 用光

natural spring 自然泉水

livestock *n.* 牲畜；家畜

hydro-electric power 水力发电

aridity *n.* 干旱

estimate *v.* 估计；估价；评估

approximately *adv.* 大约；近似地

in comparison with... 与…相比

moisture *n.* 水分

irrigation *n.* 灌溉

rely on 依靠；依赖

underground reservoir 地下水库

vital *adj.* 生死攸关的；重大的；必需的

handout *n.* 分发的印刷品

reference *n.* 参考；参考书目

outback farm 内地牧场

Test 4

Section 1 场景：咨询住房维修服务

bathroom light 浴室照明灯

flicker *v.* 闪烁

get... done right away 立即解决…

get... done straight away 立即解决…

house agency 房屋中介

leak *v.* 漏水

lease *n.* 租期

property *n.* 房产；财产

apartment *n.* 公寓

build up 建立；树立

washing machine 洗衣机

niggling *adj.* 琐碎的

annoying *adj.* 恼人的；讨厌的

right away 立刻

Section 2 场景：旅游观光地介绍

lodge *n.* 小屋；旅舍

recreation officer 文娱活动负责人

have a great stay 住(过)得很愉快

appreciate the world 欣赏大自然的美景

balcony *n.* 阳台

be frightened of 害怕；恐惧

birds' singing 鸟儿的欢唱；鸟鸣

be much better off... …会好得多

be nervous of 对…感到紧张

rainforest *n.* (热带)雨林

beware of 小心；当心

cabin *n.* 小木屋

catch a glimpse of 瞥见

crocodile cruise 乘船出游观赏鳄鱼

depart *v.* 出发

dinner served time 用餐时间

discover *v.* 发现；探索

explorer trip 探险游历

four-wheel-drive tour 乘四轮马车游览

"get away from it all" experience "远离尘嚣"的感受

have a different focus 有不同的重点

rainforest lodge 热带雨林度假小屋

wildlife *n.* 野生生物

spotlight tour 观光游

sundown *n.* 日落

make sure 确保

interruption *n.* 中断；打断

distraction *n.* 分心；分心的事物

provided *conj.* 倘若

common sense 常识

venomous *adj.* 有毒的；分泌毒液的

irritation *n.* 发炎；过敏；疼痛

Section 3 场景：学习技巧咨询与指导

assignment *n.* 论文、作业等

general interest 大众兴趣

compulsory *adj.* 必修的，必须的

counseling session 咨询时间

course requirement 课程要求

resource centre 资料中心

revise *v.* 修改

science course 科学课程(理科课程)

剑桥雅思考试全真试题解析 3

Test 1

Section 1 场景：电话咨询租房事宜

property *n.* 房地产；财产

suburb *n.* 郊区

range *v.* (在一定范围内)变动；变化

depend on 取决于

factor *n.* 因素

garage *n.* 车库；汽车修理厂

file *n.* 档案；文件夹

suit *v.* 适合

take control of time 安排(控制)时间

premise *n.* 建筑物

independently *adv.* 独立地；单独地

leisure activity 休闲活动

systematic *adj.* 系统的；体系的

cassette recorder 录音机

appeal to 有吸引力

underline *v.* 加下划线；强调

highlight *v.* 使显著；突出

Section 4 场景：关于用车安全的调查报告

car safety 汽车安全

focus of the project 项目研究重点

in advance 预先

destination *n.* 目的地

in the majority 大多数

overtake *v.* 超车

project background 项目背景

research project 研究项目

injunction *n.* 禁令

witness *v.* 目击；目睹

interview *n.* 访问

questionnaire *n.* 调查问卷

observation *n.* 观察

proportion *n.* 比例

finding *n.* 发现；决定

straightforward *adj.* 坦率的；坦白的 *adv.* 坦率地

road rage 马路愤怒

garage *n.* 车库

motorway *n.* 高速公路

strategy *n.* 策略

improvement *n.* 改进；进步

water bill 水费账单

available *adj.* 可以使用的；(某人)有空的

availability *n.* 可用性；可得性

reference letter 介绍信；推荐信

reference letter from employer 雇主介绍信

deposit *n.* 押金

amount *n.* 总数；数额

pay for contract 付合同费

give notice of moving in 通知入住日期

house agency 房屋中介

location *n.* 位置

make an enquiry 咨询

telephone rental 电话租费

Section 2 场景：家庭主妇谈论英国医疗体制

settle in 安家

removal *n.* 搬家

van *n.* 运货车；搬运车

bother *v.* 打扰

get hold of 找到；得到；抓到

well *adj.* 健康的

register *v.* 挂号；登记

practice *n.* 医务所

practice *v.* （律师、医生等）开业

general practitioner 全科医生

well off 富裕的

comparison *n.* 对比；对照

in comparison with 与…相比较

old-fashioned *adj.* 老式的

proper *adj.* 合适的

appointment *n.* 约会；预约

appointment system 预约制度

make an appointment 预约

receptionist *n.* 前台接待人员

fill in 填写

brilliant *adj.* 卓越的；出色的

be used to 习惯于…

tend *v.* 倾向于

see patients 看病人

impatient *adj.* 不耐烦的

the other day 前几天

clinic *n.* 诊所

emergency *n.* 急诊

surgery *n.* 外科

prescribe *v.* 开药

prescription *n.* 处方

write medication 开处方

charge for medication 诊断费

chemist *n.* 药剂师

chemist's shop 药店

unemployed people 失业人员

retired *adj.* 退休的

pregnant *adj.* 怀孕的

consultation *n.* 咨询

consultation with the doctor 医生诊断

consulting time/open time 就诊时间

completely *adv.* 完全地

back trouble/problem 背痛

be good with elderly people 善待老年患者

efficient *adj.* 高效的

family doctor 家庭医生

free medication 免费开药；免费诊断

health system 医疗服务体制

resident *n.* 居民

Section 3 场景：求职面试

interview *n.* 面试

group interview 小组面试

talk through 详细地讨论

application form 申请表

academic degree 学位

to date 迄今为止

economics *n.* 经济学

major *adj.* 主要的

strand *n.* （重要的）组成部分

graduate *v.* 毕业

volunteer *n.* 志愿者

volunteer teacher 教师志愿者

in total 总共

organization *n.* 组织

operate *v.* 运作；发挥作用

rural *adj.* 农村的

co-operative *n.* 合作社

a variety of 各种各样的

form *n.* 年级

geography *n.* 地理

agriculture *n.* 农业

agriculture science 农业科学

run *v.* 经营

run school farm 经营学校农场

homesick *adj.* 想家的

frustrating *adj.* 令人沮丧的

teaching resources 教学资源

useful resources 有用的资源

extend *v.* 延伸

look up 好转，改善

set up 建立

successful *adj.* 成功的

project *n.* 项目

breed *v.* 喂养

cattle *n.* 牛

local *adj.* 当地的

fund *n.* 资金

see something through 办好某事

realize *v.* 意识到

obtain funds for farm buildings 获得资金建农场

application *n.* 应用

stage *n.* 阶段；舞台

Section 4 场景：健康讲座——关于背痛的起因与防治

counsel *n.* 讨论会；商议

present *v.* 提供；做演讲

chief *adj.* 首要的

counsellor *n.* 顾问

clinic *n.* 诊所

suffer *v.* 遭受（痛苦）

chronic *adj.* 慢性的；长期的

affect *v.* 影响

all walks of life 各行各业

incapacitate *v.* 使…失去能力；使…残废

solution *n.* 解决办法

majority *n.* 大多数

vulnerable *adj.* 脆弱的

pregnancy *n.* 怀孕

osteoporosis *n.* 骨质疏松症

remedy *n.* 治疗法

unique benefit 特别之好处

beneficial *adj.* 有益的

relaxation therapy 放松疗法

specialist *n.* 专家

mishandle *v.* 处理不当

lead to 导致

menace *n.* 具有危害性的事物

strain *n.* 劳损

blow *n.* 打击；殴打

limb *n.* 肢体

resolve *v.* 解决

injury *n.* 受伤

counter-productive *adj.* 起反作用的

strike *v.* 打击

attempt *v.* 试图

immobile *adj.* 固定的

muscle *n.* 肌肉

spasm *n.* 痉挛

twist *v.* 扭曲

spine *n.* 脊椎

extreme *adj.* 极端的

recognize *v.* 认可

overweight *n.* 超重

stone *n.* 重量单位，＝14磅

diet *n.* 饮食

particularly *adv.* 尤其地

blame *v.* 指责

average *adj.* 普通的；平均的

aggravation *n.* （病情、负担）加重

slouched *adj.* 无精打采的

ligament *n.* 韧带

heal *v.* 愈合

conclusion *n.* 结论

orthopaedic *adj.* 整形外科的

posture *n.* 姿势

alignment *n.* 矫正

mattress *n.* 床垫

spring slatted bed 弹簧床

hazard *n.* 危险

heel strike 脚跟触地

effectiveness *n.* 效果；有效性

absolutely *adv.* 绝对地

relief *n.* 减轻疼痛

battery *n.* 电池

gadget *n.* 小设备

deliver *v.* 传送

subliminal *adj.* 微小的

pulse *n.* 脉搏

indicate *v.* 表明

remedy *n.* 疗法

Test 2

Section 1 场景：新生报到——入校后首日活动安排

at some stage 在某一阶段

booklet *n.* 小册子

find the level of English 确定英语水平

course *n.* 课程

offer *v.* 提供

outline *n.* 提纲

program *n.* 活动安排

gather *v.* 聚集

meet the principal and staff 与校长和教职员工见面

morning's event 上午的活动

last *v.* 持续

director *n.* 主管

requirement *n.* 要求

adviser *n.* 导师

various services and activities 各种服务和活动

placement test 分班考试

schedule *n.* 日程表

reception *n.* 接待处

facility *n.* 设施

laboratory *n.* 实验室

immediately *adv.* 立即

opposite *prep.* 在…对面

common room 休息室

mention *v.* 提及

corridor *n.* 走廊

tea and coffee facilities 茶水设施

Section 2 场景：大学新生热线求助电话

informal *adj.* 非正式的

university helpline 大学生求助热线

the Students Union 学生会

aim *v.* 旨在

provide *v.* 提供

unfamiliar *adj.* 不熟悉的

financial *adj.* 财政的

financial matter 有关理财方面的问题

grant *n.* 助学金

insufficient *adj.* 不足的；不充分的

see sb through 帮助…渡过困难

query *v.* 对…表示疑问

regarding *prep.* 关于

overseas *adj.* 海外的

outcome *n.* 结果

domestic *adj.* 家庭的

nursery *n.* 托儿所

straight away 马上

academic issue 学术方面的问题

arise *v.* 发生

essay deadline 论文上交期限

participate *v.* 参加

pursue *v.* 追求

outing *n.* 郊游

detail *n.* 细节

full-time *adj.* 专职的

employee *n.* 职员

welfare *n.* 福利

student welfare officer 学生福利负责人

provision *n.* 供应

social life 社交生活

Section 3 场景：导师指导的讨论课——讨论员工招聘策略和方法

aspect *n.* 方面

applicant *n.* 申请人

tutorial *n.* 辅导

match *v.* 搭配

supervisor *n.* 管理者

theoretical *adj.* 理论上的

qualification *n.* 资格

certificate *n.* 证书

similar *adj.* 相似的

environment *n.* 环境

get along with 与…相处融洽

contrast *v.* 对比

contrasting view 相左的观点

back *v.* 支持

loser *n.* 失败者

carry out the task 执行任务

Chinese traditional approach 中国传统方法

resistant *adj.* 对…拒绝的

candidate *n.* 求职者

involve *v.* 涉及

arguably *adv.* 有论据地，可论证地

character *n.* 性格

questionnaire *n.* 调查问卷

procedure *n.* 过程

apparently *adv.* 显然地

ancient *adj.* 古代的

civil servant 公务员

military *adj.* 军队的

appropriate *adj.* 恰当的

nature *n.* 本性

compile/write test 出题

expert *n.* 专家

indicator *n.* 指标

roughly *adv.* 基本上

truthful *adj.* 真实的

forward-looking *adj.* 有远见的

personality *n.* 性格

fit into the team or group 融入到集体或团队中

have faith in colleagues' ability 相信同事的能力

interview *n.* 面试

keep deadlines 赶上规定期限

personal information 个人信息

question technique 提问技巧

select new staff 选拔新员工

selection procedure 选拔程序

selection technique 选拔技巧

staff selection 人员选拔

Section 4 场景：课堂报告——关于手工艺品帽子的制作

presentation *n.* 课堂报告

project *n.* 课题

secondary school 中学

subject *n.* 课程

pupil *n.* 小学生

adapt *v.* 改变；使适应

roll *n.* 卷

wallpaper *n.* 墙纸

conical *adj.* 圆锥形的

overlap the cut 将切口处重叠

complicated *adj.* 复杂的

flap *n.*（帽）沿，边

bend *v.* 弯曲

stick *v.* 粘贴

glue *n.* 胶水

cover *n.* 桌布

pillbox *n.* 药盒

variation *n.* 变化

combination *n.* 结合

phase *n.* 阶段

design phase 设计阶段

two-dimensional *adj.* 二维的

small-scale *adj.* 小规模的

three-dimensional 三维的

experiment *v.* 做实验

impose *v.* 把…强加于

constraint *n.* 限制

pliable *adj.* 易弯的；柔韧的

grey *adj.* 灰色的

reflect *v.* 反映

enjoyable *adj.* 令人开心的

circular *adj.* 圆形的

stairway *n.* 楼梯

strip *n.* 条；带

crown *n.* 王冠

fairly *adv.* 相当地

castle *n.* 城堡

turret *n.* 塔楼

Test 3

Section 1 场景：同事间讨论预定圣诞大餐

sort out 弄清楚

hang over（不愉快的事情）困扰

definite *adj.* 肯定的；确定的

work out 计算出

straightforward *adj.* 简单的；直接的

book *v.* 预定

hopeless *adj.* 绝望的

be bound to 一定…的

pack *v.* 塞满

back-up *n.* 候补

reliable *adj.* 可靠的

ring *v.* 打电话

decent *adj.* 像样的

vegetarian food 素食

non-smoking section 无烟区

remind *v.* 提醒

onion *n.* 洋葱

roast *adj.* 烘烤的

lentil *n.* 扁豆，用于食物

curry *n.* 咖喱

tasty *adj.* 美味的

dessert *n.* 甜点

plum *n.* 葡萄干

pudding *n.* 布丁

plus *prep.* 加上

deposit *n.* 押金

confirm *v.* 确认

confirmation *n.* 确认

in advance 提前

guarantee *n.* 保证

bet *n.* 打赌

notice board 公告栏

newsletter *n.* 新闻通报

café *n.* 咖啡馆

Section 2 场景：校园运动设施介绍

facility *n.* 设施

membership *n.* 会员资格

appeal *v.* 呼吁

register *v.* 登记

passport-size photograph *n.* 护照规格的照片

issue *v.* 发放

opening hours 开放时间

discount *n.* 折扣

session *n.* 会期，课程

volleyball *n.* 排球

badminton *n.* 羽毛球

aerobics *n.* 有氧运动

dance studio 舞蹈室

intimate *adj.* 亲密的

ballet *n.* 芭蕾

martial arts 武术

separate *adj.* 分开的

car park *n.* 停车场

squash court 壁球场

tennis court 网球场

fitness room 健身房

annual fee 年费

be entitled to 有…的资格

cheque *n.* 支票

main hall 大厅

reception *n.* 接待处

sports centre 体育中心

Section 3 场景：课外讨论——申报参加青年电子工程师大赛

entry n 进入；登录

engineer *n.* 工程师

competition *n.* 比赛

jigsaw puzzle *n.* 拼图玩具

beeper *n.* 传呼机

designer *n.* 设计者

electronics *n.* 电路

surname *n.* 姓

visually *adv.* 视觉上的

handicapped *adj.* 残疾的

equipment *n.* 设备

length *n.* 长度

width *n.* 宽度

depth *n.* 深度

approximate *adj.* 大概的

electronic supply 电力供应

the mains *n.* 电源

battery *n.* 电池

special feature 特色

educational *adj.* 有教育意义的

brilliant *adj.* 棒极了的

comment *n.* 评论

envisage *v.* 设想

make plastic pieces 制作塑料部件

dimension *n.* [常作-s]尺寸；规格

handicap *v.* 加障碍于

range *n.* 范围

Section 4 场景：专题报告——鸵鸟的食用价值与驯养

rear *v.* 饲养

unusual type of livestock 特种家禽

rear sheep and poultry 饲养羊群和家禽

poultry *n.* 家禽

concentrate *v.* 集中注意力

domesticated *adj.* 驯养的

ostrich *n.* 鸵鸟

association *n.* 协会

breed *v.* 饲养

beef *n.* 牛肉

lamb *n.* 羊肉

pork *n.* 猪肉

kangaroo *n.* 袋鼠

slightly *adv.* 轻微地

tough *adj.* 硬的；艰苦的

crocodile *n.* 鳄鱼

pale *adj.* 苍白的

tender *adj.* 嫩的

fashionable *adj.* 时髦的

fatty *adj.* 含脂肪的；胖的

increasingly *adv.* 日益增加地

texture *n.* 质地

have similar taste and texture of beef 有牛肉的口味和质感

feather *n.* 羽毛

feather fan 羽毛扇

tribal *adj.* 部落的

ceremonial dress 礼服

good profit margin 丰厚的利润空间

out of fashion 过时的

hide *n.* 兽皮

square metre 平方米

leather *n.* 皮革

delicate *adj.* 精细的

delicate/good quality leather 精细/优质皮制品

stuff *n.* 东西

biltong *n.* 晒干的肉条

recognize *v.* 承认；认可

protein *n.* 蛋白质

low in fats and cholesterol 低脂低胆固醇

hindquarter *n.* 后臀及后腿

high in protein 高蛋白

embark on 从事；着手

mature *adj.* 成熟的

fertilized *adj.* 受精的

capital *n.* 资本

incubator *n.* 恒温箱

dependent *adj.* 依赖的

minder *n.* 照看者

intensively *adv.* 加强地

calf *n.* 小牛

hatch *v.* 孵化

nourish *v.* 滋养

nourished *adj.* 有营养的

initial *adj.* 最初的

outlay *n.* 花费

export *v.* 出口

look after 照顾

make good farming sense 农业投资价值高

Test 4

Section 1 场景：礼物选择——庆祝婴儿诞生

detail *n.* 细节；详情

weigh *v.* 给…称重

kilo *n.* 千（克）

centimetre *n.* 厘米

mass *n.* 块；团

curly black hair 黑色的卷发

pick up 接某人

refresh *v.* 使恢复；使清新

garage *n.* 车库；修车厂

last *v.* 持续

pot plant 盆栽

water *v.* 浇水

baby shampoo 婴儿洗发香波

talcum powder 爽身粉

birth statistics 出生资料

teddy bear 泰迪熊

soft toy 布娃娃

Section 2 场景：电视导购——家用器具

exhibition *n.* 展览

household gadget 家用器具

resident expert 常驻专家

investigate *v.* 调查

household *adj.* 家庭的

realistic *adj.* 逼真的

contain no glass 非玻璃制造

therefore *adv.* 因此

unbreakable *adj.* 不会破的

intent *n.* 意图

purpose *n.* 目的

stainless steel 不锈钢

unfortunately *adv.* 不幸地

recommendation *n.* 建议

natty *adj.* 整洁漂亮的

device *n.* 装置

whistle *n.* 口哨

holder *n.* 钥匙夹

basically *adv.* 基本上

pitch *n.* 音高

flash *v.* 闪光

press *v.* 挤压

button *v.* 按钮

keyhole *n.* 钥匙孔

unpleasant *adj.* 不舒服的

metal *n.* 金属

cushion *n.* 坐垫

masterpiece *n.* 杰作

gizmo *n.* 小发明

squeeze *v.* 挤压

handle *n.* 手柄

generate *v.* 产生

objective *n.* 目的

decoy *n.* 圈套

fake *adj.* 假的

scare *v.* 吓唬

burglar *n.* 窃贼

burglary *n.* 入室盗窃

vacuum flask 真空保温瓶

give off a weak light 发出微弱的光

guarantee *v.* 投保

maintain heat 保温

manufacture *n.* 制造业

on the down/weaker side 缺点

outdoor activities 户外活动

popular science 大众科学

sort out 区分

underwater *adv.* 在水下

Section 3 场景：课外研讨——论文撰写与修改

faculty *n.* 全体教员

anxious *adj.* 焦急的

chapter *n.* 章节

stand out 比同类事物好

amazing *adj.* 令人惊奇的

dash *v.* 猛冲

par *n.* 常态

division *n.* 分类

heading *n.* 标题

margin *n.* 边缘

relevant *adj.* 相关的

be relevant to 与…相关

approach *n.* 方法

valuable *adj.* 有价值的

complex *adj.* 复杂的

chronology *n.* 年表

simplistic *adj.* 简单化的

represent *v.* 表示

proof reading 校对

laser-printed *adj.* 激光打印的

faculty office 系办公室

draft *n.* 草稿

better choice 更好的选择

broad divisions 宽泛的分类

dash the writing off 匆忙完稿

do general research 做一般性研究

in/on the margin 在边缘空白处

information of housing 关于住宅的信息

interview data 采访数据

keep unchanged 保持不变

local housing 地方住宅

make a change 作改动

make some suggestions 提出一些建议

make the data clear 澄清数据

open well 开头开得好

revise *v.* 修改

rewrite *v.* 重写

start with 从…开始

support tutor 导师

That's about par for the course. 那是意料中的事。

Section 4 场景：学术讲座——关于噪音污染

environmental *adj.* 环境的

effect *n.* 影响

estate *n.* 房产

particularly *adv.* 尤其

highway *n.* 公路

somewhat *adv.* 稍微

abate *v.* 减少

extent *n.* 程度

modification *n.* 改动

significant *adj.* 重要的

developer *n.* 发展商

be about to do sth. 马上要做某事

outline *v.* 勾画轮廓

desirable *adj.* 令人渴望的

background *n.* 背景

propose *v.* 提议

perimeter *n.* 周长

normal noise threshold 正常噪音容忍度

decibel *n.* 分贝

construction *n.* 建设

modify *v.* 修饰；修改

specialized double glazing 特殊双层玻璃窗

glazing *n.* 上釉

acoustic *adj.* 听觉的

seal *n.* 密封

exterior wall 外墙

hinge *n.* 铰链

adjacent *adj.* 附近的

density *n.* 密度

intersection *n.* 十字路口

ceiling *n.* 天花板

plaster *n.* 石膏

plaster board *n.* 石膏板

mechanical *adj.* 机械的

ventilation *n.* 通风

install *v.* 安装

absorber *n.* 消音装置

air conditioning 空调

substantially *adv.* 实质上

millimeter *n.* 毫米

pane *n.* 窗户玻璃

essential *adj.* 必要的

minimum *n.* 最小值

take...into account 考虑

layout of the house 住宅的布局

interior bedroom wall 卧室内墙

laundry *n.* 洗衣房

block *n.* 街区

insulation *n.* 绝缘

air gap 气缝

at a significant cost 以昂贵的代价

cut out noise 切断噪音

double brick 双层砖

double thickness plasterboard 双层石膏板

go astray 迷路

home buyer 房屋买主

inner glass 内层玻璃

least traffic 车流量最少

less noisy area 低噪音区

light road traffic 车流量少

living area 起居地带

noise factor 噪音因素

noise level 噪音级别

outer glass 外层玻璃

overhead *adv.* 在头顶上

planned housing estate 已规划的住宅房产

private housing 私人住宅

sealed window 密封窗

剑桥雅思考试全真试题解析 4

Test 1

Section 1 场景：有关学校组织的旅游活动的咨询

cancel *v.* 取消

coach *n.* 长途汽车

confirm *v.* 确认

departure *n.* 出发

reserve *v.* 预定

（full）refund *n.* （全额）退款

schedule *n.* 时间表

vary *v.* 变化，不同

guided tours 有导游的游览

in advance 提前

notice board 公告栏

places of historical interest 历史古迹

sixteen-seater minibus 16座小巴

Section 2 场景：导游介绍古代村落遗址

a brief account 简要介绍

roam *v.* 闲逛，漫游

manufacture *v.* 制造

availability *n.* 可用性

raw materials 原材料

mineral *n.* 矿物，矿石

iron ore 铁矿石

abundance *n.* 充裕

fuel *n.* 燃料

coal *n.* 煤

craftsman *n.* 工匠

iron forge 铁匠铺

the bend in the river 河流的转弯处

water mill 水磨

steam engine 蒸汽机

plan *n.* （在地图题中指）平面图

entrance *n.* 入口

Ticket Office 售票处

Gift Shop 纪念品店

showroom 陈列室

on display 展出

grind *v.* 打磨

furnace *n.* 炉子

smelt *v.* 冶炼

cast *v.* 铸造

antique *n.* 古物

cottage *n.* 村舍

Section 3 场景：师生间就作业展开的讨论

assignment *n.* 作业

due *adj.* 到期的

extension *n.* 延期

medical or compassionate reasons 疾病或亲人病重或去世等原因

reference *n.* 参考书目

submit *v.* 提交（作业、论文）

research methodology 研究方法论

journal *n.* 期刊

relevant *adj.* 相关的

essential *adj.* 实质性的

bar graph 柱状图

photocopy *n.* 复印件

indicate *v.* 指出

proximity *n.* 临近

tenant *n.* 房客

Section 4 场景：关于树木对城市地貌影响的讲座

urban *adj.* 城市的

landscape *n.* 地形

vegetation *n.* 植被

significant impact 重大影响

as a whole 总体上

humid *adj.* 湿润的

inland city 内陆城市

on the local scale 在局部范围内

shady *adj.* 多荫的

internal *adj.* 内在的

mechanism *n.* 机制

temperature *n.* 温度

regulate *v.* 控制

evaporate *v.* 蒸发

humidify *v.* 使潮湿

property *n.* 特性

exploit *v.* 开发；利用

filter *v.* 过滤

considerably *adv.* 相当地

gust *n.* 阵风

built-up areas 建筑物密集的区域

intensify *v.* 加强

a belt of trees 林带

vehicle *n.* 车辆

surrounding *n.* 周围环境

frequency *n.* 频率

canyon *n.* 峡谷

high-rise *adj. & n.* 高楼（的）

enclose *v.* 装入

Test 2

Section 1 场景：讨论旅游行程

guidebook *n.* 旅行指南

chilled *adj.* 冰镇的

mineral water 矿泉水

cash *v.* 兑现

travellers cheque 旅行支票

exchange rate 汇率

teller *n.* 出纳员

temporarily *adv.* 临时地

transaction *n.* 交易

architect *n.* 建筑师

snack *n.* 小吃

sightseeing *n.* 观光

cathedral *n.* 大教堂

castle *n.* 城堡

Hang on!（英式英语口语）稍等！

art gallery 美术馆

botanical garden 植物园

church services 教堂礼拜仪式

charge *n.* 收费

spectacular *n.* 壮观

picnic *n.* 野餐

swan *n.* 天鹅

Section 2 场景：介绍学校咨询服务的讲座

counselling service 咨询服务

arise *v.* 出现

chase up 提醒某人尽快做某事

tutor *n.* 导师

feedback *n.* 反馈

stress *n.* 压力

adjust *v.* 调整

mounting pressure 日益增加的压力

deadline *n.* 最终期限

creep up on sb. 某事不期将至

cope with 应付

social network 社会关系网

social contacts 交往的人（如熟人、家人、朋友等）

anxiety *n.* 焦虑

trigger *v.* 引发

interrupted personal relationships 中断的个人关系

break off 中断，断绝

unmotivated *adj.* 没有动力的

concentrate *v.* 集中

resident *adj.* 常驻的

chaplain *n.*（军队、团体、医院里的）牧师

drop out 放弃

self-esteem *n.* 自尊

resit *v.* 重考，补考

anthropology *n.* 人类学

sympathetic *adj.* 同情的

dietary problems 饮食问题

to one's liking 合乎某人的喜好

upset *v.* 使不适

dietician *n.* 饮食专家

low-interest loan 低息贷款

musical instrument 乐器

welfare service 福利服务

staff cuts 裁员

appeal *n.* 要求，诉请

launch *v.* 发起

on behalf of 代表

understaffed *adj.* 人手不足的

Section 3 场景：课外研讨场景

assignment *n.* 作业

task *n.* 任务；作业

data *n.* 数据

assess *v.* 评估

social science 社会科学（研究社会中的人的科学，如政治、社会学等）

carry out 实施

subject *n.* 研究对象

questionnaire *n.* 调查问卷

interview *n.* 采访

time-consuming *adj.* 费时的

reckon *v.* （英式口语）猜想，估计

wording *n.* 措词

response *n.* 回应

reliable *adj.* 可靠的

drawback *n.* 缺点

response rate 回收率

reveal *v.* 揭示

sample *n.* 样本，例子

survey *n.* 调查

tutorial *n.* 辅导课

reading list 阅读数目

Section 4 场景：关于企业犯罪的讲座

contemporary *adj.* 当代的

preoccupation *n.* 关注之事

unique *adj.* 独特的

massive *adj.* 巨大的

corporate *adj.* 企业的

illegal *adj.* 非法的

in accordance with 与…一致

quote...unquote 用于引用语前后，表示如实引用

commit a crime 犯罪

theft *n.* 偷窃

embezzlement *n.* 盗用公款

fraud *n.* 欺骗

exclude *v.* 把…排除在外

excusable *adj.* 可原谅的

conventional *adj.* 常规的

ignore *v.* 忽视

mass media 大众传媒

under-reported *adj.* 报道不足的

in comparison with 跟…相比

academic circles 学术圈

specialist knowledge 专业知识

unaware *adj.* 不知道的，没察觉的

misfortune *n.* 不幸

dilute *v.* 冲淡

concentration *n.* （饮料）浓度

carton *n.* 硬纸盒，塑料盒

deception *n.* 欺骗

be deprived of 被夺取

undermine *v.* 破坏

illustrate *v.* 举例说明

reference to 关于

oil tanker 油轮

crew *n.* （船上或飞机上）全体工作人员

inquiry *n.* 调查

lay blame on 归咎于…

deliberately *adv.* 故意地

indifference *n.* 漠然

innocent *adj.* 无辜的

loophole *n.* 漏洞

Test 3

Section 1 场景：一女生咨询 homestay 租房事宜

move into 搬（家）进去

homestay *n.* 在当地居民家居住

particular *n.* 细节，详细 *adj.* 特殊的，详细的

post code 邮政编码

general English 普通英语

academic English 学术（专业）英语

get into sth. 进入某个领域

sound good 听起来不错

move out 搬出

accommodation *n.* 住处，膳宿

save sb. money 给某人省钱

single person 单身

company *n.* 陪伴；公司

be used to sth. 惯常，惯于

swimming pool 游泳池

pet *n.* 宠物 *adj.* 宠爱的，亲昵的

quite a bit 相当多（一般做副词修饰谓语动词）

deposit *n.* 存款；押金 *v.* 存放

insurance *n.* 保险，保险单

cash *n.* 现金

cheque/check *n.* 支票

proportion *n.* 比例

honour system 信用制度（出于信任而不加监督的制度，如学校的无监考考试制）

monthly *adj.* 每月的 *n.* 月刊

Section 2 场景：介绍一个 Summer Festival 以及其中的一些表演项目

fill sb. in on sth. 在某方面给某人提供信息

in store 贮藏着，准备着

timing *n.* 适时；时间选择

a couple of 两个；几个

allow *v.* 允许，承认

recover from 恢复

sensational *adj.* 非常好的；耸人听闻的

art exhibition 艺术展览

in particular 特别，尤其

circus *n.* 马戏团

plenty of 许多

distinct *adj.* 明显的；独特的

marquee *n.* 大帐篷；华盖

canvas *n.* 帆布

portable *adj.* 便携式的

green space 有草坪的绿地

car park 停车场

stadium *n.* 露天大型运动场

in spite of 不管

clown *n.* 小丑，粗鲁愚蠢的人

acrobatic *adj.* 杂技的，特技的

purist *n.* 纯化论者

showcase *n.* （商店或博物馆的玻璃）陈列橱

aerial display 航空展

feature *n.* 特征

well worth doing 值得做

puppet *n.* 木偶

routine *n.* 例行公事，常规

formation dancing 编队舞蹈

be taken with(by) 被征服

Section 3 场景：学生咨询学习技能课程

refer to 查阅；提到

enquire about 询问

refresher course 复习课程，进修课程

build up 树立；增进

undergraduate *n. / adj.* （尚未取得学位的）大学生（的）

postgraduate *n.* 研究生 *adj.* 毕业后的

art *n.* 艺术；文科

science *n.* 科学；理科

intensive *adj.* 精深的；透彻的

aim at 瞄准；针对

wide range of approaches 多方面的方法

strategy *n.* 策略

tip *n.* 技巧；小费

get the most from 最大限度地利用

presentation *n.* 介绍；课堂演示

motivational *adj.* 鼓励性的

take up 拿起；开始从事，占据

manage to 达成；设法

procrastination *n.* 延迟，拖延

leisure *n.* 空闲，闲暇

enrollment fee 报名费

morning tea 早茶

ahead of 在…前面

convenor *n.* 会议召集人

upgrade *n. / v.* 升级

cope with 与…竞争；应付

focus on 集中

stress management 压力管理

be better off 境况好

in line with 符合

registration form 登记表

Section 4 场景：报告——关于学生会活动中心选址问题

grateful *adj.* 感激的

Student Union 学生会

feasible *adj.* 可行的

ultimate beneficiary 终极受益者

facility *n.* 设施，工具

arrive at 到达，达到

option *n.* 选项，选择

submit *v.* 提交

questionnaire *n.* 调查问卷

approximately *adv.* 近似地；大约

collate *v.* 比较；核对

draw up 草拟

key point 关键点

in broad terms 宽泛地说

consensus *n.* 共识

crucial *adj.* 至关紧要的

outskirts *n.* 边界，（尤指）市郊

hall of residence 学校公寓

cite *vt.* 引用

lecture rooms 报告厅

access *n.* 通路，途径确*vt.* 存取；接近

living quarters 住宅，住舱

premise *n.* 前提

table games 桌上游戏（桥牌、桌球等）

gym *n.* (gymnasium)体育馆

travel agency 旅行社

insurance centre 保险中心

Student Counselling Centre 学生咨询中心

refectory *n.* (修道院\学院等处的)食堂，餐厅

largish *adj.* 相当大的

elitist *n.* /*adj.* 优秀人才(的)，杰出者(的)

surveillance *n.* 监视，监督

security personnel 安全(部门)人员

Test 4

Section 1 场景：准备一个同事的退休告别晚会

farewell *n.* 辞别

double the work 事倍功半

take notes 做笔记

near the time 时间紧迫

dinning room 餐厅

ought to 应该

office staff 办公室全体职员

faculty head 系主任

draw the line 划一界线，划定最后界限

handy *adj.* 手边的，便利的

have a little think 曾经想过

a set of 一套

social fund 社会活动基金

tape deck 录音机

later on 稍后

set up 设立

student leader 学生干部

Section 2 场景：旅游信息——自动电话咨询

deal with 处理；涉及

appropriate *adj.* 适当的

latest price list 最新的价格表

complaint *n.* 诉苦；投诉

discerning traveller 精明的(有分辨力的)旅行者

Western Europe 西欧

watch out 密切注视，提防

in detail 详细地

guarantee *n.* /*vt.* 保证

cater for 供应伙食；迎合

pride *n.* 自豪 *v.* 使自豪，使自夸

communal tables 公共餐桌

on top of 在…之上；另外

plus *prep.* 加上

Section 3 场景：学生讨论5个与儿童有关的实验

get hold of 抓住，得到

hovercraft *n.* 气垫船，水翼船

balloon *n.* 气球

engine *n.* 发动机；机车

cushion of air 气垫

paperclip *n.* 曲别针

units of measurement 度量衡单位

rock salt 岩盐，石盐

copper sulphate 硫酸铜

dissolve *v.* 溶解；解散

crystal *n.* 水晶，结晶

segment *n.* 段 *v.* 分割

merge *v.* 合并

ordinary light 自然光

equipment *n.* 装备

hand drill 手钻

pin *n.* 大头针

bolt *n.* 门闩，螺钉

tame *adj.* （口语）无聊的

amplifier *n.* 扩音器，放大器

go through 经历，经受

turn sb. off 让某人失去兴趣

for good 永久地；一劳永逸地

fortnight *n.* 两星期

halfway decent 还算不错的

write up 详细描写

babyish *adj.* 稚气的

cut out 切掉

age group 年龄段

start off 出发；开始

end up 最后，以…为结果

store sth. for later 留到以后

Section 4 场景：讲座——澳大利亚的鲨鱼与捕鲨网

reputation *n.* 名誉，名声

hunt one's pray 打猎，猎取食物（猎物）

dangerous creature 危险的生物

essentially *adv.* 本质上，本来

breed *v.*（使）繁殖 *n.* 品种，种类

acute *adj.* 敏锐的，[医]急性的

sense of smell 嗅觉

剑桥雅思考试全真试题解析 5

Test 1

Section 1 场景：旅游度假咨询

operate *v.* 管理；操作

coast *n.* 海岸

whale *n.* 鲸鱼

coach *n.* 长途汽车

run *v.* 组织；运营

at most 最多

main beach 最大的海滩

bushwalk *n.* 丛林徒步旅行

extra *n.* 额外的收费

snake *n.* 蛇

tennis court 网球场

table tennis 乒乓球

cancellation *n.* 取消

deposit *n.* 押金

provisional booking 临时预定

tour *n.* 游览

in particular 尤其

beach *n.* 海滩

minibus *n.* 小巴士

peak times 高峰期

sighting *n.* 观看

cruise *n.*（口语）游览，旅行，周游

skeleton *n.* 骨架，骨骼

cartilage *n.* 软骨

meshing *n.* 网孔

pliable *adj.* 易弯曲的，柔软的

be crowded with 充满，满是

scale *n.* 刻度；鱼鳞

Tahiti *n.* 塔希提岛（位于南太平洋，法属波利尼西亚的经济活动中心）

barb *n.* 鱼钩

maximum temperature 最高温度

big seas 汹涌的大海

sandpaper *n.* 砂纸

rolling waves 波涛汹涌

underneath *adv.* 在下面 *prep.* 在…的下面

strong currents 巨浪

fin *n.* 鳍，鱼翅

less effective 不太有效

scavenge *v.* 打扫；以（腐肉）为食

fishing trip 钓鱼旅行

reptile *n.* 爬行动物

pool *n.* 游泳池

by the hour 按小时

accommodation package 膳宿一揽子计划

booking *n.* 预约

credit card 信用卡

reference number 查询号码

Section 2 场景：产品介绍

programme *n.* 广播电视节目

baby cot 婴儿床

feature *v.* 描述特征

recommend *v.* 推荐

brake *n.* 刹车

concern *vi.* 担心，关心

trap *v.* 卡住

minus side 负面（因素）

hazard *n.* 危害；冒险

dangerous *adj.* 危险的

niggle *v.* 为小事花时间操心

discontinue *v.* 终止，停止

comfort *n.* 舒适

bent in 向内弯曲

sharp *adj.* 尖锐的

tip *n.* 秘诀；警告

budget price 廉价

verdict *n.* 评判，评语

slight problems 小毛病

matter *vi.* 要紧，有重大关系

side bar 侧柱

satisfactory *adj.* 令人满意的

pick up 搭人；抱起

label *v.* 贴标签

convenient *adj.* 方便的

detach *v.* 分开，分离，拆开

best buy 最好卖的商品

rust *v.* 生锈

edging *n.* 镶边，磨边；(衣服)边饰

toddler *n.* 蹒跚学步的人，婴儿

Section 3 场景：选课

management *n.* 管理

prospectus *n.* 大纲，计划书

intensive *adj.* (课程)强化的

advantage *n.* 优势，好处

financial circumstance 财政状况

relevant *adj.* 相关的

personnel management 人事管理

keen *adj.* 渴望的

modular course 单元课程

involve *v.* 涉及

discussion *n.* 讨论

essay *n.* 论文

report *n.* 报告

diploma course 学位课程

full-time *adj.* 专职的，全部时间的

part-time *adj.* 兼职的，非全日的

disadvantage *n.* 劣势，坏处

administration *n.* 管理

focus on 集中，聚焦

current *adj.* 目前的

unpaid leave 无薪假期

flexible *adj.* 灵活的

seminar *n.* 研究小组，研讨会

workshop *n.* 学术专题研讨会

assessment *n.* 评估

Section 4 场景：关于不同性别省钱的讲座

attitude *n.* 态度

social *adj.* 社会的

gender *n.* 性别

intelligent *adj.* 聪明的

essential *adj.* 本质的

assumption *n.* 假设，假定

save up 储蓄

retirement *n.* 退休

furthermore *adv.* 而且

pension *n.* 退休金，补助金

confidence *n.* 自信

initiative *n.* 第一步，着手；主动精神

various *adj.* 不同的

cultural *adj.* 文化的

basically *adv.* 基本上

therefore *adv.* 因此，所以

pretension *n.* 抱负，意图；自负

fundamental *adj.* 基础的

surprisingly *adv.* 令人惊讶地

nursing care 照料

crisis *n.* 恐慌，危机；转折，转变期

effectively *adv.* 有效地

low-risk investment 低风险投资

consequence *n.* 后果

Test 2

Section 1 场景：图书馆信息咨询

minimum joining age 最低加入年龄

document *n.* 文献；证件

bank statement 银行报告单(结单)

current *adj.* 现在的；通用的

reference book 参考书

fiction *n.* 小说

in place 适当的

nominal *adj.* 名义上的，微不足道的

advisable *adj.* 可取的

database *n.* 数据库

The Guardian《卫报》

The Independent《独立报》

photocopying *n.* 复印

black-and-white *adj.* 黑白的

fill out 填入

driving licence 驾照

otherwise *adv.* 否则

local library 当地图书馆

external *adj.* 外部的

fine *n. / v.* 罚款

logging on 登录（网站等）

thereafter *adv.* 此后

notice *n.* 通知

access *n.* 接近；门路 *v.* 接近

The Observer《观察报》

The Times《泰晤士报》

facilities *n.* 设施

along *adv.* 往前；一起

Section 2 场景：介绍一个慈善机构

charity *n.* 慈善事业，慈善机构

contact *n.* 接触；联系；交涉

developing countries 发展中国家

adventure *n.* 冒险，奇遇；商业投机

carry out 进行，实施

come to an end 结束

whereas *adv.* 但是

carpenter *n.* 木匠

distribute *v.* 分配，分发

enormous *adj.* 巨大的

container *n.* 集装箱；容器

run out 花完，用完（钱等）

donate *v.* 捐献

spare part 备用零件

export *v.* 出口

Ecuador *n.* 厄瓜多尔

voluntary organization 志愿者组织

survey *n.* 研究

rural *adj.* 乡下的，农村的

unusually *adv.* 通常

radius *n.* 半径，半径范围

for free 免费的

constant *adj.* 固定的，稳定的；不屈不挠的

Amsterdam *n.* 阿姆斯特丹

profile *n.* 外形，形象

strip...down 拆下来

consignment *n.* 交付；托卖

Section 3 场景：讨论作业

tutorial *n.* 有老师辅导的讨论

camera *n.* 摄像机

instruction *n.* 指导，指令

cooperate *v.* 合作

experiment *n./v.* 实验

focus *n.* 焦距

feedback session 信息反馈课

film *n./v.*（拍摄）影片

slang *n.* 俚语

compromise *v.* 和解，对…妥协

angle *n.* 角度

semester *n.* 学期

Section 4 场景：讲座

remarkable *adj.* 奇异的

Antarctica *n.* 南极洲

hostile *adj.* 不友善的

permanent *adj.* 永久的

survival *adj.* 生存的

extreme *n.* 极端

fresh water 淡水

iceberg *n.* 冰山

cost-effective *adj.* 节省成本的

all-year-round *adj.* 整年的

well-equipped *adj.* 装备好的

keep fit 保持身体健康

ice-shelf *n.* 冰层

build-up *n.* 上升，增高

extendable *adj.* 可延长的

carbohydrate *n.* 碳水化合物

compact *adj.* 协议，条约

insufficient *adj.* 不足的

capacity *n.* 身份，资格；吸引力

crucial *adj.* 关键的

monitor *v.* 监视

indicator *n.* 标识

index *n.* 指数

vacancy *n.* 空缺

continent *n.* 大陆

remote *adj.* 遥远的

uninhabited *adj.* 无人居住的

ultimate *adj.* 极限的

wilderness *n.* 旷野

ice-cap *n.* 冰盖

category *n.* 范畴

integrate *v.* 使成为整体

summer-only *adj.* 仅仅在夏天的

self-contained *adj.* 不爱说话的；独立的

gym *n.* 体育馆

satellite link 卫星链接

sledge *n.* 雪橇

come up with 作出决定

kilocalorie *n.* 千卡

ration *n.* 定额

freeze-drying *n.* 冷冻干燥

cutting edge 最前沿

marine biologist 海洋生物学家

profound *adj.* 深奥的

ozone layer 臭氧层

ultra-violet radiation 紫外线辐射

administrative *adj.* 管理的

insight *n.* 洞察力

Test 3

Section 1 场景：买车

make *n.* 样式，款式；制造

power *n.* 动力

gear *n.* 排挡，齿轮

manual *adj.* 手动的

shade *n.* 色度，(颜色)浓淡深浅

terms *n.* 价钱；条款

valuation *n.* 评估

postcode *n.* 邮政编码

mileage *n.* 英里数

metallic grey 金属灰

engine *n.* 发动机

do *v.* 行，可以；适合

presume *v.* 假定，认为

automatic *adj.* 自动的

go for 喜欢

arrangement *n.* 安排，料理

full name 全名

get hold of 找到，得到

roughly *adv.* 大概地

call in 来访

Section 2 场景：介绍学校

physical *adj.* 自然的，天然的

capability *n.* 能力

engineering *n.* 工科；工程学

geography *n.* 地理学，地理

sip *n.* 啜饮，呷

reference *n.* 推荐人

move along 向前进行

phone sb. up 给某人打电话

concern *n.* 关心的事情

norm *n.* 规范，准则

adjust *v.* 调整，适应

priority *n.* 优先权

category *n.* 范畴，种类

sort out 弄清楚，整理；解决

in advance 提前

in good time 及时地

make allowance for 体谅

geographical *adj.* 地理的

assessment *n.* 测试；评估

science *n.* 理科；自然科学

sales talk 销售演讲，招揽买卖的话

hold-up *n.* 延迟

keep in touch 保持联络

devise *v.* 设计，策划

liaise *v.* 与某人建立联系，保持联络

awful *adj.* 可怕的；极坏的

take a while 花一段时间

body *n.* 团体；主要部分

allocation *n.* 配给，分配

exceed *v.* 超过

snap up 抢先做某事

agency *n.* 代理

on one's behalf 为…的利益；代表

audience *n.* 听众

Section 3 场景：课程评价

feedback *n.* 反馈

communication *n.* 交流；通讯；书信

outline *n.* 提纲

dead *adv.* 绝对地，完全地

whole load of 大量，大批

on a course 学习一门课程

key text 重要课文

evaluation *n.* 评分，评价

presentation *n.* 陈述，表达

clarity *n.* 明确，清晰

course code 课程编码

gosh *int.* 天啊

session *n.* 学期；一段时间；会议期

all of a sudden 突然

course delivery 课程讲授

handout *n.* 讲义，小册子

reserve *n.* 储备（物）

assignment *n.* 作业，任务

criteria *n.* 标准

stressful *adj.* 产生压力的

Section 4 场景：废物回收

project *n.* 项目

recycle *v.* 回收，重复利用，再循环

target *n.* 目标

emission *n.* 放出物，发射物

greenhouse *n.* 温室

incineration plant 焚化植物

drop-off *n.* 丢弃；下降

remove *v.* 移动

oddly *adv.* 奇怪地

fiberglass *n.* 玻璃纤维

filtration *n.* 过滤

conditioner *n.* 调节器

alternative *adj.* 交替的，二选一的

bumper *n.* 保险杠

scheme *n.* 计划，方案

polystyrene *n.* 聚苯乙烯

sum up 总结

household *adj.* 家庭的 *n.* 家庭

shock *v.* 震惊

carbon dioxide 二氧化碳

virgin material 原材料

landfill site 垃圾填埋地

come up 发生，出现

bale *v.* 打包

toughen *v.* 使强韧，使困难

import *v.* 进口

manufacture *n.* 生产

stationery *n.* 文具

ban *v.* 禁止

deal with 处理

container *n.* 容器；集装箱

vend *v.* 贩卖，出售

polycup *n.* 聚苯乙烯杯子

Test 4

Section 1 场景：寄宿家庭咨询与申请

fix sb. up with... 为某人提供某物

host family 寄宿家庭

address *n.* 地址

extension *n.* 延期

permit *n.* 许可

occupation *n.* 职业

advanced *adj.* （英语学习水平）高级的

intermediate *adj.* （英语学习水平）中级的

particular requirement 特别要求

vegetarian *n.* 素食主义者

facility *n.* 设备

en suite 套间（即卧室含卫生间）

move in 搬进去

approximately *adv.* 大约

Section 2 场景：足球俱乐部会议上的发言

soccer *n.* 足球

season *n.* 赛季

competition *n.* 比赛

picnic *n.* 野餐会

presentation of prizes 颁奖

training sessions 训练课

committee *n.* 委员会

president *n.* 主席

treasurer *n.* （组织、俱乐部等）财务主管

fee *n.* 费用，收费

equipment *n.* 设备

volunteer *v.* 自愿

newsletter *n.* （组织、俱乐部等内部）新闻摘要

regularly *adv.* 按时地

Head Coach 主教练

refreshments *n.* （会议、运动赛事期间提供的）食品饮料

Section 3 场景：师生讨论商业案例

case study 案例分析

exam assessment 考试评估

summarise *v.* 总结

take... on board 完全理解；接受

advertising campaign 广告宣传活动

on top of 在…之外

immediate *adj.* 直接的

competition *n.* 竞争

get to grips 理解或解决某些难题

be stalled by 被…所拖累、耽搁

colossal *adj.* 巨大的

be set back 受挫

interest rates 利率

market share 市场份额
be credited to 归因于
favourable terms 优惠条件
cautious *adj.* 谨慎的
assume *v.* 假定
dramatic *adj.* 巨大的；突然的
a simple fix 简单的解决办法
go under 破产
intrinsic *adj.* 固有的，内在的
innovative *adj.* 有创新的
foregone conclusion 定局
stock market 股市
realistic expectations 现实的期望值
kick-start *v.* 起动
come up with 想到

Section 4 场景：对大学图书馆的介绍
guidance *n.* 引导
guided tour 带导游的参观
muddle *v.* 使…迷惑
computer literate 会使用计算机的

剑桥雅思考试全真试题解析 6

Test 1

Section 1 场景：健身中心入会咨询
membership *n.* 成员资格，会员身份
facility *n.* 设备，设施
tennis court 网球场
primarily *adv.* 首要地；根本上
badminton *n.* 羽毛球
vice versa 反之亦然
keep-fit *n.* 健身
judo *n.* 柔道
yoga *n.* 瑜伽
fully-licensed 完全获得许可的
option *n.* 自由选择，选择权
scheme *n.* 计划；系统
annual *adj.* 每年的
subscription *n.* 签名承诺，同意
assessment *n.* 测试；估定
instructor *n.* 教官；教师
trial *n.* 试验，试用

Section 2 场景：剧场重开营业的采访
redevelopment *n.* 再开发

outline *n.* 概要，框架
available *adj.* 可以被使用的
permanently *adj.* 永久地
debatable *adj.* 值得商榷的，有争议的
critical *adj.* 批判性的，有鉴别能力的
MLA （Modern Language Association）文科或人文科
学中普遍采用的论文写作及标注格式
accessible *adj.* 容易使用的
phase... out 逐渐停止使用某物
eventually *adv.* 最终地
restricted *adj.* 有限制的
supervisor *n.* 管理者，负责人
oversee *v.* 监督，监管
induction *n.* 入门
initial *adj.* 最初的
dissertation *n.* 论文
relevant *adj.* 相关的
at the outset 在一开始的时候
bibliography *n.* 书目
register *v.* 注册

foyer *n.* 门厅；走廊
repainted *adj.* 重新刷漆的
box office 售票处
reoriented *adj.* 重定方位的
access *n.* 进入；接近
premises *n.* 地基
suitable *adj.* 合适的，恰当的
audience *n.* 观众
auditorium *n.* 听众席，观众席
leg-room *n.* 坐椅间的空档
stuffy *adj.* 闷的；乏味的
wheelchair *n.* 轮椅
lift *n.* 电梯
performer *n.* 表演者
backstage *n.* 后台
convert *n.* 改建
airy *adj.* 空气充足的
electronic *adj.* 电的
lighting *n.* 照明
install *v.* 安装
experiment *n.* 试验

curtain *n.* 幕布，窗帘

Section 3 场景：课程咨询

tutor *n.* 导师，老师

enroll *n.* 注册

part-time *adj.* 业余的

recommend *v.* 推荐

integrate *v.* 合而为一；综合

particular *adj.* 特别的

presumably *adv.* 推测地，假定地

refectory *n.* 餐厅，食堂

allergy *n.* 过敏

in advance 提前

eligible *adj.* 合适的，合格的

nursery *n.* 幼儿园

supervise *v.* 监督，监管

qualified *adj.* 有资格的

stock *v.* 贮存，储藏

journal *n.* 期刊

audio-visual *adj.* 视听的

cassette *n.* 磁带

manual *n.* 手册

hire *v.* 租用

laptop *n.* 手提电脑

queue up 排队

Section 4 场景：伦敦东部历史的讲座

East End 伦敦东部

head *v.* 朝…走去

livestock *n.* 家畜

feed *v.* 喂养

invasion *n.* 侵略

tribe *n.* 部落

leather *n.* 皮革，皮革制品

conquer *v.* 征服，克服

prosperous *adj.* 繁荣的，兴旺的

restriction *n.* 限制

newcomer *n.* 新来的人

merchant *n.* 商人

money-lender *n.* 借款人，债主

dock *n.* 船坞

construct *v.* 建造，建设

eventually *adv.* 最终地

economically *adv.* 经济地

alternative *n.* 选择

marshland *n.* 沼泽地

drained *adj.* 已排水的

port *n.* 港口

poverty *n.* 贫困

suffer *v.* 折磨

appalling *adj.* 令人毛骨悚然的

sanitary *adj.* 卫生的

tenant *n.* 佃户；房客

landlord *n.* 房主，房东

electricity *n.* 电

implication *n.* 含义，暗指

nutrition *n.* 营养

Test 2

Section 1 场景：关于博物馆营业时间及服务范围的电话咨询

craft *n.* 手工艺

accompany *v.* 陪伴，伴随

adult *n.* 成人

cavern *n.* 大洞穴

label *v.* 标注，加标签

glue *n.* 胶水

decoration *n.* 装饰

splash *v.* 泼

Section 2 场景：电话咨询火车运营时间

leaflet *n.* 宣传单

commuter line 上下班线路

buffet car（火车）餐车

refreshments *n.* 茶点，便餐，饮料

open ticket 不限时间的票

discount *n.* /*v.* 打折，优惠

fascinating *adj.* 迷人的，醉人的

excursion *n.* 游览，短途旅行

surround *v.* 围绕

acclaim *v.* 喝彩，欢呼；称赞

climbing wall 攀岩壁

aquarium *n.* 水族馆

anticipate *v.* 期待，热望

Section 3 场景：论文

dissertation *n.* 论文

tutorial *n.* 导师辅导

target *n.* 目标

analysis *n.* 分析

catalogue *n.* 目录

survey *n.* 调查

discipline *n.* 知识领域；(尤指大学的)学科，科目

loan *n.* 借出；贷款

statistics *n.* 数据

draft *v.* 打草稿；*n.* 草稿

embark *v.* 着手

Section 4 场景：关于电影发展史的讲座

hoof (pl. hooves) *n.* 蹄

gallop *v.* 奔跑

succession *n.* 连续

fellow *n.* 伙计，同伴

primitive *adj.* 原始的；简单的

motion *n.* 动作，动态

projection device 投影设备

line up 排队

rival *n.* 对手

tendency *n.* 趋势

tension *n.* 紧张

loop *n.* 圈

sensation *n.* 感觉能力，感觉

faint *v.* 晕

craze *n.* 一时兴起的强烈兴趣

sound effect 声效

subtitle *n.* 字幕；副标题

compensate *v.* 补偿

Test 3

Section 1 场景：银行开户

account *n.* 账户

current *adj.* 流动的

application *n.* 申请

spelling *n.* 拼写

previous *adj.* 上一个的，以前的

profession *n.* 专业，职业

security *n.* 安全

minimum *n./adj.* 最小(的)，最小量(的)

statement *n.* 银行存取款记录

insurance *n.* 保险

detail *n.* 细节

deposit *n./v.* 存款

leaflet *n.* 传单；活页

joint *adj.* 联合的

occupation *n.* 职业

identity *n.* 身份

Indonesian *n.* 印度尼西亚人 *adj.* 印度尼西亚的

transfer *v.* 转；转账

register *v.* 注册

Section 2 场景：景点介绍

tenant *n.* 房客

running water 自来水

haven *n.* 避难所

mullion *n./v.* (用)窗框竖棂(分开)

tile *n.* 瓦

chimney stack 烟囱群

oak *n.* 橡树

greenhouse *n.* 温室

mulberry *n.* 桑葚

souvenir *n.* 纪念品

estate *n.* 房产

footbridge *n.* 人行桥，步行桥

welcome *adj.* 受欢迎的；好的

mill *n.* 磨房

hesitation *n.* 犹豫

devastate *v.* 使不知所措

privacy *n.* 隐私

sandstone *n.* 砂岩

brick *n.* 砖

clay *n.* 红土，黏土

orchard *n.* 果园

exotic *adj.* 外国的；奇异的

wander *v.* 漫游，漫步

far side 远端

signpost *n.* 广告柱；路标

woodland *n.* 林地

shade *n.* 阴凉处

stunning *adj.* 惊人的

Section 3 场景：作业——市场调查

assignment *n.* 作业

instruction *n.* 指令

industry *n.* 产业

questionnaire *n.* 调查问卷

observation *n.* 观察资料，观察数据

pop *n.* 流行音乐

folk *n.* 民间音乐 *adj.* 民族的；民间的

concert *n.* 音乐会

department store 百货商店

pub *n.* 酒馆

opera house 歌剧厅

leave...out 省略；排除

carry out 进行，开始

entertainment *n.* 娱乐

branch *n.* 分支

face-to-face *adj.* 面对面的

preference *n.* 偏爱；优先权

jazz *n.* 爵士乐

classical *n./adj.* 古典音乐(的)

live music 现场直播的音乐表演等

disco *n.* 迪斯科舞厅

club *n.* 俱乐部

karaoke bar 卡拉OK酒吧

time-scale *n.* （用以表示事件发生或发展一段时间的）时标

Section 4 场景：新石器时代讲座

hunter-gatherer *n.* 以狩猎采集为生者

Neolithic *adj.* 新石器时代的

hypothesis *n.* 假说，假设；前提

archaeological *adj.* 考古学的

add up （口语）说得通，加起来得到理想的结果

practical *adj.* 实用的

continental *adj.* 大陆的

sufficient *adj.* 足够的

viable *adj.* 能独立生存的，能独立发展的

scatter *v.* 散开

sustain *v.* 保持

descend *v.* 下来；遗传

species *n.* 物种

assume *v.* 假设

exceed *v.* 超过

severely *adv.* 严重地

restrict *v.* 限制

colonise *v.* 开拓为殖民地，使聚居

fleet *n.* 舰队，船队

cereal *n.* 谷物

wheat *n.* 小麦

barley *n.* 大麦

pottery *n.* 陶器

embed *v.* 嵌入；包围

botanist *n.* 生物学家

plough *v.* 耕地，犁地

excavation *n.* 发掘

cultivation *n.* 开垦农田

husbandry *n.* 农业，饲养业

shelter *n./v.* 庇护(所)

permanent *adj.* 永久的

dwelling *n.* 居住地

axe *n.* 斧子

systematically *adv.* 系统地

exploit *v.* 使用；剥削

quarry *n.* 采石场

ample *adj.* 丰富的

innovation *n.* 革新

hollow *adj.* 空的 *v.* (使)空，挖空

thickness *n.* 厚度

stitch *n.* 针

Test 4

Section 1 场景：预订会议室

conference *n.* 会议

reservation *n.* 预订

option *n.* 选择

arrange *v.* 安排

delegate *n.* 代表团

demand *n./v.* 要求

wh.huh *inter.* 啊

pack *n.* 打包

otherwise *conj.* 否则的话

straight *adj.* 直接的

Section 2 场景：展览中心的准备活动

staff *n.* 工作人员

exhibition *n.* 展览

recruit *v.* 招募

color-coded *adj.* 以颜色为代码的

handle *v.* 解决，处理

stamp *v.* 盖章

publicity *n.* 宣传；广告

information booth 咨询台

hospitality *n.* 好客，热情

chef *n.* 大厨

monitor *v.* 监管

considerable *adj.* 相当多的

orientation *n.* 方向；适应；熟悉

temporary *adj.* 临时的

tax *n.* 税

presentation *n.* 展示

buffet *n.* 自助餐

delay *v.* 延误

Section 3 场景：图书馆

site n. 地点

castle n. 城堡

online adj. 在线的

database n. 数据库

reference n. 参考

sociology n. 社会学

secondary adj. 中学的

primary adj. 小学的

familiarize v. 熟悉

resource n. 资源

periodical n. 期刊

CD-ROM n. 压缩光盘

hang on to 保留，保有

renew v. 续借

overdue adj. 过期的

recall v. 召回，收回；回忆

workshop n. 研讨会，讲习班

dissertation n. 论文

academic adj. 学术的

convention n. 习惯；规律

bibliography n. 参考书目

Section 4 场景：介绍亚洲狮

roam v. 漫游

vast adj. 巨大的；广袤的

globe n. 地球

habitat n. 居住地

sub-species n. 亚种

fold n. 褶子

underside n. 下面；腹部

sanctuary n. 禁猎区，保护区

vulnerable adj. 易受伤的

gene n. 基因

split off 分开，分离

decline v. 减少

steadily adv. 稳定地

mane n.（马、狮的）鬃

noticeably adv. 引人注意地

pool n. 共用物；（基因）库

die out 消亡

vitality n. 活力

livestock n. 牲畜，家畜

drought n. 干旱

剑桥雅思考试全真试题解析 7

Test 1

Section 1　场景：行程路线咨询

transport information 交通信息（咨询中心）

airport n. 机场

rent n. 租金 v. 租

option n. 选择

at least 至少

public transport　公共交通

comfortable adj. 舒适的

cab n. 出租车

available adj. 可用的

greyhound n. 灰狗巴士

shuttle n. 往返汽车；航天飞机

budget n. 预算

whereabouts adv. 在何处 n. 行踪，下落

departure n. 离开

depend on 取决于

flight n. 航班

hang on 稍等

private address 私人地址

reserve v. 预定

fill out 填表

time of arrival 到达时间

baggage n. 行李

fare n. 费用

in advance 提前

词汇拓展

airport fee 机场费

international airport 国际机场

domestic airport 国内机场

airport terminal 机场候机楼

international terminal 国际候机楼

international departure 国际航班出港

domestic departure 国内航班出港

satellite n. 卫星楼

arrival n. 进站（进港、到达）

customs n. 海关

gate/departure gate 登机口

departure lounge 候机室

flight number 航班号

arriving from 来自……

scheduled time (SCHED) 预计时间

actual time 实际时间

delay *n.* 延误

boarding *n.* 登机

currency exchange 货币兑换处

baggage claim 行李领取处

transfer correspondence 中转处

nothing to declare 不需报关

goods to declare 报关物品

Section 2 场景：旅行社介绍

audience *n.* 观众

background information 背景信息

retail chain 连锁零售

camping *n.* 露营

campsite *n.* 露营地

continental *adj.* 大陆的

exclusive *adj.* 严格限制的；独有的

majority *n.* 大多数

expand *v.* 扩大；扩张

particularly *adv.* 特别是

mountainous *adj.* 多山的，山地的

region *n.* 地区

considerably *adv.* 非常地；相当地

original *adj.* 原始的；原来的

superb *adj.* 极好的，一流的

facility *n.* 设施

occupy *v.* 占有，占用；忙于

take advantage of 利用

well-qualified *adj.* 高素质的

enthusiastic *adj.* 热心的

mime *n.* 模仿表演，哑剧表演

competition *n.* 比赛；竞赛

model making 模型制作

child-friendly *adj.* 方便儿童使用的

occasionally *adv.* 偶尔

insurance *n.* 保险

reservation *n.* 预订

recommend *v.* 推荐

regular *adj.* 经常的；定期的

special offer 特价

luxury *n.* 奢侈，高级

tent *n.* 帐篷

standard adj. 标准的 *n.* 标准

high-quality *adj.* 高质量的

barbecue *n.* 烧烤架；烧烤

blanket *n.* 毯子

mop *n.* 墩布，拖把

bucket *n.* 桶

词汇拓展

keepsake *n.* 纪念品

knick-knack *n.* 小饰品

local guide 地陪

marine life 海洋生物

meadow *n.* 草地，牧场

parachuting *n.* 跳伞

ramble *n.* 漫游

rainforest *n.* 热带雨林

resort *n.* 胜地，常去处

package tour 打包旅行

spotlight tour 集中精华游

outing *n.* 短途外出

Section 3 场景：关于管理学调研的研究

workplace *n.* 工作场所

individualism *n.* 个人主义

family business 本国企业

multinational company 跨国公司

fundamentally *adv.* 基本地

contribute *v.* 作贡献

attitude *n.* 态度

diversity *n.* 多样性，差异

behave *v.* 行为，表现

personality *n.* 个性

gender *n.* 性别

variation *n.* 差异

encourage *v.* 鼓励

creativity *n.* 创造性

unfortunately *adv.* 不幸地

conflict *n.* 冲突

utilize *v.* 利用，使用

identify *v.* 识别；辨认，区分

in fashion 风行，流行

neglect *v.* 忽略，忽视

responsibility *n.* 责任，职责

individuality *n.* 个性，独特处，个人特质

co-operation *n.* 合作

conformity *n.* 顺从，服从；一致性

personnel department 人事部门

applicant *n.* 申请人（者）

psychological *adj.* 心理学的，心理上的

convince *v.* 说服

overrate *v.* 评价过高，高估

demonstrate *v.* 展示，表现

recognition *n.* 认可，承认

priority *n.* 优先，优先权

词汇拓展

flexibility *n.* 灵活性

adaptability *n.* 适应性

competitive *adj.* 竞争激烈的

team-work spirit 团队合作精神

a fat salary 收入颇丰

sense of responsibility 责任感

material gains 物质待遇

promising future 前途大好

bright prospect 光明的前景

upgrade oneself 提升自我

inspiring *n.* 鼓舞人心的

motivation *n.* 动机

workaholic *n.* 工作狂

working environment 工作环境

work overtime 加班

social recognition 社会认可

promotion opportunity 提升机会

Section 4 场景：关于纳米比亚考古的讲座

seminar *n.* （小型）学术研讨会

archaeological *adj.* 考古的，考古学的

fieldwork *n.* 野外实地调查

fantastically *adv.* 绝妙地，极好地

participation *n.* 参与；出勤

introduction *n.* 概括，介绍

contemporary *adj.* 当今的，当代的

interpretation *n.* 翻译，理解

engraving *n.* 石刻

footprint *n.* 足迹

scholar *n.* 学者

track *n.* 轨迹，足迹

mystery *n.* 秘密；谜团

illustration *n.* 说明

accurate *adj.* 正确的

identifiable *adj.* 可辨认的

unrealistic *adj.* 非现实的

researcher *n.* 研究人员

complex *adj.* 复杂的

unintentional *adj.* 非故意的，无意的

observe *v.* 观察

disrespectful *adj.* 忽视 不尊重

priceless *adj.* 无价的

fragile *adj.* 物价的

precious *adj.* 珍贵的

intact *adj.* 未开发的，原封不动的，完整的

词汇拓展

field observation 实地观察

field of view 视野；视场

field size 农地面积

field sketching 实地描绘

field study 实地考察

field survey 实地调查

environmental conservation 环境保护

environmental constraint 环境限制

environmental degradation 环境退化

environmental improvement 环境改善

environmental lapse rate 环境递减率

environmental risk 环境风险

humid climate 湿润气候

humidity *n.* 湿度

humification 腐殖质化〔作用〕

marine climate 海洋气候

mountain climate 山地气候

mountain range 山脉

Test 2

Section 1 场景：关于购买汽车保险的问询

insurance *n.* 保险

daytime *adj.* 日间的

dentist *n.* 牙医

model *n.* 型号

relationship *n.* 关系

brother-in-law *n.* 小舅子（妻子的兄弟）

quote *n.* 报价

词汇拓展

insurance company 保险公司

sum insured 保险金额

policy-holder *n.* 保险客户，投保人

branch of insurance 保险类别

insurer/underwriter *n.* 保险业者，保险商

termination of risk 保险责任中止

coverage *n.* 保险范围

insured/assured *n.* 被保险人

survey *n.* 调查（收入等）

notice of loss 损害通知书

to renew 续保

null and void 宣告无效

deposit premium 预付保险费

reinsurance *n.* 再保险，分保

natural loss 自然损耗

natural calamities 自然灾害

Section 2 场景：景点介绍

stopping points 停靠地（点）

palace *n.* 宫殿

residence *n.* 居所，住处

refreshment *n.* 茶点，点心

commercial *adj.* 商业的

shallow *adj.* 浅的

arcade *n.* 拱廊，有拱廊的街道

commentary *n.* 解说

departure *n.* 出发，离开

hop-on hop-off 随上随下

词汇拓展

art museum 美术馆

art gallery 画廊

botanical garden 植物园

monument *n.* 纪念碑

public telephone 公共电话

public lavatory 公共厕所

national highway 国道

traffic light 交通灯

barracks *n.* 兵营

metropolis *n.* 大都市

shopping centre 商业区

municipality *n.* 市政当局

municipal *adj.* 市的，市政的

district *n.* 区

residential area 居民区，住宅区

urban *adj.* 市区的

suburb *n.* 近郊区

outskirts *n.* 郊区

slum *n.* 贫民窟，贫民区

shantytown *n.* 贫民区

Section 3 场景：关于南极科考的采访

Antarctic *adj.* 南极的

Antarctica *n.* 南极

complementary *adj.* 互补的

historical *adj.* 历史的

expedition *n.* 探险，远征

scientific base 科考基地

supply *v. / n.* 提供，供给

warehouse *n.* 仓库

specialist *n.* 专家

airforce *n.* 空军

recreate *n.* 再现

atmosphere *n.* 环境

showcase *n.* 陈列柜

co-operation *n.* 合作

awesome *adj.* 令人敬畏的

magnificent *adj.* 壮丽的，美妙的

continent *n.* 大陆

treaty *n.* 条约

propose *v.* 提议

territory *n.* 土地，领土，领地

prohibit *v.* 禁止

explosion *n.* 爆炸

词汇拓展

hemisphere *n.* 半球

humid *adj.* 潮湿的，湿润的

hurricane *n.* 飓风，狂风

hydrological cycle 水分循环

icecap *n.* （高山等上的）常积不消的冰，冰盖

inadvertent *adj.* 疏忽的，无意中做的

industrial production 工业生产

industrial revolution 工业革命

industrialization *n.* 工业化

industrialized *adj.* 工业化的

atmosphere *n.* 大气，空气

atmospheric *adj.* 大气的

atmospheric temperatures 大气温度

Section 4 场景：用手习惯对人在音乐和体育方面的影响

handedness *n.* 用手习惯

relevance *n.* 关联，相关性

psychologist *n.* 心理学家

sheer *adj.* 纯粹的，全然的

observation *n.* 观察

insight *n.* 洞察力

capacity *n.* 能力

musician *n.* 音乐家

instrument *n.* 乐器

regularity *n.* 规律性

undertake *v.* 承担；接受

keyboard *n.* 键盘

proportion *n.* 比例

consistently *adv.* 一贯地，坚持地

refer to 意指

dominant *adj.* 占优势的，支配的

laterality *n.* 偏侧化

opposite *adj.* 相对的，相反的

hockey stick 曲棍球棒

invisible *adj.* 看不见的，无形的

gymnastics *n.* 体操

predominant *adj.* 占主导地位的

词汇拓展

growth *n.* 生长

maturation *n.* 成熟

adaptation *n.* 适应

adjustment *n.* 调整

congenital attribute 先天属性

transition *n.* 转换

imitation *n.* 模仿

instinctive behavior *n.* 本能行为

habituation *n.* 习惯化

equilibrium *n.* 平衡

babyhood *n.* 婴儿期

childhood *n.* 童年期

preschool period 学前期

juvenile period 少年期

adolescence *n.* 青少年期

genius *n.* 天才

gifted child 天才儿童

Test 3

Section 1 场景：找兼职工作

available *adj.* 可得到的

register *v.* 注册

degree *n.* 学位

student card 学生证

take...off (某段时间)休假、休息

position *n.* 职位

appeal *v.* (对某人)有吸引力，使(某人)感兴趣

clerical *adj.* 职员的，办公室人员的

involve *v.* 包括，涉及

hang on 稍等

manage *v.* 做成(某事)

come up 发生，出现

hall of residence (大学的)学生宿舍

administrative *adj.* 行政的

enquiry *n.* 问询

词汇拓展

job hunting 找工作

waiter *n.*(饭店、旅馆等的)服务员

waitress *n.*女服务员

supervisor *n.* 监督人；监察员；管理者

warehouse *n.* 货仓

hairdresser *n.*(尤指为女子服务的)理发师

barber *n.*(给男子剪发和刮胡子的)理发师

laundry *n.* 洗衣店

grocery *n.* 杂货店

nosh bar 小吃店，快餐店

tuck shop(尤指在学校附近的)小吃店，糖果店

Section 2 场景：关于徒步募捐的介绍

charity *n.* 慈善；慈善团体

sponsor *v./n.* 赞助(人)

donate *v.* 捐赠

guarantee *v./n.* 保证(人)

disabled *adj.* 肢体有残疾的

the disabled 残疾人

certificate *n.* 证书

daunt *v.* 使(某人)气馁

spectacular *adj.* 壮观的

bedding *n.* 铺盖

rucksack *n.*(远足者、登山者用的)背包

marvelous *adj.* 极好的，绝妙的

historic *adj.* 历史上著名的或重要的

weave *v.* 编织

deliberately *adv.* 故意地

leaflet *n.* 散页印刷品；(通常指)传单

itinerary *n.* 旅行路线

acclimatize *v.* (使)适应新环境；服水土

culminate *v.* 终于获得某种结局或结果

gorgeous *adj.* 极好的；非常漂亮的

词汇拓展

Scout *n.* 童子军

pass the hat 募捐

charitable institution 慈善机构

philanthropist *n.* 慈善家

charity ball 慈善舞会

good works 慈善行为

hospital *n.* [用于机构名称中]慈善收养院

charity school 慈善学校

Section 3 场景：关于海洋研究的讨论

robotic *adj.* 机器人的，自动的

profile *n.* 轮廓；侧面

launch *v.* 发射；投掷；提出（抗议等）；发出（命令等）

Indonesia *n.* 印度尼西亚

impressive *adj.* 给人深刻印象的

activate *v.* 激活

satellite *n.* 卫星

variation *n.* 变化，变动，变异（的程度）

salinity *n.* 盐分；盐浓度，咸度；含盐量

meteorological *adj.* 气象学的

El Nino 厄尔尼诺

ozone *n.* 臭氧

depletion *n.* 削减，消耗

prevail *v.* 胜（过），优胜

rescue *v./n.* 援救

implication *n.* 含意；暗示，暗指

preserve *v.* 保护，维持；把……圈为禁猎地

sustainable *adj.* 能维持的

词汇拓展

Arctic Ocean 北冰洋

Indian Ocean 印度洋

Atlantic Ocean 大西洋

Pacific Ocean 太平洋

Oceania 大洋洲

America 美洲

Africa 非洲

Asia 亚洲

Europe 欧洲

Section 4 场景：有关旅馆设施和服务的发言

hospitality *n.* 殷勤的款待

disorient *v.* 使迷失方向；使神智迷乱

dispirit *v.* 使气馁，使沮丧

opulent *adj.* 富裕的；丰富的，丰饶的

contemporary *adj.* 当代的

external *adj.* 外面的

investigate *v.* 调查

chic *n./adj.* 漂亮（的）；潇洒（的）；时髦（的）

boutique *n.* 精品店；镶嵌珠宝（或镀金）的日用品（或奢侈品）

mansion *n.* 大厦

luxury *n.* 奢侈（品）

dispense with 省却，免除

maximize *v.* 使最大化

sleek *adj.* 雅致的；时髦的；豪华的

underpin *v.* 加强……的基础；[喻]支持，巩固

hotelier *n.* 旅馆老板

predictability *n.* 可预测性

indulge *v.* 使（自己）沉迷；使满足；纵容

pamper *v.* 纵容，娇养

spoil *v.* 溺爱

treat *v.* 对待；款待

  n. 款待；难得的乐事

miniscule *adj.* 很小的

词汇拓展

lease *n.* 租约

furniture *n.* 家具

stereo *n.* 立体音响装置

fridge *n.* 电冰箱

radiator *n.* 暖气

microwave stove 微波炉

quilt *n.* 被子

pillow *n.* 枕头

sheet *n.* 床单

towel *n.* 毛巾

bed-linen *n.* 床单及枕套

closet *n.* 壁橱

Test 4

Section 1 场景：租房

homestay *n.* 在当地人家里寄宿

enroll *v.* 报名，注册

advanced English 高级英语

preference *n.* 喜好；优选

veterinarian *n.* 兽医

vegetarian *n./a.* 素食主义者（的）

handball *n.* 手球

词汇拓展

cricket *n.* 板球

rugby *n.* 英式橄榄球

football *n.* 美式橄榄球

soccer *n.* 英式足球

hockey *n.* 曲棍球

squash *n.* 壁球

baseball *n.* 棒球

softball *n.* 垒球

ice hockey 冰球

Section 2 场景：公园介绍

bicentennial *a.* 200年的，持续200年的

demolition *n.* 爆破；破坏

derelict *a.* 被抛弃了的

warehouse *n.* 仓库

storehouse *n.* 仓库，栈房

housing *n.* 住房

complex *n.* 综合（体育馆）

formal park 以规则的几何图形布局的公园

feature *n.* 地势，地形

fantastic *a.* 极好的

arena *n.* 体育馆，竞技馆

gymnastics *n.* 体操

synchronized swimming 花样游泳

diving *n.* 跳水

ornamental *a.* 装饰性的

shed *n.* 棚屋，小屋

mangrove *n.* （热带沿海生长的）红树

accessible *a.* 可以进入的

boardwalk *n.* 木板路

far end 远端

refuge *n.* 保护区

shelter *n.* 棚子；庇护所 *v.* 保护

binoculars *n.* 双筒望远镜，双目显微镜

词汇拓展

valley *n.* 山谷

dale *n.* 溪谷

rocky *a.* 多石的

cave *n.* 洞穴

hike *v.* 远足，徒步旅行

hike out 露营

villa *n.* 别墅

manor *n.* 庄园

kiwi *n.* 几维鸟

ostrich *n.* 鸵鸟

cobra *n.* 眼镜蛇

poisonous spider 毒蜘蛛

crocodile *n.* 鳄鱼

chameleon *n.* 变色龙

scuba diving 潜水

barbecue *n.* 烧烤

cave exploiting 洞穴探险

mountain climbing 攀岩

sailing *n.* 航海；帆船运动

drifting *n.* 漂流

rose *n.* 玫瑰

lily *n.* 百合

carnation *n.* 康乃馨

pomelo *n.* 柚子

grapefruit *n.* 葡萄柚

Section 3 场景：老师布置展示作业

presentation *n.* 针对某一专题发表的演讲

assess *v.* 评估

historical *a.* 历史的

geographical *a.* 地理的

overview *n.* 综述

nope *ad.* （口语）不

seminar *n.* 研讨会

positive *a.* 确定的，肯定的

overhead projector 投影仪

scale *n.* 规模

resource *n.* 资源

brochure *n.* 小册子

literacy *n.* 识字，读写能力；有学问

encyclopaedia *n.* 百科全书

enthusiastic *a.* 有激情的，热情的

tutorial *n.* 指导课，个别指导

词汇拓展

assignment *n.* 作业

deadline *n.* 最后期限，截止日期

extension *n.* 延期

survey *n.* 调查，研究

questionnaire *n.* 调查问卷

Section 4 场景：关于味精的介绍

monosodium Glutamate 味精

enhancer *n.* 促进剂

cuisine *n.* 烹饪，烹调法

seaweed *n.* 海草，海藻

extraction *n.* 提取

amino acid 氨基酸

commercially *ad.* 商业地

crisp *n.* 油炸马铃薯

intensify *v.* 加剧

evolutionary *a.* 进化的

associate professor 副教授

protein *n.* 蛋白质

carbohydrate *n.* 碳水化合物

toxin *n.* 毒素

spoilage *n.* 损坏，腐烂

词汇拓展

leek *n.* 葱

ginger *n.* 姜

garlic *n.* 蒜

pepper *n.* 花椒

hot pepper 辣椒

rosemary *n.* 迷迭香

Great literature is simply language charged with meaning to the utmost possible degree。

幽默被人正确地解释为"以诚挚表达感受，寓深思于嬉笑"。

——美国诗人 庞德 *E*(*Ezra Poud, American poet*)

附录3：阅读真题认知词汇

Ⓐ

a cluster of 一系列

a cross-section of 代表；横切面

a false dawn 空欢喜

abdomen *n.* 腹，腹部

absenteeism *n.* 旷课，旷工

accepting *adj.* 易于接受的；赞同的

accreditation *n.* 认证

acoustic *adj.* 声学的；有关声音的

acquisition *n.* 获得；获得物

acre *n.* 英亩

activation *n.* 活化；激活

acupuncturist *n.* 针灸医生

adage *n.* 格言，谚语

adjunct *n.* 附属物；辅助物

adornment *n.* 装饰品

advantageous *adj.* 有利的；有益的

aeration *n.* 暴露在空气中

aeronautical *adj.* 航空学的

aesthetic *adj.* 审美的

affiliation *n.* 联系

afflict *v.* 使痛苦，折磨

ageless *adj.* 不老的；永恒的

ailment *n.* 疾病（尤指微恙）

airborne *adj.* 飞行中的；在飞行的

albeit *conj.* 虽然（即使）

aldehyde *n.* 醛，乙醛

alga *n.* （pl. algae）海藻

alienation *n.* 疏远；转让

alluvial *adj.* 冲积的，淤积的

alphabetical *adj.* 按字母顺序的

altitude tent 高原帐篷

altruistic *adj.* 无私的，利他的

aluminium *n.* 铝

ambassador *n.* 大使

amber *n.* 琥珀

ambiguity *n.* 含糊不清

amidst *prep.* 在…之中

ammonia *n.* ［化］氨

amongst *prep.* 在…中间

analogous *adj.* 类似的，相似的；可比拟的

anatomy *n.* 解剖学

ancestral *adj.* 祖传的；祖先的

anthropological *adj.* 人类学的

anthropologist *n.* 人类学家

antidote *n.* 解毒剂

antiquated *adj.* 陈旧的

antiquity *n.* 古老；古代

apace *adv.* 快速地

appeasement *n.* 缓解；平息

appreciably *adv.* 略微，有一点

approachability *n.* 可亲近

aptitude *n.* 天资

aquaculture *n.* 水产养殖业

archipelago *n.* 群岛

archive *n.* 档案

Arctic *n.* 北极

Aristotle 亚里士多德

arteriosclerosis *n.* 动脉硬化

arthritis *n.* 关节炎

artwork *n.* 艺术品，美术品

as per 按照，根据

asbestos *n.* 石棉

assemblage *n.* 与会者；聚集

assimilation *n.* 同化

assortment *n.* 混杂物，混杂体

asthma *n.* 哮喘

astronaut *n.* 宇航员

astronomy *n.* 天文学

atmospheric *adj.* 大气的

ATP *n.* 三磷酸腺苷

audacious *adj.* 大胆的，鲁莽的

aura *n.* 气氛

authenticate *v.* 鉴别

autoimmune *adj.* 自体免疫的

autonomous *adj.* 自治的

availability *n.* 可用性，有效性

avant-garde *n.* 先锋派，前卫

backlash *n.* 反撞；强烈反对

bacterial *adj.* 细菌的

bakelite *n.* 酚醛塑料，酚醛电木

baleen *n.* 鲸须

balk *v.* 犹豫，畏缩不前

banal *adj.* 平凡的；老一套的

bang *v.* 猛敲，猛撞；发出砰的响声

Bangalore 班加罗尔：印度中南部马德拉斯以西一城市

barrage *n.* 拦河坝；连续质问

basalt *n.* 玄武岩

beam *n.* 束

Beiji *n.* 白鳍豚

benevolent *adj.* 仁慈的

bent *adj.* 弯曲的

bereavement *n.* （亲人）丧亡

bilingualism *n.* 双语制；两种语言的使用

biomass *n.* （在一个单位面积或体积内的）生物量

biomechanics *n.* 生物力学

biometrics *n.* 生物测定学

black powder 黑色火药

blast *v.* 炸毁，摧毁 *n.* 爆炸，爆破

blind alley 死胡同

blink *n.* 眨眼

blonde *adj.* 金发碧眼的女人

blowhole *n.* （鲸等的）呼吸孔；喷水孔

board game 棋类游戏

Bolivia *n.* 玻利维亚

bottlenose dolphin 宽吻海豚

boulder *n.* 巨石

bounce *v.* 反射；反弹

bout *n.* 一段时间；一回合

Boutu *n.* 亚马逊海豚

bower *n.* 树荫处；闺房，卧室；凉亭

bowhead whale 北极露脊鲸，弓头鲸

breakneck *adj.* 高速而危险的

breeder *n.* 饲养者；栽培者

brittle *adj.* 脆的；易损坏的；冷淡的

bronchitis *n.* 支气管炎

brood *n.* 一窝；孩子们

budding *adj.* 发展中的

buffalo *n.* 水牛

bug *n.* 虫子

bureaucratic *adj.* 官僚政治的

burrow into 掘地洞；翻找

buzzer *n.* 蜂鸣器，警报器

bypass *v.* 绕过，避开

c. = circa 大约，左右

calf *n.* 幼崽

camel *n.* 骆驼

camouflage *v.* 伪装

campaigner *n.* 活动家

canal *n.* 沟渠，水道

canary *n.* 金丝雀

cancer-causing *adj.* 致癌的

candida *n.* 假丝酵母，念珠菌

candlewax *n.* 烛蜡

cannon *n.* 大炮，加农炮

capriciousness *n.* 任性；善变

capsize *v.* （尤指船）倾覆

captive *adj.* 被俘房的；被束缚的；可引申为"人工饲养的"

captivity *n.* 囚禁；监禁

carbon dioxide 二氧化碳

cardiovascular *adj.* 心脏血管的

cargo handling 货物装卸

carpeting *n.* 地毯；地毯织料

car pool 合伙用车

cartography *n.* 地图制作法，制图学

cartoonist *n.* 漫画家

cash management 现金管理

casualty *n.* 伤亡

catalyst *n.* 催化剂

cause *n.* 运动

cavort *vi.* 欢腾；雀跃；嬉戏

centimeter *n.* 公分，厘米

cervical *adj.* 子宫颈的

cetacean *n.* 鲸类动物，鲸

CFC *n.* chlorofluorocarbon 氟利昂

chalk *v.* 用粉笔在…上做记号

charcoal *n.* 木炭

chef *n.* 厨师长

chimpanzee *n.* 猩猩

chiropractor *n.* 按摩师；脊椎指压治疗师

chorus *n.* 合唱

churn *n.* 搅乳器

cipher *n.* 密码

circuit *n.* 环路；电路

circumscribe *v.* 限制，约束

clash *n.* 冲突

clear-cut *adj.* 明确的

clerical *adj.* 职员（工作）的

clerk *n.* 办事员

clientele *n.* 客户；委托人

coffer *n.* 资金

cognitive *adj.* 认知的

cognitive *adj.* 认知的；感知的

cohesion *n.* 内聚力

collaborative *adj.* 合作的，协作的

colonise *v.* 拓殖，殖民

combustion *n.* 燃烧

comet *n.* 彗星

communal *adj.* 公共的；公社的

comparatively *adv.* 比较地

compendium *n.* 纲要，概略

complexity *n.* 复杂性；复杂度

computational *adj.* 计算的；计算机的

conceptual *adj.* 概念的；概念上的

concur *v.* 同意，赞同

confer on 给予，授予头衔、荣誉勋章等

configuration *n.* 构造，结构

Confucius 孔子

conical *adj.* 圆锥形的

consequential *adj.* 结果的

conservatism *n.* 保守主义

consolidation *n.* 巩固

consortium *n.* 社团，协会，联盟，（国际）财团

consultant *n.* 顾问

consumerism *n.* 消费主义

containerisation *n.* 集装箱化

continually *adv.* 不断地

controller *n.* 控制者

convection *n.* 传达；对流

coolant-lined 流线型散热

Copernicus 哥白尼

coracle *n.* 小圆舟

cornerstone *n.* 基石；基础

corps *n.* 部队

corpus *n.* 一批资料；词料

cortex *n.* 脑皮层，皮层

cortical *adj.* 脑皮层的

cortisol *n.* 皮质醇（肾上腺皮脂激素）

counselor *n.* 顾问

counting house （昔日的）账房，会计室

countless *adj.* 无数的

courier *n.* 信使；信差

course *v.* 流动

courtship *n.* 求爱；求偶

cowpat 牛粪

coyote *n.* 土狼；山狗

crane *n.* 起重机

crater *n.* 火山口；弹坑

Cretaceous *n./adj.* 白垩系（的），白垩纪（的）

cropland *n.* 农田

crossbow *n.* 弩

crust *n.* 地壳

crystalline *adj.* 水晶的，晶体状的

cub *n.* 幼兽；幼崽

cubic meter 立方米

culprit *n.* 犯人；犯过失的人

curative *adj.* 医疗的，有疗效的

curator *n.* 监督人，负责人；馆长

cyan *n.* 蓝绿色，青色

cybernetics *n.* 控制论

cylinder *n.* 圆柱体

cylindrical *adj.* 圆柱体的

cystic *adj.* 胞囊的

D

dairy farm 乳牛场

dash *n.* 破折号

dearth *n.* 缺乏；不足

decipher *v.* 译解（密码等）

decompose *v.* 分解

decrepit *adj.* 破旧的；衰老的

deed *n.* 行为；行动

defendant *n.* 保护；被告

deficit *n.* 赤字

deforestation *n.* 滥砍滥伐

degenerate *v.* 退化；衰退

delta *n.* 三角洲

dementia *n.* 痴呆

demographer *n.* 人口统计学家

denounce *v.* 谴责，指责

deplete *v.* 耗尽；使衰竭

depletion *n.* 损耗

desalination *n.* 海水淡化

desert *v.* 离弃，抛弃

deter *v.* 阻止

digitize *v.* 将资料数字化

dire *adj.* 可怕的；迫切的

discharge *n.* 发射

disenchantment *n.* 觉醒；清醒

disfigure *v.* 损毁…的外貌

disjunction *n.* 分离，分裂

disparate *adj.* 根本不同的，不能比拟的

dispense *v.* 分发，分配

dispenser *n.* 药剂师；分发器

dispersal *n.* 分散

disposable *adj.* 一次性的，可任意使用的

disproportionately *adv.* 不成比例地

disruption *n.* 中断；分裂

disruptive *adj.* 使破裂的；干扰的

distaste *n.* 反感，厌恶

diversification *n.* 经营多样化

diversify *v.* 多样化

divert *v.* 转移，使转向

division *n.* 部门

dock *n.* 码头

doctoral *adj.* 博士的；博士学位的

dolphin *n.* 海豚

Dominican Republic *n.* 多米尼加共和国：西印度群岛
上位于伊斯帕尼奥拉岛东部的一个国家

drab *adj.* 单调的，乏味的

drainage *n.* 排水系统

drastically *adv.* 非常地

dredge *v.* 挖掘

dredger *n.* 挖泥机，挖泥船

droppings *n.* 粪

dung *n.* 粪

dung beetle 屎壳郎

dwindling *adj.* 日益减少的

dyke *n.* 堤，坝

dystrophy *n.* 营养失调

earnings *n.* 收益

earth-shattering *adj.* 惊天动地的

earthwork *n.* 建筑；土木工程

earthworm *n.* 蚯蚓

eccentricity *n.* 古怪，异乎寻常

echolocation *n.* 回声定位法

ecologist *n.* 生态学者

educationalist *n.* 教育家

ejection *n.* 喷出

El Nino *n.* 厄尔尼诺现象

elicitation *n.* 引出，诱出；抽出

elixir *n.* 灵丹妙药；长生不老药

Elizabethan *adj.* 伊丽莎白女王一世时代的

elucidate *v.* 阐明，说明，解释

embed *v.* 使插入；使嵌入

emblazon *v.* 用纹章装饰；炫示

emergent *adj.* 浮现的；新兴的；有民族意识的

emeritus *adj.* 荣誉退休的，退休的

emphysema *n.* 肺气肿

encapsulate *v.* 涵盖；概括

encase *v.* 装入；包住

encircle *vt.* 环绕，围绕

encode *v.* 破译

enfranchise *v.* 给予…选举权

enfranchisement *n.* 给予…选举权

engross *v.* (使)全神关注；吸引

entomologist *n.* 昆虫学家

entrepreneurship *n.* 企业家身份

epidemiologist *n.* 流行病学家

epitomize *v.* 作为…的缩影；代表

equation *n.* 相等；平衡

erroneous *adj.* 错误的；由错误得出的

erupt *vi.* (火山等)迸发，爆发

ethanol *n.* 乙醇

ethereal *adj.* 缥缈的，引申为"不切实际的"

ethnography *n.* 民族志学；人种学

eugenics *n.* 优生学；人种改良学

evoke *v.* 引发，引起

evolutionarily *adv.* 逐渐地

evolutionary *adj.* 演变的；进化论的

exacerbate *v.* 使加深

excavation *n.* 挖掘，发掘

exceptional *adj.* 例外的；异常的

exhale *v.* 呼气

exodus *n.* 大批离去

expletive *n.* 污言秽语；咒语

exploitative *adj.* 剥削的；榨取的

extrusion *n.* 挤出，推出，赶出

exuberant *adj.* 充满活力的；精力旺盛的

eye-catching *adj.* 引人注目的

F

facsimile *n.* 摹本；精确的复制品

fairground *n.* 露天马戏场，集市场地

fallow *adj.* 犁过而未播种的

fertilize *v.* 施肥

fertilizer *n.* 肥料

fibrosis *n.* 纤维化

finitude *n.* 界限，限制

firefly *n.* 萤火虫

fireworks *n.* 烟火

fixed assets 固定资产

fluid *n.* 液体

fluorescent *adj.* 荧光的；发亮的

fluster *v.* 使不安，使紧张；使困惑

foam *n.* 泡沫

focal *adj.* 焦点的

foetus *n.* 胎儿

folklore *n.* 民间传说，民俗

footage *n.* （影片的）连续镜头；片段

forage *n.* 觅食

foreland *n.* 海角；前沿地

forgo *v.* 放弃

formaldehyde *n.* 甲醛

formative *adj.* 格式化的；发展的

formulation *n.* 公式

fossil *n.* 化石

fourfold *adj./adv.* 四倍（的），四重（的）

fraught *adj.* 使人忧虑的

free radical 自由基

free-ranging *adj.* 自由放养的

freeway *n.* 高速公路

freshwater *adj.* 淡水的；内河的

Freud 弗洛伊德

fringe *n.* 边缘，外围

frock *n.* 连衣裙，女装

frost *n.* 冰冻，严寒；霜；结霜 *v.* （使）结霜，下霜

froth *n.* 泡，泡沫，琐物

frown upon 不同意，不许可

fruitless *adj.* 不结果实的

fumes *n.* 烟，气体

fur seal 海狗

G

garret *n.* 阁楼，顶楼小屋

gear *n.* 齿轮；传动装置

gene pool 基因库

genetic *adj.* 遗传的

genetical *adj.* 遗传的

genetics *n.* 遗传学

genome *n.* 基因组

genre *n.* 风格，格调；类型

germ-free *adj.* 无菌的

Giant's Causeway 巨人之路

gimmick *n.* 小玩意儿；花招，把戏

given *adj.* 指定的；特定的

glacial *adj.* 冰的，冰状的

gland *n.* 腺；密封管

gloomy *adj.* 阴暗的；忧郁的

glucose *n.* 葡萄糖

grail *n.* 圣杯

granite *n.* 花岗岩

granular *adj.* 颗粒状的

grapple *v.* 格斗，搏斗；努力设法解决

greenhouse effect 温室效应

grenade *n.* 手榴弹

grim *adj.* 严酷的

grind *v.* 磨，碾碎

Guatemala *n.* 危地马拉

H

habitat *n.* （动植物的）生活环境

haemoglobin *n.* 血红蛋白

halfway *adv.* 到一半，中途

hallmark *n.* 特点

hamster n. 仓鼠

hand in glove 同某人密切合作（尤指勾结）

handicap n. 障碍，不利条件

hard-core adj. 中坚的；死硬的，顽固不化的

hard-wired adj. 密切相关的；硬接线的

hard-won adj. 难得的，来之不易的

harridan n. 形容枯槁的老妇人；名声不好的老泼妇

haul v. 拖运

Hawaiian Islands 夏威夷群岛

head for 很可能遭受

head start n. （赛跑或竞争中）起步前的优势，有利开端

hectare n. 公顷（等于1万平方米）

helium n. 氦

helix n. 螺旋（形）

herbal adj. 草药的；草本植物的

herbalism n. 草药学；草本植物学

herbalist n. 草药医生

herdsman n. 牧人

heroic adj. 宏大的，宏伟的；英勇的

heyday n. 全盛时期

hiccup n. 打嗝；短暂的中断；间歇

hinterland n. 内地；内陆

hit-list n. 打击对象名单

hive n. 蜂巢

home visit 家访

homogeneous adj. 同种类的

honking n. 雁叫声

hormone n. 荷尔蒙，激素

hum n. 嗡嗡声

humpback whale 座头鲸

hurl v. 猛投，猛掷

hut n. 小屋

hybrid n. 混血儿；混合物

hydrogen n. 氢

hype n. 大肆宣传，天花乱坠的宣传

hypnotic adj. 催眠的

hypothetical adj. 假设的

ice-skate v. 滑冰

idiosyncratic adj. 特质的，异质的；特殊的

igloo n. 冰屋

ignite v. 点燃；引发

immunoglobulin n. 免疫球蛋白

impersonal adj. 冷淡的；无感情的

impetus n. 动力，促进物

impinge v. 侵犯

impoverished adj. 贫困的；赤贫的

in earnest 认真的（地）

in the light of 按照

in the pink 满面红光，身体健康

inaugurate v. 创立

incendiary adj. 能引起燃烧的

incendiary projectile 燃烧弹

inch n. 英寸；少许，一点儿 v. 慢慢地移动

incompatible adj. 不和谐的；无法共存的

incongruity n. 不合适，不合时宜

Indian susu 印度河中的一种小海豚

Indonesia n. 印度尼西亚

inedible adj. 不可食的

inescapable adj. 不可逃避的

infirmity n. 衰弱

influenza n. 流感

informant n. （为语言学调查）提供数据的讲本地话的人；资料提供人；线人

infra-red adj. 红外线的

inhalation n. 吸入

inheritance n. 遗传；遗产

inn n. 小旅馆，小酒馆

insomnia n. 失眠（症）

insularity n. 与外界隔绝的生活状况；（思想、观点等的）偏狭

insulating adj. 绝缘的

insulation n. 绝缘

insulin n. 胰岛素

interface n. 分界面；界面

intermix v. 混合

intermodal adj. 联合运输的

interpersonal adj. 人与人之间的，人际关系的

introspection n. 内省，反省

intruder n. 入侵者

inventory n. 存货清单；财产清单

invert v. 使颠倒

inverted commas 单引号，（英）引号

invoice n. 发票

Ireland n. 爱尔兰（共和国）

iris n. 虹膜

irrevocable *adj.* 不能取消的

irritability *n.* 过敏性，兴奋性；易怒

irritable *adj.* 易怒的

jerk *vi.* 颠簸；猝然一动

jeweler *n.* 珠宝商

jostle *v.* 挤，推；争夺

judicious *adj.* 明智的

Jupiter *n.* 木星

kaleidoscope *n.* 万花筒；变化多端；千变万化

Kant 康德

karoo *n.* 非洲南部的干旱高原

kayak *n.* (爱斯基摩人用的)皮船

kidney *n.* 肾

kitten *n.* 小猫

Krakatau *n.* 喀拉喀托火山(印度尼西亚一火山)

lagoon *n.* 咸水湖；潟海湖

largely *adv.* 大半

larva *n.* (pl. larvae)幼虫

lava *n.* 熔岩

lead *n.* 铅

leap *vi.* 跳跃；跳起

legitimacy *n.* 合法性，合理性

leopard *n.* 美洲豹

lethal *adj.* 致命的

leukemia *n.* 白血病

lexical *adj.* 词汇的

lexicographer *n.* 词典编纂者

like-minded *adj.* 志趣相投的

liken *v.* 把…比作

linger *v.* 继续存留

lingual *adj.* 舌状的；语言的；舌音的

lip *n.* 坑的边缘

lipread *v.* 观察人的嘴唇动作来理解话意

lizard *n.* 蜥蜴

locomotive *n.* 火车头；机车

logging *n.* 伐木业

long-buried *adj.* 被长期渴望的

longitudinal *adj.* 经度的

loot *v.* 掠夺，抢劫，劫掠

lopsidedness *n.* 不平衡，倾斜

ludicrousness *n.* 滑稽，可笑

lunar *adj.* 月亮的

lunatic *adj.* 疯狂的，疯癫的

luxuriant *adj.* 丰富的；富饶的

machete *n.* 弯刀

machinery *n.* (总称)机械，机器；机构

magenta *n.* 红紫色，洋红

magma *n.* 岩浆；糊剂，糊

magnetic resonance 磁共振

make-believe *n.* 虚幻；想象；缩造

malevolent *adj.* 恶毒的，狠毒的

malleable *adj.* 有延展性的

mammal *n.* 哺乳动物

managerial *adj.* 管理的

Manila *n.* 马尼拉

manioc *n.* 树薯(原产美洲热带)

mantle *n.* 地幔

Maori *n.* 毛利人；毛利语

marathon *n.* 马拉松赛跑

markedly *adv.* 显著地；明显地

marker *n.* 记号，标记

marketplace *n.* 市场

marsupial *n.* 有袋动物

matchstick *n.* 火柴杆

mate *v.* 成配偶；交配

materialise *v.* 变为现实

meagre *adj.* 瘦的；不足的

measurement *n.* 测量

megacity *n.* 大城市

melatonin *n.* 褪黑激素

mercury *n.* 汞，水银

metabolic *adj.* 新陈代谢的

meteorite *n.* 陨星，流星

methane *n.* 甲烷，沼气

metropolis *n.* 大城市

Mexico *n.* 墨西哥

microcosm *n.* 微观世界；缩影

microscope *n.* 显微镜

militant *adj.* 激进的；好战的

millimeter *n.* 毫米

mimetic *adj.* 模仿的，模拟的

mining *n.* 采矿

misjudge *v.* 判断错

mobility *n.* 灵活性

moisture *n.* 水分，湿气

molten *adj.* 熔化的；炽热的；铸造的

money-making *adj.* 赚钱的

monoculture *n.* 单作，单一栽培

monograph *n.* 学术专著，专论，专题著作

monoxide *n.* 一氧化物

monsoon *n.* 季候风，季风；（印度等地的）雨季

moody *adj.* 喜怒无常的

mother tongue 母语，本国语

motor *n.* 发动机

mould *n.* 模具

muddle *n./v.* 糊涂，混乱

muggy *adj.* 闷热的

multicultural *adj.* 多元文化的

multifaceted *adj.* 多方面的

mundane *adj.* 世界的；世俗的；平凡的

murky *adj.* 黑暗的

musculo-skeletal *adj.* 肌肉及骨骼的

Native American 印第安人；印第安人的

native speaker 说本族语的人

naturalistic *adj.* 自然的；自然主义的；博物学的

naturopath *n.* 自然疗法医师；理疗家

Navajo *n.* 纳瓦霍人（散居于新墨西哥州，亚利桑那州和犹他州的北美印第安人）

neatness *n.* 整洁

necessarily *adv.* 必定；必然地

neural *adj.* 神经系统的；神经中枢的

neuron *n.* 神经元

neuroscientist *n.* 精神科学家

neurotrophic *adj.* 神经营养的

New Zealand's National Party 新西兰国家党

newsprint *n.* 新闻用纸

newsreel *n.* 新闻短片

nicotine *n.* 尼古丁

nitrogen *n.* 氮

nitrogen dioxide 二氧化氮

nitrous *adj.* 氮的；含氮的

nomadic *adj.* 游牧的

non-existent *adj.* 不存在的

non-porous *adj.* 防渗的

non-verbal *adj.* 非用言语的；非语言性的

notable *adj.* 著名的

notational *adj.* 符号的

number plate 牌照

nutrient *n.* 营养品

oboe *n.* 双簧管

occultation *n.* 隐藏

ocean floor 海底基岩

octagonal-shaped *adj.* 八边形的

offender *n.* 犯罪者，违法者

officially *adv.* 正式地

oily *adj.* 油的；多油的；含油的

onwards *adv.* 向前地；在先地

ooze *n.* 软泥，泥浆

opinion poll 民意测验，民意调查

optimum *adj.* 最佳的；最适宜的

opulence *n.* 富裕

order *n.* 种类；[生物]目

ore *n.* 矿石，含有金属的岩石

orthography *n.* 正确拼字法

osteopath *n.* 整骨医生

outcrop *n.* 露出地面的岩层；露头

outer *adj.* 外部的，外层的

outward *adj.* 外表的；表面的

overlie *v.* 躺…上面

overstaff *v.* 为…配备人员过多

overstock *v.* 进货过多，库存过多

overuse 使用过度；滥用

oxygen *n.* 氧气

oxygenated *adj.* 被氧饱和的，氧化的

ozone *n.* 臭氧

pair up 把…配成一对

pancreatic *adj.* 胰腺的

panting *adj.* 气喘吁吁的

paralyse *v.* 麻痹；瘫痪

pastel *n.* 柔和的淡色彩

paster *n.* 贴纸

pasture *n.* 牧场

patch *n.* 补丁；小块区域

pathway *n.* 路径；神经纤维链

patronage *n.* 赞助，帮助

pedigree *n.* 家谱；起源，由来

penetration *n.* 穿过，渗透

pent-up *adj.* 被抑制的，不能自由表达的

per capita 每人

per se 本身，本质上

perimeter *n.* 周(边)，周长

periphery *n.* 外围

permafrost *n.* 永久冰冻；永冻土层，永冻层

perpetual *adj.* 永恒的

perpetuate *v.* 延续，保持

perquisite *n.* 特权

perverse *adv.* 荒谬的，变态的；任性的

pest *n.* 害虫

petrol *n.* 汽油

pharmaceuticals *n.* 药剂；药物；药品

phenolic resin 酚醛树脂

Philippines *n.* 菲律宾共和国，菲律宾群岛

photographic *adj.* 摄影的，照片的

physiological *adj.* 生理学的；生理学上的

pilot *n.* 飞行员 *adj.* 试点的

pineal *adj.* 松球状的

pip *n.* 军装上表示军官等级的星

pit *n.* 深坑；深渊

planner *n.* 策划者

plant *n.* 工厂

platelet *n.* 血小板

Plato 柏拉图

playful *adj.* 爱嬉戏的；顽皮的

playfulness *n.* 玩耍；嬉戏；顽皮

playing card 扑克牌

playmate *n.* 玩伴

plot *n.* 小块地

plough *n.* 犁

plyometrics *n.* 增强式训练

pneumonia *n.* 肺炎

pointless *adj.* 无意义的

Polynesian *adj.* 波利尼西亚的；波利尼西亚人的

populate *v.* 使人居住于；移民

porpoise *n.* 海豚

portrayal *n.* 描画，描写

power-based *adj.* 以电力为基础的，耗电的

pragmatic *adj.* 务实的，实际的

precarious *adj.* 不确定的，危险的

precipitation *n.* 降水(量)

predation *n.* 捕食；捕猎

predator *n.* 捕食者；食肉动物

predatory *adj.* 掠食的；食肉的

predispose *v.* 使倾向于；使易于患

prefrontal *adj.* 前额的，前额骨的

pregnancy *n.* 怀孕

premier *adj.* 首要的

pretender *n.* 冒充者；伪装者

prodigious *adj.* 巨大的；惊人的

projectile *n.* 射弹

propellant *n.* 推进剂

prototype *n.* 原型，模范，样本

prowess *n.* 杰出的才能；高超的技巧

proximity *n.* 接近；亲近

psychiatric *adj.* 精神病学的

psychiatrist *n.* 精神科医生

psychic *adj.* 精神的；心灵的

psycholinguistics *n.* 心理语言学

pterosaur *n.* 翼龙

puff *n.* 吸，抽；(烟、气等的)一缕

pull for 热情支持

pulverize *v.* 研磨成粉；摧毁

pumice *n.* 轻石，浮石

punch line *n.* 故事、戏剧、笑话中的妙句；关键句

punch *v.* 冲孔，打孔

puncture *v.* 戳破；化解

pup *n.* 幼崽；幼年

pupation *n.* 化蛹

pyrotechnic *adj.* 烟火的

quartile *n.* 四分位数

questionable *adj.* 可疑的

quota *n.* 配额

race-course 赛马场

racketeer *n.* 诈骗者；非法获取钱财者

rebound *v.* 重新跃起；回升

recalcitrant *adj.* 反抗的，顽抗的

recession *n.* 撤回，退回

recipient *n.* 容纳者，容器；接受者

reciprocity *n.* 互惠；相互依存；相关性

recourse *n.* 依靠；依赖；求助

reed *n.* 芦苇

reel *n.* 卷轴

reflex *n.* 反射，反射作用

regenerate *v.* 新生；重建；改革

regurgitate *v.* (使)涌回；(使)反刍

rehabilitate *v.* 使复原

rehabilitation *n.* 改造犯人；使恢复原状

rekindle *v.* 重新点燃；使复苏

remnant *n.* 残余物，剩余的东西

remuneration *n.* 报酬

rendition *n.* 处理；表演；翻译

rental *adj.* 租赁的

repack *n.* 重新打包

repatriate *v.* 遣返

repeatedly *adv.* 再三，一再；多次

repertoire *n.* 全部本领；全部功能

repetitive *adj.* 重复的，反复性的

reptile *n.* 爬行动物

reshape *v.* 改造；再成形

residue *n.* 残留物

respiratory *adj.* 呼吸的；与呼吸有关的

responsiveness *n.* 敏感度；敏感性

retailing *n.* 零售业

retard *v.* 延迟；使减速

retina *n.* 视网膜

retrenchment *n.* 费用削减；紧缩开支

revert *v.* 返回

revolutionise *v.* 宣传革命；大事改革

revolve *v.* (使)旋转；考虑

revulsion *n.* 厌恶，强烈的反感

rhesus *n.* 恒河猴

rheumatoid *adj.* 类风湿的

rickety *adj.* 不牢固的，快要散架的

rift *n.* 裂缝，隙缝 *v.* 使断裂；使裂开

right whale 露脊鲸

rigorously *adv.* 残酷地

rink *n.* 溜冰场

rocketry *n.* 火箭学；火箭技术

Rockies *n.* 落基山脉

roster *n.* 花名册

rub *v.* 摩擦；擦

rudimentary *adj.* 未完全发育的；未成熟的

rumble *v.* 发出隆隆声；辘辘行驶；低沉地说

runny *adj.* 松软的；水分过多的

runoff *n.* 流走之物；决胜投票

saber *n.* 马刀

sailplane *n.* 滑翔机

saliva *n.* 唾液

saltpeter *n.* 硝石

sampling theory 抽样法理论，抽查法理论

sanitation *n.* 卫生设施，公共卫生

sawdust *n.* 锯木屑

scamper *v.* 奔跳

scanner *n.* 扫描仪

scepticism *n.* 怀疑主义

scholarly *adj.* 博学的，学问精深的

scour *v.* 冲洗

scourge *v.* 鞭打，痛斥；折磨

scout *n.* 侦察

scrap *v.* 废弃

scrub *n.* 低矮丛林

scrupulous *adj.* 谨慎小心的，细心的

scrutinize *v.* 细察

scuffle *n.* 扭打；混战

seabed *n.* 海底，海床

sediment *n.* 沉积物

seed *n.* 种子；萌芽

self-evident *adj.* 不言而喻的；不言自明的

self-proclaimed *adj.* 自称的

semantic *adj.* 语义的

sensor *n.* 传感器

sensory *adj.* 感官的

serotonin *n.* 复合胺

set-up *n.* (事物的)安排，计划，方案

severity *n.* 严重性

sewage *n.* 下水道；污水

shaft *n.* 杆，柄

shredder *n.* 切碎机；碎纸机

shrewd *adj.* 精明的

sickle *n.* 镰刀

siesta *n.* 午睡

signification *n.* 字词的含义；意义

silt *n.* 淤泥；残渣

sinew *n.* 精力，体力；要害之处

size up 估计

sizeable *adj.* 相当大的

skills-training *n.* 技能训练

slapstick *n.* 闹剧，趣剧

sled *n.* 雪橇

slit *n.* 裂缝；狭缝

slop *v.* 溢出；溅出

slurp *n.* 啧啧吃的声音 *v.* 啜食

small-scale *adj.* 小规模的；小型的

smother *v.* 厚厚地覆盖；使窒息

snapshot *n.* 快照

sniff *v.* 用力吸，嗅

snowmobile *n.* 雪地汽车

social setting 社会环境

sociobiologist *n.* 社会生物学家

socio-economic *adj.* 社会经济学的；涉及社会和经济因素的

soft-boiled *adj.* 半熟的

soluble *adj.* 可溶的

South Africa 南非

spectrometer *n.* 分光计

sperm whale 抹香鲸

spoke *n.* (车轮上的)辐条

sponge *n.* 海绵，海绵状物 *v.* 海绵般吸收

sporadically *adv.* 不时发生地

sprawl *v.* 四肢伸开地坐(或卧)；爬行

sprint *n.* 短跑

squash *n.* 壁球

squeak *n.* 尖叫

squishy *adj.* 湿软的；黏乎乎的

stabilize *v.* 使稳定

stagnant *adj.* 不流动的

stall *n.* 货摊

standing *n.* 地位；身份；级别

starchy *adj.* 淀粉的；含淀粉的

stark *adj.* 刻板的，十足的 *adv.* 完全地

starkly *adv.* 明显地

stereoscopic *adj.* 有立体感的；有立体视觉的

stereoscopic vision 立体视觉；体视

sterilisable *adj.* 可消毒的

stigmatise *v.* 打烙印；诬蔑

stockpile *v.* 储蓄，贮存

stout *adj.* 结实矮胖的

stratosphere *n.* 同温层；平流层

streamlined *adj.* 流线型的

stringent *adj.* 严厉的

stripe *n.* 条纹

stumble *v.* 绊倒；使困惑

sub-category *n.* 亚类

subgroup *n.* 亚群；副族

subliminal *adj.* 潜意识的

subsoil *n.* 底土

substantially *adv.* 充分地

subtropical *adj.* 副热带的

suckling stage 哺乳期

Sudan *n.* 苏丹：非洲东北部一国家，位于埃及南部

Sudan Straits *n.* 苏丹海峡

sufferer *n.* 受害者；患病者

suffrage *n.* 选举权

suffragette *n.* 主张妇女参政权的女子

suited *adj.* 合适的

sulphur *n.* 硫磺

sulphur dioxide 二氧化硫

superficially *adv.* 表面地；表面性地

supersede *v.* 代替，接替

supplier *n.* 供应者

surge *n.* 汹涌，澎湃；激增 *vi.* 汹涌，涌动

swivel *v.* 旋转

synthesis *n.* 整合

synthetic *adj.* 综合的，合成的；人造的

syrup *n.* 糖浆

tablet *n.* 药片；写字板，便笺簿

tail-wagging *n.* 摇尾巴

tangibly *adv.* 可触知地，明白地

taper *v.* （逐渐）变细，变尖

tariff *n.* 关税

taste bud 味蕾

taunt *v.* 辱骂，嘲弄

tectonic *adj.* 构造的，建筑的；地壳构造的

temporal lobes 颞叶

tenable *adj.* 可维持的

terminology *n.* 术语学

terrain *n.* 地带

terrestrial *adj.* 陆生的；陆栖的；非水生的

textile *n.* 纺织品

thalassaemia *n.* 地中海贫血症

thatch *n.* 盖屋的材料；茅草屋顶

thaw *n.* 融雪

the European Renaissance 欧洲文艺复兴

the food chain 食物链

the learned 学者

the Nile Delta 尼罗河三角洲

the republic of letters 文学界，文坛

the Royal Society 英国皇家学会

therapist *n.* （特定治疗法的）治疗专家

thermo- 热的，与热有关的

thermosetting *adj.* 热定型的，热固的

Thule *n.* 古人相信存在于世界北端的国家，极北之地

tie up 占用（资金等）

tissue *n.* 纸巾，（生物学）组织

to and fro 往复地

to hand 随手可用，在手边

tobacco *n.* 烟草

toll *n.* 过桥过路费

tongue *n.* 语言

toothed *adj.* 有牙齿的

topography *n.* 地形学，地形

topsoil *n.* 表土

tortoiseshell *n.* 龟甲；玳瑁壳

tout *v.* 吹捧

trackage *n.* 铁路轨道线路

transcribe *v.* 记录；用音标记下…的语音

transient *adj.* 暂时的，短暂的

trappings *n.* 服饰；马饰

treacle *n.* 糖浆；糖蜜

treadmill *n.* 繁重的劳动；跑步机

trekker *n.* 背包客

trend-setting *adj.* 引领潮流的

Triassic *n./adj.* 三叠纪（的），三叠系（的），三叠纪岩石（的）

triglyceride *n.* 甘油三酸酯

trinket *n.* 小装饰物

troll *v.* 拖拉

tropical *adj.* 热带的

tropospheric ozone 对流层臭氧

tuck *v.* 隐藏；蜷缩

tungsten *n.* 钨

turbid *adj.* 混浊的；脏的

turn out 生产

turnover *n.* 营业额；成交量

tweak *v.* 扭，用力拉

two-fold *adj.* 双重的

typhoon *n.* [气] 台风

ultraclean *adj.* 超净的

ultrasonic *adj.* 超声波的

ultraviolet *adj.* 紫外线的

unbelievably *adv.* 难以置信地

uncompromising *adj.* 不妥协的

unconquerable *adj.* 不可征服的

under-achieving *adj.* 未能实现的

understandably *adv.* 可理解地；合乎情理地

undistinguished *adj.* 未经区分的；平凡的

undue *adj.* 不应有的

unobtrusive *adj.* 不显眼的，不醒目的

unorthodox *adj.* 非正统的，异端的

unpredictable *adj.* 不可预测的；不可预知的

unsaid *adj.* 未说出的

unwittingly *adv.* 不知不觉地

unwritten *adj.* 未成文的；口头的

upstream *adv.* 向上游

Uranus *n.* 天王星

utilitarian *adj.* 功利的

utterance *n.* 说话方式；发声；吐露；表达

V

verbal ability 口头表达能力

vertebrate *n.* 脊椎动物

vertical *adj.* 垂直的，直立的

vessel *n.* 船；容器

vested interest 既得利益

vicinity *n.* 邻近

vicissitude *n.* 变故，变迁，兴衰，浮沉

viral *adj.* 滤过性毒菌的，滤过性毒菌引起的

viscous *adj.* 黏滞的，粘稠的

vocal *adj.* 喜欢畅所欲言的，直言不讳的

vocalisation *n.* 发声，发嗓音

voiceprint *n.* 声波纹

volatile *adj.* 动荡不安的；易挥发的

volcanic *adj.* 火山的

volt *n.* （电压单位）伏

vulcanism *n.* 火山活动；火山作用

vulcanologist *n.* 火山学家

W

waggle *v.* 来回摇动，摆动

Wales 威尔士

war chest 专用资金；专款

warm-blooded *adj.* 温血的；恒温的

waterfront *n.* 滨水地区

waterways *n.* 水道，河道

wean *v.* 使丢弃

wear off 消退

whilst ＝while *conj.* 当…时候

wig *n.* 假发

wittingly *adv.* 故意地

wobble *n.* 摆动，动摇；不稳定；变度

woodflour *n.* 碎木屑

woodland *n.* 林地

workforce *n.* 工人总数

workwear *n.* 工作服

world-beating *adj.* 举世瞩目的

writhe *v.* 因剧痛而蠕动、扭动身体

Y

yolk *n.* 蛋黄，卵黄

Z

Zambia *n.* 赞比亚：非洲中南部一国家

zinc *n.* 锌

In music one must think with the heart and feel with the brains. Victor Hugo, French writer Jazz tickles your muscles, symphonies stretch your soul.

爵士乐使你的肌肉发痒，交响乐能舒展你的灵魂。

——美国指挥家 怀特曼 P（PaulWhiteman, American conductor）

新东方独家引进

《剑桥雅思考试全真试题集 8》

（含光盘 2 张）

剑桥大学考试委员会　编著

定价：110 元　开本：16 开　页码：176 页

《剑桥雅思考试全真试题集 7》

（含光盘 2 张）

剑桥大学考试委员会　编著

定价：110 元　开本：16 开　页码：176 页

《剑桥雅思考试全真试题集 6》

（含光盘 2 张）

剑桥大学考试委员会　编著

定价：110 元　开本：16 开　页码：176 页

《剑桥雅思考试全真试题集 5》

（含光盘 2 张）

剑桥大学考试委员会　编著

定价：110 元　开本：16 开　页码：176 页

◎ 4 套完整的学术类雅思全真试题

◎ 2 套培训类雅思阅读与写作全真试题

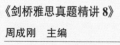

《剑桥雅思真题精讲 8》

周成刚　主编

定价：28 元　开本：16 开　页码：208 页

《剑桥雅思考试全真试题集 7 精讲》

周成刚　主编

定价：28 元　开本：16 开　页码：234 页

《剑桥雅思真题精讲 4、5、6》

周成刚　主编

定价：55 元　开本：16 开　页码：500 页

◎ 洞悉雅思出题规律，精确剖析雅思真题

◎ 针对中国雅思考生的特点和需求，分题型全面破解

《剑桥雅思常见错误透析》

Pauline Cullen，Julie Moore　编著

定价：18 元　开本：32 开　页码：136 页

《剑桥雅思语法》（附 MP3）

Diana Hopkins，Pauline Cullen　编著

定价：45 元　开本：16 开　页码：272 页

◎ 雅思备考资料官方出版机构推出的权威雅思语法教程

◎ 剑桥资深语法专家为全球雅思考生量身定做

《剑桥雅思词汇》（附 MP3）

Pauline Cullen　编著

◎ 错误警示：帮助考生避免常见错误

◎ 单元测试：协助考生检验自己的进步

◎ 试题练习：涵盖学术类、培训类阅读以及写作、听力测试内容

定价：40 元　开本：16 开　页码：180 页

《剑桥雅思写作高分范文》（附 MP3）

刘巍巍　方林　编著

◎ 收集十年雅思写作题目，全部写作话题一网打尽

◎ 从雅思写作题目出发，全面提高考生写作能力

定价：38 元　开本：16 开　页码：248 页

《剑桥雅思 12 周完全攻略——听力》

（附 MP3）　　　　王超伟　编著

◎ 针对中国雅思考生的学习特点，制定 12 周科学备考方案

◎ 覆盖雅思听力考试核心话题，提供权威答案，帮助考生有的放矢地备考

定价：29.8 元　开本：16 开　页码：184 页

《剑桥雅思 12 周完全攻略——口语》

（附 MP3）　　　　孙涛　王冬　编著

◎ 针对中国雅思考生的学习特点，制定 12 周科学备考方案

◎ 覆盖雅思口语考试核心话题，提供权威答案，帮助考生有的放矢地备考

定价：29 元　开本：16 开　页码：204 页

《雅思词汇词根+联想记忆法(加强版)》

(附 MP3)　　　　俞敏洪　编著

◎ 完整收录雅思常考词汇，大量真题例句

◎ "词根 + 联想"实用有趣，配有插图，加深记忆

◎ 按字母顺序编排，增加返记菜单，便于考生进行自测

定价: 58 元　开本: 16 开　页码: 528 页

《雅思词汇词根+联想记忆法(乱序版)》

(附 MP3)　　　　俞敏洪　编著

◎ 完整收录雅思常考词汇，大量真题例句

◎ "词根 + 联想"实用有趣，配有插图，加深记忆

◎ 增加返记菜单和索引，便于查找定位

定价: 58 元　开本: 16 开　页码: 528 页

《雅思词汇词根+联想记忆法》

(附 MP3)　　　　俞敏洪　编著

◎ 原汁原味的真题例句，收词全面，涵盖雅思四大题型词汇

◎ 标出听力、口语单词，有针对性进行记忆

定价: 28 元　开本: 32 开　页码: 456 页

《雅思词汇词根+联想记忆法——写作》

(附 MP3)　　　　俞敏洪　编著

定价: 12 元　开本: 64 开　页码: 200 页

《雅思词汇词根+联想记忆法——听力》

(附 MP3)　　　　俞敏洪　编著

定价: 12 元　开本: 64 开　页码: 160 页

《雅思词汇词根+联想记忆法——口语》

(附 MP3)　　　　俞敏洪　编著

定价: 12 元　开本: 64 开　页码: 192 页

《雅思词汇词根+联想记忆法——阅读》

(附 MP3)　　　　俞敏洪　编著

定价: 12 元　开本: 64 开　页码: 232 页

◎ "词根 + 联想"实用有趣，配有插图，加深记忆

◎ 涵盖雅思阅读词汇，收词全面，分类科学

《雅思考官口语实战指导》

(附 MP3)　　　　Mat Clark　编著

◎ 分析中国考生的成绩现状，阐释评分系统的逐项要求

◎ 详尽介绍考试三部分程式，收录最新问题与话题卡片

定价: 35 元　开本: 16 开　页码: 212 页

《雅思听力胜经》(附 MP3)

新东方教育科技集团雅思研发团队　编著

◎ 以雅思听力真题为蓝本，细分常见题型和场景

◎ 提供大量听写和分项练习，帮助考生提高听力单项技能

定价: 30 元　开本: 16 开　页码: 170 页

《雅思口语胜经》(附 MP3)

新东方教育科技集团雅思研发团队　编著

◎ 收录口语考试最新问题和卡片话题

◎ 精选口语考试常用词汇和句型

定价: 35 元　开本: 16 开　页码: 216 页

《雅思阅读胜经》

新东方教育科技集团雅思研发团队　编著

◎ 词汇、语法、语篇三大层次剖析雅思阅读

◎ 精选 16 篇时文，全真模拟雅思阅读考试情境

定价: 30 元　开本: 16 开　页码: 224 页

《雅思写作胜经》

新东方教育科技集团雅思研发团队　编著

◎ 系统说明写作准备过程及步骤

◎ 提供同题各档次作文比较，方便考生自测自学

定价: 25 元　开本: 16 开　页码: 188 页